Lecture Notes in Computer Science   12389

Advanced Research in Computing and Software Science
Subline of Lecture Notes in Computer Science

More information about this subseries at http://www.springer.com/series/7408

David Pichardie · Mihaela Sighireanu (Eds.)

Static Analysis

27th International Symposium, SAS 2020
Virtual Event, November 18–20, 2020
Proceedings

 Springer

Editors
David Pichardie ⓘ
Inria, IRISA
ENS Rennes
Bruz, France

Mihaela Sighireanu ⓘ
LSV
ENS Paris-Saclay
Gif-sur-Yvette, France

ISSN 0302-9743 ISSN 1611-3349 (electronic)
Lecture Notes in Computer Science
ISBN 978-3-030-65473-3 ISBN 978-3-030-65474-0 (eBook)
https://doi.org/10.1007/978-3-030-65474-0

LNCS Sublibrary: SL2 – Programming and Software Engineering

This Springer imprint is published by the registered company Springer Nature Switzerland AG
The registered company address is: Gewerbestrasse 11, 6330 Cham, Switzerland

Preface

This volume contains the proceedings of the 27th edition of the International Static Analysis Symposium 2020 (SAS 2020), held during November 18–20, 2020, as a co-located event of SPLASH, the ACM SIGPLAN conference on Systems, Programming, Languages, and Applications: Software for Humanity. The COVID-19 pandemic forced us to organize the event online.

Static analysis is widely recognized as a fundamental tool for program verification, bug detection, compiler optimization, program understanding, and software maintenance. The SAS series has served as the primary venue for the presentation of theoretical, practical, and application advances in the area. Previous symposia were held in Porto, Freiburg, New York, Edinburgh, Saint-Malo, Munich, Seattle, Deauville, Venice, Perpignan, Los Angeles, Valencia, Kongens Lyngby, Seoul, London, Verona, San Diego, Madrid, Paris, Santa Barbara, Pisa, Aachen, Glasgow, and Namur.

SAS 2020 called for papers on topics including, but not limited to: abstract domains, abstract interpretation, automated deduction, data flow analysis, debugging, deductive methods, emerging applications, model-checking, program transformations, predicate abstraction, security analysis, tool environments and architectures, type checking. Authors were also encouraged to submit artifacts accompanying their papers to strengthen evaluations and reproducibility of results in static analysis.

The conference employed a double-blind review process with an author-response period. Within the review period, the Program Committee used an internal two-round review process where each submission received three first-round reviews to drive the possible selection of additional expert reviews as needed before the author response period. There were 34 submissions authored by researchers from countries including China, France, Germany, Hungary, India, Iran, Israel, Italy, Japan, Singapore, Spain, Sweden, Switzerland, the UK, and the USA. 15 submissions also presented an artifact. The author response period was followed by a Program Committee discussion period and culminated in a synchronous, virtual Program Committee meeting on July 16, 2020, to finalize the selection of papers. After thoroughly evaluating the relevance and quality of each paper, the Program Committee decided to accept 14 contributions. Each of the artifacts was evaluated by three members of the Artifact Evaluation Committee, whose comments were available to the Program Committee. Five artifacts were accepted. The artifacts are available on the FTP server of the staticanalysis.org website.

We were also honored to welcome four invited talks by the following distinguished researchers during the conference:

- Gogul Balakrishnan (Google, USA) on "Static analysis for privacy-preserving artificial intelligence"
- Ezgi Çiçek (Facebook, UK) on "Static resource analysis at scale"
- Manuel Hermenegildo (IMDEA Software Institute, Spain) on "Cost analysis of smart contracts via parametric resource analysis"

- James Worrell (University of Oxford, UK) on "Polynomial invariants for affine programs"

The last three speakers provided an extended abstract of their work in these proceedings. SAS 2020 featured two associated workshops held online on November 17, 2020:

- 11th Workshop on Tools for Automatic Program Analysis (TAPAS 2020)

  • Chairs: Hakjoo Oh (Korea University, South Korea) and Yulei Sui (University of Technology Sydney, Australia)

- 9th Workshop on Numerical and Symbolic Abstract Domains (NSAD 2020)

  • Chairs: Liqian Chen (National University of Defense Technology, China) and Khalil Ghorbal (Inria, France)

This program would not have been possible without the substantial efforts of many people, whom we sincerely thank. The Program Committee, Artifact Evaluation Committee, subreviewers, and external expert reviewers worked tirelessly to select the strongest possible program while simultaneously offering constructive and supportive comments in their reviews. The Organizing Committee of SPLASH, chaired by Hridesh Rajan (Iowa State University, USA), were tremendous. We also graciously thank the SPLASH Virtualization Committee chaired by Alex Potanin and Jan Vitek for the online organization. The SAS Steering Committee was very helpful, providing to us leadership and timely advice. Finally, we thank our sponsors Google and Facebook for supporting this event, as well as Springer for publishing these proceedings.

October 2020

David Pichardie
Mihaela Sighireanu
Jyothi Vedurada

Organization

Program Chairs

David Pichardie   IRISA, ENS Rennes, France
Mihaela Sighireanu   IRIF, Université de Paris, France

Program Committee

Josh Berdine   Facebook, UK
Bor-Yuh Evan Chang   University of Colorado Boulder, Amazon, USA
Patrick Cousot   New York University, USA
Jerome Feret   Inria, ENS Paris, France
Samir Genaim   Universidad Complutense de Madrid, Spain
Arie Gurfinkel   University of Waterloo, USA
Suresh Jagannathan   Purdue University, USA
Murali Krishna   Uber Technologies Inc., USA
Francesco Logozzo   Facebook, USA
Antoine Miné   Sorbonne Université, France
Anders Møller   Aarhus University, Denmark
Kedar Namjoshi   Nokia Bell Labs, USA
Sylvie Putot   Ecole Polytechnique, France
Francesco Ranzato   University of Padova, Italy
Xavier Rival   Inria, ENS Paris, France
Helmut Seidl   Technical University of Munich, Germany
Caterina Urban   Inria, France
Tomáš Vojnar   Brno University of Technology, Czech Republic
Kwangkeun Yi   Seoul National University, South Korea
Enea Zaffanella   University of Parma, Italy
Florian Zuleger   Vienna University of Technology, Austria

Artifact Evaluation Chair

Jyothi Vedurada   Microsoft Research, India

Artifact Evaluation Committee

Umair Z. Ahmed   National University of Singapore, Singapore
Marc Chevalier   PSL University, France
Pritam Gharat   Imperial College, UK
Timothée Haudebourg   ENS Rennes, France
Maxime Jacquemin   CEA LIST, France
Nicolas Jeannerod   Université de Paris, France

Raphaël Monat	Sorbonne Université, France
Rashmi Mudduluru	University of Washington, USA
Suvam Mukherjee	Microsoft Research, India
Olivier Nicole	CEA LIST, France
Guillermo Román-Díez	Universidad Politécnica de Madrid, Spain
Devika Sondhi	IIIT Delhi, India
Pedro Valero	IMDEA Software, Spain
Marco Zanella	University of Padova, Italy

Steering Committee

Bor-Yuh Evan Chang	University of Colorado Boulder, Amazon, USA
Andreas Podelski	University of Freiburg, Germany
Francesco Ranzato	University of Padova, Italy
Xavier Rival	Inria, France
Thomas Jensen	Inria, France
Sandrine Blazy	University of Rennes 1, France
Patrick Cousot	New York University, USA

Additional Reviewers

Ahmed Bouajjani
Thao Dang
Alastair Donaldson
Julian Erhard
Pablo Gordillo
Lukáš Holík
Anastasiia Izycheva
Ondrej Lengal
Richard Mayr
Nikita Mehrotra
Adam Rogalewicz

Polynomial Invariants for Affine Programs
(Invited Talk)

James Worrell

University of Oxford, Department of Computer Science, Parks Road,
Oxford OX1 3QD, UK
james.worrell@cs.ox.ac.uk

Invariants are one of the most fundamental and useful notions in the quantitative sciences, appearing in a wide range of contexts, from dynamical systems, and control theory in physics, mathematics, and engineering, to program verification, static analysis, abstract interpretation, and programming language semantics (among others) in computer science. In spite of decades of scientific work and progress, automated invariant synthesis remains a topic of active research, particularly in the fields of theorem proving and program analysis, and plays a central role in methods and tools seeking to establish correctness properties of computer programs; see, e.g., [10], and particularly Section 8 therein.

In this talk we survey a number of results concerning the synthesis of invariants for affine programs. Affine programs are a simple kind of nondeterministic imperative program, with a finite collection of locations in which the only instructions are assignments whose right-hand sides are affine expressions, such as $x_3 := x_1 - 3x_2 + 7$. Such programs can variously be seen as counter programs in which conditionals have been over-approximated by nondeterminism, or as types of weighted automata. Affine programs enable one to reason about more complex programs (see, e.g., [14]). An even more simple subclass of affine programs that have been studied from the point of view of loop termination and computing meta-transitions are (single-path) affine loops, which are essentially affine programs with a single location with a single selfloop (see, e.g., [8]).

An algorithm due to Michael Karr in 1976 [9] computes the strongest affine invariant of an affine program, that is, the strongest invariant that is defined by linear equations on program variables. The strongest such invariant can alternatively be characterised as the affine hull of the set of reachable program configurations in each location. A more efficient reformulation of Karr's algorithm was given by MuÕller-Olm and Seidl [13], who moreover showed that if the class of affine programs is augmented with equality guards then it becomes undecidable whether or not a given affine relation holds at a particular program location. A randomised algorithm for discovering affine relations was proposed by Gulwani and Necula [6].

In the first part of the talk we consider algebraic invariants for affine programs, that is, invariants defined by polynomial equations on program variables. A given affine program has a smallest (or strongest) algebraic invariant. Whereas the strongest affine invariant corresponds to the affine hull of the set of reachable program configurations in each location, the strongest algebraic invariant is the Zariski closure of the set of program configurations in each location. This gives rise to the computational problem of, given an affine program, computing a finite set of polynomials that define its strongest algebraic invariant. We describe a solution to this problem from [7], by reducing it to (and solving) a closely related problem of independent interest: compute the Zariski closure of a given finitely generated semigroup of matrices.

Algebraic invariants are stronger (i.e., more precise) than affine invariants. Various other types of domains have been considered in the setting of abstract interpretation, e.g., intervals, octagonal sets, and convex polyhedra (see, e.g., [3, 4, 11] and references in [2]). The precision of such domains in general is incomparable to that of algebraic invariants. Unlike with algebraic and affine invariants, there need not be a strongest convex polyhedral invariant for a given affine program. A natural decision problem in this setting is to ask for an inductive invariant that is disjoint from a given set of states (which one would like to show is not reachable). The version of this decision problem for convex invariants on affine programs was proposed by Monniaux [12] and remains open; if the convexity requirement is dropped, the problem is shown to be undecidable in [5].

In the second half of this talk we consider the class of semi-algebraic invariants, i.e., those defined by Boolean combinations of polynomial inequalities. These subsume all the classes of invariants mentioned so far. Here again there is no strongest invariant, and so the natural invariant synthesis problem takes as input not only the affine program but also a semi-algebraic target set of configurations, and the problem asks to decide whether there is a semi-algebraic invariant that is disjoint from the target set. Similar to the case of (non-convex) polyhedra, this problem is undecidable for general affine programs. Here we describe work from [1] that shows how to compute semi-algebraic invariants for affine loops.

Given an affine loop, while there is no strongest semi-algebraic invariant, there is something that is almost as good—namely a parameterised family $\mathcal{F}$ of invariants that is uniformly definable in the first-order theory of $\mathfrak{R}_{exp}$ (the real field with exponential function), such that (i) $\sim$ every semi-algebraic invariant contains some member of $\mathcal{F}$, and (ii) $\sim$ one can decide whether there is some member of $\mathcal{F}$ that is disjoint from the target set of configurations[1]. From the existence of this canonical family, we derive the decidability of the synthesis problem for semi-algebraic invariants. In proving this result we moreover show a strong completeness result for the class of semi-algebraic invariants on affine loops—if an affine loop and semi-algebraic target admits an invariant that is disjoint from the target and that is definable in some o-minimal expansion of $\mathfrak{R}_{exp}$, then there already exists a semi-algebraic invariant that avoids the target. Extending these results to richer classes of programs is the subject of ongoing work.

---

[1] While the theory of $\mathfrak{R}_{exp}$ is decidable assuming Schanuel's conjecture, for the special class of properties considered here we have unconditional decidability.

References

1. Almagor, S., Chistikov, D., Ouaknine, J., Worrell, J.: O-minimal invariants for linear loops. In: 45th International Colloquium on Automata, Languages and Programming, ICALP. LIPIcs, Schloss Dagstuhl - Leibniz-Zentrum fuer Informatik (2018)
2. Bradley, A.R., Manna, Z.: The calculus of computation - decision procedures with applications to verification. Springer, Heidelberg. https://doi.org/10.1007/978-3-540-74113-8 (2007)
3. Cousot, P., Cousot, R.: Abstract interpretation: a unified lattice model for static analysis of programs by construction or approximation of fixpoints. In: Conference Record of the Fourth ACM Symposium on Principles of Programming Languages. pp. 238–252 (1977)
4. Cousot, P., Halbwachs, N.: Automatic discovery of linear restraints among variables of a program. In: Conference Record of the Fifth Annual ACM Symposium on Principles of Programming Languages. pp. 84–96 (1978)
5. Fijalkow, N., Lefaucheux, E., Ohlmann, P., Ouaknine, J., Pouly, A., Worrell, J.: On the Monniaux problem in abstract interpretation. In: Chang, B.Y., (eds.) SAS 2019. LNCS, vol. 11822. Springer, Cham (2019). https://doi.org/10.1007/978-3-030-32304-2_9
6. Gulwani, S., Necula, G.C.: Discovering affine equalities using random interpretation. In: Conference Record of POPL 2003: The 30th SIGPLAN-SIGACT Symposium on Principles of Programming Languages. pp. 74–84. ACM (2003)
7. Hrushovski, E., Ouaknine, J., Pouly, A., Worrell, J.: Polynomial invariants for affine programs. In: Proceedings of the 33rd Annual ACM/IEEE Symposium on Logic in Computer Science, LICS. pp. 530–539. ACM (2018)
8. Jeannet, B., Schrammel, P., Sankaranarayanan, S.: Abstract acceleration of general linear loops. In: Jagannathan, S., Sewell, P., (eds.) The 41st Annual ACM SIGPLAN-SIGACT Symposium on Principles of Programming Languages, POPL. pp. 529–540. ACM (2014)
9. Karr, M.: Affine relationships among variables of a program. Acta Inf. 6, 133–151 (1976). https://doi.org/10.1007/BF00268497
10. Kincaid, Z., Cyphert, J., Breck, J., Reps, T.W.: Non-linear reasoning for invariant synthesis. PACMPL 2(POPL), 54:1–54:33 (2018)
11. Miné, A.: The octagon abstract domain. In: Proceedings of the Eighth Working Conference on Reverse Engineering, WCRE 2001, Stuttgart, Germany, 2–5 October 2001 (2001)
12. Monniaux, D.: On the decidability of the existence of polyhedral invariants in transition systems. Acta Inf. **56**(4), 385–389 (2019). https://doi.org/10.1007/s00236-018-0324-y
13. Müller-Olm, M., Seidl, H.: A Note on Karr's Algorithm. In: Díaz, J., Karhumäki, J., Lepistö, A., Sannella, D., (eds) ICALP 2004. LNCS, vol. 3142. Springer, Berlin, Heidelberg (2004). https://doi.org/10.1007/978-3-540-27836-8_85
14. Müller-Olm, M., Seidl, H.: Precise interprocedural analysis through linear algebra. In: Proceedings of the 31st ACM SIGPLAN-SIGACT Symposium on Principles of Programming Languages, POPL. pp. 330–341. ACM (2004)

Contents

Invited Talks

Static Resource Analysis at Scale
(Extended Abstract)

Ezgi Çiçek[1]([⊠]), Mehdi Bouaziz[2], Sungkeun Cho[1], and Dino Distefano[1]

[1] Facebook Inc., Menlo Park, USA
{ezgi,scho,ddino}@fb.com
[2] Nomadic Labs, Paris, France
mehdi@nomadic-labs.com

1 Introduction

Programs inevitably contain bugs. Fortunately, recent research and engineering efforts across the industry and academia made significant advances in static analysis techniques allowing automatic detection of bugs that cause a program to crash or to produce an unintended result. In many settings, it is not enough for a program to execute without errors. Programs must also finish executing within expected resource bounds and adhere to a sensible resource usage. At the very least, we expect the resource usage of programs to not deteriorate significantly as the source code evolves, hurting the experience of the users or even making the program unusable.

There are many static analysis techniques for estimating and verifying the resource usage of a program, ranging from static worst-case execution time (WCET) analyses (see [13] for a detailed survey) to typed-based approaches and program logics [2,5–7,10–12]. Research in static WCET analysis has been widely applied to validation and certification of embedded systems in safety critical systems. To estimate hard real-time bounds, these analyses must be tuned carefully to take into account abstract models of caching, scheduling and pipeline behavior of the embedded system. On the other hand, type based analyses and program logics are often more abstract but require sophisticated type checking/inference algorithms or specialized tools like proof assistants which make them unsuitable to be used on big codebases without specialist proof engineers.

In our work, we turn our attention to big codebases for mobile applications. We observe that although many static analysis techniques have been deployed to detect functional correctness bugs, not much attention is given to statically detecting performance regressions in industrial codebases. Most often, developers in such codebases deal with performance regressions through dynamic analysis techniques by relying on a combination of performance tests and profilers. Considering that these applications are developed in a continuous way where developers regularly add new features or modify existing code, only a limited amount of testing and monitoring can effectively be done before the code runs in production. Moreover, once a performance regression is introduced, it may take several days or even weeks for it to be detected by production monitoring

D. Pichardie and M. Sighireanu (Eds.): SAS 2020, LNCS 12389, pp. 3–6, 2020.
https://doi.org/10.1007/978-3-030-65474-0_1

systems. Once the regression is observed, tracking it back to its root cause is also a very time consuming task: The release of an application has normally thousands of code changes and singling out the changes responsible for the performance regression is like finding a "needle in the haystack". This whole process of *identifying* and *fixing* performance regressions is costly not only for the application and its users, but also in terms of engineering time. In fact it requires multiple developers to interact, coordinate, and finally verify that fix improves the performance.

2   Static Complexity Analysis with Infer

Motivated by these issues, we have developed an inter-procedural static analysis technique to automatically detect a class of performance regressions early in the development cycle. Our analysis is based on an abstract-interpretation technique [3,9] which computes symbolic upper bounds on the resource usage of programs—execution cost being the main resource we consider. These costs are expressed in terms of polynomials describing the asymptotic complexity of procedures with respect to their input sizes. The main input of the analysis is the source file which is then translated to an intermediate language along with the control-flow graph of the program. The analysis then operates on this intermediate language in several phases: 1) a numerical value analysis based on InferBo [1] computes value ranges for instructions accessing memory, 2) a loop bound analysis determines upper bounds for the number of iterations of loops and generates constraints for nodes in the control-flow graph, and 3) a constraint solving step resolves the constraints generated in the second step and computes an upper bound on the execution cost. The analysis assumes a simple sequential model with an abstract cost semantics: each primitive instruction in the intermediate language is assumed to incur a unit execution cost. The analysis is not limited to inferring bounds for just execution cost. In order to statically detect regressions in other types of resource usage, we have generalized the analysis to account costs for different types of resources such as memory allocations.

3   Diff-Time Deployment at Scale

We implemented the analysis on top of the Infer Static Analyser [8], which is used at Facebook to detect various errors related to memory safety, concurrency, and many more specialized errors suggested by Facebook developers. Infer hooks up to the continuous integration mechanism with the internal code review system where it is run on any code change (diff) over Facebook's Android codebase [4,8]. For our diff-based analysis, we rely on this mechanism and infer polynomial bounds for the original and the updated procedures. Whenever there is an increase in the degree of the complexity from the original to the modified version (e.g. from constant to linear or from linear to quadratic), we report a warning to the developer with a trace explaining where and how the complexity increase occurred.

Since the tool was deployed, thousands of complexity increase warnings were issued in Facebook's Android codebase where hundreds of these were fixed before the code was committed. Unlike functional correctness bugs where fix-rate is a good indicator of whether the issues found by the analyser are useful to the developer, we do not solely rely on fix-rate as a metric to measure the effectiveness of asymptotic complexity increase signal. This is because, unsurprisingly, not all complexity increase warnings point to an actual performance regression: a) the complexity increase could be intended or the input sizes used in production could be small enough to have no effect on the performance and b) the warning could also be a false positive due to limitations of the analyzer. To alleviate these, we follow a two-pronged approach. First, we ask developers to provide feedback on whether a warning is good-catch, expected, or wrong (potentially pointing to a false-positive). Only a small fraction of developers provide such feedback but they are still useful: the most frequent feedback is that the warning was expected. Wrong warnings are very rare (a few times a week) and we follow up these warnings closely to fix weaknesses of the analyzer. Secondly, to help developers evaluate the severity of the warning, we incorporate different types of contextual information that surface e.g. whether the procedure with the complexity increase runs on the critical path or main (UI) thread, which critical user interactions the procedure occurs on, and some dynamic profiling info (e.g. avg CPU time of the original procedure) when available. We observe that warnings with such contextual information are fixed (and marked as good-catch) more frequently in comparison to vanilla complexity increase warnings.

Thanks to the compositional nature of the analysis that enables us to generate execution costs of procedures independently of calling contexts, it can scale to large codebases and work incrementally on frequent code modifications. We believe that there is much unlocked potential and future work opportunities for applying this type of static performance analysis. Although not all complexity increase signal could be considered an actual performance regression, we observed that surfacing them to developers is still useful for code quality and regression prevention.

We are currently working on extending the analysis to detect out-of-memory errors, combining static analysis with dynamic techniques, and adding support for handling other languages such as C++ and Objective-C.

References

1. Inferbo: Infer-based numerical buffer overrun analyzer (2017). https://research.fb.com/blog/2017/02/inferbo-infer-based-buffer-overrun-analyzer/
2. Atkey, R.: Amortised resource analysis with separation logic. Log. Methods Comput. Sci (2011)
3. Bygde, S.: Static WCET analysis based on abstract interpretation and counting of elements. Ph.D. thesis (2010)
4. Calcagno, C., Distefano, D.: Infer: an automatic program verifier for memory safety of C programs. In: Dubois, M., Havelund, K., Holzmann, G.J., Joshi, R. (eds.) NFM 2011. LNCS, vol. 6617, pp. 459–465. Springer, Heidelberg (2011). https://doi.org/10.1007/978-3-642-20398-5_33

5. Çiçek, E., Barthe, G., Gaboardi, M., Garg, D., Hoffmann, J.: Relational cost analysis. In: Proceedings of the 44th ACM SIGPLAN Symposium on Principles of Programming Languages. POPL 2017, Association for Computing Machinery, New York, NY, USA (2017)
6. Crary, K., Weirich, S.: Resource bound certification. POPL 2000, Association for Computing Machinery, New York (2000)
7. Danielsson, N.A.: Lightweight semiformal time complexity analysis for purely functional data structures. In: Proceedings of the 35th Annual ACM SIGPLAN-SIGACT Symposium on Principles of Programming Languages. POPL 2008, New York (2008)
8. Distefano, D., Fähndrich, M., Logozzo, F., O'Hearn, P.W.: Scaling static analyses at facebook. Commun. ACM (2019)
9. Ermedahl, A., Sandberg, C., Gustafsson, J., Bygde, S., Lisper, B.: Loop bound analysis based on a combination of program slicing, abstract interpretation, and invariant analysis. In: Proceedings 7th International Workshop on Worst-Case Execution Time Analysis (WCET 2007) 6 (2007)
10. Hoffmann, J., Das, A., Weng, S.C.: Towards automatic resource bound analysis for ocaml. SIGPLAN Not (2017)
11. Knoth, T., Wang, D., Reynolds, A., Hoffmann, J., Polikarpova, N.: Liquid resource types. Proc. ACM Program. Lang. (ICFP) (2020)
12. Wang, P., Wang, D., Chlipala, A.: Timl: A functional language for practical complexity analysis with invariants 1(OOPSLA) (2017)
13. Wilhelm, R., et al.: The worst-case execution-time problem–overview of methods and survey of tools. ACM Trans. Embed. Comput, Syst (2008)

Cost Analysis of Smart Contracts Via Parametric Resource Analysis

Víctor Pérez[1,2]([✉]), Maximiliano Klemen[1,2], Pedro López-García[1,3], José Francisco Morales[1], and Manuel Hermenegildo[1,2]

[1] IMDEA Software Institute, Madrid, Spain
{victor.perez,maximiliano.klemen,pedro.lopez,josef.morales,
manuel.hermenegildo}@imdea.org
[2] Universidad Politécnica de Madrid (UPM), Madrid, Spain
[3] Spanish Council for Scientific Research (CSIC), Madrid, Spain

Abstract. The very nature of smart contracts and blockchain platforms, where program execution and storage are replicated across a large number of nodes, makes resource consumption analysis highly relevant. This has led to the development of analyzers for specific platforms and languages. However, blockchain platforms present significant variability in languages and cost models, as well as over time. Approaches that facilitate the quick development and adaptation of cost analyses are thus potentially attractive in this context. We explore the application of a generic approach and tool for cost analysis to the problem of static inference of gas consumption bounds in smart contracts. The approach is based on *Parametric Resource Analysis*, a method that simplifies the implementation of analyzers for inferring safe bounds on different resources and with different resource consumption models. In addition, to support different input languages, the approach also makes use of translation into a Horn clause-based intermediate representation. To assess practicality we develop an analyzer for the Tezos platform and its Michelson language. We argue that this approach offers a rapid, flexible, and effective method for the development of cost analyses for smart contracts.

Keywords: Blockchain · Smart contracts · Parametric Resource Analysis · Static analysis · Constraint horn clauses · Program transformation

1 Introduction

Due to the nature of blockchain platforms [6,63], smart contracts [60] and their storage are replicated in every node running the chain, and any call to a contract

Partially funded by MICINN PID2019-108528RB-C21 *ProCode* and Madrid P2018/TCS-4339 *BLOQUES-CM*. Thanks to Vincent Botbol, Mehdi Bouaziz, and Raphael Cauderlier from Nomadic Labs, and Patrick Cousot, for their comments.

D. Pichardie and M. Sighireanu (Eds.): SAS 2020, LNCS 12389, pp. 7–31, 2020.
https://doi.org/10.1007/978-3-030-65474-0_2

is executed on every client. This fact has led many smart contract platforms to include upper bounds on execution time and storage, as well as fees associated with running a contract or increasing its storage size. More concretely, in order to limit execution time, smart contract platforms make use of a concept called "gas," so that each instruction of the smart contract language usually has an associated cost in terms of this resource. If a transaction exceeds its allowed *gas* consumption, its execution is stopped and its effects reverted. However, even if a transaction does not succeed because of *gas* exhaustion, it is included in the blockchain and the fees are taken. Similarly, there are limitations and costs related to *storage size*. The cost of running a contract can then be expressed in terms of these two resources, *gas* consumed and *storage*.

In this context, knowing the cost of running a contract beforehand can be useful, since it allows users to know how much they will be charged for the transaction, and whether *gas* limits will be exceeded or not. However, this is not straightforward in general. Many smart contract platforms do provide users with simulators which allow performing dry runs of smart contracts in their own node before performing actual transactions. But this of course returns cost data only for specific input values, and provides no hard guarantees on the costs that may result from processing the arbitrary inputs that the contract may receive upon deployment. Ideally, one would like to be able to obtain instead guaranteed bounds on this cost statically, or at least through a combination of static and dynamic methods.

Thus, formal verification of smart contracts, and in particular analysis and verification of their resource consumption, is receiving increased attention. At the same time, many different blockchain platforms now exist, using different languages and cost models, which often take into account different resources and count them in different, platform-specific ways. Furthermore, within each platform, the models can also evolve over time. As a consequence, the few existing resource analysis tools for smart contracts, such as GASTAP [5], GASOL [4], or MadMax [22], tend to be quite specific, focusing on just a single platform or language, or on small variations thereof.[1] This makes approaches that would allow quick development of new cost analyses or easily adapting existing ones potentially attractive in this context.

Parametric Resource Analysis (also referred to as user-defined resource analysis) [51,52,59] is an approach that simplifies the implementation of analyzers that infer safe functional bounds on different related resources and with different resource consumption models. Our objective in this paper is to explore the application of this general approach to the rapid and effective development of static analyses for gas consumption in smart contracts. To this end, we use the implementation of the method in the `CiaoPP` [29] framework, and apply it to the Tezos platform [6] and its Michelson language [1] as a proof of concept.

In the rest of the paper we start by providing an overview of the general approach (Sect. 2), and then we illustrate successively the translation process (Sect. 3), how the cost model is encoded (Sect. 4), and how the analysis is per-

---

[1] We discuss this and other relevant related work further in Sect. 7.

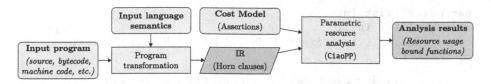

Fig. 1. Overview of the Parametric Resource Analysis approach.

formed (Sect. 5), first in general and then applied to the Michelson language. We also provide some experimental results in Sect. 6. Section 7 then discusses other related work and Sect. 8 presents our conclusions and future work.

2   The Parametric Resource Analysis Approach

We start by providing an overview of the approach (Fig. 1). Before getting into the resource analysis itself, a basic technique used in the model, in order to support different input languages, is to translate input programs to a Horn clause-based intermediate representation [46], that we refer to as the "CHC IR," a technique used nowadays in many analysis and verification tools [13,18,20,21,25,27,35,46,54]. The CHC IR is handled uniformly by the analyzers, and the results are then reflected back to the input language. To perform the Parametric Resource Analysis, assertions are used to define the resources of interest, including compound resources, and the consumption that basic elements of the input language (e.g., commands, instructions, bytecodes, built-ins, etc.) make of such resources. This constitutes the *cost model*. This model is normally generated once for each input language, and is the part modified if the costs change or different resources need to be inferred. Given an input program and the cost model, the parametric analyzer then infers, for each program point (block, procedure, etc.), safe resource usage bound *functions* that depend on data sizes and possibly other parameters. Both the resource consumption expressions inferred and those appearing in the cost models can include e.g., polynomial, summation, exponential, and logarithmic, as well as multi-variable functions. This overall approach, pioneered and supported by the `CiaoPP` framework, has been successfully applied to the analysis, verification, and optimization of resource consumption for languages ranging from source to machine code, and resources ranging from execution time to energy consumption [39–42,47,50,51].

3   Translating into the CHC IR

As mentioned above, in order to support different programming languages and program representations at different compilation levels, each input language is translated into a Horn clause-based intermediate program representation, the CHC IR [46]. A (Constrained) Horn clause ((C)HC) is a formula of first-order predicate logic (generalized with constraints) of the form $\forall (S_1 \wedge \ldots \wedge S_n \rightarrow S_0)$

```
parameter (list int);
storage (list int);
code { CAR; NIL int; SWAP; ITER { CONS }; NIL operation;
    PAIR }
```

Listing 1.1. A Michelson contract that reverses a list.

where all variables in the clause are universally quantified over the whole formula, and $S_0, S_1, \ldots, S_n$ are atomic formulas, also called literals, or constraints. CHCs are usually written: $S_0 \; : - \; S_1, \ldots, S_n$, where S_0 is referred to as the *head* and $S_1, \ldots, S_n$ as the *body*. Given a program p in an input language L_p, plus a definition of the semantics of L_p, the objective is to translate p into a set of Horn clauses that capture the semantics of p. Two main styles are generally used for encoding the operational semantics of L_p [18]: small-step (structural operational semantics) [55], as in [54], or big-step (natural semantics) [34], as in [46]. We will be concerned herein with the latter, among other reasons because the big-step approach is very direct for the case of a language that is structured and defined functionally, such as Michelson.

Typically, a CHC interpreter of L_p, I, in one of the styles above, together with a term-based representation of p and its store, would suffice to reflect the program semantics. However, precise analyses often require a tighter correspondence between predicates and body literals in the CHCs and the *blocks* (e.g., in a control-flow graph) and statements (e.g., *calls* and *built-ins*) for p. For example, for an imperative program, the CHCs typically encode a set of connected code *blocks*, so that each block is represented by a CHC: $\langle block\_id \rangle(\langle params \rangle) \; : - \; S_1, \; \ldots \; , S_n$. The *head* represents the entry point to the block and its parameters, and the *body* the sequence of steps in the block. Each of these S_i steps (or *literals*) is either a *call* to another (or the same) block or a call to one of the basic operations implemented by the interpreter I. Thus, depending on the input language, literals can represent bytecode instructions, machine instructions, calls to built-ins, constraints, compiler IR instructions, etc.

Techniques such as partial evaluation and program specialization offer powerful methods to obtain such translations. In particular, using the first Futamura projection [17], I can be specialized for a given input program p, which, with appropriate simplifications, results in a set of predicates with the desired correspondences. A direct, automatic translator can be obtained by specializing a CHC partial evaluator for I (second Futamura projection), which can then be applied to any program p. In general, these transformations may be automatic, manual, or use a combination of techniques. Also, preliminary transformations may be required to express the semantics at the right abstraction level, e.g., making all variable scoping explicit, using Static Single Assignment (SSA), reducing control constructs, etc. [46].

The Michelson Language and Its Semantics. Michelson is the "native" language used by the Tezos platform. It is interpreted, strongly-typed, and stack-based. Despite being a low-level language, Michelson provides some high-level data structures such as lists, sets, maps, and arbitrary precision integers.

$$
\begin{array}{ll}
\textsf{CAR:}\ (pair\ ta\ \_) : A \to ta : A & \textsf{NIL}\ t:\ A \to (list\ t) : A \\[4pt]
\qquad (a, \_) : S \mapsto a : S & \qquad S \mapsto ([\,]) : S \\[8pt]
\textsf{SWAP:}\ a : b : A \to b : a : A & \textsf{PAIR:}\ a : b : A \to (pair\ a\ b) : A \\[4pt]
\qquad x : y : S \mapsto y : x : S & \qquad x : y : S \mapsto (x, y) : S \\[8pt]
\textsf{ITER}\ body : (list\ t) : A \to A & \textsf{CONS:}\ t : list\ t : A \to list\ t : A \\[4pt]
\qquad body : t : A \to A & \qquad a : b : S \mapsto (a : b) : S \\[8pt]
\end{array}
$$

$$
l : S \mapsto \textsf{ITER}(l : S) = \begin{cases} S & \text{if } l = [\,] \\ \textsf{ITER}(l' : body(el : S)) & \text{if } l = el : l' \end{cases}
$$

Fig. 2. Semantics of some Michelson instructions.

Michelson contracts consist of three sections. The *parameter* and *storage* sections stipulate the types of the input argument and the storage. E.g., in Listing 1.1 both are described as lists of Michelson integers. The *code* section contains the sequence of instructions to be executed by the Michelson interpreter. This interpreter can be seen as a pure function that receives a stack and returns a result stack without altering its environment. The input stack contains just a pair consisting of the *parameter* and the contract *storage*. The output stack will contain just a pair consisting of the *list of blockchain operations* to be executed after the contract returns and the *updated storage*, to be used as storage value in the following call to the contract. I.e.:

$$
Interpreter: (pair\ parameter\ storage) : [\,] \to (pair\ (list\ operation)\ storage) : [\,]
$$
$$
(p, s) : [\,] \mapsto (l, s') : [\,]
$$

The Michelson instructions can also be seen as pure functions receiving an input stack and returning a result stack. Figure 2 shows the semantics of the Michelson instructions used in Listing 1.1—overall, there are 116 typed instructions and 23 macros. Continuing with the example, its purpose is to reverse the list passed as a parameter and store it. First, CAR discards the storage of the contract, as only the list passed as parameter is needed for the computation. Then, the NIL instruction inserts an empty list on top of the stack. The type of the elements that will fill the resulting list needs to be provided, in this case integers. SWAP simply exchanges the top two elements of the stack. After running these instructions, the stack will have the following shape: $parameter : ([\,]) : [\,]$.

The interpreter will now iterate over the input list, prepending each of its elements to the new list and reversing the former in the process. This action is carried out by the ITER instruction, which traverses the elements of a list, performing the action indicated by its argument: a macro or a sequence of instructions; in our case, just { CONS }. CONS receives a stack whose top is an element and a list of the same type, and returns a stack with just the list on top, but where the list has the element prepended, while the rest of the stack is unchanged.

```
car([(A, _)|S], [A|S]).                          nil(_, S, [[]|S]).

swap([A, B|S], [B, A|S]).                         pair([A, B|S], [(A, B)|S]).

iter(Body, [L|S0], S1) ← iter(L, Body, S0, S1).  cons([X, Xs|S], [[X|Xs]|S]).

iter([], _, S, S).
iter([X|Xs], Body, S0, S2) ← run(Body, [X|S0], S1), iter(Xs, Body, S1, S2).
```

Fig. 3. Semantics of the instructions of Fig. 2 in CHC.

Taking into account the semantics of CONS, the semantics of the loop within the contract can be defined as:

$$l_a : l_b : S \mapsto \text{ITER}(l_a : l_b : S) = \begin{cases} l_b : S & \text{if } l_a = [] \\ \text{ITER}(l'_a : (el : l_b) : S) & \text{if } l_a = el : l'_a \end{cases}$$

There are other instructions which receive code as an argument: the control structures in the language, e.g., IF or LOOP, are instructions which receive one or two *blocks* of code. Likewise, other instructions receive other kinds of arguments, such as NIL, which as we saw receives the type of the list to build; or PUSH, which receives the type and value of the element to place on top of the stack. Once the list has been reversed, the contract inserts a list of operations on top of the stack, via the NIL instruction, and builds a pair from the two elements left in the stack, using the PAIR instruction. This way, the result stack will have the required type, i.e., length and type of its elements:

$$(pair\ (list\ operation)\ storage) : [], \text{ where } storage \equiv (list\ int)$$

As a concrete example, a call to this contract with the list of numbers from 1 to 3 as parameter would present the following input (S_0) and output (S_1) stacks:

$$S_0 = ((1 : 2 : 3), \_) : [] \mapsto S_1 = ([], (3 : 2 : 1)) : []$$

Note that, as the first instruction in the contract discards the storage, its value is irrelevant to obtain the result of the computation.

As mentioned before, in addition to performing operations over terms in the stack, Michelson instructions can also return *external operations* (i.e., instructions that perform actions at the blockchain level) to be added to the list of operations in the return stack. Lack of space prevents us from going into details, but these operations can be: *transactions* (operations to transfer tokens and parameters to a smart contract), *originations* (to create new smart contracts given the required arguments), or *delegations* (operations that assign a number of tokens to the stake of another account, without transferring them).

CHC Encoding. We implement the Michelson semantics as a big-step recursive interpreter, via a direct transliteration of the semantics into CHCs (using the

Ciao system [28]). Figure 3, shows the CHC encoding of the instructions of Fig. 2. Data structures are represented in the usual way with Herbrand terms.[2] The interpreter in turn is encoded by the following clauses:[3]

```
run([], S0, S) :- S=S0.
run([Ins|Insns], S0, S) :- ins(Ins, S0, S1), run(Insns, S1, S).
% Dispatcher (one clause for each I/n instruction)
ins(<<I>>(A1,...,An), S0, S) :- <<I>>(A1,...,An,S0,S).
```

Predicate run/3 takes the input program and the initial stack (S0), and reduces it by executing the sequence of Michelson instructions to obtain the resulting stack S1. ins/3 is the instruction dispatcher, which connects each instruction term (e.g., push(X)) with its CHC definition (e.g., push(X,S0,S)) (see Fig. 3).

The Michelson to CHC IR Translation. We derive a simple translator, based on a specialization of a CHC partial evaluation algorithm for this particular recursive interpreter. In this process special care is taken to materialize stack prefixes as actual predicate arguments.

Preliminary Transformations. As preliminary transformations we introduce *labeled* blocks for sequences of instructions in the program, to help in later steps of partial evaluation. For the sake of clarity, we consider them simply as new predicate definitions (we obviate for conciseness some additional information needed to trace back blocks to the original program points). We also rely on a simple implementation within the system of Michelson type checking, which makes knowing the type of the stack (and thus of the operands) at each program point a decidable problem. This allows us to specialize polymorphic instructions, depending on the type of the passed arguments. This is particularly useful to specify (as we will see later) the semantics and cost of each instruction variant, which can vary depending on those static types. E.g., the ADD instruction is translated into one of seven possible primitive operations, depending on the type of the addends:

$$ADD[A,B] \rightarrow \begin{cases} \text{add\_intint} & \text{if } int(A), int(B) \\ \text{add\_intnat} & \text{if } int(A), nat(B) \\ \text{add\_natint} & \text{if } nat(A), int(B) \\ \text{add\_natnat} & \text{if } nat(A), nat(B) \\ \text{add\_timestamp\_to\_seconds} & \text{if } timestamp(A), int(B) \\ \text{add\_seconds\_to\_timestamp} & \text{if } int(A), timestamp(B) \\ \text{add\_tez} & \text{if } mutez(A), mutez(B) \end{cases} \quad (1)$$

Translation Using Partial Evaluation. Based on our interpreter, we derive stepwise a simple translator which combines a hand-written specializer for the run/3

---

[2] We do not include the types in Fig. 3 for brevity; they will be present however in the cost model assertions of Sect. 4.
[3] In the actual code, state variables are made implicit by using Definite Clause Grammar (DCG) syntax. We have left all variables explicit however for clarity.

```
parameter (pair int (list int)) ;
storage int ;
code { CAR ;
       UNPAIR ;
       DUP ;
       SUB ;
       DIIP { PUSH int 0 } ;
       IFNEQ { ITER { ADD } } { DROP } ;
       NIL operation ;
       PAIR }
```

Listing 1.2. A Michelson contract suitable for partial evaluation.

predicate, a stack deforestation pass (including each stack element instead of the stack itself as predicate arguments), and a generic partial evaluation for the primitive instruction definitions (e.g., evaluate conditions, arithmetic instructions, etc.). Michelson control-flow instructions receive both the control condition and the code to execute as inputs, e.g.:

```
if(Bt,Bf,[B|S0],S) :- '$if', if_(B,Bt,Bf,S0,S).
if_(true, Bt,_Bf,S0,S) :- run(Bt,S0,S).
if_(false,_Bt,Bf,S0,S) :- run(Bf,S0,S).
```

By construction, the code arguments are bound, as explained in the preliminary transformations, to new constants representing code blocks dispatched from ins/3. For each call, partial evaluation will unfold if(Bt,Bf,S0,S2) as '$if', S0=[B|S1], if_0(B,S1,S2) and generate new instances, e.g.:

```
if__0(true, S0,S) :- ... % unfolded run(<<Bt>>,S0,S).
if__0(false,S0,S) :- ... % unfolded run(<<Bf>>,S0,S).
```

The stack deforestation step is specially useful in the output of control-flow instructions, which receive $n+m$ arguments instead of the lists of variables, where n is the size of the input stack and m of the output stack. This transformation is possible thanks to Michelson's semantics, which forbids changes to the type of the stack in loops and forces the type of both output stacks in branch instructions to match. E.g., for the simple branch instruction IF:

```
if__0(true, I0,I1,...,In,O0,O1,...,Om) :- ...
if__0(false,I0,I1,...,In,O0,O1,...,Om) :- ...
```

Following the idea of abstracting away the stack, the translation also abstracts away simple data structures, such as pairs, whenever possible.

Cost-Preserving Encoding. In order to precisely capture the actual cost of instructions, while allowing aggressive program transformations such as unfolding, partial evaluation, and replacing the stack arguments by actual parameters, the instruction definitions are extended to introduce *cost markers*, e.g.:

```
:- pred code/5 : int * list(int) * int * var * var.

code(A,B,C,D,E) :-
    '$car', '$dup', '$car', '$dip', '$cdr', '$dup',
    sub_intint(A,A,F),
    '$dip'(2), '$push'(0),
    neq(F,G),
    '$if',
    if__0(G,[B,0],[E]),
    nil(D),
    '$pair'.

if__0(true,[A,B],[C]) :-
    iter__1(A,[B],[C]).
if__0(false,[A,B],[B]) :-
    '$drop'(A).

iter__1([],[A],[A]) :-
    '$iter_end'.
iter__1([A|B],[C],[D]) :-
    '$iter',
    add_intint(A,C,E),
    iter__1(B,[E],[D]).
```

Listing 1.3. CHC IR representation of Listing 1.2.

```
swap([A,B|S],[B,A|S]) :- '$swap'.
drop([X|S],S) :- '$drop'(X).
if(Bt,Bf,[B|S0],S) :- '$if', if_(B,Bt,Bf,S0,S).
if(true, Bt,_Bf,S0,S) :- run(Bt,S0,S).
if(false,_Bt,Bf,S0,S) :- run(Bf,S0,S).
```

Partial evaluation will replace each of the primitive operations (from a very reduced set) by its CHC definition in the output CHC IR, while the cost makers, whose main end is to keep a record of the consumed resources at each step, will be preserved. Note that as as a result of the transformations, some Michelson

```
:- pred code/5 : int * list(int) * int * var * var.

code(A,B,C,[],0) :-
    '$car', '$dup', '$car', '$dip', '$cdr', '$dup',
    sub_intint(A,A,0),
    '$dip'(2), '$push'(0),
    neq(0,false),
    '$if', '$drop'(B),
    nil([]),
    '$pair'.
```

Listing 1.4. CHC IR representation of Listing 1.2 with partial evaluation enabled.

instructions that simply modify/access the stack will not even be represented in the output CHC IR, only their cost markers, if relevant.

Translation Example. To illustrate all the steps described in this section, we show the resulting CHC representation for the contract shown in Listing 1.2. The direct translation of this contract can be found in Listing 1.3, whereas Listing 1.4 takes advantage of partial evaluation to perform significant, yet valid transformations, both in terms of semantics and resource semantics.

Another useful transformation performed by the translation is the inclusion of explicit arithmetic comparison operations in the contract. This way, Boolean conditions in control-flow predicates can be replaced by arithmetic tests, which not only makes the contract more readable for the human eye, but also easier to analyze. An example of this can be seen in Listing 1.5 and its CHC IR representation, Listing 1.6. In this contract one of the comparison operations and the evaluation of its result are performed in different predicates. This information can be encoded by attaching information about how they have been generated to the results of both `COMPARE` and `GT` instructions, which will propagate throughout the translation process inside the stack.

4   Defining Resources and Cost Models

After addressing in the previous section the parametricity of the approach w.r.t. the programming language, we now address parametricity w.r.t. resources and cost models. As mentioned before, the role of the *cost model* in parametric resource analysis is to provide information about the resource consumption of the basic elements of the input language, which is then used by the analysis to infer the resource usage of higher-level entities of programs such as procedures, functions, loops, blocks, and the whole code. We start by describing a subset of the assertions proposed in [52] for describing such models, which are part of the multi-purpose assertion language of the `Ciao/CiaoPP` framework [9,28,56], used in our experiments. First, the resources of interest have to be defined and given a name as follows:

$$\texttt{:- resource } \langle resname \rangle.$$

Then, we can express how each operation of the analyzed language affects the use of such resource, by means of assertions with `trust` status:

$$\texttt{:- trust pred } \langle operation \rangle \texttt{ + cost}(\langle approx \rangle, \langle resname \rangle, \langle arithexpr \rangle).$$

where $\langle arithexpr \rangle$ expresses the resource usage as a function that depends on data sizes and possibly other parameters, and which, as mentioned before, can be polynomial, summation, exponential, or logarithmic, as well as multi-variable. The $\langle approx \rangle$ field states whether $\langle arithexpr \rangle$ is providing an upper bound (`ub`), a lower bound (`lb`), a "big O" expression, i.e., with only the order information (`oub`), or an Ω asymptotic lower bound (`olb`). Such assertions can also be used to describe the resource usage of builtins, libraries, external procedures (e.g.,

```
parameter (pair int int) ;
storage int ;
code { UNPPAIIR ;
       DIIP { DUP } ;
       DUUUP ;
       SWAP ;
       CMPGT ;
       DIP CMPGT ;
       IF ASSERT FAIL ;
       NIL operation ;
       PAIR }
```

Listing 1.5. A Michelson contract with arithmetic comparisons.

defined in another language), etc. Assertions can also include a *calls* field, preceded by :, stating properties that hold at call time. This allows writing several assertions for the same predicate to deal with polymorphic predicates whose resource semantics may differ depending on the call states. E.g., for **add** we can have assertions with call fields **int * int * var** and **flt * flt * var** with possibly different costs. An optional *success field*, preceded by **=>**, can also be used to state properties that hold for the arguments on success. Additionally, size metric information can be provided by users if needed using **size_metric**(Var,$\langle sz\_metric \rangle$) properties, although in practice such metrics are generally derived automatically from the inferred types and shapes. These are the metrics used to measure data sizes, e.g.: list length, term depth, term size, actual value of a number, number of steps of the application of a type definition, etc. (see [52,59] and the use therein of *sized types*). It is also possible to declare relationships between the data sizes of the inputs and outputs of procedures, as well as provide types and actual sizes (**size**(Var,$\langle approx \rangle$,$\langle sz\_metric \rangle$,$\langle arithexpr \rangle$)). In addition to those presented, [52] proposes some additional mechanisms for defining other aspects of cost models, but they are not required for our presentation.

The Cost Model for the Tezos Platform. We now illustrate how to define the resources and cost model for our test case, the Tezos platform and its Michelson language, using the **Ciao** assertion language. The Tezos/Michelson cost model varies somewhat with each version of the protocol, which, as mentioned before, is one of the motivations for our approach. The model that we present has been derived from the OCaml source for the *Carthage* protocol. *Gas* is a *compound resource* that can be defined as a function of other *basic resources*:

```
:- pred code/5 : int * int * int * var * var.

code(A,B,C,[],D) :-
    '$dup', '$car', '$dip', '$cdr', '$dup', '$car', '$dip',
    '$cdr', '$dip'(2), '$dup', '$dip'(2), '$dup', '$dig'(3),
    '$swap',
    compare_int(A,C,E),
    gt(E,F),
    '$dip',
    compare_int(B,C,G),
    gt(G,H),
    '$if',
    if__0(A,C,B,C,H,C,D),
    nil([]),
    '$pair'.

if__0(A,B,C,D,E,F,G) :-
    A>B,
    '$if',
    if__1(C,D,F,G).
if__0(A,B,C,D,E,F,failed('()')) :-
    A=<B,
    '$push'('()'),failwith('()').

if__1(A,B,C,C) :-
    A>B.
if__1(A,B,C,failed('()')) :-
    A=<B,
    '$push'('()'),failwith('()').
```

Listing 1.6. CHC IR representation of Listing 1.5.

$$gas(allocations, steps, reads, writes, bytes\_read, bytes\_written) =$$

$$= 2^{-7} * \begin{pmatrix} allocations \\ steps \\ reads \\ writes \\ bytes\_read \\ bytes\_written \end{pmatrix} \times \begin{pmatrix} 2 \\ 1 \\ 100 \\ 160 \\ 10 \\ 15 \end{pmatrix} \tag{2}$$

In our cost model we first name the resources (Listing 1.7), and then define michelson_gas as a compound resource following Eq. 2 (Listing 1.8).

Each Michelson instruction will consume one or more of these basic resources, so the next step is to declare this consumption. Since in most cases not all resources will be consumed by every instruction, we include in the model some default cost assertions establishing, for example, that the consumption of these

```
:- resource michelson_allocations.
:- resource michelson_steps
:- resource michelson_reads.
:- resource michelson_writes.
:- resource michelson_bytes_read.
:- resource michelson_bytes_written.
```

Listing 1.7. Assertions to declare the resources to study.

```
:- resource michelson_gas.
:- compound_resource(michelson_gas, 2**(-7) * (
   michelson_allocations * 2
   + michelson_steps
   + michelson_reads * 100
   + michelson_writes * 160
   + michelson_bytes_read * 10
   + michelson_bytes_written * 15 )).
```

Listing 1.8. Assertions to declare *gas* as a compound resource.

basic resources is 0 by default. This avoids having to provide information for all resources in the cost assertions for every instruction.[4]

We illustrate the process of declaring specific resource consumptions using the ADD instruction. Listing 1.9 shows the definition of this basic operation in the (OCaml) code of the Michelson interpreter, which contains not only the semantics of the instruction, but also its cost semantics. As mentioned before, this is a polymorphic instruction, so it may be transformed into different predicates in the translation process. In this case, we will focus on the instance dealing with integers, which was called **add_intint** in Eq. 1. Comparing Eq. 1 and Listing 1.9 we can see that our translation process closely matches the Tezos internal representation of Michelson instructions.

The corresponding cost expression, as found in the Tezos source code, is shown in Listing 1.10, which is given in turn in terms of **atomic_step_cost**, Listing 1.11. This function is used to express the cost of a great number of operations, which, as in this case, can be given as a function of their arguments. Using this definition and that of **int_bytes**:

$$int\_bytes(x) = 1 + \left\lfloor \frac{\log_2 |x|}{8} \right\rfloor \tag{3}$$

we can simplify **add_intint**'s cost expression:

$$
\begin{aligned}
cost_{add\_intint}(A, B) &= 2 * \left(51 + \frac{\max\left(1 + \left\lfloor \frac{\log_2 |A|}{8} \right\rfloor, 1 + \left\lfloor \frac{\log_2 |B|}{8} \right\rfloor\right)}{62} \right) \\
&= 102 + \frac{1 + \left\lfloor \frac{\log_2 \max\left(|A|, |B|\right)}{8} \right\rfloor}{31}
\end{aligned}
\tag{4}
$$

```
| (Add_intint, Item (x, Item (y, rest))) ->
    consume_gas_binop
      descr (Script_int.add, x, y)
      Interp_costs.add rest ctxt
| (Add_intnat, Item (x, Item (y, rest))) ->
    consume_gas_binop
      descr (Script_int.add, x, y)
      Interp_costs.add rest ctxt
```

Listing 1.9. Some of the definitions for ADD.

```
let add i1 i2 =
  atomic_step_cost
    (51 +
      (Compare.Int.max
        (int_bytes i1) (int_bytes i2) / 62) )
```

Listing 1.10. Cost definition for add_intint.

The assertion used to include this cost in our CiaoPP model is shown in Listing 1.12. It expresses the exact cost of this instruction in terms of its inputs. Both an upper and a lower bound are given. Since they are the same, the cost is exact—this can also be expressed with the **exact** keyword. Note that these assertions can also include properties of instruction arguments. In this case we state the types and sizes of the arguments of the add_intint predicate on success, as well as other information such as non-failure, determinacy, or cardinality, which increase the precision of the resource analysis. In fact, since every Michelson instruction is a deterministic function defined in all of its domain, they never fail and they always return one solution. Note the direct correspondence between the arithmetic expression that defines the cost of the instruction and Eq. 4, which contributes to the readability of the model.

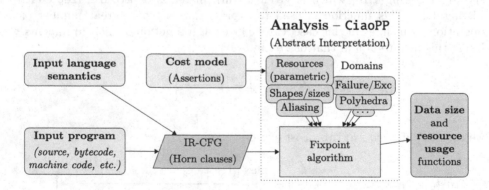

Fig. 4. Overview of analysis in the Parametric Resource Analysis approach.

---

[4] We do not include examples of default assertions due to space constraints.

```
let atomic_step_cost n =
  { allocations = Z.zero;
    steps = Z.of_int (2 * n);
    reads = Z.zero;
    writes = Z.zero;
    bytes_read = Z.zero;
    bytes_written = Z.zero; }
```

Listing 1.11. atomic_step_cost definition.

```
:- trust pred add_intint(A,B,C)
   => ( int(A), int(B), int(C),
        size(ub,C,int(A)+int(B)),
        size(lb,C,int(A)+int(B)) )
   + ( not_fails, covered, is_det, cardinality(1,1),
cost(lb,michelson_steps,102+(1+log2(max(int(A),int(B)))/8)/31),
cost(ub,michelson_steps,102+(1+log2(max(int(A),int(B)))/8)/31)).
```

Listing 1.12. Cost assertion for add_intint in the cost model.

5   Performing the Resource Analysis

As already mentioned in Sect. 2, the input to the the parametric resource analyzer is the program in CHC IR form and the resource model (Fig. 1). The core
analyzer is based on an approach in which recursive equations (cost relations),
representing the resource consumption of the program, are extracted from the
program and solved, obtaining upper- and lower-bound cost functions in terms
of the program's inputs [2,15,16,59,62]. As mentioned before, these functions
can be polynomial, exponential or logarithmic, etc., and they express the cost
for each Horn clause (block) in the CHC IR, which can then be reflected back to
the input language. Space restrictions prevent us from describing the process in
detail; we provide an overview of the tasks performed by the analyzer (Fig. 4):

1. Perform all the required **supporting analyses**. This includes typically,
   among others: a) *sized types/shapes* analysis for inferring size metrics (for
   heap manipulating programs), to simplify the control-flow graph, and to
   improve overall precision (e.g., class hierarchy analysis); b) pointer *shar-
   ing/aliasing* analysis for correctness and precision; c) *Non-failure* (no exceptions) analysis, needed for inferring non-trivial lower bounds; d) *Determinacy*
   and *mutual exclusion* analyses to obtain tighter bounds; e) other instrumental
   analyses such as, e.g., *polyhedra* for handling constraints.
2. **Size analysis**: a) Set up recurrence equations representing the size of each
   (relevant) output argument as a function of input data sizes, based on data
   dependency graphs that determine the relative sizes of variable contents at
   different program points. The size metrics are derived from the inferred shape
   (type) information. Then, b) compute bounds to the solutions of these recurrence equations to obtain output argument sizes as functions of input sizes.
   We use a hierarchical recurrence solver that classifies the equations and dis-
   patches them to an internal solver or interfaces with existing tools like Mathe-

```
:- pred code/4 : list(int) * list(int) * var * var.

code(A,B,[],C) :-
    '$car',
    nil([]),
    '$swap',
    iter__0(A,[],C),
    nil([]),
    '$pair'.

iter__0([],A,A) :-
    '$iter_end'.
iter__0([A|B],C,D) :-
    '$iter',
    cons(A,C,[A|C]),
    iter__0(B,[A|C],D).
```

Listing 1.13. CHC IR representation of contract 1.1.

```
:- true pred code(A,B,C,D)
   : ( list(int,A), list(int,B), var(C), var(D) )
   => ( list(int,A), list(int,B), list(C), list(D),
        size(lb,A,length(A)), size(lb,B,length(B)),
        size(lb,C,0), size(lb,D,0) )
   + ( cost(lb,michelson_gas,0.6875*length(A)+1.21875),
       cost(lb,michelson_steps,80*length(A)+140) ).

:- true pred code(A,B,C,D)
   : ( list(int,A), list(int,B), var(C), var(D) )
   => ( list(int,A), list(int,B), list(C), list(D),
        size(ub,A,length(A)), size(ub,B,length(B)),
        size(ub,C,inf), size(ub,D,inf) )
   + ( cost(ub,michelson_gas,0.6875*length(A)+1.21875),
       cost(ub,michelson_steps,80*length(A)+140) ).
```

Listing 1.14. Analysis output for contract 1.1.

matica, PURRS, PUBS, Matlab, etc., and also combine with techniques such as ranking functions.

3. **Resource analysis**: Use the size information to set up recurrence equations representing the resource consumptions of each version of each predicate (block), and again compute bounds to their solutions, as above, to obtain the output resource usage bound functions.

In the CiaoPP implementation all of these analysis tasks are performed by the PLAI abstract interpretation framework [30,49] of CiaoPP, using different *abstract domains* (Fig. 4). The generic resource analysis is also fully based on abstract interpretation [12] and defined as a PLAI-style abstract domain of piecewise functions and equations [59]. This brings in features such as *multivariance*, efficient fixpoints, assertion-based verification and user interaction, etc.

Michelson Contract Analysis Example. As an example of the analysis process, we analyze the contract of Listing 1.1. In the CHC IR representation of the contract in Listing 1.13, we can observe how the translation has generated a predicate with two clauses that emulates the semantics of the ITER instruction: it takes the list over which to iterate as a parameter and performs the CONS action specified by the body of the ITER instruction. In both clauses the translation tool includes a cost marker to measure the cost of each iteration step, and of leaving the loop. The output from CiaoPP, after performing analyses for shapes/measures, sharing, non-failure, sizes, and resources is shown in Listing 1.14. The cost in *gas* of this contract is inferred to be linear w.r.t. the length of the input list.

6   Some Experimental Results

We have constructed a prototype which transforms Michelson contracts to CHC IR, as well as the cost model that provides CiaoPP with the required information on the Michelson instructions. This cost model contains 97 cost assertions, covering a large percentage of Michelson instructions, and is easy to extend, as shown in Sect. 4.

Regarding the translator, it is 700 lines long, of which 190 correspond to instruction definitions, transliterated from the specification, and 175 to instruction metadata. The whole system was developed in about two months. In our prototype and experiments we have concentrated on the gas cost of *executing* a contract. However, we believe that the framework can be instantiated to other costs such as *type checking* or *storage size*, using the *sized types*-based analyses in the system [58,59].

We have tested this prototype on a wide range of contracts, a few self-made and most of them published, both in Michelson's "*A contract a day*" examples and the Tezos blockchain itself. Results for a selection are listed in Table 1. In this selection, we have tried to cover a reasonable range of Michelson data structures and control-flow instructions, as well as different cost functions using different metrics.[5] Column **Contract** lists the contracts, and **Metrics** shows the metrics used to measure the parameter and the storage. The metrics used are: *value* for the numeric value of an integer, *length* for the length of a list, and *size* which maps every ground term to the number of constants and functions appearing in it. Column **Resource A**(nalysis) shows for brevity just the order of the resource usage function inferred by the analysis in terms of the sizes of the parameter (α) and the storage (β) or k if the inferred function is constant. However, the actual expressions inferred also include the constants. For complex metrics, sub-indices starting from *1* are used to refer to the size of each argument; e.g., α_2 refers to the size of the second argument of the parameter. Finally, **Time** shows the time taken to perform all the analyses using the different abstract domains provided by CiaoPP, version 1.19 on a medium-loaded 2.3 GHz Dual-Core Intel Core i5, 16 GB of memory, running macOS Catalina 10.15.6. Many optimizations and improvements are possible, as well as more comprehensive benchmarking, but we believe that the results shown suggest that relevant bounds can be obtained in reasonable times, which, given the relative simplicity of development of the tool, seem to support our expectations regarding the advantages of the approach.

---

[5] The benchmarks themselves are briefly explained in Table 2 in the Appendix.

Table 1. Results of analysis for selected Michelson contracts.

Contract	Metrics		Resource A.	Time
	Parameter (α)	Storage (β)	*gas*	(ms)
reverse	*length*	*length*	α	216
addition	*value*	*value*	$\log \alpha$	147
michelson_arith	*value*	*value*	$\log (\alpha^2 + 2 * \beta)$	208
bytes	*value*	*length*	β	229
list_inc	*value*	*length*	β	273
lambda	*value*	*value*	$\log \alpha$	99
lambda_apply	(*value, size*)	*size*	k	114
inline	*size*	*value*	$\log \beta$	870
cross_product	(*length, length*)	*value*	$\alpha_1 + \alpha_2$	424
lineal	*value*	*value*	α	244
assertion_map	(*value, size*)	*length*	$\log \beta * \log \alpha_1$	393
quadratic	*length*	*length*	$\alpha * \beta$	520
queue	*size*	(*value, size, length*)	$\log \beta_1 * \log \beta_3$	831
king_of_tez	*size*	(*value, value, size*)	k	635
set_management	*length*	*length*	$\alpha * \log \beta$	357
lock	*size*	(*value, value, size*)	k	421
max_list	*length*	*size*	α	473
zipper	*length*	(*length, length, length*)	k	989
auction	*size*	(*value, value, size*)	k	573
union	(*length, length*)	*length*	$\alpha_1 * \log \alpha_2$	486
append	(*length, length*)	*length*	α_1	371
subset	(*length, length*)	*size*	$\alpha_1 * \log \alpha_2$	389

7 Related Work

As mentioned in the introduction, the tools that have been proposed to date for resource analysis of smart contracts are platform- and language-specific. GASPER [10] and MadMax [22] are both aimed at identifying parts of contracts that have high gas consumption in order to optimize them or to avoid gas-related vulnerabilities. GASPER is based on recognizing control-flow patterns using symbolic computation while MadMax searches for both control- and data-flow patterns. Marescotti et al. [44] also use a limited-depth path exploration approach to estimate worst-case gas consumption. These tools are useful programmer aids for finding bugs, but cannot provide safe cost bounds. GASPER and MadMax are specific to contracts written for the Ethereum platform [63], in Solidity, and translated to Ethereum Virtual Machine (EVM) bytecode. The Solidity compiler can generate gas bounds, but these bounds can only be constant, i.e., they cannot depend on any input parameters, or if they do the bound generated is infinite. This tool is of course also specific to the Ethereum platform.

Closer to our work are GASTAP [5] and its extension GASOL [4]. These tools infer upper bounds for gas consumption, using similar theoretical underpinnings as those used by CiaoPP, i.e., recurrence relation solving, combined with ranking functions, etc. GASOL is a more evolved version of GASTAP that includes optimization and allows users to choose between a number of predefined configuration options, such as counting particular types of instructions or storage. These are powerful tools that have been proven effective at inferring accurate gas bounds with reasonable analysis times, in a good percentage of cases. However, they are also specific to Ethereum Solidity contracts and EVM.

Parametric Resource Analysis (also referred to as user-defined resource analysis) was proposed in [52] and developed further in [51,59]. The approach builds on Wegbreit's seminal work [62] and the first full analyzers for upper bounds, in the context of task granularity control in automatic program parallelization [14,15]. This in turn evolved to cover other types of approximations (e.g., lower bounds [16]), and to the idea of supporting resources defined at the user level [51,52]. This analysis was extended to be fully based on abstract interpretation [12] and integrated into the PLAI multi-variant framework, leading to context-sensitive resource analyses [59]. Other extensions include static profiling [43], static bounding of run-time checking overhead [38], or analysis of parallel programs [37]. Other applications include the previously mentioned analyses of platform-dependent properties such as time or energy [39–42,47,50,51].

Resource analysis has received considerable additional attention lately [3, 7, 8, 11, 19, 23, 24, 26, 31, 31–33, 36, 45, 48, 53, 57, 61]. While these approaches are not based on the same idea of user-level parametricity that is instrumental in the approach proposed herein, we believe the parametric approach is also relevant for these analyses.

8 Conclusions and Future Work

We have explored the application of a generic approach and tool for resource consumption analysis to the problem of static inference of gas consumption bounds in smart contracts. The objective has been to provide a quick development path for cost analyses for new smart contract platforms and languages, or easily adapting existing ones to changes. To this end, we have used the techniques of Parametric Resource Analysis and translation to Horn clause-based intermediate representations, using the Ciao/CiaoPP system as tool and the Tezos platform and its Michelson language as test cases. The Horn clause translator together with the cost model and Ciao/CiaoPP constitute a gas consumption analyzer for Tezos smart contracts. We also applied this tool to a series of smart contracts obtaining relevant bounds with reasonable processing times. We believe our experience and results are supportive of our hypothesis that this general approach allows rapid, flexible, and effective development of cost analyses for smart contracts, which can be specially useful in the rapidly changing environment in blockchain technologies, where new languages arise frequently and cost models are modified with each platform iteration. In fact, while preparing the final version of this paper, a new protocol, *Delphi*, was released and we were able to update the cost model in less than a day by modifying just the cost assertions. As a final remark, we would also like to point out that the approach and tools that we have used bring in much additional functionality beyond that discussed herein, which is inherited from the `Ciao`/`CiaoPP` framework used, such as resource usage certification, static debugging of resource consumption, static profiling, or abstraction-carrying code.

A   Brief Description of Selected Michelson Contracts

Table 2. Overview of the selected Michelson contracts.

Contract	Overview
`reverse`	Reverses the input list and stores the result
`addition`	Performs a simple Michelson addition
`michelson_arith`	Calculates the function: $f(x, y) = x^2 + 2 * y + 1$
`bytes`	Slices the bytes storage according to the provided parameter
`list_inc`	Increments list of numbers in the storage by the provided parameter
`lambda`	Runs a lambda function passing the parameter as argument
`lambda_apply`	Specializes the provided lambda function and creates a Michelson operation
`inline`	Runs a lambda function several times passing different arguments
`cross_product`	Performs the cross product of the lists passed as parameters
`linear`	Loops over a number
`assertion_map`	Performs a series of operations on a Michelson map
`quadratic`	Loops over the parameter and storage lists
`queue`	Implements a queue in which calls can push or pop elements
`king_of_tez`	Stores the identity of the highest bidder
`set_management`	Iterates the input list from left to right and removes from the storage set those elements already in it and inserts those which are not present yet
`lock`	Implements a lock on a contract
`max_list`	Obtains the largest number in a list
`zipper`	Implements a zipper data structure
`auction`	Implements a distributed auction with a time limit
`union`	Calculates the union of two sets
`append`	Appends two input lists
`subset`	States whether an input set is a subset of the other

References

1. The Michelson Language Site. https://www.michelson-lang.com
2. Albert, E., Arenas, P., Genaim, S., Puebla, G.: Closed-form upper bounds in static cost analysis. J. Autom. Reason. **46**(2), 161–203 (2011)
3. Albert, E., Genaim, S., Masud, A.N.: More precise yet widely applicable cost analysis. In: Jhala, R., Schmidt, D. (eds.) VMCAI 2011. LNCS, vol. 6538, pp. 38–53. Springer, Heidelberg (2011). https://doi.org/10.1007/978-3-642-18275-4_5
4. Albert, E., Correas, J., Gordillo, P., Román-Díez, G., Rubio, A.: GASOL: gas analysis and optimization for ethereum smart contracts. In: Tools and Algorithms for the Construction and Analysis of Systems, TACAS 2020. LNCS, vol. 12079, pp. 118–125. Springer, Heidelberg (2020). https://doi.org/10.1007/978-3-030-45237-7_7
5. Albert, E., Gordillo, P., Rubio, A., Sergey, I.: Running on fumes - preventing out-of-gas vulnerabilities in ethereum smart contracts using static resource analysis. In: VECoS 2019. LNCS, vol. 11847, pp. 63–78. Springer, October 2019. DOI: https://doi.org/10.1007/978-3-030-35092-5_5
6. Allombert, V., Bourgoin, M., Tesson, J.: Introduction to the tezos blockchain. CoRR abs/1909.08458 (2019). http://arxiv.org/abs/1909.08458
7. Avanzini, M., Lago, U.D.: Automating sized-type inference for complexity analysis. Proc. ACM Program. Lang. **1**(ICFP), 43:1–43:29 (2017). https://doi.org/10.1145/3110287
8. Blazy, S., Pichardie, D., Trieu, A.: Verifying constant-time implementations by abstract interpretation. In: European Symposium on Research in Computer Security - ESORICS 2017. Lecture Notes in Computer Science, vol. 10492, pp. 260–277. Springer, September 2017. https://doi.org/10.1007/978-3-319-66402-6_16
9. Bueno, F., Cabeza, D., Carro, M., Hermenegildo, M.V., Lopez-Garcia, P., Puebla-(Eds.), G.: The Ciao System. Ref. Manual (v1.13). Tech. rep., School of Computer Science, T.U. of Madrid (UPM) (2009). http://ciao-lang.org
10. Chen, T., Li, X., Luo, X., Zhang, X.: Under-optimized smart contracts devour your money. In: IEEE 24th International Conference on Software Analysis, Evolution and Reengineering, SANER 2017. pp. 442–446. IEEE Computer Society, February 2017 https://doi.org/10.1109/SANER.2017.7884650
11. Çiçek, E., Barthe, G., Gaboardi, M., Garg, D., Hoffmann, J.: Relational cost analysis. In: Castagna, G., Gordon, A.D. (eds.) Principles of Programming Languages, POPL 2017, pp. 316–329. ACM (2017). http://dl.acm.org/citation.cfm?id=3009858
12. Cousot, P., Cousot, R.: Abstract interpretation: a unified lattice model for static analysis of programs by construction or approximation of fixpoints. In: ACM Symposium on Principles of Programming Languages (POPL 1977), pp. 238–252. ACM Press (1977)
13. De Angelis, E., Fioravanti, F., Pettorossi, A., Proietti, M.: Semantics-based generation of verification conditions by program specialization. In: 17th International Symposium on Principles and Practice of Declarative Programming, pp. 91–102. ACM (July 2015). https://doi.org/10.1145/2790449.2790529
14. Debray, S.K., Lin, N.W.: Cost analysis of logic programs. ACM Trans. Program. Lang. Syst. **15**(5), 826–875 (1993)
15. Debray, S.K., Lin, N.W., Hermenegildo, M.V.: Task granularity analysis in logic programs. In: Proceedings 1990 ACM Conference on Programming Language Design and Implementation (PLDI), pp. 174–188. ACM Press (June 1990)

16. Debray, S.K., Lopez-Garcia, P., Hermenegildo, M.V., Lin, N.W.: Lower bound cost estimation for logic programs. In: 1997 International Logic Programming Symposium, pp. 291–305. MIT Press, Cambridge, MA (October 1997)
17. Futamura, Y.: Partial evaluation of computation process - an approach to a compiler-compiler. Systems, Computers, Controls **2**(5), 45–50 (1971)
18. Gallagher, J., Hermenegildo, M.V., Kafle, B., Klemen, M., Lopez-Garcia, P., Morales, J.: From big-step to small-step semantics and back with interpreter specialization (invited paper). In: International WS on Verification and Program Transformation (VPT 2020). pp. 50–65. EPTCS, Open Publishing Association (2020). http://eptcs.web.cse.unsw.edu.au/paper.cgi?VPTHCVS2020.4
19. Giesl, J., Ströder, T., Schneider-Kamp, P., Emmes, F., Fuhs, C.: Symbolic evaluation graphs and term rewriting: a general methodology for analyzing logic programs. In: Proceedings of PPDP 2012, pp. 1–12. ACM (2012)
20. Gómez-Zamalloa, M., Albert, E., Puebla, G.: Decompilation of java bytecode to prolog by partial evaluation. JIST **51**, 1409–1427 (2009)
21. Grebenshchikov, S., Lopes, N.P., Popeea, C., Rybalchenko, A.: Synthesizing software verifiers from proof rules. In: Vitek, J., Lin, H., Tip, F. (eds.) ACM SIGPLAN Conference on Programming Language Design and Implementation, PLDI 2012, pp. 405–416. ACM (2012). https://doi.org/10.1145/2254064.2254112
22. Grech, N., Kong, M., Jurisevic, A., Brent, L., Scholz, B., Smaragdakis, Y.: MadMax: surviving out-of-gas conditions in ethereum smart contracts. PACMPL **2**(OOPSLA), 116:1–116:27 (2018). https://doi.org/10.1145/3276486
23. Grobauer, B.: Cost recurrences for DML programs. In: Proceedings of ICFP 2001, pp. 253–264. ACM, New York (2001). https://doi.org/10.1145/507635.507666, http://doi.acm.org/10.1145/507635.507666
24. Gulwani, S., Mehra, K.K., Chilimbi, T.M.: SPEED: precise and efficient static estimation of program computational complexity. In: The 36th Symposium on Principles of Programming Languages (POPL 2009), pp. 127–139. ACM (2009)
25. Gurfinkel, A., Kahsai, T., Komuravelli, A., Navas, J.A.: The seahorn verification framework. In: International Conference on Computer Aided Verification, CAV 2015, pp. 343–361. No. 9206 in LNCS, Springer (July 2015)
26. Handley, M.A.T., Vazou, N., Hutton, G.: Liquidate your assets: reasoning about resource usage in liquid haskell. Proc. ACM Program. Lang. **4**(POPL), 24:1–24:27 (2020). https://doi.org/10.1145/3371092
27. Henriksen, K.S., Gallagher, J.P.: Abstract interpretation of pic programs through logic programming. In: SCAM 2006. pp. 184–196. IEEE Computer Society (2006)
28. Hermenegildo, M.V., et al.: An overview of Ciao and its design philosophy. TPLP **12**(1–2), 219–252 (2012). http://arxiv.org/abs/1102.5497
29. Hermenegildo, M.V., Puebla, G., Bueno, F., Lopez-Garcia, P.: Integrated program debugging, verification, and optimization using abstract interpretation (and the Ciao system preprocessor). Sci. Comput. Program. **58**(1–2), 115–140 (2005). https://doi.org/10.1016/j.scico.2005.02.006
30. Hermenegildo, M.V., Puebla, G., Marriott, K., Stuckey, P.: Incremental analysis of constraint logic programs. ACM TOPLAS **22**(2), 187–223 (2000)
31. Hoffmann, J., Aehlig, K., Hofmann, M.: Multivariate amortized resource analysis. ACM TOPLAS **34**(3), 14:1–14:62 (2012)
32. Hofmann, M., Moser, G.: Multivariate amortised resource analysis for term rewrite systems. In: Altenkirch, T. (ed.) 13th International Conference on Typed Lambda Calculi and Applications. LIPIcs, vol. 38, pp. 241–256. Schloss Dagstuhl - Leibniz-Zentrum für Informatik (July 2015). https://doi.org/10.4230/LIPIcs.TLCA.2015.241

33. Igarashi, A., Kobayashi, N.: Resource usage analysis. In: Symposium on Principles of Programming Languages, pp. 331–342. ACM (2002). http://www.citeseer.ist. psu.edu/igarashi02resource.html

34. Kahn, G.: Natural semantics. Lecture Notes in Computer Science, vol. 247, pp. 22–39. Springer, Cham, February 1987. https://doi.org/10.1007/BFb0039592

35. Kahsai, T., Rümmer, P., Sanchez, H., Schäf, M.: JayHorn: a framework for verifying Java programs. In: Chaudhuri, S., Farzan, A. (eds.) Computer Aided Verification - 28th International Conference, CAV 2016. LNCS, vol. 9779, pp. 352–358. Springer, Cham, July 2016. https://doi.org/10.1007/978-3-319-41528-4_19

36. Kincaid, Z., Breck, J., Cyphert, J., Reps, T.W.: Closed forms for numerical loops. Proc. ACM Program. Lang. 3(POPL), 55:1–55:29 (2019). https://doi.org/10.1145/3290368

37. Klemen, M., Lopez-Garcia, P., Gallagher, J., Morales, J., Hermenegildo, M.V.: A general framework for static cost analysis of parallel logic programs. In: International Symposium on Logic-based Program Synthesis and Transformation (LOPSTR'19). LNCS, vol. 12042, pp. 19–35. Springer, Heidelberg, April 2020. https://doi.org/10.1007/978-3-030-45260-5_2

38. Klemen, M., Stulova, N., Lopez-Garcia, P., Morales, J.F., Hermenegildo, M.V.: Static performance guarantees for programs with run-time checks. In: International Symposium on Principles and Practice of Declarative Programming (PPDP 2018). ACM, September 2018. https://doi.org/10.1145/3236950.3236970

39. Liqat, U., Banković, Z., Lopez-Garcia, P., Hermenegildo, M.V.: Inferring energy bounds via static program analysis and evolutionary modeling of basic blocks. In: Logic-Based Program Synthesis and Transformation - 27th International Symposium. LNCS, vol. 10855. Springer (2018)

40. Liqat, U., et al.: Inferring parametric energy consumption functions at different software levels: ISA vs. LLVM IR. In: Proceedings of FOPARA. LNCS, vol. 9964, pp. 81–100. Springer, Heidelberg (2016). https://doi.org/10.1007/978-3-319-46559-3_5

41. Liqat, U., et al.: Energy consumption analysis of programs based on XMOS ISA-level models. In: Proceedings of LOPSTR 2013. LNCS, vol. 8901, pp. 72–90. Springer, New York (2014). https://doi.org/10.1007/978-3-319-14125-1_5

42. Lopez-Garcia, P., Darmawan, L., Klemen, M., Liqat, U., Bueno, F., Hermenegildo, M.V.: Interval-based Resource Usage Verification by Translation into Horn Clauses and an Application to Energy Consumption. Theory and Practice of Logic Programming, Special Issue on Computational Logic for Verification 18(2), 167–223 (March 2018), https://arxiv.org/abs/1803.04451

43. Lopez-Garcia, P., Klemen, M., Liqat, U., Hermenegildo, M.V.: A general framework for static profiling of parametric resource usage. TPLP (ICLP 2016 Special Issue) 16(5–6), 849–865 (2016). https://doi.org/10.1017/S1471068416000442

44. Marescotti, M., Blicha, M., Hyvärinen, A.E.J., Asadi, S., Sharygina, N.: Computing exact worst-case gas consumption for smart contracts. In: Leveraging Applications of Formal Methods, Verification and Validation (ISoLA 2018). LNCS, vol. 11247, pp. 450–465. Springer, Cham, November 2018. https://doi.org/10.1007/978-3-030-03427-6_33

45. Maroneze, A.O., Blazy, S., Pichardie, D., Puaut, I.: A formally verified WCET estimation tool. In: Workshop on Worst-Case Execution Time Analysis - WCET 2014. OASICS, vol. 39, pp. 11–20. Schloss Dagstuhl (2014). https://doi.org/10.4230/OASIcs.WCET.2014.11

46. Méndez-Lojo, M., Navas, J., Hermenegildo, M.: A flexible (C)LP-based approach to the analysis of object-oriented programs. In: LOPSTR. LNCS, vol. 4915, pp. 154–168. Springer, Heidelberg, August 2007. https://doi.org/10.1007/978-3-540-78769-3_11
47. Mera, E., Lopez-Garcia, P., Carro, M., Hermenegildo, M.V.: Towards execution time estimation in abstract machine-based languages. In: PPDP 2008, pp. 174–184. ACM Press, July 2008. https://doi.org/10.1145/1389449.1389471
48. Moser, G., Schneckenreither, M.: Automated amortised resource analysis for term rewrite systems. Sci. Comput. Program. **185** (2020). https://doi.org/10.1016/j.scico.2019.102306
49. Muthukumar, K., Hermenegildo, M.: Compile-time derivation of variable dependency using abstract interpretation. J. Logic Program. **13**(2/3), 315–347 (1992)
50. Navas, J., Méndez-Lojo, M., Hermenegildo, M.: Safe upper-bounds inference of energy consumption for java bytecode applications. In: The Sixth NASA Langley Formal Methods Workshop (LFM 2008). pp. 29–32, April 2008. Extended Abstract
51. Navas, J., Méndez-Lojo, M., Hermenegildo, M.V.: User-definable resource usage bounds analysis for java bytecode. In: BYTECODE 2009. ENTCS, vol. 253, pp. 6–86. Elsevier, March 2009. http://www.cliplab.org/papers/resources-bytecode09.pdf
52. Navas, J., Mera, E., Lopez-Garcia, P., Hermenegildo, M.: User-definable resource bounds analysis for logic programs. In: Proceedings of ICLP 2007. LNCS, vol. 4670, pp. 348–363. Springer, New York (2007). https://doi.org/10.1007/978-3-540-74610-2_24
53. Nielson, F., Nielson, H.R., Seidl, H.: Automatic complexity analysis. In: Le Métayer, D. (ed.) ESOP 2002. LNCS, vol. 2305, pp. 243–261. Springer, Heidelberg (2002). https://doi.org/10.1007/3-540-45927-8_18
54. Peralta, J., Gallagher, J., Sağlam, H.: Analysis of imperative programs through analysis of constraint logic programs. In: Levi, G. (ed.) Static Analysis. 5th International Symposium, SAS 1998, Pisa. LNCS, vol. 1503, pp. 246–261 (1998)
55. Plotkin, G.: A structural approach to operational semantics. Technical report DAIMI FN-19, Computer Science Department, Aarhus University, Denmark (1981)
56. Puebla, G., Bueno, F., Hermenegildo, M.V.: An assertion language for constraint logic programs. In: Analysis and Visualization Tools for Constraint Programming, pp. 23–61. No. 1870 in LNCS, Springer, New York (2000)
57. Qu, W., Gaboardi, M., Garg, D.: Relational cost analysis for functional-imperative programs. Proc. ACM Program. Lang. **3**(ICFP), 92:1–92:29 (2019). https://doi.org/10.1145/3341696
58. Serrano, A., Lopez-Garcia, P., Bueno, F., Hermenegildo, M.V.: Sized type analysis for logic programs (technical communication). In: Swift, T., Lamma, E. (eds.) Theory and Practice of Logic Programming, 29th International Conference on Logic Programming (ICLP 2013) Special Issue, On-line Supplement, vol. 13, pp. 1–14. Cambridge University Press, August 2013
59. Serrano, A., Lopez-Garcia, P., Hermenegildo, M.V.: Resource usage analysis of logic programs via abstract interpretation using sized types. TPLP, ICLP 2014 Special Issue **14**(4–5), 739–754 (2014). https://doi.org/10.1017/S147106841400057X
60. Szabo, N.: Formalizing and securing relationships on public networks. First Monday **2**(9) (1997). https://doi.org/10.5210/fm.v2i9.548
61. Vasconcelos, P.B., Hammond, K.: Inferring cost equations for recursive, polymorphic and higher-order functional programs. In: Trinder, P., Michaelson, G.J., Peña, R. (eds.) IFL 2003. LNCS, vol. 3145, pp. 86–101. Springer, Heidelberg (2004). https://doi.org/10.1007/978-3-540-27861-0_6

62. Wegbreit, B.: Mechanical program analysis. Commun. ACM **18**(9), 528–539 (1975)
63. Wood, G.: Ethereum: A secure decentralised generalised transaction ledger (2016). https://gavwood.com/paper.pdf

Regular Papers

Memory-Efficient Fixpoint Computation

Sung Kook Kim[1]([✉]) [iD], Arnaud J. Venet[2], and Aditya V. Thakur[1] [iD]

[1] University of California, Davis, CA 95616, USA
{sklkim,avthakur}@ucdavis.edu
[2] Facebook, Inc., Menlo Park, CA 94025, USA
ajv@fb.com

Abstract. Practical adoption of static analysis often requires trading precision for performance. This paper focuses on improving the memory efficiency of abstract interpretation without sacrificing precision or time efficiency. Computationally, abstract interpretation reduces the problem of inferring program invariants to computing a fixpoint of a set of equations. This paper presents a method to minimize the memory footprint in Bourdoncle's iteration strategy, a widely-used technique for fixpoint computation. Our technique is agnostic to the abstract domain used. We prove that our technique is optimal (i.e., it results in minimum memory footprint) for Bourdoncle's iteration strategy while computing the same result. We evaluate the efficacy of our technique by implementing it in a tool called MIKOS, which extends the state-of-the-art abstract interpreter IKOS. When verifying user-provided assertions, MIKOS shows a decrease in peak-memory usage to 4.07% (24.57×) on average compared to IKOS. When performing interprocedural buffer-overflow analysis, MIKOS shows a decrease in peak-memory usage to 43.7% (2.29×) on average compared to IKOS.

1 Introduction

Abstract interpretation [14] is a general framework for expressing static analysis of programs. Program invariants inferred by an abstract interpreter are used in client applications such as program verifiers, program optimizers, and bug finders. To extract the invariants, an abstract interpreter computes a fixpoint of an equation system approximating the program semantics. The efficiency and precision of the abstract interpreter depends on the *iteration strategy*, which specifies the order in which the equations are applied during fixpoint computation.

The *recursive iteration strategy* developed by Bourdoncle [10] is widely used for fixpoint computation in academic and industrial abstract interpreters such as NASA IKOS [11], Crab [32], Facebook SPARTA [16], Kestrel Technology CodeHawk [48], and Facebook Infer [12]. Extensions to Bourdoncle's approach that improve precision [1] and time efficiency [26] have also been proposed.

This paper focuses on improving the memory efficiency of abstract interpretation. This is an important problem in practice because large memory requirements can prevent clients such as compilers and developer tools from using

© Springer Nature Switzerland AG 2020
D. Pichardie and M. Sighireanu (Eds.): SAS 2020, LNCS 12389, pp. 35–64, 2020.
https://doi.org/10.1007/978-3-030-65474-0_3

sophisticated analyses. This has motivated approaches for efficient implementations of abstract domains [4, 25, 44], including techniques that trade precision for efficiency [5, 17, 24].

This paper presents a technique for memory-efficient fixpoint computation. Our technique minimizes the memory footprint in Bourdoncle's recursive iteration strategy. Our approach is agnostic to the abstract domain and does not sacrifice time efficiency. We prove that our technique exhibits optimal peak-memory usage for the recursive iteration strategy while computing the same fixpoint (Sect. 3). Specifically, our approach does not change the iteration order but provides a mechanism for early deallocation of abstract values. Thus, there is no loss of precision when improving memory performance. Furthermore, such "backward compatibility" ensures that existing implementations of Bourdoncle's approach can be replaced without impacting clients of the abstract interpreter, an important requirement in practice.

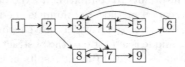

Fig. 1. Control-flow graph G_1

Suppose we are tasked with proving assertions at program points 4 and 9 of the control-flow graph $G_1(V, \rightarrow)$ in Fig. 1. Current approaches (Sect. 2.1) allocate abstract values for each program point during fixpoint computation, check the assertions at 4 and 9 after fixpoint computation, and then deallocate all abstract values. In contrast, our approach deallocates abstract values and checks the assertions during fixpoint computation while guaranteeing that the results of the checks remain the same and that the peak-memory usage is optimal.

We prove that our approach deallocates abstract values as soon as they are no longer needed during fixpoint computation. Providing this theoretical guarantee is challenging for arbitrary irreducible graphs such as G_1. For example, assuming that node 8 is analyzed after 3, one might think that the fixpoint iterator can deallocate the abstract value at 2 once it analyzes 8. However, 8 is part of the strongly-connected component $\{7, 8\}$, and the fixpoint iterator might need to iterate over node 8 multiple times. Thus, deallocating the abstract value at 2 when node 8 is first analyzed will lead to incorrect results. In this case, the earliest that the abstract value at 2 can be deallocated is after the stabilization of component $\{7, 8\}$.

Furthermore, we prove that our approach performs the assertion checks as early as possible during fixpoint computation. Once the assertions are checked, the associated abstract values are deallocated. For example, consider the assertion check at node 4. Notice that 4 is part of the strongly-connected components $\{4, 5\}$ and $\{3, 4, 5, 6\}$. Checking the assertion the first time node 4 is analyzed could lead to an incorrect result because the abstract value at 4 has not converged. The earliest that the check at node 4 can be executed is after the convergence of the component $\{3, 4, 5, 6\}$. Apart from being able to deallocate abstract values earlier, early assertion checks provide partial results on timeout.

The key theoretical result (Theorem 1) is that our iteration strategy is memory-optimal (i.e., it results in minimum memory footprint) while computing the same result as Bourdoncle's approach. Furthermore, we present an almost-linear time algorithm to compute this optimal iteration strategy (Sect. 4).

We have implemented this memory-optimal fixpoint computation in a tool called MIKOS (Sect. 5), which extends the state-of-the-art abstract interpreter for C/C++, IKOS [11]. We compared the memory efficiency of MIKOS and IKOS on the following tasks:

T1 Verifying user-provided assertions. Task T1 represents the program-verification client of a fixpoint computation. We performed interprocedural analysis of 784 SV-COMP 2019 benchmarks [6] using reduced product of Difference Bound Matrix with variable packing [17] and congruence [20] domains.

T2 Proving absence of buffer overflows. Task T2 represents the bug-finding and compiler-optimization client of fixpoint computation. In the context of bug finding, a potential buffer overflow can be reported to the user as a potential bug. In the context of compiler optimization, code to check buffer-access safety can be elided if the buffer access is verified to be safe. We performed interprocedural buffer overflow analysis of 426 open-source programs using the interval abstract domain.

On Task T1, MIKOS shows a decrease in peak-memory usage to 4.07% (24.57×) on average compared to IKOS. For instance, peak-memory required to analyze the SV-COMP 2019 benchmark `ldv-3.16-rc1/205_9a-net-rtl8187` decreased from 46 GB to 56 MB. Also, while `ldv-3.14/usb-mxl111sf` spaced out in IKOS with 64 GB memory limit, peak-memory usage was 21 GB for MIKOS. On Task T2, MIKOS shows a decrease in peak-memory usage to 43.7% (2.29×) on average compared to IKOS. For instance, peak-memory required to analyze a benchmark `ssh-keygen` decreased from 30 GB to 1 GB.

The contributions of the paper are as follows:

- A memory-optimal technique for Bourdoncle's recursive iteration strategy that does not sacrifice precision or time efficiency (Sect. 3).
- An almost-linear time algorithm to construct our memory-efficient iteration strategy (Sect. 4).
- MIKOS, an interprocedural implementation of our approach (Sect. 5).
- An empirical evaluation of the efficacy of MIKOS using a large set of C benchmarks (Sect. 6).

Sect. 2 presents necessary background on fixpoint computation, including Bourdoncle's approach; Sect. 7 presents related work; Sect. 8 concludes.

2 Fixpoint Computation Preliminaries

This section presents background on fixpoint computation that will allow us to clearly state the problem addressed in this paper (Sect. 2.3). This section is not meant to capture all possible approaches to implementing abstract interpretation. However, it does capture the relevant high-level structure of abstract-interpretation implementations such as IKOS [11].

Consider an equation system Φ whose dependency graph is $G(V, \rightarrow)$. The graph G typically reflects the control-flow graph of the program, though this is not always true. The aim is to find the fixpoint of the equation system Φ:

$$\text{PRE}[v] = \bigsqcup \{\text{POST}[p] \mid p \rightarrow v\} \qquad\qquad v \in V \qquad (1)$$
$$\text{POST}[v] = \tau_v(\text{PRE}[v]) \qquad\qquad v \in V$$

The maps $\text{PRE} \colon V \rightarrow \mathcal{A}$ and $\text{POST} \colon V \rightarrow \mathcal{A}$ maintain the abstract values at the beginning and end of each program point, where $\mathcal{A}$ is an abstract domain. The abstract transformer $\tau_v \colon \mathcal{A} \rightarrow \mathcal{A}$ overapproximates the semantics of program point $v \in V$. After fixpoint computation, $\text{PRE}[v]$ is an invariant for $v \in V$.

Client applications of the abstract interpreter typically query these fixpoint values to perform assertion checks, program optimizations, or report bugs. Let $V_C \subseteq V$ be the set of program points where such checks are performed, and let $\varphi_v \colon \mathcal{A} \rightarrow bool$ represent the corresponding functions that performs the check for each $v \in V_C$. To simplify presentation, we assume that the check function merely returns **true** or **false**. Thus, after fixpoint computation, the client application computes $\varphi_v(\text{PRE}[v])$ for each $v \in V_C$.

The exact least solution of the system Eq. 1 can be computed using Kleene iteration provided $\mathcal{A}$ is Noetherian. However, most interesting abstract domains require the use of *widening* (∇) to ensure termination followed by *narrowing* to improve the post solution. In this paper, we use "fixpoint" to refer to such an approximation of the least fixpoint. Furthermore, for simplicity of presentation, we restrict our description to a simple widening strategy. However, our implementation (Sect. 5) uses more sophisticated widening and narrowing strategies implemented in state-of-the-art abstract interpreters [1,11].

An *iteration strategy* specifies the order in which the individual equations are applied, where widening is used, and how convergence of the equation system is checked. For clarity of exposition, we introduce a *Fixpoint Machine (FM)* consisting of an imperative set of instructions. An FM program represents a particular iteration strategy used for fixpoint computation. The syntax of Fixpoint Machine programs is defined by the following grammar:

$$Prog ::= \textbf{exec } v \mid \textbf{repeat } v \ [Prog] \mid Prog \, \text{\textruncated} \, Prog \, , v \in V \qquad (2)$$

Informally, the instruction **exec** v applies τ_v for $v \in V$; the instruction **repeat** v [P_1] repeatedly executes the FM program P_1 until convergence and performs widening at v; and the instruction $P_1 \, \text{\textruncated} \, P_2$ executes FM programs P_1 and P_2 in sequence.

The syntax (Eq. 2) and semantics (Fig. 2) of the Fixpoint Machine are sufficient to express Bourdoncle's recursive iteration strategy (Sect. 2.1), a widely-
used approach for fixpoint computation [10]. We also extend the notion of iteration strategy to perform memory management of the abstract values as well as
perform checks during fixpoint computation (Sect. 2.2).

2.1 Bourdoncle's Recursive Iteration Strategy

In this section, we review Bourdoncle's recursive iteration strategy [10] and show
how to generate the corresponding FM program.

Bourdoncle's iteration strategy relies on the notion of *weak topological ordering (WTO)* of a directed graph $G(V, \to)$. A WTO is defined using the notion of
a *hierarchical total ordering (HTO)* of a set.

Definition 1. *A hierarchical total ordering $\mathcal{H}$ of a set S is a well parenthesized
permutation of S without two consecutive "(".* ∎

An HTO $\mathcal{H}$ is a string over the alphabet S augmented with left and right paren-
thesis. Alternatively, we can denote an HTO $\mathcal{H}$ by the tuple $(S, \preceq, \omega)$, where $\preceq$
is the total order induced by $\mathcal{H}$ over the elements of S and $\omega \colon V \to 2^V$. The
elements between two matching parentheses are called a *component*, and the first
element of a component is called the *head*. Given $l \in S$, $\omega(l)$ is the set of heads
of the components containing l. We use $\mathcal{C} \colon V \to 2^V$ to denote the mapping from
a head to its component.

Example 1. Let $V = \{1, 2, 3, 4, 5, 6, 7, 8, 9\}$. An example HTO $\mathcal{H}_1(V, \preceq, \omega)$ is
1 2 (3 (4 5) 6) (7 8) 9. $\omega(3) = \{3\}$, $\omega(5) = \{3, 4\}$, and $\omega(1) = \emptyset$. It has components $\mathcal{C}(4) = \{4, 5\}$, $\mathcal{C}(7) = \{7, 8\}$ and $\mathcal{C}(3) = \{3, 6\} \cup \mathcal{C}(4)$. ∎

A weak topological ordering (WTO) $\mathcal{W}$ of a directed graph $G(V, \to)$ is an
HTO $\mathcal{H}(V, \preceq, \omega)$ satisfying certain constraints listed below:

Definition 2. *A weak topological ordering $\mathcal{W}(V, \preceq, \omega)$ of a directed graph
$G(V, \to)$ is an HTO $\mathcal{H}(V, \preceq, \omega)$ such that for every edge $u \to v$, either (i) $u \prec v$,
or (ii) $v \preceq u$ and $v \in \omega(u)$.* ∎

Example 2. HTO $\mathcal{H}_1$ in Example 1 is a WTO $\mathcal{W}_1$ of the graph G_1 (Fig. 1). ∎

Given a directed graph $G(V, \to)$ that represents the dependency graph of the
equation system, Bourdoncle's approach uses a WTO $\mathcal{W}(V, \preceq, \omega)$ of G to derive
the following *recursive iteration strategy*:

- The total order $\preceq$ determines the order in which the equations are applied.
  The equation after a component is applied only after the component stabilizes.
- The stabilization of a component $\mathcal{C}(h)$ is determined by checking the stabi-
  lization of the head h.
- Widening is performed at each of the heads.

We now show how the WTO can be represented using the syntax of our Fixpoint Machine (FM) defined in Eq. 2. The following function genProg: WTO → *Prog* maps a given WTO $\mathcal{W}$ to an FM program:

$$\text{genProg}(\mathcal{W}) := \begin{cases} \text{repeat } v \text{ [genProg}(\mathcal{W}')] & \text{if } \mathcal{W} = (v \ \mathcal{W}') \\ \text{genProg}(\mathcal{W}_1) \, ; \, \text{genProg}(\mathcal{W}_2) & \text{if } \mathcal{W} = \mathcal{W}_1 \ \mathcal{W}_2 \qquad (3) \\ \text{exec } v & \text{if } \mathcal{W} = v \end{cases}$$

Each node $v \in V$ is mapped to a single FM instruction by genProg; we use Inst[v] to refer to this FM instruction corresponding to v. Note that if $v \in V$ is a head, then Inst[v] is an instruction of the form repeat v [...], else Inst[v] is exec v.

Example 3. The WTO $\mathcal{W}_1$ of graph G_1 (Fig. 1) is 1 2 (3 (4 5) 6) (7 8) 9. The corresponding FM program is P_1 = genProg($\mathcal{W}_1$) = exec 1 ; exec 2 ; repeat 3 [repeat 4 [exec 5] ; exec 6] ; repeat 7 [exec 8] ; exec 9. The colors used for brackets and parentheses are to more clearly indicate the correspondence between the WTO and the FM program. Note that Inst[1] = exec 1, and Inst[4] = repeat 4 [exec 5].   ∎

Ignoring the text in gray, the semantics of the FM instructions shown in Fig. 2 capture Bourdoncle's recursive iteration strategy. The semantics are parameterized by the graph $G(V, \rightarrow)$ and a WTO $\mathcal{W}(V, \preceq, \omega)$.

2.2   Memory Management During Fixpoint Computation

In this paper, we extend the notion of iteration strategy to indicate when abstract values are deallocated and when checks are executed. The gray text in Fig. 2 shows the semantics of the FM instructions that handle these issues. The right-hand side of ⇒ is executed if the left-hand side evaluates to true. Recall that the set $V_C \subseteq V$ is the set of program points that have assertion checks. The map CK: $V_C \rightarrow$ bool records the result of executing the check $\varphi_u(\text{PRE}[u])$ for each $u \in V_C$. Thus, the *output of the FM program* is the map CK. In practice, the functions φ_u are expensive to compute. Furthermore, they often write the result to a database or report the output to a user. Consequently, we assume that only the first execution of φ_u is recorded in CK.

The *memory configuration* $\mathcal{M}$ is a tuple (DPOST, ACHK, DPOST$^\ell$, DPRE$^\ell$) where

- The map DPOST: $V \rightarrow V$ controls the deallocation of values in POST that have no further use. If $v = \text{DPOST}[u]$, POST[u] is deallocated after the execution of Inst[v].
- The map ACHK: $V_C \rightarrow V$ controls when the check function φ_u corresponding to $u \in V_C$ is executed, after which the corresponding PRE value is deallocated. If ACHK[u] = v, assertions in u are checked and PRE[u] is subsequently deallocated after the execution of Inst[v].

$G(V, \to)$, WTO $\mathcal{W}(V, \preceq, \omega)$,

$V_C \subseteq V$,   memory configuration $\mathcal{M}(\mathrm{DPOST}, \mathrm{ACHK}, \mathrm{DPOST}^\ell, \mathrm{DPRE}^\ell)$

$[\![\mathbf{exec}\ v]\!]_{\mathcal{M}} \stackrel{\mathrm{def}}{=} \mathrm{PRE}[v] \leftarrow \bigsqcup \{\mathrm{POST}[p] \mid p \to v\}$

> **foreach** $u \in V : v = \mathrm{DPOST}[u] \Rightarrow$ **free** $\mathrm{POST}[u]$
> $\mathrm{POST}[v] \leftarrow \tau_v(\mathrm{PRE}[v])$
>
> $v \notin V_C \Rightarrow$ **free** $\mathrm{PRE}[v]$
> **foreach** $u \in V_C : v = \mathrm{ACHK}[u] \Rightarrow \mathrm{CK}[u] \leftarrow \varphi_u(\mathrm{PRE}[u]);$
> $\qquad\qquad\qquad\qquad\qquad\qquad\qquad\qquad$ **free** $\mathrm{PRE}[u]$

$[\![\mathbf{repeat}\ v\ [P]]\!]_{\mathcal{M}} \stackrel{\mathrm{def}}{=} tpre \leftarrow \bigsqcup \{\mathrm{POST}[p] \mid p \to v \wedge v \notin \omega(p)\}$ $\}$ Preamble

> **do** {
>
> > **foreach** $u \in V : v = \mathrm{DPOST}^\ell[u] \Rightarrow$ **free** $\mathrm{POST}[u]$
> > **foreach** $u \in V_C : v = \mathrm{DPRE}^\ell[u] \Rightarrow$ **free** $\mathrm{PRE}[u]$
> >
> > $\mathrm{PRE}[v], \mathrm{POST}[v] \leftarrow tpre, \tau_v(tpre)$
> >
> > $[\![P]\!]_{\mathcal{M}}$
> >
> > $tpre \leftarrow \mathrm{PRE}[v] \triangledown \bigsqcup \{\mathrm{POST}[p] \mid p \to v\}$
>
> } **while**($tpre \not\sqsubseteq \mathrm{PRE}[v]$) $\}$ Loop
>
> **foreach** $u \in V : v = \mathrm{DPOST}[u] \Rightarrow$ **free** $\mathrm{POST}[u]$
> $v \notin V_C \Rightarrow$ **free** $\mathrm{PRE}[v]$
> **foreach** $u \subset V_C : v = \mathrm{ACHK}[u] \Rightarrow \mathrm{CK}[u] \leftarrow \varphi_u(\mathrm{PRE}[u]);$ $\}$ Postamble
> $\qquad\qquad\qquad\qquad\qquad\qquad\qquad\qquad$ **free** $\mathrm{PRE}[u]$

$[\![P_1 \,\mathring{,}\, P_2]\!]_{\mathcal{M}} \stackrel{\mathrm{def}}{=} [\![P_1]\!]_{\mathcal{M}}$

$\qquad\qquad\quad [\![P_2]\!]_{\mathcal{M}}$

Fig. 2. The semantics of the Fixpoint Machine (FM) instructions of Eq. 2.

- The map $\mathrm{DPOST}^\ell : V \to 2^V$ control deallocation of POST values that are recomputed and overwritten in the loop of a **repeat** instruction before its next use. If $v \in \mathrm{DPOST}^\ell[u]$, POST$[u]$ is deallocated in the loop of Inst$[v]$.
- The map $\mathrm{DPRE}^\ell : V_C \to 2^V$ control deallocation of PRE values that recomputed and overwritten in the loop of a **repeat** instruction before its next use. If $v \in \mathrm{DPRE}^\ell[u]$, PRE$[u]$ is deallocated in the loop of Inst$[v]$.

To simplify presentation, the semantics in Fig. 2 does not make explicit the allocations of abstract values: if a POST or PRE value that has been deallocated is accessed, then it is allocated and initialized to $\bot$.

2.3   Problem Statement

Two memory configurations are *equivalent* if they result in the same values for each check in the program:

Definition 3. *Given an FM program P, memory configuration $\mathcal{M}_1$ is equivalent to $\mathcal{M}_2$, denoted by $[\![P]\!]_{\mathcal{M}_1} = [\![P]\!]_{\mathcal{M}_2}$, iff for all $u \in V_C$, we have $\mathrm{C}\mathrm{K}_1[u] = \mathrm{C}\mathrm{K}_2[u]$, where $\mathrm{C}\mathrm{K}_1$ and $\mathrm{C}\mathrm{K}_2$ are the check maps corresponding to execution of P using $\mathcal{M}_1$ and $\mathcal{M}_2$, respectively.* ∎

The *default memory configuration* $\mathcal{M}_{dflt}$ performs checks and deallocations at the end of the FM program after fixpoint has been computed.

Definition 4. *Given an FM program P, the* default memory configuration $\mathcal{M}_{dflt}$ *$(\mathrm{DPOST}_{dflt}, \mathrm{ACHK}_{dflt}, \mathrm{DPOST}^\ell{}_{dflt}, \mathrm{DPRE}^\ell{}_{dflt})$ is $\mathrm{DPOST}_{dflt}[v] = z$ for all $v \in V$, $\mathrm{ACHK}_{dflt}[c] = z$ for all $c \in V_C$, and $\mathrm{DPOST}^\ell{}_{dflt} = \mathrm{DPRE}^\ell{}_{dflt} = \emptyset$, where z is the last instruction in P.* ∎

Example 4. Consider the FM program P_1 from Example 3. Let $V_C = \{4, 9\}$. $\mathrm{DPOST}_{dflt}[v] = 9$ for all $v \in V$. That is, all POST values are deallocated at the end of the fixpoint computation. Also, $\mathrm{ACHK}_{dflt}[4] = \mathrm{ACHK}_{dflt}[9] = 9$, meaning that assertion checks also happen at the end. $\mathrm{DPOST}^\ell{}_{dflt} = \mathrm{DPRE}^\ell{}_{dflt} = \emptyset$, so the FM program does not clear abstract values whose values will be recomputed and overwritten in a loop of **repeat** instruction. ∎

Given an FM program P, a memory configuration $\mathcal{M}$ is *valid* for P iff it is equivalent to the default configuration; i.e., $[\![P]\!]_{\mathcal{M}} = [\![P]\!]_{\mathcal{M}_{dflt}}$.

Furthermore, a valid memory configuration $\mathcal{M}$ is *optimal* for a given FM program iff memory footprint of $[\![P]\!]_{\mathcal{M}}$ is smaller than or equal to that of $[\![P]\!]_{\mathcal{M}'}$ for all valid memory configuration $\mathcal{M}'$. The problem addressed in this paper can be stated as:

> Given an FM program P, find an optimal memory configuration $\mathcal{M}$.

An optimal configuration should deallocate abstract values during fixpoint computation as soon they are no longer needed. The challenge is ensuring that the memory configuration remains valid even without knowing the number of loop iterations for **repeat** instructions. Sect. 3 gives the optimal memory configuration for the FM program P_1 from Example 3.

3   Declarative Specification of Optimal Memory Configuration $\mathcal{M}_{opt}$

This section provides a declarative specification of an optimal memory configuration $\mathcal{M}_{opt}(\mathrm{DPOST}_{opt}, \mathrm{ACHK}_{opt}, \mathrm{DPOST}^\ell{}_{opt}, \mathrm{DPRE}^\ell{}_{opt})$. The proofs of the theorems in this section can be found in Appendix A. Sect. 4 presents an efficient algorithm for computing $\mathcal{M}_{opt}$.

Definition 5. *Given a WTO $\mathcal{W}(V, \preceq, \omega)$ of a graph $G(V, \rightarrow)$, the nesting relation N is a tuple $(V, \preceq_N)$ where $x \preceq_N y$ iff $x = y$ or $y \in \omega(x)$ for $x, y \in V$.* ∎

Let $\lfloor v \rceil_{\preceq_{\mathsf{N}}} \stackrel{\text{def}}{=} \{ w \in V \mid v \preceq_{\mathsf{N}} w \}$; that is, $\lfloor v \rceil_{\preceq_{\mathsf{N}}}$ equals the set containing v and the heads of components in the WTO that contain v. The nesting relation $\mathsf{N}(V, \preceq_{\mathsf{N}})$ is a *forest*; i.e. a partial order such that for all $v \in V$, $(\lfloor v \rceil_{\preceq_{\mathsf{N}}}, \preceq_{\mathsf{N}})$ is a chain (Theorem 4, Appendix A.1).

Example 5. For the WTO $\mathcal{W}_1$ of G_1 in Example 2, $\mathsf{N}_1(V, \preceq_{\mathsf{N}})$ is:

$$
\begin{array}{ccccc}
1 & 2 & 3 & & 7 \quad 9 \\
 & & \vert\backslash & & \vert \\
 & & 4 \quad 6 & & 8 \\
 & & \vert & & \\
 & & 5 & &
\end{array}
$$

Note that $\lfloor 5 \rceil_{\preceq_{\mathsf{N}}} = \{5, 4, 3\}$, forming a chain $5 \preceq_{\mathsf{N}} 4 \preceq_{\mathsf{N}} 3$. ∎

3.1 Declarative Specification of $\mathrm{DPOST}_{\mathrm{opt}}$

$\mathrm{DPOST}_{\mathrm{opt}}[u] = v$ implies that v is the earliest instruction at which $\mathrm{POST}[u]$ can be deallocated while ensuring that there are no subsequents reads of $\mathrm{POST}[u]$ during fixpoint computation. We cannot conclude $\mathrm{DPOST}_{\mathrm{opt}}[u] = v$ from a dependency $u \rightarrow v$ as illustrated in the following example.

Example 6. Consider the FM program P_1 from Example 3, whose graph $G_1(V, \rightarrow)$ is in Fig. 1. Although $2 \rightarrow 8$, memory configuration with $\mathrm{DPOST}[2] = 8$ is not valid: $\mathrm{POST}[2]$ is read by $\mathrm{Inst}[8]$, which is executed repeatedly as part of $\mathrm{Inst}[7]$; if $\mathrm{DPOST}[2] = 8$, $\mathrm{POST}[2]$ is deallocated the first time $\mathrm{Inst}[8]$ is executed, and subsequent executions of $\mathrm{Inst}[8]$ will read $\bot$ as the value of $\mathrm{POST}[2]$. ∎

In general, for a dependency $u \rightarrow v$, we must find the head of maximal component that contains v but not u as the candidate for $\mathrm{DPOST}_{\mathrm{opt}}[u]$. By choosing the head of *maximal* component, we remove the possibility of having a larger component whose head's `repeat` instruction can execute $\mathrm{Inst}[v]$ after deallocating $\mathrm{POST}[u]$. If there is no component that contains v but not u, we simply use v as the candidate. The following `Lift` operator gives us the candidate of $\mathrm{DPOST}_{\mathrm{opt}}[u]$ for $u \rightarrow v$:

$$
\mathtt{Lift}(u, v) \stackrel{\text{def}}{=} \max_{\preceq_{\mathsf{N}}} ((\lfloor v \rceil_{\preceq_{\mathsf{N}}} \setminus \lfloor u \rceil_{\preceq_{\mathsf{N}}}) \cup \{v\}) \tag{4}
$$

$\lfloor v \rceil_{\preceq_{\mathsf{N}}}$ gives us v and the heads of components that contain v. Subtracting $\lfloor u \rceil_{\preceq_{\mathsf{N}}}$ removes the heads of components that also contain u. We put back v to account for the case when there is no component containing v but not u and $\lfloor v \rceil_{\preceq_{\mathsf{N}}} \setminus \lfloor u \rceil_{\preceq_{\mathsf{N}}}$ is empty. Because $\mathsf{N}(V, \preceq_{\mathsf{N}})$ is a forest, $\lfloor v \rceil_{\preceq_{\mathsf{N}}}$ and $\lfloor u \rceil_{\preceq_{\mathsf{N}}}$ are chains, and hence, $\lfloor v \rceil_{\preceq_{\mathsf{N}}} \setminus \lfloor u \rceil_{\preceq_{\mathsf{N}}}$ is also a chain. Therefore, maximum is well-defined.

Example 7. Consider the nesting relation $\mathsf{N}_1(V, \preceq_{\mathsf{N}})$ from Example 5. $\mathtt{Lift}(2, 8) = \max_{\preceq_{\mathsf{N}}}((\{8, 7\} \setminus \{2\}) \cup \{8\}) = 7$. We see that 7 is the head of the maximal component containing 8 but not 2. Also, $\mathtt{Lift}(5, 4) = \max_{\preceq_{\mathsf{N}}}((\{4, 3\} \setminus \{5, 4, 3\}) \cup \{4\}) = 4$. There is no component that contains 4 but not 5. ∎

For each instruction u, we now need to find the last instruction from among the candidates computed using `Lift`. Notice that deallocations of POST values are at a postamble of `repeat` instructions in Fig 2. Therefore, we cannot use the total order $\preceq$ of a WTO to find the last instruction: $\preceq$ is the order in which the instruction begin executing, or the order in which *preambles* are executed.

S. K. Kim et al.

Example 8. Let $\text{DPOST}_{to}[u] \overset{\text{def}}{=} \max_{\preceq}\{\text{Lift}(u,v) \mid u \to v\}, u \in V$, an incorrect variant of $\text{DPOST}_{\text{opt}}$ that uses the total order $\preceq$. Consider the FM program P_1 from Example 3, whose graph $G_1(V, \to)$ is in Fig. 1 and nesting relation $N_1(V, \preceq_N)$ is in Example 5. $\text{POST}[5]$ has dependencies $5 \to 4$ and $5 \to 3$. $\text{Lift}(5,4) = 4$, $\text{Lift}(5,3) = 3$. Now, $\text{DPOST}_{to}[5] = 4$ because $3 \preceq 4$. However, a memory configuration with $\text{DPOST}[5] = 4$ is not valid: $\text{Inst}[4]$ is nested in $\text{Inst}[3]$. Due to the deletion of $\text{POST}[5]$ in $\text{Inst}[4]$, $\text{Inst}[3]$ will read $\perp$ as the value of $\text{POST}[5]$. ■

To find the order in which the instructions finish executing, or the order in which *postambles* are executed, we define the relation $(V, \le)$, using the total order $(V, \preceq)$ and the nesting relation $(V, \preceq_N)$:

$$x \le y \overset{\text{def}}{=} x \preceq_N y \vee (y \npreceq_N x \wedge x \preceq y) \tag{5}$$

In the definition of $\le$, the nesting relation $\preceq_N$ takes precedence over $\preceq$. $(V, \le)$ is a total order (Theorem 5, Appendix A.1). Intuitively, the total order $\le$ moves the heads in the WTO to their corresponding closing parentheses ')'.

Example 9. For G_1 (Fig. 1) and its WTO W_1, 1 2 (3 (4 5) 6) (7 8) 9, we have $1 \le 2 \le 5 \le 4 \le 6 \le 3 \le 8 \le 7 \le 9$. Note that $3 \preceq 6$ while $6 \le 3$. Postamble of `repeat 3 [...]` is executed after $\text{Inst}[6]$, while preamble of `repeat 3 [...]` is executed before $\text{Inst}[6]$. ■

We can now define $\text{DPOST}_{\text{opt}}$. Given a nesting relation $N(V, \preceq_N)$ for the graph $G(V, \to)$, $\text{DPOST}_{\text{opt}}$ is defined as:

$$\text{DPOST}_{\text{opt}}[u] \overset{\text{def}}{=} \max_{\le}\{\text{Lift}(u,v) \mid u \to v\}, u \in V \tag{6}$$

Example 10. Consider the FM program P_1 from Example 3, whose graph $G_1(V, \to)$ is in Fig. 1 and nesting relation $N_1(V, \preceq_N)$ is in Example 5. An optimal memory configuration $\mathcal{M}_{\text{opt}}$ defined by Eq. 6 is:

$\text{DPOST}_{\text{opt}}[1] = 2$, $\text{DPOST}_{\text{opt}}[2] = \text{DPOST}_{\text{opt}}[3] = \text{DPOST}_{\text{opt}}[8] = 7$, $\text{DPOST}_{\text{opt}}[4] = 6$, $\text{DPOST}_{\text{opt}}[5] = \text{DPOST}_{\text{opt}}[6] = 3$, $\text{DPOST}_{\text{opt}}[7] = \text{DPOST}_{\text{opt}}[9] = 9$.

Successors of u are first lifted to compute $\text{DPOST}_{\text{opt}}[u]$. For example, to compute $\text{DPOST}_{\text{opt}}[2]$, 2's successors, 3 and 8, are lifted to $\text{Lift}(2,3) = 3$ and $\text{Lift}(2,8) = 7$. To compute $\text{DPOST}_{\text{opt}}[5]$, 5's successors, 3 and 4, are lifted to $\text{Lift}(5,3) = 3$ and $\text{Lift}(5,4) = 4$. Then, the maximum (as per the total order $\le$) of the lifted successors is chosen as $\text{DPOST}_{\text{opt}}[u]$. Because $3 \le 7$, $\text{DPOST}_{\text{opt}}[2] = 7$. Thus, $\text{POST}[2]$ is deleted in $\text{Inst}[7]$. Also, because $4 \le 3$, $\text{DPOST}_{\text{opt}}[5] = 3$, and $\text{POST}[5]$ is deleted in $\text{Inst}[3]$. ■

3.2 Declarative Specification of $\textsc{Achk}_{\text{opt}}$

$\textsc{Achk}_{\text{opt}}[u] = v$ implies that v is the earliest instruction at which the assertion check at $u \in V_C$ can be executed so that the invariant passed to the assertion check function φ_u is the same as when using $\mathcal{M}_{\text{dflt}}$. Thus, guaranteeing the same check result $\textsc{Ck}$.

Because an instruction can be executed multiple times in a loop, we cannot simply execute the assertion checks right after the instruction, as illustrated by the following example.

Example 11. Consider the FM program P_1 from Example 3. Let $V_C = \{4, 9\}$. A memory configuration with $\textsc{Achk}[4] = 4$ is not valid: $\texttt{Inst}[4]$ is executed repeatedly as part of $\texttt{Inst}[3]$, and the first value of $\textsc{Pre}[4]$ may not be the final invariant. Consequently, executing $\varphi_4(\textsc{Pre}[4])$ in $\texttt{Inst}[4]$ may not give the same result as executing it in $\texttt{Inst}[9]$ ($\textsc{Achk}_{\text{dflt}}[4] = 9$). ∎

In general, because we cannot know the number of iterations of the loop in a **repeat** instruction, we must wait for the convergence of the maximal component that contains the assertion check. After the maximal component converges, the FM program never visits the component again, making $\textsc{Pre}$ values of the elements inside the component final. Only if the element is not in any component can its assertion check be executed right after its instruction.

Given a nesting relation $\textsf{N}(V, \preceq_\textsf{N})$ for the graph $G(V, \rightarrow)$, $\textsc{Achk}_{\text{opt}}$ is defined as:

$$\textsc{Achk}_{\text{opt}}[u] \overset{\text{def}}{=} \max_{\preceq_\textsf{N}} \lfloor u \rfloor_{\preceq_\textsf{N}}, u \in V_C \tag{7}$$

Because $\textsf{N}(V, \preceq_\textsf{N})$ is a forest, $(\lfloor u \rfloor_{\preceq_\textsf{N}}, \preceq_\textsf{N})$ is a chain. Hence, $\max_{\preceq_\textsf{N}}$ is well-defined.

Example 12. Consider the FM program P_1 from Example 3, whose graph $G_1(V, \rightarrow)$ is in Fig. 1 and nesting relation $\textsf{N}_1(V, \preceq_\textsf{N})$ is in Example 5. Suppose that $V_C = \{4, 9\}$. $\textsc{Achk}_{\text{opt}}[4] = \max_{\preceq_\textsf{N}}\{4, 3\} = 3$ and $\textsc{Achk}_{\text{opt}}[9] = \max_{\preceq_\textsf{N}}\{9\} = 9$. ∎

3.3 Declarative Specification of $\textsc{Dpost}^\ell{}_{\text{opt}}$

$v \in \textsc{Dpost}^\ell[u]$ implies that $\textsc{Post}[u]$ can be deallocated at v because it is recomputed and overwritten in the loop of a **repeat** instruction before a subsequent use of $\textsc{Post}[u]$.

$\textsc{Dpost}^\ell{}_{\text{opt}}[u]$ must be a subset of $\lfloor u \rfloor_{\preceq_\textsf{N}}$: only the instructions of the heads of components that contain v recompute $\textsc{Post}[u]$. We can further rule out the instruction of the heads of components that contain $\textsc{Dpost}_{\text{opt}}[u]$, because $\texttt{Inst}[\textsc{Dpost}_{\text{opt}}[u]]$ deletes $\textsc{Post}[u]$. We add back $\textsc{Dpost}_{\text{opt}}[u]$ to $\textsc{Dpost}^\ell{}_{\text{opt}}$ when u is contained in $\textsc{Dpost}_{\text{opt}}[u]$, because deallocation by $\textsc{Dpost}_{\text{opt}}$ happens after the deallocation by $\textsc{Dpost}^\ell{}_{\text{opt}}$.

Given a nesting relation $\textsf{N}(V, \preceq_\textsf{N})$ for the graph $G(V, \rightarrow)$, $\textsc{Dpost}^\ell{}_{\text{opt}}$ is defined as:

$$\textsc{Dpost}^\ell{}_{\text{opt}}[u] \overset{\text{def}}{=} (\lfloor u \rfloor_{\preceq_\textsf{N}} \setminus \lfloor d \rfloor_{\preceq_\textsf{N}}) \cup (u \preceq_\textsf{N} d \,?\, \{d\} : \emptyset), u \in V \tag{8}$$

where $d = \text{DPOST}_{\text{opt}}[u]$ as defined in Eq. 6, and $(\!|\text{b} \mathbin{?} \text{x} \mathbin{\text{\textsection}} \text{y}|\!)$ is the ternary conditional choice operator.

Example 13. Consider the FM program P_1 from Example 3, whose graph $G_1(V, \rightarrow)$ is in Fig. 1, nesting relation $N_1(V, \preceq_N)$ is in Example 5, and $\text{DPOST}_{\text{opt}}$ is in Example 10.

$$\text{DPOST}^{\ell}_{\text{opt}}[1] = \{1\}, \ \text{DPOST}^{\ell}_{\text{opt}}[2] = \{2\}, \ \text{DPOST}^{\ell}_{\text{opt}}[3] = \{3\},$$

$$\text{DPOST}^{\ell}_{\text{opt}}[4] = \{4\}, \ \text{DPOST}^{\ell}_{\text{opt}}[5] = \{3, 4, 5\}, \ \text{DPOST}^{\ell}_{\text{opt}}[6] = \{3, 6\},$$

$$\text{DPOST}^{\ell}_{\text{opt}}[7] = \{7\}, \ \text{DPOST}^{\ell}_{\text{opt}}[8] = \{7, 8\}, \ \text{DPOST}^{\ell}_{\text{opt}}[9] = \{9\}.$$

For 7, $\text{DPOST}_{\text{opt}}[7] = 9$. Because $7 \npreceq_N 9$, $\text{DPOST}^{\ell}_{\text{opt}}[7] = \lfloor 7 \rfloor_{\preceq_N} \setminus \lfloor 9 \rfloor_{\preceq_N} = \{7\}$. Therefore, $\text{POST}[7]$ is deleted in each iteration of the loop of $\text{Inst}[7]$. While $\text{Inst}[9]$ reads $\text{POST}[7]$ in the future, the particular values of $\text{POST}[7]$ that are deleted by $\text{DPOST}^{\ell}_{\text{opt}}[7]$ are not used in $\text{Inst}[9]$. For 5, $\text{DPOST}_{\text{opt}}[5] = 3$. Because $5 \preceq_N 3$, $\text{DPOST}^{\ell}_{\text{opt}}[5] = \lfloor 5 \rfloor_{\preceq_N} \setminus \lfloor 3 \rfloor_{\preceq_N} \cup \{3\} = \{5, 4, 3\}$. ∎

3.4   Declarative Specification of $\text{DPRE}^{\ell}_{\text{opt}}$

$v \in \text{DPRE}^{\ell}[u]$ implies that $\text{PRE}[u]$ can be deallocated at v because it is recomputed and overwritten in the loop of a **repeat** instruction before a subsequent use of $\text{PRE}[u]$.

$\text{DPRE}^{\ell}_{\text{opt}}[u]$ must be a subset of $\lfloor u \rfloor_{\preceq_N}$: only the instructions of the heads of components that contain v recompute $\text{PRE}[u]$. If $\text{Inst}[u]$ is a **repeat** instruction, $\text{PRE}[u]$ is required to perform widening. Therefore, u must not be contained in $\text{DPRE}^{\ell}_{\text{opt}}[u]$.

Example 14. Consider the FM program P_1 from Example 3. Let $V_C = \{4, 9\}$. A memory configuration with $\text{DPRE}^{\ell}[4] = \{3, 4\}$ is not valid, because $\text{Inst}[4]$ would read $\perp$ as the value of $\text{POST}[4]$ when performing widening. ∎

Given a nesting relation $N(V, \preceq_N)$ for the graph $G(V, \rightarrow)$, $\text{DPRE}^{\ell}_{\text{opt}}$ is defined as:

$$\text{DPRE}^{\ell}_{\text{opt}}[u] \stackrel{\text{def}}{=} \lfloor u \rfloor_{\preceq_N} \setminus \{u\} \ , u \in V_C \tag{9}$$

Example 15. Consider the FM program P_1 from Example 3, whose graph $G_1(V, \rightarrow)$ is in Fig. 1 and nesting relation $N_1(V, \preceq_N)$ is in Example 5. Let $V_C = \{4, 9\}$. $\text{DPRE}^{\ell}_{\text{opt}}[4] = \{4, 3\} \setminus \{4\} = \{3\}$ and $\text{DPRE}^{\ell}_{\text{opt}}[9] = \{9\} \setminus \{9\} = \emptyset$. Therefore, $\text{PRE}[4]$ is deleted in each loop iteration of $\text{Inst}[3]$. ∎

The following theorem is proved in Appendix A.2:

Theorem 1. *The memory configuration* $\mathcal{M}_{\text{opt}}(\text{DPOST}_{\text{opt}}, \text{ACHK}_{\text{opt}}, \text{DPOST}^{\ell}_{\text{opt}}, \text{DPRE}^{\ell}_{\text{opt}})$ *is optimal.*

Algorithm 1: GenerateFMProgram(G)

Input: Directed graph $G(V, \rightarrow)$
Output: FM program pgm, $\mathcal{M}_{\mathrm{opt}}$(DPOST$_{\mathrm{opt}}$, ACHK$_{\mathrm{opt}}$, DPOST$^{\ell}{}_{\mathrm{opt}}$, DPRE$^{\ell}{}_{\mathrm{opt}}$)

```
 1  D := DepthFirstForest(G)                        29  def generateFMInstruction(h):
 2  →ʙ := back edges in D                            30    Nₕ, Bₕ := findNestedSCCs(h)
 3  →CF := cross & forward edges in D                31    if Bₕ = ∅ then
 4  →' := → \ →ʙ                                      32      Inst[h] := exec h
 5  for v ∈ V do rep(v) := v; R[v] := ∅              33      return
 6  P := ∅
 7  removeAllCrossFwdEdges()                         34    for v ∈ Nₕ in desc. postDFNᴅ do
 8  for h ∈ V in descending DFNᴅ do                  35      Inst[h] := Inst[h] ⨾ Inst[v]
 9    restoreCrossFwdEdges(h)                     *36      for u s.t. u →' v do
10    generateFMInstruction(h)                    *37        DPOSTₒₚₜ[u] := v
                                                   *38        T[u] := rep(u)
11  pgm := connectFMInstructions()
12  return pgm, ℳₒₚₜ                                  39    Inst[h] := repeat h [Inst[h]]
                                                   *40    for u s.t. u →ʙ h do
13  def removeAllCrossFwdEdges():                  *41      DPOSTₒₚₜ[u] := T[u] := h
14    for (u, v) ∈ →CF do
15      →' := →' \ {(u, v)}                          42    for v ∈ Nₕ do
          ▷ Lowest common ancestor.                  43      merge(v, h); P := P ∪ {(v, h)}
16      R[lcaᴅ(u, v)] := R[lcaᴅ(u, v)] ∪ {(u, v)}
                                                     44  def connectFMInstructions():
17  def restoreCrossFwdEdges(h):                     45    pgm := ε              ▷ Empty program.
18    →' := →' ∪ {(u, rep(v)) | (u, v) ∈ R[h]}       46    for v ∈ V in desc. postDFNᴅ do
                                                     47      if rep(v) = v then
19  def findNestedSCCs(h):                           48        pgm := pgm ⨾ Inst[v]
20    Bₕ := {rep(p) | (p, h) ∈ B}                  *49        for u s.t. u →' v do
21    Nₕ := ∅       ▷ Nested SCCs except h.        *50          DPOSTₒₚₜ[u] := v
22    W := Bₕ \ {h}           ▷ Worklist.          *51          T[u] := rep(u)
23    while there exists v ∈ W do
24      W, Nₕ := W \ {v}, Nₕ ∪ [v]                 *52      if v ∈ V_C then
25      for u s.t. u →' v do                       *53        ACHKₒₚₜ[v] := rep(v)
26        if rep(u) ∉ Nₕ ∪ {h} ∪ W then            *54        DPRE^ℓₒₚₜ[v] := ⌊v, rep(v)⌉ₚ* \ {v}
27          W := W ∪ {rep(u)}
                                                   *55    for v ∈ V do
                                                   *56      DPOST^ℓₒₚₜ[v] := ⌊v, T[v]⌉ₚ*
28    return Nₕ, Bₕ
                                                     57    return pgm
```

---

4   Efficient Algorithm to Compute $\mathcal{M}_{\mathrm{opt}}$

Algorithm GenerateFMProgram (Algorithm 1) is an almost-linear time algorithm for computing an FM program P and optimal memory configuration $\mathcal{M}_{\mathrm{opt}}$ for a given directed graph $G(V, \rightarrow)$. Algorithm 1 adapts the bottom-up WTO construction algorithm presented in Kim et al. [26]. In particular, Algorithm 1 applies the genProg rules (Eq. 3) to generate the FM program from a WTO. Line 32 generates exec instructions for non-heads. Line 39 generates repeat instructions for heads, with their bodies ([ ]) generated on Line 35. Finally, instructions are merged on Line 48 to construct the final output P.

Algorithm GenerateFMProgram utilizes a disjoint-set data structure. Operation rep(v) returns the representative of the set that contains v. In Line 5, the sets are initialized to be rep(v) = v for all $v \in V$. Operation merge(v, h) on Line 43 merges the sets containing v and h, and assigns h to be the representative for the combined set. lca$_{\mathrm{D}}(u, v)$ is the lowest common ancestor of u, v in the depth-first forest D [47]. Cross and forward edges are initially removed from $\rightarrow'$

on Line 7, making the graph $(V, \rightarrow' \cup \rightarrow_B)$ reducible. Restoring it on Line 9 when $h = \texttt{lca}_D(u, v)$ restores some reachability while keeping $(V, \rightarrow' \cup \rightarrow_B)$ reducible.

Lines indicated by $\star$ in Algorithm 1 compute $\mathcal{M}_{opt}$. Lines 37, 41, and 50 compute $\textsc{Dpost}_{opt}$. Due to the specific order in which the algorithm traverses G, $\textsc{Dpost}_{opt}[u]$ is overwritten with greater values (as per the total order $\leq$) on these lines, making the final value to be the maximum among the successors. $\texttt{Lift}$ is implicitly applied when restoring the edges in $\texttt{restoreCrossFwdEdges}$: edge $u \rightarrow v$ whose $\texttt{Lift}(u, v) = h$ is replaced to $u \rightarrow' h$ on Line 9.

$\textsc{Dpost}^{\ell}_{opt}$ is computed using an auxiliary map $\texttt{T}: V \rightarrow V$ and a relation $\texttt{P}: V \times V$. At the end of the algorithm, $\texttt{T}[u]$ will be the maximum element (as per $\preceq_N$) in $\textsc{Dpost}^{\ell}_{opt}[u]$. That is, $\texttt{T}[u] = \max_{\preceq_N}((\lfloor u \rfloor_{\preceq_N} \setminus \lfloor d \rfloor_{\preceq_N}) \cup (\llbracket u \preceq_N d \text{ ? } \{d\} \text{ : } \emptyset \rrbracket))$, where $d = \textsc{Dpost}_{opt}[u]$. Once $\texttt{T}[u]$ is computed by lines 38, 41, and 51, the transitive reduction of $\preceq_N$, $\texttt{P}$, is used to find all elements of $\textsc{Dpost}^{\ell}_{opt}[u]$ on Line 56. $\texttt{P}$ is computed on Line 43. Note that $\texttt{P}^* = \preceq_N$ and $\llbracket x, y \rrbracket_{\texttt{P}^*} \overset{\text{def}}{=} \{v \mid x \texttt{ P}^* v \wedge v \texttt{ P}^* y\}$. $\textsc{Achk}$ and $\textsc{Dpre}^{\ell}$ are computed on Lines 53 and 54, respectively. An example run of the algorithm on graph G_1 can be found in the extended version of this paper [27].

The proofs of the following theorems are in Appendix A.3:

Theorem 2. *GenerateFMProgram correctly computes* $\mathcal{M}_{opt}$, *defined in Sect. 3.*

Theorem 3. *Running time of GenerateFMProgram is almost-linear.*

5   Implementation

We have implemented our approach in a tool called Mikos, which extends NASA's IKOS [11], a WTO-based abstract-interpreter for C/C++. Mikos inherits all abstract domains and widening-narrowing strategies from IKOS. It includes the localized narrowing strategy [1] that intertwines the increasing and decreasing sequences.

Abstract Domains in IKOS. IKOS uses the state-of-the-art implementations of abstract domains comparable to those used in industrial abstract interpreters such as Astrée. In particular, IKOS implements the interval abstract domain [14] using functional data-structures based on Patricia Trees [35]. Astrée implements intervals using OCaml's map data structure that uses balanced trees [8, Section 6.2]. As shown in [35, Section 5], the Patricia Trees used by IKOS are more efficient when you have to merge data structures, which is required often during abstract interpretation. Also, IKOS uses memory-efficient variable packing Difference Bound Matrix (DBM) relational abstract domain [17], similar to the variable packing relational domains employed by Astrée [5, Section 3.3.2].

Interprocedural Analysis in IKOS. IKOS implements context-sensitive interprocedural analysis by means of dynamic inlining, much like the semantic expansion of function bodies in Astrée [15, Section 5]: at a function call, formal and actual parameters are matched, the callee is analyzed, and the return value at the call site is updated after the callee returns; a function pointer is resolved to a set of callees and the results for each call are joined; IKOS returns top for a callee when a cycle is found in this dynamic call chain. To prevent running the entire interprocedural analysis again at the assertion checking phase, invariants at exits of the callees are additionally cached during the fixpoint computation.

Interprocedural Extension of MIKOS. Although the description of our iteration strategy focused on intraprocedural analysis, it can be extended to interprocedural analysis as follows. Suppose there is a call to function f1 from a basic block contained in component C. Any checks in this call to f1 must be deferred until we know that the component C has stabilized. Furthermore, if function f1 calls the function f2, then the checks in f2 must also be deferred until C converges. In general, checks corresponding to a function call f must be deferred until the maximal component containing the call is stabilized.

When the analysis of callee returns in MIKOS, only PRE values for the deferred checks remain. They are deallocated when the checks are performed or when the component containing the call is reiterated.

6   Experimental Evaluation

The experiments in this section were designed to answer the following questions:

RQ0 [Accuracy] Does MIKOS (Sect. 5) have the same analysis results as IKOS?
RQ1 [Memory footprint] How does the memory footprint of MIKOS compare to that of IKOS?
RQ2 [Runtime] How does the runtime of MIKOS compare to that of IKOS?

Experimental Setup. All experiments were run on Amazon EC2 r5.2 × large instances (64 GiB memory, 8 vCPUs, 4 physical cores), which use Intel Xeon Platinum 8175M processors. Processors have L1, L2, and L3 caches of sizes 1.5 MiB (data: 0.75 MiB, instruction: 0.75 MiB), 24 MiB, and 33 MiB, respectively. Linux kernel version 4.15.0-1051-aws was used, and gcc 7.4.0 was used to compile both MIKOS and IKOS. Dedicated EC2 instances and BenchExec [7] were used to improve reliability of the results. Time and space limit were set to an hour and 64 GB, respectively. The experiments can be reproduced using https://github. com/95616ARG/mikos_sas2020. Further experimental data can be found in the extended version of this paper [27].

Benchmarks. We evaluated MIKOS on two tasks that represent different client applications of abstract interpretation, each using different benchmarks described in Sects. 6.1 and 6.2. In both tasks, we excluded benchmarks that did not complete in *both* IKOS and MIKOS given the time and space budget. There were no benchmarks for which IKOS succeeded but MIKOS failed to complete. Benchmarks for which IKOS took less than 5 s were also excluded. Measurements for benchmarks that took less than 5 s are summarized in Appendix B of our extended paper [27].

Metrics. To answer RQ1, we define and use *memory reduction ratio (MRR)*:

$$\text{MRR} \overset{\text{def}}{=} \text{Memory footprint of Mikos} / \text{Memory footprint of IKOS} \qquad (10)$$

The smaller the MRR, the greater reduction in peak-memory usage in Mikos. If MRR is less than 1, Mikos has smaller memory footprint than IKOS.

For RQ2, we report the *speedup*, which is defined as below:

$$\text{Speedup} \overset{\text{def}}{=} \text{Runtime of IKOS} / \text{Runtime of Mikos} \qquad (11)$$

The larger the speedup, the greater reduction in runtime in Mikos. If speedup is greater than 1, Mikos is faster than IKOS.

RQ0: Accuracy of Mikos. As a sanity check for our theoretical results, we experimentally validated Theorem 1 by comparing the analysis results reported by IKOS and Mikos. Mikos used a valid memory configuration, reporting the same analysis results as IKOS. Recall that Theorem 1 also proves that the fixpoint computation in Mikos is memory-optimal (, it results in minimum memory footprint).

6.1   Task T1: Verifying User-Provided Assertions

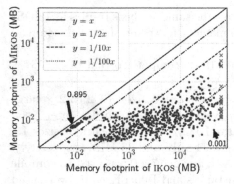 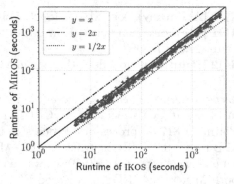

(a) Min MRR: 0.895. Max MRR: 0.001. Geometric means: (i) 0.044 (when ×s are ignored), (ii) 0.041 (when measurements until timeout/spaceout are used for ×s). 29 non-completions in IKOS.

(b) Min speedup: 0.87×. Max speedup: 1.80×. Geometric mean: 1.29×. Note that ×s are ignored as they space out fast in IKOS compared to in Mikos where they complete.

Fig. 3. Task T1. Log-log scatter plots of (a) memory footprint and (b) runtime of IKOS and Mikos, with an hour timeout and 64 GB spaceout. Benchmarks that did not complete in IKOS are marked ×. All ×s completed in Mikos. Benchmarks below $y = x$ required less memory or runtime in Mikos.

Benchmarks. For Task T1, we selected all 2928 benchmarks from DeviceDriversLinux64, ControlFlow, and Loops categories of SV-COMP 2019 [6]. These categories are well suited for numerical analysis, and have been used in recent works [26,45,46]. From these benchmarks, we removed 435 benchmarks that timed out in both MIKOS and IKOS, and 1709 benchmarks that took less than 5 s in IKOS. That left us with **784** SV-COMP 2019 benchmarks.

Abstract Domain. Task T1 used the reduced product of Difference Bound Matrix (DBM) with variable packing [17] and congruence [20]. This domain is much richer and more expressive than the interval domain used in task T2.

Task. Task T1 consists of using the results of interprocedural fixpoint computation to prove user-provided assertions in the SV-COMP benchmarks. Each benchmark typically has one assertion to prove.

RQ1: Memory footprint of MIKOS *compared to IKOS.* Figure 3(a) shows the measured memory footprints in a log-log scatter plot. For Task T1, the MRR (Eq. 10) ranged from 0.895 to 0.001. That is, the memory footprint decreased to 0.1% in the best case. For all benchmarks, MIKOS had smaller memory footprint than IKOS: MRR was less than 1 for all benchmarks, with all points below the $y = x$ line in Fig. 3(a). On average, MIKOS required only 4.1% of the memory required by IKOS, with an MRR 0.041 as the geometric mean.

As Fig. 3(a) shows, reduction in memory tended to be greater as the memory footprint in the baseline IKOS grew. For the top 25% benchmarks with largest memory footprint in IKOS, the geometric mean of MRRs was 0.009. While a similar trend was observed in task T2, the trend was significantly stronger in task T1. Our extended paper has more detailed numbers [27].

RQ2: Runtime of MIKOS *compared to IKOS.* Figure 3(b) shows the measured runtime in a log-log scatter plot. We measured both the speedup (Eq. 11) and the difference in the runtimes. For fair comparison, we excluded 29 benchmarks that did not complete in IKOS. This left us with 755 SV-COMP 2019 benchmarks. Out of these 755 benchmarks, 740 benchmarks had speedup > 1. The speedup ranged from 0.87× to 1.80×, with geometric mean of 1.29×. The difference in runtimes (runtime of IKOS − runtime of MIKOS) ranged from −7.47 s to 1160.04 s, with arithmetic mean of 96.90 s. Our extended paper has more detailed numbers [27].

6.2 Task T2: Proving Absence of Buffer Overflows

Benchmarks. For Task T2, we selected all 1503 programs from the official Arch Linux core packages that are primarily written in C and whose LLVM bitcodes are obtainable by gllvm [19]. These include, but are not limited to, `coreutils`, `dhcp`, `gnupg`, `inetutils`, `iproute`, `nmap`, `openssh`, `vim`, etc. From these benchmarks, we removed 76 benchmarks that timed out and 8 benchmarks that spaced out in both MIKOS and IKOS. Also, 994 benchmarks that took less than 5 s in IKOS were removed. That left us with **426** open-source benchmarks.

Abstract Domain. Task T2 used the interval abstract domain [14]. Using a richer domain like DBM caused IKOS and MIKOS to timeout on most benchmarks.

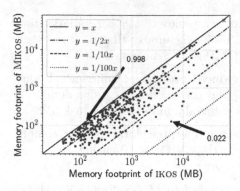
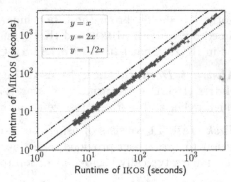

(a) Min MRR: 0.998. Max MRR: 0.022. Geometric means: (i) 0.436 (when ×s are ignored), (ii) 0.437 (when measurements until timeout/spaceout are used for ×s). 1 non-completions in IKOS.

(b) Min speedup: 0.88×. Max speedup: 2.83×. Geometric mean: 1.08×. Note that ×s are ignored as they space out fast in IKOS compared to in MIKOS where they complete.

Fig. 4. Task T2. Log-log scatter plots of (a) memory footprint and (b) runtime of IKOS and MIKOS, with an hour timeout and 64 GB spaceout. Benchmarks that did not complete in IKOS are marked ×. All ×s completed in MIKOS. Benchmarks below $y = x$ required less memory or runtime in MIKOS.

Task. Task T2 consists of using the results of interprocedural fixpoint computation to prove the safety of buffer accesses. In this task, most program points had checks.

RQ1: Memory footprint of MIKOS compared to IKOS. Figure 4(a) shows the measured memory footprints in a log-log scatter plot. For Task T2, MRR (Eq. 10) ranged from 0.998 to 0.022. That is, the memory footprint decreased to 2.2% in the best case. For all benchmarks, MIKOS had smaller memory footprint than IKOS: MRR was less than 1 for all benchmarks, with all points below the $y = x$ line in Fig. 4(a). On average, MIKOS's memory footprint was less than half of that of IKOS, with an MRR 0.437 as the geometric mean. Our extended paper has more detailed numbers [27].

RQ2: Runtime of MIKOS compared to IKOS. Figure 4(b) shows the measured runtime in a log-log scatter plot. We measured both the speedup (Eq. 11) and the difference in the runtimes. For fair comparison, we excluded 1 benchmark that did not complete in IKOS. This left us with 425 open-source benchmarks. Out of these 425 benchmarks, 331 benchmarks had speedup > 1. The speedup ranged from 0.88× to 2.83×, with geometric mean of 1.08×. The difference in runtimes (runtime of IKOS − runtime of MIKOS) ranged from −409.74 s to 198.39 s, with arithmetic mean of 1.29 s. Our extended paper has more detailed numbers [27].

7   Related Work

Abstract interpretation has a long history of designing time and memory efficient algorithms for specific abstract domains, which exploit variable packing and clustering and sparse constraints [13,18,22,24,43–46]. Often these techniques represent a trade-off between precision and performance of the analysis. Nonetheless, such techniques are orthogonal to the abstract-domain agnostic approach discussed in this paper. Approaches for improving precision via sophisticated widening and narrowing strategies [2,3,21] are also orthogonal to our memory-efficient iteration strategy. MIKOS inherits the interleaved widening-narrowing strategy implemented in the baseline IKOS abstract interpreter.

As noted in Sect. 1, Bourdoncle's approach [10] is used in many industrial and academic abstract interpreters [11,12,16,32,48]. Thus, improving memory efficiency of WTO-based exploration is of great applicability to real-world static analysis. Astrée is one of the few, if not only, industrial abstract interpreters that does not use WTO exploration, because it assumes that programs do not have gotos and recursion [8, Section 2.1], and is targeted towards a specific class of embedded C code [5, Section 3.2]. Such restrictions makes is easier to compute when an abstract value will not be used anymore by naturally following the abstract syntax tree [29, Section 3.4.3]. In contrast, MIKOS works for general programs with goto and recursion, which requires the use of WTO-based exploration.

Generic fixpoint-computation approaches for improving running time of abstract interpretation have also been explored [26,30,52]. Most recently, Kim et al. [26] present the notion of weak partial order (WPO), which generalizes the notion of WTO that is used in this paper. Kim et al. describe a parallel fixpoint algorithm that exploits maximal parallelism while computing the same fixpoint as the WTO-based algorithm. Reasoning about correctness of concurrent algorithms is complex; hence, we decided to investigate an optimal memory management scheme in the sequential setting first. However, we believe it would be possible to extend our WTO-based result to one that uses WPO.

The nesting relation described in Sect. 3 is closely related to the notion of Loop Nesting Forest [36,37], as observed in Kim et al. [26]. The almost-linear time algorithm GenerateFMProgram is an adaptation of LNF construction algorithm by Ramalingam [36]. The Lift operation in Sect. 3 is similar to the outermost-loop-excluding (OLE) operator introduced by Rastello [38, Section 2.4.4].

Seidl et al. [42] present time and space improvements to a generic fixpoint solver, which is closest in spirit to the problem discussed in this paper. For improving space efficiency, their approach recomputes values during fixpoint computation, and does not prove optimality, unlike our approach. However, the setting discussed in their work is also more generic compared to ours; we assume a static dependency graph for the equation system.

Abstract interpreters such as Astrée [8] and CodeHawk [48] are implemented in OCaml, which provides a garbage collector. However, merely using a reference counting garbage collector will not reduce peak memory usage of fixpoint computation. For instance, the reference count of $\text{PRE}[u]$ can be decreased to zero only after the final check/assert that uses $\text{PRE}[u]$. If the checks are all conducted at the end of the analysis (as is currently done in prior tools), then using a reference counting garbage collector will not reduce peak memory usage. In contrast, our approach lifts the checks as early as possible enabling the analysis to free the abstract values as early as possible.

Symbolic approaches for applying abstract transformers during fixpoint computation [23,28,40,41,49–51] allow the entire loop body to be encoded as a single formula. This might appear to obviate the need for PRE and POST values for individual basic blocks within the loop; by storing the PRE value only at the header, such a symbolic approach might appear to reduce the memory footprint. First, this scenario does not account for the fact that PRE values need to be computed and stored if basic blocks in the loop have checks. Note that if there are no checks within the loop body, then our approach would also only store the PRE value at the loop header. Second, such symbolic approaches only perform intraprocedural analysis [23]; additional abstract values would need to be stored depending on how function calls are handled in interprocedural analysis. Third, due to the use of SMT solvers in such symbolic approaches, the memory footprint might not necessarily reduce, but might increase if one takes into account the memory used by the SMT solver.

Sparse analysis [33,34] and database-backed analysis [54] improve the memory cost of static analysis. For specific classes of static analysis such as the IFDS framework [39], there have been approaches for improving the time and memory efficiency [9,31,53,55].

8 Conclusion

This paper presented an approach for memory-efficient abstract interpretation that is agnostic to the abstract domain used. Our approach is memory-optimal and produces the same result as Bourdoncle's approach without sacrificing time efficiency. We extended the notion of iteration strategy to intelligently deallocate abstract values and perform assertion checks during fixpoint computation. We provided an almost-linear time algorithm that constructs this iteration strategy. We implemented our approach in a tool called MIKOS, which extended the abstract interpreter IKOS. Despite the use of state-of-the-art implementation of abstract domains, IKOS had a large memory footprint on two analysis tasks. MIKOS was shown to effectively reduce it. When verifying user-provided assertions in SV-COMP 2019 benchmarks, MIKOS showed a decrease in peak-memory usage to 4.07% (24.57×) on average compared to IKOS. When performing interprocedural buffer-overflow analysis of open-source programs, MIKOS showed a decrease in peak-memory usage to 43.7% (2.29×) on average compared to IKOS.

A   Proofs

This section provides proofs of theorems presented in the paper.

A.1   Nesting forest $(V, \preceq_N)$ and total order $(V, \leq)$ in Sect. 3

This section presents the theorems and proofs about $\preceq_N$ and $\leq$ defined in Sect. 3.

A partial order (S, R) is a forest if for all $x \in S$, $(\llbracket x \rrbracket_R, R)$ is a chain, where $\llbracket x \rrbracket_R \overset{\text{def}}{=} \{y \in S \mid x \, R \, y\}$.

Theorem 4. $(V, \preceq_N)$ *is a forest.*

Proof. First, we show that $(V, \preceq_N)$ is a partial order. Let x, y, z be a vertex in V.

- Reflexivity: $x \preceq_N x$. This is true by the definition of $\preceq_N$.
- Transitivity: $x \preceq_N y$ and $y \preceq_N z$ implies $x \preceq_N z$. (i) If $x = y$, $x \preceq_N z$. (ii) Otherwise, by definition of $\preceq_N$, $y \in \omega(x)$. Furthermore, (ii-1) if $y = z$, $z \in \omega(x)$; and hence, $x \preceq_N z$. (ii-2) Otherwise, $z \in \omega(y)$, and by definition of HTO, $z \in \omega(x)$.
- Anti-symmetry: $x \preceq_N y$ and $y \preceq_N x$ implies $x = y$. Suppose $x \neq y$. By definition of $\preceq_N$ and premises, $y \in \omega(x)$ and $x \in \omega(y)$. Then, by definition of HTO, $x \prec y$ and $y \prec x$. This contradicts that $\preceq$ is a total order.

Next, we show that the partial order is a forest. Suppose there exists $v \in V$ such that $(\llbracket v \rrbracket_{\preceq_N}, \preceq_N)$ is not a chain. That is, there exists $x, y \in \llbracket v \rrbracket_{\preceq_N}$ such that $x \not\preceq_N y$ and $y \not\preceq_N x$. Then, by definition of HTO, $\mathcal{C}(x) \cap \mathcal{C}(y) = \emptyset$. However, this contradicts that $v \in \mathcal{C}(x)$ and $v \in \mathcal{C}(y)$. $\square$

Theorem 5. $(V, \leq)$ *is a total order.*

Proof. We prove the properties of a total order. Let x, y, z be a vertex in V.

- Connexity: $x \leq y$ or $y \leq x$. This follows from the connexity of the total order $\preceq$.
- Transitivity: $x \leq y$ and $y \leq z$ implies $x \leq z$. (i) Suppose $x \preceq_N y$. (i-1) If $y \preceq_N z$, by transitivity of $\preceq_N$, $x \preceq_N z$. (ii-2) Otherwise, $z \not\preceq_N y$ and $y \preceq z$. It cannot be $z \preceq_N x$ because transitivity of $\preceq_N$ implies $z \preceq_N y$, which is a contradiction. Furthermore, it cannot be $z \prec x$ because $y \preceq z \prec x$ and $x \preceq_N y$ implies $y \in \omega(z)$ by the definition of HTO. By connexity of $\preceq$, $x \preceq z$. (ii) Otherwise $y \not\preceq_N x$ and $x \preceq y$. (ii-1) If $y \preceq_N z$, $z \not\preceq_N x$ because, otherwise, transitivity of $\preceq_N$ will imply $y \preceq_N x$. By connexity of $\preceq$, it is either $x \preceq z$ or $z \prec x$. If $x \preceq z$, $x \leq z$. If $z \prec x$, by definition of HTO, $z \in \omega(z)$.
- Anti-symmetry: $x \leq y$ and $y \leq x$ implies $x = y$. (i) If $x \preceq_N y$, it should be $y \preceq_N x$ for $y \leq x$ to be true. By anti-symmetry of $\preceq_N$, $x = y$. (ii) Otherwise, $y \not\preceq_N x$ and $x \preceq y$. For $y \leq x$ to be true, $x \not\preceq_N y$ and $x \preceq y$. By anti-symmetry of $\preceq$, $x = y$.

□

Theorem 6. *For $u, v \in V$, if $\textit{Inst}[v]$ reads $\text{POST}[u]$, then $u \leq v$.*

Proof. By the definition of the mapping $\textit{Inst}$, there must exists $v' \in V$ such that $u \rightarrow v'$ and $v' \preceq_{\mathsf{N}} v$ for $\textit{Inst}[v]$ to read $\text{POST}[u]$. By the definition of WTO, it is either $u \prec v'$ and $v' \notin \omega(u)$, or $v' \preceq u$ and $v' \in \omega(u)$. In both cases, $u \leq v'$. Because $v' \preceq_{\mathsf{N}} v$, and hence $v' \leq v$, $u \leq v$.   □

A.2   Optimality of $\mathcal{M}_{\text{opt}}$ in Sect. 3

This section presents the theorems and proofs about the optimality of $\mathcal{M}_{\text{opt}}$ described in Sect. 3. The theorem is divided into optimality theorems of the maps that constitute $\mathcal{M}_{\text{opt}}$.

Given $\mathcal{M}(\text{DPOST}, \text{ACHK}, \text{DPOST}^{\ell}, \text{DPRE}^{\ell})$ and a map DPOST_0, we use $\mathcal{M} \wr \text{DPOST}_0$ to denote the memory configuration $(\text{DPOST}_0, \text{ACHK}, \text{DPOST}^{\ell}, \text{DPRE}^{\ell})$. Similarly, $\mathcal{M} \wr \text{ACHK}_0$ means $(\text{DPOST}, \text{ACHK}_0, \text{DPOST}^{\ell}, \text{DPRE}^{\ell})$, and so on. For a given FM program P, each map X that constitutes a memory configuration is valid for P iff $\mathcal{M} \wr X$ is valid for every valid memory configuration $\mathcal{M}$. Also, X is optimal for P iff $\mathcal{M} \wr X$ is optimal for an optimal memory configuration $\mathcal{M}$.

Theorem 7. DPOST_{opt} *is valid. That is, given an FM program P and a valid memory configuration $\mathcal{M}$, $[\![P]\!]_{\mathcal{M} \wr \text{DPOST}_{opt}} = [\![P]\!]_{\mathcal{M}}$.*

Proof. Our approach does not change the iteration order and only changes where the deallocations are performed. Therefore, it is sufficient to show that for all $u \rightarrow v$, $\text{POST}[u]$ is available whenever $\textit{Inst}[v]$ is executed.

Suppose that this is false: there exists an edge $u \rightarrow v$ that violates it. Let d be $\text{DPOST}_{opt}[u]$ computed by our approach. Then, the execution trace of P has execution of $\textit{Inst}[v]$ after the deallocation of $\text{POST}[u]$ in $\textit{Inst}[d]$, with no execution of $\textit{Inst}[u]$ in between.

Because $\leq$ is a total order, it is either $d < v$ or $v \leq d$. It must be $v \leq d$, because $d < v$ implies $d < v \leq \textit{Lift}(u, v)$, which contradicts the definition of $\text{DPOST}_{opt}[u]$. Then, by definition of $\leq$, it is either $v \preceq_{\mathsf{N}} d$ or $(d \npreceq_{\mathsf{N}} v) \wedge (v \preceq d)$. In both cases, the only way $\textit{Inst}[v]$ can be executed after $\textit{Inst}[d]$ is to have another head h whose repeat instruction includes both $\textit{Inst}[d]$ and $\textit{Inst}[v]$. That is, when $d \prec_{\mathsf{N}} h$ and $v \prec_{\mathsf{N}} h$. By definition of WTO and $u \rightarrow v$, it is either $u \prec v$, or $u \preceq_{\mathsf{N}} v$. It must be $u \prec v$, because if $u \preceq_{\mathsf{N}} v$, $\textit{Inst}[u]$ is part of $\textit{Inst}[v]$, making $\textit{Inst}[u]$ to be executed before reading $\text{POST}[u]$ in $\textit{Inst}[v]$. Furthermore, it must be $u \prec h$, because if $h \preceq u$, $\textit{Inst}[u]$ is executed before $\textit{Inst}[v]$ in each iteration over $\mathcal{C}(h)$. However, that implies $h \in (\lfloor v \rfloor_{\preceq_{\mathsf{N}}} \setminus \lfloor u \rfloor_{\preceq_{\mathsf{N}}})$, which combined with $d \prec_{\mathsf{N}} h$, contradicts the definition of $\text{DPOST}_{opt}[u]$. Therefore, no such edge $u \rightarrow v$ can exist and the theorem is true.   □

Theorem 8. DPOST_{opt} *is optimal. That is, given an FM program P, memory footprint of $[\![P]\!]_{\mathcal{M} \wr \text{DPOST}_{opt}}$ is smaller than or equal to that of $[\![P]\!]_{\mathcal{M}}$ for all valid memory configuration $\mathcal{M}$.*

Proof. For $\text{DPOST}_{\text{opt}}$ to be optimal, deallocation of POST values must be determined at earliest positions as possible with a valid memory configuration $\mathcal{M}\nmid\text{DPOST}_{\text{opt}}$. That is, there should not exists $u, b \in V$ such that if $d = \text{DPOST}_{\text{opt}}[u]$, $b \neq d$, $\mathcal{M}\nmid(\text{DPOST}_{\text{opt}}[u \leftarrow b])$ is valid, and $\text{Inst}[b]$ deletes $\text{POST}[u]$ earlier than $\text{Inst}[d]$.

Suppose that this is false: such u, b exists. Let d be $\text{DPOST}_{\text{opt}}[u]$, computed by our approach. Then it must be $b < d$ for $\text{Inst}[b]$ to be able to delete $\text{POST}[u]$ earlier than $\text{Inst}[d]$. Also, for all $u \to v$, it must be $v \leq b$ for $\text{Inst}[v]$ to be executed before deleting $\text{POST}[u]$ in $\text{Inst}[b]$.

By definition of $\text{DPOST}_{\text{opt}}$, $v \leq d$ for all $u \to v$. Also, by Theorem 6, $u \leq v$. Hence, $u \leq d$, making it either $u \preceq_N d$, or $(d \npreceq_N u) \wedge (u \preceq d)$. If $u \preceq_N d$, by definition of Lift, it must be $u \to d$. Therefore, it must be $d \leq b$, which contradicts that $b < d$. Alternative, if $(d \npreceq_N u) \wedge (u \preceq d)$, there must exist $v \in V$ such that $u \to v$ and $\text{Lift}(u, v) = d$. To satisfy $v \leq b$, $v \preceq_N d$, and $b < d$, it must be $b \preceq_N d$. However, this makes the analysis incorrect because when stabilization check fails for $\mathcal{C}(d)$, $\text{Inst}[v]$ gets executed again, attempting to read $\text{POST}[u]$ that is already deleted by $\text{Inst}[b]$. Therefore, no such u, b can exist, and the theorem is true. $\qquad\square$

Theorem 9. ACHK_{opt} *is valid. That is, given an* FM *program* P *and a valid memory configuration* $\mathcal{M}$, $[\![P]\!]_{\mathcal{M}\nmid\text{ACHK}_{opt}} = [\![P]\!]_{\mathcal{M}}$

Proof. Let $v = \text{ACHK}_{\text{opt}}[u]$. If v is a head, by definition of ACHK_{opt}, $\mathcal{C}(v)$ is the largest component that contains u. Therefore, once $\mathcal{C}(v)$ is stabilized, $\text{Inst}[u]$ can no longer be executed, and $\text{PRE}[u]$ remains the same. If v is not a head, then $v = u$. That is, there is no component that contains u. Therefore, $\text{PRE}[u]$ remains the same after the execution of $\text{Inst}[u]$. In both cases, the value passed to CK_u are the same as when using $\text{ACHK}_{\text{dflt}}$. $\qquad\square$

Theorem 10. ACHK_{opt} *is optimal. That is, given an* FM *program* P, *memory footprint of* $[\![P]\!]_{\mathcal{M}\nmid\text{ACHK}_{opt}}$ *is smaller than or equal to that of* $[\![P]\!]_{\mathcal{M}}$ *for all valid memory configuration* $\mathcal{M}$.

Proof. Because PRE value is deleted right after its corresponding assertions are checked, it is sufficient to show that assertion checks are placed at the earliest positions with ACHK_{opt}.

Let $v = \text{ACHK}_{\text{opt}}[u]$. By definition of ACHK_{opt}, $u \preceq_N v$. For some b to perform assertion checks of u earlier than v, it must satisfy $b \prec_N v$. However, because one cannot know in advance when a component of v would stabilize and when $\text{PRE}[u]$ would converge, the assertion checks of u cannot be performed in $\text{Inst}[b]$. Therefore, our approach puts the assertion checks at the earliest positions, and it leads to the minimum memory footprint. $\qquad\square$

Theorem 11. $\text{DPOST}^{\ell}_{opt}$ *is valid. That is, given an* FM *program* P *and a valid memory configuration* $\mathcal{M}$, $[\![P]\!]_{\mathcal{M}\nmid\text{DPOST}^{\ell}_{opt}} = [\![P]\!]_{\mathcal{M}}$.

Proof. Again, our approach does not change the iteration order and only changes where the deallocations are performed. Therefore, it is sufficient to show that for all $u \rightarrow v$, $\text{POST}[u]$ is available whenever $\text{Inst}[v]$ is executed.

Suppose that this is false: there exists an edge $u \rightarrow v$ that violates it. Let d' be element in $\text{DPOST}^{\ell}{}_{\text{opt}}[u]$ that causes this violation. Then, the execution trace of P has execution of $\text{Inst}[v]$ after the deallocation of $\text{POST}[u]$ in $\text{Inst}[d']$, with no execution of $\text{Inst}[u]$ in between. Because $\text{POST}[u]$ is deleted inside the loop of $\text{Inst}[d']$, $\text{Inst}[v]$ must be nested in $\text{Inst}[d']$ or be executed after $\text{Inst}[d']$ to be affected. That is, it must be either $v \preceq_{\text{N}} d'$ or $d' \prec v$. Also, because of how $\text{DPOST}^{\ell}{}_{\text{opt}}[u]$ is computed, $u \preceq_{\text{N}} d'$.

First consider the case $v \preceq_{\text{N}} d'$. By definition of WTO and $u \rightarrow v$, it is either $u \prec v$ or $u \preceq_{\text{N}} v$. In either case, $\text{Inst}[u]$ gets executed before $\text{Inst}[v]$ reads $\text{POST}[u]$. Therefore, deallocation of $\text{POST}[u]$ in $\text{Inst}[d']$ cannot cause the violation.

Alternatively, consider $d' \prec v$ and $v \npreceq_{\text{N}} d'$. Because $u \preceq_{\text{N}} d'$, $\text{POST}[u]$ is generated in each iteration over $\mathcal{C}(d')$, and the last iteration does not delete $\text{POST}[u]$. Therefore, $\text{POST}[u]$ will be available when executing $\text{Inst}[v]$. Therefore, such u, d' does not exists, and the theorem is true. □

Theorem 12. $\text{DPOST}^{\ell}{}_{opt}$ *is optimal. That is, given an FM program P, memory footprint of $[\![P]\!]_{\mathcal{M} \sharp \text{DPOST}^{\ell}{}_{opt}}$ is smaller than or equal to that of $[\![P]\!]_{\mathcal{M}}$ for all valid memory configuration $\mathcal{M}$.*

Proof. Because one cannot know when a component would stabilize in advance, the decision to delete intermediate $\text{POST}[u]$ cannot be made earlier than the stabilization check of a component that contains u. Our approach makes such decisions in all relevant components that contains u.

If $u \preceq_{\text{N}} d$, $\text{DPOST}^{\ell}{}_{\text{opt}}[u] = \lfloor u \rfloor_{\preceq_{\text{N}}} \cap \lfloor d \rfloor_{\preceq_{\text{N}}}$. Because $\text{POST}[u]$ is deleted in $\text{Inst}[d]$, we do not have to consider components in $\lfloor d \rfloor_{\preceq_{\text{N}}} \setminus \{d\}$. Alternatively, if $u \npreceq_{\text{N}} d$, $\text{DPOST}^{\ell}{}_{\text{opt}}[u] = \lfloor u \rfloor_{\preceq_{\text{N}}} \setminus \lfloor d \rfloor_{\preceq_{\text{N}}}$. Because $\text{POST}[u]$ is deleted $\text{Inst}[d]$, we do not have to consider components in $\lfloor u \rfloor_{\preceq_{\text{N}}} \setminus \lfloor d \rfloor_{\preceq_{\text{N}}}$. Therefore, $\text{DPOST}^{\ell}{}_{\text{opt}}$ is optimal. □

Theorem 13. $\text{DPRE}^{\ell}{}_{opt}$ *is valid. That is, given an FM program P and a valid memory configuration $\mathcal{M}$, $[\![P]\!]_{\mathcal{M} \sharp \text{DPRE}^{\ell}{}_{opt}} = [\![P]\!]_{\mathcal{M}}$.*

Proof. $\text{PRE}[u]$ is only used in assertion checks and to perform widening in $\text{Inst}[u]$. Because u is removed from $\text{DPRE}^{\ell}[u]$, the deletion does not affect widening.

For all $v \in \text{DPRE}^{\ell}[u]$, $v \preceq_{\text{N}} \text{ACHK}_{\text{opt}}[u]$. Because $\text{PRE}[u]$ is not deleted when $\mathcal{C}(v)$ is stabilized, $\text{PRE}[u]$ will be available when performing assertion checks in $\text{Inst}[\text{ACHK}_{\text{opt}}[u]]$. Therefore, DPRE^{ℓ} is valid. □

Theorem 14. $\text{DPRE}^{\ell}{}_{opt}$ *is optimal. That is, given an FM program P, memory footprint of $[\![P]\!]_{\mathcal{M} \sharp \text{DPRE}^{\ell}{}_{opt}}$ is smaller than or equal to that of $[\![P]\!]_{\mathcal{M}}$ for all valid memory configuration $\mathcal{M}$.*

Proof. Because one cannot know when a component would stabilize in advance, the decision to delete intermediate $\text{PRE}[u]$ cannot be made earlier than the stabilization check of a component that contains u. Our approach makes such decisions in all components that contains u. Therefore, $\text{DPRE}^{\ell}_{\text{opt}}$ is optimal.   □

Theorem 1. *The memory configuration* $\mathcal{M}_{\text{opt}}(\text{DPOST}_{\text{opt}}, \text{ACHK}_{\text{opt}}, \text{DPOST}^{\ell}_{\text{opt}}, \text{DPRE}^{\ell}_{\text{opt}})$ *is optimal.*

Proof. This follows from theorems Theorem 11 to 14.   □

A.3   Correctness and efficiency of `GenerateFMProgram` in Sect. 4

This section presents the theorems and proofs about the correctness and efficiency of `GenerateFMProgram` (Algorithm 1, Sect. 4).

Theorem 2. *GenerateFMProgram correctly computes* $\mathcal{M}_{opt}$, *defined in Sect. 3.*

Proof. We show that each map is constructed correctly.

- $\text{DPOST}_{\text{opt}}$: Let v' be the value of $\text{DPOST}_{\text{opt}}[u]$ before overwritten in Line 50, 37, or 41. Descending post DFN ordering corresponds to a topological sorting of the nested SCCs. Therefore, in Line 50 and 37, $v' \prec v$. Also, because $v \preceq_{\mathsf{N}} h$ for all $v \in N_h$ in Line 41, $v' \preceq_{\mathsf{N}} v$. In any case, $v' \leq v$. Because $\text{rep}(v)$ essentially performs $\text{Lift}(u, v)$ when restoring the edges, the final $\text{DPOST}_{\text{opt}}[u]$ is the maximum of the lifted successors, and the map is correctly computed.
- $\text{DPOST}^{\ell}_{\text{opt}}$: The correctness follows from the correctness of T. Because the components are constructed bottom-up, $\text{rep}(u)$ in Line 51 and 38 returns $\max_{\preceq_{\mathsf{N}}}(\lfloor u \rfloor_{\preceq_{\mathsf{N}}} \setminus \lfloor \text{DPOST}_{\text{opt}}[u] \rfloor_{\preceq_{\mathsf{N}}})$. Also, $\mathsf{N}^* =\preceq_{\mathsf{N}}$. Thus, $\text{DPOST}^{\ell}_{\text{opt}}$ is correctly computed.
- ACHK_{opt}: At the end of the algorithm $\text{rep}(v)$ is the head of maximal component that contains v, or v itself when v is outside of any components. Therefore, ACHK_{opt} is correctly computed.
- $\text{DPRE}^{\ell}_{\text{opt}}$: Using the same reasoning as in ACHK_{opt}, and because $\mathsf{N}^* =\preceq_{\mathsf{N}}$, $\text{DPRE}^{\ell}_{\text{opt}}$ is correctly computed.

□

Theorem 3. *Running time of GenerateFMProgram is almost-linear.*

Proof. The base WTO-construction algorithm is almost-linear time [26]. The starred lines in Algorithm 1 visit each edge and vertex once. Therefore, time complexity still remains almost-linear time.   □

References

1. Amato, G., Scozzari, F.: Localizing widening and narrowing. In: Static Analysis - 20th International Symposium, SAS 2013, Seattle, WA, USA, June 20–22, 2013. Proceedings. pp. 25–42 (2013). https://doi.org/10.1007/978-3-642-38856-9_4
2. Amato, G., Scozzari, F., Seidl, H., Apinis, K., Vojdani, V.: Efficiently intertwining widening and narrowing. Sci. Comput. Program. **120**, 1–24 (2016). https://doi.org/10.1016/j.scico.2015.12.005
3. Apinis, K., Seidl, H., Vojdani, V.: Enhancing top-down solving with widening and narrowing. In: Probst, C.W., Hankin, C., Hansen, R.R. (eds.) Semantics, Logics, and Calculi - Essays Dedicated to Hanne Riis Nielson and Flemming Nielson on the Occasion of Their 60th Birthdays. Lecture Notes in Computer Science, vol. 9560, pp. 272–288. Springer, Heidelberg (2016). https://doi.org/10.1007/978-3-319-27810-0_14
4. Bagnara, R., Hill, P.M., Zaffanella, E.: The parma polyhedra library: toward a complete set of numerical abstractions for the analysis and verification of hardware and software systems. Sci. Comput. Program. **72**(1–2), 3–21 (2008). https://doi.org/10.1016/j.scico.2007.08.001
5. Bertrane, J., et al.: Static analysis by abstract interpretation of embedded critical software. ACM SIGSOFT Softw. Eng. Notes **36**(1), 1–8 (2011). https://doi.org/10.1145/1921532.1921553
6. Beyer, D.: Automatic verification of C and java programs: SV-COMP 2019. In: Tools and Algorithms for the Construction and Analysis of Systems - 25 Years of TACAS: TOOLympics, Held as Part of ETAPS 2019, Prague, Czech Republic, April 6–11, 2019, Proceedings, Part III, pp. 133–155 (2019). https://doi.org/10.1007/978-3-030-17502-3_9
7. Beyer, D., Löwe, S., Wendler, P.: Reliable benchmarking: requirements and solutions. Int. J. Softw. Tools Technol. Transfer **21**(1), 1–29 (2017). https://doi.org/10.1007/s10009-017-0469-y
8. Blanchet, B., et al.: Design and implementation of a special-purpose static program analyzer for safety-critical real-time embedded software. In: Mogensen, T.Æ., Schmidt, D.A., Sudborough, I.H. (eds.) The Essence of Computation, Complexity, Analysis, Transformation. Essays Dedicated to Neil D. Jones [on occasion of his 60th birthday]. Lecture Notes in Computer Science, vol. 2566, pp. 85–108. Springer, Cham (2002). https://doi.org/10.1007/3-540-36377-7_5
9. Bodden, E.: Inter-procedural data-flow analysis with IFDS/IDE and soot. In: Bodden, E., Hendren, L.J., Lam, P., Sherman, E. (eds.) Proceedings of the ACM SIGPLAN International Workshop on State of the Art in Java Program analysis, SOAP 2012, Beijing, China, June 14, 2012, pp. 3–8. ACM (2012). https://doi.org/10.1145/2259051.2259052
10. Bourdoncle, F.: Efficient chaotic iteration strategies with widenings. In: Bjørner, D., Broy, M., Pottosin, I.V. (eds.) FMP&TA 1993. LNCS, vol. 735, pp. 128–141. Springer, Heidelberg (1993). https://doi.org/10.1007/BFb0039704
11. Brat, G., Navas, J.A., Shi, N., Venet, A.: IKOS: A framework for static analysis based on abstract interpretation. In: Software Engineering and Formal Methods - 12th International Conference, SEFM 2014, Grenoble, France, September 1–5, 2014. Proceedings, pp. 271–277 (2014). https://doi.org/10.1007/978-3-319-10431-7_20
12. Calcagno, C., Distefano, D.: Infer: An automatic program verifier for memory safety of C programs. In: Bobaru, M.G., Havelund, K., Holzmann, G.J., Joshi, R. (eds.)

NASA Formal Methods - Third International Symposium, NFM 2011, Pasadena, CA, USA, April 18–20, 2011. Proceedings. Lecture Notes in Computer Science, vol. 6617, pp. 459–465. Springer, Heidelberg (2011). https://doi.org/10.1007/978-3-642-20398-5_33

13. Chawdhary, A., King, A.: Compact difference bound matrices. In: Chang, B.E. (ed.) Programming Languages and Systems - 15th Asian Symposium, APLAS 2017, Suzhou, China, November 27–29, 2017, Proceedings. Lecture Notes in Computer Science, vol. 10695, pp. 471–490. Springer (2017). https://doi.org/10.1007/978-3-319-71237-6_23

14. Cousot, P., Cousot, R.: Abstract interpretation: a unified lattice model for static analysis of programs by construction or approximation of fixpoints. In: Conference Record of the Fourth ACM Symposium on Principles of Programming Languages, Los Angeles, California, USA, January 1977, pp. 238–252 (1977). https://doi.org/10.1145/512950.512973

15. Cousot, P., Cousot, R., Feret, J., Mauborgne, L., Miné, A., Monniaux, D., Rival, X.: The astreé analyzer. In: Sagiv, S. (ed.) Programming Languages and Systems, 14th European Symposium on Programming, ESOP 2005, Held as Part of the Joint European Conferences on Theory and Practice of Software, ETAPS 2005, Edinburgh, UK, April 4–8, 2005, Proceedings. Lecture Notes in Computer Science, vol. 3444, pp. 21–30. Springer, Cham (2005). https://doi.org/10.1007/978-3-540-31987-0_3

16. Facebook: Sparta. https://github.com/facebookincubator/SPARTA (2020)

17. Gange, G., Navas, J.A., Schachte, P., Søndergaard, H., Stuckey, P.J.: An abstract domain of uninterpreted functions. In: Verification, Model Checking, and Abstract Interpretation - 17th International Conference, VMCAI 2016, St. Petersburg, FL, USA, January 17–19, 2016. Proceedings. pp. 85–103 (2016). https://doi.org/10.1007/978-3-662-49122-5_4

18. Gange, G., Navas, J.A., Schachte, P., Søndergaard, H., Stuckey, P.J.: Exploiting sparsity in difference-bound matrices. In: Rival, X. (ed.) Static Analysis - 23rd International Symposium, SAS 2016, Edinburgh, UK, September 8–10, 2016, Proceedings. Lecture Notes in Computer Science, vol. 9837, pp. 189–211. Springer, Heidelberg (2016). https://doi.org/10.1007/978-3-662-53413-7_10

19. gllvm. https://github.com/SRI-CSL/gllvm (2020)

20. Granger, P.: Static analysis of arithmetical congruences. Int. J. Comput. Math. **30**(3–4), 165–190 (1989). https://doi.org/10.1080/00207168908803778

21. Halbwachs, N., Henry, J.: When the decreasing sequence fails. In: Static Analysis - 19th International Symposium, SAS 2012, Deauville, France, September 11–13, 2012. Proceedings, pp. 198–213 (2012). https://doi.org/10.1007/978-3-642-33125-1_15

22. Halbwachs, N., Merchat, D., Gonnord, L.: Some ways to reduce the space dimension in polyhedra computations. Formal Methods Syst. Des. **29**(1), 79–95 (2006). https://doi.org/10.1007/s10703-006-0013-2

23. Henry, J., Monniaux, D., Moy, M.: PAGAI: a path sensitive static analyser. Electron. Notes Theor. Comput. Sci. **289**, 15–25 (2012). https://doi.org/10.1016/j.entcs.2012.11.003

24. Heo, K., Oh, H., Yang, H.: Learning a variable-clustering strategy for octagon from labeled data generated by a static analysis. In: Rival, X. (ed.) Static Analysis - 23rd International Symposium, SAS 2016, Edinburgh, UK, September 8–10, 2016, Proceedings. Lecture Notes in Computer Science, vol. 9837, pp. 237–256. Springer, Cham (2016). https://doi.org/10.1007/978-3-662-53413-7_12

25. Jeannet, B., Miné, A.: Apron: A library of numerical abstract domains for static analysis. In: Bouajjani, A., Maler, O. (eds.) Computer Aided Verification, 21st International Conference, CAV 2009, Grenoble, France, June 26 - July 2, 2009. Proceedings. Lecture Notes in Computer Science, vol. 5643, pp. 661–667. Springer, Heidelberg (2009). https://doi.org/10.1007/978-3-642-02658-4_52

26. Kim, S.K., Venet, A.J., Thakur, A.V.: Deterministic parallel fixpoint computation. PACMPL **4**(POPL), 14:1–14:33 (2020). https://doi.org/10.1145/3371082

27. Kim, S.K., Venet, A.J., Thakur, A.V.: Memory-efficient fixpoint computation (2020). https://arxiv.org/abs/2009.05865

28. Li, Y., Albarghouthi, A., Kincaid, Z., Gurfinkel, A., Chechik, M.: Symbolic optimization with SMT solvers. In: Jagannathan, S., Sewell, P. (eds.) The 41st Annual ACM SIGPLAN-SIGACT Symposium on Principles of Programming Languages, POPL 2014, San Diego, CA, USA, January 20–21, 2014. pp. 607–618. ACM (2014). https://doi.org/10.1145/2535838.2535857

29. Miné, A.: Tutorial on static inference of numeric invariants by abstract interpretation. Found. Trends Program. Lang. **4**(3–4), 120–372 (2017). https://doi.org/10.1561/2500000034

30. Monniaux, D.: The parallel implementation of the astrée static analyzer. In: Programming Languages and Systems, Third Asian Symposium, APLAS 2005, Tsukuba, Japan, November 2–5, 2005, Proceedings, pp. 86–96 (2005). https://doi.org/10.1007/11575467_7

31. Naeem, N.A., Lhoták, O., Rodriguez, J.: Practical extensions to the IFDS algorithm. In: Gupta, R. (ed.) Compiler Construction, 19th International Conference, CC 2010, Held as Part of the Joint European Conferences on Theory and Practice of Software, ETAPS 2010, Paphos, Cyprus, March 20–28, 2010. Proceedings. Lecture Notes in Computer Science, vol. 6011, pp. 124–144. Springer, Heidelberg (2010). https://doi.org/10.1007/978-3-642-11970-5_8

32. Navas, J.A.: Crab: Cornucopia of abstractions: a language-agnostic library for abstract interpretation. https://github.com/seahorn/crab (2019)

33. Oh, H., Heo, K., Lee, W., Lee, W., Park, D., Kang, J., Yi, K.: Global sparse analysis framework. ACM Trans. Program. Lang. Syst. **36**(3), 8:1–8:44 (2014). https://doi.org/10.1145/2590811

34. Oh, H., Heo, K., Lee, W., Lee, W., Yi, K.: Design and implementation of sparse global analyses for c-like languages. In: ACM SIGPLAN Conference on Programming Language Design and Implementation, PLDI 2012, Beijing, China - June 11–16, 2012, pp. 229–238 (2012). https://doi.org/10.1145/2254064.2254092

35. Okasaki, C., Gill, A.: Fast mergeable integer maps. In: Workshop on ML, pp. 77–86 (1998)

36. Ramalingam, G.: Identifying loops in almost linear time. ACM Trans. Program. Lang. Syst. **21**(2), 175–188 (1999). https://doi.org/10.1145/316686.316687

37. Ramalingam, G.: On loops, dominators, and dominance frontiers. ACM Trans. Program. Lang. Syst. **24**(5), 455–490 (2002). https://doi.org/10.1145/570886.570887

38. Rastello, F.: On Sparse Intermediate Representations: Some Structural Properties and Applications to Just-In-Time Compilation. University works, Inria Grenoble Rhône-Alpes (Dec 2012). https://hal.inria.fr/hal-00761555, habilitation à diriger des recherches, École normale supérieure de Lyon

39. Reps, T.W., Horwitz, S., Sagiv, M.: Precise interprocedural dataflow analysis via graph reachability. In: Conference Record of POPL 1995: 22nd ACM SIGPLAN-SIGACT Symposium on Principles of Programming Languages, San Francisco, California, USA, January 23–25, 1995, pp. 49–61 (1995). https://doi.org/10.1145/199448.199462

40. Reps, T.W., Sagiv, S., Yorsh, G.: Symbolic implementation of the best transformer. In: Steffen, B., Levi, G. (eds.) Verification, Model Checking, and Abstract Interpretation, 5th International Conference, VMCAI 2004, Venice, Italy, January 11–13, 2004, Proceedings. Lecture Notes in Computer Science, vol. 2937, pp. 252–266. Springer, New York (2004). https://doi.org/10.1007/978-3-540-24622-0_21
41. Reps, T.W., Thakur, A.V.: Automating abstract interpretation. In: Jobstmann, B., Leino, K.R.M. (eds.) Verification, Model Checking, and Abstract Interpretation - 17th International Conference, VMCAI 2016, St. Petersburg, FL, USA, January 17–19, 2016. Proceedings. Lecture Notes in Computer Science, vol. 9583, pp. 3–40. Springer, Heidelberg (2016). https://doi.org/10.1007/978-3-662-49122-5_1
42. Seidl, H., Vogler, R.: Three improvements to the top-down solver. In: Sabel, D., Thiemann, P. (eds.) Proceedings of the 20th International Symposium on Principles and Practice of Declarative Programming, PPDP 2018, Frankfurt am Main, Germany, September 03–05, 2018, pp. 21:1–21:14. ACM (2018). https://doi.org/10.1145/3236950.3236967
43. Singh, G., Püschel, M., Vechev, M.T.: Making numerical program analysis fast. In: Proceedings of the 36th ACM SIGPLAN Conference on Programming Language Design and Implementation, Portland, OR, USA, June 15–17, 2015, pp. 303–313 (2015). https://doi.org/10.1145/2737924.2738000
44. Singh, G., Püschel, M., Vechev, M.T.: Fast polyhedra abstract domain. In: Castagna, G., Gordon, A.D. (eds.) Proceedings of the 44th ACM SIGPLAN Symposium on Principles of Programming Languages, POPL 2017, Paris, France, January 18–20, 2017, pp. 46–59. ACM (2017). https://doi.org/10.1145/3009837.3009885
45. Singh, G., Püschel, M., Vechev, M.T.: Fast numerical program analysis with reinforcement learning. In: Computer Aided Verification - 30th International Conference, CAV 2018, Held as Part of the Federated Logic Conference, FloC 2018, Oxford, UK, July 14–17, 2018, Proceedings, Part I. pp. 211–229 (2018). https://doi.org/10.1007/978-3-319-96145-3_12
46. Singh, G., Püschel, M., Vechev, M.T.: A practical construction for decomposing numerical abstract domains. In: Proceedings ACM Programming Language 2(POPL), 55:1–55:28 (2018). https://doi.org/10.1145/3158143
47. Tarjan, R.E.: Applications of path compression on balanced trees. J. ACM 26(4), 690–715 (1979). https://doi.org/10.1145/322154.322161
48. Technology, K.: Codehawk. https://github.com/kestreltechnology/codehawk (2020)
49. Thakur, A.V., Elder, M., Reps, T.W.: Bilateral algorithms for symbolic abstraction. In: Miné, A., Schmidt, D. (eds.) Static Analysis - 19th International Symposium, SAS 2012, Deauville, France, September 11–13, 2012. Proceedings. Lecture Notes in Computer Science, vol. 7460, pp. 111–128. Springer, Cham (2012). https://doi.org/10.1007/978-3-642-33125-1_10
50. Thakur, A.V., Lal, A., Lim, J., Reps, T.W.: Posthat and all that: automating abstract interpretation. Electron. Notes Theor. Comput. Sci. 311, 15–32 (2015). https://doi.org/10.1016/j.entcs.2015.02.003
51. Thakur, A.V., Reps, T.W.: A method for symbolic computation of abstract operations. In: Madhusudan, P., Seshia, S.A. (eds.) Computer Aided Verification - 24th International Conference, CAV 2012, Berkeley, CA, USA, July 7–13, 2012 Proceedings. Lecture Notes in Computer Science, vol. 7358, pp. 174–192. Springer, Heeidelberg (2012). https://doi.org/10.1007/978-3-642-31424-7_17

52. Venet, A., Brat, G.P.: Precise and efficient static array bound checking for large embedded C programs. In: Proceedings of the ACM SIGPLAN 2004 Conference on Programming Language Design and Implementation 2004, Washington, DC, USA, June 9–11, 2004 pp. 231–242 (2004). https://doi.org/10.1145/996841.996869
53. Wang, K., Hussain, A., Zuo, Z., Xu, G.H., Sani, A.A.: Graspan: A single-machine disk-based graph system for interprocedural static analyses of large-scale systems code. In: Proceedings of the Twenty-Second International Conference on Architectural Support for Programming Languages and Operating Systems, ASPLOS 2017, Xi'an, China, April 8–12, 2017, pp. 389–404 (2017). https://doi.org/10.1145/3037697.3037744
54. Weiss, C., Rubio-González, C., Liblit, B.: Database-backed program analysis for scalable error propagation. In: 37th IEEE/ACM International Conference on Software Engineering, ICSE 2015, Florence, Italy, May 16–24, 2015, vol. 1. pp. 586–597 (2015). https://doi.org/10.1109/ICSE.2015.75
55. Zuo, Z., Gu, R., Jiang, X., Wang, Z., Huang, Y., Wang, L., Li, X.: Bigspa: an efficient interprocedural static analysis engine in the cloud. In: 2019 IEEE International Parallel and Distributed Processing Symposium, IPDPS 2019, Rio de Janeiro, Brazil, May 20–24, 2019, pp. 771–780. IEEE (2019). https://doi.org/10.1109/IPDPS.2019.00086

Abstract Neural Networks

Matthew Sotoudeh$^{(\boxtimes)}$ (ID) and Aditya V. Thakur (ID)

University of California, Davis, USA
{masotoudeh,avthakur}@ucdavis.edu

Abstract. Deep Neural Networks (DNNs) are rapidly being applied
to safety-critical domains such as drone and airplane control, motivating techniques for verifying the safety of their behavior. Unfortunately,
DNN verification is NP-hard, with current algorithms slowing exponentially with the number of nodes in the DNN. This paper introduces
the notion of Abstract Neural Networks (ANNs), which can be used
to soundly overapproximate DNNs while using fewer nodes. An ANN
is like a DNN except weight matrices are replaced by values in a given
abstract domain. We present a framework parameterized by the abstract
domain and activation functions used in the DNN that can be used to
construct a corresponding ANN. We present necessary and sufficient conditions on the DNN activation functions for the constructed ANN to
soundly over-approximate the given DNN. Prior work on DNN abstraction was restricted to the interval domain and ReLU activation function.
Our framework can be instantiated with other abstract domains such
as octagons and polyhedra, as well as other activation functions such as
Leaky ReLU, Sigmoid, and Hyperbolic Tangent.

Keywords: Deep Neural Networks · Abstraction · Soundness

1 Introduction

Deep Neural Networks (DNNs), defined formally in Sect. 3, are loop-free computer programs organized into *layers*, each of which computes a linear combination of the layer's inputs, then applies some *non-linear activation function*
to the resulting values. The activation function used varies between networks,
with popular activation functions including ReLU, Hyperbolic Tangent, and
Leaky ReLU [13]. DNNs have rapidly become important in a variety of applications, including image recognition and safety-critical control systems, motivating
research into the problem of verifying properties about their behavior [9,18].

Although they lack loops, the use of non-linear activation functions introduces *exponential branching behavior* into the DNN semantics. It has been shown
that DNN verification is NP-hard [18]. In particular, this exponential behavior
scales with the number of *nodes* in a network. DNNs in practice have very large
numbers of nodes, e.g., the aircraft collision-avoidance DNN ACAS Xu [17] has
300 and a modern image recognition network has tens of thousands [20]. The
number of nodes in modern networks has also been growing with time as more
effective training methods have been found [3].

© Springer Nature Switzerland AG 2020
D. Pichardie and M. Sighireanu (Eds.): SAS 2020, LNCS 12389, pp. 65–88, 2020.
https://doi.org/10.1007/978-3-030-65474-0_4

One increasingly common way of addressing this problem is to compress the DNN into a smaller proxy network which can be analyzed in its place. However, most such approaches usually do not guarantee that properties of the proxy network hold in the original network (they are unsound). Recently, Prabhakar et al. [29] introduced the notion of *Interval Neural Networks* (INNs), which can produce a smaller proxy network that is *guaranteed* to over-approximate the behavior of the original DNN. While promising, soundness is only guaranteed with a particular activation function (ReLU) and abstract domain (intervals).

In this work, we introduce *Abstract Neural Networks* (ANNs), which are like DNNs except weight matrices are replaced with values in an abstract domain. Given a DNN and an abstract domain, we present an algorithm for constructing a corresponding ANN with fewer nodes. The algorithm works by merging groups of nodes in the DNN to form corresponding abstract nodes in the ANN. We prove necessary and sufficient conditions on the activation functions used for the constructed ANN to over-approximate the input DNN. If these conditions are met, the smaller ANN can be soundly analyzed in place of the DNN. Our formalization and theoretical results generalize those of Prabhakar et al. [29], which are an instantiation of our framework for ReLU activation functions and the interval domain. Our results also show how to instantiate the algorithm such that sound abstraction can be achieved with a variety of different abstract domains (including polytopes and octagons) as well as many popular activation functions (including Hyperbolic Tangent, Leaky ReLU, and Sigmoid).

Outline. In this paper, we aim to lay strong theoretical foundations for research into abstracting neural networks for verification. Section 2 gives an overview of our technique. Section 3 defines preliminaries. Section 4 defines *Abstract Neural Networks* (ANNs). Section 5 presents an algorithm for constructing an ANN from a given DNN. Section 6 motivates our theoretical results with a number of examples. Section 7 proves our soundness theorem. Section 8 discusses related work, while Sect. 9 concludes with a discussion of future work. Code implementing our framework can be found at https://doi.org/10.5281/zenodo.4031610. Detailed proofs of all theorems are in the extended version of this paper [34].

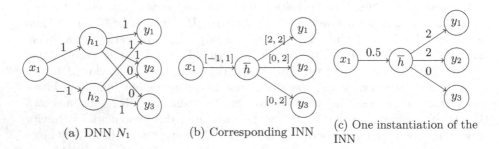

(a) DNN N_1 (b) Corresponding INN   (c) One instantiation of the INN

Fig. 1. Example DNN to INN and one of many instantiations of the INN.

2   Motivation

DNNs are often denoted by a graph of the form shown in Fig. 1a. The input node x_1 is assigned the *input value*, then the values of h_1 and h_2 are computed by first a linear combination of the values of the previous layer (in this case x_1) followed by some *non-linear activation function*. The behavior of the network is dependent on the non-linear activation function used. We will assume that the output layer with nodes y_1, y_2, and y_3 uses the identity activation function $I(x) = x$. For the hidden layer with nodes h_1 and h_2 we will consider two scenarios, each using one of the following two activation functions:

$$\sigma(x) = \begin{cases} x & \text{if } x \geq 0 \\ 0 & \text{otherwise.} \end{cases} \qquad \phi(x) = \begin{cases} x & \text{if } x \geq 0 \\ 0.5x & \text{otherwise.} \end{cases}$$

Using σ as the activation function for the hidden layer, when $x_1 = 1$ we have $h_1 = \sigma(1x_1) = 1$ and $h_2 = \sigma(-1x_1) = 0$. That in turn gives us $y_1 = I(1h_1 + 1h_2) = 1$, $y_2 = I(1h_1 + 0h_2) = 1$, and $y_3 = I(0h_1 + 1h_2) = 0$.

Using σ as the activation function for the hidden layer, when $x_1 = 1$, we have

$$h_1 = \sigma(1x_1) = 1 \qquad h_2 = \sigma(-1x_1) = 0$$
$$y_1 = I(1h_1 + 1h_2) = 1 \quad y_2 = I(1h_1 + 0h_2) = 1 \quad y_3 = I(0h_1 + 1h_2) = 0.$$

Using ϕ as the activation function for the hidden layer, when $x_1 = 1$, we have

$$h_1 = \phi(1) = 1 \qquad h_2 = \phi(-1) = -0.5$$
$$y_1 = 0.5 \qquad\qquad y_2 = 1 \qquad\qquad\qquad y_3 = -0.5.$$

2.1   Merging Nodes

Our goal is to *merge* nodes and their corresponding weights in this DNN to produce a smaller network that over-approximates the behavior of the original one. One way of doing this was proposed by Prabhakar et al. [29], where nodes within a layer can be merged and the *weighted interval hull* of their edge weights is taken. For example, if we merge all of the h_i nodes together into a single $\bar{h}$ node, this process results in an *Interval Neural Network* (INN) shown in Fig. 1b.

Intuitively, given this new INN we can form a *DNN instantiation* by picking any weight within the interval for each edge. We can then find the output of this DNN instantiation on, say, $x_1 = 1$. We take the *output of the INN* on an input x_1 to be the set of *all* such (y_1, y_2, y_3) triples outputted by some such instantiated DNN on x_1.

For example, we can take the instantiation in Fig. 1c. Using the σ activation function, this implies $(y_1 = 1, y_2 = 1, y_3 = 0)$ is in the output set of the INN on input $x_1 = 1$. In fact, the results of Prabhakar et al. [29] show that, if the σ activation function is used, then for any input x_1 we will have some assignment to the weights which produces the same output as the original DNN (although many assignments will produce different outputs—the output set is an *over-approximation* of the behavior of the original network).

However, something different happens if the network were using the ϕ activation function, a case that was not considered by Prabhakar et al. [29]. In that scenario, the original DNN had an output of $(0.5, 1, -0.5)$, so if the INN were to soundly over-approximate it there would need to be some instantiation of the weights where y_1 and y_3 could have opposite signs. But this cannot happen—both will have the same (or zero) sign as $\bar{h}$!

These examples highlight the fact that the soundness of the algorithm from Prabhakar et al. [29] is specific to the ReLU activation function (σ above) and Interval abstract domain. Their results make no statement about whether INNs over-approximate DNNs using different activation functions (such as ϕ above), or if abstractions using different domains (such as the *Octagon* Neural Networks defined in Definition 11) also permit sound DNN over-approximation.

This paper develops a general framework for such DNN abstractions, parameterized by the abstract domain and activation functions used. In this framework, we prove *necessary and sufficient* conditions on the activation functions for a *Layer-Wise Abstraction Algorithm* generalizing that of Prabhakar et al. [29] to produce an ANN soundly over-approximating the given DNN. Finally, we discuss ways to modify the abstraction algorithm in order to soundly over-approximate common DNN architectures that fail the necessary conditions, extending the applicability of model abstraction to almost all currently-used DNNs.

These results lay a solid theoretical foundation for research into Abstract Neural Networks. Because our algorithm and proofs are parameterized by the abstract domain and activation functions used, our proofs allow practitioners to experiment with different abstractions, activation functions, and optimizations without having to re-prove soundness for their particular instantiation (which, as we will see in Sect. 7, is a surprisingly subtle process).

3 Preliminaries

In this section we define Deep Neural Networks and a number of commonly-used activation functions.

3.1 Deep Neural Networks

In Sect. 2, we represented neural networks by *graphs*. While this is useful for intuition, in Sect. 4 we will talk about, e.g., *octagons of layer weight matrices*, for which the graph representation makes significantly less intuitive sense. Hence, for the rest of the paper we will use an entirely equivalent *matrix representation* for DNNs, which will simplify the definitions, intuition, and proofs considerably. With this notation, we think of nodes as *dimensions* and layers of nodes as *intermediate spaces*. We then define a *layer* to be a transformation from one intermediate space to another.

Definition 1. *A DNN layer from n to m dimensions is a tuple (W, σ) where W is an $m \times n$ matrix and $\sigma : \mathbb{R} \to \mathbb{R}$ is an arbitrarily-chosen* activation function.

We will often abuse notation such that, for a vector $\boldsymbol{v}$, $\sigma(\boldsymbol{v})$ is the vector formed by applying σ to each component of $\boldsymbol{v}$.

Definition 2. *A Deep Neural Network (DNN) with layer sizes $s_0, s_1, \ldots, s_n$ is a collection of n DNN layers $(W^{(1)}, \sigma^{(1)}), \ldots, (W^{(n)}, \sigma^{(n)})$, where the $(W^{(i)}, \sigma^{(i)})$ layer is from s_{i-1} to s_i dimensions.*

Every DNN has a corresponding *function*, defined below.

Definition 3. *Given a DNN from s_0 to s_n dimensions with layers $(W^{(i)}, \sigma^{(i)})$, the* function corresponding to the DNN *is the function $f : \mathbb{R}^{s_0} \to \mathbb{R}^{s_n}$ given by $f(\boldsymbol{v}) = \boldsymbol{v}^{(n)}$, where $\boldsymbol{v}^{(i)}$ is defined inductively by $\boldsymbol{v}^{(0)} = \boldsymbol{v}$ and $\boldsymbol{v}^{(i)} = \sigma^{(i)}(W^{(i)}(\boldsymbol{v}^{(i-1)}))$.*

Where convenient, we will often refer to the corresponding function as the DNN or vice-versa.

Example 1. The DNN N_1 from Fig. 1a, when using the σ hidden-layer activation function, is represented by the layers $\left(\begin{bmatrix} 1 \\ -1 \end{bmatrix}, \sigma \right)$ and $\left(\begin{bmatrix} 1 & 1 \\ 1 & 0 \\ 0 & 1 \end{bmatrix}, I \right)$. The *function corresponding to the DNN* is given by $N_1(x_1) = \begin{bmatrix} 1 & 1 \\ 1 & 0 \\ 0 & 1 \end{bmatrix} \sigma \left(\begin{bmatrix} 1 \\ -1 \end{bmatrix} [x_1] \right)$.

3.2 Common Activation Functions

There are a number of commonly-used activation functions, listed below.

Definition 4. *The* Leaky Rectified Linear Unit *(LReLU) [22]*, Rectified Linear Unit *(ReLU)*, Hyperbolic Tangent *(tanh), and* Threshold *(thresh) activation functions are defined:*

$$\text{LReLU}(x; \mathsf{c}) := \begin{cases} x & x \geq 0 \\ \mathsf{c}x & x < 0 \end{cases}, \qquad \text{ReLU}(x) := \text{LReLU}(x; 0),$$

$$\tanh := \frac{e^{2x} - 1}{e^{2x} + 1}, \qquad \text{thresh}(x; \mathsf{t}, \mathsf{v}) := \begin{cases} x & \text{if } x \geq \mathsf{t} \\ \mathsf{v} & \text{otherwise} \end{cases}.$$

Here LReLU *and* thresh *actually represent families of activation functions parameterized by the constants $\mathsf{c}, \mathsf{t}, \mathsf{v}$. The constants used varies between networks. $\mathsf{c} = 0$ is a common choice for the* LReLU *parameter, hence the explicit definition of* ReLU.

All of these activation functions are present in standard deep-learning toolkits, such as Pytorch [26]. Libraries such as Pytorch also enable users to implement new activation functions. This variety of activation functions used in practice will motivate our study of necessary and sufficient conditions on the activation function to permit sound over-approximation.

4   Abstract Neural Networks

In this section, we formalize the syntax and semantics of Abstract Neural Networks (ANNs). We also present two types of ANNs: Interval Neural Networks (INNs) and Octagon Neural Networks (ONNs).

An ANN is like a DNN except the weights in each layer are represented by an abstract value in some abstract domain. This is formalized below.

Definition 5. *An* $n \times m$ *weight set abstract domain is a lattice* $\mathcal{A}$ *with Galois connection* $(\alpha_{\mathcal{A}}, \gamma_{\mathcal{A}})$ *with the powerset lattice* $\mathcal{P}(\mathbb{R}^{n \times m})$ *of* $n \times m$ *matrices.*

Definition 6. *An ANN layer from* n *to* m *dimensions is a triple* $(\mathcal{A}, A, \sigma)$ *where* A *is a member of the weight set abstraction* $\mathcal{A}$ *and* $\sigma : \mathbb{R} \to \mathbb{R}$ *is an arbitrarily-chosen activation function.*

Thus, we see that each ANN layer $(\mathcal{A}, A, \sigma)$ is associated with a set of weights $\gamma_{\mathcal{A}}(A)$. Finally, we can define the notion of an ANN:

Definition 7. *An Abstract Neural Network (ANN) with layer sizes* $s_0, s_1, \ldots, s_n$ *is a collection of* n *ANN layers* $(\mathcal{A}^{(i)}, A^{(i)}, \sigma^{(i)})$, *where the* ith *layer is from* s_{i-1} *to* s_i *dimensions.*

We consider the output of the ANN to be the set of outputs of all *instantiations* of the ANN into a DNN, as illustrated in Fig. 2.

Definition 8. *We say a DNN with layers* $(W^{(i)}, \sigma^{(i)})$ *is an instantiation of an ANN* T *with layers* $(\mathcal{A}^{(i)}, A^{(i)}, \sigma^{(i)})$ *if each* $W^{(i)} \in \gamma_{\mathcal{A}^{(i)}}(A^{(i)})$. *The set of all DNNs that are instantiations of an ANN* T *is given by* $\gamma(T)$.

The semantics of an ANN naturally lift those of the DNN instantiations.

Definition 9. *For an ANN* T *from* s_0 *to* s_n *dimensions, the* function corresponding to T *is the set-valued function* $T : \mathbb{R}^{s_0} \to \mathcal{P}(\mathbb{R}^{s_n})$ *defined by* $T(\boldsymbol{v}) := \{g(\boldsymbol{v}) \mid g \in \gamma(T)\}$.

Space constraints prevent us from defining a full Galois connection here, however one can be established between the lattice of ANNs of a certain *architecture* and the powerset of DNNs of the same architecture.

The definition of an ANN above is agnostic to the actual abstract domain(s) used. For expository purposes, we now define two particular types of ANNs: *Interval Neural Networks* (INNs) and *Octagon Neural Networks* (ONNs).

Definition 10. *An* Interval Neural Network (INN) *is an ANN with layers* $(\mathcal{A}^{(i)}, A^{(i)}, \sigma^{(i)})$, *where each* $\mathcal{A}^{(i)}$ *is an interval hull domain [5]. The interval hull domain represents sets of matrices by their* component-wise interval hull.

Notably, the definition of INN in Prabhakar et al. [29] is equivalent to the above, except that they further assume every activation function $\sigma^{(i)}$ is the ReLU function.

$$
\begin{array}{ccccccc}
\boldsymbol{v} & A^{(1)} & \sigma^{(1)} & A^{(2)} & \sigma^{(2)} & A^{(3)} & \sigma^{(3)}\ T(\boldsymbol{v}) \\
\end{array}
$$

$$
\boldsymbol{v} \xrightarrow{H^{(1,1)}} \boldsymbol{w}^{(1,1)} \xrightarrow{\sigma^{(1)}} \boldsymbol{v}^{(1,1)} \xrightarrow{H^{(1,2)}} \boldsymbol{w}^{(1,2)} \xrightarrow{\sigma^{(2)}} \boldsymbol{v}^{(1,2)} \xrightarrow{H^{(1,3)}} \boldsymbol{w}^{(1,3)} \xrightarrow{\sigma^{(3)}} \boldsymbol{v}^{(1,3)} \in T(\boldsymbol{v})
$$

$$
\boldsymbol{v} \xrightarrow{H^{(2,1)}} \boldsymbol{w}^{(2,1)} \xrightarrow{\sigma^{(1)}} \boldsymbol{v}^{(2,1)} \xrightarrow{H^{(2,2)}} \boldsymbol{w}^{(2,2)} \xrightarrow{\sigma^{(2)}} \boldsymbol{v}^{(2,2)} \xrightarrow{H^{(2,3)}} \boldsymbol{w}^{(2,3)} \xrightarrow{\sigma^{(3)}} \boldsymbol{v}^{(2,3)} \in T(\boldsymbol{v})
$$

$$
\vdots \qquad\qquad \vdots \qquad\qquad \vdots
$$

$$
\boldsymbol{v} \xrightarrow{H^{(j,1)}} \boldsymbol{w}^{(j,1)} \xrightarrow{\sigma^{(1)}} \boldsymbol{v}^{(j,1)} \xrightarrow{H^{(j,2)}} \boldsymbol{w}^{(j,2)} \xrightarrow{\sigma^{(2)}} \boldsymbol{v}^{(j,2)} \xrightarrow{H^{(j,3)}} \boldsymbol{w}^{(j,3)} \xrightarrow{\sigma^{(3)}} \boldsymbol{v}^{(j,3)} \in T(\boldsymbol{v})
$$

$$
\vdots \qquad\qquad \vdots \qquad\qquad \vdots
$$

Fig. 2. Visualization of ANN semantics for a 3-layer ANN T (first row). Different DNN *instantiations* (other rows) of T are formed by replacing each abstract weight matrix $A^{(i)}$ by some concrete weight matrix $H^{(j,i)} \in \gamma(A^{(i)})$. $\boldsymbol{v}^{(j,3)}$ is the output of each instantiation on the input $\boldsymbol{v}$. The set of all such outputs producable by some valid instantiation is taken to be the output $T(\boldsymbol{v})$ of the ANN on vector $\boldsymbol{v}$.

Example 2. We first demonstrate the interval hull domain: $\gamma_{\text{Int}}\left(\begin{bmatrix} [-1,1] & [0,2] \\ [-3,-2] & [1,2] \end{bmatrix}\right) = \left\{ \begin{bmatrix} a & b \\ c & d \end{bmatrix} \mid a \in [-1,1], b \in [0,2], c \in [-3,-2], d \in [1,2] \right\}$. We can thus define a two-layer INN $f(\boldsymbol{v}) := \begin{bmatrix} [0,1] & [0,1] \end{bmatrix} \text{ReLU}\left(\begin{bmatrix} [-1,1] & [0,2] \\ [-3,-2] & [1,2] \end{bmatrix} \boldsymbol{v}\right)$. We can instantiate this network in a variety of ways, for example $g(\boldsymbol{v}) := \begin{bmatrix} 0.5 & 1 \end{bmatrix} \text{ReLU}\left(\begin{bmatrix} 0 & 2 \\ -2.5 & 1.5 \end{bmatrix} \boldsymbol{v}\right) \in \gamma(f)$. Taking arbitrarily $(1,1)^T$ as an example input, we have $g((1,1)^T) = \begin{bmatrix} 1 \end{bmatrix} \in f((1,1)^T)$. In fact, $f((1,1)^T)$ is the set of *all* values that can be achieved by such instantiations, which in this case is the set given by $f((1,1)^T) = \begin{bmatrix} [0,3] \end{bmatrix}$.

Definition 11. *An* Octagon Neural Network (ONN) *is an ANN with layers* $(A^{(i)}, A^{(i)}, \sigma^{(i)})$, *where each* $A^{(i)}$ *is an* octagon hull domain *[23]. The octagon hull domain represents sets of matrices by octagons in the space of their components.*

Example 3. Octagons representing a set of $n \times m$ matrices can be thought of exactly like an octagon in the vector space $\mathbb{R}^{n \cdot m}$. Unfortunately, this is particularly difficult to visualize in higher dimensions, hence in this example we will stick to the case where $nm = 2$.

Let O_1, O_2 be octagons such that

$$
\gamma_{\text{Oct}}(O_1) = \left\{ \begin{bmatrix} a \\ b \end{bmatrix} \mid a - b \le 1, -a + b \le 1, a + b \le 2, -a - b \le 2 \right\},
$$

$$
\gamma_{\text{Oct}}(O_2) = \left\{ \begin{bmatrix} a & b \end{bmatrix} \mid a - b \le 2, -a + b \le 3, a + b \le 4, -a - b \le 5 \right\}.
$$

We can thus define a two-layer ONN $f(\boldsymbol{v}) := O_2 \text{ReLU}(O_1 \boldsymbol{v})$. One instantiation of this ONN f is the DNN $g(\boldsymbol{v}) := \begin{bmatrix} 3 & 1 \end{bmatrix} \text{ReLU}\left(\begin{bmatrix} 0.5 \\ 1.5 \end{bmatrix} \boldsymbol{v}\right) \in \gamma(f)$. We can confirm that $g(1) = \begin{bmatrix} 3 \end{bmatrix} \in f(1)$.

We can similarly define Polyhedra Neural Networks (PNNs) using the polyhedra domain [6].

5   Layer-Wise Abstraction Algorithm

Given a large DNN, how might we construct a smaller ANN which soundly *over-approximates* that DNN? We define over-approximation formally below.

Definition 12. *An ANN T* over-approximates *a DNN N if, for every $\boldsymbol{v} \in \mathbb{R}^n$, $N(\boldsymbol{v}) \in T(\boldsymbol{v})$.*

Remark 1. By Definition 9, then, T over-approximates N if, for every $\boldsymbol{v}$ we can find some instantiation $T_{\boldsymbol{v}} \in \gamma(T)$ such that $T_{\boldsymbol{v}}(\boldsymbol{v}) = N(\boldsymbol{v})$.

Algorithm 3 constructs a small ANN that, under certain assumptions discussed in Sect. 2, soundly over-approximates the large DNN given. The basic idea is to *merge* groups of dimensions together, forming an ANN where each dimension in the ANN represents a collection of dimensions in the original DNN. We formalize the notion of "groups of dimensions" as a *layer-wise partitioning*.

Definition 13. *Given a DNN with layer sizes $s_0, s_1, \ldots, s_n$, a* layer-wise partitioning $\mathbb{P}$ *of the network is a set of partitionings $\mathbb{P}^{(0)}, \mathbb{P}^{(1)}, \ldots, \mathbb{P}^{(n)}$ where each $\mathbb{P}^{(i)}$ partitions $\{1, 2, \ldots, s_i\}$. For ease of notation, we will write partitionings with set notation but assume they have some intrinsic ordering for indexing.*

Remark 2. To maintain the same number of input and output dimensions in our ANN and DNN, we assume $\mathbb{P}^{(0)} = \{\{1\}, \{2\}, \ldots, \{s_0\}\}$ and $\mathbb{P}^{(n)} = \{\{1\}, \{2\}, \ldots, \{s_n\}\}$.

Example 4. Consider the DNN corresponding to the function
$$f(x_1) = \begin{bmatrix} 1 & 1 \\ 1 & 0 \\ 0 & 1 \end{bmatrix} \text{ReLU}\left(\begin{bmatrix} 1 \\ -1 \end{bmatrix} [x_1]\right).$$ The layer sizes are $s_0 = 1, s_1 = 2, s_2 = 3$. Hence, one valid layer-wise partitioning is to merge the two inner dimensions: $\mathbb{P}^{(0)} = \{\{1\}\}$ $\mathbb{P}^{(1)} = \{\{1, 2\}\}$ $\mathbb{P}^{(2)} = \{\{1\}, \{2\}, \{3\}\}$. Here we have, e.g., $\mathbb{P}_1^{(0)} = \{1\}$, $\mathbb{P}_1^{(1)} = \{1, 2\}$, and $\mathbb{P}_3^{(2)} = \{3\}$.

Algorithm 1: $\widehat{\alpha}(M, \mathcal{P}^{in}, \mathcal{P}^{out}, \mathcal{A})$	Algorithm 2: $\widehat{\alpha}_{bin}(M, \mathcal{P}^{in}, \mathcal{P}^{out}, \mathcal{A})$
Input: Matrix M. Partitionings $\mathcal{P}^{in}$, $\mathcal{P}^{out}$ with $|\mathcal{P}^{in}| = k$. Abstract domain $\mathcal{A}$.	**Input:** Matrix M. Partitionings $\mathcal{P}^{in}$, $\mathcal{P}^{out}$ with $|\mathcal{P}^{in}| = k$. Abstract domain $\mathcal{A}$.
Output: Abstract element representing all merges of M.	**Output:** Abstract element representing all binary merges of M

Algorithm 1:

1 $S \leftarrow \{\}$
2 $w \leftarrow (|\mathcal{P}_1^{in}|, |\mathcal{P}_2^{in}|, \ldots, |\mathcal{P}_k^{in}|)$
3 **for** $C \in \text{PCMs}(\mathcal{P}^{in})$ **do**
4   **for** $D \in \text{PCMs}(\mathcal{P}^{out})$ **do**
5          $S \leftarrow S \cup \{\text{ScaleCols}(D^T M C, w))\}$
6 **return** $\alpha_{\mathcal{A}}(S)$

Algorithm 2:

1 $S \leftarrow \{\}$
2 $w \leftarrow (|\mathcal{P}_1^{in}|, |\mathcal{P}_2^{in}|, \ldots, |\mathcal{P}_k^{in}|)$
3 **for** $C \in \text{BinPCMs}(\mathcal{P}^{in})$ **do**
4   **for** $D \in \text{BinPCMs}(\mathcal{P}^{out})$ **do**
5          $S \leftarrow S \cup \{\text{ScaleCols}(D^T M C, w))\}$
6 **return** $\alpha_{\mathcal{A}}(S)$

Algorithm 3: $\text{AbstractLayerWise}\langle \mathfrak{A}, \Sigma \rangle(N, \mathbb{P}, \mathcal{A})$

Input: DNN N consisting of n layers $(W^{(i)}, \sigma^{(i)})$ with each $\sigma^{(i)} \in \Sigma$. Layer-wise partitioning $\mathbb{P}$ of N. List of n abstract weight domains $\mathcal{A}^{(i)} \in \mathfrak{A}$.
Output: An ANN with layers $(\mathcal{A}^{(i)}, A^{(i)}, \sigma^{(i)})$ where $A^{(i)} \in \mathcal{A}^{(i)} \in \mathfrak{A}$.

1 $A \leftarrow [\ \ ]$
2 **for** $i \in \{1, 2, \ldots, n\}$ **do**
3      $A^{(i)} \leftarrow \widehat{\alpha}(W^{(i)}, \mathbb{P}^{(i-1)}, \mathbb{P}^{(i)}, \mathcal{A}^{(i)})$
4      $A.\text{append}((\mathcal{A}^{(i)}, A^{(i)}, \sigma^{(i)}))$
5 **return** A

Our layer-wise abstraction algorithm is shown in Algorithm 3. For each layer in the DNN, we will call Algorithm 1 to abstract the set of *mergings* of the layer's weight matrix. This abstract element becomes the abstract weight $A^{(i)}$ for the corresponding layer in the constructed ANN.

The functions PCMs and ScaleCols are defined more precisely below.

Definition 14. *Let P be some partition, i.e., non-empty subset, of $\{1, 2, \ldots, n\}$. Then a vector $c \in \mathbb{R}^n$ is a* partition combination vector *(PCV) if (i) each component c_i is non-negative, (ii) the components of c_i sum to one, and (iii) $c_i = 0$ whenever $i \notin P$.*

Definition 15. *Given a partitioning $\mathcal{P}$ of $\{1, 2, \ldots, n\}$ with $|\mathcal{P}| = k$, a partitioning combination matrix (PCM) is a matrix $C = \begin{bmatrix} | & | & & | \\ c_1 & c_2 & \cdots & c_k \\ | & | & & | \end{bmatrix}$, where each c_i is a PCV of partition $\mathcal{P}_i$. We refer to the set of all such PCMs for a partitioning $\mathcal{P}$ by $\text{PCMs}(\mathcal{P})$.*

Definition 16. *A PCM is* binary *if each entry is either 0 or 1. We refer to the set of all binary PCMs for a partitioning $\mathcal{P}$ as* BinPCMs($\mathcal{P}$).

Definition 17. *For an $n \times m$ matrix M, PCM C of partitioning $\mathcal{P}^{in}$ of $\{1, 2, \ldots, m\}$, and PCM D for partitioning $\mathcal{P}^{out}$ of $\{1, 2, \ldots, n\}$, we call $D^T M C$ a* merging *of M.*

The jth column in MC is a convex combination of the columns of M that belong to partition $\mathcal{P}_j^{in}$, weighted by the jth column of C. Similarly, the ith row in $D^T M$ is a convex combination of the rows in M that belong to partition $\mathcal{P}_i^{out}$. In total, the i, jth entry of merged matrix $D^T M C$ is a convex combination of the entries of M with indices in $\mathcal{P}_i^{out} \times \mathcal{P}_j^{in}$. This observation will lead to Theorem 1 in Sect. 5.1.

Definition 18. *Given a matrix M, the* column-scaled matrix *formed by weights $w_1, w_2, \ldots, w_k$ is the matrix with entries given component-wise by* $\mathrm{ScaleCols}(M, (w_1, \ldots, w_k))_{i,j} := M_{i,j} w_j$.

Intuitively, column-scaling is needed because what were originally n dimensions contributing to an input have been collapsed into a single representative dimension. This is demonstrated nicely for the specific case of Interval Neural Network and ReLU activations by Figs. 3 and 4 in Prabhakar et al. [29].

Example 5. Given the matrix $M = \begin{bmatrix} m_{1,1} & m_{1,2} & m_{1,3} \\ m_{2,1} & m_{2,2} & m_{2,3} \\ m_{3,1} & m_{3,2} & m_{3,3} \\ m_{4,1} & m_{4,2} & m_{4,3} \end{bmatrix}$, partitioning $\mathbb{P}^{(0)} = \{\{1,3\}, \{2\}\}$ of the input dimensions and $\mathbb{P}^{(1)} = \{\{2,4\}, \{1,3\}\}$ of the output dimensions, we can define a PCM for $\mathbb{P}^{(0)}$ as $C := \begin{bmatrix} 0.25 & 0 \\ 0 & 1 \\ 0.75 & 0 \end{bmatrix}$ and a PCM for $\mathbb{P}^{(1)}$ as: $D := \begin{bmatrix} 0 & 0.99 \\ 0.4 & 0 \\ 0 & 0.01 \\ 0.6 & 0 \end{bmatrix}$. We can then compute the *column–merged matrix*

$MC = \begin{bmatrix} 0.25m_{1,1} + 0.75m_{1,3} & m_{1,2} \\ 0.25m_{2,1} + 0.75m_{2,3} & m_{2,2} \\ 0.25m_{3,1} + 0.75m_{3,3} & m_{3,2} \\ 0.25m_{4,1} + 0.75m_{4,3} & m_{4,2} \end{bmatrix}$, and furthermore the *column-row–merged matrix*

$D^T MC = \begin{bmatrix} 0.4(0.25m_{2,1} + 0.75m_{2,3}) + 0.6(0.25m_{4,1} + 0.75m_{4,3}) & 0.4m_{2,2} + 0.6m_{4,2} \\ 0.99(0.25m_{1,1} + 0.75m_{1,3}) + 0.01(0.25m_{3,1} + 0.75m_{3,3}) & 0.99m_{1,2} + 0.01m_{3,2} \end{bmatrix}$.

Finally, we can column-scale this matrix like so:

$\mathrm{ScaleCols}(D^T MC, (2, 2))$

$= \begin{bmatrix} 0.8(0.25m_{2,1} + 0.75m_{2,3}) + 1.2(0.25m_{4,1} + 0.75m_{4,3}) & 0.8m_{2,2} + 1.2m_{4,2} \\ 1.98(0.25m_{1,1} + 0.75m_{1,3}) + 0.02(0.25m_{3,1} + 0.75m_{3,3}) & 1.98m_{1,2} + 0.02m_{3,2} \end{bmatrix}$.

5.1 Computability

In general, there are an infinite number of mergings. Hence, to actually compute $\widehat{\alpha}$ (Algorithm 1) we need some non-trivial way to compute the abstraction of the infinite set of mergings. If the abstract domain $\mathcal{A}^{(i)}$ is *convex*, it can be shown that one only needs to iterate over the binary PCMs, of which there are finitely many, producing a computationally feasible algorithm.

Definition 19. *A weight set abstract domain $\mathcal{A}$ is* convex *if, for any set S of concrete values, $\gamma_A(\alpha_A(S))$ is convex.*

Many commonly-used abstractions—including intervals [5], octagons [23], and polyhedra [6]—are convex.

Theorem 1. *If $\mathcal{A}$ is convex, then $\widehat{\alpha}(M, \mathcal{P}^{in}, \mathcal{P}^{out}, A) = \widehat{\alpha}_{bin}(M, \mathcal{P}^{in}, \mathcal{P}^{out}, A)$.*

Remark 3. Consider PCMs C and D corresponding to merged matrix $D^T W^{(i)} C$. We may think of C and D as vectors in the vector space of matrices. Then their outer product $D \otimes C$ forms a convex coefficient matrix of the binary mergings R of $W^{(i)}$, such that $(D \otimes C)R = D^T W^{(i)} C$. From this intuition, it follows that the converse to Theorem 1 *does not* hold, as every matrix E cannot be decomposed into vectors $D \otimes C$ as described (i.e., not every matrix has rank 1). Hence, the convexity condition may be slightly weakened. However, we are not presently aware of any abstract domains that satisfy such a condition but not convexity.

Example 6. Let $W^{(i)} = \begin{bmatrix} 1 & -2 & 3 \\ 4 & -5 & 6 \\ 7 & -8 & 9 \end{bmatrix}$ and consider $\mathbb{P}^{(i-1)} = \{\{1,2\}, \{3\}\}$ and $\mathbb{P}^{(i)} = \{\{1,3\}, \{2\}\}$. Then we have the binary PCMs $\text{BinPCMs}(\mathbb{P}^{(i-1)}) = \left\{ \begin{bmatrix} 1 & 0 \\ 0 & 0 \\ 0 & 1 \end{bmatrix}, \begin{bmatrix} 0 & 0 \\ 1 & 0 \\ 0 & 1 \end{bmatrix} \right\}$ and $\text{BinPCMs}(\mathbb{P}^{(i)}) = \left\{ \begin{bmatrix} 1 & 0 \\ 0 & 1 \\ 0 & 0 \end{bmatrix}, \begin{bmatrix} 0 & 0 \\ 0 & 1 \\ 1 & 0 \end{bmatrix} \right\}$. These correspond to the column-scaled binary mergings $\left\{ \begin{bmatrix} 2 & 3 \\ 8 & 6 \end{bmatrix}, \begin{bmatrix} -4 & 3 \\ -10 & 6 \end{bmatrix}, \begin{bmatrix} 14 & 9 \\ 8 & 6 \end{bmatrix}, \begin{bmatrix} -16 & 9 \\ -10 & 6 \end{bmatrix} \right\}$.

We can take any PCMs such as $C = \begin{bmatrix} 0.75 & 0 \\ 0.25 & 0 \\ 0 & 1 \end{bmatrix}$ for $\mathbb{P}^{(i-1)}$ as well as $D = \begin{bmatrix} 0.5 & 0 \\ 0 & 1 \\ 0.5 & 0 \end{bmatrix}$ for $\mathbb{P}^{(i)}$, resulting in the scaled merging $\text{ScaleCols}(D^T W^{(i)} C, (2,1)) = \begin{bmatrix} 3.5 & 6 \\ 3.5 & 6 \end{bmatrix}$. According to Theorem 1, we can write this as a convex combination of the four column-scaled binary merged matrices. In particular, we find the combination

$$\begin{bmatrix} 3.5 & 6 \\ 3.5 & 6 \end{bmatrix} = (1.5/2)(1)(0.5)(1) \begin{bmatrix} 2 & 3 \\ 8 & 6 \end{bmatrix} + (0.5/2)(1)(0.5)(1) \begin{bmatrix} -4 & 3 \\ -10 & 6 \end{bmatrix}$$
$$+ (1.5/2)(1)(0.5)(1) \begin{bmatrix} 14 & 9 \\ 8 & 6 \end{bmatrix} + (0.5/2)(1)(0.5)(1) \begin{bmatrix} -16 & 9 \\ -10 & 6 \end{bmatrix}.$$

We can confirm that this is a convex combination, as

$$(1.5/2)(1)(0.5)(1) + (0.5/2)(1)(0.5)(1) + (1.5/2)(1)(0.5)(1) + (0.5/2)(1)(0.5)(1) = 1.$$

Because we can find such a convex combination for any such non-binary merging in terms of the binary ones, and because the abstract domain is assumed to be convex, including only the binary mergings will ensure that *all* mergings are represented by the abstract element $A^{(i)}$.

5.2 Walkthrough Example

Example 7. Consider again the DNN from Example 4 corresponding to $f(x_1) = \begin{bmatrix} 1 & 1 \\ 1 & 0 \\ 0 & 1 \end{bmatrix} \sigma \left(\begin{bmatrix} 1 \\ -1 \end{bmatrix} [x_1] \right)$, the partitioning $\mathbb{P}^{(0)} = \{\{1\}\}, \mathbb{P}^{(1)} = \{\{1,2\}\}, \mathbb{P}^{(2)} =$

$\{\{1\}, \{2\}, \{3\}\}$, which collapses the two hidden dimensions, and assume the abstract domains $\mathcal{A}^{(i)}$ are all convex.

For the input layer, we have $w = (1)$, because the only partition in $\mathbb{P}^{(0)}$ has size 1. Similarly, the only binary PCM for $\mathbb{P}^{(0)}$ is $C = \begin{bmatrix} 1 \end{bmatrix}$. However, there are two binary PCMs for $\mathbb{P}^{(1)}$, namely $D = \begin{bmatrix} 1 \\ 0 \end{bmatrix}$ or $D = \begin{bmatrix} 0 \\ 1 \end{bmatrix}$. These correspond to the binary merged matrices $\begin{bmatrix} 1 \end{bmatrix}$ and $\begin{bmatrix} -1 \end{bmatrix}$. Hence, we get $A^{(1)} = \alpha_{\mathcal{A}^{(1)}}(\{\begin{bmatrix} 1 \end{bmatrix}, \begin{bmatrix} -1 \end{bmatrix}\})$, completing the first layer.

For the output layer, we have $w = (2)$, because the only partition in $\mathbb{P}^{(1)}$ contains *two* nodes. Hence, the column scaling will need to play a role: because we have merged two dimensions in the domain, we should interpret any value from that dimension as being from *both* of the dimensions that were merged. We have two binary mergings, namely $\begin{bmatrix} 1 \\ 1 \\ 0 \end{bmatrix}$ and $\begin{bmatrix} 1 \\ 0 \\ 1 \end{bmatrix}$, which after rescaling gives us

$$A^{(2)} = \alpha_{\mathcal{A}^{(2)}}\left(\left\{\begin{bmatrix} 2 \\ 2 \\ 0 \end{bmatrix}, \begin{bmatrix} 2 \\ 0 \\ 2 \end{bmatrix}\right\}\right).$$

In total then, the returned ANN can be written $(A^{(1)}, \sigma)$, $(A^{(2)}, x \mapsto x)$ or in a more functional notation as $g(x) = A^{(2)}\sigma(A^{(1)}x)$, where in either case $A^{(1)} = \alpha_{\mathcal{A}^{(1)}}(\{\begin{bmatrix} 1 \end{bmatrix}, \begin{bmatrix} -1 \end{bmatrix}\})$, and $A^{(2)} = \alpha_{\mathcal{A}^{(2)}}\left(\left\{\begin{bmatrix} 2 \\ 2 \\ 0 \end{bmatrix}, \begin{bmatrix} 2 \\ 0 \\ 2 \end{bmatrix}\right\}\right).$

Note in particular that, while the operation of the algorithm was agnostic to the exact abstract domains $\mathfrak{A}$ and activation functions Σ used, the semantics of the resulting ANN depend *entirely* on these. Hence, correctness of the algorithm will depend on the abstract domain and activation functions satisfying certain conditions. We will discuss this further in Sect. 6.

6   Layer-Wise Abstraction: Instantiations and Examples

This section examines a number of examples. For some DNNs, Algorithm 3 will produce a soundly over-approximating ANN. For others, the ANN will provably *not* over-approximate the given DNN. We will generalize these examples to necessary and sufficient conditions on the activation functions Σ used in order for AbstractLayerWise$\langle \mathfrak{A}, \Sigma \rangle(N, \mathbb{P}, \mathcal{A})$ to soundly over-approximate N.

6.1   Interval Hull Domain with ReLU Activation Functions

Consider again the DNN from Example 7 given by $f(x_1) = \begin{bmatrix} 1 & 1 \\ 1 & 0 \\ 0 & 1 \end{bmatrix}$ ReLU $\left(\begin{bmatrix} 1 \\ -1 \end{bmatrix} [x_1]\right)$ and partitioning which merges the two intermediate dimensions. Using the interval hull domain in Example 7 gives the corresponding INN:
$g(x_1) = \begin{bmatrix} [2,2] \\ [0,2] \\ [0,2] \end{bmatrix}$ ReLU $([[-1,1]] [x_1])$.

In fact, because the ReLU activation function and interval domain was used, it follows from the results of Prabhakar et al. [29] that g in fact over-approximates

f. To see this, consider two cases. If $x_1 > 0$, then the second component in the hidden dimension of f will always become 0 under the activation function. Hence,

$$f(x_1) = \begin{bmatrix} 1 \\ 1 \\ 0 \end{bmatrix} \text{ReLU} \left([1]\, [x_1] \right) = \begin{bmatrix} 2 \\ 2 \\ 0 \end{bmatrix} \text{ReLU} \left([0.5]\, [x_1] \right), \text{ which is a valid instantiation}$$

of the weights in g. Otherwise, if $x_1 \leq 0$, we find $f(x_1) = \begin{bmatrix} 2 \\ 0 \\ 2 \end{bmatrix} \text{ReLU} \left([-0.5]\, [x_1] \right)$,

which is again a valid instantiation. Hence in all cases, the true output $f(x_1)$ can be made by some valid instantiation of the weights in g. Therefore, $f(x_1) \in g(x_1)$ for all x_1 and so g over-approximates f.

Sufficiency Condition. The soundness of this particular instantiation can be generalized to a sufficiency theorem, Theorem 2, for soundness of the layer-wise abstraction algorithm. Its statement relies on the activation function satisfying the *weakened intermediate value property*, which is defined below:

Definition 20. *A function* $f : \mathbb{R} \to \mathbb{R}$ *satisfies the* Weakened Intermediate Value Property (WIVP) *if, for every* $a_1 \leq a_2 \leq \cdots \leq a_n \in \mathbb{R}$, *there exists some* $b \in [a_1, a_n]$ *such that* $f(b) = \frac{\sum_i f(a_i)}{n}$.

Every continuous function satisfies the IVP and hence the WIVP. Almost all commonly-used activation functions, except for thresh, are continuous and, therefore, satisfy the WIVP. However, the WIVP is not equivalent to the IVP, as the below proof shows by constructing a function f such that $f((a,b)) = \mathbb{Q}$ for any non-empty open interval (a, b).

We now state the soundness theorem below, which is proved in Sect. 7.

Theorem 2. *Let* $\mathfrak{A}$ *be a set of weight set abstract domains and* Σ *a set of activation functions. Suppose (i) each* $\sigma \in \Sigma$ *has entirely non-negative outputs, and (ii) each* $\sigma \in \Sigma$ *satisfies the Weakened Intermediate Value Property (Definition 20). Then* $T = \text{AbstractLayerWise}\langle \mathfrak{A}, \Sigma \rangle(N, \mathbb{P}, \mathcal{A})$ *(Algorithm 3) soundly over-approximates the DNN* N.

6.2 Interval Hull Domain with *Leaky* ReLUs

Something different happens if we slightly modify f in Example 7 to use an activation function producing *negative values* in the intermediate dimensions. This is quite common of activation functions like Leaky ReLU and tanh, and was not mentioned by Prabhakar et al. [29]. For example, we will take the Leaky ReLU function (Definition 4) with $c = 0.5$ and consider the DNN $f(x_1) = \begin{bmatrix} 1 & 1 \\ 0 & 1 \end{bmatrix} \text{LReLU} \left(\begin{bmatrix} 1 \\ -1 \end{bmatrix} [x_1]; 0.5 \right)$. Using the same partitioning gives us the INN $g(x_1) = \begin{bmatrix} [2,2] \\ [0,2] \\ [0,2] \end{bmatrix} \text{LReLU} \left([[-1,1]]\, [x_1]; 0.5 \right)$.

Surprisingly, this small change to the activation function in fact makes the constructed ANN no longer over-approximate the original DNN. For example, note that $f(1) = \begin{bmatrix} 0.5 & 1 & -0.5 \end{bmatrix}^T$ and consider $g(1)$. In g, the output of the LReLU is one-dimensional, hence, it will have either positive, negative, or zero sign. But no matter how the weights in the final matrix are instantiated, every component of $g(1)$ will have *the same (or zero) sign*, and so $f(1) \not\subseteq g(1)$, because $f(1)$ has mixed signs.

Necessary Condition: Non-negative Values. We can generalize this counterexample to the following necessary condition on soundness:

Theorem 3. *Suppose some $\sigma \in \Sigma$ is an activation function with neither entirely non-negative nor entirely non-positive outputs, and every $A \in \mathfrak{A}$ is at least as precise as the interval hull abstraction. Then there exists a neural network N that uses σ and a partitioning $\mathbb{P}$ such that $T = \mathrm{AbstractLayerWise}\langle\mathfrak{A}, \Sigma\rangle(N, \mathbb{P}, A)$ does not over-approximate N.*

Handling Negative Values. Thankfully, there is a workaround to support sometimes-negative activation functions. The constructive theorem below implies that a given DNN can be modified into a *shifted* version of itself such that the input-output behavior on any arbitrary bounded region is retained, but the intermediate activations are all non-negative.

Theorem 4. *Let N be a DNN and suppose that, on some input region R, the output of the activation functions are lower-bounded by a constant C. Then, there exists another DNN N', with at most one extra dimension per layer, which satisfies (i) $N'(x) = N(x)$ for any $x \in R$, (ii) N' has all non-negative activation functions, and (iii) the new activation functions σ' are of the form $\sigma'(x) = \max(\sigma(x) + |C|, 0)$.*

Notably, the proof of this theorem is *constructive* with a straightforward construction. The one requirement is that a lower-bound C be provided for the output of the nodes in the network. This lower-bound need not be tight, and can be computed quickly using the same procedure discussed for upper bounds immediately following Eq. 1 in Prabhakar et al. [29]. For tanh in particular, its output is always lower-bounded by -1 so we can immediately take $C = -1$ for a network using only tanh activations.

6.3   Interval Hull Abstraction with Non-continuous Functions

Another way that the constructed ANN may not over-approximate the DNN is if the activation function does not satisfy the Weakened Intermediate Value Property (WIVP) (Definition 20). For example, consider the threshold activation function (Definition 4) with parameters $t = 1$, $v = 0$ and the same overall network, i.e. $f(x_1) = \begin{bmatrix} 1 & 1 \\ 1 & 0 \\ 0 & 1 \end{bmatrix} \mathrm{thresh}\left(\begin{bmatrix} 1 \\ -1 \end{bmatrix}[x_1]; 1, 0\right)$ and the same partitioning. We get the INN $g(x_1) = \begin{bmatrix} [2,2] \\ [0,2] \\ [0,2] \end{bmatrix} \mathrm{thresh}([[-1,1]][x_1]; 1, 0)$. We have $f(1) = \begin{bmatrix} 1 & 1 & 0 \end{bmatrix}^T$, however, in $g(1)$, no matter how we instantiate the $[-1, 1]$ weight, the output of the thresh unit will either be 0 or 1. But then the output of the first output component must be either 0 or 2, neither of which is 1, and so g does *not* over-approximate f.

Necessary Condition: WIVP. We can generalize this example to the following necessary condition:

Theorem 5. *Suppose some $\sigma \in \Sigma$ is an activation function which does not satisfy the WIVP, and every $A \in \mathfrak{A}$ is at least as precise as the interval hull abstraction. Then there exists a neural network N using only the identity and σ activation functions and partitioning $\mathbb{P}$ such that $T = $ AbstractLayerWise$\langle \mathfrak{A}, \Sigma \rangle (N, \mathbb{P}, A)$ does not over-approximate N.*

While this is of some theoretical curiosity, in practice almost all commonly-used activation functions do satisfy the WIVP. Nevertheless, if one does wish to use such a function, one way to soundly over-approximate it with an ANN is to replace the *scalar* activation function with a *set-valued* one. The ANN semantics can be extended to allow picking any output value from the activation function in addition to any weight from the weight set.

For example, consider again the thresh$(x; 1, 0)$ activation function. It can be completed to a set-valued activation function which satisfies the WIVP such as

$$\text{thresh}'(x; 1, 0) := \begin{cases} \{x\} & \text{if } x > 1 \\ \{a \mid a \in [0, 1]\} & \text{if } x = 1 \\ \{0\} & \text{otherwise} \end{cases}.$$ The idea is that we "fill the gap" in

the graph. Whereas in the original threshold function we had an issue because there was no $x \in [0, 1]$ which satisfied thresh$(x; 1, 0) = \frac{f(0) + f(1)}{2} = \frac{1}{2}$, on the set-valued function we can take $x = 1 \in [0, 1]$ to find $\frac{1}{2} \in \text{thresh}'(1; 1, 0)$.

6.4   Powerset Abstraction, ReLU, and $\widehat{\alpha}_{bin}$

Recall that $\widehat{\alpha}$ (Algorithm 1) requires abstracting the, usually-infinite, set of *all* merged matrices $D^T W^{(i)} C$. However, in Sect. 5.1 we showed that for convex abstract domains it suffices to only consider the finitely-many *binary* mergings. The reader may wonder if there are abstract domains for which it is *not* sufficient to consider only the binary PCMs. This section presents such an example.

Suppose we use the same ReLU DNN f as in Sect. 6.1, for which we noted before the corresponding INN over-approximates it. However, suppose instead of intervals we used the *powerset* abstract domain, i.e., $\alpha(S) = S$ and $A \sqcup B = A \cup B$. If we (incorrectly) used $\widehat{\alpha}_{bin}$ instead of $\widehat{\alpha}$, we would get the powerset

ANN $g(x_1) = \left\{ \begin{bmatrix} 2 \\ 2 \\ 0 \end{bmatrix}, \begin{bmatrix} 2 \\ 0 \\ 2 \end{bmatrix} \right\} \text{ReLU} (\{[1], [-1]\} [x_1])$. Recall that $f(1) = [1 \ 1 \ 0]^T$.

However, with $g(1)$, the first output will always be either 0 or 2, so g does *not* over-approximate f. The basic issue is that to get the correct output, we need to instantiate the inner weight to 0.5, which is in the convex hull of the original weights, but is not either one of the original weights itself.

Note that, in this particular example, it is possible to find an ANN that over-approximates the DNN using only finite sets for the abstract weights. However, this is only because ReLU is piecewise-linear, and the size of the sets needed will grow exponentially with the number of dimensions. For other activation functions, e.g., tanh infinite sets are required in general.

In general, non-convex abstract domains will need to use some other method of computing an over-approximation of $\widehat{\alpha}$. One general-purpose option is to use techniques such as those developed for symbolic abstraction [36] to iteratively compute an over-approximation of the true $A^{(i)}$ and use that instead.

7   Proof of Sufficient Conditions

We now prove Theorem 2, which provides sufficient conditions on the activation functions for which Algorithm 3 produces an ANN that soundly over-approximates the given DNN.

The structure of the proof is illustrated in Fig. 3. To show that ANN T over-approximates DNN N, we must show that $N(v) \in T(v)$ for every v. This occurs, by definition, only if there exists some *instantiation* $T_v \in \gamma(T)$ of T for which $N(v) = T_v(v)$. Recall that an instantiation of an ANN is a DNN formed by replacing each abstract weight $A^{(i)}$ with a concrete weight matrix $H^{(i)} \in \gamma(A^{(i)})$. In particular, our proof will proceed layer-by-layer. On an input $v = v^{(0)}$, the ith layer of DNN N maps $v^{(i-1)}$ to $v^{(i)}$ until the output $v^{(n)}$ is computed. We will prove that, for each abstract layer $(A^{(i)}, \sigma^{(i)}, \mathcal{A}^{(i)})$, there is a matrix $H^{(i)} = \overline{\gamma}(A^{(i)}, v^{(i-1)}) \in \gamma(A^{(i)})$ for which the instantiated layer $(H^{(i)}, \sigma^{(i)})$, roughly speaking, also maps $v^{(i-1)}$ to $v^{(i)}$. However, by design the abstract layer will have fewer dimensions, hence the higher-dimensional $v^{(i-1)}$ and $v^{(i)}$ may not belong to its domain and range (respectively). We resolve this by associating with each vector $v^{(i)}$ in the intermediate spaces of N a *mean representative* vector $v^{(i)}{}_{/\mathbb{P}^{(i)}}$ in the intermediate spaces of T_v. Then we can rigorously prove that the instantiated layer $(H^{(i)}, \sigma^{(i)})$ maps $v^{(i-1)}{}_{/\mathbb{P}^{(i-1)}}$ to $v^{(i)}{}_{/\mathbb{P}^{(i)}}$. Applying this fact inductively gives us $T_v(v_{/\mathbb{P}^{(0)}}) = (N(v))_{/\mathbb{P}^{(n)}}$. Because $\mathbb{P}^{(0)}$ and $\mathbb{P}^{(n)}$ are the singleton partitionings, this gives us exactly the desired relationship $T_v(v) = N(v)$.

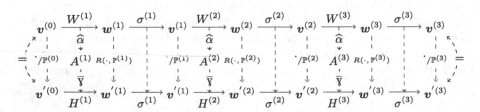

Fig. 3. Visualization of the relationships between concrete, abstract, and instantiated elements in the soundness proof. The original DNN's action on an input vector $v^{(0)}$ is shown on the top row. This DNN is abstracted to an ANN, represented by the $A^{(i)}$s on the middle row. We will show that we can instantiate the ANN such that the instantiation has the same output as the original DNN on $v^{(0)}$.

Algorithm 4: $\overline{y}(M, \mathcal{P}^{in}, \mathcal{P}^{out}, \boldsymbol{v}, \boldsymbol{w}')$

Input: An $n \times m$ matrix M. Partitionings $\mathcal{P}^{in}$, $\mathcal{P}^{out}$. A vector $\boldsymbol{v}$ with non-negative entries. A vector $\boldsymbol{w}' \in R(M\boldsymbol{v}, \mathcal{P}^{out})$.

Output: A matrix $H \in \gamma(\widehat{\alpha}(M, \mathcal{P}^{in}, \mathcal{P}^{out}))$ such that $H(\boldsymbol{v}_{/\mathcal{P}^{in}}) = \boldsymbol{w}'$.

1 $C, D \leftarrow 0_{|\mathcal{P}^{in}| \times n}, 0_{|\mathcal{P}^{out}| \times m}$
2 **for** $i = 1, 2, \ldots, |\mathcal{P}^{in}|$ **do**
3 $\quad$ **for** $j \in \mathcal{P}_i^{in}$ **do**
4 $\quad\quad$ $C_{j,i} \leftarrow v_j / (\sum_{k \in \mathcal{P}_i^{in}} v_k)$

5 $\boldsymbol{w} \leftarrow M\boldsymbol{v}$
6 **for** $i = 1, 2, \ldots, |\mathcal{P}^{out}|$ **do**
7 $\quad$ $a, b \leftarrow \operatorname{argmax}_{p \in \mathcal{P}_i^{out}} w_p, \operatorname{argmin}_{p \in \mathcal{P}_i^{out}} w_p$
8 $\quad$ $D_{a,i} \leftarrow (w'_i - w_b)/(w_a - w_b)$
9 $\quad$ $D_{b,i} \leftarrow 1 - D_{a,i}$
10 $\boldsymbol{s} \leftarrow (|\mathcal{P}_1^{in}|, \ldots, |\mathcal{P}_{|\mathcal{P}^{in}|}^{in}|)$
11 **return** ScaleCols$\left(D^T M C, \boldsymbol{s}\right)$

7.1 Vector Representatives

Our proof relies heavily on the concept of representatives.

Definition 21. *Given a vector* $\boldsymbol{v} = (v_1, v_2, \ldots, v_n)$ *and a partitioning* $\mathcal{P}$ *of* $\{1, 2, \ldots, n\}$ *with* $|\mathcal{P}| = k$, *we define the* convex representative set *of* $\boldsymbol{v}$ *under* $\mathcal{P}$ *to be* $R(\boldsymbol{v}, \mathcal{P}) = \left\{ (z_1, z_2, \ldots, z_k) \mid \forall j. \min_{h \in \mathcal{P}_j} v_h \leq z_j \leq \max_{h \in \mathcal{P}_j} v_h \right\}$.

$R(\boldsymbol{v}, \mathcal{P})$ is referred to as $AV(\boldsymbol{v})$ in Prabhakar et al. [29], and is always a box in $\mathbb{R}^k$.

One representative will be particularly useful, so we give it a specific notation:

Definition 22. *Given a vector* $(v_1, v_2, \ldots, v_n)$ *and a partitioning* $\mathcal{P}$ *of* $\{1, 2, \ldots, n\}$ *with* $|\mathcal{P}| = k$, *we define the* mean representative *of* v *under* $\mathcal{P}$ *to be* $v_{/\mathcal{P}} = \left(\frac{\sum_{j \in \mathcal{P}_1} v_j}{|\mathcal{P}_1|}, \ldots, \frac{\sum_{j \in \mathcal{P}_k} v_j}{|\mathcal{P}_k|} \right)$

Example 8. Consider the vector $\boldsymbol{v} := (5, 6, 11, 2, 1)$ and the partitioning $\mathcal{P} = \{\{1, 3\}, \{2, 4, 5\}\}$. Then we have $\boldsymbol{v}_{/\mathcal{P}} = ((5 + 11)/2, (6 + 2 + 1)/3) = (8, 3)$ and $R(\boldsymbol{v}, \mathcal{P}) = \{(z_1, z_2) \mid z_1 \in [5, 11], z_2 \in [1, 6]\}$.

7.2 Proof of Soundness Theorem

The operation $\overline{y}$ presented in Algorithm 4 shows how to instantiate an abstract weight matrix such that it has input/output behavior corresponding to that of the original DNN layer. We now prove the correctness of Algorithm 4.

Lemma 1. *Given any $w' \in R(Mv, \mathcal{P}^{in})$, a vector v with non-negative entries, and $H = \overline{\mathfrak{y}}(M, \mathcal{P}^{in}, \mathcal{P}^{out}, v, w')$, then $H \in \gamma(\widehat{\alpha}(M, \mathcal{P}^{in}, \mathcal{P}^{out}))$ and $H(v_{/\mathcal{P}^{in}}) = w'$.*

Proof. To prove correctness of Algorithm 4, it suffices to show that (i) C and D are PCMs, and (ii) the returned matrix H satisfies the equality $H(v_{/\mathcal{P}^{in}}) = w'$.

C is a PCM by construction: The ith column only has non-zero entries for rows that are in the ith partition. The sum of all entries in a column is $\sum_{j \in \mathcal{P}_i^{in}} v_j / (\sum_{k \in \mathcal{P}_i^{in}} v_k) = 1$. All entries are non-negative by assumption on v.

D is also a PCM: The ith column only has two entries. It suffices to show that $D_{a,i}$ is in $[0, 1]$, which follows because $w' \in R(Mv, \mathcal{P}^{out})$ implies w'_i is in between the minimum b and maximum a.

By associativity, line 11 is equivalent to returning $H = D^T M E$ where $E = \text{ScaleCols}(C, s)$. Thus, to show that $H(v_{/\mathcal{P}^{in}}) = w'$, it suffices to show (i) that $E(v_{/\mathcal{P}^{in}}) = v$, and (ii) that $D^T M v = w'$.

Note that here $E_{j,i} = C_{j,i} |\mathcal{P}_i^{in}|$. Then to show (i), consider any index $j \in \mathcal{P}_i^{in}$. Then we find that the jth output component of $E(v_{/\mathcal{P}^{in}})$ is $(v_j / (\sum_{k \in \mathcal{P}_i^{in}} v_k)) |\mathcal{P}_i^{in}| ((\sum_{k \in \mathcal{P}_i^{in}} v_k) / |\mathcal{P}_i^{in}|) = v_j$. Hence, the entire output vector is v.

To show (ii), note that each column of D is exactly the convex combination that produces the output w'_i from the maximum/minimum indices of Mv.

In total then, the returned matrix is in $\gamma(\widehat{\alpha}(M, \mathcal{P}^{in}, \mathcal{P}^{out}))$ and satisfies $H(v_{/\mathcal{P}^{in}}) = w'$. $\square$

The next lemma implies that we can always find such a $w' \in R(Mv, \mathcal{P}^{in})$ satisfying the relations in Fig. 3.

Lemma 2. *Let σ be an activation function satisfying the WIVP, w any vector, and $\mathcal{P}$ a partitioning the dimensions of w. Then there exists a vector $w' \in R(w, \mathcal{P})$ such that $\sigma(w') = (\sigma(w))_{/\mathcal{P}}$.*

Proof. Because $\sigma^{(i)}$ is defined to be a component-wise activation function, we can assume WLOG that $\mathbb{P}^{(i)}$ has only a single partition, i.e., $\mathbb{P}^{(i)} = \{\{1, 2, \ldots, s^{(i)}\}\}$.

In that case, label the components of $w^{(i)}$ such that $w_1^{(i)} \leq w_2^{(i)} \leq \ldots \leq w_n^{(i)}$. Then the statement of the lemma is equivalent to the assertion that there exists some $b \in [w_1^{(i)}, w_n^{(i)}]$ such that $\sigma^{(i)}(b) = (\sum_j w_j^{(i)})/n$. But this is exactly the definition of the WIVP. Hence, by assumption that $\sigma^{(i)}$ satisfies the WIVP, we complete the proof. $\square$

We are finally prepared to prove the soundness theorem. It is restated here for clarity.

Theorem 2. *Let $\mathfrak{A}$ be a set of weight set abstract domains and Σ a set of activation functions. Suppose (i) each $\sigma \in \Sigma$ has entirely non-negative outputs, and (ii) each $\sigma \in \Sigma$ satisfies the Weakened Intermediate Value Property (Definition 20). Then $T = \text{AbstractLayerWise}\langle \mathfrak{A}, \Sigma \rangle(N, \mathbb{P}, \mathcal{A})$ (Algorithm 3) soundly over-approximates the DNN N.*

Proof. A diagram of the proof is provided in Fig. 3.

Consider the ith layer. By Lemma 2, there exists some vector $\boldsymbol{w}'^{(i)} \in R(\boldsymbol{w}^{(i)}, \mathbb{P}^{(i)})$ such that $\sigma^{(i)}(\boldsymbol{w}'^{(i)}) = \boldsymbol{v}_{/\mathbb{P}^{(i)}}$. Furthermore, by Lemma 1 there exists some $H^{(i)} \in \gamma(A^{(i)})$ such that $H^{(i)}(\boldsymbol{v}^{(i-1)}_{/\mathbb{P}^{(i-1)}}) = \boldsymbol{w}'^{(i)}$. Therefore, in total we can instantiate the ith abstract layer to $(H^{(i)}, \sigma^{(i)})$, which maps $\boldsymbol{v}^{(i-1)}_{/\mathbb{P}^{(i-1)}}$ to $\boldsymbol{v}^{(i)}_{/\mathbb{P}^{(i)}}$.

By applying this construction to each layer, we find an instantiation of the ANN that maps $\boldsymbol{v}^{(0)}_{/\mathbb{P}^{(0)}}$ to $\boldsymbol{v}^{(n)}_{/\mathbb{P}^{(n)}}$. Assuming $\mathbb{P}^{(0)}$ and $\mathbb{P}^{(n)}$ are the singleton partitionings, then, we have that the instantiation maps $\boldsymbol{v}^{(0)} = \boldsymbol{v}$ to $\boldsymbol{v}^{(n)} = N(\boldsymbol{v})$, as hoped for. Hence, $N(\boldsymbol{v}) \in T(\boldsymbol{v})$ for any such vector $\boldsymbol{v}$, and so the ANN overapproximates the original DNN.   □

8 Related Work

The recent results by Prabhakar et al. [29] are the closest to this paper. Prabhakar et al. introduce the notion of Interval Neural Networks and a sound quotienting (abstraction) procedure when the ReLU activation function is used. Prabhakar et al. also proposed a technique for verification of DNNs using ReLU activation functions by analyzing the corresponding INN using a MILP encoding. Prabhakar et al. leaves open the question of determining the appropriate partitioning of the nodes, and their results assume the use of the ReLU activation function and interval domain. We have generalized their results to address the subtleties of other abstract domains and activation functions as highlighted in Sect. 6.

There exists prior work [2,8,27] on models using interval-weighted neural networks. The goal of such approaches is generally to represent uncertainty, instead of improve analysis time of a corresponding DNN. Furthermore, their semantics are defined using interval arithmetic instead of the more-precise semantics we give in Sect. 4. Nevertheless, we believe that future work may consider applications of our more general ANN formulation and novel abstraction algorithm to the problem of representing uncertainty.

There have been many recent approaches exploring formal verification of DNNs using abstractions. ReluVal [38] computes interval bounds on the outputs of a DNN for a given input range. Neurify [37] extends ReluVal by using symbolic interval analysis. Approaches such as DeepPoly [33] and AI^2 [9] perform abstract interpretation of DNNs using more expressive numerical domains such as polyhedra and zonotopes. In contrast, Abstract Neural Networks introduced in this paper use abstract values to represent the weight matrices of a DNN, and are a different way of applying abstraction to DNN analysis.

This paper builds upon extensive literature on numerical abstract domains [5,6,23,24], including libraries such as APRON [16] and PPL [1]. Of particular relevance are techniques for verification of floating-point computation [4,28,28].

Techniques for compression of DNNs reduce their size using heuristics [7,14, 15]. They can degrade accuracy of the network, and do not provide theoretical guarantees. Gokulanathan et al. [12] use the Marabou Verification Engine [19] to simplify neural networks so that the simplified network is equivalent to the given network. Shriver et al. [32] refactor the given DNN to aid verification, though the refactored DNN is not guaranteed to be an overapproximation.

9   Conclusion and Future Directions

We introduced the notion of an *Abstract Neural Network (ANN)*. The weight matrices in an ANN are represented using numerical abstract domains, such as intervals, octagons, and polyhedra. We presented a framework, parameterized by abstract domain and DNN activation function, that performs layer-wise abstraction to compute an ANN given a DNN. We identified necessary and sufficient conditions on the abstract domain and the activation function that ensure that the computed ANN is a sound over-approximation of the given DNN. Furthermore, we showed how the input DNN can be modified in order to soundly abstract DNNs using rare activation functions that do not satisfy the sufficiency conditions are used. Our framework is applicable to DNNs that use activation functions such as ReLU, Leaky ReLU, and Hyperbolic Tangent. Our framework can use convex abstract domains such as intervals, octagons, and polyhedra. Code implementing our framework can be found at https://doi.org/10.5281/ zenodo.4031610. Detailed proofs of all theorems are in the extended version of this paper [34].

The results in this paper provide a strong theoretical foundation for further research on abstraction of DNNs. One interesting direction worth exploring is the notion of completeness of abstract domains [11] in the context of Abstract Neural Networks. Our framework is restricted to convex abstract domains; the use of non-convex abstract domains, such as modulo intervals [25] or donut domains [10], would require a different abstraction algorithm. Algorithms for computing symbolic abstraction might show promise [21,30,31,35,36].

This paper focused on feed-forward neural networks. Because convolutional neural networks (CNNs) are special cases of feed-forward neural networks, future work can directly extend the theory in this paper to CNN models as well. Such future work would need to consider problems posed by non-componentwise activation functions such as MaxPool, which do not fit nicely into the framework presented here. Furthermore, extensions for recursive neural networks (RNNs) and other more general neural-network architectures seems feasible.

On the practical side of things, it would be worth investigating the impact of abstracting DNNs on the verification times. Prabhakar et al. [29] demonstrated that their abstraction technique improved verification of DNNs. The results in this paper are a significant generalization of the results of Prabhakar et al., which were restricted to interval abstractions and ReLU activation functions. We believe that our approach would similarly help scale up verification of DNNs.

Acknowledgments. We thank the anonymous reviewers and Cindy Rubio González for their feedback on this work.

References

1. Bagnara, R., Hill, P.M., Zaffanella, E.: The parma polyhedra library: toward a complete set of numerical abstractions for the analysis and verification of hardware and software systems. Sci. Comput. Program. **72**(1–2), 3–21 (2008). https://doi.org/10.1016/j.scico.2007.08.001
2. Beheshti, M., Berrached, A., de Korvin, A., Hu, C., Sirisaengtaksin, O.: On interval weighted three-layer neural networks. In: Proceedings 31st Annual Simulation Symposium (SS 1998), 5–9 April 1998, Boston, MA, USA. pp. 188–194. IEEE Computer Society (1998). https://doi.org/10.1109/SIMSYM.1998.668487
3. Brown, T.B., et al.: Language models are few-shot learners. CoRR abs/2005.14165 (2020). https://arxiv.org/abs/2005.14165
4. Chen, L., Miné, A., Cousot, P.: A sound floating-point polyhedra abstract domain. In: Ramalingam, G. (ed.) APLAS 2008. LNCS, vol. 5356, pp. 3–18. Springer, Heidelberg (2008). https://doi.org/10.1007/978-3-540-89330-1_2
5. Cousot, P., Cousot, R.: Abstract interpretation: a unified lattice model for static analysis of programs by construction or approximation of fixpoints. In: Graham, R.M., Harrison, M.A., Sethi, R. (eds.) Conference Record of the Fourth ACM Symposium on Principles of Programming Languages, Los Angeles, California, USA, January 1977, pp. 238–252. ACM (1977). https://doi.org/10.1145/512950.512973
6. Cousot, P., Halbwachs, N.: Automatic discovery of linear restraints among variables of a program. In: Aho, A.V., Zilles, S.N., Szymanski, T.G. (eds.) Conference Record of the Fifth Annual ACM Symposium on Principles of Programming Languages, Tucson, Arizona, USA, January 1978, pp. 84–96. ACM Press (1978). https://doi.org/10.1145/512760.512770
7. Deng, L., Li, G., Han, S., Shi, L., Xie, Y.: Model compression and hardware acceleration for neural networks: a comprehensive survey. Proc. IEEE **108**(4), 485–532 (2020). https://doi.org/10.1109/JPROC.2020.2976475
8. Garczarczyk, Z.A.: Interval neural networks. In: IEEE International Symposium on Circuits and Systems, ISCAS 2000, Emerging Technologies for the 21st Century, Geneva, Switzerland, 28–31 May 2000, Proceedings. pp. 567–570. IEEE (2000). https://doi.org/10.1109/ISCAS.2000.856123
9. Gehr, T., Mirman, M., Drachsler-Cohen, D., Tsankov, P., Chaudhuri, S., Vechev, M.T.: AI2: safety and robustness certification of neural networks with abstract interpretation. In: 2018 IEEE Symposium on Security and Privacy, SP 2018, Proceedings, 21–23 May 2018, San Francisco, California, USA, pp. 3–18. IEEE Computer Society (2018). https://doi.org/10.1109/SP.2018.00058
10. Ghorbal, K., Ivančić, F., Balakrishnan, G., Maeda, N., Gupta, A.: Donut domains: efficient non-convex domains for abstract interpretation. In: Kuncak, V., Rybalchenko, A. (eds.) VMCAI 2012. LNCS, vol. 7148, pp. 235–250. Springer, Heidelberg (2012). https://doi.org/10.1007/978-3-642-27940-9_16
11. Giacobazzi, R., Ranzato, F., Scozzari, F.: Making abstract interpretations complete. J. ACM **47**(2), 361–416 (2000). https://doi.org/10.1145/333979.333989
12. Gokulanathan, S., Feldsher, A., Malca, A., Barrett, C.W., Katz, G.: Simplifying neural networks with the marabou verification engine. CoRR abs/1910.12396 (2019). http://arxiv.org/abs/1910.12396
13. Goodfellow, I.J., Bengio, Y., Courville, A.C.: Deep Learning. Adaptive Computation and Machine Learning. MIT Press (2016). http://www.deeplearningbook.org/

14. Han, S., Mao, H., Dally, W.J.: Deep compression: Compressing deep neural network with pruning, trained quantization and huffman coding. In: Bengio, Y., LeCun, Y. (eds.) 4th International Conference on Learning Representations, ICLR 2016, San Juan, Puerto Rico, May 2–4, 2016, Conference Track Proceedings (2016). http://arxiv.org/abs/1510.00149

15. Iandola, F.N., Moskewicz, M.W., Ashraf, K., Han, S., Dally, W.J., Keutzer, K.: Squeezenet: Alexnet-level accuracy with 50x fewer parameters and <1mb model size. CoRR abs/1602.07360 (2016). http://arxiv.org/abs/1602.07360

16. Jeannet, B., Miné, A.: APRON: a library of numerical abstract domains for static analysis. In: Bouajjani, A., Maler, O. (eds.) CAV 2009. LNCS, vol. 5643, pp. 661–667. Springer, Heidelberg (2009). https://doi.org/10.1007/978-3-642-02658-4_52

17. Julian, K.D., Kochenderfer, M.J., Owen, M.P.: Deep neural network compression for aircraft collision avoidance systems. CoRR abs/1810.04240 (2018). http://arxiv.org/abs/1810.04240

18. Katz, G., Barrett, C., Dill, D.L., Julian, K., Kochenderfer, M.J.: Reluplex: an efficient SMT solver for verifying deep neural networks. In: Majumdar, R., Kunčak, V. (eds.) CAV 2017. LNCS, vol. 10426, pp. 97–117. Springer, Cham (2017). https://doi.org/10.1007/978-3-319-63387-9_5

19. Katz, G., et al.: The marabou framework for verification and analysis of deep neural networks. In: Dillig, I., Tasiran, S. (eds.) CAV 2019. LNCS, vol. 11561, pp. 443–452. Springer, Cham (2019). https://doi.org/10.1007/978-3-030-25540-4_26

20. Krizhevsky, A., Sutskever, I., Hinton, G.E.: Imagenet classification with deep convolutional neural networks. In: Bartlett, P.L., Pereira, F.C.N., Burges, C.J.C., Bottou, L., Weinberger, K.Q. (eds.) Advances in Neural Information Processing Systems 25: 26th Annual Conference on Neural Information Processing Systems 2012. Proceedings of a meeting held December 3–6, 2012, Lake Tahoe, Nevada, United States, pp. 1106–1114 (2012). http://papers.nips.cc/paper/4824-imagenet-classification-with-deep-convolutional-neural-networks

21. Li, Y., Albarghouthi, A., Kincaid, Z., Gurfinkel, A., Chechik, M.: Symbolic optimization with SMT solvers. In: Jagannathan, S., Sewell, P. (eds.) The 41st Annual ACM SIGPLAN-SIGACT Symposium on Principles of Programming Languages, POPL 2014, San Diego, CA, USA, January 20–21, 2014. pp. 607–618. ACM (2014). https://doi.org/10.1145/2535838.2535857

22. Maas, A., Hannun, A., Ng, A.: Rectifier nonlinearities improve neural network acoustic models. In: Proceedings of the International Conference on Machine Learning (2013)

23. Miné, A.: The octagon abstract domain. High. Order Symb. Comput. 19(1), 31–100 (2006). https://doi.org/10.1007/s10990-006-8609-1

24. Miné, A.: Tutorial on static inference of numeric invariants by abstract interpretation. Found. Trends Program. Lang. 4(3–4), 120–372 (2017). https://doi.org/10.1561/2500000034

25. Nakanishi, T., Joe, K., Polychronopoulos, C.D., Fukuda, A.: The modulo interval: a simple and practical representation for program analysis. In: Proceedings of the 1999 International Conference on Parallel Architectures and Compilation Techniques, Newport Beach, California, USA, October 12–16, 1999, pp. 91–96. IEEE Computer Society (1999). https://doi.org/10.1109/PACT.1999.807422

26. Paszke, A., et al.: Pytorch: An imperative style, high-performance deep learning library. In: Wallach, H.M., Larochelle, H., Beygelzimer, A., d'Alché-Buc, F., Fox, E.B., Garnett, R. (eds.) Advances in Neural Information Processing Systems 32: Annual Conference on Neural Information Processing Systems 2019, NeurIPS 2019, 8–14 December 2019, Vancouver, BC, Canada, pp. 8024–8035 (2019). http://papers.nips.cc/paper/9015-pytorch-an-imperative-style-high-performance-deep-learning-library

27. Patiño-Escarcina, R.E., Callejas Bedregal, B.R., Lyra, A.: Interval computing in neural networks: one layer interval neural networks. In: Das, G., Gulati, V.P. (eds.) CIT 2004. LNCS, vol. 3356, pp. 68–75. Springer, Heidelberg (2004). https://doi.org/10.1007/978-3-540-30561-3_8

28. Ponsini, O., Michel, C., Rueher, M.: Verifying floating-point programs with constraint programming and abstract interpretation techniques. Autom. Softw. Eng. 23(2), 191–217 (2016). https://doi.org/10.1007/s10515-014-0154-2

29. Prabhakar, P., Afzal, Z.R.: Abstraction based output range analysis for neural networks. In: Wallach, H.M., Larochelle, H., Beygelzimer, A., d'Alché-Buc, F., Fox, E.B., Garnett, R. (eds.) Advances in Neural Information Processing Systems 32: Annual Conference on Neural Information Processing Systems 2019, NeurIPS 2019, 8–14 December 2019, Vancouver, BC, Canada, pp. 15762–15772 (2019). http://papers.nips.cc/paper/9708-abstraction-based-output-range-analysis-for-neural-networks

30. Reps, T., Sagiv, M., Yorsh, G.: Symbolic implementation of the best transformer. In: Steffen, B., Levi, G. (eds.) VMCAI 2004. LNCS, vol. 2937, pp. 252–266. Springer, Heidelberg (2004). https://doi.org/10.1007/978-3-540-24622-0_21

31. Reps, T., Thakur, A.: Automating abstract interpretation. In: Jobstmann, B., Leino, K.R.M. (eds.) VMCAI 2016. LNCS, vol. 9583, pp. 3–40. Springer, Heidelberg (2016). https://doi.org/10.1007/978-3-662-49122-5_1

32. Shriver, D., Xu, D., Elbaum, S.G., Dwyer, M.B.: Refactoring neural networks for verification. CoRR abs/1908.08026 (2019). http://arxiv.org/abs/1908.08026

33. Singh, G., Gehr, T., Püschel, M., Vechev, M.T.: An abstract domain for certifying neural networks. Proc. ACM Program. Lang. 3(POPL), 411–4130 (2019). https://doi.org/10.1145/3290354

34. Sotoudeh, M., Thakur, A.V.: Abstract neural networks. CoRR abs/2009.05660 (2020). http://arxiv.org/abs/2009.05660

35. Thakur, A., Elder, M., Reps, T.: Bilateral algorithms for symbolic abstraction. In: Miné, A., Schmidt, D. (eds.) SAS 2012. LNCS, vol. 7460, pp. 111–128. Springer, Heidelberg (2012). https://doi.org/10.1007/978-3-642-33125-1_10

36. Thakur, A., Reps, T.: A method for symbolic computation of abstract operations. In: Madhusudan, P., Seshia, S.A. (eds.) CAV 2012. LNCS, vol. 7358, pp. 174–192. Springer, Heidelberg (2012). https://doi.org/10.1007/978-3-642-31424-7_17

37. Wang, S., Pei, K., Whitehouse, J., Yang, J., Jana, S.: Efficient formal safety analysis of neural networks. In: Bengio, S., Wallach, H.M., Larochelle, H., Grauman, K., Cesa-Bianchi, N., Garnett, R. (eds.) Advances in Neural Information Processing Systems 31: Annual Conference on Neural Information Processing Systems 2018, NeurIPS 2018, 3–8 December 2018, Montréal, Canada, pp. 6369–6379 (2018). http://papers.nips.cc/paper/7873-efficient-formal-safety-analysis-of-neural-networks
38. Wang, S., Pei, K., Whitehouse, J., Yang, J., Jana, S.: Formal security analysis of neural networks using symbolic intervals. In: Enck, W., Felt, A.P. (eds.) 27th USENIX Security Symposium, USENIX Security 2018, Baltimore, MD, USA, August 15–17, 2018, pp. 1599–1614. USENIX Association (2018). https://www.usenix.org/conference/usenixsecurity18/presentation/wang-shiqi

Termination of Polynomial Loops

Florian Frohn[1] , Marcel Hark[2(✉)] , and Jürgen Giesl[2]

[1] Max Planck Institute for Informatics and Saarland Informatics Campus,
Saarbrücken, Germany
[2] LuFG Informatik 2, RWTH Aachen University, Aachen, Germany
marcel.hark@cs.rwth-aachen.de

Abstract. We consider the termination problem for triangular weakly non-linear loops (*twn*-loops) over some ring S like $\mathbb{Z}$, $\mathbb{Q}$, or $\mathbb{R}$. Essentially, the guard of such a loop is an arbitrary Boolean formula over (possibly non-linear) polynomial inequations, and the body is a single assignment $\begin{bmatrix} x_1 \\ \cdots \\ x_d \end{bmatrix} \leftarrow \begin{bmatrix} c_1 \cdot x_1 + p_1 \\ \cdots \\ c_d \cdot x_d + p_d \end{bmatrix}$ where each x_i is a variable, $c_i \in S$, and each p_i is a (possibly non-linear) polynomial over S and the variables $x_{i+1}, \ldots, x_d$.

We present a reduction from the question of termination to the existential fragment of the first-order theory of S and $\mathbb{R}$. For loops over $\mathbb{R}$, our reduction entails decidability of termination. For loops over $\mathbb{Z}$ and $\mathbb{Q}$, it proves semi-decidability of non-termination.

Furthermore, we present a transformation to convert certain non-*twn*-loops into *twn*-form. Then the original loop terminates iff the transformed loop terminates over a specific subset of $\mathbb{R}$, which can also be checked via our reduction. This transformation also allows us to prove *tight* complexity bounds for the termination problem for two important classes of loops which can *always* be transformed into *twn*-loops.

1 Introduction

Let $\mathbb{R}_A$ denote the real algebraic numbers. We consider loops of the form

$$\textbf{while } \varphi \textbf{ do } \vec{x} \leftarrow \vec{a}. \tag{1}$$

Here, $\vec{x}$ is a vector[1] of $d \geq 1$ pairwise different variables that range over a ring $\mathbb{Z} \leq S \leq \mathbb{R}_A$, where $\leq$ denotes the subring relation. Moreover, $\vec{a} \in (S[\vec{x}])^d$ where

---

[1] We use row- and column-vectors interchangeably to improve readability.

Funded by the Deutsche Forschungsgemeinschaft (DFG, German Research Foundation) - 389792660 as part of TRR 248, by the Deutsche Forschungsgemeinschaft (DFG, German Research Foundation) 235050644 (Project GI 274/6-2), and by the DFG Research Training Group 2236 UnRAVeL.

© Springer Nature Switzerland AG 2020
D. Pichardie and M. Sighireanu (Eds.): SAS 2020, LNCS 12389, pp. 89–112, 2020.
https://doi.org/10.1007/978-3-030-65474-0_5

$\mathcal{S}[\vec{x}]$ is the set of all polynomials over $\vec{x}$ with coefficients from $\mathcal{S}$. The condition φ is an arbitrary propositional formula over the atoms $\{p \triangleright 0 \mid p \in \mathcal{S}[\vec{x}], \triangleright \in \{\geq, >\}\}$.[2]

We require $\mathcal{S} \leq \mathbb{R}_\mathbb{A}$ instead of $\mathcal{S} \leq \mathbb{R}$, as it is unclear how to represent transcendental numbers on computers. However, in Sect. 5 we will see that the loops considered in this paper terminate over $\mathbb{R}$ iff they terminate over $\mathbb{R}_\mathbb{A}$. Thus, our results immediately carry over to loops where the variables range over $\mathbb{R}$. Hence, we sometimes also consider loops over $\mathcal{S} = \mathbb{R}$. However, even then we restrict ourselves to loops (1) where all constants in φ and $\vec{a}$ are algebraic.

We often represent a loop (1) by the tuple $(\varphi, \vec{a})$ of the *loop condition* φ and the *update* $\vec{a} = (a_1, \ldots, a_d)$. Unless stated otherwise, $(\varphi, \vec{a})$ is always a loop on $\mathcal{S}^d$ using the variables $\vec{x} = (x_1, \ldots, x_d)$ where $\mathbb{Z} \leq \mathcal{S} \leq \mathbb{R}_\mathbb{A}$. A *linear-update loop* has the form $(\varphi, A \cdot \vec{x} + \vec{b})$ and it has *real spectrum* if A has real eigenvalues only. A *linear loop* is a linear-update loop where φ is linear (i.e., its atoms are only linear[3] inequations). A *conjunctive loop* is a loop $(\varphi, \vec{a})$ where φ does not contain disjunctions.

There exist several decidability results for the termination of linear loops [6,8,15,24,34,37,41,53], but there are only very few results on the decidability of termination for certain forms of non-linear loops [35,36,38,55]. Moreover, all of these previous works only consider conjunctive loops besides [38] which only allows for loop conditions defining compact sets. In this paper, we regard (linear and non-linear) loops with arbitrary conditions, i.e., they may also contain disjunctions and define non-compact sets. Furthermore, we study the decidability of termination for non-linear loops over $\mathbb{Z}$, $\mathbb{Q}$, $\mathbb{R}_\mathbb{A}$, and $\mathbb{R}$, whereas the existing decidability results for non-linear loops are restricted to loops over $\mathbb{R}$. So we identify new sub-classes of loops of the form (1) where (non-)termination is (semi-)decidable. Moreover, we also investigate the complexity of the termination problem.

Contributions: We study a sub-class of loops of the form (1) (so-called *twn-loops* (Sect. 2)), and present an (incomplete) transformation *Tr* from non-*twn*-loops to *twn*-loops (Sect. 3). Then we show that termination of *twn*-loops over $\mathbb{R}_\mathbb{A}$ and $\mathbb{R}$ is decidable and that non-termination over $\mathbb{Z}$ and $\mathbb{Q}$ is semi-decidable (Sect. 4 and 5). For those classes of non-*twn*-loops where our transformation *Tr* is complete, we obtain analogous decidability results. For all other loops of the form (1), our (semi-)decision procedures still apply if *Tr* is applicable.

Finally, we prove Co-NP-completeness of termination of linear loops over $\mathbb{Z}$, $\mathbb{Q}$, $\mathbb{R}_\mathbb{A}$, and $\mathbb{R}$ with real spectrum and $\forall\mathbb{R}$-completeness of termination of linear-update loops with real spectrum over $\mathbb{R}_\mathbb{A}$ and $\mathbb{R}$ (Sect. 6).

All missing proofs can be found in [16].

2   Preliminaries

For any entity s, $s[x/t]$ is the entity that results from s by replacing all free occurrences of x by t. Similarly, if $\vec{x} = (x_1, \ldots, x_d)$ and $\vec{t} = (t_1, \ldots, t_d)$, then

---

[2] Note that negation is syntactic sugar in our setting, as, e.g., $\neg(p > 0)$ is equivalent to $-p \geq 0$. So w.l.o.g. φ is built from atoms, $\wedge$, and $\vee$.

[3] In this paper "linear" refers to "linear polynomials" and thus includes *affine* functions.

$s[\vec{x}/\vec{t}]$ results from s by replacing all free occurrences of x_i by t_i, for each $1 \leq i \leq d$.

Any vector of polynomials $\vec{a} \in (\mathcal{S}[\vec{x}])^d$ can also be regarded as a function $\vec{a} : (\mathcal{S}[\vec{x}])^d \rightarrow (\mathcal{S}[\vec{x}])^d$, where for any $\vec{p} \in (\mathcal{S}[\vec{x}])^d$, $\vec{a}(\vec{p}) = \vec{a}[\vec{x}/\vec{p}]$ results from *applying* the polynomials $\vec{a}$ to the polynomials $\vec{p}$. In a similar way, we can also apply a formula to polynomials $\vec{p} \in (\mathcal{S}[\vec{x}])^d$. To this end, we define $\psi(\vec{p}) = \psi[\vec{x}/\vec{p}]$ for first-order formulas ψ with free variables $\vec{x}$. As usual, function application associates to the left, i.e., $\vec{a}(\vec{b})(\vec{p})$ stands for $(\vec{a}(\vec{b}))(\vec{p})$. However, since applying polynomials only means that one instantiates variables, we obviously have $(\vec{a}(\vec{b}))(\vec{p}) = \vec{a}(\vec{b}(\vec{p}))$.

Definition 1 formalizes the intuitive notion of termination for a loop $(\varphi, \vec{a})$.

Definition 1 (Termination). *The loop $(\varphi, \vec{a})$ is non-terminating (over $\mathcal{S}$) if*

$$\exists \vec{c} \in \mathcal{S}^d. \ \forall n \in \mathbb{N}. \ \varphi(\vec{a}^n(\vec{c})).$$

Then $\vec{c}$ is a witness *for non-termination. Otherwise, $(\varphi, \vec{a})$ terminates (over $\mathcal{S}$).*

Here, $\vec{a}^n$ denotes the n-fold application of $\vec{a}$, i.e., $\vec{a}^0(\vec{c}) = \vec{c}$ and $\vec{a}^{n+1}(\vec{c}) = \vec{a}(\vec{a}^n(\vec{c}))$. Termination (which is sometimes also called *universal* termination) is not to be confused with the *halting problem*, where one is interested in termination w.r.t. a *given* input. In contrast, Definition 1 considers termination w.r.t. *all* inputs.

For any entity s, let $\mathcal{V}(s)$ be the set of all free variables that occur in s. Given an assignment $\vec{x} \leftarrow \vec{a}$, the relation $\succ_{\vec{a}} \in \mathcal{V}(\vec{a}) \times \mathcal{V}(\vec{a})$ is the transitive closure of $\{(x_i, x_j) \mid i, j \in \{1, \ldots, d\}, i \neq j, x_j \in \mathcal{V}(a_i)\}$. We call $(\varphi, \vec{a})$ *triangular* if $\succ_{\vec{a}}$ is well founded. So the restriction to triangular loops prohibits "cyclic dependencies" of variables (e.g., where the new values of x_1 and x_2 both depend on the old values of x_1 and x_2). For example, a loop with the body $\begin{bmatrix} x_1 \\ x_2 \end{bmatrix} \leftarrow \begin{bmatrix} x_1 + x_2^2 \\ x_2 - 1 \end{bmatrix}$ is triangular since $\succ = \{(x_1, x_2)\}$ is well founded, whereas a loop with the body $\begin{bmatrix} x_1 \\ x_2 \end{bmatrix} \leftarrow \begin{bmatrix} x_1 + x_2^2 \\ x_1 - 1 \end{bmatrix}$ is not triangular. Triangularity is used to compute a *closed form* for the n-fold application of the loop update $\vec{a}$, i.e., a vector $\vec{q}$ of d expressions over the variables $\vec{x}$ and n such that $\vec{q} = \vec{a}^n$. From a practical point of view, the restriction to triangular loops seems quite natural. For example, in [18], 1511 polynomial loops were extracted from the *Termination Problems Data Base* [54], the benchmark collection which is used at the annual *Termination and Complexity Competition* [21], and only 26 of them were non-triangular.

The loop $(\varphi, \vec{a})$ is *weakly non-linear* if for no i, x_i occurs in a non-linear monomial of a_i. So for example, a loop with the body $\begin{bmatrix} x_1 \\ x_2 \end{bmatrix} \leftarrow \begin{bmatrix} x_1 + x_2^2 \\ x_2 - 1 \end{bmatrix}$ is weakly non-linear, whereas a loop with the body $\begin{bmatrix} x_1 \\ x_2 \end{bmatrix} \leftarrow \begin{bmatrix} x_1 \cdot x_2 \\ x_2 - 1 \end{bmatrix}$ is not. Together with triangularity, weak non-linearity ensures that we can always compute closed forms. In particular, weak non-linearity excludes loops like $(\varphi, x \leftarrow x^2)$ that need exponential space, as the values of some variables grow doubly exponentially.

A *twn*-loop is <u>t</u>riangular and <u>w</u>eakly <u>n</u>on-linear. So in other words, by permuting variables every *twn*-loop can be transformed to the form

$$\begin{bmatrix} x_1 \\ \ldots \\ x_d \end{bmatrix} \leftarrow \begin{bmatrix} c_1 \cdot x_1 + p_1 \\ \ldots \\ c_d \cdot x_d + p_d \end{bmatrix}$$

where $c_i \in \mathcal{S}$ and $p_i \in \mathcal{S}[x_{i+1}, \ldots, x_d]$. If $(\varphi, \vec{a})$ is weakly non-linear and x_i's coefficient in a_i is non-negative for all $1 \leq i \leq d$, then $(\varphi, \vec{a})$ is *non-negative*. A *tnn*-loop is triangular and non-negative (and thus, also weakly non-linear).

Our *twn*-loops are a special case of *solvable loops* [48].

Definition 2 (Solvable Loops). *A loop* $(\varphi, \vec{a})$ *is solvable if there is a partitioning* $\mathcal{J} = \{J_1, \ldots, J_k\}$ *of* $\{1, \ldots, d\}$ *such that for each* $1 \leq i \leq k$ *we have*

$$\vec{a}_{J_i} = A_i \cdot \vec{x}_{J_i} + \vec{p}_i,$$

where $\vec{a}_{J_i}$ *is the vector of all* a_j *with* $j \in J_i$ *(and* $\vec{x}_{J_i}$ *is defined analogously),* $d_i = |J_i|$, $A_i \in \mathcal{S}^{d_i \times d_i}$, *and* $\vec{p}_i \in (\mathcal{S}[\vec{x}_{J_{i+1}}, \ldots, \vec{x}_{J_k}])^{d_i}$. *The eigenvalues of a solvable loop are defined as the union of the eigenvalues of all* A_i.

So solvable loops allow for blocks of variables with linear dependencies, and *twn*-loops correspond to the case that each such block has size 1. While our approach could easily be generalized to solvable loops with real eigenvalues, in Sect. 3 we show that such a generalization does not increase its applicability.

For a ring $\mathbb{Z} \leq \mathcal{S} \leq \mathbb{R}_\mathbb{A}$, the *existential fragment of the first-order theory of* $\mathcal{S}$ is the set $\mathrm{Th}_\exists(\mathcal{S})$ of all formulas $\exists \vec{y} \in \mathcal{S}^k. \psi$, where ψ is a propositional formula over the atoms $\{p \triangleright 0 \mid p \in \mathbb{Q}[\vec{y}, \vec{z}], \triangleright \in \{\geq, >\}\}$ and $k \in \mathbb{N}$ [44,51]. Here, $\vec{y}$ and $\vec{z}$ are pairwise disjoint vectors of variables (i.e., the variables $\vec{z}$ are *free*). Moreover, $\mathrm{Th}_\exists(\mathcal{S}, \mathbb{R}_\mathbb{A})$ is the set of all formulas $\exists \vec{y}' \in \mathbb{R}_\mathbb{A}^{k'}, \vec{y} \in \mathcal{S}^k. \psi$, with a propositional formula ψ over $\{p \triangleright 0 \mid p \in \mathbb{Q}[\vec{y}', \vec{y}, \vec{z}], \triangleright \in \{\geq, >\}\}$ where $k', k \in \mathbb{N}$ and the variables $\vec{y}'$, $\vec{y}$, and $\vec{z}$ are pairwise disjoint. As usual, a formula without free variables is *closed*. In the following, we also consider formulas over inequations $p \triangleright 0$ where p's coefficients are from $\mathbb{R}_\mathbb{A}$ to be elements of $\mathrm{Th}_\exists(\mathbb{R}_\mathbb{A})$ (resp. $\mathrm{Th}_\exists(\mathcal{S}, \mathbb{R}_\mathbb{A})$). The reason is that real algebraic numbers are $\mathrm{Th}_\exists(\mathbb{R}_\mathbb{A})$-definable.

Finally, note that validity of formulas from $\mathrm{Th}_\exists(\mathcal{S})$ or $\mathrm{Th}_\exists(\mathcal{S}, \mathbb{R}_\mathbb{A})$ is decidable if $\mathcal{S} \in \{\mathbb{R}_\mathbb{A}, \mathbb{R}\}$ and semi-decidable if $\mathcal{S} \in \{\mathbb{Z}, \mathbb{Q}\}$ [11,52]. By undecidability of Hilbert's Tenth Problem, validity is undecidable for $\mathcal{S} = \mathbb{Z}$. While validity of full first-order formulas (i.e., also containing universal quantifiers) over $\mathcal{S} = \mathbb{Q}$ is undecidable [45], it is still open whether validity of formulas from $\mathrm{Th}_\exists(\mathbb{Q})$ or $\mathrm{Th}_\exists(\mathbb{Q}, \mathbb{R}_\mathbb{A})$ is decidable. However, validity of *linear* formulas from $\mathrm{Th}_\exists(\mathcal{S})$ or $\mathrm{Th}_\exists(\mathcal{S}, \mathbb{R}_\mathbb{A})$ is decidable for all $\mathcal{S} \in \{\mathbb{Z}, \mathbb{Q}, \mathbb{R}_\mathbb{A}, \mathbb{R}\}$.

3   Transformation to Triangular Weakly Non-linear Form

We first show how to handle loops that are not yet *twn*. To this end, we introduce a transformation of loops via *polynomial automorphisms* in Sect. 3.1 and show that our transformation preserves (non-)termination (Theorem 10). In Sect. 3.2, we use results from algebraic geometry to show that the question whether a loop can be transformed into *twn*-form is reducible to validity of $\mathrm{Th}_\exists(\mathbb{R}_\mathbb{A})$-formulas (Theorem 20). Moreover, we show that it is decidable whether a *linear* automorphism can transform a loop into a special case of the *twn*-form (Theorem 23).

3.1   Transforming Loops

Clearly, the *polynomials* $x_1, \ldots, x_d$ are *generators* of the $\mathcal{S}$-algebra $\mathcal{S}[\vec{x}]$, i.e., every polynomial from $\mathcal{S}[\vec{x}]$ can be obtained from $x_1, \ldots, x_d$ and the operations of the algebra (i.e., addition and multiplication). So far, we have implicitly chosen a special "representation" of the loop based on the generators $x_1, \ldots, x_d$.

We now change this representation, i.e., we use a different set of d polynomials which are also generators of $\mathcal{S}[\vec{x}]$. Then the loop has to be modified accordingly in order to adapt it to this new representation. This modification does not affect the loop's termination behavior, but it may transform a non-*twn*-loop into *twn*-form.

The desired change of representation is described by $\mathcal{S}$-*automorphisms* of $\mathcal{S}[\vec{x}]$. As usual, an $\mathcal{S}$-*endomorphism* of $\mathcal{S}[\vec{x}]$ is a mapping $\eta : \mathcal{S}[\vec{x}] \to \mathcal{S}[\vec{x}]$ which is $\mathcal{S}$-linear and multiplicative.[4] We denote the ring of $\mathcal{S}$-endomorphisms of $\mathcal{S}[\vec{x}]$ by $\mathrm{End}_{\mathcal{S}}(\mathcal{S}[\vec{x}])$ (where the operations on this ring are pointwise addition and function composition $\circ$). The group of $\mathcal{S}$-automorphisms of $\mathcal{S}[\vec{x}]$ is $\mathrm{End}_{\mathcal{S}}(\mathcal{S}[\vec{x}])$'s group of units, and we denote it by $\mathrm{Aut}_{\mathcal{S}}(\mathcal{S}[\vec{x}])$. So an $\mathcal{S}$-automorphism of $\mathcal{S}[\vec{x}]$ is an $\eta \in \mathrm{End}_{\mathcal{S}}(\mathcal{S}[\vec{x}])$ that is *invertible*. Thus, there exists an $\eta^{-1} \in \mathrm{End}_{\mathcal{S}}(\mathcal{S}[\vec{x}])$ such that $\eta \circ \eta^{-1} = \eta^{-1} \circ \eta = id_{\mathcal{S}[\vec{x}]}$, where $id_{\mathcal{S}[\vec{x}]}$ is the identity function on $\mathcal{S}[\vec{x}]$.

Example 3 (Automorphism). Let $\eta \in \mathrm{End}_{\mathcal{S}} (\mathcal{S}[x_1, x_2])$ with $\eta(x_1) = x_2$, $\eta(x_2) = x_1 - x_2^2$. Then $\eta \in \mathrm{Aut}_{\mathcal{S}} (\mathcal{S}[x_1, x_2])$, where $\eta^{-1}(x_1) = x_1^2 + x_2$ and $\eta^{-1}(x_2) = x_1$.

As $\mathcal{S}[\vec{x}]$ is free on the generators $\vec{x}$, an endomorphism $\eta \in \mathrm{End}_{\mathcal{S}}(\mathcal{S}[\vec{x}])$ is uniquely determined by the images of the variables, i.e., by $\eta(x_1), \ldots, \eta(x_d)$. Hence, we have a one-to-one correspondence between elements of $(\mathcal{S}[\vec{x}])^d$ and $\mathrm{End}_{\mathcal{S}}(\mathcal{S}[\vec{x}])$. In particular, every tuple $\vec{a} = (a_1, \ldots, a_d) \in (\mathcal{S}[\vec{x}])^d$ corresponds to the unique endomorphism $\tilde{a} \in \mathrm{End}_{\mathcal{S}}(\mathcal{S}[\vec{x}])$ with $\tilde{a}(x_i) = a_i$ for all $1 \leq i \leq d$. So for any $p \in \mathcal{S}[\vec{x}]$ we have $\tilde{a}(p) = p(\vec{a})$. Thus, the update of a loop induces an endomorphism which operates on polynomials.

Example 4 (Updates as Endomorphisms). Consider the loop

$$\textbf{while } x_2^3 + x_1 - x_2^2 > 0 \textbf{ do } (x_1, x_2) \leftarrow (a_1, a_2)$$

where $a_1 = ((-x_2^2 + x_1)^2 + x_2)^2 - 2 \cdot x_2^2 + 2 \cdot x_1$ and $a_2 = (-x_2^2 + x_1)^2 + x_2$, i.e., $\varphi = (x_2^3 + x_1 - x_2^2 > 0)$ and $\vec{a} = (a_1, a_2)$. Then $\vec{a}$ induces the endomorphism $\tilde{a}$ with $\tilde{a}(x_1) = a_1$ and $\tilde{a}(x_2) = a_2$. So we have $\tilde{a}(2 \cdot x_1 + x_2^3) = (2 \cdot x_1 + x_2^3)(\vec{a}) = 2 \cdot a_1 + a_2^3$.

For tuples of numbers (e.g., $\vec{c} = (5, 2)$), the endomorphism $\tilde{c}$ is $\tilde{c}(x_1) = 5$ and $\tilde{c}(x_2) = 2$. Thus, we have $\tilde{c}(x_2^3 + x_1 - x_2^2) = (x_2^3 + x_1 - x_2^2)(5, 2) = 2^3 + 5 - 2^2 = 9$.

We extend the application of endomorphisms $\eta : \mathcal{S}[\vec{x}] \to \mathcal{S}[\vec{x}]$ to vectors of polynomials $\vec{a} = (a_1, \ldots, a_d)$ by defining $\eta(\vec{a}) = (\eta(a_1), \ldots, \eta(a_d))$ and to formulas $\varphi \in \mathrm{Th}_{\exists}(\mathcal{S})$ by defining $\eta(\varphi) = \varphi(\eta(\vec{x}))$, i.e., $\eta(\varphi)$ results from φ by applying η to all polynomials that occur in φ. This allows us to transform $(\varphi, \vec{a})$ into a new loop $Tr_{\eta}(\varphi, \vec{a})$ using any automorphism $\eta \in \mathrm{Aut}_{\mathcal{S}}(\mathcal{S}[\vec{x}])$.

---

[4] So we have $\eta(c \cdot p + c' \cdot p') = c \cdot \eta(p) + c' \cdot \eta(p')$, $\eta(1) = 1$, and $\eta(p \cdot p') = \eta(p) \cdot \eta(p')$ for all $c, c' \in \mathcal{S}$ and all $p, p' \in \mathcal{S}[\vec{x}]$.

Definition 5 (*Tr*). *Let* $\eta \in \text{Aut}_\mathcal{S}(\mathcal{S}[\vec{x}])$. *We define* $Tr_\eta(\varphi, \vec{a}) = (\varphi', \vec{a}')$ *where*[5]

$$\varphi' = \eta^{-1}(\varphi) \qquad and \qquad \vec{a}' = (\eta^{-1} \circ \tilde{a} \circ \eta)(\vec{x}).$$

Example 6 (Transforming Loops). We transform the loop $(\varphi, \vec{a})$ from Example 4 with the automorphism η from Example 3. We obtain $Tr_\eta(\varphi, \vec{a}) = (\varphi', \vec{a}')$ where

$$\varphi' = \eta^{-1}(\varphi) = ((\eta^{-1}(x_2))^3 + \eta^{-1}(x_1) - (\eta^{-1}(x_2))^2 > 0)$$

$$= (x_1^3 + x_1^2 + x_2 - x_1^2 > 0) = (x_1^3 + x_2 > 0) \qquad \text{and}$$

$$\vec{a}' = ((\eta^{-1} \circ \tilde{a} \circ \eta)(x_1), (\eta^{-1} \circ \tilde{a} \circ \eta)(x_2)) = (\eta^{-1}(\tilde{a}(x_2)), \eta^{-1}(\tilde{a}(x_1 - x_2^2)))$$

$$= \qquad (\eta^{-1}(a_2), \eta^{-1}(a_1 - a_2^2)) \qquad = \qquad (x_1 + x_2^2, 2 \cdot x_2).$$

So the resulting transformed loop is $(x_1^3 + x_2 > 0, (x_1 + x_2^2, 2 \cdot x_2))$. Note that while the original loop $(\varphi, \vec{a})$ is neither triangular nor weakly non-linear, the resulting transformed loop is *twn*. Also note that we used a *non-linear* automorphism with $\eta(x_2) = x_1 - x_2^2$ for the transformation.

While the above example shows that our transformation can indeed transform non-*twn*-loops into *twn*-loops, it remains to prove that this transformation preserves (non-)termination. Then we can use our techniques for termination analysis of *twn*-loops for *twn-transformable*-loops as well, i.e., for all loops $(\varphi, \vec{a})$ where $Tr_\eta(\varphi, \vec{a})$ is *twn* for some automorphism η. (The question how to find such automorphisms will be addressed in Sect. 3.2.)

As a first step, by Lemma 7, our transformation is "compatible" with the operation $\circ$ of the group $\text{Aut}_\mathcal{S}(\mathcal{S}[\vec{x}])$, i.e., it is an *action*.

Lemma 7. *Tr is an* action *of* $\text{Aut}_\mathcal{S}(\mathcal{S}[\vec{x}])$ *on loops, i.e., for* $\eta_1, \eta_2 \in \text{Aut}_\mathcal{S}(\mathcal{S}[\vec{x}])$

$$Tr_{id_{\mathcal{S}[\vec{x}]}}(\varphi, \vec{a}) = (\varphi, \vec{a}) \quad and \quad Tr_{\eta_1 \circ \eta_2}(\varphi, \vec{a}) = Tr_{\eta_2}(Tr_{\eta_1}(\varphi, \vec{a})).$$

The next lemma shows that a witness for non-termination of $(\varphi, \vec{a})$ is transformed by $\eta(\vec{x})$ into a witness for non-termination of $Tr_\eta(\varphi, \vec{a})$.

Lemma 8. *If* $\vec{c}$ *witnesses non-termination of* $(\varphi, \vec{a})$*, then* $\hat{\eta}(\vec{c})$ *witnesses non-termination of* $Tr_\eta(\varphi, \vec{a})$. *Here,* $\hat{\eta} : \mathcal{S}^d \to \mathcal{S}^d$ *maps* $\vec{c}$ *to* $\hat{\eta}(\vec{c}) = \tilde{c}(\eta(\vec{x})) = (\eta(\vec{x}))(\vec{c})$.

Example 9 (Transforming Witnesses). For the tuple $\vec{c} = (5, 2)$ from Example 4 and the automorphism η from Example 3 with $\eta(x_1) = x_2$ and $\eta(x_2) = x_1 - x_2^2$, we obtain

$$\hat{\eta}(\vec{c}) = (\eta(x_1), \eta(x_2)) (\vec{c}) = (2, 5 - 2^2) = (2, 1).$$

As $\vec{c} = (5, 2)$ witnesses non-termination of Example 4, $\hat{\eta}(\vec{c}) = (2, 1)$ witnesses non-termination of $Tr_\eta(\varphi, \vec{a})$ due to Lemma 8.

---

[5] In other words, we have $\vec{a}' = (\eta(\vec{x})) (\vec{a}) (\eta^{-1}(\vec{x}))$, since $(\eta^{-1} \circ \tilde{a} \circ \eta)(\vec{x}) = \eta^{-1}(\eta(\vec{x})[\vec{x}/\vec{a}]) = \eta(\vec{x})[\vec{x}/\vec{a}][\vec{x}/\eta^{-1}(\vec{x})] = (\eta(\vec{x}))(\vec{a})(\eta^{-1}(\vec{x}))$.

Finally, Theorem 10 states that transforming a loop preserves (non-)termination.

Theorem 10 (*Tr* Preserves Termination). *If $\eta \in \text{Aut}_{\mathcal{S}}(\mathcal{S}[\vec{x}])$, then $(\varphi, \vec{a})$ terminates iff $Tr_\eta(\varphi, \vec{a})$ terminates. Furthermore, $\widehat{\eta}$ is a bijection between the respective sets of witnesses for non-termination.*

Up to now, we only transformed a loop $(\varphi, \vec{a})$ on $\mathcal{S}^d$ using elements of $\text{Aut}_{\mathcal{S}}(\mathcal{S}[\vec{x}])$. However, we can also transform it into the loop $Tr_\eta(\varphi, \vec{a})$ on $\mathbb{R}_{\mathbb{A}}^d$ using an automorphism $\eta \in \text{Aut}_{\mathbb{R}_{\mathbb{A}}}(\mathbb{R}_{\mathbb{A}}[\vec{x}])$. Nevertheless, our goal remains to prove termination on $\mathcal{S}^d$ instead of $\mathbb{R}_{\mathbb{A}}^d$, which is not equivalent in general. Thus, in Sect. 5 we will show how to analyze termination of loops on certain subsets F of $\mathbb{R}_{\mathbb{A}}^d$. This allows us to analyze termination of $(\varphi, \vec{a})$ on $\mathcal{S}^d$ by checking termination of $Tr_\eta(\varphi, \vec{a})$ on the subset $\widehat{\eta}(\mathcal{S}^d) \subseteq \mathbb{R}_{\mathbb{A}}^d$ instead.

By our definition of loops over a ring $\mathcal{S}$, we have $\vec{a}(\vec{c}) \in \mathcal{S}^d$ for all $\vec{c} \in \mathcal{S}^d$, i.e., $\mathcal{S}^d$ is $\vec{a}$-*invariant*. This property is preserved by our transformation.

Definition 11 ($\vec{a}$-Invariance). *Let $(\varphi, \vec{a})$ be a loop on $\mathcal{S}^d$ and let $F \subseteq \mathcal{S}^d$. We call F $\vec{a}$-invariant or update-invariant if for all $\vec{c} \in F$ we have $\vec{a}(\vec{c}) \in F$.*

Lemma 12. *Let $(\varphi, \vec{a})$ be a loop on $\mathcal{S}^d$, let $F \subseteq \mathcal{S}^d$ be $\vec{a}$-invariant, and let $\eta \in \text{Aut}_{\mathbb{R}_{\mathbb{A}}}(\mathbb{R}_{\mathbb{A}}[\vec{x}])$. Furthermore, let $Tr_\eta(\varphi, \vec{a}) = (\varphi', \vec{a}')$. Then $\widehat{\eta}(F)$ is $\vec{a}'$-invariant.*

Recall that our goal is to reduce termination to a $\text{Th}_\exists(\mathcal{S}, \mathbb{R}_{\mathbb{A}})$-formula. Clearly, *termination on F* cannot be encoded with such a formula if F cannot be defined via $\text{Th}_\exists(\mathcal{S}, \mathbb{R}_{\mathbb{A}})$. Thus, we require that F is $\text{Th}_\exists(\mathcal{S}, \mathbb{R}_{\mathbb{A}})$-*definable*.

Definition 13 ($\text{Th}_\exists(\mathcal{S}, \mathbb{R}_{\mathbb{A}})$-Definability). *A set $F \subseteq \mathbb{R}_{\mathbb{A}}^d$ is $\text{Th}_\exists(\mathcal{S}, \mathbb{R}_{\mathbb{A}})$-definable if there is a $\psi \in \text{Th}_\exists(\mathcal{S}, \mathbb{R}_{\mathbb{A}})$ with free variables $\vec{x}$ such that for all $\vec{c} \in \mathbb{R}_{\mathbb{A}}^d$*

$$\vec{c} \in F \quad \text{iff} \quad \psi(\vec{c}) \text{ is valid.}$$

An example for a $\text{Th}_\exists(\mathbb{Z}, \mathbb{R}_{\mathbb{A}})$-definable set is $\{(a, 0, a) \mid a \in \mathbb{Z}\}$, which is characterized by the formula $\exists a \in \mathbb{Z}. \; x_1 = a \wedge x_2 = 0 \wedge x_3 = a$.

To analyze termination of $(\varphi, \vec{a})$ on $\mathcal{S}^d$, we can analyze termination of $Tr_\eta(\varphi, \vec{a})$ on $\widehat{\eta}(\mathcal{S}^d) \subseteq \mathbb{R}_{\mathbb{A}}^d$ instead. The reason is that $\vec{c} \in \mathcal{S}^d$ witnesses non-termination of $(\varphi, \vec{a})$ iff $\widehat{\eta}(\vec{c})$ witnesses non-termination of $Tr_\eta(\varphi, \vec{a})$ due to Theorem 10, i.e., $\mathcal{S}^d$ contains a witness for non-termination of $(\varphi, \vec{a})$ iff $\widehat{\eta}(\mathcal{S}^d)$ contains a witness for non-termination of $Tr_\eta(\varphi, \vec{a})$. While $\mathcal{S}^d$ is clearly $\text{Th}_\exists(\mathcal{S}, \mathbb{R}_{\mathbb{A}})$-definable, the following lemma shows that $\widehat{\eta}(\mathcal{S}^d)$ is $\text{Th}_\exists(\mathcal{S}, \mathbb{R}_{\mathbb{A}})$-definable, too. More precisely, $\text{Th}_\exists(\mathcal{S}, \mathbb{R}_{\mathbb{A}})$-definability is preserved by polynomial endomorphisms.

Lemma 14. *Let $\mathbb{Z} \leq \mathcal{S} \leq \mathbb{R}_{\mathbb{A}}$ and let $\eta \in \text{End}_{\mathbb{R}_{\mathbb{A}}}(\mathbb{R}_{\mathbb{A}}[\vec{x}])$. If $F \subseteq \mathbb{R}_{\mathbb{A}}^d$ is $\text{Th}_\exists(\mathcal{S}, \mathbb{R}_{\mathbb{A}})$-definable then so is $\widehat{\eta}(F)$.*

Example 15. The set $\mathbb{Z}^2$ is $\text{Th}_\exists(\mathbb{Z}, \mathbb{R}_{\mathbb{A}})$-definable, as we have $(x_1, x_2) \in \mathbb{Z}^2$ iff

$$\exists a, b \in \mathbb{Z}. \; x_1 = a \wedge x_2 = b.$$

Let $\eta \in \mathrm{End}_{\mathbb{R}_A}(\mathbb{R}_A[\vec{x}])$ with $\eta(x_1) = \frac{1}{2} \cdot x_1^2 + x_2^2$ and $\eta(x_2) = x_2^2$. Then $\widehat{\eta}(\mathbb{Z}^2)$ is also $\mathrm{Th}_\exists(\mathbb{Z}, \mathbb{R}_A)$-definable, because for $x_1, x_2 \in \mathbb{R}_A$, we have $(x_1, x_2) \in \eta(\mathbb{Z}^2)$ iff

$$\exists y_1, y_2 \in \mathbb{R}_A, \, a, b \in \mathbb{Z}. \; y_1 = a \wedge y_2 = b \, \wedge \, x_1 = \frac{1}{2} \cdot y_1^2 + y_2^2 \wedge x_2 = y_2^2.$$

The following theorem shows that instead of regarding *solvable loops* [48], w.l.o.g. we can restrict ourselves to *twn*-loops. The reason is that every solvable loop with real eigenvalues can be transformed into a *twn*-loop by a *linear* automorphism η, i.e., the degree $\deg(\eta)$ of η is 1, where $\deg(\eta) = \max_{1 \leq i \leq d} \deg(\eta(x_i))$.

Theorem 16. *Let $(\varphi, \vec{a})$ be a solvable loop with real eigenvalues. Then one can compute a linear automorphism $\eta \in \mathrm{Aut}_{\mathbb{R}_A}(\mathbb{R}_A[\vec{x}])$ such that $Tr_\eta(\varphi, \vec{a})$ is twn.*

We recapitulate our most important results on Tr in the following corollary.

Corollary 17 (Properties of Tr). *Let $(\varphi, \vec{a})$ be a loop, $\eta \in \mathrm{Aut}_{\mathbb{R}_A}(\mathbb{R}_A[\vec{x}])$, $Tr_\eta(\varphi, \vec{a}) = (\varphi', \vec{a}')$, and $F \subseteq \mathcal{S}^d$ be $\vec{a}$-invariant and $\mathrm{Th}_\exists(\mathcal{S}, \mathbb{R}_A)$-definable. Then*

1. *$\widehat{\eta}(F) \subseteq \mathbb{R}_A^d$ is $\vec{a}'$-invariant and $\mathrm{Th}_\exists(\mathcal{S}, \mathbb{R}_A)$-definable,*
2. *$(\varphi, \vec{a})$ terminates on F iff $(\varphi', \vec{a}')$ terminates on $\widehat{\eta}(F)$, and*
3. *$\vec{c} \in F$ witnesses non-termination of $(\varphi, \vec{a})$ iff $\widehat{\eta}(\vec{c}) \in \widehat{\eta}(F)$ witnesses non-termination of $(\varphi', \vec{a}')$.*

3.2   Finding Automorphisms to Transform Loops into *twn*-Form

The goal of the transformation from Sect. 3.1 is to transform $(\varphi, \vec{a})$ into *twn*-form, such that termination of the resulting loop $Tr_\eta(\varphi, \vec{a})$ can be analyzed by the technique which will be presented in Sect. 4 and 5. Hence, the remaining challenge is to find a suitable automorphism $\eta \in \mathrm{Aut}_{\mathbb{R}_A}(\mathbb{R}_A[\vec{x}])$ such that $Tr_\eta(\varphi, \vec{a})$ is *twn*. In this section, we will present two techniques to check the existence of such automorphisms *constructively*, i.e., these techniques can also be used to compute such automorphisms.

Note that the search for suitable automorphisms is closely related to the question if a polynomial endomorphism can be conjugated into a "de Jonquiéres"-automorphism, a difficult question from algebraic geometry [14]. So future advances in this field may help to improve the results of the current section.

The first technique (Theorem 20) reduces the search for a suitable automorphism *of bounded degree* to $\mathrm{Th}_\exists(\mathbb{R}_A)$. It is known that for any automorphism the degree of its inverse has an upper bound in terms of the length d of $\vec{x}$, see [14, Cor. 2.3.4].

Theorem 18. *Let $\eta \in \mathrm{Aut}_{\mathbb{R}_A}(\mathbb{R}_A[\vec{x}])$. Then we have $\deg(\eta^{-1}) \leq (\deg(\eta))^{d-1}$.*

By Theorem 18, checking if an endomorphism is indeed an automorphism can be reduced to $\mathrm{Th}_\exists(\mathbb{R}_A)$. To do so, one encodes the existence of suitable coefficients of the polynomials $\eta^{-1}(x_1), \ldots, \eta^{-1}(x_d)$, which all have at most degree $(\deg(\eta))^{d-1}$.

Lemma 19. *Let* $\eta \in \mathrm{End}_{\mathbb{R}_A}(\mathbb{R}_A[\vec{x}])$. *Then the question whether* $\eta \in \mathrm{Aut}_{\mathbb{R}_A}(\mathbb{R}_A[\vec{x}])$ *holds is reducible to* $\mathrm{Th}_\exists(\mathbb{R}_A)$.

Based on Lemma 19, we now present our first technique to find an automorphism η that transforms a loop into *twn*-form.

Theorem 20 (*Tr* with Automorphisms of Bounded Degree). *For any* $\delta \geq 0$, *the question whether there exists an* $\eta \in \mathrm{Aut}_{\mathbb{R}_A}(\mathbb{R}_A[\vec{x}])$ *with* $\deg(\eta) \leq \delta$ *such that* $Tr_\eta(\varphi, \vec{a})$ *is* twn *is reducible to* $\mathrm{Th}_\exists(\mathbb{R}_A)$.

So if the degree of η is bounded a priori, then it is decidable whether there exists an $\eta \in \mathrm{Aut}_{\mathbb{R}_A}(\mathbb{R}_A[\vec{x}])$ such that $Tr_\eta(\varphi, \vec{a})$ is *twn*, since $\mathrm{Th}_\exists(\mathbb{R}_A)$ is decidable.

We call a loop *twn-transformable* if there is an $\eta \in \mathrm{Aut}_{\mathbb{R}_A}(\mathbb{R}_A[\vec{x}])$ such that $Tr_\eta(\varphi, \vec{a})$ is *twn*. By Theorem 20, *twn*-transformability is *semi-decidable*, since one can increment δ until a suitable automorphism is found. So in other words, any loop which is transformable to a *twn*-loop can be transformed via Theorem 20.

We call our transformation *Tr complete* for a class of loops if *every* loop from this class is *twn*-transformable. For such classes of loops, a suitable automorphism is *computable* by Theorem 20. Together with Theorem 16, we get the following corollary.

Corollary 21. *Tr is complete for solvable loops with real eigenvalues.*

Note that for solvable loops $(\varphi, \vec{a})$, instead of computing η using Theorem 20, the proof of Theorem 16 yields a more efficient way to compute a linear automorphism η such that $Tr_\eta(\varphi, \vec{a})$ is *twn*. To this end, one computes the Jordan normal form of each A_i (see Definition 2), which is possible in polynomial time (see e.g., [19, 46]).

Our second technique to find suitable automorphisms for our transformation is restricted to *linear* automorphisms. In this case, it is decidable whether a loop can be transformed into a *twn*-loop $(\varphi', \vec{a}')$ where the monomial for x_i has the coefficient 1 in each a_i'. The decision procedure checks whether a certain Jacobian matrix is *strongly nilpotent*, i.e., it is not based on a reduction to $\mathrm{Th}_\exists(\mathbb{R}_A)$.

Definition 22 (Strong Nilpotence). *Let* $J \in (\mathbb{R}_A[\vec{x}])^{d \times d}$ *be a matrix of polynomials. For all* $1 \leq i \leq d$, *let* $\vec{y}^{(i)}$ *be a vector of fresh variables. J is strongly nilpotent if* $\prod_{i=1}^{d} J[\vec{x}/\vec{y}^{(i)}] = 0^{d \times d}$, *where* $0^{d \times d} \in (\mathbb{R}_A[\vec{x}])^{d \times d}$ *is the zero matrix.*

Our second technique is formulated in the following theorem which follows from an existing result in linear algebra [13, Thm. 1.6.].

Theorem 23 (*Tr* with Linear Automorphisms [13, Thm. 1.6.]). *Let* $(\varphi, \vec{a})$ *be a loop. The Jacobian matrix* $(\frac{\partial(a_i - x_i)}{\partial x_j})_{1 \leq i, j \leq d} \in (\mathbb{R}_A[\vec{x}])^{d \times d}$ *is strongly nilpotent iff there exists a linear automorphism* $\eta \in \mathrm{Aut}_{\mathbb{R}_A}(\mathbb{R}_A[\vec{x}])$ *with*

$$Tr_\eta(\varphi, \vec{a}) = (\varphi', (x_1 + p_1, \ldots, x_d + p_d)) \tag{2}$$

and $p_i \in \mathbb{R}_A[x_{i+1}, \ldots, x_d]$. *Thus,* $Tr_\eta(\varphi, \vec{a})$ *is* twn.

As strong nilpotence of the Jacobian matrix is clearly decidable, Theorem 23 gives rise to a decision procedure for the existence of a linear automorphism that transforms $(\varphi, \vec{a})$ to the form (2).

Example 24 (Finding Automorphisms). The following loop on $\mathcal{S}^3$ shows how our results enlarge the class of loops where termination is reducible to $\mathrm{Th}_\exists(\mathcal{S}, \mathbb{R}_\mathbb{A})$.

$$\textbf{while } 4 \cdot x_2{}^2 + x_1 + x_2 + x_3 > 0 \textbf{ do } (x_1, x_2, x_3) \leftarrow (a_1, a_2, a_3) \qquad (3)$$

with $\quad a_1 = x_1 + 8 \cdot x_1 \cdot x_2{}^2 + 16 \cdot x_2{}^3 + 16 \cdot x_2{}^2 \cdot x_3$

$$a_2 = x_2 - x_1{}^2 - 4 \cdot x_1 \cdot x_2 - 4 \cdot x_1 \cdot x_3 - 4 \cdot x_2{}^2 - 8 \cdot x_2 \cdot x_3 - 4 \cdot x_3{}^2$$

$$a_3 = x_3 - 4 \cdot x_1 \cdot x_2{}^2 - 8 \cdot x_2{}^3 - 8 \cdot x_2{}^2 \cdot x_3 + x_1{}^2 + 4 \cdot x_1 \cdot x_2 +$$
$$4 \cdot x_1 \cdot x_3 + 4 \cdot x_2{}^2 + 8 \cdot x_2 \cdot x_3 + 4 \cdot x_3{}^2$$

It is clearly *not* in *twn*-form. To transform it, we use Theorem 23. The Jacobian matrix J of $(a_1 - x_1, a_2 - x_2, a_3 - x_3)$ is:

$$\begin{bmatrix} 8 \cdot x_2^2 & 16 \cdot x_1 \cdot x_2 + 48 \cdot x_2^2 + 32 \cdot x_2 \cdot x_3 & 16 \cdot x_2^2 \\ -2 \cdot x_1 - 4 \cdot x_2 - 4 \cdot x_3 & -4 \cdot x_1 - 8 \cdot x_2 - 8 \cdot x_3 & -4 \cdot x_1 - 8 \cdot x_2 - 8 \cdot x_3 \\ -4 \cdot x_2^2 + 2 \cdot x_1 + 4 \cdot x_2 + 4 \cdot x_3 & -8 \cdot x_1 \cdot x_2 - 24 \cdot x_2^2 - 16 \cdot x_2 \cdot x_3 + 4 \cdot x_1 + 8 \cdot x_2 + 8 \cdot x_3 & -8 \cdot x_2^2 + 4 \cdot x_1 + 8 \cdot x_2 + 8 \cdot x_3 \end{bmatrix}$$

One easily checks that J is strongly nilpotent. Thus, by Theorem 23 the loop can be transformed into *twn*-form by a linear automorphism. Indeed, consider the linear automorphism $\eta \in \mathrm{Aut}_{\mathbb{R}_\mathbb{A}}(\mathbb{R}_\mathbb{A}[\vec{x}])$ induced by the matrix $M = \begin{bmatrix} 1 & 1 & 1 \\ 0 & 2 & 0 \\ 1 & 2 & 2 \end{bmatrix}$, i.e.,

$$x_1 \mapsto x_1 + x_2 + x_3, \quad x_2 \mapsto 2 \cdot x_2, \quad x_3 \mapsto x_1 + 2 \cdot x_2 + 2 \cdot x_3$$

with its inverse η^{-1}

$$x_1 \mapsto 2 \cdot x_1 - x_3, \quad x_2 \mapsto \tfrac{1}{2} \cdot x_2, \quad x_3 \mapsto -x_1 - \tfrac{1}{2} \cdot x_2 + x_3.$$

If we transform our loop with η, we obtain the following *twn*-loop:

$$\textbf{while } x_1 + x_2^2 > 0 \textbf{ do } \begin{bmatrix} x_1 \\ x_2 \\ x_3 \end{bmatrix} \leftarrow \begin{bmatrix} x_1 + x_2^2 \cdot x_3 \\ x_2 - 2 \cdot x_3^2 \\ x_3 \end{bmatrix} \qquad (4)$$

If $\mathcal{S} = \mathbb{R}_\mathbb{A}$, then (4) terminates on $\mathbb{R}_\mathbb{A}^3$ iff (3) terminates on $\mathbb{R}_\mathbb{A}^3$ by Theorem 10. Now assume $\mathcal{S} = \mathbb{Z}$, i.e., we are interested in termination of (3) on $\mathbb{Z}^3$ instead of $\mathbb{R}_\mathbb{A}^3$. Note that $\hat{\eta}$ maps $\mathbb{Z}^3$ to the set of all $\mathbb{Z}$-linear combinations of columns of M, i.e.,

$$\hat{\eta}(\mathbb{Z}^3) = \{a \cdot (1, 0, 1) + b \cdot (1, 2, 2) + c \cdot (1, 0, 2) \mid a, b, c \in \mathbb{Z}\}.$$

By Corollary 17, (4) terminates on $\hat{\eta}(\mathbb{Z}^3)$ iff (3) terminates on $\mathbb{Z}^3$. Moreover, $\hat{\eta}(\mathbb{Z}^3)$ is $\mathrm{Th}_\exists(\mathbb{Z}, \mathbb{R}_\mathbb{A})$-definable: We have $(x_1, x_2, x_3) \in \hat{\eta}(\mathbb{Z}^3)$ iff

$$\exists a, b, c \in \mathbb{Z}. \; x_1 = a \cdot 1 + b \cdot 1 + c \cdot 1 \wedge x_2 = b \cdot 2 \wedge x_3 = a \cdot 1 + b \cdot 2 + c \cdot 2.$$

In the following sections, we will see how to analyze termination of loops like (4) on sets that can be characterized by such formulas.

To summarize, if a loop is *twn*-transformable, then we can *always* find a suitable automorphism via Theorem 20. So whenever Theorem 23 is applicable, a suitable linear automorphism can also be obtained by using Theorem 20 for some fixed degree $\delta \geq 1$. Hence, our first technique from Theorem 20 subsumes our second one from Theorem 23. However, while Theorem 20 is *always* applicable, Theorem 23 is *easier* to apply. The reason is that for Theorem 20 one has to check validity of a possibly *non-linear* formula over the reals, where the degree of the occurring polynomials depends on δ and the update $\vec{a}$ of the loop. So even when searching for a linear automorphism, one may obtain a non-linear formula if the loop is non-linear. In contrast, Theorem 23 only requires linear algebra. So it is preferable to first check whether the loop can be transformed into a *twn*-loop $(\varphi', (x_1 + p_1, \ldots, x_d + p_d))$ with $x_i \notin \mathcal{V}(p_i)$ via a linear automorphism. This check is *decidable* due to Theorem 23.

Note that the proof of Theorem 20 and the proof of [13, Thm. 1.6.] which implies Theorem 23 are constructive. Thus, we can not only check the existence of a suitable automorphism, but we can also compute it whenever its existence can be proven.

4 Computing Closed Forms

Now we show how to reduce the termination problem of a *twn*-loop on a $\mathrm{Th}_\exists(\mathcal{S}, \mathbb{R}_A)$-definable set to validity of a formula from $\mathrm{Th}_\exists(\mathcal{S}, \mathbb{R}_A)$. Our reduction exploits that for *twn*-loops $(\varphi, \vec{a})$, there is a closed form for the n-fold application of $\vec{a}$ which can be represented as a vector of *poly-exponential expressions*.

As in [15], we restrict ourselves to *tnn*-loops (instead of *twn*-loops), because each *twn*-loop can be transformed into a *tnn*-loop via *chaining*.

Definition 25 (Chaining). Chaining *a loop* $(\varphi, \vec{a})$ *yields* $(\varphi \wedge \varphi(\vec{a}), \vec{a}(\vec{a}))$.

Clearly, $(\varphi, \vec{a})$ terminates iff $(\varphi \wedge \varphi(\vec{a}), \vec{a}(\vec{a}))$ terminates. Moreover, if $(\varphi, \vec{a})$ is a *twn*-loop then $(\varphi \wedge \varphi(\vec{a}), \vec{a}(\vec{a}))$ is a *tnn*-loop, i.e., the coefficient of each x_i in $a_i(\vec{a})$ is non-negative. Thus, analogous to [15], we obtain the following theorem.

Theorem 26. *Termination of twn-loops is reducible to termination of tnn-loops.*

It is well known that closed forms for *tnn*-loops are computable, see, e.g., [28]. The reason is that the bodies of *tnn*-loops correspond to a special case of *C-finite recurrences*, which are known to be solvable [26]. The resulting closed forms may contain polynomial arithmetic and exponentiation w.r.t. n (as, e.g., $x_1 \leftarrow 2 \cdot x_1$ has the closed form $x_1 \cdot 2^n$) as well as certain piecewise defined functions. For example, the closed form of $x_1 \leftarrow 1$ is $x_1^{(n)} = x_1$ if $n = 0$ and $x_1^{(n)} = 1$, otherwise.

We use *poly-exponential expressions* [15][6] to represent closed forms where piecewise defined functions are simulated via *characteristic functions*. Given a

---

[6] Our definition of poly-exponential expressions slightly generalizes [15, Def. 9] (e.g., we allow polynomials over the variables $\vec{x}$ instead of just linear combinations).

formula ψ over n, its characteristic function $[\![\psi]\!] : \mathbb{N} \rightarrow \{0,1\}$ evaluates to 1 iff ψ is satisfied (i.e., $[\![\psi]\!](c) = 1$ if $\psi[n/c]$ holds and $[\![\psi]\!](c) = 0$, otherwise). In this way, we avoid handling piecewise defined functions via disjunctions (as done in the closed form of [28]). Poly-exponential expressions are sums of arithmetic terms over the variables $\vec{x}$ and the additional designated variable n, where it is always clear which addend determines the asymptotic growth of the whole expression when increasing n. This is crucial for our reducibility proof in Sect. 5. In the following, for any set $X \subseteq \mathbb{R}$, any $k \in X$, and $\triangleright \in \{\geq, >\}$, let $X_{\triangleright k} = \{x \in X \mid x \triangleright k\}$.

Definition 27 (Poly-Exponential Expressions). *Let $\mathcal{C}$ be the set of all finite conjunctions over $\{n = c, n \neq c \mid c \in \mathbb{N}\}$ where n is a designated variable. The set of all* poly-exponential expressions *with the variables $\vec{x}$ is*

$$\mathbb{PE}[\vec{x}] = \left\{ \sum_{j=1}^{\ell} [\![\psi_j]\!] \cdot \alpha_j \cdot n^{a_j} \cdot b_j^n \ \middle| \ \ell, a_j \in \mathbb{N}, \ \psi_j \in \mathcal{C}, \ \alpha_j \in \mathbb{R}_A[\vec{x}], \ b_j \in (\mathbb{R}_A)_{>0} \right\}.$$

So an example for a poly-exponential expression is

$$[\![n \neq 0 \wedge n \neq 1]\!] \cdot (\tfrac{1}{2} \cdot x_1^2 + \tfrac{3}{4} \cdot x_2 - 1) \cdot n^3 \cdot 3^n + [\![n = 1]\!] \cdot (x_1 - x_2).$$

Note that the restriction to triangular loops ensures that the closed form does not contain complex numbers. For example, for arbitrary matrices $A \in \mathcal{S}^{d \times d}$, the update $\vec{x} \leftarrow A \cdot \vec{x}$ is known to admit a closed form as in Definition 27 with complex b_j's, whereas real numbers suffice for triangular matrices. Moreover, non-negativity is required to ensure $b_j > 0$ (e.g., the non-*tnn* loop $x_1 \leftarrow -x_1$ has the closed form $x_1 \cdot (-1)^n$). So together with triangularity, weak non-linearity ensures that for every *tnn*-loop, one can compute a closed form $\vec{q} \in (\mathbb{PE}[\vec{x}])^d$ with $\vec{q} = \vec{a}^n$.

Example 28 (Closed Forms). Reconsider the loop (4) from Example 24. This loop is *tnn* as $\succ_{(4)} = \{(x_1, x_2), (x_1, x_3), (x_2, x_3)\}$ is well founded. Moreover, every variable x_i occurs with a non-negative coefficient in its corresponding update a_i. A closed form for the update after $n \in \mathbb{N}$ loop iterations is:

$$\vec{q} = \begin{bmatrix} \tfrac{4}{3} \cdot x_3^5 \cdot n^3 + (-2 \cdot x_3^5 - 2 \cdot x_2 \cdot x_3^3) \cdot n^2 + (x_2^2 \cdot x_3 + \tfrac{2}{3} \cdot x_3^5 + 2 \cdot x_2 \cdot x_3^3) \cdot n + x_1 \\ -2 \cdot x_3^2 \cdot n + x_2 \\ x_3 \end{bmatrix}$$

5 Reducing Termination of *tnn*-Loops to $\mathrm{Th}_\exists(\mathcal{S}, \mathbb{R}_A)$

It is known that the bodies of *tnn*-loops can be linearized [39], i.e., one can reduce termination of a *tnn*-loop $(\varphi, \vec{a})$ to termination of a linear-update *tnn*-loop $(\varphi', \vec{a}')$ where φ' may be *non*-linear. Moreover, [55] showed decidability of termination for certain classes of conjunctive linear-update loops over $\mathbb{R}$, which cover conjunctive linear-update *tnn*-loops. So, by combining the results of [39] and [55], one can conclude that termination for *conjunctive tnn*-loops over $\mathbb{R}$ is decidable.

However, we will now present a reduction of termination of tnn-loops to $\mathrm{Th}_\exists(\mathcal{S}, \mathbb{R}_A)$ which applies to tnn-loops over *any* ring $\mathbb{Z} \leq \mathcal{S} \leq \mathbb{R}$ and can handle also *disjunctions* in the loop condition. Moreover, our reduction yields tight complexity results on termination of linear loops over $\mathbb{Z}$, $\mathbb{Q}$, $\mathbb{R}_A$, and $\mathbb{R}$, and on termination of linear-update loops over $\mathbb{R}_A$ and $\mathbb{R}$ (Sect. 6).

The idea of our reduction is similar to [15]. However, in [15], we considered conjunctive linear loops over $\mathbb{Z}$. In contrast, we now analyze termination of $(\varphi, \vec{a})$ on an $\vec{a}$-invariant $\mathrm{Th}_\exists(\mathcal{S}, \mathbb{R}_A)$-definable subset of $\mathbb{R}_A^d$ and allow arbitrary propositional formulas and *non*-linearity in the condition. So the correctness proofs differ substantially from [15]. For reasons of space, we only show the major steps of our reduction and refer to [16] for more details.

In the following, let $(\varphi, \vec{a})$ be tnn, let $F \subseteq \mathbb{R}_A^d$ be $\vec{a}$-invariant and $\mathrm{Th}_\exists(\mathcal{S}, \mathbb{R}_A)$-definable by the formula ψ_F, and let $\vec{q} \in (\mathbb{PE}[\vec{x}])^d$ be the closed form of $\vec{a}^n$.

We now show how to encode termination of $(\varphi, \vec{a})$ on F into a $\mathrm{Th}_\exists(\mathcal{S}, \mathbb{R}_A)$-formula. More precisely, we show that there is a function with the following specification that is computable in polynomial time:

$$\begin{aligned} \text{Input}: \quad & (\varphi, \vec{a}), \ \vec{q}, \text{ and } \psi_F \text{ as above} \\ \text{Result}: \quad & \text{a closed formula } \chi \in \mathrm{Th}_\exists(\mathcal{S}, \mathbb{R}_A) \text{ such that} \\ & \chi \text{ is valid iff } (\varphi, \vec{a}) \text{ does not terminate on } F \end{aligned} \tag{5}$$

We use the concept of *eventual non-termination* [8,53], where the loop condition may be violated finitely often, i.e., $\vec{c}$ witnesses eventual non-termination of $(\varphi, \vec{a})$ if $\vec{a}^{n_0}(\vec{c})$ witnesses non-termination for some $n_0 \in \mathbb{N}$. Clearly, $(\varphi, \vec{a})$ is non-terminating iff it is eventually non-terminating [41]. The formula χ in (5) will encode the existence of a witness for eventual non-termination.

By the definition of $\vec{q}$, $(\varphi, \vec{a})$ is eventually non-terminating on F iff

$$\exists \vec{x} \in F, \ n_0 \in \mathbb{N}. \ \forall n \in \mathbb{N}_{>n_0}. \ \varphi(\vec{q}). \tag{6}$$

Example 29. Continuing Examples 24 and 28, (4) is eventually non-terminating on

$$F = \widehat{\eta}(\mathbb{Z}^3) = \{ a \cdot (1,0,1) + b \cdot (1,2,2) + c \cdot (1,0,2) \mid a,b,c \in \mathbb{Z} \}$$

iff there is a corresponding witness $\vec{c} = (x_1, x_2, x_3)$, i.e., iff

$$\exists x_1, x_2, x_3 \in F, \ n_0 \in \mathbb{N}. \ \forall n \in \mathbb{N}_{>n_0}. \ p > 0, \qquad \text{where} \tag{7}$$

$$\begin{aligned} p = \left(\tfrac{4}{3} \cdot x_3^5 \right) \cdot n^3 &+ \left(-2 \cdot x_3^5 - 2 \cdot x_2 \cdot x_3^3 + 4 \cdot x_3^4 \right) \cdot n^2 & + \\ \left(x_2^2 \cdot x_3 + \tfrac{2}{3} \cdot x_3^5 + 2 \cdot x_2 \cdot x_3^3 - 4 \cdot x_2 \cdot x_3^2 \right) \cdot n & & + \left(x_1 + x_2^2 \right). \end{aligned}$$

Let $\vec{q}_{norm}$ be like $\vec{q}$, but each factor $[\![\psi]\!]$ is replaced by 0 if it contains an equation and by 1, otherwise. The reason is that for large enough n, equations in ψ become false and negated equations become true. Thus, (6) is equivalent to

$$\exists \vec{x} \in F, \ n_0 \in \mathbb{N}. \ \forall n \in \mathbb{N}_{>n_0}. \ \varphi(\vec{q}_{norm}). \tag{8}$$

In this way, we obtain *normalized* poly-exponential expressions.

Definition 30 (Normalized PEs). *We call* $p \in \mathrm{PE}[\vec{x}]$ normalized *if it is in*

$$\mathrm{NPE}[\vec{x}] = \left\{ \sum_{j=1}^{\ell} \alpha_j \cdot n^{a_j} \cdot b_j^n \ \middle| \ \ell, a_j \in \mathbb{N}, \ \alpha_j \in \mathbb{R}_\mathbb{A}[\vec{x}], \ b_j \in (\mathbb{R}_\mathbb{A})_{>0} \right\}.$$

W.l.o.g., we always assume $(b_i, a_i) \neq (b_j, a_j)$ *if* $i \neq j$. *We define* $\mathrm{NPE} = \mathrm{NPE}[\varnothing]$.

As φ is a propositional formula over $\mathbb{R}_\mathbb{A}[\vec{x}]$-inequations, $\varphi(\vec{q}_{norm})$ is a propositional formula over $\mathrm{NPE}[\vec{x}]$-inequations. By (8), we need to check if there is an $\vec{x} \in F$ such that $\varphi(\vec{q}_{norm})$ is valid for large enough n. To do so, we generalize [15, Lemma 24]. As usual, $g : \mathbb{N} \to \mathbb{R}$ dominates $f : \mathbb{N} \to \mathbb{R}$ asymptotically ($f \in o(g)$) if for all $m > 0$ there is an $n_0 \in \mathbb{N}$ such that $|f(n)| < m \cdot |g(n)|$ for all $n \in \mathbb{N}_{>n_0}$.

Lemma 31. *Let* $b_1, b_2 \in (\mathbb{R}_\mathbb{A})_{>0}$ *and* $a_1, a_2 \in \mathbb{N}$. *If* $(b_2, a_2) >_{lex} (b_1, a_1)$, *then* $n^{a_1} \cdot b_1^n \in o(n^{a_2} \cdot b_2^n)$, *where* $(b_2, a_2) >_{lex} (b_1, a_1)$ *iff* $b_2 > b_1$ *or* $b_2 = b_1 \wedge a_2 > a_1$.

In the following, let $p \geq 0$ or $p > 0$ occur in $\varphi(\vec{q}_{norm})$. Then we can order the coefficients of p according to the asymptotic growth of their addends w.r.t. n.

Definition 32 (Ordering Coefficients). Marked coefficients *are of the form* $\alpha^{(b,a)}$ *where* $\alpha \in \mathbb{R}_\mathbb{A}[\vec{x}], b \in (\mathbb{R}_\mathbb{A})_{>0}$, *and* $a \in \mathbb{N}$. *We define* unmark $(\alpha^{(b,a)}) = \alpha$ *and* $\alpha_2^{(b_2,a_2)} \succ_{coef} \alpha_1^{(b_1,a_1)}$ *if* $(b_2, a_2) >_{lex} (b_1, a_1)$. *Let* $p = \sum_{j=1}^{\ell} \alpha_j \cdot n^{a_j} \cdot b_j^n \in \mathrm{NPE}[\vec{x}]$, *where* $\alpha_j \neq 0$ *for all* $1 \leq j \leq \ell$. *Then the marked coefficients of* p *are*

$$\mathrm{coefs}(p) = \{0^{(1,0)}\} \ \textit{if} \ \ell = 0 \ \textit{and} \ \mathrm{coefs}(p) = \{\alpha_j^{(b_j,a_j)} \mid 0 \leq j \leq \ell\}, \ \textit{otherwise}.$$

Example 33. Continuing Example 29, $\mathrm{coefs}(p)$ is $\{\alpha_1^{(1,3)}, \alpha_2^{(1,2)}, \alpha_3^{(1,1)}, \alpha_4^{(1,0)}\}$ where:

$$\alpha_1 = \tfrac{4}{3} \cdot x_3^5 \qquad\qquad\qquad \alpha_2 = -2 \cdot x_3^5 - 2 \cdot x_2 \cdot x_3^3 + 4 \cdot x_3^4$$
$$\alpha_3 = x_2^2 \cdot x_3 + \tfrac{2}{3} \cdot x_3^5 + 2 \cdot x_2 \cdot x_3^3 - 4 \cdot x_2 \cdot x_3^2 \qquad \alpha_4 = x_2^2 + x_1$$

Note that $p(\vec{c}) \in \mathrm{NPE}$ for any $\vec{c} \in \mathbb{R}_\mathbb{A}^d$, i.e., the only variable in $p(\vec{c})$ is n. Now the $\succ_{coef}$-maximal addend determines the asymptotic growth of $p(\vec{c})$:

$$o(p(\vec{c})) = o(k \cdot n^a \cdot b^n) \qquad \text{where } k^{(b,a)} = \max_{\succ_{coef}} (\mathrm{coefs}(p(\vec{c}))). \qquad (9)$$

Note that (9) would be incorrect for the case $k = 0$ if we replaced $o(p(\vec{c})) = o(k \cdot n^a \cdot b^n)$ with $o(p(\vec{c})) = o(n^a \cdot b^n)$ as $o(0) = \varnothing \neq o(1)$. Obviously, (9) implies

$$\exists n_0 \in \mathbb{N}. \ \forall n \in \mathbb{N}_{>n_0}. \ \mathrm{sign}(p(\vec{c})) = \mathrm{sign}(k) \qquad (10)$$

where $\mathrm{sign}(0) = 0$, $\mathrm{sign}(k) = 1$ if $k > 0$, and $\mathrm{sign}(k) = -1$ if $k < 0$. This already allows us to reduce eventual non-termination to $\mathrm{Th}_\exists(\mathcal{S}, \mathbb{R}_\mathbb{A})$ if φ is an atom.

Lemma 34. *Given* $p \in \mathrm{NPE}[\vec{x}]$ *and* $\triangleright \in \{\geq, >\}$, *one can reduce validity of*

$$\exists \vec{x} \in F, \ n_0 \in \mathbb{N}. \ \forall n \in \mathbb{N}_{>n_0}. \ p \triangleright 0 \qquad (11)$$

to validity of a closed formula from $\mathrm{Th}_\exists(\mathcal{S}, \mathbb{R}_\mathbb{A})$ *in polynomial time.*[7]

---

[7] More precisely, the reduction of Lemma 34 and of the following Theorem 36 takes polynomially many steps in the size of the input of the function in (5).

More precisely, (11) can be reduced to a formula $\exists \vec{x} \in \mathbb{R}_{\mathbb{A}}^d.\ \psi_F \wedge \mathrm{red}(p \triangleright 0)$, where $\mathrm{red}(p \triangleright 0)$ is constructed as follows. By (10), we have $p(\vec{c}) > 0$ for large enough values of n iff the coefficient of the asymptotically fastest-growing addend $\alpha(\vec{c}) \cdot n^a \cdot b^n$ of p that does not vanish (i.e., where $\alpha(\vec{c}) \neq 0$) is *positive*. Similarly, we have $p(\vec{c}) < 0$ for large enough n iff $\alpha(\vec{c}) < 0$. If *all* addends of p vanish when instantiating $\vec{x}$ with $\vec{c}$, then $p(\vec{c}) = 0$. In other words, (11) holds iff there is a $\vec{c} \in F$ such that $\mathrm{unmark}\left(\max_{\succ_{coef}}(\mathrm{coefs}(p(\vec{c})))\right) \triangleright 0$. To express this in $\mathrm{Th}_{\exists}(\mathcal{S}, \mathbb{R}_{\mathbb{A}})$, let $\alpha_1, \ldots, \alpha_\ell$ be the coefficients of p, ordered according to the asymptotic growth of the respective addends where α_1 belongs to the fastest-growing addend. Then

$$\mathrm{red}(p > 0) \quad \text{is} \quad \bigvee_{j=1}^{\ell}\left(\alpha_j > 0 \wedge \bigwedge_{i=1}^{j-1} \alpha_i = 0\right)$$

and $\quad \mathrm{red}(p \geq 0) \quad$ is $\quad \mathrm{red}(p > 0) \vee \bigwedge_{i=1}^{\ell} \alpha_i = 0.$

Hence, (11) is equivalent to $\exists \vec{x} \in \mathbb{R}_{\mathbb{A}}^d.\ \psi_F \wedge \mathrm{red}(p \triangleright 0)$.

Example 35 (Reducing Eventual Non-Termination to $\mathrm{Th}_{\exists}(\mathcal{S}, \mathbb{R}_{\mathbb{A}})$*).* We finish Example 33 resp. Example 24 for $\mathcal{S} = \mathbb{Z}$, where $\mathrm{unmark}\left(\max_{\succ_{coef}}(\mathrm{coefs}(p))\right) = \frac{4}{3} \cdot x_3^5$ and ψ_F is

$$\exists a, b, c \in \mathbb{Z}.\ x_1 = a + b + c \wedge x_2 = b \cdot 2 \wedge x_3 = a + b \cdot 2 + c \cdot 2.$$

Thus, (7) is valid iff $\exists x_1, x_2, x_3 \in \mathbb{R}_{\mathbb{A}}.\ \psi_F \wedge \mathrm{red}(p > 0)$ is valid where

$$\mathrm{red}(p > 0) = \quad \alpha_1 > 0 \qquad\qquad \vee\ (\alpha_2 > 0 \wedge \alpha_1 = 0)$$
$$\vee\ (\alpha_3 > 0 \wedge \alpha_1 = \alpha_2 = 0) \vee (\alpha_4 > 0 \wedge \alpha_1 = \alpha_2 = \alpha_3 = 0).$$

Then $[x_1/1, x_2/0, x_3/1]$ satisfies $\psi_F \wedge \alpha_1 > 0$ as $(1, 0, 1) \in F$ (see Example 29) and $\left(\frac{4}{3} \cdot x_3^5\right)[x_1/1, x_2/0, x_3/1] > 0$. Thus, $(1, 0, 1)$ witnesses eventual non-termination of (4). So the original loop (3) is non-terminating on $\mathbb{Z}^3$ by Corollary 17 resp. Theorem 10.

Now we lift our reduction to propositional formulas. Note that a version of the following Theorem 36 that only covers conjunctions is a direct corollary of Lemma 34. To handle disjunctions, the proof of Theorem 36 exploits the crucial additional insight that a *tnn*-loop $(\varphi \vee \varphi', \vec{a})$ terminates iff $(\varphi, \vec{a})$ and $(\varphi', \vec{a})$ terminate, which is not true in general (as, e.g., witnessed by the loop $(x > 0 \vee -x > 0, -x)$).

Theorem 36. *Given a propositional formula ξ over the atoms $\{p \triangleright 0 \mid p \in \mathrm{NPE}[\vec{x}], \triangleright \in \{\geq, >\}\}$, one can reduce validity of*

$$\exists \vec{x} \in F, n_0 \in \mathbb{N}.\ \forall n \in \mathbb{N}_{>n_0}.\ \xi \tag{12}$$

to validity of a formula $\exists \vec{x} \in \mathbb{R}_{\mathbb{A}}^d.\ \psi_F \wedge \mathrm{red}(\xi) \in \mathrm{Th}_{\exists}(\mathcal{S}, \mathbb{R}_{\mathbb{A}})$ in polynomial time.

Here, $\mathrm{red}(\xi)$ results from replacing each atom $p \triangleright 0$ in ξ by $\mathrm{red}(p \triangleright 0)$.

Theorem 36 shows that the function (5) is computable (in polynomial time). This leads to the main result of this section.

Theorem 37 (Reducing Termination). Termination of *tnn*-loops (resp. *twn*-loops) on $\vec{a}$-invariant and $\mathrm{Th}_\exists(\mathcal{S}, \mathbb{R}_\mathbb{A})$-definable sets is reducible to $\mathrm{Th}_\exists(\mathcal{S}, \mathbb{R}_\mathbb{A})$.

However, in general this reduction is not computable in polynomial time. The reason is that closed forms $\vec{q}$ of $\vec{a}^n$ cannot be computed in polynomial time if the update $\vec{a}$ contains *non-linear* terms. For example, consider the following *tnn*-loop:

$$\textbf{while } \text{ true } \textbf{ do } \vec{x} \leftarrow (d \cdot x_1, x_1^d, \ldots, x_{d-2}^d, x_{d-1}^d) \tag{13}$$

The closed form for $x_i^{(n)}$ is $q_i = d^{\left(d^{i-1} \cdot (n-i+1)\right)} \cdot x_1^{\left(d^{i-1}\right)}$ for all $n \geq d$. Note that $\log d^{\left(d^{d-1}\right)}$ grows faster in d than any expression of the form c^d, where $c \in \mathbb{N}$. Thus, the closed form $q_d \in \mathbb{PE}[\vec{x}]$ for $x_d^{(n)}$ contains constants whose logarithm grows faster than any expression c^d. Hence, q_d cannot be computed in polynomial time. As mentioned at the beginning of this section, the bodies of *tnn*-loops could also be linearized [39]. However, since the linearization of (13) contains these constants as well, it cannot be computed in polynomial time, either.

Note that our reduction also works if $\mathcal{S} = \mathbb{R}$, i.e., termination over $\mathbb{R}$ is reducible to $\mathrm{Th}_\exists(\mathbb{R}, \mathbb{R}_\mathbb{A})$. As $\mathbb{R}$ and $\mathbb{R}_\mathbb{A}$ are *elementary equivalent*, i.e., a first-order formula is valid over $\mathbb{R}$ iff it is valid over $\mathbb{R}_\mathbb{A}$, we get the following corollary.

Corollary 38 ((Semi-)Decidability of (Non-)Termination). *Let $(\varphi, \vec{a})$ be a twn-loop and let $F \subseteq \mathbb{R}_\mathbb{A}^d$ be $\vec{a}$-invariant and $\mathrm{Th}_\exists(\mathcal{S}, \mathbb{R}_\mathbb{A})$-definable.*

(a) The loop $(\varphi, \vec{a})$ terminates over $\mathbb{R}_\mathbb{A}$ iff it terminates over $\mathbb{R}$.
(b) Termination of $(\varphi, \vec{a})$ on F is decidable if $\mathcal{S} = \mathbb{R}_\mathbb{A}$ or $\mathcal{S} = \mathbb{R}$.
(c) Non-termination of $(\varphi, \vec{a})$ on F is semi-decidable if $\mathcal{S} = \mathbb{Z}$ or $\mathcal{S} = \mathbb{Q}$.

Moreover, by Theorem 20 it is semi-decidable if a loop is *twn-transformable*. For *conjunctive twn*-loops, Corollary 38 (b) also follows from combining [39] and [55].

Our technique does not yield witnesses for non-termination, but the formula constructed by Theorem 36 describes *all* witnesses for *eventual* non-termination. So, the set of witnesses of *eventual* non-termination is $\mathrm{Th}_\exists(\mathcal{S}, \mathbb{R}_\mathbb{A})$-definable whereas in general, the set of witnesses of non-termination is not (see [12]).

Lemma 39. *Let $\xi = \varphi(\vec{q}_{norm})$. Then $\vec{c} \in \mathbb{R}_\mathbb{A}^d$ witnesses eventual non-termination of $(\varphi, \vec{a})$ on F iff $\psi_F(\vec{c}) \wedge (\mathrm{red}(\xi))(\vec{c})$.*

However, in [23] we showed how to compute witnesses for non-termination from witnesses for eventual non-termination of *twn*-loops. Thus, Lemma 39 combined with our results from [23] yields a technique to enumerate all witnesses for non-termination.

If $(\varphi, \vec{a})$ results from the original loop by first transforming it into *twn*-form (Sect. 3) and by subsequently chaining it in order to obtain a loop in *tnn*-form

(Sect. 4), then our approach can also be used to obtain witnesses for eventual non-termination of the original loop. In other words, one can compute a witness for the original loop from the witness for the transformed loop as in Corollary 17, since chaining clearly preserves witnesses for eventual non-termination. Algorithm 1 summarizes our technique to check termination of *twn*-transformable-loops.

Algorithm 1: Checking Termination

Input: a *twn*-transformable-loop $(\varphi, \vec{a})$ and $\psi_F \in \text{Th}_\exists(\mathcal{S}, \mathbb{R}_A)$
Result: $\top$ resp. $\bot$ if (non-)termination of $(\varphi, \vec{a})$ on F is proven, ? otherwise
$(\varphi, \vec{a}) \leftarrow Tr_\eta(\varphi, \vec{a})$, $\psi_F \leftarrow \psi_{\hat\eta(F)}$, such that $(\varphi, \vec{a})$ becomes *twn*
$(\varphi, \vec{a}) \leftarrow (\varphi \wedge \varphi(\vec{a}), \vec{a}(\vec{a}))$, such that $(\varphi, \vec{a})$ becomes *tnn*
$\vec{q} \leftarrow$ closed form of $\vec{a}^n$
if (un)satisfiability of $\psi_F \wedge \text{red}(\varphi(\vec{q}_{norm}))$ cannot be proven **then return** ?
if $\psi_F \wedge \text{red}(\varphi(\vec{q}_{norm}))$ is satisfiable **then return** $\bot$ **else return** $\top$

---

6   Complexity Analysis

We now analyze the complexity of our technique. We first regard *linear-update* loops, i.e., where the update is of the form $\vec{x} \leftarrow A \cdot \vec{x} + \vec{b}$ with $A \in \mathcal{S}^{d \times d}$ and $\vec{b} \in \mathcal{S}^d$. More precisely, we show that termination of linear loops with real spectrum is Co-NP-complete if $\mathcal{S} \in \{\mathbb{Z}, \mathbb{Q}, \mathbb{R}_A\}$ and that termination of linear-update loops with real spectrum is $\forall \mathbb{R}$-complete if $\mathcal{S} = \mathbb{R}_A$. Since our proof is based on a reduction to $\text{Th}_\exists(\mathcal{S}, \mathbb{R}_A)$, and $\mathbb{R}_A$ and $\mathbb{R}$ are elementary equivalent, our results also hold if the program variables range over $\mathbb{R}$.

For our complexity results, we assume the usual dense encoding of univariate polynomials, i.e., a polynomial of degree k is represented as a list of $k + 1$ coefficients. As discussed in [47], many problems which are considered to be efficiently solvable become intractable if polynomials are encoded sparsely (e.g., as lists of monomials where each monomial is a pair of its non-zero coefficient and its degree). With densely encoded polynomials, all common representations of algebraic numbers can be converted into each other in polynomial time [3].

When analyzing linear-update loops, w.l.o.g. we can assume $\vec{b} = \vec{0}$, since

$$\textbf{while } \varphi \textbf{ do } \vec{x} \leftarrow A \cdot \vec{x} + \vec{b} \qquad \text{terminates iff} \qquad (14)$$

$$\textbf{while } \varphi \wedge x_{\vec{b}} = 1 \textbf{ do } \begin{bmatrix} \vec{x} \\ x_{\vec{b}} \end{bmatrix} \leftarrow \begin{bmatrix} A & \vec{b} \\ \vec{0}^T & 1 \end{bmatrix} \cdot \begin{bmatrix} \vec{x} \\ x_{\vec{b}} \end{bmatrix} \qquad (15)$$

terminates, where $x_{\vec{b}}$ is a fresh variable (see [24,41]). Moreover, $\vec{c}$ witnesses (eventual) non-termination for (14) iff $\begin{bmatrix} \vec{c} \\ 1 \end{bmatrix}$ witnesses (eventual) non-termination for (15). Note that the only eigenvalue of $\begin{bmatrix} A & \vec{b} \\ \vec{0}^T & 1 \end{bmatrix}$ whose multiplicity increases in comparison to A is 1. Thus, to decide termination of linear-update loops with real spectrum, it suffices to decide termination of loops of the form $(\varphi, A \cdot \vec{x})$ where A has only real eigenvalues.

Such loops can *always* be transformed into *twn*-form using our transformation *Tr* from Sect. 3. To compute the required automorphism η, we compute the Jordan normal form Q of A together with the corresponding transformation matrix T, i.e., T is an invertible real matrix such that $A = T^{-1} \cdot Q \cdot T$. Then Q is a triangular real matrix whose diagonal consists of the eigenvalues $\lambda \in \mathbb{R}_A$ of A. Now we define $\eta \in \mathrm{End}_{\mathbb{R}_A}(\mathbb{R}_A[\vec{x}])$ by $\eta(\vec{x}) = T \cdot \vec{x}$. Then $\eta \in \mathrm{Aut}_{\mathbb{R}_A}(\mathbb{R}_A[\vec{x}])$ has the inverse $\eta^{-1}(\vec{x}) = T^{-1} \cdot \vec{x}$. Thus, $Tr_\eta(\varphi, A \cdot \vec{x})$ is a *twn*-loop with the update

$$(\eta(\vec{x})) \, (A \cdot \vec{x}) \, (\eta^{-1}(\vec{x})) = T \cdot A \cdot T^{-1} \cdot \vec{x} = Q \cdot \vec{x}.$$

The Jordan normal form Q as well as the matrices T and T^{-1} can be computed in polynomial time [19,46]. Hence, we can decide whether all eigenvalues are real numbers in polynomial time by checking the diagonal entries of Q. Thus, we obtain the following lemma.

Lemma 40. *Let $(\varphi, A \cdot \vec{x})$ be a linear-update loop.*

(a) It is decidable in polynomial time whether A has only real eigenvalues.
(b) If A has only real eigenvalues, then we can compute a linear $\eta \in \mathrm{Aut}_{\mathbb{R}_A}(\mathbb{R}_A[\vec{x}])$ such that $Tr_\eta(\varphi, A \cdot \vec{x})$ is a linear-update twn-loop in polynomial time.
(c) If $(\varphi, A \cdot \vec{x})$ is a linear loop, then so is $Tr_\eta(\varphi, A \cdot \vec{x})$.

Hence, the transformation from Sect. 3 is complete for linear(-update) loops with real spectrum, i.e., every such loop can be transformed into a linear(-update) *twn*-loop. Note that the first part of Lemma 40 yields an efficient check whether a given linear(-update) loop has real spectrum.

As chaining (Definition 25) can clearly be done in polynomial time, w.l.o.g. we may assume that $Tr_\eta(\varphi, A \cdot \vec{x}) = (\varphi', Q \cdot \vec{x})$ is *tnn*. Next, to analyze termination of a loop, our technique of Sect. 4 computes a closed form for the n-fold application of the update. For *tnn*-loops of the form $(\varphi', Q \cdot \vec{x})$ where Q is a triangular matrix with non-negative diagonal entries, a suitable (i.e., poly-exponential) closed form can be computed in polynomial time analogously to [28, Prop. 5.2]. This closed form is linear in $\vec{x}$.

According to our approach in Sect. 5, we now proceed as in Algorithm 1 and compute $\mathrm{red}(\varphi(\vec{q}_{norm})) \in \mathrm{Th}_\exists(\mathcal{S}, \mathbb{R}_A)$. The construction of this formula can be done in polynomial time due to Theorem 36. Hence, we get the following lemma.

Lemma 41. *Let $(\varphi, A \cdot \vec{x})$ be a linear-update loop with real spectrum. Then we can compute a formula $\psi \in \mathrm{Th}_\exists(\mathcal{S}, \mathbb{R}_A)$ in polynomial time, such that ψ is valid iff the loop is non-terminating. If φ is linear, then so is ψ.*

Note that ψ is existentially quantified. Hence, if φ (and thus, also ψ) is linear and $\mathcal{S} \in \{\mathbb{Z}, \mathbb{Q}, \mathbb{R}_A, \mathbb{R}\}$, then invalidity of ψ is in Co-NP as validity of such formulas is in NP [42]. Thus, we obtain the first main result of this section.

Theorem 42 (Co-NP-Completeness). *Termination of linear loops* $(\varphi, A \cdot \vec{x} + \vec{b})$ *with real spectrum over* $\mathbb{Z}$, $\mathbb{Q}$, $\mathbb{R}_\mathbb{A}$, *and* $\mathbb{R}$ *is* Co-NP-*complete.*

For Co-NP-hardness, let ξ be a propositional formula over the variables $\vec{x}$. Then $(\xi[x_i/(x_i > 0) \mid 1 \leq i \leq d], \vec{x})$ terminates iff ξ is unsatisfiable. So Co-NP-hardness follows from Co-NP-hardness of unsatisfiability of propositional formulas.

We now consider linear-update loops with real spectrum (and possibly non-linear loop conditions) on $\mathbb{R}_\mathbb{A}^d$ and $\mathbb{R}^d$. Here, non-termination is $\exists\mathbb{R}$-complete.

Definition 43 ($\exists\mathbb{R}$ [50,51]). Let $\text{Th}_\exists(\mathbb{R})_\top = \{\psi \in \text{Th}_\exists(\mathbb{R}) \mid \psi \text{ is satisfiable}\}$. The complexity class $\exists\mathbb{R}$ is the closure of $\text{Th}_\exists(\mathbb{R})_\top$ under poly-time-reductions.

We have $\mathsf{NP} \subseteq \exists\mathbb{R} \subseteq \mathsf{PSPACE}$. By Lemma 41, non-termination of linear-update loops with real spectrum is in $\exists\mathbb{R}$. It is also $\exists\mathbb{R}$-hard since $(\varphi, \vec{x})$ is non-terminating iff φ is satisfiable. So non-termination is $\exists\mathbb{R}$-complete, i.e., termination is Co-$\exists\mathbb{R}$-complete (where Co-$\exists\mathbb{R} = \forall\mathbb{R}$ [51]).

Theorem 44 ($\forall\mathbb{R}$-Completeness). *Termination of linear-update loops with real spectrum over* $\mathbb{R}_\mathbb{A}$ *and* $\mathbb{R}$ *is* $\forall\mathbb{R}$-*complete.*

Recall that the bodies of *tnn*-loops can be linearized [39]. The loop (13) showed that in general, this linearization is not computable in polynomial time. However, if the number of variables d is bounded by a constant D, then the linearization is in EXPTIME (see the proof of Theorem 45 in [16]). If the number of variables is bounded, then checking validity of an existential formula over the reals is in P (see [2]). So in this case, combining the fact that linearization is in EXPTIME with Lemma 41 yields Theorem 45.

Theorem 45. *Let* $D \in \mathbb{N}$ *be fixed. Termination of twn-loops over* $\mathbb{R}_\mathbb{A}$ *and* $\mathbb{R}$ *is in* EXPTIME *if the number of variables is at most* D.

7   Related Work and Conclusion

We presented a reduction from termination of *twn*-loops to $\text{Th}_\exists(\mathcal{S}, \mathbb{R}_\mathbb{A})$. This implies decidability of termination over $\mathcal{S} = \mathbb{R}_\mathbb{A}$ and $\mathcal{S} = \mathbb{R}$ and semi-decidability of non-termination over $\mathcal{S} = \mathbb{Z}$ and $\mathcal{S} = \mathbb{Q}$. Moreover, we showed how to transform certain non-*twn*-loops into *twn*-form, which generalizes our results to a wider class of loops, including *solvable loops with real eigenvalues*. We also showed that *twn*-transformability is semi-decidable. Finally, we used our results to prove Co-NP-completeness (resp. $\forall\mathbb{R}$-completeness) of termination of linear (resp. linear-update) loops with real spectrum.

Related Work: In contrast to *automated* termination analysis (e.g., [1,4,5,7, 9,10,17,20–22,30–33,43]), we investigate *decidability* of termination for certain classes of loops. Clearly, such decidability results can only be obtained for quite restricted classes of programs.

Nevertheless, many techniques used in automated tools for termination analysis (e.g., the application of ranking functions) focus on similar classes of loops, since such loops occur as sub-programs in (abstractions of) real programs. Tools based on these techniques have turned out to be very successful, also for larger classes of programs. Thus, these tools could benefit from integrating our (semi-)decision procedures and applying them instead of incomplete techniques for any sub-program that can be transformed into a *twn*-loop.

Related work on decidability of termination also considers related (and often more restricted) classes of loops. For linear conjunctive loops (where the loop condition is a conjunction), termination over $\mathbb{R}$ [34,37,53], $\mathbb{Q}$ [8], and $\mathbb{Z}$ [24] is decidable. Tiwari [53] uses the special case of our *twn*-transformation from Sect. 6 where the loop and the automorphism are linear. In contrast to these techniques, our approach applies to *non-linear* loops with *arbitrary* loop conditions over *various rings*.

Linearization is an alternative attempt to handle non-linearity. While the *update* of solvable loops can be linearized [39,49], the *guard* cannot. Otherwise, one could linearize any loop $(p = 0, \vec{x})$, which terminates over $\mathbb{Z}$ iff p has no integer root. With [24], this would imply decidability of Hilbert's Tenth Problem.

Regarding complexity, [41] proves that termination of conjunctive linear loops over $\mathbb{Z}$ with update $\vec{x} \leftarrow A \cdot \vec{x} + \vec{b}$ is in EXPSPACE if A is diagonalizable resp. in PSPACE if $|\vec{x}| \leq 4$. Moreover, [41] states that the techniques from [8,53] run in polynomial time. So termination of conjunctive linear loops over $\mathbb{Q}$ and $\mathbb{R}$ is in P.

Our Co-NP-completeness result is orthogonal to those results as we allow disjunctions in the loop condition. Moreover, Co-NP-completeness also holds for termination over $\mathbb{Z}$, whereas [8,53] only consider termination over $\mathbb{Q}$ resp. $\mathbb{R}$.

In the non-linear case, [35] proves decidability of termination for conjunctive loops on $\mathbb{R}^d$ for the case that the loop condition defines a compact and connected subset of $\mathbb{R}^d$. In [55], decidability of termination of conjunctive linear-update loops on $\mathbb{R}^d$ with the *non-zero minimum property* is shown, which covers conjunctive linear-update loops with real spectrum. In combination with [39], this yields a decision procedure for termination of conjunctive *twn*-loops over $\mathbb{R}$. For general conjunctive linear-update loops on $\mathbb{R}^d$ undecidability is conjectured. Furthermore, [38] proves that termination of (not necessarily conjunctive) linear-update loops is decidable if the loop condition describes a compact set. Finally, [56] gives sufficient criteria for (non-)termination of solvable loops and [36] introduces sufficient conditions under which termination of non-deterministic non-linear loops on $\mathbb{R}^d$ can be reduced to satisfiability of a semi-algebraic system.

For linear-update loops with real spectrum over $\mathbb{R}$, we prove $\forall\mathbb{R}$-completeness of termination, whereas [55] does not give tight complexity results. The approach from [56] is incomplete, whereas we present a complete reduction from termination to the respective first-order theory. The work in [36] is orthogonal to ours as it only applies to loops that satisfy certain non-trivial conditions. Moreover, we consider loops with arbitrary loop conditions over various rings, whereas [35,36,55] only consider conjunctive loops over $\mathbb{R}$ and [38] only considers loops over $\mathbb{R}$ where the loop condition defines a compact set.

Finally, several other works exploit the existence of closed forms for solvable (or similar classes of) loops to, e.g., analyze termination for *fixed* inputs or deduce invariants (e.g., [23,25,27–29,39,40,48,49]). While our approach covers solvable loops with real eigenvalues (by Corollary 21), it also applies to loops which are not solvable, see Example 24. Note that our transformation from Sect. 3 may also be of interest for other techniques for solvable or other sub-classes of polynomial loops, as it may be used to extend the applicability of such approaches.

Acknowledgments. We thank Alberto Fiori for help with the example loop (13) and Arno van den Essen for useful discussions.

References

1. Babić, D., Cook, B., Hu, A.J., Rakamaric, Z.: Proving termination of nonlinear command sequences. Formal Aspects Comput. **25**(3), 389–403 (2013). https://doi.org/10.1007/s00165-012-0252-5
2. Basu, S., Pollack, R., Roy, M.-F.: Algorithms in Real Algebraic Geometry, Algorithms and Computation in Mathematics, vol. 10. Springer, Heidelberg (2006). https://doi.org/10.1007/3-540-33099-2
3. Basu, S., Mishra, B.: Computational and quantitative real algebraic geometry. In: Goodman, J.E., O'Rourke, J., Tóth, C.D. (eds.) Handbook of Discrete and Computational Geometry, 3rd edn. Chapman and Hall/CRC, pp. 969–1002 (2017). https://doi.org/10.1201/9781315119601
4. Ben-Amram, A.M., Genaim, S.: On multiphase-linear ranking functions. In: Majumdar, R., Kunčak, V. (eds.) CAV 2017. LNCS, vol. 10427, pp. 601–620. Springer, Cham (2017). https://doi.org/10.1007/978-3-319-63390-9_32
5. Ben-Amram, A.M., Doménech, J.J., Genaim, S.: Multiphase-linear ranking functions and their relation to recurrent sets. In: Chang, B.-Y.E. (ed.) SAS 2019. LNCS, vol. 11822, pp. 459–480. Springer, Cham (2019). https://doi.org/10.1007/978-3-030-32304-2_22
6. Bozga, M., Iosif, R., Konecný, F.: Deciding conditional termination. Logical Meth. Comput. Sci. **10**(3) (2014). https://doi.org/10.2168/LMCS-10(3:8)2014
7. Bradley, A.R., Manna, Z., Sipma, H.B.: Termination of polynomial programs. In: Cousot, R. (ed.) VMCAI 2005. LNCS, vol. 3385, pp. 113–129. Springer, Heidelberg (2005). https://doi.org/10.1007/978-3-540-30579-8_8
8. Braverman, M.: Termination of integer linear programs. In: Ball, T., Jones, R.B. (eds.) CAV 2006. LNCS, vol. 4144, pp. 372–385. Springer, Heidelberg (2006). https://doi.org/10.1007/11817963_34
9. Brockschmidt, M., Cook, B., Fuhs, C.: Better termination proving through cooperation. In: Sharygina, N., Veith, H. (eds.) CAV 2013. LNCS, vol. 8044, pp. 413–429. Springer, Heidelberg (2013). https://doi.org/10.1007/978-3-642-39799-8_28

10. Chen, H.-Y., Cook, B., Fuhs, C., Nimkar, K., O'Hearn, P.: Proving nontermination via safety. In: Ábrahám, E., Havelund, K. (eds.) TACAS 2014. LNCS, vol. 8413, pp. 156–171. Springer, Heidelberg (2014). https://doi.org/10.1007/978-3-642-54862-8_11

11. Cohen, P.J.: Decision procedures for real and p-adic fields. Commun. Pure Appl. Math. **22**(2), 131–151 (1969). https://doi.org/10.1002/cpa.3160220202

12. Dai, L., Xia, B.: Non-termination sets of simple linear loops. In: Roychoudhury, A., D'Souza, M. (eds.) ICTAC 2012. LNCS, vol. 7521, pp. 61–73. Springer, Heidelberg (2012). https://doi.org/10.1007/978-3-642-32943-2_5

13. van den Essen, A., Hubbers, E.: Polynomial maps with strongly nilpotent Jacobian matrix and the Jacobian conjecture. Linear Algebra Appl. **247**, 121–132 (1996). https://doi.org/10.1016/0024-3795(95)00095-X

14. van den Essen, A.: Polynomial Automorphisms and the Jacobian Conjecture. Springer, Basel (2000). https://doi.org/10.1007/978-3-0348-8440-2

15. Frohn, F., Giesl, J.: Termination of triangular integer loops is decidable. In: Dillig, I., Tasiran, S. (eds.) CAV 2019. LNCS, vol. 11562, pp. 426–444. Springer, Cham (2019). https://doi.org/10.1007/978-3-030-25543-5_24

16. Frohn, F., Hark, M., Giesl, J.: On the decidability of termination for polynomial loops. CoRR abs/1910.11588 (2019). https://arxiv.org/abs/1910.11588

17. Frohn, F., Giesl, J.: Proving non-termination via loop acceleration. In: Barrett, C.W., Yang, J. (eds.) FMCAD 2019, pp. 221–230 (2019). https://doi.org/10.23919/FMCAD.2019

18. Frohn, F.: A calculus for modular loop acceleration. In: Biere, A., Parkerm D. (eds.) TACAS 2020. LNCS, vol. 12078, pp. 58–76. Springer, Cham (2020). https://doi.org/10.1007/978-3-030-45190-5_4

19. Giesbrecht, M.: Nearly optimal algorithms for canonical matrix forms. SIAM J. Comput. **24**(5), 948–969 (1995). https://doi.org/10.1137/S0097539793252687

20. Giesl, J.: Analyzing program termination and complexity automatically with AProVE. J. Autom. Reasoning **58**(1), 3–31 (2017). https://doi.org/10.1007/s10817-016-9388-y

21. Giesl, J., Rubio, A., Sternagel, C., Waldmann, J., Yamada, A.: The termination and complexity competition. In: Beyer, D., Huisman, M., Kordon, F., Steffen, B. (eds.) TACAS 2019. LNCS, vol. 11429, pp. 156–166. Springer, Cham (2019). https://doi.org/10.1007/978-3-030-17502-3_10

22. Gupta, A., Henzinger, T.A., Majumdar, R., Rybalchenko, A., Xu, R.: Proving non-termination. In: Necula, G.C., Wadler, P. (eds.) POPL 2008, pp. 147–158 (2008). https://doi.org/10.1145/1328438.1328459

23. Hark, M., Frohn, F., Giesl, J.: Polynomial loops: beyond termination. In: Albert, E., Kovács, L. (eds.) LPAR 2020. EPiC, vol. 73, pp. 279–297 (2020). https://doi.org/10.29007/nxv1

24. Hosseini, M., Ouaknine, J., Worrell, J.: Termination of linear loops over the integers. In: Baier, C., Chatzigiannakis, I., Flocchini, P., Leonardi, S. (eds.) ICALP 2019. LIPIcs, vol. 132, 118:1–118:13 (2019). https://doi.org/10.4230/LIPIcs.ICALP.2019.118

25. Humenberger, A., Jaroschek, M., Kovács, L.: Invariant generation for multi-path loops with polynomial assignments. In: Dillig, I., Palsberg, J. (eds.) VMCAI 2018. LNCS, vol. 10747, pp. 226–246. Springer, Cham (2018). https://doi.org/10.1007/978-3-319-73721-8_11

26. Kauers, M., Paule, P.: The Concrete Tetrahedron – Symbolic Sums, Recurrence Equations, Generating Functions, Asymptotic Estimates. Springer, Heidelberg (2011). https://doi.org/10.1007/978-3-7091-0445-3

27. Kincaid, Z., Cyphert, J., Breck, J., Reps, T.W.: Non-linear reasoning for invariant synthesis. Proc. ACM Program. Lang. **2**(POPL), 54:1–54:33 (2018). https://doi.org/10.1145/3158142
28. Kincaid, Z., Breck, J., Cyphert, J., Reps, T.W.: Closed forms for numerical loops. Proc. ACM Program. Lang. **3**(POPL), 55:1–55:29 (2019). https://doi.org/10.1145/3290368
29. Kovács, L.: Reasoning algebraically about p-solvable loops. In: Ramakrishnan, C.R., Rehof, J. (eds.) TACAS 2008. LNCS, vol. 4963, pp. 249–264. Springer, Heidelberg (2008). https://doi.org/10.1007/978-3-540-78800-3_18
30. Larraz, D., Oliveras, A., Rodríguez-Carbonell, E., Rubio, A.: Proving termination of imperative programs using Max-SMT. In: Jobstmann, B., Ray, S. (eds.) FMCAD 2013, pp. 218–225 (2013). https://doi.org/10.1109/FMCAD.2013.6679413
31. Larraz, D., Nimkar, K., Oliveras, A., Rodríguez-Carbonell, E., Rubio, A.: Proving non-termination Using Max-SMT. In: Biere, A., Bloem, R. (eds.) CAV 2014. LNCS, vol. 8559, pp. 779–796. Springer, Cham (2014). https://doi.org/10.1007/978-3-319-08867-9_52
32. Leike, J., Heizmann, M.: Ranking templates for linear loops. Logical Method Comput. Sci. **11**(1) (2015). https://doi.org/10.2168/LMCS-11(1:16)2015
33. Leike, J., Heizmann, M.: Geometric nontermination arguments. In: Beyer, D., Huisman, M. (eds.) TACAS 2018. LNCS, vol. 10806, pp. 266–283. Springer, Cham (2018). https://doi.org/10.1007/978-3-319-89963-3_16
34. Li, Y.: A recursive decision method for termination of linear programs. In: Zhi, L., Watt, S.M. (eds.) SNC 2014, pp. 97–106 (2014). https://doi.org/10.1145/2631948.2631966
35. Li, Y.: Termination of single-path polynomial loop programs. In: Sampaio, A., Wang, F. (eds.) ICTAC 2016. LNCS, vol. 9965, pp. 33–50. Springer, Cham (2016). https://doi.org/10.1007/978-3-319-46750-4_3
36. Li, Y.: Termination of semi-algebraic loop programs. In: Larsen, K.G., Sokolsky, O., Wang, J. (eds.) SETTA 2017. LNCS, vol. 10606, pp. 131–146. Springer, Cham (2017). https://doi.org/10.1007/978-3-319-69483-2_8
37. Li, Y.: Witness to non-termination of linear programs. Theoret. Comput. Sci. **681**, 75–100 (2017). https://doi.org/10.1016/j.tcs.2017.03
38. Neumann, E., Ouaknine, J., Worrell, J.: On ranking function synthesis and termination for polynomial programs. In: Konnov, I., Kovács, L. (eds.) CONCUR 2020. LIPIcs, vol. 171, pp. 15:1–15:15 (2020). https://doi.org/10.4230/LIPIcs.CONCUR.2020.15
39. de Oliveira, S., Bensalem, S., Prevosto, V.: Polynomial invariants by linear algebra. In: Artho, C., Legay, A., Peled, D. (eds.) ATVA 2016. LNCS, vol. 9938, pp. 479–494. Springer, Cham (2016). https://doi.org/10.1007/978-3-319-46520-3_30
40. de Oliveira, S., Bensalem, S., Prevosto, V.: Synthesizing invariants by solving solvable loops. In: D'Souza, D., Narayan Kumar, K. (eds.) ATVA 2017. LNCS, vol. 10482, pp. 327–343. Springer, Cham (2017). https://doi.org/10.1007/978-3-319-68167-2_22
41. Ouaknine, J., Pinto, J.S., Worrell, J.: On termination of integer linear loops. In: Indyk, P. (ed.) SODA 2015, pp. 957–969 (2015). https://doi.org/10.1137/19781611973730.65
42. Pia, A.D., Dey, S.S., Molinaro, M.: Mixed-integer quadratic programming is in NP. Math. Program. **162**(1–2), 225–240 (2017) https://doi.org/10.1007/s10107-016-1030-0

43. Podelski, A., Rybalchenko, A.: A complete method for the synthesis of linear ranking functions. In: Steffen, B., Levi, G. (eds.) VMCAI 2004. LNCS, vol. 2937, pp. 239–251. Springer, Heidelberg (2004). https://doi.org/10.1007/978-3-540-24622-0_20

44. Renegar, J.: On the computational complexity and geometry of the first-order theory of the reals, part I: Introduction. Preliminaries. The geometry of semi-algebraic sets. The decision problem for the existential theory of the reals. J. Symbolic Comput. **13**(3), 255–300 (1992). https://doi.org/10.1016/S0747-7171(10)80003-3

45. Robinson, J.: Definability and decision problems in arithmetic. J. Symbolic Logic **14**(2), 98–114 (1949). https://doi.org/10.2307/2266510

46. Roch, J.-L., Villard, G.: Fast parallel computation of the Jordan normal form of matrices. Parallel Process. Lett. **06**(02), 203–212 (1996). https://doi.org/10.1142/S0129626496000200

47. Roche, D.S.: What Can (and Can't) we Do with Sparse Polynomials?" In: Kauers, M., Indyk, Ovchinnikov, A., Schost, É (eds.) ISSAC 2018, pp. 25–30 (2018). https://doi.org/10.1145/3208976.3209027

48. Rodríguez-Carbonell, E., Kapur, D.: Automatic generation of polynomial loop invariants: algebraic foundation. In: Gutierrez, J. (ed.) ISSAC 2004, pp. 266–273 (2004). https://doi.org/10.1145/1005285.1005324

49. Rodríguez-Carbonell, E., Kapur, D.: Generating all polynomial invariants in simple loops. J. Symbolic Comput. **42**(4), 443–476 (2007). https://doi.org/10.1016/j.jsc.2007.01.002

50. Schaefer, M.: Complexity of some geometric and topological problems. In: Eppstein, D., Gansner, E.R. (eds.) GD 2009. LNCS, vol. 5849, pp. 334–344. Springer, Heidelberg (2010). https://doi.org/10.1007/978-3-642-11805-0_32

51. Schaefer, M., Štefankovič, D.: Fixed points, Nash equilibria, and the existential theory of the reals. Theory Comput. Syst. **60**(2), 172–193 (2017). https://doi.org/10.1007/s00224-015-9662-0

52. Tarski, A.: A decision method for elementary algebra and geometry. In: Caviness, B.F., Johnson, J.R. (eds.) Quantifier Elimination and Cylindrical Algebraic Decomposition. Originally appeared in 1951, University of California Press, Berkeley and Los Angeles, pp. 24–84. Springer, Vienna (1998). https://doi.org/10.1007/978-3-7091-9459-1_3

53. Tiwari, A.: Termination of linear programs. In: Alur, R., Peled, D.A. (eds.) CAV 2004. LNCS, vol. 3114, pp. 70–82. Springer, Heidelberg (2004). https://doi.org/10.1007/978-3-540-27813-9_6

54. TPDB (Termination Problems Data Base). http://termination-portal.org/wiki/TPDB

55. Xia, B., Zhang, Z.: Termination of linear programs with nonlinear constraints. J. Symbolic Comput. **45**(11), 1234–1249 (2010). https://doi.org/10.1016/j.jsc.2010.06.006

56. Xu, M., Li, Z.: Symbolic termination analysis of solvable loops. J. Symbolic Comput. **50**, 28–49 (2013). https://doi.org/10.1016/jjsc.2012.05.005

Stratified Guarded First-Order Transition Systems

Christan Müller and Helmut Seidl[(✉)]

TU München, Boltzmannstraße 3, Garching, Germany
seidl@in.tum.de

Abstract. First-order transition systems are a convenient formalism to specify parametric systems such as multi-agent workflows or distributed algorithms. In general, any nontrivial question about such systems is undecidable. Here, we present three subclasses of first-order transition systems where every universal invariant can effectively be decided via fixpoint iteration. These subclasses are defined in terms of syntactical restrictions: negation, stratification and guardedness. While guardedness represents a particular pattern how input predicates control existential quantifiers, stratification limits the information flow between predicates. Guardedness implies that the weakest precondition for every universal invariant is again universal, while the remaining sufficient criteria enforce that either the number of first-order variables, or the number of required instances of input predicates remains bounded, or the number of occurring negated literals decreases in every iteration. We argue for each of these three cases that termination of the fixpoint iteration can be guaranteed.

Keywords: First-order transition systems · Universal invariants · Second-order quantifier elimination · Stratification · Decidability

1 Introduction

FO transition systems (FO for First-order) are a convenient tool for specifying systems where the number of agents is not known in advance. This is very useful for modeling systems like network protocols [22] or web-based workflows like conference management, banking or commerce platforms. Consider, e.g., the specification from Fig. 1 modeling parts of the review process of a conference management system as a FO transition system.

Assume that initially, all predicates with the exception of auth are false, i.e., the property $\mathcal{H}$ given by

$$\forall x_1, x_2, p, r, d. \neg \mathsf{conf}(x_1, p) \wedge \neg \mathsf{assign}(x_1, p) \wedge \\ \neg \mathsf{report}(x_1, p, r) \wedge \neg \mathsf{discuss}(x_1, x_2, p, d) \tag{1}$$

holds. The predicates $A_1, \ldots, A_4$ are *input predicates* whose values either represent agents' decisions or actions from the environment. Intuitively, the transition

© The Author(s) 2020
D. Pichardie and M. Sighireanu (Eds.): SAS 2020, LNCS 12389, pp. 113–133, 2020.
https://doi.org/10.1007/978-3-030-65474-0_6

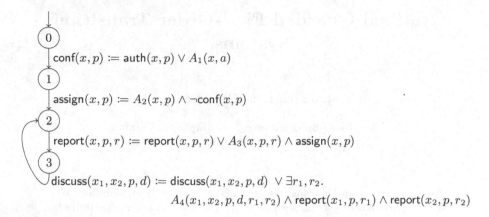

$$\text{conf}(x,p) := \text{auth}(x,p) \vee A_1(x,a)$$

$$\text{assign}(x,p) := A_2(x,p) \wedge \neg\text{conf}(x,p)$$

$$\text{report}(x,p,r) := \text{report}(x,p,r) \vee A_3(x,p,r) \wedge \text{assign}(x,p)$$

$$\text{discuss}(x_1,x_2,p,d) := \text{discuss}(x_1,x_2,p,d) \vee \exists r_1,r_2.$$
$$A_4(x_1,x_2,p,d,r_1,r_2) \wedge \text{report}(x_1,p,r_1) \wedge \text{report}(x_2,p,r_2)$$

Fig. 1. A conference management system.

system works as follows: First, each PC member x possibly declares her conflict with each paper p. Then, papers p are assigned to PC members x in such a way that the conf relation is respected. Repeatedly, reports for PC members x about papers p arrive, where a subsequent discussion between PC members x_1, x_2 on some paper p is only possible if both have received a report on that paper and may update their reviews based on the discussions. Variants of this example have already been studied in [19,25].

A useful property to ensure in this example is that a discussion between x_1 and x_2 on some paper p is only possible if neither x_1 nor x_2 are authors of p:

$$\forall x_1, x_2, p, d. \neg\text{discuss}(x_1,x_2,p,d) \vee \neg\text{auth}(x_1,p) \wedge \neg\text{auth}(x_2,p) \qquad (2)$$

As FO predicate logic is undecidable, we cannot hope to find an effective algorithm for proving an invariant such as (2) for arbitrary FO transition systems. That does not exclude, though, that at least some invariants can be proven *inductive* and thus, to be valid. Also, approximation techniques may be conceived to construct *strengthenings* of given invariants which, hopefully turn out to be inductive and thus may serve as certificates for the invariants in question.

The idea of using FO predicate logic for specifying the semantics of systems has perhaps been pioneered by abstract state machines (ASMs) [6,7,14]. Recently, it has successfully been applied for the specification and verification of software-defined networks [2,20], of network protocols [23], of distributed algorithms [22]. The corresponding approach is built into the tool IVY [18,23]. IVY is a proof assistant for systems specified in FO logic which is carefully designed around a decidable many-sorted extension of EPR (Effectively Propositional Logic, or $\exists^*\forall^*$FO logic). In the base setting, invariants are provided manually and then checked for inductiveness by the theorem prover Z3 [8]. Some effort, though, has been invested to come up with more automatic techniques for specific settings such as threshold algorithms [4] or more general FO invariant inference [15,16]. The fundamental problem thereby is that repeated application of the weakest precondition operator may introduce additional first-order variables, new instances of input predicates or existential quantifiers and thus result in formulas outside the decidable fragment of FO logic.

This problem also has been encountered in [10,11,19] where noninterference [13] is investigated for multi-agent workflows in the spirit of the conference management system from Fig. 1. In [19], the authors present a a symbolic verification approach where the agent capabilities as well as declassification and self-composition of the original system T is encoded into a FO transition system T^2. Noninterference of the original system is thus reduced to a universal invariant of the resulting system T^2. Further abstraction (i.e., strengthening of the encountered formulas) is applied in order to arrive at a practical algorithm which iteratively strengthens the initial invariant.

Only for rare cases, so far, decidability could be shown. In [21], Sagiv et al. show that inferring universal inductive invariants is decidable when the transition relation is expressed by formulas with unary predicates and a single binary predicate restricted by the background theory of singly-linked-lists. The same problem becomes undecidable when the binary symbol is not restricted by a background theory. In [19] on the other hand, syntactic restrictions are introduced under which termination at least of an *abstract* fixpoint iteration can be guaranteed. The abstraction thereby, consists in strengthening each occurring existential quantifier via appropriate instantiations (see also [9]). The syntactic restrictions proposed in [19] essentially amount to introducing a *stratification* on the predicates and restricting substitutions to be *stratified* and *guarded updates*. It is argued that these restrictions are not unrealistic in specifications of multi-agent systems where the computation proceeds in stages each of which accumulates information based on the results obtained in earlier stages. The example transition system from Fig. 1, e.g., is stratified: there is a mapping λ assigning a *level* $\lambda(R)$ to each predicate R so that the predicates occurring in right-hand sides which are distinct from the left-hand side have lower levels. In the example, λ could be given by

$$\{\mathsf{auth} \mapsto 0, \mathsf{conf} \mapsto 1, \mathsf{assign} \mapsto 2, \mathsf{report} \mapsto 3, \mathsf{discuss} \mapsto 4\}$$

Intuitively, stratification limits dependencies between predicates to be acyclic. Examples of *stratified guarded updates* on the other hand, are the two statements in the loop body of Fig. 1. *Guarded updates* only allow to extend predicates where the extensions constrain the use of existential quantifiers to the format $\varphi \vee \exists \bar{z}.A\bar{y}\bar{z} \wedge \psi$ for some input predicate A and quantifier-free subformulas φ, ψ.

The loop of the example thus satisfies the requirements of [19], implying that an *abstract* fixpoint iteration is guaranteed to terminate for every universal invariant. Here, we show that under the given assumptions, *no abstraction* is required: the *concrete* fixpoint iteration in question already terminates and returns the weakest inductive invariant, which happens to consist of universal formulas only. We conclude that universal invariants for the given class of FO transition systems are decidable.

Boyond that, we extend this class of FO transition systems by additionally allowing stratified guarded *resets* such as the two assignments before the loop in Fig. 1. Guarded stratified resets are seemingly *easier* than updates, as they define their left-hand sides solely in terms of predicates of lower levels. In full generality, though, when there are both updates and resets, we *failed* to prove that universal invariants are decidable. We only succeed so—provided further (mild) restrictions are satisfied. Our results are that jointly, stratified guarded updates and resets can be allowed

- when resets refer to predicates at the highest and at the lowest level of the stratification only; or
- when all predicates of level at least 1, occur in right-hand sides only positively; or
- when all updates are not only guarded, but *strictly* guarded.

2   Basic Definitions

Assume that we are given a finite set of predicate names $\mathcal{R}$ together with a finite set of constant names $\mathcal{C}$. A *FO structure* $s = \langle I, \rho \rangle$ over a given universe $\mathcal{U}$ consists of an *interpretation* I of the predicates in $\mathcal{R}$, i.e., a mapping which assigns to each predicate $R \in \mathcal{R}$ of arity $k \geq 0$, a k-ary relation over $\mathcal{U}$, together with a valuation $\rho : \mathcal{C} \to \mathcal{U}$ which assigns to each constant name an element in $\mathcal{U}$. The *semantics* of FO (first-order) formulas as well as SO (second-order) formulas with free occurrences of predicates and variables in $\mathcal{R}$ and $\mathcal{C}$, respectively, is defined as usual. We write $s \models \varphi$ or $I, \rho \models \varphi$ to denote that φ is valid for the given interpretation I and valuation ρ as provided by s. For FO transition systems, we distinguish between the set $\mathcal{R}_{state}$ of *state predicates* and the disjoint set $\mathcal{A}$ of *input predicates*. While the values of constants as well as the interpretation of the state predicates constitute the state attained by the system, the input predicates are used to model (unknown) input from the environment or decisions of participating agents.

At each transition of a FO transition system, the system state s' after the transition is determined in terms of the system state s before the transition via a *substitution* θ. For each state predicate $R \in \mathcal{R}_{state}$, θ provides a FO formula to specify the interpretation of R after the transition in terms of the interpretation and valuation in s.

Technically, we introduce a set $\mathcal{Y} = \{y_i \mid i \in \mathbb{N}\}$ of distinct formal parameters where $\mathcal{C} \cap \mathcal{Y} = \emptyset$. For a predicate R of arity $k \geq 0$, we write $R\bar{y}$ for the literal $R(y_1, \ldots, y_k)$ and assume that each substitution θ maps each literal $R\bar{y}$, $R \in \mathcal{R}_{state}$, to some FO formula $\theta(R\bar{y})$ with predicates in $\mathcal{R}_{state} \cup \mathcal{A}$ and free variables either from $\mathcal{C}$ or occurring among the variables in $\bar{y}$. In case that $\theta(R\bar{y}) = \psi$ and $\theta(R'\bar{y}) = R'\bar{y}$ for all $R' \in \mathcal{R}_{state} \setminus \{R\}$, we also denote θ by $R\bar{y} := \psi$.

Example 1. In the example from Fig. 1, $\mathcal{R}_{state}$ consists of the predicates conf, auth, assign, report and discuss while $\mathcal{R}_{input}$ consists of the predicates $A_1 \ldots A_4$. No constants are needed, so $\mathcal{C} = \emptyset$. The edge from node 1 to 2, e.g., specifies a substitution θ that updates assign with

$$\theta(\mathsf{assign}(x,p)) = A_2(x,p) \land \neg\mathsf{conf}(x,p)$$

but does not change literals of predicates conf, auth, report or discuss.   □

Applying θ to a FO formula φ results in the FO formula $\theta(\varphi)$ which is obtained from φ by replacing each literal $R\bar{z}$ with the FO formula $\theta(R\bar{y})[\bar{z}/\bar{y}]$. Here, $[\bar{z}/\bar{y}]$ represents the simultaneous substitution of the variables in $\bar{y}$ by the corresponding variables in $\bar{z}$.

Example 2. Consider formula φ that specifies that the author of a paper p should never be assigned to provide a review for p:

$$\varphi = \forall x, p. \neg\mathsf{assign}(x, p) \vee \neg\mathsf{auth}(x, p)$$

Applying the substitution θ from Example 1 results in

$$\theta(\varphi) = \forall x, p. \neg(A_2(x, p) \wedge \neg\mathsf{conf}(x, p)) \vee \neg\mathsf{auth}(x, p)$$

□

A FO transition system $\mathcal{T}$ (over the given sets $\mathcal{R}_{state}$ of predicates, $\mathcal{A}$ of input predicates and $\mathcal{C}$ of constant names) consists of a finite set of nodes V together with a finite set E of edges of the form $e = (u, \theta, v)$ where $u, v \in V$ and θ is a substitution of the predicates in $\mathcal{R}_{state}$. W.l.o.g., we assume that each substitution θ at some edge e always has occurrences of at most one input predicate, which we denote by A_e. For a given universe $\mathcal{U}$, a program state s attained at a program point is a FO structure for the predicates in $\mathcal{R}_{state}$ and the constants in $\mathcal{C}$ over the universe $\mathcal{U}$. Let S denote the set of all program states. A *configuration* of $\mathcal{T}$ is a pair $(v, s) \in V \times S$. A (finite) *run* τ of $\mathcal{T}$ starting in configuration (v_0, s_0) and ending at node v in state s, i.e., in configuration (v, s) is a sequence of configurations (v_i, s_i), $i = 0, \ldots, n$ where $(v_n, s_n) = (v, s)$ and for all $i = 1, \ldots, n$, there is some edge $e_i = (v_{i-1}, \theta_i, v_i) \in E$ such that for $s_{i-1} = \langle I, \rho \rangle$, $s_i = \langle I', \rho \rangle$ where for some interpretation R_i of the input predicate A_{e_i}, and every valuation ρy of the formals, $I', \rho \oplus \rho y \models R\bar{y}$ iff $I \oplus \{A_{e_i} \mapsto R_i\}, \rho \oplus \rho y \models \theta(R\bar{y})$. Assume that we are given an initial node $v_0 \in V$ together with an initial hypothesis $\mathcal{H}$, i.e., a FO formula (with predicates in $\mathcal{R}_{state}$ and free variables only in $\mathcal{C}$) characterizing all possible initial states attained at v_0.

Example 3. According to the specification in Eq. (1) for the example transition system in Fig. 1, the single initial state is a pair of state 0 and the FO structure which interprets the relations auth, assign, report and discuss with the empty relation.   □

Input predicates may take fresh interpretations whenever the substitution of the corresponding edge is executed. This should be contrasted to state predicates whose interpretations stay the same if they are not explicitly updated by the transition system. The constant interpretation of such predicates instead may be constrained by suitable background theories as provided, e.g., via conjuncts of the initial hypothesis.

Assume that Ψ assigns to each program point $v \in V$, a FO formula $\Psi[v]$. Then Ψ is a *valid invariant* (relative to the initial hypothesis $\mathcal{H}$), if every run τ

of the system starting in a configuration (v_0, s_0) with $s_0 \models \mathcal{H}$ and visiting some configuration (v, s), it holds that $s \models \Psi[v]$. Ψ is *inductive* if

$$\Psi[u] \rightarrow \theta(\Psi[v]) \qquad \text{forall } (u, \theta, v) \in E \tag{3}$$

If Ψ is inductive, then Ψ is a valid whenever

$$\mathcal{H} \rightarrow \Psi[v_0] \tag{4}$$

Indeed, it is this observation which is used in the IVY project to verify distributed algorithms such as the PAXOS protocol, essentially, by manually providing the invariant Ψ and verifying properties (3) and (4) via the theorem prover Z3 [8].

Not each valid invariant Ψ, though, is by itself inductive. If this is not yet the case, iterative *strengthenings* $\Psi^{(h)}, h \geq 0$, of Ψ may be computed as follows:

$$\Psi^{(0)}[u] = \Psi[u]$$

$$\Psi^{(h)}[u] = \Psi^{(h-1)}[u] \wedge \bigwedge_{e=(u,\theta,v)\in E} \forall A_e. \, (\theta(\Psi^{(h-1)}[v])) \quad \text{for } h > 0 \tag{5}$$

For computing the next iterate in (5), universal SO quantification over the input predicate A_e is required in order to account for *every* input possibly occurring during a run at the given edge. As, e.g., noted in [25], $s \models \Psi^{(h)}[u]$ iff every run of length at most h starting in (u, s), ends in some configuration (u', s') with $s' \models \Psi[u']$. In particular, the assignment Ψ is a valid invariant iff $\mathcal{H} \rightarrow \Psi^{(h)}[v_0]$ for all $h \geq 0$. The iteration thus can be considered as computing the *weakest pre-condition* of the given invariant Ψ – as opposed to the *collecting semantics* of the FO transition system, which corresponds to the set of all configurations reachable from the set of all initial configurations $(v_0, s), s \models \mathcal{H}$. Whenever the fixpoint iteration (5) terminates, we obtain the *weakest* strengthening of the given invariant Ψ which is inductive. We have:

Lemma 1. *Let $\mathcal{T}$ be a FO transition system and let Ψ an invariant. Assume that for some $h \geq 0$, $\Psi^{(h)} = \Psi^{(h+1)}$ holds. Then $\Psi^{(h)}$ is the* weakest *inductive invariant implying Ψ. Moreover, Ψ is valid iff $\mathcal{H} \rightarrow \Psi^{(h)}[v_0]$.*   □

In general, the required SO quantifier elimination may not always be possible, i.e., there need not always exist an equivalent FO formula [1], and even if SO quantifier elimination is always possible, the fixpoint iteration need not terminate. Non-termination may already occur when all involved predicates either have no arguments or are *monadic* [25]. Termination as well as effective computability can be enforced by applying *abstraction* (see, e.g., [24] for a general discussion). Applying an abstraction α amounts to computing a *sufficient* condition for the invariant Ψ to hold. Technically, an abstraction maps each occurring formula ψ to a formula $\alpha[\psi]$ (hopefully of a simpler form) so that $\alpha[\psi] \rightarrow \psi$. Subsequently, we list three examples for such strengthenings.

Example 4. Abstraction of existentials. In [19], formulas with universal SO quantifiers and universal as well as existential quantifiers are strengthened to formulas with universal quantifiers only. The idea is to replace an existentially quantified subformula $\exists x.\varphi$ with a disjunction $\bigvee_{y \in Y} \varphi[y/x]$ where Y is the subset of constants and those universally quantified variables in whose scope φ occurs. So, the formula $\forall y_1, y_2.\exists x.R(x)$ is abstracted by $\forall y_1, y_2.R(y_1) \vee R(y_2)$. This abstraction is particularly useful, since SO universal quantifiers can be eliminated from universally quantified formulas.

Abstraction of Universals. Fixpoint iteration for universally quantified formulas still may not terminate due to an ever increasing number of quantified variables. The universally quantified variable x in an otherwise quantifier-free formula ψ in negation normal form can be removed by replacing each literal containing x with *false*. In this way, the formula $\forall x.\ (Rx \vee \neg Sy \vee Tz) \wedge (\neg Rx \vee \neg Ty)$ is strengthened to $(\neg Sy \vee Tz) \wedge \neg Ty$.

Abstraction of Conjunctions. Assume that the quantifier-free formula ψ is a conjunction of clauses. Then ψ is implied by the single clause c consisting of all literals which all clauses in ψ have in common. The formula $(Rx \vee \neg Sy \vee Tz) \wedge (Rx \vee Tz \vee \neg Tx)$, e.g., can be strengthened to $Rx \vee Tz$.   □

In this paper, rather than focusing on using abstractions, we identify sufficient criteria when the concrete iteration (5) terminates without any further abstraction.

3   Stratification and Guardedness

Subsequently, we concentrate on initial conditions in the $\exists^* \forall^*$ fragment and *universal* invariants, i.e., where the invariant Ψ consists of *universal* FO formulas only. Already for this setting, non-termination of the inference algorithm may occur even without SO quantification when a single binary predicate is involved.

Example 5. Consider the FO transition system $\mathcal{T}$ over a monadic state predicate R, a binary state predicate E and a constant element a. $\mathcal{T}$ consists of a single state u with a single transition:

$$R(y) := R(y) \vee \exists z.\ E(y, z) \wedge R(z)$$

Consider the invariant $\Psi[u] = \neg R(a)$. Then for $h \geq 0$,

$$\Psi^{(h)}[u] = \neg R(a) \wedge \bigwedge_{k=1}^{h} \forall z_1, \ldots, z_k.\ \neg E(a, z_1) \vee \bigvee_{i=1}^{k-1} \neg E(z_i, z_{i+1}) \vee \neg R(z_k)$$

The weakest inductive invariant thus represents the set of elements which are *not* reachable from a via the edge relation E. This property is not expressible in FO predicate logic. Accordingly, $\Psi^{(h)}[u] \neq \Psi^{(h+1)}[u]$ must hold for all $h \geq 0$. □

Our goal is to identify useful non-trivial classes of FO transition systems where the fixpoint iteration is guaranteed to terminate. One ingredient for this definition is a stratification mapping $\lambda : \mathcal{R}_{state} \to \mathbb{N}$ which assigns to each state predicate R a *level* $\lambda(R)$. Intuitively, this mapping is intended to describe how the information flows between predicates. Thereby, we use the convention that $\lambda(R) = 0$ only for predicates R which are never substituted, i.e., whose values stay the same throughout each run of the transition system.

We will consider substitutions which are *guarded* and *stratified*. A substitution θ is called *guarded* if it modifies at most one predicate $R \in \mathcal{R}_{state}$ at a time and is of one of the following forms:

$$Update: \qquad R\bar{y} := R\bar{y} \vee \varphi \vee \exists \bar{z}.\, A\bar{y}\bar{z} \wedge \psi \qquad (6)$$

$$Reset: \qquad R\bar{y} := \varphi \vee \exists \bar{z}.\, A\bar{y}\bar{z} \wedge \psi \qquad (7)$$

where $A \in \mathcal{R}_{input}$ is an input predicate and φ, ψ are quantifier-free FO formulas without occurrences of predicate A. If additionally, each predicate R' occurring in φ or ψ has level less than $\lambda(R)$, then θ is called *stratified*.

According to our definition, a *guarded* substitution only updates a single predicate R. We might wonder whether the single update restriction could be lifted by additionally allowing simultaneous updates of several predicates which are coupled via the same input predicate. For this extension, however, termination can no longer be guaranteed.

Lemma 2. *There exists a FO transition system $\mathcal{T}$ using stratified simultaneous guarded updates and resets, together with some universal invariant Ψ such that for each $h \geq 0$, $\Psi^{(h)}$ is universal FO definable, but $\Psi^{(h)}[u] \not\rightarrow \Psi^{(h+1)}[u]$ for some program point u.*

Proof. Consider the FO transition system $\mathcal{T}$ as shown in Fig. 2 for some binary predicate E, together with the invariant $\Psi = \{1 \mapsto \text{error} \vee \neg\text{hull}(a,b), 0, 2 \mapsto \top\}$ for constants a, b. Initially, the predicate hull is set to $\bot$. By executing the loop h times, either the error flag error is set to $\top$, or hull receives $k$fold compositions of E for $k = 0, \ldots, h$. Still, we can assign levels to the predicates used by $\mathcal{T}$ which meet the requirements of a stratification:

$$\lambda = \{E \mapsto 0, \text{add} \mapsto 0, \text{hull} \mapsto 1, \text{error} \mapsto 2\}$$

For $h \geq 0$, we obtain $\Psi^{(h)}[1] =$

$$\bigwedge_{j=1}^{h} \forall y_1 \ldots y_j.\ \text{error} \vee \neg\text{hull}(a,b) \vee \neg\text{hull}(a, y_1) \vee \bigvee_{i=1}^{j-1} \neg E(y_i, y_{i+1}) \vee \neg E(y_j, b)$$

For the required SO quantifier elimination of A_1, A_2, we note that in order to avoid error to be set to $\top$, $\text{add}(x, y, z)$ must imply $\text{hull}(x, y) \wedge E(y, z)$. In order to falsify the invariant at program point 1 whenever possible, thus, $A_1(x, y, z)$ should be set to $\text{hull}(x, y) \wedge E(y, z)$, and $A_2(x, z, y)$ at least to $\text{add}(x, y, z)$. Altogether thus, the weakest inductive invariant for program point 0 is given by error $\vee \neg E^*(a, b)$ where E^* is the transitive closure of E. As transitive closure is not FO definable, we conclude that the fixpoint iteration cannot terminate. $\square$

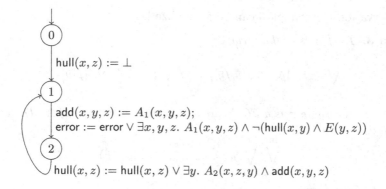

Fig. 2. FO transition system capturing transitive closure.

At the expense of slightly more complicated formulas for $\Psi^{(h)}$, the right-hand side for add could be brought into the form (6). Thus, the crucial issue which results in inexpressible weakest inductive invariants, is the use of the *same* input predicate in two simultaneous updates. In the next section, we indicate how to generally deal with SO quantifiers, once a guarded substitution has been applied.

4   Universal So Quantifier Elimination

It is well-known that universal SO quantifiers can be removed from otherwise quantifier-free formulas [12,19]. For example,

$$\forall A.\, R\bar{x} \vee A\bar{y} \vee \neg A\bar{z} \quad\longleftrightarrow\quad R\bar{x} \vee (\bar{y} = \bar{z})$$

where for $\bar{y} = (y_1, \ldots, y_k)$ and $\bar{z} = (z_1, \ldots, z_k)$, $\bar{y} = \bar{z}$ is a shortcut for the formula $(y_1 = z_1) \wedge \ldots \wedge (y_k = z_k)$. Interestingly, there are also cases where SO quantifier elimination is possible even in presence of FO existential quantifiers.

Example 6. Consider the substitution θ

$$R(y) := R(y) \vee \exists z.\, A(y, z) \wedge S(y, z)$$

In that case, $\theta(R(a) \vee \neg R(b))$ is given by

$$\forall z_1.\, R(a) \vee \exists z.\, A(a, z) \wedge S(a, z) \vee \neg R(b) \wedge (\neg A(b, z_1) \vee \neg S(b, z_1))$$
$$\longleftrightarrow \forall z_1.\, (R(a) \vee \exists z.\, A(a, z) \wedge S(a, z) \vee \neg R(b)) \wedge$$
$$(R(a) \vee (\exists z.\, A(a, z) \wedge S(a, z)) \vee \neg A(b, z_1) \vee \neg S(b, z_1))$$

A closer inspection reveals that in this case, SO quantifier elimination of A is possible where $\forall A.\, \theta(R(a) \vee \neg R(b))$ is equivalent to

$$\forall z_1.\, (R(a) \vee \neg R(b)) \wedge ((R(a) \vee (a = b) \wedge S(a, z_1)) \vee \neg S(b, z_1))$$
$$\longleftrightarrow \forall z_1.\, (R(a) \vee \neg R(b)) \wedge ((R(a) \vee (a = b) \wedge S(b, z_1)) \vee \neg S(b, z_1))$$
$$\longleftrightarrow \forall z_1.\, (R(a) \vee \neg R(b)) \wedge (R(a) \vee (a = b) \vee \neg S(b, z_1))$$
$$\longleftrightarrow \forall z_1.\, R(a) \vee R(b) \wedge ((a = b) \vee \neg S(b, z_1))$$

In particular, the resulting FO formula has universal FO quantifiers only.   □

The observation in Example 6 can be generalized.

Lemma 3. *1. If Ψ is of the form*

$$\bigvee_{i=1}^{n} (\exists \bar{z}.\, A\bar{y}_i \bar{z} \wedge \varphi[\bar{y}_i/\bar{y}]) \vee \bigvee_{j=1}^{m} (\forall \bar{z}.\neg A\bar{y}'_j \bar{z} \vee \neg\varphi[\bar{y}'_j/\bar{y}]) \tag{8}$$

for $n, m \in \mathbb{N}$ where φ is a FO formula without occurrences of A. Then $\forall A.\, \Psi$ is equivalent to

$$\bigvee_{j=1}^{m} (\bigvee_{i=1}^{n} \bar{y}_i = \bar{y}'_j) \vee (\forall \bar{z}.\neg\varphi[\bar{y}'_j/\bar{y}]) \tag{9}$$

2. If Ψ is of the form

$$\varphi' \vee \bigvee_{i=1}^{n} (\exists \bar{z}.\, A\bar{y}_i \bar{z} \wedge \varphi[\bar{y}_i/\bar{y}]) \vee \bigvee_{j=1}^{m} (\forall \bar{z}.\neg A\bar{y}'_j \bar{z} \vee \neg\varphi[\bar{y}'_j/\bar{y}]) \wedge \psi'_j \tag{10}$$

for $n, m \in \mathbb{N}$ where $\varphi, \varphi', \psi'_j$ all are FO formulas without occurrences of A. Then $\forall A.\, \Psi$ is equivalent to

$$\varphi' \vee \bigvee_{j=1}^{m} (\bigvee_{i=1}^{n} (\bar{y}_i = \bar{y}'_j) \vee (\forall \bar{z}.\neg\varphi[\bar{y}'_j/\bar{y}]) \wedge \psi'_j \tag{11}$$

Proof. For proving statement (1), we consider the negated formula $\exists A.\neg\Psi$ and apply Ackermann's lemma in order to remove existential SO quantification. We calculate:

$$
\begin{aligned}
\exists A.\neg\Psi &\longleftrightarrow \exists \bar{z}_1 \ldots \bar{z}_m.\exists A.\forall \bar{z}.\, \textstyle\bigwedge_{i=1}^{n} \bigwedge_{j=1}^{m} (\neg A\bar{y}_i \bar{z} \vee \neg\varphi[\bar{y}_i/\bar{y}]) \wedge A\bar{y}'_j \bar{z}_j \wedge \varphi[\bar{y}'_j/\bar{y}, \bar{z}_j/\bar{z}] \\
&\longleftrightarrow \exists \bar{z}_1 \ldots \bar{z}_m.\, \textstyle\bigwedge_{i=1}^{n} \bigwedge_{j=1}^{m} ((\bar{y}_i \neq \bar{y}'_j) \vee \neg\varphi[\bar{y}_i/\bar{y}, \bar{z}_j/\bar{z}]) \wedge \bigwedge_{j=1}^{m} \varphi[\bar{y}'_j/\bar{y}, \bar{z}_j/\bar{z}] \\
&\longleftrightarrow \exists \bar{z}_1 \ldots \bar{z}_m.\, \textstyle\bigwedge_{i=1}^{n} \bigwedge_{j=1}^{m} ((\bar{y}_i \neq \bar{y}'_j) \vee \neg\varphi[\bar{y}_j/\bar{y}, \bar{z}_j/\bar{z}]) \wedge \bigwedge_{j=1}^{m} \varphi[\bar{y}'_j/\bar{y}/\bar{z}_j/\bar{z}] \\
&\longleftrightarrow \exists \bar{z}_1 \ldots \bar{z}_m.\, \textstyle\bigwedge_{i=1}^{n} \bigwedge_{j=1}^{m} ((\bar{y}_i \neq \bar{y}'_j) \vee \neg\varphi[\bar{y}_j/\bar{y}]) \wedge \varphi[\bar{y}'_j/\bar{y}, /\bar{z}_j/\bar{z}] \\
&\longleftrightarrow \textstyle\bigwedge_{i=1}^{n} \bigwedge_{j=1}^{m} ((\bar{y}_i \neq \bar{y}'_j) \vee \exists \bar{z}.\, \varphi[\bar{y}'_j/\bar{y}])
\end{aligned}
$$

where the last formula is equivalent to the negation of formula (9). The second statement then follows from statement (1) by distributivity.   □

Interestingly, the same result is obtained when the existentially quantified variables $\bar{z}$ do not occur as arguments to the input predicate A.

Lemma 4. *1. If Ψ is of the form*

$$\bigvee_{i=1}^{n} A\bar{y}_i \wedge (\exists \bar{z}.\, \varphi[\bar{y}_i/\bar{y}]) \vee \bigvee_{j=1}^{m} \neg A\bar{y}'_j \vee (\forall \bar{z}.\neg\varphi[\bar{y}'_j/\bar{y}]) \tag{12}$$

for $n, m \in \mathbb{N}$ where φ is a FO formula without occurrences of A. Then $\forall A.\, \Psi$ is equivalent to

$$\bigvee_{j=1}^{m} (\bigvee_{i=1}^{n} \bar{y}_i = \bar{y}'_j) \vee (\forall \bar{z}.\neg\varphi[\bar{y}'_j/\bar{y}]) \tag{13}$$

2. *If Ψ is of the form*

$$\varphi' \vee \bigvee_{i=1}^{n} A\bar{y}_i \wedge (\exists \bar{z}. \varphi[\bar{y}_i/\bar{y}]) \vee \bigvee_{j=1}^{m} (\neg A\bar{y}'_j \vee (\forall \bar{z}. \neg\varphi[\bar{y}'_j/\bar{y}])) \wedge \psi'_j \qquad (14)$$

for $n, m \in \mathbb{N}$ where $\varphi, \varphi', \psi'_j$ all are FO formulas without occurrences of A. Then $\forall A. \Psi$ is equivalent to

$$\varphi' \vee \bigvee_{j=1}^{m} (\bigvee_{i=1}^{n} (\bar{y}_i = \bar{y}'_j) \vee (\forall \bar{z}. \neg\varphi[\bar{y}'_j/\bar{y}]) \wedge \psi'_j \qquad (15)$$

Proof. For proving statement (1), we again consider the negated formula $\exists A. \neg\Psi$ and apply Ackermann's lemma in order to remove existential SO quantification. By introducing the shortcut Φ for $\exists \bar{z}. \varphi$, we calculate:

$$\begin{aligned}
\exists A. \neg\Psi &\longleftrightarrow \exists A. \bigwedge_{i=1}^{n} \bigwedge_{j=1}^{m} (\neg A\bar{y}_i \vee \neg\Phi[\bar{y}_i/\bar{y}]) \wedge A\bar{y}'_j \wedge \neg\Phi[\bar{y}'_j/\bar{y}] \\
&\longleftrightarrow \bigwedge_{i=1}^{n} \bigwedge_{j=1}^{m} ((\bar{y}_i \neq \bar{y}'_j) \vee \neg\Phi[\bar{y}_i/\bar{y}]) \wedge \bigwedge_{j=1}^{m} \Phi[\bar{y}'_j/\bar{y}] \\
&\longleftrightarrow \bigwedge_{i=1}^{n} \bigwedge_{j=1}^{m} ((\bar{y}_i \neq \bar{y}'_j) \vee \neg\Phi[\bar{y}_j/\bar{y}]) \wedge \bigwedge_{j=1}^{m} \Phi[\bar{y}'_j/\bar{y}] \\
&\longleftrightarrow \bigwedge_{i=1}^{n} \bigwedge_{j=1}^{m} ((\bar{y}_i \neq \bar{y}'_j) \vee \neg\Phi[\bar{y}_j/\bar{y}]) \wedge \Phi[\bar{y}'_j/\bar{y}] \\
&\longleftrightarrow \bigwedge_{i=1}^{n} \bigwedge_{j=1}^{m} ((\bar{y}_i \neq \bar{y}'_j) \wedge \Phi[\bar{y}'_j/\bar{y}])
\end{aligned}$$

where the last formula is equivalent to the negation of formula (13). Again, the second statement then follows from statement (1) by distributivity. $\sqcap$

In light of Lemmas 3 and 4, we introduce simplified versions of guarded updates and resets where the input predicate no longer occurs in the scope of existential quantifiers:

Simplified Update:	$R\bar{y} := R\bar{y} \vee \varphi \vee A\bar{y} \wedge \exists \bar{z}. \psi$	(16)
Simplified Reset:	$R\bar{y} := \varphi \vee A\bar{y} \wedge \exists \bar{z}. \psi$	(17)

As a first corollary, we obtain:

Corollary 1. *Assume that θ is a guarded update of the form (6) (guarded reset of the form (7)), and that θ' is the corresponding simplified update (16) (simplified reset (17)). Then for every universal FO formula Ψ,*

$$\forall A. \theta(\Psi) \quad \longleftrightarrow \quad \forall A. \theta'(\Psi)$$

$\square$

In light of Corollary 1, we subsequently consider FO transition systems with *simplified* guarded updates and resets only.

Example 7. Consider the second update in the loop of the transition system from Fig. 1. Its simplified variant removes r_1 and r_2 from the signature of A_4:

$$\mathsf{discuss}(x_1, x_2, p, d) := \mathsf{discuss}(x_1, x_2, p, d) \vee A_4(x_1, x_2, p, d) \wedge$$
$$\exists r_1, r_2. \mathsf{report}(x_1, p, r_1) \wedge \mathsf{report}(x_2, p, r_2)$$

Let θ_4 denote this simplified update, and consider the invariant (2) from the introduction. Application of θ_4 results in the formula

$$\forall x_1, x_2, p, d, r_1, r_2. \neg\mathsf{discuss}(x_1, x_2, p, d) \wedge$$
$$(\neg A_4(x_1, x_2, p, d) \vee \neg\mathsf{report}(x_1, p, r_1) \vee \neg\mathsf{report}(x_2, p, r_2)) \vee$$
$$(\neg\mathsf{auth}(x_1, p) \wedge \neg\mathsf{auth}(x_2, p))$$

Since A_4 only occurs negatively, universal SO quantifier elimination of A_4 yields

$$\forall x_1, x_2, p, d, r_1, r_2. \neg\mathsf{discuss}(x_1, x_2, p, d) \wedge$$
$$(\neg\mathsf{report}(x_1, p, r_1) \vee \neg\mathsf{report}(x_2, p, r_2)) \vee$$
$$(\neg\mathsf{auth}(x_1, p) \wedge \neg\mathsf{auth}(x_2, p))$$

$\square$

Corollary 2. *Assume Ψ is a formula of the form (14). Then $\forall A. \Psi \longleftrightarrow \theta(\Psi)$ where θ is given by*

$$A\bar{y} := \bigwedge_{i=1}^{n} (\bar{y}_i \neq \bar{y}) \tag{18}$$

The definition (18) thus provides us with the *worst* adversarial strategy to defeat the proposed invariant. As another consequence of Lemma 3, we find that in presence of subsequent SO quantifier elimination, the effect of a guarded substitution of the forms (16) or (17) could also be simulated by the corresponding *nonuniform* substitutions:

$$R\bar{y} := R\bar{y} \vee \varphi \vee A\bar{y}$$
$$\neg R\bar{y} := \neg R\bar{y} \wedge \neg\varphi \wedge (\neg A\bar{y} \vee \forall \bar{z}.\neg\psi) \tag{19}$$

and

$$R\bar{y} := \varphi \vee A\bar{y}$$
$$\neg R\bar{y} := \neg\varphi \wedge (\neg A\bar{y} \vee \forall \bar{z}.\neg\psi) \tag{20}$$

respectively. Here, *nonuniform* means that positive and negative occurrences of literals are substituted differently. We have:

Corollary 3. *Assume that θ is a guarded substitution of the form (16) or (17). Assume that θ' is the nonuniform substitution of the corresponding form (19) or (20), respectively. Then for every universal formula Ψ,*

$$\forall A. \theta(\Psi) \quad \longleftrightarrow \quad \forall A. \theta'(\Psi)$$

$\square$

Finally, as another important consequence of Lemma 3, we obtain:

Theorem 1. *Assume that $\mathcal{T}$ is a FO transition system with guarded (simplified) updates and resets only, and Ψ a universal FO invariant.*

1. The iterates $\Psi^{(h)}[u], h \geq 0$, in (5) all are effectively equivalent to universal FO formulas.
2. The iteration terminates, i.e., $\Psi^{(h)} = \Psi^{(h+1)}$ for some $h \geq 0$, iff for each program point u, the weakest strengthening of all iterates $\Psi^{(h)}[u]$ is FO-definable.

Proof. Due to Lemmas 3 and 4, for each universal FO formula φ and each guarded (simplified) update or reset θ with input predicate A, $\forall A.\,(\theta\varphi)$ is equivalent to a universal FO formula. That implies statement (1). Now assume for for each $h \geq 0$ and each $v \in V$, $\Phi^{(h)}[v]$ is FO definable. Then due to the compactness theorem for FO predicate logic [5], there is some $h \geq 0$ such that $\Psi^{(h)}[v] \leftrightarrow \Psi^{(h+j)}[v]$ holds for all $v \in V$ and $j \geq 0$, iff for each $v \in V$, the conjunction $\bigwedge_{h \geq 0} \Psi^{(h)}[v]$ is again FO definable. □

Example 8. Consider again the specification from Fig. 1, and let $\theta_1, \theta_2, \theta_3$, and θ_4 denote the simplified substitutions occurring therein. Assume that Ψ equals the universal formula in (2), and we are interested in its validity at program point 2 of the transition system. The formula $\forall A_3.\,\theta_3(\forall A_4.\,\theta_4(\Psi))$ is given by

$$\forall A_3.\,\theta_3(\forall x_1, x_2, p, d, r_1, r_2. \neg\mathsf{discuss}(x_1, x_2, p, d) \wedge$$
$$(\neg\mathsf{report}(x_1, p, r_1) \vee \neg\mathsf{report}(x_2, p, r_2)) \vee (\neg\mathsf{auth}(x_1, p) \wedge \neg\mathsf{auth}(x_2, p))$$
$$\longleftrightarrow \forall x_1, x_2, p, d, r_1, r_2. \neg\mathsf{discuss}(x_1, x_2, p, d) \wedge$$
$$(\neg\mathsf{report}(x_1, p, r_1) \wedge \neg\mathsf{assign}(x_1, p) \vee \neg\mathsf{report}(x_2, p, r_2) \wedge \neg\mathsf{assign}(x_2, p)) \vee$$
$$(\neg\mathsf{auth}(x_1, p) \wedge \neg\mathsf{auth}(x_2, p))$$

The resulting formula Ψ' already equals the fixpoint for the loop. Since the predicate assign only occurs negatively in Ψ' and conf only negatively in the right-hand side for assign, the formula $\forall A_1.\theta_1(\forall A_2.\theta_2(\Phi'))$ construction from Ψ' via the substitution θ_{assign} defined by

$$\mathsf{assign}(y_1, y_2) := \neg\mathsf{auth}(y_1, y_2)$$

This means the formula Ψ'' for the initial node of the transition system is given by

$$\forall x_1, x_2, p, d, r_1, r_2. \neg\mathsf{discuss}(x_1, x_2, p, d) \wedge$$
$$(\neg\mathsf{report}(x_1, p, r_1) \wedge \mathsf{auth}(x_1, p) \vee \neg\mathsf{report}(x_2, p, r_2) \wedge \mathsf{auth}(x_2, p)) \vee$$
$$(\neg\mathsf{auth}(x_1, p) \wedge \neg\mathsf{auth}(x_2, p))$$

By the initial condition $\mathcal{H}$ from the introduction, $\neg\mathsf{discuss}(x_1, x_2, p, d)$ holds at the initial node of the transition system, as well as $\neg\mathsf{report}(x_1, p, r_1)$ and $\neg\mathsf{report}(x_2, p, r_2)$ for all x_1, x_2, p, d, r_1, r_2. Therefore, $\mathcal{H}$ implies Ψ'', and the property Ψ at the exit of the transition system is valid. □

In this section we have shown comprehensively how to eliminate universal SO quantifiers introduced by guarded updates in a FO transition system and introduced a non-uniform variant of any guarded updates and resets which removes all possibly introduced existential FO quantifiers. In the next two sections, we will apply these results to FO transition systems which additionally are stratified.

5 Stratified Guarded Updates

In [19], termination was announced for FO transition systems with stratified guarded updates where instantiation of existential quantifiers was applied as an *abstraction* to enforce all occurring formulas to be universal. Here, we improve on that result in two respects. First, we present a proof that termination can also be guaranteed without any abstraction. Second, we generalize the setting to allow stratified guarded resets—at least at the maximal and minimal levels.

Theorem 2. *Assume that $\mathcal{T}$ is a FO transition system where each occurring substitution is stratified guarded with the restriction that resets only occur for predicates of level 1 and the maximal level L. Then for every universal invariant Ψ, the weakest inductive invariant is again universal and can effectively be computed.*

Proof. W.l.o.g., we assume that each occurring substitution is a *simplified update* or *reset*, i.e., either of the form (16) or (17). We show that there is some $h \geq 0$, so that $\Psi^{(h+1)} = \Psi^{(h)}$. Since by Lemma 4, $\Psi^{(h)}[u]$ is a universal formula for all $h \geq 0$ and program points u, the statement of the theorem follows.

Assume that each simplified update θ of a predicate R always is specified by means of the *same* input predicate A_R. Let Θ denote the finite set of stratified guarded substitutions occurring in $\mathcal{T}$, and Φ a universal FO formula. Let $\pi = \theta_N, \ldots, \theta_1$ be any sequence of nonuniform substitutions where for each $i = 1, \ldots, N$, $\theta_i = \theta_i'[A_i/A_R]$ holds for a fresh input predicate A_i, and a nonuniform substitution θ_i' of the form (19) corresponding to a simplified update or reset $\theta'' \in \Theta$ with left-hand side $R\bar{y}$.

Lemma 5. *There is some number V only depending on Φ and Θ so that $\pi(\Phi) = \theta_N(\ldots \theta_1(\Phi) \ldots) = \bigwedge_{h=t}^{N}(\forall \bar{z}_t.c_t)$ for clauses c_t where the number of FO variables in $\bar{z}_t$ is bounded by V. In particular, V is independent of the number N of substitutions in π.*

Given Lemma 5, the number of argument tuples $\bar{z}$ of occurring literals $A_i\bar{z}$ in any c_t is bounded. Due to Corollary 2, a bounded number of substitutions of the form (18) therefore suffices to realize SO quantifier elimination of $A_1, \ldots, A_N$ in c_t. As a consequence, the number of universal FO formulas possibly occurring in each conjunct of $\forall A_1 \ldots A_N. \pi(\Phi)$, and thus also the number of conjunctions of these formulas is finite. Accordingly, there must be some $h \geq 0$ so that $\Phi^{(h+1)} = \Phi^{(h)}$, and the theorem follows. It therefore remains to prove Lemma 5.

Proof (of Lemma 5). Let us first consider the case where there is no reset of predicates at maximal level L. We introduce a dedicated class of formulas g as finite conjunctions of *generalized* clauses c which are built up according to the following abstract grammar

$$
\begin{aligned}
g &::= \top \quad | \quad c \wedge g \\
c &::= c_0 \quad | \quad A\bar{a} \vee c' \quad | \quad f_{R\bar{b}} \vee c' \quad | \quad o_{\bar{b}} \vee c' \\
f_{R\bar{b}} &::= \neg R\bar{b} \wedge \forall \bar{z}_R. \bigwedge_{n=1}^{r}(\neg A_n \bar{b} \vee c_n) \\
o_{\bar{b}} &::= \forall \bar{z}. \bigwedge_{n=1}^{r}(\neg A_n \bar{b} \vee c_n)
\end{aligned}
$$

where c_0 is an ordinary clause without occurrences of input predicates, R is a predicate, A, A_n are input predicates, $\bar{a}, \bar{b}$ are sequences of arguments, $\bar{z}_R$ is a sequence of fresh variables whose length only depends on R, and formulas $o_{\bar{b}}$ where all state predicates are of level 0. A formula $f_{R\bar{b}}$ is also called *negation tree* with head $\neg R\bar{b}$, while we call a formula $o_{\bar{b}}$ a level 0 *chunk*. Moreover,

(a) All literals occurring in the generalized clauses c_n inside the conjunction within $f_{R\bar{b}}$ are of levels less than $\lambda(R)$;

(b) For any two negation trees φ_1, φ_2 with identical head $\neg R\bar{b}$, there is some formula Δ so that either $\varphi_1 = \varphi_2 \wedge \Delta$ or vice versa, $\varphi_2 = \varphi_1 \wedge \Delta$ holds.

Φ can be brought into the form $\forall \bar{z}. \bigwedge_{t=1}^{m} c_t$ where each c_t is an ordinary clause without occurrences of input predicates, i.e., a plain disjunction of literals and (dis-)equalities. Therefore, now consider a single generalized clause c which satisfies properties (a) and (b). We show that for each nonuniform update substitution θ of the form

$$R\bar{y} := R\bar{y} \vee \varphi \vee A_h\bar{y}$$
$$\neg R\bar{y} := \neg R\bar{y} \wedge \neg\varphi \wedge (\neg A_h\bar{y} \vee \neg\forall\bar{z}.\neg\psi)$$

$\theta(c)$ can again be represented as a conjunction of generalized clauses satisfying properties (a) and (b), and whose free variables are all contained in the set of free variables from c and θ. Assume that c is of the form $c' \vee \bigvee_{i=1}^{s} R\bar{a}_i \vee \bigvee_{j=1}^{t} f_{R\bar{b}_j}$ where c' is a generalized clause without further top-level occurrences either of positive literals $R\bar{a}'$ or negation trees with head $\neg R\bar{b}'$ for any $\bar{a}', \bar{b}'$, and $f_{R\bar{b}_j} = \neg R\bar{b}_j \wedge \forall\bar{z}_R. \bigwedge_{\nu=1}^{u_j}(\neg A_{j,\nu}\bar{b}_j \vee c_{j,\nu})$ is a negation tree with head $\neg R\bar{b}_j$. Then

$$\theta(c) = \bigwedge_{c_1,\ldots,c_s \in \mathcal{C}} \bigwedge_{J \subseteq [1,t]} \bigwedge_{j \in J, \bar{c}_j \in \bar{\mathcal{C}}} \theta(c') \vee$$
$$\bigvee_{i=1}^{s} R\bar{a}_i \vee A\bar{a}_i \vee c_i[\bar{a}_i/\bar{y}] \vee \bigvee_{j \in J} \bar{c}_j[\bar{b}_j/\bar{y}] \vee$$
$$\bigvee_{j \notin J} \neg R\bar{b}_j \wedge (\forall\bar{z}_R. A\bar{b}_j \vee \psi[\bar{b}_j/\bar{y}]) \wedge \bigwedge_{\nu=1}^{u_j}(\neg A_{j,\nu}\bar{b}_j \vee \psi_{j,\nu})$$

where $\mathcal{C}$ and $\bar{\mathcal{C}}$ are the sets of clauses in the normal forms of φ and $\neg\varphi$, respectively. The resulting formula can indeed be represented as a conjunction of generalized clauses satisfying property (a). Concerning property (b), we observe that for every fresh negative literal property (b) trivially holds, while for existing negation trees, this property is preserved. If on the other hand, θ is a reset of a predicate at level 1, $\theta(c)$ is a conjunction of generalized clauses where some negation trees have been replaced by level 0 chunks. In particular, properties (a) and (b) still hold.

Assume now that we are given a generalized clause c satisfying properties (a) and (b). Then c is called *flat up to level i*, if the roots of all negation trees occurring in c with a nonempty conjunction, have level at most i, and for every predicate R of level i and every possible argument tuple $\bar{b}$, there is at most one negation tree with head $\neg R\bar{b}$. For a generalized clause c which is flat up to level i, we define the transformation $\mathsf{flatten}_i$ as follows. Assume that c is of the form

$$c' \vee \bigvee_{j=1}^{t} \neg R_j\bar{b}_j \wedge \forall\bar{z}_j. \bigwedge_{\nu=1}^{u_j}(\neg A_{j,\nu}\bar{b}_j \vee c_{j,\nu})$$

where the $\neg R_j \bar{b}_j$ represent all occurrences of negated literals of level i. Then

$$c \quad \longleftrightarrow \quad \bigwedge_{J=\{j_1<\ldots<j_k\}\subseteq[1,t]} \bigwedge_{\nu_1 \in [1,u_{j_1}],\ldots,\nu_k \in [1,u_{j_k}]}$$
$$(\forall \bar{z}_{j_1} \ldots \bar{z}_{j_k}.\, c' \vee \bigvee_{j \notin J} R_j \bar{b}_j \vee \bigvee_{l=1}^{k} \neg A_{j_l,\nu_l} \bar{b}_j \vee c_{j_l,\nu_l})$$

In each quantified clause $\forall \bar{z}_{j_1} \ldots \bar{z}_{j_k}.\, c'$ in the conjunction, all occurring negation trees have level less than i. Now due to property (2), c' can be simplified so that for each negated literal $R'\bar{b}$ where R' is of level $i-1$, there is at most one negation tree. The resulting conjunction of quantified clauses is denoted by $\mathsf{flatten}_i\, c$.

To compute a bound on the number of possible argument variables, let us introduce the following structural parameters:

v — the number of variables occurring in Φ

L — the number of levels of predicates

r — maximal arity of a predicate

m — maximal number predicates at some level i

l — maximal length of $\bar{z}$ in subformulas $\forall \bar{z}.\, \neg \psi$
occurring in the substitutions from Θ

Successive application of $\mathsf{flatten}_L, \ldots, \mathsf{flatten}_1$ allows us to construct for a generalized clause c satisfying properties (a) and (b), an equivalent conjunction of formulas $\forall \bar{z}'.\, c'$ where c' is disjunction of literals, (dis-)equalities and level 0 chunks $o_{\bar{b}}$ only, and $\bar{z}'$ is the list of globally bound variables occurring freely in c'.

For $i = L, \ldots, 1$, we inductively determine a bound V_i to the number of distinct FO variables possibly occurring as arguments of literals at level i in a clause c'. For $i = L$, we can set $V_L = v$, since the only literals at level L occurring in c' already must have occurred in Φ. Therefore, assume that $i < L$ and a bound V_{i+1} has already been found. Then V_i can be bound as follows: Given the number V_{i+1}, the number of literals of predicates at level $i+1$ can be bound by $m \cdot V_{i+1}^r$. For each of these literals, a fresh list of variables of length at most l can be provided. Accordingly,

$$V_i = V_{i+1} + l \cdot m \cdot V_{i+1}^r \leq (1 + l \cdot m) \cdot V_{i+1}^r$$

Altogether, this means that the total number of variables possibly occurring in literals of c' (outside of level 0 chunks) at level at least 0 is bounded by

$$V \leq \begin{cases} (1 + l \cdot m)^L \cdot v & \text{if } r = 1 \\ (1 + l \cdot m)^{\frac{r^L-1}{r-1}} \cdot v^{r^L} & \text{if } r > 1 \end{cases} \tag{21}$$

Now given that there is a bound V_1 to the number of variables possibly occurring as arguments of predicates at level 1, there is also only a bounded number O of non-equivalent subformulas $o_{\bar{b}}$ (after SO quantifier elimination) in any of the generalized clauses from $\mathsf{flatten}_1(\ldots \mathsf{flatten}_L(c')\ldots)$. Accordingly, $V_0 + O \cdot l$ bounds the number of variables occurring in equalities, disequalities and literals of predicates at level 0.

Let us finally also consider the case when additionally resets of predicates at maximal level L occur. Such a reset for a predicate R takes effect at most once. It thus introduces one fresh list of universally quantified variables for each occurrence $\neg R\bar{b}$ of the negated the negated literal at most once where we w.l.o.g. may even assume that the list of outside universal quantifiers of the negation tree for that literal can be reused. Thus, no further universal quantifiers are introduced. Altogether, therefore, the number of FO variables in quantified clauses $\forall \bar{z}'.c'$ contained in $\pi(\Phi)$ remains bounded. This completes the proof of Lemma 5. $\Box$

We remark that Theorem 2 remains true if there are predicates R' with stratified guarded updates as well as resets also at non-extremal levels—given that neither their updates nor their resets introduce FO variables, i.e., the variable lists $\bar{z}$ in (6) and (7) ((16) and (17)) are empty. In general, though, the proof technique of Theorem 2 cannot easily be extended to FO transition systems with arbitrary resets of the form (7), since then conjunctions of the form $o_{\bar{b}}$ with non-empty lists of quantified variables may also occur at higher levels—where it is no longer clear how to prove that their number is finite.

6   Allowing Guarded Stratified Resets

We would like to extend Theorem 2 from the last section to FO transition systems which additionally have resets at arbitrary levels. We succeed in doing so in two special cases (see Theorems 3 and 4, respectively). Let us call an update *strictly guarded* it it is of the form:

$$R\bar{y} := R\bar{y} \vee A\bar{y} \wedge \exists \bar{z}.\,\psi \tag{22}$$

for some predicate R and quantifier-free FO formula ψ without occurrences of A. Furthermore, let us call an update or reset θ *positive* if all predicates only occur positively in the right-hand side.

Theorem 3. *Consider a FO transition system T where all substitutions are stratified, guarded, and all substitutions of predicates not of level 0 are positive. Then for every universal invariant Ψ, the weakest inductive invariant is again universal and can effectively be computed.*

Proof. Let Θ denote the set of substitutions occurring in T. As in the proof of Theorem 2, let $\pi = \theta_N, \ldots, \theta_1$ be any sequence of nonuniform substitutions where for each $i = 1, \ldots, N$, $\theta_i = \theta'_i[A_i/A_R]$ holds for a fresh input predicate A_i, and a nonuniform substitution θ'_i of the form (19) corresponding to an update or reset substitution $\theta'' \in \Theta$ with left-hand side $R\bar{y}$. Let $\bigwedge_{j=1}^{M}(\forall \bar{z}_j.\,c_j)$ denote the conjunction of quantified generalized clauses for $\pi(\Phi)$—now possibly also with subformulas $o_{\bar{b}}$ holding predicates of level > 0. Then each FO variable x occurring in a positive literal $A_i \bar{a}$ in any c_j, already occurs in Φ. In light of Corollary 2, it therefore suffices to use only a globally bounded number of input predicates in each c_j. If the number of predicate symbols is bounded, then also the number of generalized clauses as well as the number of non-equivalent formulas $\forall \Lambda_1 \ldots \Lambda_N.\,\pi(\Phi)$—implying that for every universal invariant Ψ, $\Psi^{(h+1)} = \Psi^{(h)}$ for some $h \geq 0$. From that, the statement of the theorem follows. $\Box$

The proof argument for Theorem 3 cannot easily be extended to unrestricted stratified guarded substitutions. In presence of *negated* literals in substitutions, it is no longer the case that the arguments of positive literals $R\bar{a}$ occurring in $\pi(\Phi)$ have already occurred in Φ, so for the next result we have to rely on a different proof strategy.

Theorem 4. *Consider a FO transition system $\mathcal{T}$ where all substitutions are guarded and stratified. Assume furthermore that all updates are strictly guarded. Then for every universal invariant Ψ, the weakest inductive invariant is again universal and can effectively be computed.*

Proof. For this proof, it is convenient to use the notation $\Phi \ni \forall \bar{x}.\, c$ for a universal FO formula Φ, a clause c, and a list $\bar{x}$ of distinct variables so that for the prenex CNF $\forall \bar{z}.\, c_1 \wedge \ldots \wedge c_m$ of Φ, c occurs among the c_j, and $\bar{x}$ is the subsequence of variables in $\bar{z}$ which occur in c. We rely on the following technical lemma:

Lemma 6. *Assume that c is a clause and θ a stratified reset or stratified strictly guarded update with input predicate A which substitutes a predicate R with $\lambda(R) = s$. Let c' be a clause with $\forall A.\, \theta(c) \ni \forall \bar{x}.\, c'$ where $\bar{x}$ is the list of newly introduced variables in c'. Then either $c = c'$ and $\bar{x}$ is empty, or the number of literals at level s of c' is less than the corresponding number of c.*

Proof. Assume that the clause c is of the form

$$c_0 \vee R\bar{y}_1 \vee \ldots \vee R\bar{y}_n \vee \neg R\bar{y}_1' \vee \cdots \vee \neg R\bar{y}_m'$$

where c_0 does not contain the predicate R. If θ is a reset, all literals containing R are eliminated. Therefore, the assertion of the lemma trivially holds. Now assume that θ is a strictly guarded update, i.e., of the form (22). Then by Lemma 3,

$$
\begin{aligned}
\forall A.\, \theta(R_i \bar{y}) &\longleftrightarrow c_0 \vee \bigvee_{j=1}^{m} \neg R\bar{y}_j' \wedge \left(\bigvee_{i=1}^{n} (\bar{y}_i = \bar{y}_j') \vee \neg \psi[\bar{y}_j'/\bar{y}] \right) \\
&\longleftrightarrow \bigwedge_{J \subseteq [1,m]} \forall \bar{z}_J.\, \Big(c_0 \vee \bigvee_{j \notin J} \neg R\bar{y}_j' \vee \\
&\qquad\qquad \bigvee_{j \in J} \bigvee_{i=1}^{n} (\bar{y}_i = \bar{y}_j') \vee \neg \psi[\bar{y}_j'/\bar{y}, \bar{z}_j/\bar{z}] \Big)
\end{aligned}
$$

where $\bar{z}_j$ is a fresh list of FO variables of the same length as $\bar{z}$, and $\bar{z}_J$ is the concatenation of all lists $\bar{z}_j, j \in J$. In particular for $J = \emptyset$, $\bar{z}_J$ is empty and the corresponding clause equals c. If on the other hand $J \neq \emptyset$, the number of negated literals occurring in the clause has decreased. □

By Lemma 6, the number of literals at level s therefore either decreases, or the clause stays the same. Let Θ denote a finite set of stratified guarded substitutions where all updates in Θ are strictly guarded, and let c_0 denote any clause. Consider a sequence $(\theta_t, \forall \bar{x}_t.c_t), t \geq 1$, where for all $t \geq 1$, $\theta_t \in \Theta$ with some input predicate A_t, and $\forall A_t.\, (\theta_t c_{t-1}) \ni \forall \bar{x}_t.\, c_t$ holds. We claim that then there is some $t' \geq 1$ so that $c_{t'} = c_{t''}$ and $\bar{x}_{t''}$ is empty for all $t'' > t'$.

In order to prove that claim, we introduce for $t \geq 1$, the vector $v_t = (v_{t,L}, \ldots, v_{t,1}) \in \mathbb{N}^L$ where L is the maximal level of a predicate in $\mathcal{R}_{state}$, and $v_{t,i}$ is the number of literals with predicates of level i. By Lemma 6, it holds for all $t \geq 0$, that either $c_t = c_{t+1}$ and $\bar{z}_t$ is empty, or $v_t > v_{t+1}$ w.r.t. the lexicographic order on $\mathbb{N}^L$. Since the lexicographical ordering on $\mathbb{N}^L$ is well-founded, the claim follows. We conclude that the set of quantified clauses $\forall \bar{z}.c$ with $\Psi^{(h)}[u] \ni \forall \bar{z}.c$ for any u and h, is finite. From that, the statement of the theorem follows. $\quad\square$

Theorem 4 leaves open the case of transition systems with stratified guarded resets and stratified guarded updates of which some are not strictly guarded. To these, the presented proof technique cannot be easily extended. The reason is that a non-strictly guarded update θ for some predicate R, when applied to some clause c, may result in a quantified clause $\forall \bar{z}.\,c'$ with $\forall A.\theta(c) \ni \forall \bar{z}.\,c'$ so that neither $c = c'$ holds nor does the number of literals $\neg R\bar{b}$ decrease.

7 Conclusion

We have investigated FO transition systems where all substitutions are either guarded updates or guarded resets. For these, we observed that the exact weakest pre-condition of a universal FO formula is again a universal FO formula, thus allowing us to realize a fixpoint computation of iterated strengthening for proving the validity of universal invariants. In order to identify sub-classes of FO transition systems where termination can be guaranteed, we relied on a natural notion of stratification. Here, we were able to prove termination (and thus decidability) for three interesting sub-classes of stratified guarded FO transition systems. However, it remains as an open question whether termination can be proven for *all* FO transition systems with stratified guarded updates and resets.

The results of our paper can immediately be applied to the multi-agent workflow language as considered in [19] for analyzing noninterference in presence of declassification and agent coalitions. There, transformations are presented to encode noninterference properties as invariants of the *self-composition* of the given workflow [3,17]. At least for the case of *stubborn agents* [11], i.e., agents who do not participate in adversarial coalitions, the given transformation preserves both guardedness and the stratification. The same also holds true if the size of adversarial coalitions is bounded. For these cases, our novel decidability results therefore translate into decidability of noninterence.

References

1. Ackermann, W.: Untersuchungen über das Eliminationsproblem der mathematischen Logik. Math. Ann. **110**, 390–413 (1935)
2. Ball, T., et al.: Vericon: towards verifying controller programs in software-defined networks. In: ACM Sig-plan Notices number 6, vol. 49, pp. 282–293. ACM (2014)
3. Barthe, G., Crespo, J,M., Kunz, C.: Product programs and relational program logics. J. Log. Algebraic Methods Program. **85**(5), 847–859 (2016). https://doi.org/10.1016/j.jlamp.2016.05.004

4. Berkovits, I., Lazić, M., Losa, G., Padon, O., Shoham, S.: Verification of threshold-based distributed algorithms by decomposition to decidable logics. In: Dillig, I., Tasiran, S. (eds.) CAV 2019. LNCS, vol. 11562, pp. 245–266. Springer, Cham (2019). https://doi.org/10.1007/978-3-030-25543-5_15
5. Börger, E., Grädel, E., Gurevich, Y.: The Classical Decision Problem. Perspectives in Mathematical Logic. Springer, Heidelberg (1997)
6. Börger, E., Stärk, R.: History and survey of ASM research. In Abstract State Machines: A Method for High-Level System Design and Analysis, pp. 343–367. Springer, Heidelberg (2003). ISBN: 978-3-642-18216-7. https://doi.org/10.1007/978-3-642-18216-7_9
7. Böorger, E., Stäark, R.: Tool support for ASMs. In: Abstract State Machines: A Method for High-Level System Design and Analysis, pp. 313–342. Springer, Heidelberg (2003). ISBN: 978-3-642-18216-7, https://doi.org/10.1007/978-3-642-18216-7_8
8. de Moura, L., Bjørner, N.: Z3: an efficient SMT solver. In: Ramakrishnan, C.R., Rehof, J. (eds.) TACAS 2008. LNCS, vol. 4963, pp. 337–340. Springer, Heidelberg (2008). https://doi.org/10.1007/978-3-540-78800-3_24
9. Feldman, Y.M.Y., Padon, O., Immerman, N., Sagiv, M., Shoham, S.: Bounded quantifier instantiation for checking inductive invariants. Logical Methods Comput. Sci. **15**, 3 (2019). https://doi.org/10.23638/LMCS-15(3:18)2019
10. Finkbeiner, B., Müller, C., Seidl, H., Zalinescu, E.: Verifying security policies in multi-agent work OWS with loops. In: Proceedings of the 2017 ACM SIGSAC Conference on Computer and Communications Security (CCS 2017), pp. 633–645. IEEE (2017). https://doi.org/10.1145/3133956.3134080
11. Finkbeiner, B., Seidl, H., Müller, C.: Specifying and verifying secrecy in workflows with arbitrarily many agents. In: Artho, C., Legay, A., Peled, D. (eds.) ATVA 2016. LNCS, vol. 9938, pp. 157–173. Springer, Cham (2016). https://doi.org/10.1007/978-3-319-46520-3_11
12. Gabbay, D.M., Schmidt, R., Szalas, A.: Second Order Quantifier Elimination: Foundations. Computational Aspects and Applications, College Publications (2008)
13. Goguen, J.A., Meseguer, J.: Security policies and security models. In: IEEE Symposium on Security and Privacy, Oakland, CA, USA, April 26–28, 1982. IEEE Computer Society (1982). https://doi.org/10.1109/SP.1982.10014
14. Gurevich, Y.: Evolving algebras 1993: Lipari guide. arXiv preprint arXiv:1808.06255 (2018)
15. Karbyshev, A., Bjørner, N., Itzhaky, S., Rinetzky, N., Shoham, S.: Property-directed inference of universal invariants or proving their absence. J. ACM (JACM) **64**(1), 7 (2017)
16. Koenig, J.R., Padon, O., Immerman, N., Aiken, A.: [n. d.] Firstorder quantified separators. In: Proceedings of the ACM SIGPLAN Conference on Programming Language Design and Implementation (PLDI 2020) (2020, to appear)
17. Kovács, M., Seidl, H., Finkbeiner, B.: Relational abstract interpretation for the verification of 2-hypersafety properties. In: Sadeghi, A.-R., Gligor, V.D., Yung, M. (eds.) 2013 ACM SIGSAC Conference on Computer and Communications Security, CCS 2013, Berlin, Germany, November 4–8, 2013, pp. 211–222. ACM (2013). https://doi.org/10.1145/2508859.2516721
18. McMillan, K.L., Padon, O.: Deductive verification in decidable fragments with ivy. In: Podelski, A. (ed.) SAS 2018. LNCS, vol. 11002, pp. 43–55. Springer, Cham (2018). https://doi.org/10.1007/978-3-319-99725-4_4

19. Müller, C., Seidl, H., Zalinescu, E.: Inductive invariants for noninterference in multi-agent work flows. In: 31st IEEE Computer Security Foundations Symposium, (CSF 2018), pp. 247–261. IEEE (2018). https://doi.org/10.1109/CSF.2018.00025
20. Padon, O., Immerman, N., Karbyshev, A., Lahav, O., Sagiv, M., Shoham, S.: Decentralizing SDN policies. In: ACM SIGPLAN Notices, vol. 50, no. 1, pp. 663–676. ACM (2015)
21. Padon, O., Immerman, N., Shoham, S., Karbyshev, A., Sagiv, M.: Decidability of inferring inductive invariants. In: Proceedings of the 43rd Annual ACM SIGPLAN-SIGACT Symposium on Principles of Programming Languages, POPL 2016. ACM, 217–231 (2016). https://doi.org/10.1145/2837614.2837640
22. Padon, O., Losa, G., Sagiv, M., Shoham, S.: Paxos made EPR: decidable reasoning about distributed protocols. In: Proceedings of the ACM Programming Language, 1, OOPSLA, 108:1–108:31 (2017). https://doi.org/10.1145/3140568
23. Padon, O., McMillan, K.L., Panda, A., Sagiv, M., Shoham, S.: Ivy: safety verification by interactive generalization. ACM SIG- PLAN Notices **51**(6), 614–630 (2016)
24. Ranzato, F.: Decidability and synthesis of abstract inductive invariants. CoRR, abs/2004.03170. arXiv:2004.03170 (2020). https://arxiv.org/abs/2004.03170
25. Seidl, H., Müller, C., Finkbeiner, B.: How to win first-order safety games. In: Beyer, D., Zufferey, D. (eds.) VMCAI 2020. LNCS, vol. 11990, pp. 426–448. Springer, Cham (2020). https://doi.org/10.1007/978-3-030-39322-9_20

Predicate Abstraction and CEGAR
for νHFL$_\mathbb{Z}$ Validity Checking

Naoki Iwayama[1], Naoki Kobayashi[1]([✉]) [iD], Ryota Suzuki[1],
and Takeshi Tsukada[2] [iD]

[1] The University of Tokyo, Tokyo, Japan
{iwayama,koba,rsuzuki}@kb.is.s.u-tokyo.ac.jp
[2] Chiba University, Chiba, Japan
tsukada@math.s.chiba-u.ac.jp

Abstract. We propose an automated method for νHFL$_\mathbb{Z}$ validity checking. HFL$_\mathbb{Z}$ is an extension of the higher-order fixpoint logic HFL with
integers, and νHFL$_\mathbb{Z}$ is a restriction of it to the fragment without the least
fixpoint operator. The validity checking problem for HFL$_\mathbb{Z}$ has recently
been shown to provide a uniform approach to higher-order program verification. The restriction to νHFL$_\mathbb{Z}$ studied in this paper already provides
an automated method for a large class of program verification problems
including safety and non-termination verification, and also serves as a key
building block for solving the validity checking problem for full HFL$_\mathbb{Z}$.
Our approach is based on predicate abstraction and counterexample-
guided abstraction refinement (CEGAR). We have implemented the
proposed method, and applied it to program verification. According to
experiments, our tool outperforms a closely related tool called Horus in
terms of precision, and is competitive with a more specialized program
verification tool called MoCHi despite the generality of our approach.

1 Introduction

HFL$_\mathbb{Z}$ [13] is an extension of the higher-order fixpoint logic HFL [22] with integers. Kobayashi et al. [13,23] have shown that various program verification problems for functional programs can be reduced to HFL$_\mathbb{Z}$ validity checking problems.[1] For example, consider the following OCaml program.

```
let rec sum f n k = if n<=0 then k 0
                    else f n (fun x-> sum f (n-1) (fun y -> k(x+y)))
let main n = sum (fun x k -> k(x+x)) n (fun r->assert(r>=n))
```

The main function takes an integer n as an argument, computes the sum $r = \sum_{x=1}^{n}(x+x)$, and asserts that $r \geq n$ (here, the function sum is represented in the

---

[1] Kobayashi et al. [13] actually considered *model* checking problems, but it is actually sufficient to consider validity checking problems for formulas without modal
operators, as shown in a follow-up paper [23]; thus, throughout this paper, we shall
consider only validity checking for formulas without modal operators.

© Springer Nature Switzerland AG 2020
D. Pichardie and M. Sighireanu (Eds.): SAS 2020, LNCS 12389, pp. 134–155, 2020.
https://doi.org/10.1007/978-3-030-65474-0_7

continuation-passing style to make the correspondence with the formula below clear). By using the reduction of [13], the property that the assertion never fails for any integer n can be expressed by the HFL$_\mathbb{Z}$ formula $\forall n.main\ n$, where $main$ is defined by:

$$main\ n =_\nu sum\ (\lambda x.\lambda k.k(x+x))\ n\ (\lambda r.r \geq n)$$
$$sum\ f\ n\ k =_\nu (n \leq 0 \Rightarrow k\ 0) \wedge (n > 0 \Rightarrow f\ n\ (\lambda x.sum\ f\ (n-1)\ \lambda y.k(x+y))).$$

Here, the subscript ν of each equality symbol indicates that $main$ and sum are the *greatest* predicates that satisfy the equations. Notice that the formulas above (whose precise semantics will be introduced later) directly correspond to the definitions of the **main** and **sum** functions; for example, the part $n \leq 0 \Rightarrow k\ 0$ in the equation for the sum predicate corresponds to the then-part of the **sum** function. Watanabe et al. [23] have shown that verification of arbitrary regular properties (i.e., those expressible in the modal μ-calculus) of simply-typed, higher-order recursive functional programs can be reduced to HFL$_\mathbb{Z}$ validity checking in a similar (but a little more elaborated) manner: more precisely, given a closed program P and a regular property A, one can construct a closed HFL$_\mathbb{Z}$ formula $\varphi_{P,A}$ such that P satisfies A just if $\varphi_{P,A}$ is valid. Thus, an automated HFL$_\mathbb{Z}$ validity checker would yield a very general automated verification tool for higher-order functional programs.

As the first step towards the development of an automated HFL$_\mathbb{Z}$ validity checker, in the present paper, we focus on a fragment of HFL$_\mathbb{Z}$ called νHFL$_\mathbb{Z}$, and develop an automated method for validity checking of νHFL$_\mathbb{Z}$ formulas (note that our method is sound but necessarily incomplete, as the problem is undecidable). The fragment νHFL$_\mathbb{Z}$ is obtained by removing the least fixpoint operator from HFL$_\mathbb{Z}$. A νHFL$_\mathbb{Z}$ validity checker can be used for verifying various properties of higher-order functional programs, such as safety and non-termination properties. In fact, the verification of properties expressible in the ν-only fragment of the modal μ-calculus can be reduced to validity checking of a νHFL$_\mathbb{Z}$ formula. This fragment is powerful enough to verify the (un)reachability problem in the presence of both angelic and demonic branches; in contrast, most of the previous automated verification tools for higher-order programs (such as MoCHi [11]) only deal with demonic branches. A νHFL$_\mathbb{Z}$ validity checker can also be used as a building block for a (forthcoming) full HFL$_\mathbb{Z}$ validity checker (which can then be used for verification of arbitrary properties expressive in the full the modal μ-calculus, like "an event A occurs infinitely often"), by using the technique developed for a first-order fixpoint logic [10].

Our method is based on predicate abstraction and counterexample-guided abstraction refinement (CEGAR). The techniques of predicate abstraction and CEGAR have been used in the context of model checking. In this paper, we adapt them for proving the validity of a νHFL$_\mathbb{Z}$ formula. Given a νHFL$_\mathbb{Z}$ formula φ and a set of predicates on integers, we compute a *pure* HFL formula φ' without integers, as an underapproximation of φ, so that if φ' is valid, so is φ. The validity of the pure HFL formula φ' is decidable; one can use either an HFL model checker (such as HomuSat [6]) or a HORS model checker (such as [8]) based on the reduction from HORS to HFL model checking [9]. For example, suppose that we have chosen the predicate $\lambda x.x > 0$ for abstracting integers. Then, the integer predicate $\lambda x.\lambda y.x + y > 0$ can be abstracted to $\lambda b_{x>0}.\lambda b'_{y>0}.b_{x>0} \wedge b'_{y>0}$, where $b_{x>0}$ ($b'_{y>0}$, resp.) is instantiated to `true` just if the value of the original argument x (y, resp.) is positive. The formula $\lambda b_{x>0}.\lambda b'_{y>0}.b_{x>0} \wedge b'_{y>0}$ semantically represents the predicate $\lambda x.\lambda y.x > 0 \wedge y > 0$, which is an underapproximation of the original predicate $\lambda x.\lambda y.x + y > 0$. As in the ordinary predicate abstraction technique for model checking, the success of validity checking heavily depends on the choice of the predicates used for abstraction; we thus use CEGAR to refine the set of predicates in an on-demand manner, based on counterexamples. Due to the generality of νHFL$_\mathbb{Z}$ validity checking (which, as mentioned earlier, can deal with the reachability in the presence of both angelic and demonic branches), we need a more elaborate method for CEGAR than the previous methods for CEGAR for higher-order program verification.

We have implemented an automated νHFL$_\mathbb{Z}$ validity checker PAHFL based on the method above, and compared through experiments with two related tools: Horus [2] and MOCHI [11]. Horus is a satisfiability checker for HoCHC, higher-order constrained Horn clauses. As we discuss in Sect. 2, the validity checking problem for νHFL$_\mathbb{Z}$ and the satisfiability problem for HoCHC are reducible to each other; thus Horus can also be used as a νHFL$_\mathbb{Z}$ validity checker. As demonstrated through the experiments, however, Horus is not powerful enough to prove the validity of many formulas obtained from higher-order program verification problems, although Horus often terminates quickly when it succeeds. MOCHI [11] is an automated program verification tool for OCaml, developed based on HORS model checking. The original version of MOCHI is tailor-made for (non-)reachability verification, although various extensions for proving and disproving termination and fair termination have been developed later. In contrast, our νHFL$_\mathbb{Z}$ validity checker can deal with a wider class of properties than the original version of MOCHI, in a more uniform and general manner than the various extensions of MOCHI mentioned above. According to our experiments, PAHFL is competitive with MOCHI, despite the generality.

The rest of this paper is structured as follows. Section 2 reviews the definition of HFL$_\mathbb{Z}$ and its validity checking problem. Sections 3 and 4 formalize our method. Section 5 reports our implementation and experiments. Section 6 discusses related work and Sect. 7 concludes the paper.

2   Preliminaries: Higher-Order Fixed-Point Logic νHFL$_\mathbb{Z}$

This section reviews (modal-free) νHFL$_\mathbb{Z}$ and its *validity checking problem*. The logic νHFL$_\mathbb{Z}$ is a higher-order logic with arithmetic (over integers) and greatest fixed-point operators $\nu x.\psi$, hence the name. It is a fragment of HFL$_\mathbb{Z}$ [13], which is an extension of HFL [22] with arithmetic (over integers).[2]

---

[2] It is possible to further extend HFL$_\mathbb{Z}$ with other data structures such as lists and trees, and extend our predicate abstraction method accordingly, as long as the background solvers (such as SMT and CHC solvers) support them.

$$\frac{}{\Gamma, x : \tau \vdash_{\text{ST}} x : \tau} \text{ (S-Var)} \qquad \frac{b \in \{\text{true}, \text{false}\}}{\Gamma \vdash_{\text{ST}} b : \bullet} \text{ (S-Bool)} \qquad \frac{}{\Gamma \vdash_{\text{ST}} n : \text{int}} \text{ (S-Int)}$$

$$\frac{\Gamma \vdash_{\text{ST}} a_i : \text{int for each } i}{\Gamma \vdash_{\text{ST}} p(a_1, ..., a_n) : \bullet} \text{ (S-Pred)} \qquad \frac{\Gamma \vdash_{\text{ST}} a_i : \text{int for each } i}{\Gamma \vdash_{\text{ST}} op(a_1, ..., a_n) : \text{int}} \text{ (S-Op)}$$

$$\frac{\Gamma \vdash_{\text{ST}} \psi : \bar{\tau} \to \tau \qquad \Gamma \vdash_{\text{ST}} \bar{\psi} : \bar{\tau}}{\Gamma \vdash_{\text{ST}} \psi\bar{\psi} : \tau} \text{ (S-App)} \qquad \frac{\Gamma, x : \bar{\tau} \vdash_{\text{ST}} \psi : \tau}{\Gamma \vdash_{\text{ST}} \lambda x^{\bar{\tau}}.\psi : \bar{\tau} \to \tau} \text{ (S-Abs)}$$

$$\frac{\Gamma \vdash_{\text{ST}} \psi_1 : \bullet \qquad \Gamma \vdash_{\text{ST}} \psi_2 : \bullet}{\Gamma \vdash_{\text{ST}} \psi_1 \wedge \psi_2 : \bullet} \text{ (S-And)} \qquad \frac{\Gamma \vdash_{\text{ST}} \psi_1 : \bullet \qquad \Gamma \vdash_{\text{ST}} \psi_2 : \bullet}{\Gamma \vdash_{\text{ST}} \psi_1 \vee \psi_2 : \bullet} \text{ (S-Or)}$$

$$\frac{\Gamma, x : \tau \vdash_{\text{ST}} \psi : \tau}{\Gamma \vdash_{\text{ST}} \nu x^{\tau}.\psi : \tau} \text{ (S-Nu)}$$

Fig. 1. Simple typing of νHFL$_\mathbb{Z}$

The set of *types*, ranged over by τ, is defined by:

$$\tau \text{ (types)} ::= \bullet \mid \bar{\tau} \to \tau \qquad \bar{\tau} \text{ (extended types)} ::= \tau \mid \text{int}.$$

The type $\bullet$ describes propositions. Note that int can occur only on the lefthand side of $\to$; for example, $\text{int} \to \text{int}$ is invalid. Every type τ can be written in the form $\tau_1 \to \cdots \to \tau_k \to \bullet$.

The set of νHFL$_\mathbb{Z}$ formulas, ranged over ψ, is defined by:

$$\begin{aligned}
\psi \text{ (formula)} \qquad &::= x^{\tau} \mid \text{true} \mid \text{false} \mid \psi_1 \vee \psi_2 \mid \psi_1 \wedge \psi_2 \\
&\quad \mid \nu x^{\tau}.\psi \mid \lambda x^{\bar{\tau}}.\psi \mid \psi\bar{\psi} \mid p(\tilde{a}) \\
a \text{ (arithmetic expression)} &::= n \mid x^{\text{int}} \mid op(\tilde{a}) \\
\bar{\psi} \text{ (extended formula)} \quad &::= \psi \mid a
\end{aligned}$$

Here, the metavariables x, n, p, and op respectively range over the sets of variables, integers, integer predicates (such as $<$), and integer operators (such as $+$). We often use infix notations for predicates and operators. The formula $\nu x^{\tau}.\psi$ denotes the greatest fixpoint of $\lambda x^{\tau}.\psi$. We often omit the type annotation on the shoulder of a variable.

We use a standard simple type system for the λ-calculus to restrict the shape of formulas. As usual, a *type environment*, denoted by the metavariable Γ, is a finite map from a set of variables to the set of extended types. The typing relation $\Gamma \vdash_{\text{ST}} \bar{\psi} : \bar{\tau}$ is defined by the rules in Fig. 1. Henceforth, we consider only well-typed formulas.

The interpretation of a type $\bar{\tau}$ is a poset $(\mathbb{D}_{\bar{\tau}}, \sqsubseteq_{\bar{\tau}})$, inductively defined by:

$$\begin{aligned}
\mathbb{D}_\bullet &:= \{tt, ff\} & \sqsubseteq_\bullet &:= \{(ff, ff), (ff, tt), (tt, tt)\} \\
\mathbb{D}_{\text{int}} &:= \mathbb{Z} & \sqsubseteq_{\text{int}} &:= \{(n, n) \mid n \in \mathbb{Z}\} \\
\mathbb{D}_{\bar{\tau} \to \tau} &:= \mathbb{D}_{\bar{\tau}} \to \mathbb{D}_{\tau} & \sqsubseteq_{\bar{\tau} \to \tau} &:= \{(f, g) \mid \forall v \in \mathbb{D}_{\bar{\tau}}. f(v) \sqsubseteq_{\tau} g(v)\}.
\end{aligned}$$

Here, $\mathbb{D}_{\bar{\tau}} \to \mathbb{D}_{\tau}$ denotes the set of *monotone* functions from $\mathbb{D}_{\bar{\tau}}$ to $\mathbb{D}_{\tau}$. Note that $(\mathbb{D}_{\tau}, \sqsubseteq_{\tau})$ is a complete lattice (although $(\mathbb{D}_{\text{int}}, \sqsubseteq_{\text{int}})$ is not). Hence, for every function $f \in \mathbb{D}_{\tau \to \tau}$, there exists a greatest fixpoint. $\mathrm{gfp}(f)$ of f, given by: $\mathrm{gfp}(f) = \bigsqcup \{\, v \in \mathbb{D}_\tau \mid v \sqsubseteq_\tau f(v) \,\}$.

We define the interpretation of formulas. Given a type environment Γ, a *valuation for Γ* is a mapping ρ such that $\rho(x) \in \mathbb{D}_\tau$ for each $(x : \tau) \in \Gamma$. We assume that the interpretations $[\![op]\!]$ and $[\![p]\!]$ of operators and atomic predicates are given a priori. For a formula $\Gamma \vdash_{\mathrm{ST}} \psi : \tau$ and a valuation ρ for Γ, the interpretation $[\![\psi]\!]_\rho$ is defined by:

$$[\![x]\!]_\rho := \rho(x) \qquad [\![\mathbf{true}]\!]_\rho := t\!t \qquad [\![\mathbf{false}]\!]_\rho := f\!\!f \qquad [\![n]\!]_\rho := n$$

$$[\![op(a_1, \ldots, a_n)]\!]_\rho := [\![op]\!]([\![a_1]\!]_\rho, \ldots, [\![a_n]\!]_\rho)$$

$$[\![p(a_1, \ldots, a_n)]\!]_\rho := [\![p]\!]([\![a_1]\!]_\rho, \ldots, [\![a_n]\!]_\rho)$$

$$[\![\psi\, \bar{\psi}]\!]_\rho := [\![\psi]\!]_\rho([\![\bar{\psi}]\!]_\rho) \qquad [\![\lambda x^\tau.\psi]\!]_\rho = \{\, v \mapsto [\![\psi]\!]_{\rho \cup \{x \mapsto v\}} \mid v \in \mathbb{D}_{\bar{\tau}} \,\}$$

$$[\![\nu x^\tau.\psi]\!]_\rho := \mathrm{gfp}([\![\lambda x^\tau.\psi]\!]_\rho).$$

For a formula ψ of type $\bullet$, we write $\rho \models \psi$ to mean $[\![\psi]\!]_\rho = t\!t$. If $\rho \models \psi$ for every valuation ρ, we write $\models \psi$ and say that ψ is *valid*. The $\nu\mathrm{HFL}_\mathbb{Z}$ *validity checking problem* asks if a formula of type $\bullet$ is valid. Since the universal quantifiers are definable (see Examples 3 and 4 below), we can assume without loss of generality that an input of the validity checking problem is a closed formula. The validity checking problem for $\nu\mathrm{HFL}_\mathbb{Z}$ is undecidable.

Example 1. Let ψ be $\nu X.\lambda n.(n = 0 \vee (n > 0 \wedge X(n-2)))$. Then $\models \psi(n)$ holds just if n is a non-negative even number. □

Example 2. The example in Sect. 1 is expressed by $\forall n.main\ n$, where $main$ is defined by:

$$main := \lambda n^{\mathrm{int}}.sum\ (\lambda x.\lambda k.k(x+x))\ n\ (\lambda r.r \geq n)$$
$$sum := \nu sum^\tau.\lambda f^{\mathrm{int} \to (\mathrm{int} \to \bullet) \to \bullet}.\lambda n^{\mathrm{int}}.\lambda k^{\mathrm{int} \to \bullet}.(n > 0 \vee k\ 0)$$
$$\wedge (n \leq 0 \vee f\ n\ (\lambda x^{\mathrm{int}}.sum\ f\ (n-1)\ \lambda y^{\mathrm{int}}.k(x+y)))$$
$$\tau := (\mathrm{int} \to (\mathrm{int} \to \bullet) \to \bullet) \to \mathrm{int} \to (\mathrm{int} \to \bullet) \to \bullet.$$

Note that the subformula $n > 0 \vee k\ 0$ is equivalent to $n \leq 0 \Rightarrow k\ 0$, which in turn corresponds to the then-part of the sum function in the source program. We emphasize again that the formula above mimics the structure of the source program in the continuation passing style, where the answer type of the source program corresponds to the type $\bullet$ of formulas. □

Example 3. The universal quantifier over integers is definable. Let $\mathrm{forall}_{\mathrm{int}} := \lambda f^{\mathrm{int} \to \bullet}.\Big((\nu X^{\mathrm{int} \to \bullet}.\lambda y^{\mathrm{int}}.(f\ y) \wedge (X\ (y+1)) \wedge (X\ (y-1)))\ 0\Big)$. Then, given a formula of type $\mathrm{int} \to \bullet$, one has $[\![\mathrm{forall}_{\mathrm{int}}\ \psi]\!]_\rho = t\!t$ iff $\forall n \in \mathbb{Z}. [\![\psi]\!]_\rho(n) = t\!t$. □

Example 4. The universal quantifiers over predicates can be given without using the fixed-point operators. Since the interpretation of a formula is monotone, $[\![\psi]\!]_\rho(\bot_\tau) = t\!t$ if and only if $\forall v \in \mathbb{D}_\tau. [\![\psi]\!]_\rho(v) = t\!t$, where $\bot_\tau$ is the least element of $\mathbb{D}_\tau$. Since $\bot_\tau = [\![\lambda x_1.\ldots.\lambda x_k.\texttt{false}]\!]$ (where $\tau = \tau_1 \to \cdots \to \tau_k \to \bullet$), the universal quantifier can be defined by $forall_\tau := \lambda f^{\tau \to \bullet}.f\,(\lambda x_1.\ldots.\lambda x_k.\texttt{false})$. One can define existential quantifiers on predicates by the same technique, using the greatest element $\lambda x_1.\ldots.\lambda x_k.\texttt{true}$ instead of the least one.[3]   □

A νHFL *formula* is a νHFL$_\mathbb{Z}$ formula that has no arithmetic subformula. It is known that the validity checking of closed νHFL formulas is decidable. We shall use νHFL as the target of the predicate abstraction in Sect. 3.

Remark 1. The νHFL$_\mathbb{Z}$ validity checking problem is polynomial-time equivalent to the HoCHC satisfiability checking problem [2] with arithmetic as the underlying constraint language. The mutual reductions between the two problems are obtained in essentially the same way as those between the validity checking problem for the first-order fragment of νHFL$_\mathbb{Z}$ and the satisfiability problem for CHC [10]. Existential quantifiers in HoCHC correspond to universal quantifiers in νHFL$_\mathbb{Z}$, which can be expressed as discussed in Examples 3 and 4 above.   □

3   Predicate Abstraction

This section formalizes a predicate abstraction method for νHFL$_\mathbb{Z}$. It computes a pure νHFL formula φ (for which validity checking is decidable) as an underapproximation of an input νHFL$_\mathbb{Z}$ formula ψ, by abstracting information about integers. We can then check the validity of φ by using either a (pure) νHFL model checker [6], or using a reduction to HORS model checking [9]. If φ is valid, we can conclude that the original formula ψ is also valid; otherwise, we proceed to the CEGAR phase described in Sect. 4.

Following the predicate abstraction method of Kobayashi et al. [11] for higher-order functional programs, we use *abstraction types* to express how each subformula should be abstracted. The syntax of *abstraction type* is given by:

$$
\begin{array}{lll}
\text{(abstraction type) } \sigma & ::= \bullet \mid x : \texttt{int}[P_1, ..., P_k] \to \sigma \mid \sigma_1 \to \sigma_2 \\
\text{(predicate) } & P, Q ::= \texttt{true} \mid \texttt{false} \mid p(\tilde{a}) \mid P_1 \wedge P_2 \mid P_1 \vee P_2 \\
\text{(environment) } & \Sigma \quad ::= \emptyset \mid \Sigma, x : \texttt{int} \mid \Sigma, x : \sigma
\end{array}
$$

Here x in $x:\texttt{int}[P_1, \ldots, P_k] \to \sigma$ is a binding variable whose scope is $P_1, \ldots, P_k$ and σ. The type $(x : \texttt{int}[P_1, \ldots, P_n] \to \sigma)$ describes predicates whose first integer argument x should be abstracted by using the predicates $P_1, \ldots, P_n$. For example, given an abstraction type $(x : \texttt{int}[x = 0, 1 < x, x < 5] \to \bullet)$, the predicate $\lambda x.(0 \le x \wedge x \le 10)$ on integers is abstracted to the predicate $\lambda b_{x=0} b_{1<x} b_{x<5}.\big(b_{x=0} \vee (b_{1<x} \wedge b_{x<5})\big)$ on Booleans $b_{x=0}, b_{1<x}$, and $b_{x<5}$, which respectively represent underapproximations of the values of $x = 0$, $1 < x$, and $x < 5$. Thus, $(\lambda x.(0 \le x \wedge x \le 10))2$ is abstracted to $(\lambda b_{x=0} b_{1<x} b_{x<5}.b_{x=0} \vee (b_{1<x} \wedge b_{x<5}))\texttt{false}\,\texttt{true}\,\texttt{true}$, which evaluates to $t\!t$. Intuitively, the abstract Boolean predicate above corresponds to $\lambda x.(x = 0 \vee (1 < x \wedge x < 5))$, which is an underapproximation of the original predicate $\lambda x.(0 \le x \wedge x \le 10)$. As another

---

[3] In contrast, the existential quantifier over integers is not definable in this logic.

example, let us consider the higher-order predicate $\lambda x.\lambda k.k(x+x)$. Given the abstraction type $x:\text{int}[x \geq 0] \to (r:\text{int}[r \geq x] \to \bullet) \to \bullet$, $\lambda x.\lambda k.k(x+x)$ is abstracted to $\lambda b_{x \geq 0}.\lambda k'.k'\,b_{x \geq 0}$. Here, k' expects as its argument an underapproximation of $r \geq x$, where r refers to the argument $x+x$ of k in the original expression. Since $x \geq 0$ implies $x+x \geq x$, we can pass $b_{x \geq 0}$ to k' as an underapproximation of $r \geq x$. The formula $(\lambda x.\lambda k.k(x+x))1\,(\lambda r.r \geq 1)$ is then abstracted to $(\lambda b_{x \geq 0}.\lambda k'.k'\,b_{x \geq 0})\text{true}\,(\lambda b_{r \geq 1}.b_{r \geq 1})$, which evaluates to true. In contrast, by using the same abstraction type, $(\lambda x.\lambda k.k(x+x))1\,(\lambda r.r \geq 2)$ is abstracted to $(\lambda b_{x \geq 0}.\lambda k'.k'\,b_{x \geq 0})\text{true}\,(\lambda b_{r \geq 1}.\text{false})$, which is equivalent to false; note that $b_{r \geq 1}$ only gives an underapproximation of $r \geq 1$, which is not useful to conclude $r \geq 2$, although r in the original formula evaluates to 2.[4] As the last example shows, the result of predicate abstraction only provides an underapproximation of the original formula (which is equivalent to true in the last example).

In order to clarify the shapes of input and output formulas of predicate abstraction, let us define the following two translations from abstraction types to simple types:

$$\bullet^{\sharp} := \bullet \quad (x:\text{int}[P_1,...,P_k] \to \sigma)^{\sharp} = \text{int} \to \sigma^{\sharp} \quad (\sigma_1 \to \sigma_2)^{\sharp} = \sigma_1^{\sharp} \to \sigma^{\sharp}$$

$$\bullet^{\flat} = \bullet \quad (x:\text{int}[P_1,...,P_k] \to \sigma)^{\flat} = \overbrace{\bullet \to \cdots \to \bullet}^{k} \to \sigma^{\flat} \quad (\sigma_1 \to \sigma_2)^{\flat} = \sigma_1^{\flat} \to \sigma^{\flat}.$$

Given an abstraction type σ, our predicate abstraction converts a $\nu\text{HFL}_{\mathbb{Z}}$ formula of type $\sigma^{\sharp}$ to a νHFL formula of type $\sigma^{\flat}$; for instance, as in the above examples, the abstraction type $x:\text{int}[x = 0, 1 < x, x < 5] \to \bullet$ is used to abstract a formula of type $(x:\text{int}[x = 0, 1 < x, x < 5] \to \bullet)^{\sharp} = \text{int} \to \bullet$ to a formula of type $(x:\text{int}[x = 0, 1 < x, x < 5] \to \bullet)^{\flat} = \bullet \to \bullet \to \bullet \to \bullet$.

Our predicate abstraction is formalized as the *predicate abstraction relation* $\Sigma \mid \Theta \vdash \psi : \sigma \rightsquigarrow \varphi$ (where the metavariable Θ denotes a sequence of predicates $P_1, \ldots, P_k$; we sometimes use set notations for Θ when the order is not important) given in Fig. 2. It means that assuming that the free variables in ψ are abstracted according to the abstraction type environment Σ, and that underapproximations of $\Theta = P_1, \ldots, P_k$ are available as special Boolean variables $b_{P_1}, \ldots, b_{P_k}$, ψ can be abstracted to ϕ according to the abstraction type σ. The abstraction relation $\Sigma \mid P_1, \ldots, P_k \vdash \psi : \sigma \rightsquigarrow \varphi$ is used to convert a $\nu\text{HFL}_{\mathbb{Z}}$ formula ψ such that $\Sigma^{\sharp} \vdash \psi : \sigma^{\sharp}$ to a νHFL formula φ such that $\Sigma^{\flat}, b_{P_1} : \bullet, \ldots, b_{P_k} : \bullet \vdash \varphi : \sigma^{\flat}$, where $\Sigma^{\sharp}$ and $\Sigma^{\flat}$ are pointwise extensions of the corresponding translations for types, defined by:

$$\emptyset^{\sharp} := \emptyset \quad (\Sigma, x:\text{int})^{\sharp} := \Sigma^{\sharp}, x:\text{int} \quad (\Sigma, x:\sigma)^{\sharp} := \Sigma^{\sharp}, x:\sigma^{\sharp}$$

$$\emptyset^{\flat} := \emptyset \quad (\Sigma, x:\text{int})^{\flat} := \Sigma^{\flat} \quad (\Sigma, x:\sigma)^{\flat} := \Sigma^{\flat}, x:\sigma^{\flat}$$

We explain the main rules in Fig. 2. (A-PRED) translates a predicate into a corresponding Boolean variable provided that the predicate is currently available. In (A-INTABS), the integer variable x of $\lambda x.\psi$ is translated into Boolean

---

[4] We can prove the validity of $(\lambda x.\lambda k.k(x+x))1\,(\lambda r.r \geq 2)$ if we use a different abstraction type, like $x:\text{int}[\,] \to (r:\text{int}[r \geq 2x] \to \bullet) \to \bullet$ for $\lambda x.\lambda k.k(x+x)$.

$$\frac{}{\Sigma, x : \sigma \mid \Theta \vdash x : \sigma \rightsquigarrow x} \quad \text{(A-VAR)}$$

$$\frac{P \in \Theta}{\Sigma \mid \Theta \vdash P : \bullet \rightsquigarrow b_P} \quad \text{(A-PRED)}$$

$$\frac{\Sigma \mid \Theta \vdash \psi : (x : \mathtt{int}[P_1, ..., P_k] \to \sigma) \rightsquigarrow \varphi \qquad \Sigma \vdash_{\mathrm{ST}} a : \mathtt{int}}{\Sigma \mid \Theta, [a/x]\tilde{P} \vdash \psi a : [a/x]\sigma \rightsquigarrow \varphi \tilde{b}_{[a/x]P}} \quad \text{(A-INTAPP)}$$

$$\frac{\Sigma, x : \mathtt{int} \mid \Theta, \tilde{P} \vdash \psi : \sigma \rightsquigarrow \varphi}{\Sigma \mid \Theta \vdash \lambda x.\psi : (x : \mathtt{int}[\tilde{P}] \to \sigma) \rightsquigarrow \lambda \tilde{b}_P.\varphi} \quad \text{(A-INTABS)}$$

$$\frac{\Sigma \mid \Theta \vdash \psi_1 : \sigma_1 \to \sigma_2 \rightsquigarrow \varphi_1 \qquad \Sigma \mid \Theta \vdash \psi_2 : \sigma_1 \rightsquigarrow \varphi_2}{\Sigma \mid \Theta \vdash \psi_1\psi_2 : \sigma_2 \rightsquigarrow \varphi_1\varphi_2} \quad \text{(A-APP)}$$

$$\frac{\Sigma, x : \sigma_1 \mid \Theta \vdash \psi : \sigma_2 \rightsquigarrow \varphi}{\Sigma \mid \Theta \vdash \lambda x.\psi : \sigma_1 \to \sigma_2 \rightsquigarrow \lambda x.\varphi} \quad \text{(A-ABS)}$$

$$\frac{\Sigma \mid \Theta \vdash \psi_1 : \bullet \rightsquigarrow \varphi_1 \qquad \Sigma \mid \Theta \vdash \psi_2 : \bullet \rightsquigarrow \varphi_2}{\Sigma \mid \Theta \vdash \psi_1 \wedge \psi_2 \rightsquigarrow \varphi_1 \wedge \varphi_2} \quad \text{(A-AND)}$$

$$\frac{\Sigma \mid \Theta \vdash \psi_1 : \bullet \rightsquigarrow \varphi_1 \qquad \Sigma \mid \Theta \vdash \psi_2 : \bullet \rightsquigarrow \varphi_2}{\Sigma \mid \Theta \vdash \psi_1 \vee \psi_2 \rightsquigarrow \varphi_1 \vee \varphi_2} \quad \text{(A-OR)}$$

$$\frac{\Sigma, x : \sigma \mid \Theta \vdash \psi : \sigma \rightsquigarrow \varphi}{\Sigma \mid \Theta \vdash \nu x.\psi : \sigma \rightsquigarrow \nu x.\varphi} \quad \text{(A-NU)}$$

$$\frac{\Sigma \mid \Theta \vdash \psi : \sigma \rightsquigarrow \varphi \qquad \Sigma \vdash \varphi : (\Theta, \sigma) \preceq (\Theta', \sigma') \rightsquigarrow \varphi'}{\Sigma \mid \Theta' \vdash \psi : \sigma' \rightsquigarrow \varphi'} \quad \text{(A-COERCE)}$$

$$\frac{X : \bullet^k \to \bullet \vdash_{\mathrm{ST}} \xi : \bullet^l \to \bullet \qquad [\![XP_1...P_k]\!]_\rho \sqsupseteq_\bullet [\![\xi Q_1...Q_l]\!]_\rho \text{ for all } \rho \text{ s.t. } \mathrm{dom}(\rho) = \{X\} \cup \{x \mid x : \mathtt{int} \in \Sigma\}}{\Sigma \vdash \varphi : (P_1, ..., P_k, \bullet) \preceq (Q_1, ..., Q_l, \bullet) \rightsquigarrow [\lambda b_{P_1}...b_{P_k}.\varphi/X]\xi b_{Q_1}...b_{Q_l}} \quad \text{(AC-BASE)}$$

$$\frac{\Sigma, x : \mathtt{int} \vdash \varphi b_{P_1}...b_{P_k} : ((\Theta_1, P_1, ..., P_k), \sigma_1) \preceq ((\Theta_2, Q_1, ..., Q_l), \sigma_2) \rightsquigarrow \varphi'}{\Sigma \vdash \varphi : (\Theta_1, x : \mathtt{int}[P_1, ..., P_k] \to \sigma_1) \preceq (\Theta_2, x : \mathtt{int}[Q_1, ..., Q_l] \to \sigma_2) \rightsquigarrow \lambda b_{Q_1} \cdots b_{Q_l}.\varphi'} \quad \text{(AC-INTARROW)}$$

$$\frac{\Sigma, x : \sigma_1' \vdash x : (\varepsilon, \sigma_1') \preceq (\Theta', \sigma_1) \rightsquigarrow \varphi_1 \qquad \Sigma, y : \sigma_1 \vdash \varphi y : (\Theta, \sigma_2) \preceq (\Theta', \sigma_2') \rightsquigarrow \varphi_2'}{\Sigma \vdash \varphi : (\Theta, \sigma_1 \to \sigma_2) \preceq (\Theta', \sigma_1' \to \sigma_2') \rightsquigarrow \lambda x.[\varphi_1/y]\varphi_2'} \quad \text{(AC-ARROW)}$$

Fig. 2. Abstraction relation

variables $b_{P_1}, ..., b_{P_k}$ where $P_1, ..., P_k$ is predicates attached to x; the predicates $P_1, ..., P_k$, as well as corresponding variables b_{P_i}, are available in the body ψ. These Boolean variables are supplied in (A-INTAPP), which applies Boolean variables $\widetilde{b_P}$ to the abstraction φ of the function. The (A-COERCE) rule is used to change the abstraction type σ and predicates $\tilde{P}$ in a judgment. Its major premise is the coercion relation $\Sigma \vdash \varphi : (\Theta, \sigma) \preceq (\Theta', \sigma') \rightsquigarrow \varphi'$, which we shall explain below.

The *coercion relation* $\Sigma \vdash \varphi : (\Theta, \sigma) \preceq (\Theta', \sigma') \rightsquigarrow \varphi'$ transforms an abstraction φ following (Θ, σ) into another abstraction φ' following (Θ', σ'). For example, let $\Theta = (x = 0, \tilde{P})$ and $\Theta' = (x \leq 0, x \geq 0, \tilde{P})$. Then an abstraction φ following (Θ, σ) can be rewritten to another abstraction $[(b_{x \leq 0} \wedge b_{x \geq 0})/b_{x=0}]\varphi$ following (Θ', σ) since $\models x = 0 \iff (x \leq 0 \wedge x \geq 0)$; hence $\Sigma \vdash \varphi : (\Theta, \sigma) \preceq (\Theta', \sigma) \rightsquigarrow [(b_{x \leq 0} \wedge b_{x \geq 0})/b_{x=0}]\varphi$.[5] Another interesting example is

$$\Sigma \vdash \varphi : ((x \leq 0, x \geq 0), \bullet) \preceq ((), \bullet)$$
$$\rightsquigarrow ([\mathrm{true}/b_{x \leq 0}, \mathrm{false}/b_{x \geq 0}]\varphi) \wedge ([\mathrm{false}/b_{x \leq 0}, \mathrm{true}/b_{x \geq 0}]\varphi).$$

Although an abstraction following $((), \bullet)$ has no information on x, we know that $\models (x \leq 0) \vee (x \geq 0)$ and the above coercion means that it suffices to check the two cases, namely the cases that $x \leq 0$ and that $x \geq 0$.[6] The most important rule is (AC-BASE), which is a generalization of the above argument. Since $[XP_1 \cdots P_k]_\rho \sqsupseteq_\bullet [\xi Q_1 \cdots Q_l]_\rho$ for arbitrary X, substituting $\lambda \tilde{b_P}.\varphi$ for X results in the judgment of the conclusion. Note that (AC-BASE) is non-deterministic in the choice of ξ. In general, the most precise ξ is given by the following formula.

$$\xi = \lambda \widetilde{b_Q}. \bigvee_{\substack{\Phi, \Psi \\ \models \Psi(\tilde{Q}) \Longrightarrow \Phi(\tilde{P})}} \left(\Psi(\widetilde{b_Q}) \wedge \left(\bigwedge_{\substack{\tilde{v} \in \{\mathrm{true}, \mathrm{false}\}^n \\ \models \Phi(\tilde{v})}} X \tilde{v} \right) \right)$$

where n and m are the lengths of $\tilde{P}$ and $\tilde{Q}$, and Φ and Ψ range over positive Boolean formulas over n and m variables. In practice, since computing the best abstraction is too costly, we restrict the shape and size of Ψ and Φ (for example, Ψ is restricted to conjunctive formulas of a certain size, as in [1]).

We present basic properties of the proposed abstraction. The first property is soundness, as stated in the following theorem; see [7] for a proof.

Theorem 1 (Soundness of predicate abstraction). *Suppose* $\vdash \psi : \bullet \rightsquigarrow \varphi$. *If φ is valid, so is ψ.*

The second property is about expressivity. The theorem below (see [7] for a proof) says that the proposed predicate abstraction (followed by νHFL validity checking) is at least as expressive as a *refinement intersection type system* (see [7] for the definition). In particular, this result indicates that our approach is more

---

[5] More precisely there exists a formula φ' such that $\Sigma \vdash \varphi : (\Theta, \sigma) \preceq (\Theta', \sigma) \rightsquigarrow \varphi'$ and $\varphi' =_{\beta\eta} [(b_{x \leq 0} \wedge b_{x \geq 0})/b_{x=0}]\varphi$.

[6] Note that the case where both $x \leq 0$ and $x \geq 0$ hold (i.e. $x = 0$) is not problematic because of monotonicity: if $[\mathrm{true}/b_{x \leq 0}, \mathrm{false}/b_{x \geq 0}]\varphi$ is true, then $[\mathrm{true}/b_{x \leq 0}, \mathrm{true}/b_{x \geq 0}]\varphi$ is true as well.

powerful than the approach of Horus for HoCHC [2], because their approach is based on a refinement type system *without intersection types*.

Theorem 2 (Completeness with respect to refinement intersection system). *If $\vdash \psi : \text{tt}$ is provable in the refinement dependent intersection type system, then there exists a νHFL formula φ such that $\vdash \psi : \bullet \rightsquigarrow \varphi$ and φ is valid.*

As indicated in the example below, an abstraction of a valid formula is not necessarily valid. One needs to find a good abstraction type to obtain an abstraction that is valid.

Example 5. Let $\psi := \psi_0 \, 7 \, \psi_1$ where

$$\psi_0 := (\lambda n.\lambda f.(f\,5) \wedge (f\,n)) \quad \text{and} \quad \psi_1 := (\lambda y.(0 \leq y \wedge y \leq 10)).$$

It is easy to see that ψ is valid. For the abstraction type $\sigma_0 := \big(n : \text{int}[0 \leq n] \rightarrow (y : \text{int}[0 \leq y, y \leq 5] \rightarrow \bullet) \rightarrow \bullet\big)$, we obtain:

$$\vdash \psi_0 : \sigma_0 \rightsquigarrow \lambda b_{0 \leq n}.\lambda f.$$
$$f\,\text{true}\,\text{true} \wedge \big((b_{0 \leq n} \wedge f\,\text{true}\,\text{false}) \vee (f\,\text{true}\,\text{false} \wedge f\,\text{false}\,\text{true})\big).$$

Here $f\,\text{true}\,\text{true}$ is the abstraction of $f\,5$ and the remaining part of the body of the function is the abstraction of $f\,n$. This is indeed the "most precise" abstraction of ψ_0 following σ_0. An abstraction of ψ_1 following $\sigma_2 := (y : \text{int}[0 \leq y, y \leq 5] \rightarrow \bullet)$ is $\lambda b_{0 \leq y} b_{y \leq 5}.b_{0 \leq y} \wedge b_{y \leq 5}$. Hence

$$\vdash \psi_0 \, 7 \, \psi_1 : \bullet \quad \rightsquigarrow$$
$$\Big(\lambda b_{0 \leq n}.\lambda f.f\,\text{true}\,\text{true} \wedge \big((b_{0 \leq n} \wedge f\,\text{true}\,\text{false})$$
$$\vee (f\,\text{true}\,\text{false} \wedge f\,\text{false}\,\text{true}))\Big)\text{true}\,(\lambda b_{0 \leq y} b_{y \leq 5}.b_{0 \leq y} \wedge b_{y \leq 5}).$$

The result of the abstraction is invalid. This suggests that a better abstraction type is required for ψ_0. □

Example 6. Recall Example 2. Let the abstraction type σ_{sum} for *sum* be:

$$(x{:}\text{int}[x \geq 0] \rightarrow (y{:}\text{int}[y \geq x] \rightarrow \bullet) \rightarrow \bullet) \rightarrow n{:}\text{int}[] \rightarrow (r{:}\text{int}[r \geq n] \rightarrow \bullet) \rightarrow \bullet.$$

The body ψ_{sum} of *sum* can be abstracted as follows.

$$\Gamma; n > 0, n \leq 0 \vdash \psi_{sum} : \sigma_{sum} \rightsquigarrow$$
$$(b_{n>0} \vee k\,b_{n \leq 0})$$
$$\wedge (b_{n \leq 0} \vee f\,b_{n>0}\,(\lambda b_{x \geq n}.sum\,f\,(\lambda b_{y \geq n-1}.k(b_{x \geq n} \wedge b_{y \geq n-1} \wedge b_{n \leq 0})))).$$

Here, $\Gamma = sum : \sigma_{sum}, r : \text{int}, f : (y : \text{int}[y \geq r] \rightarrow \bullet) \rightarrow \bullet, n : \text{int}, k : r : \text{int}[r \geq n] \rightarrow \bullet$. By (A-COERCE) (let ξ in (AC-BASE) be $(\lambda X.X\,\text{false}\,\text{true} \vee X\,\text{true}\,\text{false})X)$, we get:

$\Gamma; \vdash \psi_{sum} : \sigma_{sum} \rightsquigarrow (\lambda X.X \text{ false true} \vee X \text{ true false})$
$(\lambda b_{n>0} b_{n\leq 0}.(b_{n>0} \vee k\, b_{n\leq 0})$
$\quad \wedge (b_{n\leq 0} \vee f\, b_{n>0}\, (\lambda b_{x\geq n}.sum\, f\, (\lambda b_{y\geq n-1}.k(b_{x\geq n} \wedge b_{y\geq n-1} \wedge b_{n>0})))))).$

The output formula can be simplified to:

$$k \text{ true} \vee f \text{ true } \lambda b_{x\geq n}.sum\, f\, \lambda b_{y\geq n-1}.k(b_{x\geq n} \wedge b_{y\geq n-1}).$$

Thus, the whole formula is abstracted to $sum'\, (\lambda b_{x\geq 0}.\lambda k.k\, b_{x\geq 0})\, \lambda b_{r\geq n}.b_{r\geq n}$, where

$$sum' := \nu sum.\lambda f.\lambda k.k \text{ true} \vee f \text{ true } \lambda b_{x\geq n}.sum\, f\, \lambda b_{y\geq n-1}.k(b_{x\geq n} \wedge b_{y\geq n-1}),$$

which is equivalent to **true** (as can be confirmed by a HFL model checker); hence, we can conclude that the original formula is also valid. $\square$

4   Counterexample-Guided Abstraction Refinement

This section describes the second component of our method, counterexample-guided abstraction refinement (CEGAR). Let φ be an abstraction of ψ, i.e. $\vdash \psi :$ $\bullet \rightsquigarrow \varphi$. If φ is valid, then ψ is valid and we are done, as discussed in the previous section. Otherwise either ψ is invalid or the abstraction is too coarse (or both). Below we first introduce the notion of a counterexample (which shows why φ is invalid) in our context in Sect. 4.1. We then discuss, in Sect. 4.2, a way to determine whether the counterexample also implies the invalidity of ψ. If that is the case, we can conclude that ψ is invalid; otherwise, we refine the abstraction by finding new predicates, as discussed in Sect. 4.3.

4.1   Counterexample

In the context of our νHFL$_{\mathbb{Z}}$ validity checking, a counterexample is a witness of the invalidity of a closed proposition. Formally the set of *candidate counterexamples* used in this paper is given by the following grammar:

$$c ::= \text{false} \mid c \wedge * \mid * \wedge c \mid c \vee c.$$

Intuitively a candidate counterexample is a sufficiently large part of a formula, which ensures the invalidity of the formula; replacing each $*$ in a counterexample to an arbitrary formula results in a false formula.

A candidate counterexample c is a *counterexample of* ψ, written $c \triangleright \psi$, if c witnesses the invalidity of ψ. Intuitively $c \triangleright \psi$ means that ψ matches the pattern of c. For example, counterexamples of

$$((1 = 0) \wedge (10 > 1)) \vee ((4 \neq 2 + 2) \wedge (3 < 0))$$

$$\frac{\models \neg p(\tilde{a})}{\textbf{false} \triangleright p(\tilde{a})} \qquad \frac{c_1 \triangleright \varphi_1}{c_1 \wedge * \triangleright \varphi_1 \wedge \varphi_2} \qquad \frac{c_2 \triangleright \varphi_2}{* \wedge c_2 \triangleright \varphi_1 \wedge \varphi_2}$$

$$\frac{c_1 \triangleright \varphi_1 \qquad c_2 \triangleright \varphi_2}{c_1 \vee c_2 \triangleright \varphi_1 \vee \varphi_2} \qquad \frac{c \triangleright ([\varphi'/x]\varphi)\,\tilde{\psi}}{c \triangleright (\lambda x.\varphi)\,\varphi'\,\tilde{\psi}} \qquad \frac{c \triangleright ([\nu x.\varphi/x]\varphi)\,\tilde{\psi}}{c \triangleright (\nu x.\varphi)\,\tilde{\psi}}$$

Fig. 3. Rules for the counterexample relation $c \triangleright \psi$

are
$$\big(\textbf{false} \wedge *\big) \vee \big(\textbf{false} \wedge *\big) \quad \text{and} \quad \big(\textbf{false} \wedge *\big) \vee \big(* \wedge \textbf{false}\big).$$

Here, the subformulas $1 = 0$, $4 \neq 2+2$, and $3 < 0$ "match" **false**, since they are equivalent to **false**. The counterexamples above evaluate to **false** irrespectively of which formula we substitute for $*$.

The relation $c \triangleright \psi$ is formally defined inductively by the rules in Fig. 3.

Example 7. Let φ be the result of the abstraction in Example 5, i.e.,

$$\vdash \psi_0\,7\,\psi_1 : \bullet \quad \rightsquigarrow$$

$$\Big(\lambda b_{0 \leq n}.\lambda f.f\,\textbf{true}\,\textbf{true} \wedge \big((b_{0 \leq n} \wedge f\,\textbf{true}\,\textbf{false})$$

$$\vee (f\,\textbf{true}\,\textbf{false} \wedge f\,\textbf{false}\,\textbf{true})\big)\Big)\textbf{true}\,(\lambda b_{0 \leq y}b_{y \leq 5}.b_{0 \leq y} \wedge b_{y \leq 5}).$$

Then $c \triangleright \varphi$ for

$$c = * \wedge \big(* \wedge (* \wedge \textbf{false})\big) \vee \big(* \wedge (\textbf{false} \wedge *)\big).$$

In fact, we have

$$c \triangleright (\textbf{true} \wedge \textbf{true}) \wedge \Big((\textbf{true} \wedge (\textbf{true} \wedge \textbf{false})) \vee ((\textbf{true} \wedge \textbf{false}) \wedge (\textbf{false} \wedge \textbf{true}))\Big),$$

from which we can derive $c \triangleright \varphi$ by using the rule for β-redexes in Fig. 3.   □

Every invalid formula has a counterexample. This follows easily from the fact that, for co-continuous arguments, $[\![\nu x^\tau.\psi]\!]_\rho$ coincides with $\prod_{i \in \omega}[\![\lambda x^\tau.\psi]\!]^i_\rho(\top^\tau)$ in the semantics of νHFL$_\mathbb{Z}$ formulas[7]; see, e.g. Lemma 14 of [12]:

Proposition 1. *For any closed νHFL$_\mathbb{Z}$ formula ψ of type $\bullet$, $[\![\psi]\!] = ff$ if and only if $c \triangleright \psi$ for some c.*

Let ψ be a νHFL$_\mathbb{Z}$ formula, and φ be a νHFL formula obtained by applying predicate abstraction to φ, and suppose that φ is invalid. The goal of the rest of this subsection is to compute a set of candidate counterexamples for ψ.

By using a model-checker for νHFL (without arithmetic), we can obtain a counterexample c for φ (i.e., c such that $c \triangleright \varphi$). Note, however, that the shape of c does not necessarily match that of ψ, due to the conjunctions and disjunctions

---

[7] This is not the case for full HFL$_\mathbb{Z}$.

that may have been introduced in the predicate abstraction phase. For example, recall φ in Example 7, which is an abstraction of the formula ψ in Example 5. The counterexample c in Example 7 is not a counterexample of ψ. In fact, the original formula has just conjunctions, and the disjunctions (and also some of the conjunctions) in c have been introduced by the abstraction.

To address the issue above, we distinguish between boolean connectives in an original formula and those introduced in the abstraction phase, by writing $\bar{\wedge}$ and $\bar{\vee}$ for the latter. We assume that the boolean connectives in (AC-BASE) (used in ξ) are $\bar{\wedge}$ and $\bar{\vee}$. A counterexample with $\bar{\wedge}$ or $\bar{\vee}$ is called an *abstract counterexample*.

An abstract counterexample c induces a set of (candidate) counterexamples $\mathcal{C}(c)$ defined by:

$$\mathcal{C}(\mathtt{false}) := \{\mathtt{false}\} \qquad \mathcal{C}(c_1 \vee c_2) := \{c_1' \vee c_2' \mid c_i' \in \mathcal{C}(c_i)\}$$
$$\mathcal{C}(* \wedge c) := \{* \wedge c' \mid c' \in \mathcal{C}(c)\} \qquad \mathcal{C}(c \wedge *) := \{c' \wedge * \mid c' \in \mathcal{C}(c)\}$$
$$\mathcal{C}(c_1 \bar{\vee} c_2) := \mathcal{C}(c_1) \cup \mathcal{C}(c_2) \qquad \mathcal{C}(* \bar{\wedge} c) := \mathcal{C}(c) \qquad \mathcal{C}(c \bar{\wedge} *) := \mathcal{C}(c).$$

Example 8. The formula in Example 7 should be written as

$$\left(\lambda b_{0 \leq n}.\lambda f.f \,\mathtt{true}\,\mathtt{true} \wedge \left((b_{0 \leq n} \bar{\wedge} f \,\mathtt{true}\,\mathtt{false})\right.\right.$$
$$\left.\left. \bar{\vee} (f \,\mathtt{true}\,\mathtt{false} \bar{\wedge} f \,\mathtt{false}\,\mathtt{true})\right)\right)\mathtt{true} \,(\lambda b_{0 \leq y} b_{y \leq 5}.b_{0 \leq y} \wedge b_{y \leq 5}).$$

and an abstract counterexample is $c = * \wedge \left((* \bar{\wedge} (* \wedge \mathtt{false})) \bar{\vee} (* \bar{\wedge} (\mathtt{false} \wedge *))\right)$. Then $\mathcal{C}(c) = \{* \wedge (* \wedge \mathtt{false}), * \wedge (\mathtt{false} \wedge *)\}$. $\square$

Assume that $\vdash \psi : \bullet \rightsquigarrow \varphi$ and φ is invalid. Then a model-checker generates an abstract counterexample c of φ. We randomly pick a candidate counterexample from $\mathcal{C}(c)$ and proceed to feasibility checking.

4.2 Feasibility Check

Let ψ be a closed formula, and c be a candidate counterexample of ψ. We would like to check whether $c \triangleright \psi$.

The rules in Fig. 3 can be seen as the definition of a procedure for checking $c \triangleright \psi$. For example, to check whether $c_1 \vee c_2 \triangleright \psi_1 \vee \psi_2$, the procedure checks whether $c_1 \triangleright \psi_1$ and $c_2 \triangleright \psi_2$. If the candidate counterexample c comes from an abstract counterexample of an abstraction of ψ, the procedure to check $c \triangleright \psi$ terminates.[8]

If $c \triangleright \psi$, then ψ is invalid. Otherwise we refine the abstraction by using c, as discussed in the next subsection.

Remark 2. In the actual implementation, we allow ψ to contain free integer variables $x_1, \ldots, x_k$, and judge the validity of $\forall x_1, \ldots, x_k.\psi$. In this case, the feasibility check is a little more involved.

---

[8] This procedure does not terminate in general. An example is $\mathtt{false} \triangleright (\nu f.\lambda x.f\,x)\,0$.

4.3   Predicate Discovery and Abstraction Refinement

Let c be an infeasible candidate counterexample c of ψ. To improve the precision of abstraction, we would like to find predicates that are useful to show the validity of ψ. Our approach is based on a refinement dependent intersection type system.

Our type system is a variant of the refinement intersection type system for higher-order functional programs [19]. An important feature of our type system is a type of the form $\neg c$, for each candidate counterexample c. Intuitively, a formula ψ has type $\neg c$ if ψ does not have c as a counterexample (i.e. if $c \not\vdash \psi$). The typing rules include:

$$\frac{\Delta \mid \Phi \vdash \psi_2 : \neg c}{\Delta \mid \Phi \vdash \psi_1 \wedge \psi_2 : \neg(* \wedge c)} \quad \text{and} \quad \frac{\Delta \mid \Phi \vdash \psi_i : \neg c_i \quad (i = 1 \text{ or } 2)}{\Delta \mid \Phi \vdash \psi_1 \vee \psi_2 : \neg(c_1 \vee c_2)}$$

where Δ is a type environment and Φ is a precondition. The former rule checks the specified branch, ignoring the discarded part (i.e. ψ_1) corresponding to $*$. So $\vdash \mathtt{false} \wedge \mathtt{true} : \neg(* \wedge \mathtt{false})$ is a valid type judgment although $\mathtt{false} \wedge \mathtt{true}$ is an invalid formula. The latter rule says that, to show $(c_1 \vee c_2) \not\vdash (\psi_1 \vee \psi_2)$, it suffices to prove either $c_1 \not\vdash \psi$ or $c_2 \not\vdash \psi_2$. The complete list of typing rules can be found in [7].

Example 9. Here is an example of a derivation in the refinement intersection type system.

$$\frac{\dfrac{y : \mathtt{int} \mid y \leq 9 \vdash (y \leq 10) \; : \; \neg(\mathtt{false})}{y : \mathtt{int} \mid y \leq 9 \vdash (0 \leq y) \wedge (y \leq 10) \; : \; \neg(* \wedge \mathtt{false})}}{\epsilon \mid \mathtt{true} \vdash \lambda y.(0 \leq y) \wedge (y \leq 10)) \; : \; y\!:\!\{\mathtt{int} \mid y \leq 9\} \rightarrow \neg(* \wedge \mathtt{false})}$$

Although the condition $y \leq 9$ does not imply that the body is true, $y \leq 9$ implies that $* \wedge \mathtt{false}$ is not a valid counterexample for the body (since the right branch of the conjunction $y \leq 10$ is actually true).   □

The abstraction refinement phase proceeds as follows. Given an infeasible candidate counterexample c of ψ, we construct a derivation $\vdash \psi : \neg c$, a proof of $c \not\vdash \psi$. Then we extract predicates from the derivation.

We can use a template-based dependent type inference [19,20] to find a derivation for $\vdash \psi : \neg c$. We first prepare a template of each refinement type, which is completely determined by ψ and c. For example, the template for the formula ψ in Example 5 with candidate counterexample $* \wedge (* \wedge \mathtt{false})$ is

$(\lambda n.\lambda f.fn) \; :$
$\quad n\!:\!\{\mathtt{int} \mid P(n)\} \rightarrow \big(y\!:\!\{\mathtt{int} \mid Q(n,y)\} \rightarrow \neg(* \wedge \mathtt{false})\big) \rightarrow \neg(* \wedge \mathtt{false})$
$(\lambda y.(0 \leq y) \wedge (y \leq 10)) \; : \; y\!:\!\{\mathtt{int} \mid R(y)\} \rightarrow \neg(* \wedge \mathtt{false})$

where P, Q and R are predicate variables. We then generate constraints on predicate variables so that the formula has type $\neg c$ if and only if the constraints are satisfied, in a manner similar to [11]. We then solve the constraints by using a CHC solver [4,20] (see the remark below) and obtain a derivation for $\vdash \psi : \neg c$.

Remark 3. The constraints generated are actually more complex than those generated in the CEGAR phase of [11]. The constraints generated in our CEGAR phase are conjunctions of clauses of the form:

$$P_1(\tilde{x}_1) \vee \cdots \vee P_k(\tilde{x}_k) \Leftarrow A_1 \wedge \cdots \wedge A_m,$$

where $k \geq 0$, and each A_i is an atom of the form $P_\ell(\tilde{y})$ or $p(\tilde{a})$. The constraints are acyclic (in the sense that there is no circular dependency like $P(x) \vee \cdots \Leftarrow Q(x) \wedge \cdots$ and $Q(x) \vee \cdots \Leftarrow P(x) \wedge \cdots$). In contrast, the constraints generated in the CEGAR phase of [11] are acyclic CHCs, obtained by imposing the restriction $k \leq 1$ to the form of constraints above. Thanks to the acyclicity, we can solve the extended constraints by invoking a CHC solver multiple times.   □

The extraction of predicates from a derivation for $\vdash \psi : \neg c$ is rather straightforward. For example, suppose a subformula $\lambda x.\psi_0$ of ψ that has simple type $\text{int} \rightarrow \tau$. Because our type system has intersection types, this subformula may have several types, say $x : \{\text{int} \mid P_i(x)\} \rightarrow \delta_i$ for each $i = 1, \ldots, k$. Then the extracted abstraction type for this subformula is $x : \text{int}[P_1, \ldots, P_k] \rightarrow \sigma$ for some σ.

Example 10. Let ψ be a formula in Example 5, i.e. $\psi = \psi_0 \, 7 \, \psi_1$ where $\psi_0 = (\lambda n.\lambda f.f5 \wedge fn)$ and $\psi_1 = (\lambda y.(0 \leq y) \wedge (y \leq 10))$. Assume that a candidate counterexample is $* \wedge (* \wedge \texttt{false})$ (cf. Example 8). A derivation of $\vdash \psi : \neg(* \wedge (* \wedge \texttt{false}))$ contains the following typing to subformulas:

$$\psi_0 : n : \{\text{int} \mid n \leq 7\} \rightarrow (y : \{\text{int} \mid y \leq 8\} \rightarrow \neg(* \wedge \texttt{false})) \rightarrow \neg(* \wedge (* \wedge \texttt{false}))$$
$$\psi_1 : y : \{\text{int} \mid y \leq 9\} \rightarrow \neg(* \wedge \texttt{false})$$

(how to infer those refinement types is briefly discussed in the paragraph below this example). The abstraction types for ψ_0 and ψ_1 extracted from this proof are

$$\sigma_0' := n : \text{int}[n \leq 7] \rightarrow (y : \text{int}[y \leq 8] \rightarrow \bullet) \rightarrow \bullet \qquad \sigma_1' := y : \text{int}[y \leq 9] \rightarrow \bullet.$$

By adding this information to the abstraction types in Example 5, one obtains

$$\sigma_0'' := n : \text{int}[0 \leq n, n \leq 7] \rightarrow (y : \text{int}[0 \leq y, y \leq 5, y \leq 8] \rightarrow \bullet) \rightarrow \bullet$$
$$\sigma_2'' := y : \text{int}[0 \leq y, y \leq 5, y \leq 9] \rightarrow \bullet.$$

After this refinement, there exists an abstraction that is true.   □

The refinement process enjoys the progress property in the following sense.

Theorem 3 (Progress). *Assume a derivation of $\vdash \psi : \neg c$ in the dependent intersection type system. Then there exists an abstraction $\vdash \psi : \bullet \rightsquigarrow \varphi$ following the abstraction types extracted from the derivation such that, for any abstract counterexample c' of φ, the set $C(c')$ contains a candidate counterexample that differs from c.*

5   Implementation and Evaluation

We have implemented a νHFL$_\mathbb{Z}$ validity checker PAHFL based on the method described so far. PAHFL uses the following tools as backend solvers:

- Z3 [15], as a backend SMT solver for computing predicate abstraction.
- HorSat2, as a backend model checker for checking the validity of (pure) νHFL formulas and extracting an abstract counterexample if there is any. (HorSat2 is a HORS model checker, but it can also be used as a νHFL model checker by using the reduction of Kobayashi et al. [9].)
- RCaml [20] and HoIce [4] as backend constraint solvers, for the predicate discovery phase.

Given a νHFL$_\mathbb{Z}$ formula, PAHFL starts with the empty set of predicates, and repeats the CEGAR loop until it succeeds to prove or disprove the validity of the formula; of course, it may run forever since the validity checking problem is undecidable.

We have conducted experiments to compare our tool with two related tools:

- A HoCHC solver called Horus [2], which solves the satisfiability of HoCHC (a higher-order extension of CHC, constrained Horn Clauses). Since the HoCHC satisfiability problem and νHFL$_\mathbb{Z}$ can be mutually reducible (recall Remark 1), Horus is a direct competitor of our tool.
- An automated higher-order program verification tool MoCHi, developed by Kobayashi et al. [11,14,17]. Since the main application of our νHFL$_\mathbb{Z}$ validity checking is higher-order program verification, MoCHi is also an (indirect) competitor of our tool. Like PAHFL, MoCHi uses predicate abstraction and CEGAR, though its main building block is HORS model checking (rather than HFL validity checking. Actually, the goal of our project has been to replace the HORS-based approach of MoCHi with the HFL-based approach, where the latter provides a more uniform approach to program verification. Thus the goal of the comparison with MoCHi is to confirm that our new tool PAHFL works at least as effectively as MoCHi, for program verification problems. There are other fully automated verification tools for functional programs, including those based on refinement type inference [3,5,24–26]. We have chosen MoCHi as the target of the experimental comparison, as the underlying technique is directly related; other tools can be indirectly compared through their experimental comparison with MoCHi found in the respective papers [3,25,26].

Both experiments were conducted on a Linux server with Intel Xeon CPU E5-2680 v3 and 64 GB of RAM with a timeout set to 180 s.

Comparison with Horus. We used two benchmark sets in this experiment: Benchmarks A and B. Benchmark A has been taken from that of Horus [2], which in turn comes from a benchmark set of MoCHi for safety property verification [11]. Benchmark B has been obtained from another benchmark set of

Table 1. Comparison of PAHFL with Horus

		Benchmark A	Benchmark B
Ours	Solved	8	50
	Timeout	0	8
Horus	Solved	7	19
	Timeout	0	3
	Unknown	1	35

MoCHi, by using our own translation (based on [13,23]). Benchmark A has 10 instances and B has 58. We used Z3 as a backend CHC solver of Horus.

The result is shown in Table 1 and Fig. 4. In the table, the row 'Unknown' means that Horus could not prove the validity of νHFL$_\mathbb{Z}$ formula due to its incompleteness; as mentioned in Sect. 1, Horus reduces HoCHC problems to CHC problems in a sound but *incomplete* manner. The "unknown" case of Horus in Benchmark A is attributed to the lack of intersection types in the type system used by Horus; recall our remark before Theorem 2. As is clear from Fig. 4, Horus is much faster than PAHFL when Horus succeeds. In fact, Horus terminated within 0.1 s in those cases. In contrast, PAHFL clearly outperforms Horus in the number of solved instances. That is more apparent for the subset of benchmarks consisting of only higher-order inputs: see [7].

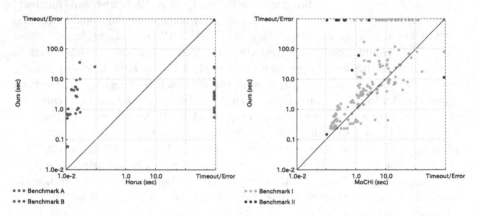

Fig. 4. Comparison of PAHFL with Horus (left) and MoCHi (right)

Comparison with MoCHi. Figure 4 shows the result of the comparison with MoCHi. We used two benchmark sets; Benchmark I consists of 258 of 262 safety property verification problems of OCaml programs used in [17] and Benchmark

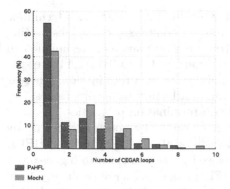

Table 2. Average percentage of time spent in each phase

	PAHFL	MOCHI
Preprocess	31.0	39.2
Abstraction	47.7	45.4
Refine	19.1	13.9
Model Checking	2.21	1.49

Fig. 5. Distribution of the number of CEGAR loops

II consists of a modified version[9] of 10 non-termination property verification problems used in [14]. All the benchmark programs are small (each around 10 lines of OCaml programs), but many of them are tricky. The νHFL$_{\mathbb{Z}}$ formulas in both benchmark sets have been obtained by using the translation used for obtaining Benchmark B. Different modes of MOCHI have been used for the two benchmark sets: the reachability verification mode [11] for Benchmark I, and the non-termination verification mode [14] for Benchmark II. PAHFL solved 221 instances for Benchmark I and 4 for II while MOCHI solved 252 for Benchmark I and 9 for II. Although PAHFL is a little inferior to MOCHI in the number of solved instances, PAHFL is competitive in terms of the running times for solved instances, as shown in Fig. 4.

Figure 5 and Table 2 respectively show the distribution of the number of CEGAR loops and the average percentage of the time spent in each phase for solved instances in Benchmark I and II. PAHFL and MOCHI have similar tendencies in both the figure and the table.

6 Related Work

Burn et al. [2] introduced higher-order constrained Horn clauses (HoCHC), and developed Horus, a type-based HoCHC satisfiability checker. As already mentioned, Horus is a direct competitor of our tool PAHFL, since the satisfiability problem for HoCHC is essentially equivalent to the validity problem for νHFL$_{\mathbb{Z}}$. As confirmed by experiments, our tool is often slower than Horus, but can solve more problem instances. Ong and Wagner [16] also studied some theoretical aspects of HoCHC, but have not developed an actual verification tool, to our knowledge.

Our technique of predicate abstraction has been inspired by the corresponding techniques developed for MOCHI [11,14]; in particular, we have borrowed the

---

[9] Existential quantifiers that arise from the original programs have been replaced with finite disjunctions.

notion of abstraction types from their work. Our predicate abstraction technique is, however, different from theirs, in that our technique is used for abstracting formulas, while their technique is for abstracting programs. Our technique can also be considered more general since the techniques of MoCHi [11,14] are specialized for the verification of either reachability or non-termination, whereas our technique can be used for the verification of arbitrary branching-time safety properties, including the reachability and non-termination properties.

Higher-order fixpoint logic (HFL) has originally been proposed by Viswanathan and Viswanathan [22]. Kobayashi et al. [13,23] introduced HFL$_\mathbb{Z}$, an extension of HFL with integers, and showed its applications to higher-order program verification. Although a pure HFL model checker has already been developed by Hosoi et al. [6], there is no automated validity checker for HFL$_\mathbb{Z}$, to our knowledge. Kobayashi et al. [10] have recently developed a validity checker for the first-order fragment of HFL$_\mathbb{Z}$, which reduces (in a sound but incomplete manner) the validity problem for the first-order fragment of HFL$_\mathbb{Z}$ to that for the ν-only, first-order fragment of HFL$_\mathbb{Z}$. We expect that the same technique can be used to obtain a full HFL$_\mathbb{Z}$ validity checker from our νHFL$_\mathbb{Z}$ validity checker.

Another major approach to automated verification of higher-order programs is a type-based one [3,5,19,24–26], some of which incorporates counterexample-guided refinement [19,24]. Most of them are restricted to verification of the (un)reachability problem in the presence of only demonic branches (except [21]), and do not support intersection types (except [19]). Our support of both kinds of (i.e., angelic and demonic) branches is crucial for building the full HFL$_\mathbb{Z}$ validity checker as mentioned above. Intersection types are also crucial for high precision. To mitigate the high cost of predicate abstraction and discovery, Sato et al. [17] combined higher-order model checking and type inference.

7   Conclusion

We have proposed a new method for automated νHFL$_\mathbb{Z}$ validity checking based on predicate abstraction and CEGAR, and developed a tool based on the proposed technique. According to our experiments on applications to program verification, our tool outperformed Horus in terms of precision, and was competitive with a more specialized program verification tool MoCHi. We plan to develop a full HFL$_\mathbb{Z}$ validity checker, by combining the present work with the work of Kobayashi et al.'s [10] for the first-order HFL$_\mathbb{Z}$ validity checker. It is also left for future work to extending the logic with data structures (such as lists and trees), which is important for verification of higher-order functional programs that manipulate data structures. To this end, we plan to exploit two approaches: one is to encode data structures as higher-order functions as in MoCHi [18], and the other is to directly handle data structures, as in the refinement-type-based approach [5,26].

Acknowledgments. We would like to thank anonymous referees for useful comments. This work was supported by JSPS KAKENHI Grant Number JP15H05706, JP20H00577 and JP20H05703.

References

1. Ball, T., Majumdar, R., Millstein, T.D., Rajamani, S.K.: Automatic predicate abstraction of C programs. In: Burke, M., Soffa, M.L. (eds.) Proceedings of the 2001 ACM SIGPLAN Conference on Programming Language Design and Implementation (PLDI), Snowbird, Utah, USA, 20–22 June 2001, pp. 203–213. ACM (2001). https://doi.org/10.1145/378795.378846

2. Burn, T.C., Ong, C.L., Ramsay, S.J.: Higher-order constrained horn clauses for verification. Proc. ACM Program. Lang. **2**(POPL), 11:1–11:28 (2018). https://doi.org/10.1145/3158099

3. Champion, A., Chiba, T., Kobayashi, N., Sato, R.: ICE-based refinement type discovery for higher-order functional programs. J. Autom. Reason. (2010, to appear). A preliminary summary appeared in Proceedings of TACAS 2018

4. Champion, A., Chiba, T., Kobayashi, N., Sato, R.: ICE-based refinement type discovery for higher-order functional programs. In: Beyer, D., Huisman, M. (eds.) TACAS 2018. LNCS, vol. 10805, pp. 365–384. Springer, Cham (2018). https://doi.org/10.1007/978-3-319-89960-2_20

5. Hashimoto, K., Unno, H.: Refinement type inference via horn constraint optimization. In: Blazy, S., Jensen, T. (eds.) SAS 2015. LNCS, vol. 9291, pp. 199–216. Springer, Heidelberg (2015). https://doi.org/10.1007/978-3-662-48288-9_12

6. Hosoi, Y., Kobayashi, N., Tsukada, T.: A type-based HFL model checking algorithm. In: Lin, A.W. (ed.) APLAS 2019. LNCS, vol. 11893, pp. 136–155. Springer, Cham (2019). https://doi.org/10.1007/978-3-030-34175-6_8

7. Iwayama, N., Kobayashi, N., Suzuki, R., Tsukada, T.: Predicate abstraction and CEGAR for νHFL$\mathbb{Z}$ validity checking (2020). A long version of this paper. https://www.kb.is.s.u-tokyo.ac.jp/~koba/papers/sas2020-long.pdf

8. Kobayashi, N.: HorSat2: a saturation-based model checker for higher-order recursion schemes (2015). https://www.kb.is.s.u-tokyo.ac.jp/~koba/horsat2/

9. Kobayashi, N., Lozes, É., Bruse, F.: On the relationship between higher-order recursion schemes and higher-order fixpoint logic. In: Castagna, G., Gordon, A.D. (eds.) Proceedings of the 44th ACM SIGPLAN Symposium on Principles of Programming Languages, POPL 2017, Paris, France, 18–20 January 2017, pp. 246–259. ACM (2017)

10. Kobayashi, N., Nishikawa, T., Igarashi, A., Unno, H.: Temporal verification of programs via first-order fixpoint logic. In: Chang, B.-Y.E. (ed.) SAS 2019. LNCS, vol. 11822, pp. 413–436. Springer, Cham (2019). https://doi.org/10.1007/978-3-030-32304-2_20

11. Kobayashi, N., Sato, R., Unno, H.: Predicate abstraction and CEGAR for higher-order model checking. In: Hall, M.W., Padua, D.A. (eds.) Proceedings of the 32nd ACM SIGPLAN Conference on Programming Language Design and Implementation, PLDI 2011, San Jose, CA, USA, 4–8 June 2011, pp. 222–233. ACM (2011). https://doi.org/10.1145/1993498.1993525

12. Kobayashi, N., Tsukada, T., Watanabe, K.: Higher-order program verification via HFL model checking. CoRR abs/1710.08614 (2017). http://arxiv.org/abs/1710.08614

13. Kobayashi, N., Tsukada, T., Watanabe, K.: Higher-order program verification via HFL model checking. In: Ahmed, A. (ed.) ESOP 2018. LNCS, vol. 10801, pp. 711 738. Springer, Cham (2018). https://doi.org/10.1007/978-3-319-89884-1_25

14. Kuwahara, T., Sato, R., Unno, H., Kobayashi, N.: Predicate abstraction and CEGAR for disproving termination of higher-order functional programs. In: Kroening, D., Păsăreanu, C.S. (eds.) CAV 2015. LNCS, vol. 9207, pp. 287–303. Springer, Cham (2015). https://doi.org/10.1007/978-3-319-21668-3_17

15. de Moura, L., Bjørner, N.: Z3: an efficient SMT solver. In: Ramakrishnan, C.R., Rehof, J. (eds.) TACAS 2008. LNCS, vol. 4963, pp. 337–340. Springer, Heidelberg (2008). https://doi.org/10.1007/978-3-540-78800-3_24

16. Ong, C.L., Wagner, D.: HoCHC: a refutationally complete and semantically invariant system of higher-order logic modulo theories. In: 34th Annual ACM/IEEE Symposium on Logic in Computer Science, LICS 2019, Vancouver, BC, Canada, 24–27 June 2019, pp. 1–14. IEEE (2019). https://doi.org/10.1109/LICS.2019.8785784

17. Sato, R., Iwayama, N., Kobayashi, N.: Combining higher-order model checking with refinement type inference. In: Hermenegildo, M.V., Igarashi, A. (eds.) Proceedings of the 2019 ACM SIGPLAN Workshop on Partial Evaluation and Program Manipulation, PEPM@POPL 2019, Cascais, Portugal, 14–15 January 2019, pp. 47–53. ACM (2019). https://doi.org/10.1145/3294032.3294081

18. Sato, R., Unno, H., Kobayashi, N.: Towards a scalable software model checker for higher-order programs. In: Albert, E., Mu, S. (eds.) Proceedings of the ACM SIGPLAN 2013 Workshop on Partial Evaluation and Program Manipulation, PEPM 2013, Rome, Italy, 21–22 January 2013, pp. 53–62. ACM (2013). https://doi.org/10.1145/2426890.2426900

19. Terauchi, T.: Dependent types from counterexamples. In: Hermenegildo, M.V., Palsberg, J. (eds.) Proceedings of the 37th ACM SIGPLAN-SIGACT Symposium on Principles of Programming Languages, POPL 2010, Madrid, Spain, 17–23 January 2010, pp. 119–130. ACM (2010). https://doi.org/10.1145/1706299.1706315

20. Unno, H., Kobayashi, N.: Dependent type inference with interpolants. In: Porto, A., López-Fraguas, F.J. (eds.) Proceedings of the 11th International ACM SIGPLAN Conference on Principles and Practice of Declarative Programming, Coimbra, Portugal, 7–9 September 2009, pp. 277–288. ACM (2009). https://doi.org/10.1145/1599410.1599445

21. Unno, H., Satake, Y., Terauchi, T.: Relatively complete refinement type system for verification of higher-order non-deterministic programs. Proc. ACM Program. Lang. 2(POPL), 12:1–12:29 (2018). https://doi.org/10.1145/3158100

22. Viswanathan, M., Viswanathan, R.: A higher order modal fixed point logic. In: Gardner, P., Yoshida, N. (eds.) CONCUR 2004. LNCS, vol. 3170, pp. 512–528. Springer, Heidelberg (2004). https://doi.org/10.1007/978-3-540-28644-8_33

23. Watanabe, K., Tsukada, T., Oshikawa, H., Kobayashi, N.: Reduction from branching-time property verification of higher-order programs to HFL validity checking. In: Hermenegildo, M.V., Igarashi, A. (eds.) Proceedings of the 2019 ACM SIGPLAN Workshop on Partial Evaluation and Program Manipulation, PEPM@POPL 2019, Cascais, Portugal, 14–15 January 2019, pp. 22–34. ACM (2019). https://doi.org/10.1145/3294032.3294077

24. Zhu, H., Jagannathan, S.: Compositional and lightweight dependent type inference for ML. In: Giacobazzi, R., Berdine, J., Mastroeni, I. (eds.) VMCAI 2013. LNCS, vol. 7737, pp. 295–314. Springer, Heidelberg (2013). https://doi.org/10.1007/978-3-642-35873-9_19

25. Zhu, H., Nori, A.V., Jagannathan, S.: Learning refinement types. In: Fisher, K., Reppy, J.H. (eds.) Proceedings of the 20th ACM SIGPLAN International Conference on Functional Programming, ICFP 2015, Vancouver, BC, Canada, 1–3 September 2015, pp. 400–411. ACM (2015). https://doi.org/10.1145/2784731. 2784766
26. Zhu, H., Petri, G., Jagannathan, S.: Automatically learning shape specifications. In: Krintz, C., Berger, E. (eds.) Proceedings of the 37th ACM SIGPLAN Conference on Programming Language Design and Implementation, PLDI 2016, Santa Barbara, CA, USA, 13–17 June 2016, pp. 491–507. ACM (2016). https://doi.org/ 10.1145/2908080.2908125

Counterexample- and Simulation-Guided Floating-Point Loop Invariant Synthesis

Anastasiia Izycheva[1(✉)], Eva Darulova[2], and Helmut Seidl[1]

[1] Fakultät für Informatik, TU München, Munich, Germany
{izycheva,seidl}@in.tum.de
[2] MPI-SWS, Kaiserslautern, Germany
eva@mpi-sws.org

Abstract. We present an automated procedure for synthesizing sound inductive invariants for floating-point numerical loops. Our procedure generates invariants of the form of a convex polynomial inequality that tightly bounds the values of loop variables. Such invariants are a prerequisite for reasoning about the safety and roundoff errors of floating-point programs. Unlike previous approaches that rely on policy iteration, linear algebra or semi-definite programming, we propose a heuristic procedure based on simulation and counterexample-guided refinement. We observe that this combination is remarkably effective and general and can handle both linear and nonlinear loop bodies, nondeterministic values as well as conditional statements. Our evaluation shows that our approach can efficiently synthesize loop invariants for existing benchmarks from literature, but that it is also able to find invariants for nonlinear loops that today's tools cannot handle.

Keywords: Invariant synthesis · Floating-point arithmetic · CEGIS · Simulation

1 Introduction

Finding and proving inductive loop invariants is one of the fundamental tasks in program verification, allowing to prove a property for all program executions even in the presence of unbounded loops. *Proving* (or disproving) that a given loop invariant is inductive is generally an easier task and can in many cases be straight-forwardly automated using off-the-shelf SMT solvers [6,31]. *Finding* a loop invariant, however, is in general difficult to do manually, and automating this process remains an important challenge [7,14,16,19].

In this paper, we focus on numerical loops over floating-point variables, which are found across domains such as embedded control systems and scientific computing. Reasoning about floating-point arithmetic is additionally complex due to its unintuitive nature: every arithmetic operation introduces a roundoff error w.r.t. the ideal real-valued execution and overflow or invalid operations introduce the special values ±infinity and Not-a-Number. For floating-point computations,

D. Pichardie and M. Sighireanu (Eds.): SAS 2020, LNCS 12389, pp. 156–177, 2020.
https://doi.org/10.1007/978-3-030-65474-0_8

it is thus of utmost importance to bound the values of variables as accurately as possible. This information is required for proving safety, absence of floating-point special values, and bounds of roundoff errors [13].

Some previous techniques for loop invariant synthesis for numerical programs require a target property to be given [19,29,38,40,43]; in most cases this is a set of unsafe states that should be proven to be unreachable. However, for floating-point loops where the goal is to compute as tight invariants as possible, specifying unsafe states essentially amounts to finding the invariant itself.

Abstract interpretation-based techniques [9] do not require a target property. Nonetheless, existing efficient linear abstract domains that rely on widening are often not strong enough to find non-trivial inductive invariants, i.e. where the bounds are not ±infinity. As our evaluation shows, even conjunctions of linear inequalities as provided by convex polyhedra [4,10] are often insufficient.

We thus require nonlinear loop invariants expressed as polynomial inequalities to handle many numerical loops. However, existing techniques each have limitations, as they require templates to be given by the user [1]; are limited to linear loops only [36]; do not always produce invariants that satisfy the precondition [33]; or require a target range in order to produce tight invariants [29].

Here, we propose a rather pragmatic approach. We use concrete executions and polynomial approximation in order to obtain candidate invariants which, when combined with counterexample-guided refinement, allows us to synthesize invariants for floating-point loops. Our approach does not require a target bound, efficiently produces tight polynomial inequality invariants, handles linear as well as nonlinear loops, and soundly takes into account floating-point roundoff errors. Our algorithm thus generates exactly the invariants we are looking for. This generality, naturally, comes at a certain cost. While previous approaches provide certain completeness guarantees [29,33,36] at the expense of the above listed limitations, our algorithm effectively trades completeness for a wider applicability. Nevertheless, we empirically observe that our proposed algorithm, despite being based on a heuristic search, is remarkably effective.

Our algorithm performs a form of iterative counterexample-guided invariant generation: it proposes a candidate invariant, checks it using an off-the-shelf SMT solver, and if the solver returns a counterexample, uses it to adjust the next candidate invariant. We cannot query the SMT solver for the polynomial coefficients directly, as such a query would require quantifiers, which neither the real-valued nor the floating-point SMT theories support well. Instead, candidate invariants are generated based on simulation, i.e. concrete executions of the loop, and polynomial approximation which guesses the shape of the invariant based on the convex hull of seen program values. Concrete executions (instead of abstractions) starting from a given precondition allow our algorithm to accurately capture the behavior of linear as well as nonlinear loop bodies, and thus to generate tight invariants. Our algorithm abstracts the floating-point semantics of the loop body by a sound roundoff error bound, adds it as nondeterministic noise, and then uses a real-valued decision procedure to verify the proposed candidate invariants. This approach is more efficient than using the currently

```
x ∈ [0.0, 0.1]
y ∈ [0.0, 0.1]

while (true) {
  x := x + 0.01 * (-2*x - 3*y + x*x)
  y := y + 0.01 * (x + y)
}
```

$$-0.03x - 0.1y + 0.44x^2 + xy + 0.86y^2 \le 0.02$$

$$x \in [-0.5, 0.3]$$
$$y \in [-0.2, 0.4]$$

(b) Generated invariant

(a) Example benchmark

Fig. 1. Running example

limited floating-point decision procedures, but at the same time accurate, as the error bound is computed based on a concrete candidate invariant, and thus adds only as much noise as is necessary.

Our approach is motivated by the fact that the numerical invariants we are looking for are robust to some noise [36], and the loops of interest do not have a single inductive invariant, but they admit *many similar* invariants. The robustness to noise is important; few developers program with the exact floating-point semantics in mind, rather they treat it as a noisy version of real arithmetic. If a loop was not robust to noise, even small changes in roundoff errors e.g. due to non-associativity, would lead to large changes in the overall loop behavior. This robustness allows us to use a heuristic search to find *one of these* invariants.

We implement our algorithm as a Python library in a tool called PINE. PINE can fully automatically handle non-nested loops with linear and nonlinear assignments, nondeterministic noise and conditional statements. In this paper, we focus on convex invariants that consist of a single polynomial inequality of degree two, and note that an extension to more complex bounded invariant shapes (non-convex shapes, disjunctive invariants, higher degrees) requires mainly engineering work to find a suitable way to fit the polynomial(s) from the simulated points. We evaluate PINE on a number of existing benchmarks from literature and show that it computes invariants that are on average 12.4x smaller than those computed by existing tools. Furthermore, we show that PINE computes invariants for nonlinear loops, which are out of reach for state-of-the-art tools.

Contributions. To summarize, our paper makes the following contributions:

- a novel algorithm for polynomial inequality invariant synthesis for linear and nonlinear floating-point loops,
- an open-source prototype implementation PINE[1], and
- a detailed evaluation on existing and new benchmarks.

---

[1] https://github.com/izycheva/pine.

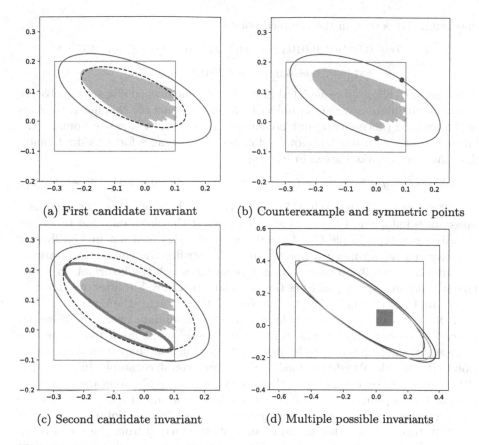

(a) First candidate invariant   (b) Counterexample and symmetric points

(c) Second candidate invariant   (d) Multiple possible invariants

Fig. 2. Nonlinear benchmark candidate invariants (Color figure online)

2 Overview

Before explaining our invariant synthesis algorithm in detail, we illustrate it at
a high-level on an example. Figure 1a shows our example loop that simulates a
dynamical system together with the precondition on the loop variables.

PINE starts by simulating the loop to collect a set of concrete points that
an inductive invariant definitely has to include. For this, PINE samples $m = 100$
random values from the input ranges $x \in [0, 0.1]$ and $y \in [0, 0.1]$, and executes
the loop $n = 1000$ times for each point. Sampled points are shown in light blue
in Fig. 2a–2b. Since we are looking for a convex invariant, PINE next computes
the convex hull of the sampled points. This reduces the number of points to
consider and gives us an initial estimate of the shape of the invariant.

We consider invariants that include variable ranges and a shape enclosing
all values expressed as an ellipsoid, i.e. a second degree polynomial inequality.
We obtain the polynomial coefficients by computing the minimum volume ellipsoid enclosing the convex hull, and the variable bounds from the minimum and

maximum values seen in the sampled points:

$$-0.0009x - 0.004y + 0.0103x^2 + 0.021xy + 0.0298y^2 \leq 5.4 \cdot 10^{-5} \wedge$$

$$x \in [-0.2098, 0.0976], \; y \in [-0.0159, 0.1723]$$

The computed ellipsoid is depicted in Fig. 2a by blue dashed ellipse. We observe that this candidate invariant is noisy. To remove (a part of) this noise, we scale and round the (normalized) polynomial coefficients and the range bounds (the latter is rounded outwards). Obtained ellipsoid and ranges form the first candidate invariant (marked green in Fig. 2a):

$$-0.03x - 0.13y + 0.35x^2 + 0.7xy + y^2 \leq 0.01 \wedge x \in [-0.3, 0.1], y \in [-0.1, 0.2]$$

PINE uses an off-the-shelf SMT solver (Z3) to check whether this candidate invariant is inductive. For our candidate invariant the check fails and the solver returns a counterexample $C_1 : (x = 0.0, y = -0.0542)$ (red dot in Fig. 2b). By counterexample, we mean a point that itself satisfies the candidate invariant, but after one loop iteration results in a point for which the invariant no longer holds. In our example C_1 satisfies the candidate invariant, but after one iteration we obtain $C_1' : (x = 0.001626, y = -0.054742)$ that violates the invariant.

PINE uses this counterexample to refine the candidate invariant. However, instead of recomputing the convex hull and ellipsoid shape immediately, we generate additional counterexamples in order to not bias the shape in a single direction that is (randomly) determined by the solver's counterexample. In particular, PINE computes counterexamples that are symmetric to C_1 along the symmetry axes of the ellipsoid and satisfy the candidate invariant. Figure 2b shows the counterexamples generated for our running example (purple dots).

PINE then uses another round of simulation, starting from the set of counterexamples, to obtain a new set of points that need to be included in an invariant (by transitivity, if a counterexample point is included after one loop iteration, then the points after additional iterations also have to be included). The new set of points is then used to generate the next candidate invariant. Figure 2c shows simulated points in red, and the new candidate invariant in green. Note that Fig. 2c contains three simulation traces - one for each counterexample, and the traces originated from the bottom left counterexample and C_1 coincide.

PINE repeats this iterative process until either an invariant is found, or a maximum number of refinement iterations is reached. For our example, PINE finds an inductive invariant (shown green in Fig. 2d) after 6 iterations.

The invariant so found holds for a real-valued loop, i.e. when the loop body is evaluated under real arithmetic. The last step of PINE's algorithm is to verify that the invariant also holds under a floating-point loop semantics. To do this, PINE uses an off-the-shelf analysis tool to get the worst-case roundoff error bound for each expression in the loop body. The errors are then added as nondeterministic noise terms to the loop, and the invariant is re-checked by the SMT solver. For our running example, this check succeeds, and the following invariant is confirmed:

$$-0.03x - 0.1y + 0.44x^2 + xy + 0.86y^2 \leq 0.02 \; \wedge x \in [-0.5, 0.3], y \in [-0.2, 0.4]$$

Figure 2d shows several invariants generated by PINE for our example, for different parameters of its algorithm. Note that these invariants are similar, but differ slightly in shape and volume. The range component of the invariant is shown by the green and blue boxes; the red box denotes the input ranges.

3   Problem Definition

The input to our algorithm is a loop body together with a precondition. We consider simple non-nested loops given by the following grammar:

```
L ::= while(true){ B }
B ::= if (G) S else S | S
S ::= ε | xᵢ := p(x₁, ..., xₙ) + uⱼ; S
G ::= * | p ≤ 0
```

In each iteration, the loop updates a set of variables $x_i \in \mathcal{X}$. The right-hand-side of each assignment consists of polynomial expressions p in the loop variables together with an (optional) nondeterministic noise term u_j, which is bounded in magnitude and that denotes any additional noise, e.g. input error from sensor values. The loop body can include a top-level conditional statement, which can also be used to express the loop exit condition. The conditions of the if-statement can either be nondeterministic choice or a polynomial inequality. We note that adding support for more complex conditions as well as nested and chained if-statements would only affect the way we parse the loop and encode it in the SMT query and is not a fundamental limitation of our algorithm.

The precondition specifies the initial ranges for all variables x_i, as well as bounds on the nondeterministic noise variables: $x_i \in [a_i, b_i]$, $u_j \in [c_j, d_j]$. The loop and noise variables take values in the set $\mathbb{F}$ of floating-point values. Then the semantics of a loop body b is given by $[\![b]\!] :: (\mathcal{X} \to \mathbb{F}) \to 2^{(\mathcal{X} \to \mathbb{F})}$, which is defined by

$$
\begin{aligned}
[\![\epsilon]\!]\, \rho &= \{\rho\} \\
[\![x_i := p + u_j; s]\!]\, \rho &= \bigcup \{[\![s]\!](\rho \oplus \{x_i \mapsto p(\rho) + u\}) \mid u \in [c_j, d_j]\} \\
[\![\text{if } (*)\, s_1 \text{ else } s_2]\!]\, \rho &= [\![s_1]\!]\, \rho \cup [\![s_2]\!]\, \rho \\
[\![\text{if } (p \leq 0)\, s_1 \text{ else } s_2]\!]\, \rho &= \{\rho_1 \in [\![s_1]\!]\, \rho \mid p(\rho) \leq 0\} \cup \\
&\quad\ \{\rho_2 \in [\![s_2]\!]\, \rho \mid p(\rho) > 0\}
\end{aligned}
$$

Here, $p(\rho)$ denotes the value of the polynomial p for the variable assignment ρ under the floating-point arithmetic semantics specified by the IEEE 754 standard [22]. The set of initial program states is given by

$$
\text{Init} = \{\rho : \mathcal{X} \to \mathbb{R} \mid \forall x_i \in \mathcal{X}.\, \rho(x_i) \in [a_i, b_i]\}
$$

Our goal is to find an inductive invariant $\mathcal{I}$ such that

$$
\text{Init} \subseteq \mathcal{I} \quad \wedge \quad \forall \rho \in \mathcal{I}.\, [\![b]\!]\, \rho \subseteq \mathcal{I} \tag{1}
$$

i.e., $\mathcal{I}$ subsumes the initial states and is preserved by each iteration of the loop. We consider convex invariants given by a polynomial inequality together with ranges for variables:

$$\mathcal{I} = \{\rho \mid \mathcal{P}(\rho) \le 0, \rho(\mathsf{x}_i) \in \mathcal{R}_i = [l_i, h_i]\}$$

The goal is thus to find the coefficients of the polynomial $\mathcal{P}$ and the lower and upper bounds (l_i, h_i) for the variables of the loop. In this paper, we consider polynomials $\mathcal{P}$ of degree two, although our algorithm generalizes to higher degrees. We observe that second degree polynomials are already sufficient for a large class of loops.

Additionally, we are interested in finding as small an invariant as possible, where we measure size by the volume enclosed by an invariant. We note that the ellipsoid (the polynomial inequality), is not only needed to prove the inductiveness of many invariants, but it can also enable more accurate verification based on our inductive invariants, for instance by techniques relying on SMT solving. For this reason, we do not only measure the volume as the size of the box described by $\mathcal{R}$, but rather as the intersection between the box and the ellipsoid shape, which can be substantially smaller.

4   Algorithm

Figure 3 shows a high-level view of our invariant synthesis algorithm. The input to the algorithm is a loop together with a precondition on the loop variables, and the output is a polynomial $\mathcal{P}$ and a set of ranges $\mathcal{R}$, a range $\mathcal{R}_i$ for each program variable x_i, that define the synthesized invariant:

$$\mathcal{P}(x_1, ..., x_n) \le 0 \land x_1 \in \mathcal{R}_1 \land ... \land x_n \in \mathcal{R}_n \tag{2}$$

The key component of our algorithm is the invariant synthesis, which infers the shape of the bounding polynomial and the variable ranges (lines 1–21). The algorithm first synthesizes an invariant assuming a real-valued semantics for the loop body (withRoundoff == False).

The synthesis starts by simulating the loop on a number of random inputs from the precondition, keeping track of all the seen points, i.e. tuples $(x_1, ..., x_n)$. From the obtained points, the algorithm next guesses the shape of a candidate invariant, i.e. a polynomial $\mathcal{P}$ and a set of ranges $\mathcal{R}$ (line 5–7). We check this candidate invariant using an off-the-shelf SMT solver (line 12). If the candidate is not an invariant or is not inductive, the solver returns a counterexample. The algorithm generalizes from the counterexample (line 16–20) and uses the newly obtained points to refine the candidate invariant. We repeat the process until either an invariant is found, or we reach a maximum number of iterations (empirically, all benchmarks required less than 100 iterations).

After the real-valued invariant is generated, the algorithm checks whether it also holds for the floating-point implementation of the loop (line 29). Should this not be the case, invariant synthesis is repeated taking floating-point roundoff

```
1   def get_real_invariant(loop, init, withRoundoff):
2     pts = simulate(loop, random.sample(init, m), n)
3     // update pts iteratively
4     for i in range(0, max_iters):
5       pts = convexHull(pts)
6       ranges = round(min(pts), max(pts), prec_range)
7       coefficients = getShape(pts, prec_poly)
8       inv = (coefficients, ranges)
9
10      if withRoundoff:
11        loop = addRoundoff(loop, ranges)
12      cex = checkInvariant(loop, inv)
13      if cex is None:
14        return inv
15      else:
16        addCex = getAdditionalCex(loop, inv, cex, cex_num, d)
17        symPts = getSymmetricPts(cex, inv)
18        nearbyPts = getNearbyPts(cex, d, inv)
19        pts = pts ∪ cex ∪ addCex ∪ symPts ∪ nearbyPts
20        pts = simulate(loop, pts, k)
21    return None
22
23  def get_fp_invariant(loop, init):
24    inv = get_real_invariant(loop, init, withRoundoff=False)
25    if inv is None:
26      return None
27    else:
28      loopFP = addRoundoff(loop, inv.ranges)
29      cex = checkInvariant(loopFP, inv)
30      if cex is None:
31        return inv
32      else:
33        return get_real_invariant(loop, init, withRoundoff=True)
```

Fig. 3. High-level invariant synthesis algorithm (parameters are in cursive)

errors into account in every refinement iteration. Since roundoff errors are usually relatively small, this recomputation is seldom necessary, so that PINE first runs real-valued invariant synthesis for performance reasons.

4.1 Simulation

The synthesis starts by simulating the loop execution. For this, PINE samples m values from the variables' input ranges Init uniformly at random, and concretely executes the loop n times for every sample. As a result, we obtain $m \times n$ points, i.e. combinations of variable values, that appear in the concrete semantics of the loop and thus have to be included in an invariant. The sampled points provide a starting point for the invariant search.

4.2   Candidate Invariant Conjecture

The invariant we are looking for has two parts: variable ranges $\mathcal{R}$ and a polynomial shape $\mathcal{P}(x)$ enclosing all variable values. To obtain $\mathcal{R}$ and $\mathcal{P}(x)$, PINE first reduces the number of samples by computing the convex hull of the sampled points. We consider invariant shapes that are convex, therefore the values inside the shape can be safely discarded. Extending our algorithm to non-convex shapes is a matter of finding an appropriate way to reduce the number of samples.

The minimum and maximum values of each loop variable x_i in the convex hull vertices determine the range $\mathcal{R}_i$.

PINE infers the shape $\mathcal{P}(x)$ enclosing the convex hull vertices using two optimization methods: minimum volume enclosing ellipsoid (MVEE), and least squares curve fitting. The minimum volume enclosing ellipsoid method computes a bounding ellipsoid such that all points are inside the shape. PINE utilizes a library that computes MVEE by solving the following optimization problem:

$$\text{minimize } \log(\det(E))$$
$$s.t. (x_i - c)^T E (x_i - c) \leq 1$$

where x_i are the individual points, c is a vector containing the center of the ellipsoid and E contains the information about the ellipsoid shape [30].

While MVEE computes the desired shape, the library that we use supports only two dimensions, and it is furthermore possible that it diverges. To support higher-dimensional loops, or when MVEE fails, we resort to using least squares. With the method of least squares, we find coefficients such that the sum of the squares of the errors w.r.t. to the given points is minimized. For a degree 2 polynomial in variables x and y, PINE transforms the points into the matrix A with entries having the values of $[1, x, y, x^2, xy]$, and a vector b which consists of the values of y^2. By solving the system of equations $Az = b$ for z, we obtain the coefficients of the polynomial. By setting $b = y^2$, we set the last coefficient to 1 in order to avoid the trivial (zero) solution. Least squares computes a tight fit, but will, in general, not include all of the points *inside* the polynomial shape, so that we additionally have to enlarge the 'radius' such that it includes all points. While we do not explore this further in this work, we note that the above sketched least-squares approach also generalizes to fit polynomials of higher degree than 2, using suitable constraints to ensure convex shapes [27].

In this paper, we only consider convex shapes described by a single polynomial inequality (and ranges). However, with a suitable fitting method it is possible to include more complex shapes. For instance, for disjunctive invariants one can first perform clustering, and then fit the polynomials using MVEE or the least squares method.

4.3   Reducing the Noise

Both methods used to infer a shape are approximate, i.e. they find a polynomial that is close to the actual shape up to a tolerance bound. Furthermore, they fit a set of points that is incomplete in that it only captures a (random) subset of all of the possible concrete executions. This makes the inferred polynomial shapes inherently noisy and unlikely to be an invariant. We reduce the noise by first normalizing and then rounding the polynomial coefficients to a predefined precision $prec_{poly}$, i.e. to a given (relatively small) number of digits after the decimal point. This effectively discards coefficients (rounds to zero) whose magnitude is significantly smaller than the largest coefficient found. For the remaining coefficients, it removes the—likely noisy—least significant digits.

Similarly, the lower and upper bounds of the computed ranges $\mathcal{R}$ capture only the values seen in simulation and are thus likely to be under-approximating the true ranges. We round the lower and upper bounds outwards to a predefined precision $prec_{range}$, thus including additional values.

The precisions (number of decimal digits) chosen for rounding the polynomial coefficients and the ranges should be high enough to not lead to too large over-approximations, but nonetheless small enough to discard most of the noise. We have empirically observed that the polynomial coefficients should be more precise than the range bounds by one digit, and that $prec_{poly} = 2$ and $prec_{range} = 1$ seems to be a good default choice.

4.4   Checking a Candidate Invariant

The obtained polynomial and variables ranges form a candidate invariant, which we check for inductiveness using an off-the-shelf SMT solver by encoding the (standard) constraint $(\text{Init} \rightarrow I(x)) \wedge (I(x) \wedge L \rightarrow I(x'))$, where $I(x) = \mathcal{P}(x) \leq 0 \bigwedge_i x_i \in \mathcal{R}_i$, L is the loop body relating the variables x before the execution of the loop body to the variables x' after.

We translate conditional statements using the SMT command ite. Non-deterministic terms receive fresh values from the user-defined range at every loop iteration. Since the ranges do not change we add constraints on the ranges of non-deterministic terms only to I and Init. We encode the above constraint in SMT-LIB using the real-valued theory [24]. The SMT solver evaluates the query and returns a counterexample if it exists. If no counterexample is returned, a candidate invariant is confirmed to be inductive and returned.

4.5   Generalizing from Counterexamples

The counterexample returned by the SMT solver is added to the existing set of points that the invariant has to cover. However, this additional point is arbitrary, depending on the internal heuristics of the solver. In order to speed up invariant synthesis, and to avoid biasing the search in a single direction and thus skewing the invariant shape, we generate additional points that also have to be covered by the next invariant candidate. We consider three different generalizations: additional counterexamples, symmetric points and nearby points.

PINE obtains additional counterexamples from the solver by extending the SMT query such that the initial counterexample is blocked and the new counterexample has to be a minimum distance d away from it. PINE will iteratively generate up to *cex_num* additional counterexamples, as long as the solver returns them within a (small) timeout (*cex_num* is a parameter of the algorithm).

Our second generalization strategy leverages the fact that the candidate invariant is an ellipsoid and thus has several axes of symmetry. PINE computes points that are symmetric to the counterexample with respect to all axes of symmetry of the ellipsoid, and adds them as additional points if they satisfy I or Init (i.e. they are also valid counterexamples).

Nearby points are the points that are at a distance d to the counterexample. PINE computes these points in all directions, i.e. $x_i \pm d$, and adds them to the set of points, if they are valid counterexamples. The rationale behind this generalization is that points in the vicinity of a counterexample are often also likely counterexamples. Adding the nearby points allows us to explore an entire area, instead of just a single point.

PINE then performs a second simulation of the loop starting from the newly added set of counterexamples for k iterations. All obtained points are added to the original sampled values and we proceed to synthesize the next candidate invariant.

4.6   Floating-Point Invariant

We encode the SMT queries to check the inductiveness of our candidate invariants using the real-valued theory. We note that it is in principle possible to encode the queries using the floating-point theory, and thus to encode the semantics of the loop body, including roundoff errors, exactly. However, despite the recent advances in floating-point decision procedures [8], we have observed that their performance is still prohibitively slow for our purpose (CVC4's state-of-the-art floating-point procedure [8] was several orders of magnitude slower than Z3's real-valued procedure [24]).

We thus use a real-valued SMT encoding and soundly over-approximate the roundoff errors in the loop body. We compute a worst-case roundoff error bound rnd for each expression in the loop body using an off-the-shelf roundoff analysis tool. Static analyses for bounding roundoff errors [12,42] assume the following abstraction of floating-point arithmetic operations: $(x \circ_{fl} y) = (x \circ y)(1 + e) + d$ $|e| \leq \epsilon, |d| \leq \eta$, where $\circ \in \{+, -, *, /\}$ and $\circ_{fl}$ is the floating-point counter-part. The so-called machine epsilon ϵ bounds the relative error for arithmetic operations on normal numbers and η bounds the absolute error on the so-called subnormal numbers (very small numbers close to zero that have a special representation). The static analyses use interval abstract domains to bound the ranges of all intermediate arithmetic expressions, and from those compute the new roundoff errors committed by each arithmetic operation, as well as their propagation through the rest of the program. These techniques compute roundoff error bounds for loop-free code, which is sufficient for our purpose, since we only need to verify that $I(x) \wedge L \to I(x')$, i.e. the executions of the (loop-free) loop body remain within the bounds given by I.

The computed roundoff error bound is added to the expression as a non-deterministic noise term bounded by $[-rnd, rnd]$. Note that unlike in existing work [36] that derives one general error bound for all programs assuming a large enough number of arithmetic operations, our roundoff error is computed on-demand for each particular candidate invariant. The magnitude of roundoff errors depends on ranges of inputs, and so by computing the roundoff error only for the invariant's ranges, we are able to add only as little noise as is necessary.

Our algorithm first finds a real-valued invariant and then verifies whether it also holds under a floating-point loop semantics. If not, we restart the invariant synthesis and take roundoff errors into account for each candidate invariant, recomputing a new tight roundoff error in each iteration of our algorithm (line 11). We do not include roundoff errors in the first run of the synthesis for better performance, since in practice, we rarely need to recompute the invariant.

Except for the roundoff error analysis, our algorithm is agnostic to the finite precision used for the implementation of the loop. By choosing to compute round-off errors w.r.t. different precisions, it thus supports in particular both single and double floating-point precision, but also fixed-point arithmetic of different bit lengths [12], which is particular relevant for embedded platforms that do not have a floating-point unit.

4.7 Implementation

We have implemented the algorithm from Fig. 3 in the tool PINE as a Python library in roughly 1600 lines of code, relying on the following main libraries and tools: the Qhull library for computing the convex hull[2], a library for computing the minimum volume ellipsoid[3], the least-squares function from scipy (scipy.linalg.lstsq), the Python API for the Z3 SMT solver version 4.8.7, and the Daisy tool [12] for computing roundoff errors. Simulations of the loop are performed in 64-bit floating-point arithmetic.

5 Experimental Evaluation

We evaluate PINE on a set of benchmarks from scientific computing and control theory domains. We aim to answer the following research questions:

RQ1: How does PINE compare with state-of-the-art tools?
RQ2: How quickly does PINE generate invariants?
RQ3: How sensitive is PINE's algorithm to parameter changes?

5.1 State-of-the-Art Techniques

We compare the invariants synthesized by PINE to those generated by two state-of-the-art tools: Pilat [33] and SMT-AI [36]. These two tools are the only ones

---

[2] www.qhull.org.
[3] https://github.com/minillinim/ellipsoid.

that compute polynomial inequality invariants for floating-point loops without requiring a target condition to be given.

Pilat reduces the generation of invariants of a loop body f to computing the eigenvector ϕ of f that is associated to the eigenvalue 1, i.e. $f(\phi) = \phi$ and ϕ is thus an invariant. Pilat can, in principle, handle nonlinear loops by introducing a new variable for each nonlinear term and thus effectively linearizing it. This transformation is similar to how we use least-squares to fit a polynomial (Sect. 4.2). Pilat handles floating-point roundoff errors by (manually) including nondeterministic noise for each floating-point operation that captures the roundoff error: $(x \circ y) \cdot \delta$, where $\circ \in \{+, -, \times, /\}$ and $|\delta| \leq \epsilon$ is bounded by the machine epsilon. For simplicity, we ignore errors due to subnormal numbers.

SMT-AI [36] and Adje et al. [1] implement policy iteration using the ellipsoid abstract domain. The approach by Adje et al. requires the ellipsoid template to be provided, while SMT-AI generates templates automatically. For our comparison we therefore consider the more general approach of SMT-AI. SMT-AI generates the ellipsoid templates from Lyapunov functions [3], which are functions known from control theory for proving that equilibrium points of dynamical systems are stable. These functions prove that a loop is bounded and thus the shape effectively serves as an invariant. It is known that for linear loops one can generate the polynomial shapes automatically using semi-definite programming. Since such an automated method does not exist for nonlinear functions, SMT-AI is limited to linear loops. Semi-definite programming can compute different polynomial shapes, and SMT-AI selects shapes to be tight using a binary search. SMT-AI first computes a real-valued invariant, like PINE, and then verifies that it also satisfies a floating-point loop. Unlike PINE, SMT-AI derives one generic roundoff error bound for all (reasonably-sized) loops, and does not recompute the invariant if the floating-point verification fails. We were unfortunately not able to install SMT-AI, so that we perform our comparison on the benchmarks used by SMT-AI, comparing to the (detailed) results reported in the paper [35,36].

Interproc [18] is a static analyzer based on abstract interpretation. It infers numerical invariants using boxes, octagons, linear congruences and convex polyhedra. A user can choose between two libraries that implement these domains: APRON [23] and Parma Polyhedra Library [4]. We tried Interproc on our set of benchmarks, and on 2 benchmarks it produced some bounds for a subset of the program variables. However, the invariants were not convex, and we could not compute their volume. We therefore exclude Interproc from the comparison.

Another potential competitor is an approach by Mine et al. [29] that combines interval and octagon abstract domains with constraint solving. The invariants discovered are effectively ellipsoids, i.e. second-degree polynomial inequalities. However, their approach fundamentally requires target bounds. Since the goal of PINE is to find such tight bounds, and not only prove that they are inductive, we do not compare with Mine et al. [29].

5.2 Experimental Setup

Our set of benchmarks contains both linear and nonlinear loops. Each benchmark consists of a loop body which iterates an infinite number of times. The linear benchmarks *filter_goubault, filter_mine*, arrow_hurwicz, harmonic, symplectic* are taken from related work [1,29] and implement linear filters and oscillators. Benchmarks *ex** are taken from the evaluation of SMT-AI [35] and comprise linear controllers, found for instance in embedded systems.

We additionally include the nonlinear benchmark *pendulum**, that simulates a simple pendulum and *rotation**, which repeatedly rotates a 2D vector by an (small) angle that is nondeterministically picked in each iteration. Both benchmarks use the sine function, which we approximate using a Taylor approximation. The *nonlin_example** are nonlinear dynamical systems collected from textbook examples on Lyapunov functions.

Three of our benchmarks contain operations on nondeterministic noise terms. Most benchmarks are 2-dimensional, except for *ex4**, which has 3 variables, *ex2** and *ex5**, which have 4 variables, and *ex6** that has 5 variables.

We run our evaluation on a MacBook Pro with an 3.1 GHz Intel Core i5 CPU, 16 GB RAM, and macOS Catalina 10.15.3.

5.3 Comparison with State-of-the-Art

Each tool generates an invariant with an elliptic shape, and PINE and SMT-AI provide additionally ranges for variables. We compare the inductive invariants generated by each tool based on their volume. The volume of an invariant is given by the set of points satisfying $\mathcal{P}(x) \leq 0 \wedge \bigwedge_i x_i \in \mathcal{R}_i$, where the variable ranges may intersect with the ellipsoid. We compute this intersection (approximately) using a Monte-Carlo simulation with $3 \cdot 10^6$ samples, by comparing how many samples are within the invariant to how many are inside the variable ranges (for the latter we know the volume exactly). Our volume estimates are accurate to two decimal digits.

We run PINE with a default set of parameters, that we determined empirically (see Sect. 5.5). In order to compare with other tools that only support single floating-point precision, PINE computes roundoff errors (and invariants) for 32-bit floating-point precision.

Columns 2–4 in Table 1 show the volumes of the invariants generated by SMT-AI, Pilat, and PINE. '-' denotes the cases where a tool did not generate an invariant. Benchmarks for which we did not have data for SMT-AI are marked as 'undef'. 'PF' denotes cases where an invariant was generated, but it did not satisfy the given precondition. 'TO' marks cases when a tool took longer than 20 min to generate an invariant. Here, smaller volume is better, the best volumes are marked bold.

Due to the inherent randomness in its algorithm, we run PINE 4 times and compute the average volume and running time across the runs. The last column shows variations in volume with respect to the average (i.e. (max - min)/average).

Table 1. Volumes of invariants generated by PINE, Pilat and SMT-AI, PINE's average running time and variation in invariant volumes across 4 runs

	Benchmark	SMT-AI	Pilat	PINE	PINE avg time, s	Volume variation
Non-linear	pendulum-approx	undef	-	**12.92**	21.09	30.03%
	rot.nondet-small	undef	-	**5.97**	30.13	16.25%
	rot.nondet-large	undef	-	**6.67**	33.78	10.87%
	nonlin-ex1	undef	-	**0.23**	14.43	18.51%
	nonlin-ex2	undef	-	**0.56**	7.32	5.23%
	nonlin-ex3	undef	-	**7.07**	12.45	3.35%
Linear	arrow-hurwitz	undef	-	**4.40**	4.75	7.00%
	harmonic	undef	18.41	**3.52**	10.81	9.70%
	symplectic	undef	PF	**2.32**	7.71	12.11%
	filter-goubault	undef	PF	**1.84**	4.94	1.31%
	filter-mine1	undef	PF	**6.32**	7.18	1.58%
	filter-mine2	undef	1.16	**0.49**	4.48	71.92%
	filter-mine2-nondet	undef	4.92	**4.45**	10.70	66.38%
	pendulum-small	undef	12.53	**9.10**	7.11	7.51%
	ex1- filter	**475.06**	498.37	-	43.61	-
	ex1-reset-filter	**475.98**	-	-	45.95	-
	ex2-2order	17.37	**1.07**	4.92	7.45	46.73%
	ex2-reset-2order	17.36	-	**3.08**	6.28	6.65%
	ex3-leadlag	-	-	-	46.68	-
	ex3-reset-leadlag	-	-	-	44.56	-
	ex4-gaussian	0.61	-	**0.22**	16.93	46.16%
	ex4-reset-gaussian	17.05	-	**1.45**	23.10	137.47%
	ex5-coupled-mass	5,538.47	TO	**100.61**	8.63	9.48%
	ex5-reset-coupled-mass	5,538.34	-	**81.02**	8.44	27.54%
	ex6-butterworth	65.25	-	**25.43**	16.34	272.89%
	ex6-reset-butterworth	700.06	-	**10.30**	219.34	0.00%
	ex7-dampened	**12.17**	-	18.68	19.96	15.71%
	ex7-reset-dampened	**12.17**	-	-	39.70	-
	ex8-harmonic	5.75	-	**2.32**	6.99	9.77%
	ex8-reset-harmonic	5.75	-	**2.85**	7.15	28.08%
	ex5+6	**6,927.12**	TO	TO	TO	-

We observe that PINE produces the tightest invariants on 17/24 (70%) of the linear benchmarks. Additionally, PINE generates invariants for all nonlinear benchmarks in our set, whereas Pilat was not able to generate invariants for any of them. PINE produces invariants that are in the best case on average 20x tighter than the ones by SMT-AI, and 2.7x tighter than the ones by Pilat (compared on the 6 benchmarks, for which it was able to generate an invariant). In the worst case (observed over our 4 runs), the factors decrease to 13.8x and 1.8x respectively. Only for the benchmarks *ex6-butterworth* and *filter-mine2-nondet*, the worst-case volumes computed by PINE become 1.9x and 1.6x larger than the ones computed by SMT-AI and Pilat, respectively, and are thus still of the same order of magnitude.

Table 2. Top-5 minimum volume configurations

m	n	cex_num	d	k	symPts	nearbyPts	volume
100	1000	0	0.5	500	✓		2.283
100	1000	0	0.5	100		✓	2.297
100	10000	5	0.25	100	✓	✓	2.311
100	1000	2	0.25	100		✓	2.314
100	10000	1	0.5	500		✓	2.335

5.4 Efficiency

PINE generates invariants in on average 25, and at most 220 s; the largest running time is also the benchmark with the largest number of variables. PINE was able to confirm the real-valued invariant also for the floating-point semantics for all but two *rotation** benchmarks, for which it had to recompute the invariants two out of four times. We consider the running times to be acceptably low such that it is feasible to re-run PINE several times for an input loop, in order to obtain a smaller invariant, if needed.

5.5 Parameter Sensitivity

We now evaluate the influence of different parameter settings on the performance of our proposed algorithm in terms of its ability to find tight inductive invariants. For this, we explored the parameter space of our algorithm on 13 of our benchmarks that include (non-)linear infinite loops without branching. We evaluate the different combinations of varying the following parameters:

- whether or not symmetric points are used
- whether or not nearby points are used
- number of random inputs and loop iterations for initial simulation (algorithm parameter m–n): 100–1k, 1k–1k, 100–10k
- number of loop iterations for counterexamples simulation (k): 0, 100, 500
- number of additional counterexamples (cex_num): 0, 1, 2, 5 (when $cex\_num = 0$, no additional counterexample is generated)
- distance to nearby points (in % of the range) (d): 10%, 25%, 50%
- three different precisions for rounding: ($prec_{poly} = 1, prec_{range} = 0$), ($prec_{poly} = 2, prec_{range} = 1$), ($prec_{poly} = 3, prec_{range} = 2$), where $prec_{poly}$, $prec_{range}$ give the number of decimal digits for the polynomial coefficients and the variable ranges, respectively.

In total, we obtain 1296 configurations. We run PINE with each of them once.

Default Configuration. 185 parameter configurations were successful on all of the 13 benchmarks. From these, we select the configuration that generates invariants with the smallest average volume across the benchmarks as our default configuration: $prec_{poly} = 2, prec_{range} = 1, m = 100, n = 1000, k = 500$. To generalize from counterexamples the default configuration uses only symmetric points.

172   A. Izycheva et al.

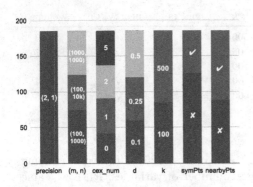

Benchmark	min	avg	max
pendulum-approx	9.88	12.03	20.21
rot.nondet-small	4.76	5.78	8.07
rot.nondet-large	6.27	6.92	11.43
nonlin-ex1	0.06	0.20	0.83
nonlin-ex2	0.55	0.56	0.59
nonlin-ex3	6.84	7.04	7.27
harmonic	3.28	3.84	4.46
symplectic	2.12	2.21	2.68
filter-goubault	1.82	1.83	1.85
filter-mine1	6.29	6.40	8.72
filter-mine2	0.28	1.03	3.83
filter-mine2-nondet	1.74	2.44	11.37
pendulum-small	8.61	10.14	24.55

Fig. 4. Proportion of parameters appearing in successful configurations

Fig. 5. Volumes of invariants with successful configurations

Table 2 shows the 5 best configurations, according to average volume (we normalized the volume across benchmarks). We note that the differences between volumes for successful configurations are small, so that we could have chosen any of these configurations as the default.

Successful Configurations. We study the 185 successful configurations to see which parameter values appear the most frequently, and thus seem most successful in finding invariants. Figure 4 shows the distribution of the different parameters in the set of successful configurations. For instance, the precisions $(prec_{poly} = 1, prec_{range} = 0)$ and $(prec_{poly} = 3, prec_{range} = 2)$ do not appear at all in the successful configurations, i.e. only $(prec_{poly} = 2, prec_{range} = 1)$ was able to find invariants for all benchmarks. On the other hand, nearby points are included in the generalization in roughly half of the configurations.

From Fig. 4, we conclude that simulating the loop starting from counterexamples (line 21 in Fig. 3) is crucial in finding an invariant - none of the configurations without this additional simulation worked on all benchmarks. On the other hand, whether this simulation runs 100 or 500 loop iterations seems to make less of a difference.

For the remaining parameters, we do not observe a strong significance; they are roughly equally distributed among the successful configurations. From this we conclude that our algorithm is not sensitive to particular parameter settings, and will find invariants successfully for many different parameter configurations.

The choice of parameters does, however, influence the size of the invariants generated, at least for certain benchmarks. Figure 5 shows the minimum, maximum and average volumes for each benchmark across successful configurations. While for some benchmarks, the variation is small, for others the best configuration produces invariants that are half the size from the worst one.

Across the 1296 configurations, we observe that if a real-valued invariant is found, it is also confirmed in 89% of cases, and thus has to be re-computed in only 11% of cases. The only outlier that needs recomputation more often is *rotation-nondet-large*, which rotates a vector by a larger angle, and therefore is understandably more sensitive to enlarging the coordinates with some noise.

Last but not least, we used PINE's default configuration to generate invariants for fixed-point precision with uniform 16 bit length for all our 30 benchmarks (including ex^*). The smaller bit length results in larger roundoff errors, so that PINE had to recompute an invariant for 5 additional benchmarks (i.e. where the real-valued invariant was not confirmed), but was able to find an inductive invariant for as many loops as with floating-point implementation.

6 Related Work

Many tools and libraries [23] infer invariants over program variables using abstract interpretation. The abstract domains range from efficient and imprecise intervals [11], over octagons [28], to more expensive and expressive polyhedra [4,41]. For programs with elliptic invariants most linear abstract domains are insufficient to express an invariant [36].

Ellipsoid domains have been defined that work for specific types of programs, e.g. digital filters [17] and programs where variables grow linearly with respect to the enclosing loop counters [34]. Performing abstract interpretation using policy iterations instead of widening allows the use of the ellipsoid abstract domain more generally [1,20]. This approach requires templates of the ellipsoids to be given, however. Recent works [33,36] are able to discover ellipsoid inductive loop invariants without the need for templates, but being based on semidefinite programming and linear algebra, respectively, are fundamentally limited to linear loops only. Alternatively, Bagnara et.al. [5] have explored an abstract domain that approximates polynomial inequalities by convex polyhedra and leverages the operations, including widening, of polyhedra. Sankaranarayanan et.al. [37] show how to generate polynomial equality invariants by reducing the problem to a constraint satisfaction problem.

Our algorithm builds on several ideas that have been explored in loop invariant synthesis previously, including the use of concrete executions to derive polynomial templates and counter-example based refinement. Floating-point loops and in particular the uncertainties introduced due to roundoff errors pose unique challenges that existing techniques cannot handle, as we discuss next.

Several works have explored the use of machine-learning in teacher-learner frameworks [19,43]: the learner guesses a candidate invariant from a set of examples, and the teacher checks whether the invariant is inductive. If it is not, the teacher provides feedback to the learner in form of additional (counter)examples. These approaches rely on a target property to be given (to provide negative examples) and are thus not immediately applicable to synthesizing floating-point inequality invariants. The framework C2I [38] employs a learner-teacher framework, but where the learner uses a randomized search to generate candidate

174 A. Izycheva et al.

invariants. While surprisingly effective, the approach is, however, limited to a
a fixed search, e.g. linear inequalities with a finite set of given constants as
coefficients. Sharma et.al. [40] present a learning based algorithm to generate
invariants that are arbitrary boolean combinations of polynomial inequalities,
but require a set of good and bad states and thus an assertion to be given.

The tool InvGen [21] generates integer linear invariants from linear templates, using concrete program executions to derive constraints on the template
parameters. The tool NumInv [32] and the Guess-And-Check algorithm [39]
generate polynomial equality invariants using a similar approach. For integer
programs and in particular equality constraints, this approach is exact. In our
setting with floating-point programs and inequalities such constraints cannot be
solved exactly and thus require a different, approximate, approach. NumInv and
Guess-And-Check furthermore employ counterexamples returned by the solver
for refinement of the invariant. These counterexamples are program inputs, however, due to the complexity of the floating-point or real-arithmetic decision procedures, this technique does not scale to our target numerical programs. We are
thus restricted to counterexamples to the invariant property.

Abductive inference in the tool Hola [14] and enumerative synthesis in FreqHorn [15] are two further techniques that have been used to generate invariants
for numerical programs, but are unfortunately not applicable to generate the
invariants we are looking for. Hola relies on quantifier elimination which solvers
do not support (well) for floating-points and reals; FreqHorn generates the invariant grammar from the program's source code, but for our invariants the terms
do not appear in the program itself.

Allamigeon et al. [2] extend ellipsoidal analyses to generate disjunctive and
non-convex invariants for switched linear systems. We do not consider disjunctive
invariants in this work and leave their exploration to future work.

Recurrence-based techniques [25, 26] generate loop invariants that exactly
capture the behavior of a numerical integer loop. While these techniques work for
arbitrary conditional branches, imperative code and nested loops, they generate
invariants of a different form, i.e. in general not polynomial inequalities and are
thus orthogonal to our approach.

7   Conclusion

We propose a novel algorithm for synthesizing polynomial inequality invariants
for floating-point loops. For this, we show how to extend the well-know technique
of counterexample-guided invariant synthesis to handle the uncertainties arising
from finite-precision arithmetic. The key insight to make our iterative refinement
work is that a single counterexample is not sufficient and the algorithm has
to explore the space of counterexamples more evenly in order to successfully
generalize. While the resulting algorithm is heuristic in nature, it proved to be
remarkably effective on existing benchmarks as well as on handling benchmarks
out of reach of existing tools.

Acknowledgements. We would like to thank Sebastian Bruggisser for helping to debug our ellipsoids.

References

1. Adjé, A., Gaubert, S., Goubault, E.: Coupling policy iteration with semi-definite relaxation to compute accurate numerical invariants in static analysis. Logical Methods Comput. Sci. **8**(1), 23–42 (2012)
2. Allamigeon, X., Gaubert, S., Goubault, E., Putot, S., Stott, N.: A fast method to compute disjunctive quadratic invariants of numerical programs. ACM Trans. Embedded Comput. Syst. **16**(5s), 166:1–166:19 (2017)
3. Astrom, K.J., Murray, R.M.: Feedback Systems: An Introduction for Scientists and Engineers. Princeton University Press, Princeton (2008)
4. Bagnara, R., Hill, P.M., Zaffanella, E.: The Parma Polyhedra library: toward a complete set of numerical abstractions for the analysis and verification of hardware and software systems. Sci. Comput. Program. **72**(1), 3–21 (2008)
5. Bagnara, R., Rodríguez-Carbonell, E., Zaffanella, E.: Generation of basic semi-algebraic invariants using convex polyhedra. In: Hankin, C., Siveroni, I. (eds.) SAS 2005. LNCS, vol. 3672, pp. 19–34. Springer, Heidelberg (2005). https://doi.org/10.1007/11547662_4
6. Barrett, C., et al.: CVC4. In: Gopalakrishnan, G., Qadeer, S. (eds.) CAV 2011. LNCS, vol. 6806, pp. 171–177. Springer, Heidelberg (2011). https://doi.org/10.1007/978-3-642-22110-1_14
7. Bradley, A.R.: SAT-based model checking without unrolling. In: Jhala, R., Schmidt, D. (eds.) VMCAI 2011. LNCS, vol. 6538, pp. 70–87. Springer, Heidelberg (2011). https://doi.org/10.1007/978-3-642-18275-4_7
8. Brain, M., Schanda, F., Sun, Y.: Building better bit-blasting for floating-point problems. In: Vojnar, T., Zhang, L. (eds.) TACAS 2019. LNCS, vol. 11427, pp. 79–98. Springer, Cham (2019). https://doi.org/10.1007/978-3-030-17462-0_5
9. Cousot, P., Cousot, R.: Abstract interpretation: a unified lattice model for static analysis of programs by construction or approximation of fixpoints. In: Fourth ACM Symposium on Principles of Programming Languages (1977)
10. Cousot, P., Halbwachs, N.: Automatic discovery of linear restraints among variables of a program. In: 5th ACM SIGACT-SIGPLAN Symposium on Principles of Programming Languages, POPL 1978 (1978)
11. Cousot, P., Radhia, C.: Static determination of dynamic properties of programs. In: ISOP (1976)
12. Darulova, E., Izycheva, A., Nasir, F., Ritter, F., Becker, H., Bastian, R.: Daisy - framework for analysis and optimization of numerical programs (tool paper). In: Beyer, D., Huisman, M. (eds.) TACAS 2018. LNCS, vol. 10805, pp. 270–287. Springer, Cham (2018). https://doi.org/10.1007/978-3-319-89960-2_15
13. Darulova, E., Kuncak, V.: Towards a compiler for reals. ACM Trans. Program. Lang. Syst. **39**(2), 8:1–8:28 (2017)
14. Dillig, I., Dillig, T., Li, B., McMillan, K.L.: Inductive invariant generation via abductive inference. In: Object Oriented Programming Systems Languages & Applications (OOPSLA) (2013)
15. Fedyukovich, G., Bodík, R.: Accelerating syntax guided invariant synthesis. In: Beyer, D., Huisman, M. (eds.) TACAS 2018. LNCS, vol. 10805, pp. 251–269. Springer, Cham (2018). https://doi.org/10.1007/978-3-319-89960-2_14

16. Fedyukovich, G., Kaufman, S.J., Bodík, R.: Sampling invariants from frequency distributions. In: FMCAD (Formal Methods in Computer Aided Design) (2017)
17. Feret, J.: Static analysis of digital filters. In: Schmidt, D. (ed.) ESOP 2004. LNCS, vol. 2986, pp. 33–48. Springer, Heidelberg (2004). https://doi.org/10.1007/978-3-540-24725-8_4
18. Gal Lalire, M. Argoud, B.J.: A web interface to the interproc analyzer. http://pop-art.inrialpes.fr/interproc/interprocwebf.cgi
19. Garg, P., Löding, C., Madhusudan, P., Neider, D.: ICE: a robust framework for learning invariants. In: Biere, A., Bloem, R. (eds.) CAV 2014. LNCS, vol. 8559, pp. 69–87. Springer, Cham (2014). https://doi.org/10.1007/978-3-319-08867-9_5
20. Gawlitza, T.M., Seidl, H.: Numerical invariants through convex relaxation and max-strategy iteration. Formal Methods Syst. Des. **44**(2), 101–148 (2014)
21. Gupta, A., Rybalchenko, A.: InvGen: an efficient invariant generator. In: Bouajjani, A., Maler, O. (eds.) CAV 2009. LNCS, vol. 5643, pp. 634–640. Springer, Heidelberg (2009). https://doi.org/10.1007/978-3-642-02658-4_48
22. IEEE Computer Society: IEEE Standard for Floating-Point Arithmetic. IEEE Std 754-2008 (2008)
23. Jeannet, B., Miné, A.: APRON: a library of numerical abstract domains for static analysis. In: Bouajjani, A., Maler, O. (eds.) CAV 2009. LNCS, vol. 5643, pp. 661–667. Springer, Heidelberg (2009). https://doi.org/10.1007/978-3-642-02658-4_52
24. Jovanović, D., de Moura, L.: Solving non-linear arithmetic. In: Gramlich, B., Miller, D., Sattler, U. (eds.) IJCAR 2012. LNCS (LNAI), vol. 7364, pp. 339–354. Springer, Heidelberg (2012). https://doi.org/10.1007/978-3-642-31365-3_27
25. Kincaid, Z., Cyphert, J., Breck, J., Reps, T.W.: Non-linear reasoning for invariant synthesis. Proc. ACM Program. Lang. **2**(POPL), 54:1–54:33 (2018)
26. Kovács, L.: Reasoning algebraically about p-solvable loops. In: Ramakrishnan, C.R., Rehof, J. (eds.) TACAS 2008. LNCS, vol. 4963, pp. 249–264. Springer, Heidelberg (2008). https://doi.org/10.1007/978-3-540-78800-3_18
27. Magnani, A., Lall, S., Boyd, S.: Tractable fitting with convex polynomials via sum-of-squares. In: Proceedings of the 44th IEEE Conference on Decision and Control (2005)
28. Miné, A.: The octagon abstract domain. High. Order Symb. Comput. **19**(1), 31–100 (2006). https://doi.org/10.1007/s10990-006-8609-1
29. Miné, A., Breck, J., Reps, T.: An algorithm inspired by constraint solvers to infer inductive invariants in numeric programs. In: Thiemann, P. (ed.) ESOP 2016. LNCS, vol. 9632, pp. 560–588. Springer, Heidelberg (2016). https://doi.org/10.1007/978-3-662-49498-1_22
30. Moshtagh, N.: Minimum Volume Enclosing Ellipsoid (2020). https://www.mathworks.com/matlabcentral/fileexchange/9542-minimum-volume-enclosing-ellipsoid. Accessed 21 May 2020
31. de Moura, L., Bjørner, N.: Z3: an efficient SMT solver. In: Ramakrishnan, C.R., Rehof, J. (eds.) TACAS 2008. LNCS, vol. 4963, pp. 337–340. Springer, Heidelberg (2008). https://doi.org/10.1007/978-3-540-78800-3_24
32. Nguyen, T., Antonopoulos, T., Ruef, A., Hicks, M.: Counterexample-guided approach to finding numerical invariants. In: Foundations of Software Engineering (ESEC/FSE) (2017)
33. de Oliveira, S., Bensalem, S., Prevosto, V.: Synthesizing invariants by solving solvable loops. In: D'Souza, D., Narayan Kumar, K. (eds.) ATVA 2017. LNCS, vol. 10482, pp. 327–343. Springer, Cham (2017). https://doi.org/10.1007/978-3-319-68167-2_22

34. Oulamara, M., Venet, A.J.: Abstract interpretation with higher-dimensional ellipsoids and conic extrapolation. In: Kroening, D., Păsăreanu, C.S. (eds.) CAV 2015. LNCS, vol. 9206, pp. 415–430. Springer, Cham (2015). https://doi.org/10.1007/978-3-319-21690-4_24

35. Roux, P., Garoche, P.-L.: Integrating policy iterations in abstract interpreters. In: Van Hung, D., Ogawa, M. (eds.) ATVA 2013. LNCS, vol. 8172, pp. 240–254. Springer, Cham (2013). https://doi.org/10.1007/978-3-319-02444-8_18

36. Roux, P., Garoche, P.: Practical policy iterations - a practical use of policy iterations for static analysis: the quadratic case. Formal Methods Syst. Des. **46**(2), 163–196 (2015)

37. Sankaranarayanan, S., Sipma, H.B., Manna, Z.: Non-linear loop invariant generation using gröbner bases. In: Principles of Programming Languages, POPL (2004)

38. Sharma, R., Aiken, A.: From invariant checking to invariant inference using randomized search. In: Biere, A., Bloem, R. (eds.) CAV 2014. LNCS, vol. 8559, pp. 88–105. Springer, Cham (2014). https://doi.org/10.1007/978-3-319-08867-9_6

39. Sharma, R., Gupta, S., Hariharan, B., Aiken, A., Liang, P., Nori, A.V.: A data driven approach for algebraic loop invariants. In: Felleisen, M., Gardner, P. (eds.) ESOP 2013. LNCS, vol. 7792, pp. 574–592. Springer, Heidelberg (2013). https://doi.org/10.1007/978-3-642-37036-6_31

40. Sharma, R., Gupta, S., Hariharan, B., Aiken, A., Nori, A.V.: Verification as learning geometric concepts. In: Logozzo, F., Fähndrich, M. (eds.) SAS 2013. LNCS, vol. 7935, pp. 388–411. Springer, Heidelberg (2013). https://doi.org/10.1007/978-3-642-38856-9_21

41. Singh, G., Püschel, M., Vechev, M.: A practical construction for decomposing numerical abstract domains. Proc. ACM Program. Lang. **2**(POPL), 1–28 (2017)

42. Solovyev, A., Jacobsen, C., Rakamaric, Z., Gopalakrishnan, G.: Rigorous estimation of floating-point round-off errors with symbolic Taylor expansions. In: Formal Methods (FM) (2015)

43. Zhu, H., Magill, S., Jagannathan, S.: A data-driven CHC solver. In: Programming Language Design and Implementation (PLDI) (2018)

Formal Framework for Reasoning About the Precision of Dynamic Analysis

Mila Dalla Preda[✉], Roberto Giacobazzi, and Niccoló Marastoni

Dipartimento di Informatica, University of Verona, Verona, Italy
{mila.dallapreda,roberto.giacobazzi,niccolo.marastoni}@univr.it

Abstract. Dynamic program analysis is extremely successful both in code debugging and in malicious code attacks. Fuzzing, concolic, and monkey testing are instances of the more general problem of analysing programs by dynamically executing their code with selected inputs. While static program analysis has a beautiful and well established theoretical foundation in abstract interpretation, dynamic analysis still lacks such a foundation. In this paper, we introduce a formal model for understanding the notion of precision in dynamic program analysis. It is known that in sound-by-construction static program analysis the precision amounts to completeness. In dynamic analysis, which is inherently unsound, precision boils down to a notion of coverage of execution traces with respect to what the observer (attacker or debugger) can effectively observe about the computation. We introduce a topological characterisation of the notion of coverage relatively to a given (fixed) observation for dynamic program analysis and we show how this coverage can be changed by semantic preserving code transformations. Once again, as well as in the case of static program analysis and abstract interpretation, also for dynamic analysis we can morph the precision of the analysis by transforming the code. In this context, we validate our model on well established code obfuscation and watermarking techniques. We confirm the efficiency of existing methods for preventing control-flow-graph extraction and data exploit by dynamic analysis, including a validation of the potency of fully homomorphic data encodings in code obfuscation.

1 Introduction

Program analysis allows us to infer information on programs behaviour (semantics). It is well known from the Rice theorem that, in general, it is not possible to decide whether a given program satisfies a semantic property. For this reason analysts recur to approximation either by static or dynamic analysis. Static analysis computes an over-approximation of program semantics, while dynamic analysis under-approximates program semantics. In both cases, we have a decidable evaluation of the semantic property on an approximation of program semantics. For this reason what we can conclude regarding the semantic property of programs has to take into account false positives for static analysis and false negatives for dynamic analysis. Static analysis is precise when it is complete (no

D. Pichardie and M. Sighireanu (Eds.): SAS 2020, LNCS 12389, pp. 178–199, 2020.
https://doi.org/10.1007/978-3-030-65474-0_9

false positives) and this relates to the well studied notion of completeness in abstract interpretation [10,11,20]. Dynamic analysis is precise when it is sound (no false negatives), this happens when the execution traces considered by the dynamic analysis exhibit all the behaviours of the program that are relevant wrt the semantic property of interest. Code coverage is the metric typically used by dynamic analysis to evaluate its soundness, namely the amount of false negatives [1].

Program analysis has been originally developed for program verification and debugging and researchers have put a great effort in developing efficient analysis techniques and tools that reduce the number of both false positives and false negatives. In this setting, analysis precision relates to the ability of identifying bugs and vulnerabilities that may lead to unexpected behaviours, or that may be exploited by an adversary for malicious purposes.

Software protection is another interesting scenario where program analysis plays a central role but in a dual way. Indeed, in the software protection scenario program analysis is used by adversaries to reverse engineer proprietary code and then illicitly reuse portions of the code or tamper with the code in some unauthorised way. Here, the intellectual property and integrity of programs is guaranteed when the analysis is imprecise or very expensive since this complicates the attacks. In this setting, researchers have developed program transformations, called code obfuscations, with the explicit intent of complicating program analysis. In the last years many different kinds of obfuscation techniques and tools have been proposed [5]. Code obfuscation proved its efficiency in degrading the results of static program analysis while it is less efficient with respect to dynamic program analysis [28].

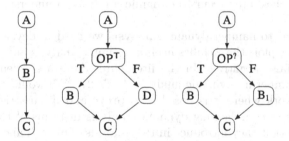

Fig. 1. Code obfuscation

For example, consider a program whose control flow graph is depicted on the left of Fig. 1 where we have three blocks of sequential instructions A, B and C executed in the order specified by the arrows $A \to B \to C$. A true opaque predicate OP^T is a predicate that always evaluates to *true*, but this invariant behaviour is not known to the attacker that considers as possible also the execution of the false branch [6]. In the middle of Fig. 1 we can see what happens to the control flow graph when we insert a true opaque predicate, where block D has to be considered in the static analysis of the control flow even if it is never executed at runtime. Thus, $A \rightarrow OP^{\top} \rightarrow D \rightarrow C$ is a false positive path added by obfuscation to static analysis, while no imprecision is added to dynamic analysis since all executions follow the path $A \rightarrow OP^{\top} \rightarrow B \rightarrow C$. On the right of Fig. 1 we have the control flow graph of the program obtained inserting an unknown opaque predicate. An unknown opaque predicate $OP^?$ is a predicate that sometimes evaluates to *true* and sometimes evaluates to *false*. These predicates are used to diversify program execution by inserting in the true and false branches sequences of instructions that are different but functionally equivalent (e.g. blocks B and B_1) [6]. Observe that this transformation adds confusion to dynamic analysis: a dynamic analyser has to consider more execution traces in order to observe all possible program behaviours. Indeed, if the dynamic analysis observes only traces that follow the original path $A \rightarrow OP^? \rightarrow B \rightarrow C$ it may not be sound as it misses the traces that follow $A \rightarrow OP^? \rightarrow B_1 \rightarrow C$ (false negative).

The abstract interpretation framework has been used to formally prove the efficiency of code obfuscation in making static analysers imprecise [13]. Indeed, code obfuscation hampers static analysis by exploiting its conservative nature, namely by increasing its imprecision (false positives) while preserving the program intended behaviour. It has been observed that adding false positives to the analysis can be formalised in terms of incompleteness in the analysis of the transformed program [13,14,18,21]. Observe that, in general, the imprecision added by these obfuscating transformations in order to confuse a static analyzer is not able to confuse a dynamic attacker that looks at the real program execution and thus cannot be deceived by false positives. Indeed, dynamic analysis observes only paths that are actually executed. For this reason common deobfuscation approaches often recur to dynamic analysis to understand obfuscated code [3,7,31,38].

It is clear that to hamper dynamic analysis we need to develop obfuscation techniques that exploit the Achilles heel of dynamic analysis and that increases the number of false negatives. In the literature, there are defense techniques that focus on hampering dynamic analysis [2,25–27]. We would like to provide a formal framework where it is possible to prove and discuss the efficiency of these techniques in complicating dynamic analysis in terms of the imprecision (false negatives) that they introduce in the analysis. This will allow us to better understand the potential and limits of code obfuscation against dynamic program analysis. We start by providing a formalisation of dynamic analysis and software protection techniques in terms of program semantics and equivalence reactions over semantic domains, and we characterise when a program transformation hampers a dynamic analysis in terms of topological features.

The contribution of this work are: (1) formal specification for dynamic analysis/attacks based on program semantics and equivalence relations; (2) formal definition of software-based protection transformations against dynamic attacks that induce imprecision in dynamic analysis (false negatives); (3) validation of the model on some known software-based defense strategies.

2 Preliminaries

Basic Lattice and Fix-Point Theory: Given two sets S and T, we denote with $\wp(S)$ the powerset of S, with $S \times T$ the Cartesian product of S and T, with $S \subset T$ strict inclusion, with $S \subseteq T$ inclusion, with $S \subseteq_F T$ the fact that S is a finite set. $\langle C, \leqslant, \vee, \wedge, \top, \bot \rangle$ denotes a complete lattice on the set C, with ordering $\leqslant$, least upper bound (*lub*) $\vee$, greatest lower bound (*glb*) $\wedge$, greatest element (top) $\top$, and least element (bottom) $\bot$. Let C and D be complete lattices. Then, $C \xrightarrow{m} D$ and $C \xrightarrow{c} D$ denote, respectively, the set and the type of all monotone and (Scott-)continuous functions from C to D. Recall that $f \in C \xrightarrow{c} D$ if and only if f preserves *lub*'s of (nonempty) chains if and only if f preserves *lub*'s of directed subsets. Let $f : C \rightarrow C$ be a function on a complete lattice C, we denote with *lfp*(f) the least fix-point, when it exists, of function f on C. The well-known Knaster-Tarski's theorem states that any monotone operator $f : C \xrightarrow{m} C$ on a complete lattice C admits a least fix point. It is known that if $f : C \xrightarrow{c} C$ is continuous then $lfp(f) = \vee_{i \in \mathbb{N}} f^i(\bot_C)$, where, for any $i \in \mathbb{N}$ and $x \in C$, the i-th power of f in x is inductively defined as follows: $f^0(x) = x$; $f^{i+1}(x) = f(f^i(x))$.

Given a relation $\mathcal{R} \subseteq C \times D$ between two sets C and D, and two elements $x \in C$ and $y \in D$, then $(x, y) \in \mathcal{R}$ denotes that the pair (x, y) belongs to the relation $\mathcal{R}$. A binary relation $\mathcal{R}$ on a set C, namely $\mathcal{R} \subseteq C \times C$, is an *equivalence relation* if $\mathcal{R}$ is reflexive $\forall x \in C : (x, x) \in \mathcal{R}$, symmetric $\forall x, y \in C : (x, y) \in \mathcal{R} \Rightarrow (y, x) \in \mathcal{R}$ and transitive $\forall x, y, z \in C : (x, y) \in \mathcal{R} \wedge (y, z) \in \mathcal{R} \Rightarrow (x, z) \in \mathcal{R}$. Given a set C equipped with an equivalence relation $\mathcal{R}$, we consider for each element $x \in C$ the subset $[x]_{\mathcal{R}}$ of C containing all the elements of C in equivalence relation with x, i.e., $[x]_{\mathcal{R}} = \{y \in C \mid (x, y) \in \mathcal{R}\}$. The sets $[x]_{\mathcal{R}}$ are called equivalence classes of C wrt relation R. Let *eq*(C) be the set of equivalence relations over the set C. The equivalence classes of an equivalence relation $\mathcal{R} \in eq(C)$ form a partition of the set C, namely $\forall x, y \in C : [x]_{\mathcal{R}} = [y]_{\mathcal{R}} \vee [x]_{\mathcal{R}} \cap [y]_{\mathcal{R}} = \emptyset$ and $\cup\{[x]_{\mathcal{R}} \mid x \in C\} = C$. The partition of C induced by the set of equivalence classes of relation $\mathcal{R}$ is called the quotient set of C and it is denoted by $C/_{\mathcal{R}}$. A partition $C/_{\mathcal{R}_1}$ is a refinement of a partition $C/_{\mathcal{R}_2}$, namely $\mathcal{R}_1$ if finer than $\mathcal{R}_2$ or $\mathcal{R}_2$ is coarser than $\mathcal{R}_1$, if every equivalence class in $C/_{\mathcal{R}_1}$ is a subset of some equivalence class in $C/_{\mathcal{R}_2}$. We denote with $\mathcal{R}_1 \sqsubseteq \mathcal{R}_2$ the fact that the equivalence relation $\mathcal{R}_1$ is finer than the equivalence relation $\mathcal{R}_2$. Given a subset $S \subseteq C$ we denote with $\mathcal{R}(S)$ the set of equivalence classes of the elements of S, namely $\mathcal{R}(S) = \{[x]_{\mathcal{R}} \mid x \in S\}$, and with $S/_{\mathcal{R}}$ the partition of the subset S induced by the equivalence relation $\mathcal{R}$, namely $S/_{\mathcal{R}} = \{[x]_{\mathcal{R}} \cap S \mid x \in S\}$.

Program Semantics: Let *Prog* be a set of programs ranged over by P. Let $v \in \mathbb{I}$ denote a possible input and let $\mathbb{I}^*$ denote the set of input sequences ranged over by $\mathcal{I}$, let *PP* denote the set of program points ranged over by *pp*, let *Com* denote the set of program statements ranged over by C and let *Mem* denote the set of memory maps that associates values to variables ranged over by $m : Var \rightarrow Values$. $\Sigma = \mathbb{I}^* \times PP \times Com \times Mem$ is the set of program states. Thus, a program state $s \in \Sigma$ is a tuple $s = \langle \mathcal{I}, pp, C, m \rangle$ where $\mathcal{I}$ denotes the sequence of inputs that still needs to be consumed to terminate the execution, *pp* denotes the program point of the next instruction C that has to be executed, and m is the current memory. We denote with $C_1; C_2$ the sequential composition of statements and we refer to *skip* as the identity statement whose execution has no effects on memory. Given a program P we denote with $\mathbb{I}_P \subseteq \mathbb{I}^*$ the set of the initial input sequences for the execution of program P, and with $Init_P = \{s \in \Sigma \mid s = \langle \mathfrak{I}, pp, C, m \rangle, \mathfrak{I} \in \mathbb{I}_P\}$ the set of its initial states. We use Σ^* to denote the set of all finite and infinite sequences or traces of states, where $\epsilon \in \Sigma^*$ is the empty sequence, $|\sigma|$ the length of sequence $\sigma \in \Sigma^*$. $\Sigma^+ \subset \Sigma^*$ denotes the set of finite sequences of elements of Σ. We denote the concatenation of sequences $\sigma, \nu \in \Sigma^*$ as $\sigma\nu$. Given $\sigma, \nu \in \Sigma^*$, $\nu \preceq \sigma$ means that ν is a subsequence of σ, namely that there exists $\sigma_1, \sigma_2 \in \Sigma^*$ such that $\sigma = \sigma_1\nu\sigma_2$. Given $s \in \Sigma$ we write $s \in \sigma$ when s is an element occurring in sequence σ, and we denote with $\sigma_0 \in \Sigma$ the first element of sequence σ and with σ_f the final element of the finite sequence $\sigma \in \Sigma^+$. Let $R \subseteq \Sigma \times \Sigma$ denote the transition relation between program states, thus $(s, s') \in R$ means that state s' can be obtained from state s in one computational step. The *(finite) trace semantics* of a program P is defined, as usual, as the least fix-point computation of function $\mathcal{F}_P : \wp(\Sigma^*) \rightarrow \wp(\Sigma^*)$ [9]:

$$\mathcal{F}_P(X) \stackrel{\text{def}}{=} Init_P \cup \{ \sigma s_i s_{i+1} \mid (s_i, s_{i+1}) \in R, \sigma s_i \in X \}$$

The trace semantics of P is $[\![P]\!] = \mathit{lfp}(\mathcal{F}_P) = \bigcup_{i \in \mathbb{N}} \mathcal{F}_P^i(\bot_C)$. $Den[\![P]\!]$ denotes the denotational (finite) semantics of program P which abstracts away the history of the computation by observing only the input-output relation of finite traces. Therefore we have $Den[\![P]\!] = \{\sigma \in \Sigma^+ \mid \exists \eta \in [\![P]\!] : \eta_0 = \sigma_0, \eta_f = \sigma_f\}$.

3   Topological Characterisation of the Precision of Dynamic Analysis

We start our investigation by considering dynamic analysis that observes features of single execution traces, as for example: the order of successive accesses to memory, the order of execution of instructions, the location of the first instruction of a function, the target of jumps, function location, possible data values at certain program points, etc. The extension of the framework to properties of sets of traces (hyper-properties) and relational properties among traces is left as future work.

The simplest way to model properties of single traces is in terms of equivalence relations over program traces. Indeed, an equivalence relation $\mathcal{R} \in eq(\Sigma^*)$ groups together all those execution traces that are equivalent wrt the property used to establish the equivalence for $\mathcal{R}$. In this setting, each equivalence class $[\sigma]_{\mathcal{R}} \subseteq \Sigma^*$ represents the set of execution traces that are equivalent to σ wrt $\mathcal{R}$, namely all those execution traces that $\mathcal{R}$ is not able to distinguish from σ. In general, given a program $P \in Prog$ and an equivalence relation $\mathcal{R} \in eq(\Sigma^*)$ it may not be possible to precisely observe property $\mathcal{R}$ of program semantics, namely the set $\mathcal{R}([\![P]\!]) = \{[\sigma]_{\mathcal{R}} \mid \sigma \in [\![P]\!]\}$ may not be precisely observable. This means that it may not be possible to decide whether $\mathcal{R}([\![P]\!]) \subseteq \Pi$, for some $\Pi \in \wp(\Sigma^*/_{\mathcal{R}})$, a set of equivalence classes representing a possible feature of program execution that can be expressed in terms of $\mathcal{R}$. In order to verify these features, analysts resort to approximation either by static or dynamic analysis.

Example 1. Consider function $\iota : \Sigma \to \mathbb{I}$ that observes the first input value $v \in \mathbb{I}$ of a program state, namely $\iota(\langle v\mathbb{J}, pp, C, m \rangle) \stackrel{def}{=} v$. We can define the equivalence relation $\mathcal{R}_\iota$ as $(\sigma, \nu) \in \mathcal{R}_\iota$ iff $\iota(\sigma_0) = \iota(\nu_0)$, grouping together traces with the same starting input values. Based on $\mathcal{R}_\iota$ we can define features of program behaviour as for example $\Pi_1, \Pi_2 \in \wp(\Sigma^*/_{\mathcal{R}_\iota})$ where $\Pi_1 = \{[\sigma]_{\mathcal{R}_\iota} \mid \iota(\sigma) \geqslant 0\}$ observes the equivalence classes of traces whose first input value is positive, and $\Pi_2 = \{[\sigma]_{\mathcal{R}_\iota} \mid \iota(\sigma) \in [l, u]\}$ observes the equivalence classes of traces whose first input value is in the interval $[l, u]$.

We can think about relation $\mathcal{R}$ as the granularity at which the analysis observes program executions. Given $\mathcal{R}_1 \sqsubseteq \mathcal{R}_2$ we have that $\mathcal{R}_1$ describes an analysis that is more precise than $\mathcal{R}_2$ in distinguishing program traces, while $\mathcal{R}_2$ describes an analysis that groups together more traces than $\mathcal{R}_1$. The equivalence classes can then be combined to describe properties of programs at different levels of abstraction.

In the literature there exists a formal investigation of the effects of code obfuscation to the precision of static analysis [13,14,18,21]. This has lead to a better understanding of the potential and limits of obfuscation, and it has been useful in the design of obfuscation techniques that target specific program properties [14,18,19].

In the following we apply a similar approach to dynamic analysis. To this end we formalise the absence of false negatives, namely the precision of dynamic analysis, in terms of topological properties of program trace semantics and of the equivalence relation $\mathcal{R}$ modelling the property to be observed. False negatives happen when the set of traces considered by dynamic analysis misses some traces that would modify the equivalence classes observed by property $\mathcal{R}$. We show how to transform a program in order to hinder the dynamic analysis of a property $\mathcal{R}$, namely in order to make the dynamic analysis of the transformed program not sound.

3.1   Modelling Dynamic Program Analysis

Dynamic analysis observes a finite subset of finite execution traces of a program and from this partial observation tries to drive conclusions on the whole program behaviour.

Definition 1 (Dynamic Execution). *The execution traces of program* P *with initial states in* $T_P \subseteq_F Init_P$ *and with time limits* $t \in \mathbb{N}$, *are defined as:*

$$Exe(P, T_P, t) \stackrel{def}{=} \{ \sigma \in [\![P]\!] \mid |\sigma| \leqslant t, \sigma = s_0\sigma', s_0 \in T_P \}$$

Note that $Exe(P, T_P, t)$ is a finite set and that each trace in $Exe(P, T_P, t)$ is finite (it has at most t states). This correctly implies that: $Exe(P, T_P, t) \subseteq_F [\![P]\!]$.

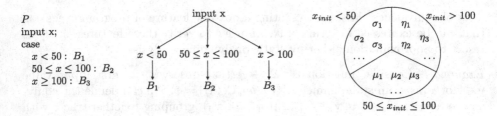

Fig. 2. Dynamic analysis and soundness

The goal of dynamic analysis is to derive knowledge of a semantic property of a program by observing a finite subset $Exe(P, T_P, t)$ of its execution traces. Dynamic analysis is therefore specified as the set of observed execution traces $Exe(P, T_P, t)$ and of an equivalence relation on traces $\mathcal{R} \in eq(\Sigma^*)$.

Definition 2 (Dynamic Analysis). *A dynamic analysis of property* $\mathcal{R} \in eq(\Sigma^*)$ *of program* $P \in Prog$, *is defined as a pair* $\langle \mathcal{R}, Exe(P, T_P, t) \rangle$.

Let us consider program P on the left of Fig. 2 where the block of code to execute depends on the input value of x. Consider a property of traces $\bar{\mathcal{R}} \in eq(\Sigma^*)$ that observes which block B_1, B_2 or B_3 of program P is executed. On the right of Fig. 2 we represent the partition of the traces of program P induced by property $\bar{\mathcal{R}}$ where x_{Init} denotes the input value of variable x.

Dynamic analysis $\langle \mathcal{R}, Exe(P, T_P, t) \rangle$ can precisely observe property $\mathcal{R}$ of the semantics of P (no false negatives) when $Exe(P, T_P, t)$ contains at least one trace for each one of the equivalence classes of the traces of $[\![P]\!]$.

Definition 3 (Soundness). *Given* $P \in Prog$ *and* $\mathcal{R} \in eq(\Sigma^*)$ *a dynamic analysis* $\langle \mathcal{R}, Exe(P, T_P, t) \rangle$ *is sound if* $\forall x \in [\![P]\!] : [x]_{\mathcal{R}} \in \mathcal{R}(Exe(P, T_P, t))$.

When a dynamic analysis $\langle \mathcal{R}, Exe(P, T_P, t) \rangle$ is sound we have no false negatives, namely $\forall y \in [\![P]\!] : [y]_{\mathcal{R}} \in \mathcal{R}(Exe(P, T_P, t))$. When this happens, all the behaviours of program P that relation $\mathcal{R}$ is able to distinguish are taken into account by the partial observation of program behaviour $Exe(P, T_P, t)$. In the example in Fig. 2 we have that a dynamic analysis $\langle \bar{\mathcal{R}}, Exe(P, T_P, t) \rangle$ is sound if $Exe(P, T_P, t)$ contains at least one execution trace for each one of the three equivalence classes depicted on the right of Fig. 2.

Definition 4 (Covers). *Given* $P \in Prog$, *and* $\mathcal{R} \in eq(\Sigma^*)$, *we say that* $S \subseteq [\![P]\!]$ *covers* P *wrt* $\mathcal{R}$ *when:* $\mathcal{R}(S) = \mathcal{R}([\![P]\!])$.

It is clear that when S covers P wrt $\mathcal{R}$ we have that the partial observation S of the behaviours of P is sound wrt $\mathcal{R}$, since it allows us to observe all the equivalence classes of $\mathcal{R}$ that we would observe by having access to all the traces in $[\![P]\!]$ (no false negatives). Thus, in the example in Fig. 2 we have that the set of traces $\{\sigma_1, \eta_1\}$ does not cover P wrt $\bar{\mathcal{R}}$, while the set of traces $\{\sigma_1, \eta_1, \eta_2, \mu_2\}$ does. The following theorem comes straight from the definitions.

Theorem 1. *Given* $P \in Prog$ *and* $\mathcal{R} \in eq(\Sigma^*)$, *if* $Exe(P, T_P, t)$ *covers* P *wrt* $\mathcal{R}$ *then the dynamic analysis* $\langle \mathcal{R}, Exe(P, T_P, t) \rangle$ *is sound (no false negatives).*

The goal of dynamic analysis of a property $\mathcal{R}$ on a program P, is to identify the set T_P of inputs, and the length t that induce a partial observation of program semantics that makes the analysis sound (no false negatives) wrt $\mathcal{R}$. Thus, a possible way to hamper dynamic analysis is to transform programs in order to increase the number of traces that it is necessary to observe to ensure soundness. Indeed, by tying the precision of dynamic analysis to the observation of a wider set of traces (worst case being the observation of all possible traces) we are limiting the advantages of using dynamic analysis.

In order to formalise this idea, in the following we provide a characterisation of the set of traces that are needed to guarantee the soundness of the dynamic analysis of a program P wrt a semantic property $\mathcal{R}$. We use this characterisation to formalise what it means for a software-based defense transformation to harm dynamic analysis. We validate our model by showing how it naturally relates to the notion of code coverage of dynamic analysis, and by showing how existing techniques for hindering dynamic analysis fit in our framework.

3.2   Harming Dynamic Analysis

Given an equivalence relation $\mathcal{R} \in eq(\Sigma^*)$ concerning what we can observe and a set of equivalence classes $X \in \wp(\Sigma^*/_\mathcal{R})$ we would like to characterise the minimal sets of traces that the relation $\mathcal{R}$ maps to X.

Definition 5 (Core). *Consider* $\mathcal{R} \in eq(\Sigma^*)$ *and* $X \in \wp(\Sigma^*/_\mathcal{R})$:

$$Core(X, \mathcal{R}) \stackrel{def}{=} \left\{ T = \{\sigma \in \Sigma^* \mid [\sigma]_\mathcal{R} \in X\} \left| \begin{array}{l} \forall \sigma_1, \sigma_2 \in T, \sigma_1 \neq \sigma_2 \Rightarrow [\sigma_1]_\mathcal{R} \neq [\sigma_2]_\mathcal{R} \\ \forall [v]_\mathcal{R} \in X : \exists \sigma \in T : [\sigma]_\mathcal{R} = [v]_\mathcal{R} \end{array} \right. \right\}$$

Theorem 2. *Consider* $\mathcal{R} \in eq(\Sigma^*)$ *and* $X \in \wp(\Sigma^*/_\mathcal{R})$:

1. *Given* $T \in Core(X, \mathcal{R})$ *we have that:* $\mathcal{R}(T) = X$
2. $\forall S \in \wp(\Sigma^*)$: *If* $\mathcal{R}(S) = X$ *then* $\exists T \in Core(X, \mathcal{R}) : T \subseteq S$

This means that $Core(\mathcal{R}([\![P]\!]), \mathcal{R})$ characterises the minimal sets of execution traces that provide a sound dynamic analysis of property $\mathcal{R}$ for program P. In the example in Fig. 2 we have that $Core([\![P]\!], \bar{\mathcal{R}})$ identifies those sets of trace that have exactly three traces: one trace with $x_{init} < 50$, one trace with $50 \leqslant x_{init} \leqslant 100$ and one trace with $x_{init} > 100$.

Corollary 1. *Given* $P \in Prog$ *and* $\mathcal{R} \in eq(\Sigma^*)$ *we have that:*

- $\forall T \in Core(\mathcal{R}([\![P]\!]), \mathcal{R})$ *we have that* T *covers* $[\![P]\!]$ *wrt* $\mathcal{R}$.
- *Given* $T_P \sqsubseteq_\Gamma Init_P$ *and* $t \subset \mathbb{N}$ *the dynamic analysis* $\langle \mathcal{R}, Exe(P, I_P, t) \rangle$ *is sound iff* $\exists T \in Core(\mathcal{R}([\![P]\!]), \mathcal{R})$ *such that* $T \subseteq Exe(P, T_P, t)$.

- *For every semantic feature* $\Pi \in \wp(\Sigma^*/_\mathcal{R})$ *expressed in terms of equivalence classes of* $\mathcal{R}$, *we have that if* $Exe(\mathsf{P},\mathsf{T}_\mathsf{P},\mathsf{t})$ *covers* $[\![\mathsf{P}]\!]$ *wrt* $\mathcal{R}$ *then we can precisely evaluate* $[\![\mathsf{P}]\!] \subseteq \Pi$ *by evaluating* $Exe(\mathsf{P},\mathsf{T}_\mathsf{P},\mathsf{t}) \subseteq \Pi$.

Thus, a dynamic analysis $\langle \mathcal{R}, Exe(\mathsf{P},\mathsf{T}_\mathsf{P},\mathsf{t}) \rangle$ is sound if $Exe(\mathsf{P},\mathsf{T}_\mathsf{P},\mathsf{t})$ observes at least one execution trace for each one of the equivalence classes of the traces in $[\![\mathsf{P}]\!]$ for the relation $\mathcal{R}$. In the worst case we have a different equivalence class for every execution trace of P. When this happens, a sound dynamic analysis of property $\mathcal{R}$ on program P has to observe all possible execution traces, which is unfeasible in the general case. Thus, if we want to protect a program from a dynamic analysis that is interested in the property $\mathcal{R}$, we have to diversify property $\mathcal{R}$ as much as possible among the execution traces of the program.

This allows us to define when a program transformation is *potent* wrt a dynamic analysis, namely when a program transformation forces a dynamic analysis to observe a wider set of traces in order to be sound. See [5] for the general notion of potency of a program transformation, i.e., a program transformation that foils a given attack (in our case a dynamic analysis).

Definition 6 (Potency). *A program transformation* $\mathcal{T} : Prog \rightarrow Prog$ *that preserves the denotational semantics of programs is potent for a program* $\mathsf{P} \in Prog$ *wrt an observation* $\mathcal{R} \in eq(\Sigma^*)$ *if the following two conditions hold:*

1. $\forall \sigma_1, \sigma_2 \in [\![\mathcal{T}(\mathsf{P})]\!] : [\sigma_1]_\mathcal{R} = [\sigma_2]_\mathcal{R}$ *we have that* $\forall v_1, v_2 \in [\![\mathsf{P}]\!] : Den(v_1) = Den(\sigma_1) \wedge Den(v_2) = Den(\sigma_2)$ *then* $[v_1]_\mathcal{R} = [v_2]_\mathcal{R}$
2. $\exists v_1, v_2 \in [\![\mathsf{P}]\!] : [v_1]_\mathcal{R} = [v_2]_\mathcal{R}$ *for which* $\exists \sigma_1, \sigma_2 \in [\![\mathcal{T}(\mathsf{P})]\!] : Den(v_1) = Den(\sigma_1) \wedge Den(v_2) = Den(\sigma_2)$ *such that* $[\sigma_1]_\mathcal{R} \neq [\sigma_2]_\mathcal{R}$

Figure 3 provides a graphical representation of the notion of potency. On the left we have the traces of the original program P partitioned according to the equivalence relation $\mathcal{R}$, while on the right we have the traces of the transformed program $\mathcal{T}(\mathsf{P})$ partitioned according to $\mathcal{R}$. Traces that are denotationally equivalent have the same shape (triangle, square, circle, oval), but are filled differently since they are in general different traces. The first condition means that the traces of $\mathcal{T}(\mathsf{P})$ that property $\mathcal{R}$ maps to the same equivalence class (triangle and square), are denotationally equivalent to traces of P that property $\mathcal{R}$ maps to the same equivalence class. This means that what is grouped together by $\mathcal{R}$ on $[\![\mathcal{T}(\mathsf{P})]\!]$ was grouped together by $\mathcal{R}$ on $[\![\mathsf{P}]\!]$, modulo the denotational equivalence of traces. The second condition requires that there are traces of P (circle and oval) that property $\mathcal{R}$ maps to the same equivalence class and whose denotationally equivalent traces in $\mathcal{T}(\mathsf{P})$ are mapped by $\mathcal{R}$ to different equivalence classes. This means that a defense technique against dynamic analysis wrt a property $\mathcal{R}$ is successful when it transforms a program into a functionally equivalent one for which property $\mathcal{R}$ is more diversified among execution traces. This implies that it is necessary to collect more execution traces in order for the analysis to be precise. At the limit we have an optimal defense technique when $\mathcal{R}$ varies at every execution trace.

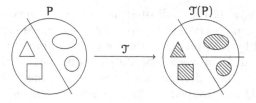

Fig. 3. Transformation potency

Example 2. Consider the following programs P and Q that compute the sum of natural numbers from $x \geqslant 0$ to 49 (we assume that the inputs values for x are natural numbers).

P
input x;
sum := 0;
while x < 50
• ⸲ X = [0, 49] ⸲
    sum := sum + x;
    x := x + 1;

Q
input x;
n : = select(N,x)
x := x * n;
sum := 0;
while x < 50 * n
• ⸲ X = [0, n * 50 − 1] ⸲
    sum := sum + x/n;
    x := x + n;
    x := x/n;

Consider a dynamic analysis that observes the maximal value assumed by x at program point •. For every possible execution of program P we have that the maximal value assumed by x at program point • is 49. Consider a state $s \in \Sigma$ as a tuple $\langle \mathcal{I}, pp, C, [val_x, val_{sum}] \rangle$, where val_x and val_{sum} denote the current values of variables x and sum respectively. We define a function $\tau : \Sigma \to \mathbb{N}$ that observes the value assumed by x at state s when s refers to program point •, and function $Max : \Sigma^* \to \mathbb{N}$ that observes the maximal value assumed by x at • along an execution trace:

$$\tau(s) \overset{\text{def}}{=} \begin{cases} val_x & \text{if } pp = \bullet \\ \emptyset & \text{otherwise} \end{cases} \qquad Max(\sigma) \overset{\text{def}}{=} max(\{\tau(s) \mid s \in \sigma\})$$

This allows us to define the equivalence relation $\mathcal{R}_{Max} \in eq(\Sigma^*)$ that observes traces wrt the maximal value assumed by x at •, as $(\sigma, \sigma') \in \mathcal{R}_{Max}$ iff $Max(\sigma) = Max(\sigma')$. The equivalence classes of $\mathcal{R}_{Max}$ are the sets of traces with the same maximal value assumed by x at •. We can observe that all the execution traces of P belong to the same equivalence class of $\mathcal{R}_{Max}$. In this case, a dynamic analysis $\langle \mathcal{R}_{Max}, Exe(\mathsf{P}, \mathsf{T_P}, t) \rangle$ is sound if $Exe(\mathsf{P}, \mathsf{T_P}, t)$ contains at least one execution trace of P. This happens because the property that we are looking for is an invariant property of program executions and it can be observed on any execution trace.

Let us now consider program Q. Q is equivalent to P, i.e., $Den[\![\mathsf{P}]\!] = Den[\![\mathsf{Q}]\!]$, but the value of x is diversified by multiplying it by the parameter n. The guard and the body of the while are adjusted in order to preserve the functionality of the program. When observing property $\mathcal{R}_{Max}$ on Q, we have that the maximal value assumed by x at program point $\bullet$ is determined by the parameter n generated in the considered trace. The statement n:=select(N,x) assigns to n a value in the range $[0, N]$ depending on the input value x. We have that the traces of program Q are grouped by $\mathcal{R}_{Max}$ depending on the value assumed by n. Thus, $\mathcal{R}(\llbracket Q \rrbracket)$ contains an equivalence class for every possible value assumed by n during execution. This means that the transformation that rewrites P into Q is potent according to Definition 6. Dynamic analysis $\langle \mathcal{R}_{Max}, Exe(Q, T_Q, t) \rangle$ is sound if $Exe(Q, T_Q, t)$ contains at least one execution trace for each of the possible values of n generated during execution.

4 Model Validation

In this section we show how the proposed framework can be used to model existing code obfuscation techniques. In particular we model the way these transformations deceive dynamic analysis of control flow and data flow properties of programs. We also show how the measures of code coverage used by dynamic analysis tools can be naturally interpreted in the proposed framework.

4.1 Control Flow Analysis

Dynamic Extraction of the Control Flow Graph. The control flow graph CFG of a program P is a graph $CFG_P = (V, E)$ where each node $v \in V$ is a pair (pp, C) denoting a statement C at program point pp in P, and $E \subseteq V \times V$ is the set of edges such that $(v_1, v_2) \in E$ means that the statement in v_2 could be executed after the statement in v_1 when running P. Thus, we define the domain of nodes as $Nodes \stackrel{\text{def}}{=} PP \times Com$, and the domain of edges as $Edges \stackrel{\text{def}}{=} Nodes \times Nodes$. It is possible to dynamically construct the CFG of a program by observing the commands that are executed and the edges that are traversed when the program runs. Let us define $\eta : \Sigma \rightarrow Nodes$ that observes the command to be executed together with its program point, namely $\eta(s) = \eta(\langle \mathfrak{I}, pp, C, m \rangle) \stackrel{\text{def}}{=} (pp, C)$. By extending this function on traces we obtain function $path : \Sigma^* \rightarrow Nodes \times Edges$ that extracts the path of the CFG corresponding to the considered execution trace, abstracting from the number of times that an edge is traversed or a node is computed:

$$path(\sigma) \stackrel{\text{def}}{=} (\{\eta(s) \mid s \in \sigma\}, \{(\eta(s), \eta(s')) \mid ss' \preceq \sigma\})$$

where $s \in \sigma$ means that s is a state that appears in trace σ and $ss' \preceq \sigma$ means that s and s' are successive states in σ. This allows us to define the equivalence relation $\mathcal{R}_{CFG} \in eq(\Sigma^*)$ that observes traces up to the path that they define, as $(\sigma, \sigma') \in \mathcal{R}_{CFG}$ iff $path(\sigma) = path(\sigma')$. Indeed, $\mathcal{R}_{CFG}$ groups together those traces that execute the same set of nodes and traverse the same set of edges, abstracting from the number of times that nodes are executed and edges are traversed.

The CFG of a program P can be defined as the union of the paths of its execution traces, namely $CFG_P = \bigsqcup\{path(\sigma) \mid \sigma \in [\![P]\!]\}$, where the union of graphs is defined as $(V_1, E_1) \sqcup (V_2, E_2) = (V_1 \cup V_2, E_1 \cup E_2)$. The dynamic extraction of the CFG of a program P from the observation of a set $X \subseteq_F [\![P]\!]$ of execution traces, is given by $\bigsqcup\{path(\sigma) \mid \sigma \in X\}$. In the general case we have $\bigsqcup\{path(\sigma) \mid \sigma \in X\} \subseteq CFG_P$.

Preventing Dynamic CFG Extraction. Control code obfuscations are program transformations that modify the program's control flow in order to make it difficult for an adversary to analyse the flow of control of programs [5]. According to Sect. 3.2, a program transformation $\mathcal{T} : Prog \to Prog$ is a potent defence against the dynamic extraction of the CFG of a program P when $\mathcal{T}$ diversifies the paths taken by the execution traces of $\mathcal{T}(P)$ wrt the paths taken by the traces of P. In the following, we show how two known defence techniques for preventing dynamic analysis actually work by diversifying program traces with respect to property $\mathcal{R}_{CFG}$.

Range Dividers: Range Divider (RD) is a transformation designed to prevent dynamic symbolic execution and it is an efficient protection against the dynamic extraction of the CFG [2]. RD relies on the existence of n program transformations $\mathcal{T}_i : Prog \to Prog$ with $i \in [1, n]$ that:

1. Preserve the denotational semantics of programs:
$$\forall P \in Prog, i \in [1, n] : Den[\![P]\!] = Den[\![\mathcal{T}_i(P)]\!]$$
2. Modify the paths of the CFG of programs in different ways:
$$\forall P \in Prog, \forall i, j \in [1, n]: \quad \mathcal{R}_{CFG}([\![\mathcal{T}_i(P)]\!]) = \mathcal{R}_{CFG}([\![\mathcal{T}_j(P)]\!]) \Rightarrow i = j.$$

Given a program P, the RD transformation works by inserting a `switch` control statement with n cases and whose condition depends on program inputs. Every case of the `switch` contains a semantically equivalent version $\mathcal{T}_i(P)$ of P that is specialised wrt the input values. Thus, depending on the input values we

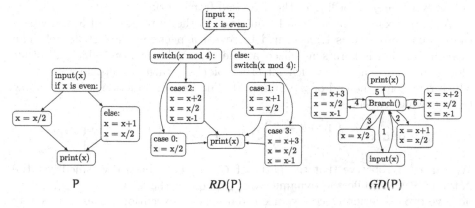

Fig. 4. CFG of P, RD(P) and GD(P)

would execute one of the diversified programs $\mathcal{T}_1(P), \ldots, \mathcal{T}_n(P)$. Since for each variant $\mathcal{T}_i(P)$ with $i \in [1, n]$ the set of execution traces are mapped by $\mathcal{R}_{CFG}$ into different equivalent classes, we have that property $\mathcal{R}_{CFG}$ has been diversified among the traces of $RD(P)$. Thus, the transformation RD is potent wrt $\mathcal{R}_{CFG}$ and harms the dynamic extraction of the CFG.

A simple example is provided in Fig. 4 where on the left we have the CFG of the original program P. P verifies the parity of the input value and then computes the integer division. The second graph in Fig. 4 represents the CFG of program P transformed by RD. The CFG of program $RD(P)$ has four different paths depending on the value of the input variable x. Each one of these paths is functionally equivalent to the corresponding path in P (case 0 and case 2 are equivalent to the path taken when x is even, while case 1 and case 3 are equivalent to the path taken when x is odd). We can easily observe that in this case the paths of $RD(P)$ have been diversified wrt the paths of P. Indeed, a dynamic analysis has to observe two execution traces to precisely build the CFG for P, while four traces are need to precisely build the CFG of $RD(P)$.

Gadget Diversification: In [27] the authors propose a program transformation, denoted $GD : Prog \rightarrow Prog$ that hinders the dynamic CFG analysis. GD starts by identifying a sequence Q_{seq} of sequential command (no branches) in program P. Next, GD assumes to have access to a set of diversifying transformations $\mathcal{T}_i :$ $Prog \rightarrow Prog$ with $i \in [1, n]$ that diversify command sequences while preserving their functionality. These transformations are then applied to portions of Q_{seq} in order to generate a wide set $S_{seq} = \{Q_1..Q_m\}$ of command sequences where each $Q_j \in S_{seq}$ is functionally equivalent to Q_{seq}, while every pair $Q_j, Q_l \in S_{seq}$ are such that $\mathcal{R}_{CFG}([\![Q_j]\!]) \neq \mathcal{R}_{CFG}([\![Q_l]\!])$. This means that each execution trace generated by the run of a sequence in S_{seq} belongs to a different equivalence class wrt relation $\mathcal{R}_{CFG}$, while being denotationally equivalent by definition.

Transformation GD proceeds by adding a **branching function** to the original program P that, depending on the input values, deviates the control flow to one of the sequences of commands in S_{seq}. Thus, depending on the input values, GD diversifies the path that is executed. This makes the transformation GD potent wrt $\mathcal{R}_{CFG}$ according to the proposed framework.

A simple example of GD can be observed in the third graph of Fig. 4, where the original program is transformed to reveal a peculiar CFG structure. The **branch** function is here symbolized as the central block from which all other blocks are called and to which all other blocks return (except for **print(x)** which represents the end of the program). The **branch** function will only allow the following sequences of edges:

$$\text{odd}(x) \rightarrow \left\{ \begin{array}{c} 1 \rightarrow 2 \rightarrow 5 \\ 1 \rightarrow 4 \rightarrow 5 \end{array} \right\} \qquad \text{even}(x) \rightarrow \left\{ \begin{array}{c} 1 \rightarrow 3 \rightarrow 5 \\ 1 \rightarrow 6 \rightarrow 5 \end{array} \right\}$$

We can easily observe that the paths of $GD(P)$ have been diversified wrt the paths of P and while the dynamic construction of the CFG for P requires to observe two execution traces, we need to observe 4 execution traces to precisely build the CFG of $GD(P)$.

4.2   Code Coverage

Most dynamic algorithms use code coverage to measure the potential soundness of the analysis [1]. Intuitively, given a program P and a partial observation $Exe(P, T_P, t)$ of its execution traces, code coverage wants to measure the amount of program behaviour considered by $Exe(P, T_P, t)$ wrt the set of all possible behaviours $[\![P]\!]$. In the following we describe some known code coverage measures.

Statement coverage considers the statements of the program that have been executed by the traces in $Exe(P, T_P, t)$. This is a function $st : \Sigma^* \to Nodes$ that collects commands annotated with their program point, that are executed along a considered trace: $st(\sigma) \stackrel{\text{def}}{=} \{\eta(s) \mid s \in \sigma\}$. This allows us to define the equivalence relation $\mathcal{R}_{st} \in eq(\Sigma^*)$ that groups together traces that execute the same set of statements.

Count-Statement coverage considers how many times each statement of the program has been executed by the traces in $Exe(P, T_P, t)$. Thus, it can be formalised in terms of an equivalence relation $\mathcal{R}_{st}^+ \in eq(\Sigma^*)$ that groups together traces that execute the same set of statements the same amount of times. It is clear that relation $\mathcal{R}_{st}^+$ is finer than relation $\mathcal{R}_{st}$, namely $\mathcal{R}_{st}^+ \sqsubseteq \mathcal{R}_{st}$.

Path coverage observes the nodes executed and edges traversed by the traces in $Exe(P, T_P, t)$. This precisely corresponds to the observation of property $\mathcal{R}_{CFG} \in eq(\Sigma^*)$ defined above, where the paths of the CFG are observed by abstracting form the number of times that edges are traversed. It is clear that relation $\mathcal{R}_{CFG}$ is finer than relation $\mathcal{R}_{st}$, namely $\mathcal{R}_{CFG} \sqsubseteq \mathcal{R}_{st}$.

Count-Path coverage considers the different paths in $Exe(P, T_P, t)$, where the number of times that edges are traversed in a trace is taken into account. This can be formalised in terms of an equivalence relation $\mathcal{R}_{CFG}^+ \in eq(\Sigma^*)$ that groups together traces that execute and traverse the same nodes and edges the same number of times. It is clear that relation $\mathcal{R}_{CFG}^+$ is finer than relation $\mathcal{R}_{CFG}$, namely $\mathcal{R}_{CFG}^+ \sqsubseteq \mathcal{R}_{CFG}$.

Trace coverage considers the traces of commands that have been executed abstracting from the memory map. In this case we can define the code coverage in terms of function $trace : \Sigma^* \to Com \times PP$ defined as $trace(\epsilon) \stackrel{\text{def}}{=} \epsilon$ and $trace(s\sigma) \stackrel{\text{def}}{=} \eta(s)trace(\sigma)$. The equivalence relation $\mathcal{R}_{trace} \in eq(\Sigma^*)$ is such that $(\sigma, \sigma') \in \mathcal{R}_{trace}$ if $trace(\sigma) = trace(\sigma')$. This equivalence relation is finer than $\mathcal{R}_{CFG}^+$ since it keeps track of the order of execution of the edges.

In order to avoid false negatives, dynamic algorithms automatically look for inputs whose execution traces have to exhibit new behaviours with respect to the code coverage metric used (e.g., they have to execute new statements or execute them a different number of times, traverse new edges or change the number of times edges are traversed, or execute nodes in a different order). This can be naturally formalised in our framework. Given a set $Exe(P, T_P, t)$ of observed traces, an automatically generated input increases the code coverage measured as $\mathcal{R}_{st}$ (or $\mathcal{R}_{st}^+, \mathcal{R}_{CFG}, \mathcal{R}_{CFG}^+, \mathcal{R}_{trace}$) if the execution trace σ generated by the input is mapped in a new equivalence class of $\mathcal{R}_{st}$ (or $\mathcal{R}_{st}^+, \mathcal{R}_{CFG}, \mathcal{R}_{CFG}^+, \mathcal{R}_{trace}$), namely in an equivalence class that was not observed by traces in $Exe(P, T_P, t)$, namely if $[\sigma]_{\mathcal{R}_{st}} \notin \mathcal{R}_{st}(Exe(P, T_P, t))$ (analogously for $\mathcal{R}_{st}^+, \mathcal{R}_{CFG}, \mathcal{R}_{CFG}^+, \mathcal{R}_{trace}$).

We have seen above that some of the common measures for code coverage can be expressed in terms of semantic program properties with different degrees of precision $id \sqsubseteq \mathcal{R}_{traces} \sqsubseteq \mathcal{R}_{CFG}^{+} \sqsubseteq \mathcal{R}_{CFG} \sqsubseteq \mathcal{R}_{st}$. This means, for example, that automatically generated inputs could add coverage for $\mathcal{R}_{CFG}^{+}$ but not for $\mathcal{R}_{st}$. Indeed, a new input generates a new behaviour depending on the metric used for code coverage.

Fuzzing and dynamic symbolic execution are typical techniques used by dynamic analysis to automatically generate inputs in order to extend code coverage. The metrics that fuzzing and symbolic execution use to measure code coverage are sometimes a slight variations of the ones mentioned earlier.

Fuzzing: The term fuzzing refers to a family of automated input generating techniques that are widely used in the industry to find vulnerabilities and bugs in all kinds of software [35]. In general, a fuzzer aims at discovering inputs that generate new behaviors, thus one measure of success for fuzzer is code coverage. Simple statement coverage is rarely a good choice, since crashes do not usually depend on a single program statement, but on a specific sequence of statements [39]. Most fuzzing algorithms choose to define their own code coverage metric. American Fuzzy Lop (AFL) is a state of the art fuzzer that has seen extensive use in the industry in its base form, while new fuzzers are continuously built on top of it [32]. The measure used by AFL for code coverage lays between path and count-path coverage as it approximates the number of times that edges are traversed by specified intervals of natural numbers ([1], [2], [3], [4–7], [8–15], [16–31], [32–127], [128, ∞]). Libfuzzer [30] and Honggfuzz [36] employ count-statement coverage. To the best our knowledge trace coverage is never used as it is infeasible in practice [16].

Dynamic Symbolic Execution: DSE is a well known dynamic analysis technique that combines concrete and symbolic execution [22]. DSE typically starts by executing a program on a random input and then generates branch conditions that take into account the executed branches. When execution ends, DSE looks at the last branch condition generated and uses a theorem prover to solve the negated predicate in order to explore the branch that was not executed. This is akin to symbolic execution, but DSE can use the concrete values obtained in the execution to simplify the job of the theorem prover. The ideal goal of DSE is to reach path coverage, which is always guaranteed if the conditions in the target program only contain linear arithmetics [22]. Thus, the efficacy of DSE in generating new inputs is measured in terms of path coverage formalised as $\mathcal{R}_{CFG}$ in our framework.

Let us denote with $\mathcal{R} \in eq(\Sigma^{*})$ the equivalence relation modelling the code coverage metric used either by fuzzing or symbolic execution or any other algorithm for input generation. When $Exe(\mathsf{P}, \mathsf{T_P}, t)$ covers P wrt $\mathcal{R}$, we have that the fuzzer or symbolic execution algorithm has found all the inputs that allow us to observe the different behaviours of P wrt $\mathcal{R}$. In general, a dynamic analysis may be interested in a property $\mathcal{R}_A \in eq(\Sigma^{*})$ that is different from the property $\mathcal{R}$ used to measure code coverage. When $\mathcal{R} \sqsubseteq \mathcal{R}_A$ we have that if $Exe(\mathsf{P}, \mathsf{T_P}, t)$

covers P wrt $\mathcal{R}$, then $Exe(\mathsf{P}, \mathsf{T_P}, t)$ covers P also wrt $\mathcal{R_A}$ and this means that the code coverage metric $\mathcal{R}$ can help in limiting the number of false negative of the dynamic analysis $\langle \mathcal{R_A}, Exe(\mathsf{P}, \mathsf{T_P}, t) \rangle$. When $\mathcal{R} \not\sqsubseteq \mathcal{R_A}$ then a different metric for code coverage should be used (for example $\mathcal{R_A}$ itself).

4.3 Harming Dynamic Data Analysis

Data obfuscation transformations change the representation of data with the aim of hiding both variable content and usage. Usually, data obfuscation requires the program code to be modified, so that the original data representation can be reconstructed at runtime. Data obfuscation is often achieved through data encoding [5,28]. More specifically, in [15,23] data encoding for a variable x is formalised as a pair of statements: encoding statement $C_{enc} = x := f(x)$ and decoding statement $C_{dec} = x := g(x)$ for some function f and g, such that $C_{dec}; C_{enc} = skip$. According to [15,23] a program transformation $\mathcal{T}(\mathsf{P}) \overset{\text{def}}{=} C_{dec}; t_x(\mathsf{P}); C_{enc}$ is a data obfuscation for x where t_x adjusts the computations involving x in order to preserve program's functionality, namely $Den[\![\mathsf{P}]\!] = Den[\![C_{dec}; t_x(\mathsf{P}); C_{enc}]\!]$. In Fig. 5 we provide a simple example of data obfuscation from [15,23] where $C_{enc} = x := 2 * x$ and $C_{dec} = x := x/2$ and $\mathcal{T}(\mathsf{P}) = x := x/2; t_x(\mathsf{P}); x := 2 * x$ and program P is the one considered in Example 2. This data transformation induces imprecision in the static analysis of the possible values assumed by x at program point •. Indeed, the static analysis of the interval of values of x at program point • in $\mathcal{T}(\mathsf{P})$ is different and wider (it contains spurious values) than the interval of possible values of x at • in P. However, the dynamic analysis of properties on the values assumed by x during execution at the different program points (e.g., maximal/minimal value, number of possible values, interval of possible values) has not been hardened in $\mathcal{T}(\mathsf{P})$. The values assumed by x at • in $\mathcal{T}(\mathsf{P})$ are different from the values assumed by x at • in P but these properties on the values assumed by x are precisely observable by dynamic analysis on $\mathcal{T}(\mathsf{P})$. Transformation $\mathcal{T}(\mathsf{P})$ changes the properties of data values wrt P, but it does it in an invariant way: during every execution of $\mathcal{T}(\mathsf{P})$ we have that x is iteratively incremented by 2 and the guard of the loop becomes $x < 2 * 50 - 1$, and this is observable on any execution of $\mathcal{T}(\mathsf{P})$. This means that by dynamic analysis we could learn that the maximal value assumed by x is $99 (= 2 * 50 - 1)$. Thus, transformation $\mathcal{T}$ is not potent wrt properties of data values according to Definition 6 since it does not diversify the properties of values assumed by variables among traces. In order to hamper dynamic analysis we need to diversify data among traces, thus forcing dynamic analysis to observe more execution traces to be sound. We could do this by making the encoding and decoding statements parametric on some natural number n as described by the third program $\mathcal{T}_n(\mathsf{P}) = x := x/n; t_{x,n}(\mathsf{P}); x := n * x$ in Fig. 5 (which is the same as Q in Example 2). Indeed, the parametric transformation $\mathcal{T}_n(\mathsf{P})$ is potent wrt properties that observe data values since it diversifies the values assumed by x among different executions thanks to the parameter n. For example, to observe the maximal value assumed by x in $\mathcal{T}_n(\mathsf{P})$ we should observe an execution for every possible value of n.

$$
\begin{array}{llll}
 & \mathcal{T}(\mathsf{P}) & \mathcal{T}_n(\mathsf{P}) & \mathcal{T}_H(\mathsf{P}) \\
\mathsf{P} & \text{input x;} & \text{input x;} & \text{input x;} \\
\text{input x;} & \text{x := 2*x;} & \text{x := n*x;} & \text{n := select(N,x);} \\
\text{sum := 0;} & \text{sum := 0;} & \text{sum := 0;} & \text{x := } \mathsf{H}^e(\text{n,x}); \\
\text{while x < 50} & \text{while x < 2*50} & \text{while x < n*50} & \text{sum := } \mathsf{H}^e(\text{n,0}); \\
\bullet\ X = [\text{x}, 49] & \bullet\ X = [\text{x}, 2*50-1] & \bullet\ X = [\text{x}, n*50-1] & \text{while x} <_H \mathsf{H}^e(\text{n,50}) \\
\quad \text{sum := sum + x;} & \quad \text{sum := sum + x/2;} & \quad \text{sum := sum + x/n;} & \bullet\ X = [\text{x}, \mathsf{H}^e(\text{n}, 50)-1] \\
\quad \text{x := x + 1;} & \quad \text{x := x + 2;} & \quad \text{x := x + n;} & \quad \text{sum := sum} +_H \text{x;} \\
 & \quad \text{x:= x/2;} & \quad \text{x:= x/n;} & \quad \text{x := x} +_H \mathsf{H}^e(\text{n,1}); \\
 & & & \quad \text{x:= } \mathsf{H}^d(\text{x});
\end{array}
$$

Fig. 5. From the left: programs P, $\mathcal{T}(\mathsf{P})$, $\mathcal{T}_n(\mathsf{P})$ and $\mathcal{T}_H(\mathsf{P})$

This confirms what observed [28]: existing data obfuscation makes static analysis imprecise but it is less effective against dynamic analysis. Interpreting data obfuscation in our framework allows us to see that, in order to hamper dynamic analysis, data encoding needs to diversify among traces. This can be done by making the existing data encoding techniques parametric.

Homomorphic Encryption: As argued above, in order to preserve program functionality the original program code needs to be adapted to the encoding. In general, automatically deriving the modified code $t_x(\mathsf{P})$ for a given encoding on every possible program may be complicated. In this setting, an ideal situation is the one provided by fully homomorphic encryption where any operation on the original data has its respective for the encrypted data. It has been proven that fully homomorphic encryption is possible on any circuit [17]. Let H^e and H^d be the fully homomorphic encryption and decryption procedures. We could design a data obfuscation for the variables in P as $\mathsf{H}^d; \mathsf{P}_H; \mathsf{H}^e$ where the program variables are encrypted with H^e, the computation is carried on the encrypted values by using homomorphic operations (denoted with subscript $_H$), and at the end the final values of the variables are decrypted with H^d. Thus, the original program P and P_H are exactly the same programs where the operations have been replaced by their homomorphic version. In Fig. 5 on the right we show how a homomorphic encoding of program P would work, where the subscript $_H$ denotes the homomorphic operations on the encrypted values. Encryption and decryption procedures have a random nature and use a key (that may be dependent on input values). Thus, the values of encrypted data varies among program traces. Moreover, since successive encryptions of the same values would lead to different encrypted values, we have that re-runs on the same values would generate different encrypted values. This proves that homomorphic encryption could be useful to design a potent data obfuscation against dynamic analysis: as it can diversify the encrypted data values among traces and the original values are retrieved only at the end of the computation.

Abstract Software Watermarking: In [12] the authors propose a sophisticated software watermarking algorithm and prove its resilience against static program analysis. The watermark can be extracted only by analysing the program on a specific congruence domain that acts like a secret key. The authors discuss some possible countermeasures against dynamic analysis that could reveal the existence of the watermark (and then remove it). Interestingly, the common idea behind these countermeasures is diversification of the property of data values that the dynamic analyses observe.

5 Related Works

To the best of our knowledge we are the first to propose a formal framework for dynamic analysis efficacy based on semantic properties. Other works have proposed more empirical ways to assess the impact of dynamic analysis.

Evaluating Reverse Engineering. Program comprehension guided by dynamic analysis has been evaluated with specific test cases, quantitative measures and the involvement of human subjects [8]. For example, comparing the effectiveness of static analysis and dynamic analysis towards the feature location task has been carried out through experiments involving 2 teams of analysts solving the same problem with a static analysis and a dynamic analysis approach respectively [37]. In order to compare the effectiveness of different reverse engineering techniques (which often employ dynamic analysis), Sim et al. propose the use of common benchmarks [34]. The efficacy of protections against human subjects has been evaluated in a set of experiments by Ceccato et al., finding that program executions are important to understand the behavior of obfuscated code [4]. Our approach characterizes dynamic attacks and protections according to their semantic properties which is an orthogonal work that can be complemented by more empirical approaches.

Obfuscations Against Dynamic Analysis. One of the first works tackling obfuscations specifically geared towards dynamic analysis is by Schrittwieser and Katzenbeisser [27]. Their approach adopts some principles of software diversification in order to generate additional paths in the CFG that are dependent on program input (i.e. they do not work for other inputs). Similar to this approach, Pawlowski et al. [26] generate additional branches in the CFG but add non-determinism in order to decide the executed path at runtime. Both of these works empirically evaluate their methodology and classify it with potency and resilience, two metrics introduced by Collberg et al. [6]. Banescu et al. empirically evaluated some obfuscations against dynamic symbolic execution (DSE) [2], finding that DSE does not suffer from the addition of opaque branches since they do not depend on program input. To overcome this limitation they propose the Range Dividers obfuscation that we illustrated in Sect. 4. A recent work by Ollivier et al. refines the evaluation of protections against dynamic symbolic execution with a framework that enables the optimal design of such protections [25]. All these works share with us the intuition that dynamic analysis suffers from insufficient path exploration and they prove this intuition with extensive experimentation. Our work aims at enabling the formal study of these approaches.

Formal Systems. Dynamic taint analysis has been formalized by making explicit the taint information in the program semantics [29]. Their work focuses on writing correct algorithms and shows some possible pitfalls of the various approaches. Ochoa et al. [24] use game theory to quantify and compare the effectiveness of different probabilistic countermeasures with respect to remote attacks that exploit memory-safety vulnerabilities. In our work we model MATE attacks. Shu et al. introduce a framework that formalizes the detection capability in existing anomaly detection methods [33]. Their approach equates the detection capability to the expressiveness of the language used to characterize normal program traces.

6   Discussion and Future Works

This work represents the first step towards a formal investigation of the precision of dynamic analysis in relation with dynamic code attack and defences. The results that we have obtained so far confirm the initial intuition: *diversification is the key for harming dynamic analysis*. Dynamic analysis generalises what it learns from a partial observation of program behaviour, diversification makes this generalisation less precise (dynamic analysis cannot consider what it has not observed). We think that this work would be the basis for further interesting investigations. Indeed, there are many aspects that still need to be understood for the development of a complete framework for the formal specification of the precision of dynamic analysis (no false negatives), and for the systematic development of program transformations that induce imprecision.

We plan to consider more sophisticated properties than the ones that can be expressed as equivalence relations. It would be interesting to generalise the proposed framework wrt to any semantic property that can be formalised as a closure operator on trace semantics. The properties that we have considered so far correspond to the set of atomistic closures where the abstract domain is additive. We would like to generalise our framework to properties modelled as abstract domains and where the precision of dynamic analysis is probably characterised in terms of the join-irreducible elements of such domains. A further investigation would probably lead to a classification of the properties usually considered by dynamic analysis: properties of traces, properties of sets of traces, relational properties, hyper-properties, together with a specific characterisation of the precision of the analysis and of the program transformations that can reduce it. This unifying framework would provide a common ground where to interpret and compare the potency of different software protection techniques in harming dynamic analysis.

We can view dynamic analysis as a learner that observes properties of some execution traces (training set) and then generalises what it has observed, where the generalisation process is the identity function. We wonder what would happen if we consider more sophisticated generalisation processes such as the ones used by machine learning. Would it be possible to define what is learnable? Would it be possible to formally define robustness in the adversarial setting? We think that this is an intriguing research direction and we plan to pursue it.

Acknowledgments. The research has been partially supported by the project "Dipartimenti di Eccellenza 2018–2022" funded by the Italian Ministry of Education, Universities and Research (MIUR).

References

1. Ammann, P., Offutt, J.: Introduction to Software Testing. Cambridge University Press, Cambridge (2016)
2. Banescu, S., Collberg, C., Ganesh, V., Newsham, Z., Pretschner, A.: Code obfuscation against symbolic execution attacks. In: Proceedings of the 32nd Annual Conference on Computer Security Applications, pp. 189–200 (2016)
3. Blazytko, T., Contag, M., Aschermann, C., Holz, T.: Syntia: synthesizing the semantics of obfuscated code. In: 26th USENIX Security Symposium, USENIX Security 2017, Vancouver, BC, Canada, 16–18 August 2017, pp. 643–659. USENIX Association (2017)
4. Ceccato, M., Di Penta, M., Falcarin, P., Ricca, F., Torchiano, M., Tonella, P.: A family of experiments to assess the effectiveness and efficiency of source code obfuscation techniques. Empir. Softw. Eng. **19**(4), 1040–1074 (2013). https://doi.org/10.1007/s10664-013-9248-x
5. Collberg, C., Nagra, J.: Surreptitious Software: Obfuscation, Watermarking, and Tamperproofing for Software Protection. Addison-Wesley Professional, Boston (2009)
6. Collberg, C., Thomborson, C., Low, D.: Manufacturing cheap, resilient, and stealthy opaque constructs. In: Proceedings of the 25th ACM SIGPLAN-SIGACT Symposium on Principles of Programming Languages, POPL 1998, pp. 184–196. ACM Press (1998)
7. Coogan, K., Lu, G., Debray, S.K.: Deobfuscation of virtualization-obfuscated software: a semantics-based approach. In: Proceedings of the 18th ACM Conference on Computer and Communications Security, CCS 2011, Chicago, Illinois, USA, 17–21 October 2011, pp. 275–284. ACM (2011)
8. Cornelissen, B., Zaidman, A., Van Deursen, A., Moonen, L., Koschke, R.: A systematic survey of program comprehension through dynamic analysis. IEEE Trans. Softw. Eng. **35**(5), 684–702 (2009)
9. Cousot, P.: Constructive design of a hierarchy of semantics of a transition system by abstract interpretation. Theor. Comput. Sci. **277**(1–2), 47–103 (2002)
10. Cousot, P., Cousot, R.: Abstract interpretation: a unified lattice model for static analysis of programs by construction or approximation of fixpoints. In: Conference Record of the 4th ACM Symposium on Principles of Programming Languages, POPL 1977, pp. 238–252. ACM Press (1977)
11. Cousot, P., Cousot, R.: Systematic design of program analysis frameworks. In: Conference Record of the 6th ACM Symposium on Principles of Programming Languages, POPL 1979, pp. 269–282. ACM Press (1979)
12. Cousot, P., Cousot, R.: An abstract interpretation-based framework for software watermarking. In: Conference Record of the Thirtyfirst Annual ACM SIGPLAN-SIGACT Symposium on Principles of Programming Languages, pp. 173–185. ACM Press, New York (2004)
13. Dalla Preda, M., Giacobazzi, R.: Semantic-based code obfuscation by abstract interpretation. J. Comput. Secur. **17**(6), 855–908 (2009)
14. Dalla Preda, M., Mastroeni, I.: Characterizing a property-driven obfuscation strategy. J. Comput. Secur. **26**(1), 31–69 (2018)

15. Drape, S., Thomborson, C., Majumdar, A.: Specifying imperative data obfusca-
    tions. In: Garay, J.A., Lenstra, A.K., Mambo, M., Peralta, R. (eds.) ISC 2007.
    LNCS, vol. 4779, pp. 299–314. Springer, Heidelberg (2007). https://doi.org/10.
    1007/978-3-540-75496-1_20
16. Gan, S., et al.: Collafl: path sensitive fuzzing. In: 2018 IEEE Symposium on Security
    and Privacy (SP), pp. 679–696. IEEE (2018)
17. Gentry, C., Boneh, D.: A Fully Homomorphic Encryption Scheme, vol. 20. Stanford
    University, Stanford (2009)
18. Giacobazzi, R.: Hiding information in completeness holes - new perspectives in
    code obfuscation and watermarking. In: Proceedings of the 6th IEEE International
    Conferences on Software Engineering and Formal Methods, SEFM 2008, pp. 7–20.
    IEEE Press (2008)
19. Giacobazzi, R., Jones, N.D., Mastroeni, I.: Obfuscation by partial evaluation of
    distorted interpreters. In: Kiselyov, O., Thompson, S. (eds.) Proceedings of the
    ACM SIGPLAN Symposium on Partial Evaluation and Semantics-Based Program
    Manipulation, PEPM 2012, pp. 63–72. ACM Press (2012)
20. Giacobazzi, R., Ranzato, F., Scozzari, F.: Making abstract interpretation complete.
    J. ACM 47(2), 361–416 (2000)
21. Giacobazzi, R., Mastroeni, I., Dalla Preda, M.: Maximal incompleteness as obfus-
    cation potency. Formal Aspects Comput. 29(1), 3–31 (2016). https://doi.org/10.
    1007/s00165-016-0374-2
22. Godefroid, P., Klarlund, N., Sen, K.: DART: directed automated random testing.
    In: Proceedings of the 2005 ACM SIGPLAN Conference on Programming Language
    Design and Implementation, pp. 213–223 (2005)
23. Majumdar, A., Drape, S.J., Thomborson, C.D.: Slicing obfuscations: design, cor-
    rectness, and evaluation. In: DRM 2007: Proceedings of the 2007 ACM Workshop
    on Digital Rights Management, pp. 70–81. ACM (2007)
24. Ochoa, M., Banescu, S., Disenfeld, C., Barthe, G., Ganesh, V.: Reasoning about
    probabilistic defense mechanisms against remote attacks. In: 2017 IEEE European
    Symposium on Security and Privacy, EuroS&P 2017, Paris, France, 26–28 April
    2017, pp. 499–513. IEEE (2017)
25. Ollivier, M., Bardin, S., Bonichon, R., Marion, J.-Y.: How to kill symbolic deob-
    fuscation for free (or: unleashing the potential of path-oriented protections). In:
    Proceedings of the 35th Annual Computer Security Applications Conference, pp.
    177–189 (2019)
26. Pawlowski, A., Contag, M., Holz, T.: Probfuscation: an obfuscation approach using
    probabilistic control flows. In: Caballero, J., Zurutuza, U., Rodríguez, R.J. (eds.)
    DIMVA 2016. LNCS, vol. 9721, pp. 165–185. Springer, Cham (2016). https://doi.
    org/10.1007/978-3-319-40667-1_9
27. Schrittwieser, S., Katzenbeisser, S.: Code obfuscation against static and dynamic
    reverse engineering. In: Filler, T., Pevný, T., Craver, S., Ker, A. (eds.) IH 2011.
    LNCS, vol. 6958, pp. 270–284. Springer, Heidelberg (2011). https://doi.org/10.
    1007/978-3-642-24178-9_19
28. Schrittwieser, S., Katzenbeisser, S., Kinder, J., Merzdovnik, G., Weippl, E.R.: Pro-
    tecting software through obfuscation: can it keep pace with progress in code anal-
    ysis? ACM Comput. Surv. 49(1), 4:1–4:37 (2016)
29. Schwartz, E.J., Avgerinos, T., Brumley, D.: All you ever wanted to know about
    dynamic taint analysis and forward symbolic execution (but might have been afraid
    to ask). In: 2010 IEEE Symposium on Security and Privacy, pp. 317–331. IEEE
    (2010)

30. Serebryany, K.: Continuous fuzzing with libfuzzer and addresssanitizer. In: 2016 IEEE Cybersecurity Development (SecDev), pp. 157–157. IEEE (2016)
31. Sharif, M.I., Lanzi, A., Giffin, J.T., Lee, W.: Automatic reverse engineering of malware emulators. In: 30th IEEE Symposium on Security and Privacy, S&P 2009, Oakland, California, USA, 17–20 May 2009, pp. 94–109. IEEE Computer Society (2009)
32. She, D., Pei, K., Epstein, D., Yang, J., Ray, B., Jana, S.: NEUZZ: efficient fuzzing with neural program smoothing. In: 2019 IEEE Symposium on Security and Privacy (SP), pp. 803–817. IEEE (2019)
33. Shu, X., Yao, D.D., Ryder, B.G.: A formal framework for program anomaly detection. In: Bos, H., Monrose, F., Blanc, G. (eds.) RAID 2015. LNCS, vol. 9404, pp. 270–292. Springer, Cham (2015). https://doi.org/10.1007/978-3-319-26362-5_13
34. Sim, S.E., Easterbrook, S., Holt, R.C.: Using benchmarking to advance research: a challenge to software engineering. In: Proceedings of the 25th International Conference on Software Engineering, pp. 74–83. IEEE (2003)
35. Sutton, M., Greene, A., Amini, P.: Fuzzing: Brute Force Vulnerability Discovery. Pearson Education, London (2007)
36. Swiecki, R.: Honggfuzz (2016). http://code.google.com/p/honggfuzz
37. Wilde, N., Buckellew, M., Page, H., Rajlich, V., Pounds, L.T.: A comparison of methods for locating features in legacy software. J. Syst. Softw. **65**(2), 105–114 (2003)
38. Yadegari, B., Johannesmeyer, B., Whitely, B., Debray, S.: A generic approach to automatic deobfuscation of executable code. In: 2015 IEEE Symposium on Security and Privacy, SP 2015, San Jose, CA, USA, 17–21 May 2015, pp. 674–691. IEEE Computer Society (2015)
39. Zalewski, M.: Technical "whitepaper" for afl-fuzz (2014). http://lcamtuf.coredump.cx/afl/technical_details.txt

Simple and Efficient Computation of Minimal Weak Control Closure

Abu Naser Masud[✉][ID]

School of Innovation, Design and Engineering,
Mälardalen University, Vasteras, Sweden
masud.abunaser@mdh.se

Abstract. Control dependency is a fundamental concept in many program analyses, transformation, parallelization, and compiler optimization techniques. An overwhelming number of definitions of control dependency relations are found in the literature that capture various kinds of program control flow structures. Weak and strong control closure (WCC and SCC) relations capture nontermination insensitive and sensitive control dependencies and subsume all previously defined control dependency relations. In this paper, we have shown that static dependency-based program slicing requires the repeated computation of WCC and SCC. The state-of-the-art WCC algorithm provided by Danicic et al. has the cubic worst-case complexity in terms of the size of the control flow graph and is a major obstacle to be used in static program slicing. We have provided a simple yet efficient method to compute the minimal WCC which has the quadratic worst-case complexity and proved the correctness of our algorithms. We implemented ours and the state-of-the-art algorithms in the Clang/LLVM compiler framework and run experiments on a number of SPEC CPU 2017 benchmarks. Our method performs a maximum of 23.8 times and on average 10.6 times faster than the state-of-the-art method. The performance curves of our WCC algorithm for practical applications are closer to the NlogN curve in the microsecond scale. Evidently, we improve the practical performance of WCC computation by an order of magnitude.

Keywords: Control dependency · Weak control closure · Strong control closure · Program slicing · Nontermination (in)sensitive

1 Introduction

Control dependency is a fundamental concept in many program analyses, transformation, parallelization and compiler optimization techniques. It is used to express the relation between two program statements such that one decides whether the other statement can be executed or not. One of the key applications of control dependency is program slicing [20] that transforms an original program into a sliced program with respect to a so-called slicing criterion. The slicing criterion specifies the variables at a particular program point that will

© Springer Nature Switzerland AG 2020
D. Pichardie and M. Sighireanu (Eds.): SAS 2020, LNCS 12389, pp. 200–222, 2020.
https://doi.org/10.1007/978-3-030-65474-0_10

affect the execution of the sliced program. All program instructions in the original program that does not affect the slicing criterion are discarded from the sliced code. Control dependency is used to identify the program instructions that indirectly affect the slicing criterion due to the execution of conditional expressions in the loops or conditional instructions.

The standard definition of control dependency provided by Ferrante et al. [6] has been widely used for over two decades. This definition is provided at the level of the *control flow graph* (CFG) representation of a program assuming that the CFG has a unique *end* node (i.e. the program has a single exit point). Several recent articles on control dependency illustrate that this definition does not sufficiently capture the intended control dependency of programs having the modern programming language features. For instance, the *exception* or *halt* instructions cause multiple exits of the programs, or reactive systems, web services or distributed real-time systems have nonterminating program instructions without an end node. The standard definition of control dependency did not intend to handle the above systems. The possibility of having nontermination in the program code introduces two different types of control dependency relations: the *weak* and *strong* control dependencies that are nontermination insensitive and nontermination sensitive. One of the distinguishing effects between the two types of control dependencies is that an original nonterminating program remains nonterminating or may be transformed into a terminating program if the slicing method uses *strong* or *weak* control dependence respectively.

Numerous authors provided an overwhelming number of definitions of control dependencies [2,6,16,19,20] given at the level of CFG and describe computation methods to obtain such dependencies. Danicic et al. [4] unified all previously defined control dependence relations by providing the definitions and theoretical insights of *weak* and *strong control-closure* (WCC and SCC) that are most generalized and capture all non-termination insensitive and nontermination sensitive control dependence relations. Thus, WCC and SCC subsume all control dependency relations found in the literature. However, Danicic et al. provided expensive algorithms to compute WCC and SCC. In particular, the algorithms for computing WCC and SCC have the cubic and quartic worst-case asymptotic complexity in terms of the size of the CFG. We have shown that static program slicing requires the repeated computation of WCC and/or SCC. The state-of-the-art WCC and SCC algorithms are not only expensive, but the use of these algorithms in client applications such as program slicing will make these applications underperforming.

In this article, we have provided a simple and efficient method to compute WCC. We have formalized several theorems and lemmas demonstrating the soundness, minimality, and complexity of our algorithm. Our WCC algorithm has the quadratic worst-case time complexity in terms of the size of the CFG. We implemented ours and the WCC algorithm of Danicic et al. in the Clang/LLVM compiler framework [9] and performed experiments on a number of benchmarks selected from SPEC CPU 2017 [3]. Our algorithm performs a maximum of 29.8 times and on average 10.6 times faster than the WCC algorithm of Danicic et al. Moreover, the practical performance of our WCC algorithm is closer to the NlogN curve, and thus we improve the theoretical as well as the practical performance of WCC computation by an order of magnitude.

Outline. The remainder of this paper is organized as follows. Section 2 provides some notations and backgrounds on WCC, Sect. 3 illustrates the changes to be performed in static program slicing due to WCC/SCC, Sect. 4 provides the detailed description of our WCC computation method, prove the correctness, and the worst-case time complexity of our method, Sect. 5 compares the performance of ours and the WCC computation method of Danicic et al. on some practical benchmarks, Sect. 6 discusses the related works, and Sect. 7 concludes the paper.

2   Background

We provide the following formal definition of control flow graph (CFG).

Definition 1 (CFG). *A CFG is a directed graph* (N, E) *where*

1. *N is the set of nodes that includes a Start node from where the execution starts, at most one End node where the execution terminates normally, Cond nodes representing boolean conditions, and nonCond nodes; and*
2. *$E \subseteq N \times N$ is the relation describing the possible flow of execution in the graph. An End node has no successor, a Cond node n has at most one true successor and at most one false successor, and all other nodes have at most one successor.*

Like Danicic et al. [4], we assume the following:

- The CFG is deterministic. So, any *Cond* node n cannot have multiple true successors and/or multiple false successors.
- We allow *Cond* nodes to have either or both of the successors missing. We may also have non-*End* nodes having no successor (i.e. out-degree zero). An execution that reaches these nodes are silently nonterminating as it is not performing any action and does not return control to the operating system.
- If the CFG G has no *End* nodes, then all executions of G are nonterminating.
- Moreover, if a program has multiple terminating exit points, nodes representing those exit points are connected to the *End* node to model those terminations. Thus, the CFG in Definition 1 is sufficiently general to model a wide-range of real-world intraprocedural programs.

The sets of successor and predecessor nodes of any CFG node n in a CFG (N, E) are denoted by $succ(n)$ and $pred(n)$ where $succ(n) = \{m : (n, m) \in E\}$ and $pred(n) = \{m : (m, n) \in E\}$.

Definition 2 (CFG paths). *A path π is a sequence $n_1, n_2, \ldots, n_k$ of CFG nodes (denoted by $[n_1..n_k]$) such that $k \geq 1$ and $n_{i+1} \in succ(n_i)$ for all $1 \leq i \leq k - 1$.*

A path is *non-trivial* if it contains at least two nodes. We write $\pi - S$ to denote the set of all nodes in the path π that are not in the set S. The length of any path $[n_1..n_k]$ is $k - 1$. A trivial path $[n]$ has path length 0.

Definition 3 (Disjoint paths). *Two finite paths $[n_1..n_k]$ and $[m_1..m_l]$ such that $k, l \geq 1$ in any CFG G are disjoint paths if and only if no n_i is equal to m_j for all $1 \leq i \leq k$ and $1 \leq j \leq l$. In other words, the paths do not meet at a common vertex.*

Sometimes, we shall use the phrase "two disjoint paths from n" to mean that there exist two paths $n_1 = n, \ldots, n_k$ and $n'_1 = n, \ldots, n'_l$ such that $[n_2..n_k]$ and $[n'_2..n'_l]$ are disjoint paths. In other words, the paths are disjoint after the first common vertex.

Ferrante et al. [6] provided the first formal definition of control dependency relation based on *postdominator* [17] relation. Computing postdominator relations on a CFG G requires that G has a single End node n_e and there is a path from each node n in G to n_e. A node n *postdominates* a node m if and only if every path from m to n_e goes through n. Node n *strictly postdominates* m if n postdominates m and $n \neq m$. The standard *postdominator-based control dependency relation* can then be defined as follows:

Definition 4 (Control Dependency [6,19]). *Node n is control dependent on node m (written $m \overset{cd}{\to} n$) in the CFG G if (1) there exists a nontrivial path π in G from m to n such that every node $m' \in \pi - \{m, n\}$ is postdominated by n, and (2) m is not strictly postdominated by n.*

The relation $m \overset{cd}{\to} n$ implies that there must be two branches of m such that n is always executed in one branch and may not execute in the other branch.

Example 1. The CFG in Fig. 1 that we shall use as a running example is obtained from the perlbench in SPEC CPU2017 [3]. The details of the source code and the labeling of *true* and *false* branches of Cond nodes are omitted for simplicity. The control dependency graph (CDG) is computed from the CFG based on computing postdominator relations such that an edge (n, m) in the CDG represents the control dependency relation $n \overset{cd}{\to} m$.

Podgurski and Clarke [16] introduced the weak control dependence which is nontermination sensitive. A number of different nontermination sensitive and nontermination insensitive control dependency relations conservatively extending the standard relation above are defined in successive works [1,14–16,19]. Danicic et al. [4] unified all previous definitions and presented two generalizations called *weak* and *strong control closure* which are non-termination insensitive and non-termination sensitive. WCC and SCC capture all the existing non-termination (in)sensitive control dependency relations found in the literature. In this paper, we shall focus mostly on the efficient computation of WCC and occasionally mention SCC. We now recall some relevant definitions and terminologies of WCC from Danicic et al. [4].

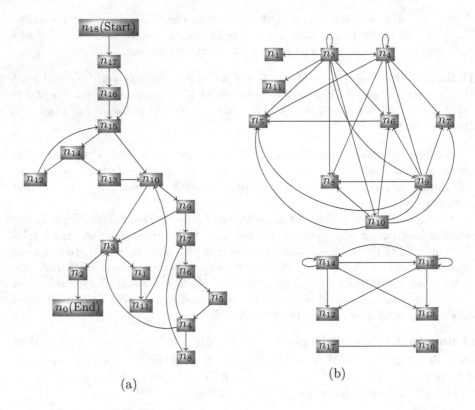

Fig. 1. (a) CFG obtained from a benchmark in SPEC CPU2017 [3] (we omit the program instructions for simplicity), (b) control dependency graph computed using postdominator relations.

Definition 5 (N'-Path). *An N'-path is a finite path $[n_1..n_k]$ in a CFG G such that $n_k \in N'$ and $n_i \notin N'$ for all $1 < i \le k-1$.*

Note that n_1 may be in N' in the above definition. Thus, an N'-path from n ends at a node in N' and no node in this path are in N' except n_1 which may or may not be in N'.

Definition 6 (N'-weakly committing vertex). *Let $G = (N, E)$ be any CFG. A node $n \in N$ is N'-weakly committing in G if all N'-paths from n have the same endpoint. In other words, there is at most one element of N' that is 'first-reachable' from n.*

Definition 7 (Weak control closure). *Let $G = (N, E)$ be any CFG and let $N' \subseteq N$. N' is weakly control-closed in G if and only if all nodes $n \in N \setminus N'$ that are reachable from N' are N'-weakly committing in G.*

The concept of weakly deciding vertices is introduced to prove that there exists minimal and unique WCC of a set of nodes $N' \subseteq N$. Since program slicing uses control dependence relations to capture all control dependent nodes affecting the slicing criterion, using minimal WCC in program slicing gives us smaller nontermination insensitive slices.

Definition 8 (Weakly deciding vertices). *A node* $n \in N$ *is* N'-*weakly deciding in* G *if and only if there exist two finite proper* N'-*paths in* G *that both start at* n *and have no other common vertices.* $WD_G(N')$ *denotes the set of all* N'-*weakly deciding vertices in* G.

Thus, if there exists an N'-weakly deciding vertex n, then n is not N'-weakly committing. The WCC of an arbitrary set $N' \subseteq N$ can be formally defined using weakly deciding vertices as follows:

$$WCC(N') = \{n : n \in WD_G(N'), n \text{ is reachable from } N' \text{ in } G\} \cup N'$$

Example 2. Consider the CFG in Fig. 1. Let $N' = \{n_5, n_8, n_{10}\}$. The N'-paths in this CFG include $n_9, \ldots, n_5$ and $n_4, \ldots, n_6, n_4, n_8$. The path n_6, n_5, n_4, n_8 is not an N'-path since $n_5 \in N'$. Nodes n_{12}, n_{13}, n_{14} and n_{15} are N'-weakly committing. However, n_9 and n_6 are not N'-weakly committing due to the N'-paths $[n_9..n_{10}]$ and $[n_9..n_5]$, and n_6, n_5 and n_6, n_4, n_8. Nodes n_9 and n_6 are thus N'-weakly deciding and N' is not weakly control closed. However, all N'-weakly deciding vertices n_4, n_6 and n_9 are reachable from N' and thus $N' \cup \{n_4, n_6, n_9\}$ is a weak control-closed set capturing all the relevant control dependencies of N'.

3   Program Slicing Using WCC and SCC

Program slicing is specified by means of a *slicing criterion* which is usually a set of CFG nodes representing program points of interest. Static backward/forward program slicing then asks to select all program instructions that directly or indirectly affect/ affected by the computation specified in the slicing criterion. Static dependence-based program slicing [7,11,20] is performed by constructing a so-called program dependence graph (PDG) [6]. A PDG explicitly represents the data and the control dependence relations in the control flow graph (CFG) of the input program. Any edge $n_1 \rightarrow n_2$ in a PDG represents either the control dependence relation $n_1 \xrightarrow{cd} n_2$ or the data dependence relation $n_1 \xrightarrow{dd} n_2$. The relation $n_1 \xrightarrow{dd} n_2$ holds if n_2 is using the value of a program variable defined at n_1. A PDG is constructed by computing all the data and the control dependence relations in the CFG of a program beforehand, and then include all edges (n, m) in the PDG if $n_1 \xrightarrow{dd} n_2$ or $n_1 \xrightarrow{cd} n_2$ holds. A forward/backward slice includes the set of all reachable nodes in the PDG from the nodes in the slicing criterion in the forward/backward direction.

The existence of the numerous kinds of control dependence in the literature puts us in the dilemma of which control dependence algorithm is to be used to construct PDG. Control dependence computation algorithms such as postdominator-based algorithms exist that cannot compute control dependencies from the following code having no exit point:

if (p) { L1: x=x+1; goto L2; } else { L2: print(x); goto L1; }

Building a PDG by using a particular control dependence computation algorithm may miss computing certain kinds of control dependencies, and the program slicing may produce unsound results. With the advent of WCC and SCC, we obtain a more generalized method to compute control closure of a wide-range of programs. However, the above approach of static program slicing is not feasible with WCC and SCC. This is due to the fact that even though WCC and SCC capture/compute the weak and strong form of control dependencies that are nontermination (in)sensitive, it is not possible to tell specifically which node is control dependent on which other nodes. Given any set N' of CFG nodes, the weak/strong control closure $cl(N')$ of N' captures all control dependencies $n_1 \xrightarrow{cd} n_2$ such that $n_2 \in cl(N')$ implies $n_1, n_2 \in cl(N')$. However, by looking into the set $cl(N')$, it is not possible to tell if the relation $n_1 \xrightarrow{cd} n_2$ holds or not for any $n_1, n_2 \in cl(N')$. Since we cannot compute all individual control dependencies $n_1 \xrightarrow{cd} n_2$ beforehand, it is not possible to compute a PDG from a CFG using weak or strong control closed sets. However, Algorithm 1 can be applied to perform the static program slicing using weak or strong control closures.

The relation $\xrightarrow{dd}^*$ denotes the transitive-reflexive closure of $\xrightarrow{dd}$. The above algorithm computes the *slice set* S for backward slicing containing all CFG nodes that affect the computation at the nodes in C. For forward slicing, the relation $\xrightarrow{dd}^*$ has to be computed in the forward direction. To compute the relation $\xrightarrow{dd}^*$, we can build a data dependency graph (DDG) capturing only the data dependency relations. Then, step 1 in Algorithm 1 can be accomplished by obtaining the set of all reachable nodes in the DDG from the nodes in S in the forward/backward direction.

Algorithm 1 illustrates that step 2 needs to be performed iteratively until a fixpoint $S = S'$ is reached. Given any CFG (N, E), Danicic et al. provided expensive algorithms to compute weak and strong control closures with worst-case time complexity $O(|N|^3)$ and $O(|N|^4)$ respectively. These algorithms are not only computationally expensive, they cause the static forward/backward program slicing practically inefficient. In the next section, we shall provide an alternative simple yet practically efficient method of computing a minimal weak control closed set.

Algorithm 1 (Slicing). *Let C be the the slicing criterion, and let $S = C$.*

1. $S' := \bigcup_{n \in S} \{m : m \xrightarrow{dd}^* n\}$
2. $S := cl(S')$
3. **if** $(S = S')$ **then EXIT**
4. **else GOTO** step 1

4 Efficient Computation of Minimal WCC

The relationship between WCC and weakly deciding vertices are the following (Lemma 51 in [4]): the set of CFG nodes $N' \subseteq N$ is weakly control-closed in the CFG $G = (N, E)$ iff all N'-weakly deciding vertices in G that are reachable from N' are in N'. Moreover, $N' \cup WD_G(N')$ is the unique minimal weakly control-closed subset of N that contains N' (Theorem 54 in [4]). We perform a simple and efficient two-step process of computing all N'-weakly deciding vertices $WD_G(N')$ followed by checking the reachability of these vertices from N' to compute the weakly control-closed subset of N containing N'.

In what follows, let $G = (N, E)$ be a CFG, let $N' \subseteq N$, and let $\mathcal{N}$ be the set of nodes such that $WD_G(N') \cup N' \subseteq \mathcal{N} \subseteq N$. The set of all N'-weakly deciding vertices $WD_G(N')$ are computed in the following two steps:

1. We compute a set of CFG nodes WD which is an overapproximation of the set of all N'-weakly deciding vertices, i.e., $WD_G(N') \subseteq WD$. The WD set includes all CFG nodes n such that n has two disjoint N'-paths. However, WD also contains spurious nodes having overlapping N'-paths or a single N' path which are not N'-weakly deciding. Thus, $\mathcal{N} = WD \cup N'$ is a weakly control-closed subset of N containing N' which is not minimal.
2. For each node $n \in WD$, the above process also indicates all CFG nodes $m \in \mathcal{N}$ such that either $[n..m]$ is an N'-path or there exists an N'-path from n that must go through m. From this information, we build a directed graph $(\mathcal{N}, \mathcal{E})$ such that any edge $(n, m) \in \mathcal{E}$ indicates that n is possibly a weakly deciding vertex, $m \in \mathcal{N}$, and there exists an $\mathcal{N}$-path $[n..m]$ in G. Next, we perform a verification process to check that each node in WD has two disjoint N'-paths using the graph $(\mathcal{N}, \mathcal{E})$ and discard all nodes in WD that do not have two such paths.

Table 1. The $\mathcal{N}$-paths discovered by our algorithm. CFG nodes are visited in two different orders denoted by S_1 and S_2. T_i represents the sequence of visited CFG nodes and P_i represents the sequence of discovered $\mathcal{N}$-paths during the corresponding visits for $1 \leq i \leq 4$. The superscript on a path denotes its length.

S_1	$T_1 = m_1 \to n_6 \to n_5 \to n_4 \to n_3 \to n_2 \to n_1 \to n_2$
	$P_1 = [m_1]^0 \quad [n_6, m_1]^1 \quad [n_5..m_1]^2 \quad [n_4..m_1]^3 \quad [n_3..m_1]^4 \quad [n_2..m_1]^5 \quad [n_1..m_1]^6$
	$T_2 = m_2 \to n_5 \to n_4 \to n_3 \to n_2 \to n_1 \to n_2$
	$P_2 = [m_2]^0 \quad [\mathbf{n_5}]^0 \quad [n_4, n_5]^1 \quad [n_3..n_5]^2 \quad [\mathbf{n_2}]^0 \quad [n_1..n_2]^1$
S_2	$T_3 = m_1 \to n_6 \to n_5 \to n_4$
	$P_3 = [m_1]^0 \quad [n_6, m_1]^1 \quad [n_5..m_1]^2 \quad [n_4..m_1]^3$
	$T_4 = m_2 \to n_5 \to n_4 \to n_3 \to n_2 \to n_1 \to n_2$
	$P_4 = [m_2]^0 \quad [\mathbf{n_5}]^0 \quad [n_4, n_5]^1 \quad [n_3..n_5]^2 \quad [n_2..n_5]^3 \quad [n_1..n_5]^4$

4.1 An Informal Account of Our Approach

In this section, we give an informal description of our algorithm to compute the N'-weakly deciding vertices. The first step of this algorithm keeps track of all

N'-paths (or $\mathcal{N}$-paths to be more specific where $\mathcal{N} = N'$ initially) in the CFG. We traverse the CFG backward from the nodes in N' and record all $\mathcal{N}$-paths at each visited node of the CFG. During this process, we discover all CFG nodes n that have more than one $\mathcal{N}$-paths ending at different CFG nodes, and n is included in WD (and thus $n \in \mathcal{N}$) as it is a potential N'-weakly deciding vertex. In the following, we illustrate this process using the CFG G in Fig. 2 where $m_1, m_2 \in N'$.

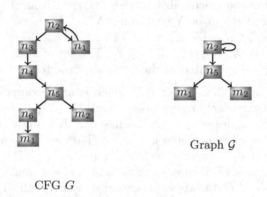

CFG G Graph $\mathcal{G}$

Fig. 2. CFG G used for the informal illustration of our approach. The graph $\mathcal{G}$ is generated by our analysis for the verification of potential N'-weakly deciding vertices.

We have trivial $\mathcal{N}$-paths $[m_1]$ and $[m_2]$ of lengths zero at CFG nodes m_1 and m_2 respectively. The $\mathcal{N}$-paths from a node are identified from the $\mathcal{N}$-paths of its successor nodes. The trivial $\mathcal{N}$-path $[m_1]$ leads to the $\mathcal{N}$-path $[n_6, m_1]$ of length 1 which in turn leads to $[n_5..m_1]$ of length 2. Similarly, $[m_2]$ leads to the $\mathcal{N}$-path $[n_5, m_2]$ of length 1. Since two $\mathcal{N}$-paths $[n_5..m_1]$ and $[n_5, m_2]$ are identified from n_5, n_5 is included in WD and a new trivial $\mathcal{N}$-path $[n_5]$ of length 0 is identified. Different orders of visiting CFG nodes may produce different $\mathcal{N}$-paths.

Table 1 presents two possible orders of visiting the CFG nodes. The sequence of $\mathcal{N}$-paths denoted by P_1 is produced due to visiting the node sequence T_1. Note that an earlier visit to n_2 has produced the $\mathcal{N}$-path $[n_2..m_1]$ of length 5, and the last visit to n_2 from n_1 (via the backward edge) in T_1 does not produce any new $\mathcal{N}$-path at n_2 as it could generate the $\mathcal{N}$-path $[n_2..m_1]$ of length 7 which is not preferred over $[n_2..m_1]$ of length 5 by our algorithm. While visiting the sequence of nodes in T_2, our algorithm identifies two $\mathcal{N}$-paths $[n_5..m_1]$ and $[n_5..m_2]$, and thus it includes n_5 in WD. Moreover, a new trivial $\mathcal{N}$-path $[n_5]$ is generated, and the successive visits to the remaining sequence of nodes replace the old $\mathcal{N}$-paths by the newly generated paths of smaller lengths. From the $\mathcal{N}$-paths $[n_3..n_5]$ and $[n_1..m_1]$ at the successor nodes of n_2, our algorithm infers that there exist two $\mathcal{N}$-paths $[n_2..m_1]$ and $[n_2..n_5]$ from n_2, and thus it includes n_2 in WD even though no two disjoint $\mathcal{N}$-paths exist in G. Thus, WD is an overapproximation of $WD_G(N')$. When CFG nodes are visited according to the order specified in S_2, our algorithm does not infer two $\mathcal{N}$-paths at n_2, and thus it becomes more precise by not including n_2 in WD. Note that this order of visiting CFG nodes does not affect the soundness (as we prove it later in this section), but the precision and performance of the first step our analysis, which is a well-known phenomenon in static program analysis. Note that our algorithm does not compute path lengths explicitly in generating $\mathcal{N}$-paths; it is accounted implicitly by our analysis.

The second step of our algorithm generates a graph $\mathcal{G}$ consisting of the set of nodes $N' \cup WD$ and the edges (n, m) such that $n \in WD$, $n' \in succ(n)$, and $[n'..m]$ is the $\mathcal{N}$-path discovered in the first step of the analysis. Thus, $[n..m]$ is an $\mathcal{N}$-path in the CFG. The graph $\mathcal{G}$ in Fig. 2 is generated from the WD set and the $\mathcal{N}$-paths generated due to visiting node sequences T_1 and T_2 in Table 1. Next, we traverse the graph $\mathcal{G}$ from N' backward; if a node $n \in WD$ is reached, we immediately know one of the $\mathcal{N}$-paths from n and explore the other unvisited branches of n to look for a second disjoint $\mathcal{N}$-path. For the graph $\mathcal{G}$ in Fig. 2, if $n_5 \in WD$ is reached from m_1, it ensures that $[n_5..m_1]$ is an $\mathcal{N}$-path in the CFG. Next, we look for a second $\mathcal{N}$-path in the other branch of n_5. In this particular case, the immediate successor of n_5 that is not yet visited is $m_2 \in N'$ such that $[n_5..m_2]$ is the second $\mathcal{N}$-path disjoint from $[n_5..m_1]$, which verifies that n_5 is an N'-weakly deciding vertex. We could have that $m_2 \notin N'$, and in that case, we traverse the graph $\mathcal{G}$ from m_2 in the forward direction to look for an $\mathcal{N}$-path different from $[n_5..m_1]$, include n_5 in $WD_G(N')$ if such a path is found, and excluded it from $WD_G(N')$ otherwise. Similarly, we discover the $\mathcal{N}$-path $[n_2..n_5]$ by reaching n_2 from n_5. However, since any $\mathcal{N}$-path from n_2 through the other branch of n_2 overlaps with $[n_2..n_5]$, n_2 is discarded to be a N'-weakly deciding vertex. When all nodes in WD are verified, we obtain the set $WD_G(N') \subseteq WD$ and the algorithm terminates.

4.2 An Overapproximation of the Weakly Deciding Vertices

We perform a backward traversal of the CFG from the nodes in N'. Initially, $\mathcal{N} = N'$. We maintain a function $A(n)$ for each CFG node $n \in N$. This function serves the following purposes:

1. If the backward traversal of the CFG visits only one $\mathcal{N}$-path $[n..m]$, then we set $A(n) = m$.
2. If two disjoint $\mathcal{N}$-paths $[n..m_1]$ and $[n..m_2]$ are visited during the backward traversal of the CFG, then we set $A(n) = n$.

We initialize the function $A(n)$ as follows:

$$A(n) = \begin{cases} \bot & n \in N \setminus N' \\ n & n \in N' \end{cases} \tag{1}$$

The valuation $A(n) = \bot$ indicates that no $\mathcal{N}$-path from n is visited yet. If we visit a CFG node $n \in N \setminus N'$ with two N'-paths (which may possibly be not disjoint due to overapproximation), then n is a potential N'-weakly deciding vertex. In this case, we set $A(n) = n$, n is included in WD (and hence $n \in \mathcal{N}$), and the function $A(n)$ will not be changed further.

If $A(n) \neq n$, then $A(n)$ may be modified multiple times during the walk of the CFG. If $A(n) = m_1$ is modified to $A(n) = m_2$ such that $n \neq m_1 \neq m_2$, then there exists a path $n, \ldots, m_2, \ldots, m_1$ in G such that $m_1, m_2 \in \mathcal{N}$ and $[n..m_2]$ is an $\mathcal{N}$-path in G. This may happen when (i) visiting the CFG discovers the $\mathcal{N}$-path $[n..m_1]$ such that $m_2 \notin \mathcal{N}$, and (ii) in a later visit to m_2, m_2 is included in WD (and in $\mathcal{N}$) that invalidates the path $[n..m_1]$ as an $\mathcal{N}$-path and obtains a new $\mathcal{N}$-path $[n..m_2]$. Note that if $[n..m]$ is an $\mathcal{N}$-path and $m \notin N'$, then there exists an N'-path from n that go through m which we prove later in this section.

Algorithm 2 computes the set WD which is an overapproximation of weakly control-closed subset of N containing N'. It uses a worklist W to keep track of which CFG nodes to visit next. Note the following observations for Algorithm 2.

- For any node n in W, $A(n) \neq \bot$ due to the initializations in Eq. 1 and steps 2(b) and 2(c).
- The set S_m in step 2(a) is never empty due to the fact that n is a successor of m and $A(n) \neq \bot$.
- If $A(m) = m$, then m will never be included in W in 2(b) and 2(c) as further processing of node m will not give us any new information.
- Since m can only be included in WD in step (2b) if $A(m) \neq m$, and $A(m) = m$ for any $m \in N'$ due to Eq. 1, we must have $WD \cap N' = \emptyset$.
- Node m can only be included in W in step 2(c) if $A(m) = x$ is updated to $A(m) = y$ such that $y \neq x$.
- If any path $[n..m]$ is traversed such that $A(m) = m$ and no node in $[n..m] - \{m\}$ is in WD, then m is transferred such that $A(n') = m$ for all $n' \in [n..m] - \{m\}$ due to step (2c). Also, note that if $A(n) = m$, then we must have $A(m) = m$.
- The functions A are both the input and the output of the algorithm. This facilitates computing WD incrementally. This incremental WD computation will improve the performance of client applications of WCC such as program slicing (see Algorithm 1). We leave the study on the impact of incremental WD computation on program slicing as a future work.

Algorithm 2 (OverapproxWD). *Input:* $G = (N, E), N', A$, *Output:* A, WD

1. *Initialization:*
   (a) *Set* $WD = \emptyset$
   (b) *Set the worklist* $W = N'$
2. *Remove an element n from W.* **Forall** $m \in pred(n)$ **do** *the following:*
   (a) *Compute* $S_m = \{A(m') : m' \in succ(m), A(m') \neq \bot\}$
       if $(|S_m| > 1)$ **then GOTO** (b) **else GOTO** (c)
   (b) **if** $(A(m) \neq m)$ **then** *insert m into W, update $A(m) = m$, and add m to WD.* **GOTO** (3).
   (c) **if** $(A(m) \neq m$ and $x \in S_m)$ **then** (i) *obtain* $y = A(m)$,
       (ii) *update* $A(m) = x$, *and* (iii) **if** $(y \neq x)$ **then** *insert m into W.*
       GOTO (3).
3. **if** $(W$ *is empty)* **then EXIT else GOTO** (2)

Theorems 1 and 2 below state the correctness of Algorithm 2 which we prove using an auxiliary lemma.

Lemma 1. *If $A(n) = m$ and $n \neq m$, then there exists an N'-path from n and all N'-paths from n must include m.*

Proof. Since $A(n) = m$, there exists a path $\pi = [n..m]$ visited in Algorithm 2 from m backward. The transfer of m to $A(n)$ is only possible if we have $S_x = \{m\}$ for all $x \in \pi - \{m\}$ and $A(x) = m$ is set in step (2c). Since $A(x) \neq x$, no node $x \in \pi - \{m\}$ is in $WD \cup N'$. Also, there exists a predecessor y of m such that $S_y = \{m\}$ which is only possible if $A(m) = m$. Thus, we must have $m \in N' \cup WD$ and π is a $(WD \cup N')$-path.

If $m \in N'$, then the lemma trivially holds. Suppose $m = m_1 \notin N'$. Then, we must have $m_1 \in WD$, and there exists a successor n_1 of m_1 such that $A(n_1) = m_2$. If $m_2 \notin N'$, then $m_2 \in WD$ and there exists a successor n_2 of m_2 such that $A(n_2) = m_3$. Thus, we obtain a subsequence of nodes $n_1, \ldots, n_k$ such that $A(n_i) = m_{i+1}$ for all $1 \leq i \leq k$ and eventually we have $m_{k+1} \in N'$ since the CFG is finite and it is traversed from the nodes in N' backward. Thus, $[n..m_{k+1}]$ is an N'-path which go through m. $\qquad\square$

Corollary 1. *If $A(n) = m$, then $m \in N' \cup WD$.*

Proof. The proof follows from the first part of the proof of Lemma 1. $\qquad\square$

Theorem 1. *For any WD computed in Algorithm 2, $WD_G(N') \subseteq WD$.*

Proof. Suppose the lemma does not hold. So, there exists an N'-weakly deciding vertex $n \in WD_G(N')$ such that $n \notin WD$. Thus, there are two disjoint N'-paths from n. Let $n_1 = n, \ldots, n_k$ and $m_1 = n, \ldots, m_l$ be two N'-paths. Since $n_k, m_l \in N'$, $A(n_k) = n_k$ and $A(m_l) = m_l$ due to Eq. 1. Algorithm 2 traverses these paths and update $A(n_i)$ and $A(m_j)$ in step (2c) such that

$$A(n_i) \neq \bot \text{ and } A(m_j) \neq \bot \text{ for all } 1 \leq i < k \text{ and } 1 \leq j < l.$$

Since $n \notin WD$, $|S_n| \leq 1$ in (2a). Node n has at most two successors according to the definition of CFG (Definition 1). Since $A(n_2) \neq \bot$ and $A(m_2) \neq \bot$, $|S_n| \leq 1$ is only possible if $A(n_2) = A(m_2)$. Let $A(n_2) = m$. Then, we must have $A(n) = m$ and all N'-paths must include m according to Lemma 1. Thus, we conclude that n is not an N'-weakly deciding vertex since the N'-paths from n are not disjoint, and we obtain the contradiction. $\qquad\square$

Theorem 2. *Algorithm 2 eventually terminates.*

Proof. Algorithm 2 iterates as long as there exist elements in W. For all $n \in N$ such that $A(n) = n$, n is included in WD and it never gets included in W again. If the value of $A(n)$ remains $\bot$, then n is never reached and included in W during the walk of the CFG. Thus the algorithm can only be nonterminating for some node n such that $A(n) \neq n \neq \bot$. According to step (2c) in the algorithm, n can only be included in W if the new value of $A(n)$ is different from the old one. Thus, in order for the algorithm to be nonterminating, there exists an infinite update to $A(n)$ by the sequence of values $m_1, \ldots, m_k, \ldots$ such that no two consecutive values are the same, i.e., $m_i \neq m_{i+1}$ for all $i \geq 1$.

According to Lemma 1, $A(n) = m_i$ implies that there exists an N'-path from n and all N'-paths from n must include m_i. Thus, there exists a path $[n..m_i]$ in the CFG. If $A(n)$ is updated by m_{i+1}, then $m_{i+1} \in WD$ and $A(m_{i+1}) = m_{i+1}$. Node m_{i+1} must be in the path $[n..m_i]$ as otherwise we eventually have $S_n = \{m_i, m_{i+1}\}$ in (2a) which will lead to $A(n) = n$. So, $A(n)$ will never become m_i again in (2c) as all N'-paths from n must go through $m_{i+1} \in WD$. Similarly, if $A(n)$ is updated by m_{i+2}, m_{i+2} must be in the path $[n..m_{i+1}]$ and $A(n)$ will never be updated by m_{i+1} again. Since the path $[n..m_{i+1}]$ has a finite number of nodes, $A(n)$ cannot be updated infinitely, and the algorithm eventually terminates. $\square$

Example 3. Let $N' = \{n_5, n_8\}$ for the CFG in Fig. 1. Algorithm 2 computes A and WD as follows:

- $A(n) = \bot$ for $n \in \{n_0, n_2\}$
- $A(n_i) = n_i$ for $i \in \{4, \ldots, 6, 8, \ldots, 10, 14, 15, 17\}$
- $A(n_i) = n_{10}$ for $i \in \{1, 3, 11, 13\}$
- $A(n_7) = n_6, A(n_{12}) = n_{15}, A(n_{16}) = n_{15}, A(n_{18}) = n_{17}$
- $WD = \{n_4, n_6, n_9, n_{10}, n_{14}, n_{15}, n_{17}\}$

Note that CFG nodes $n_9, n_{10}, n_{14}, n_{15}$, and n_{17} have no disjoint N'-paths as all N'-paths from these nodes must go through n_{10}. Thus, these nodes do not belong to $WD_G(N')$. However, we have $WD_G(N') = \{n_4, n_6\}$ and $WD_G(N') \subseteq WD$ holds.

4.3   Generating Minimal Weakly Deciding Vertices

Algorithm 2 is sound according to Theorem 1. However, as illustrated in Sect. 4.1, the WD set computed in this algorithm contains spurious nodes that are not N'-weakly deciding. In what follows, we provide a general and efficient algorithm to verify the results obtained from Algorithm 2 and discard all incorrectly identified N'-weakly deciding vertices. Thus, both algorithms together provide minimal and sound N'-weakly deciding vertices. We first represent the solutions generated by Algorithm 2 as a directed graph $\mathcal{G}$ as follows:

Definition 9. $\mathcal{G} = (\mathcal{N}, \mathcal{E})$ *is a directed graph, where*

- $\mathcal{N} = N' \cup WD$*, and*
- $\mathcal{E} = \{(n, A(m)) : n \in WD, m \in succ(n), A(m) \neq \bot\}$*.*

Note that $succ(n)$ is the set of successors of n in the CFG. In Fig. 3, $\mathcal{G} = (\mathcal{N}, \mathcal{E})$ is constructed from A and WD in Example 3 and the CFG in Fig. 1. Any graph $\mathcal{G}$ constructed according to Definition 9 has the following properties:

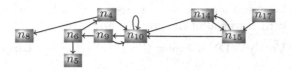

Fig. 3. Graph $\mathcal{G} = (\mathcal{N}, \mathcal{E})$ constructed according to Definition 9 from the CFG in Fig. 1, and A and WD in Example 3

- If there exists an edge (n, m) in $\mathcal{E}$ such that $m \in N'$, then there exists an N'-path $[n..m]$ in the CFG G.
- An edge (n, m) in $\mathcal{E}$ such that $m \in WD$ implies that there exists an N'-path from n going through m (from Lemma 1).
- There exist no successors of a node in N' since $WD \cap N' = \emptyset$.
- Graph $\mathcal{G}$ may be an edge-disjoint graph since there may exist N'-weakly deciding vertices and their N'-paths do not overlap.
- Since our CFG has at most two successors according to Definition 1, any node in $\mathcal{G}$ has at most two successors. However, some nodes in $\mathcal{G}$ may have self-loop or only one successor due to the spurious nodes generated in WD. Moreover, $|\mathcal{N}| \leq |N|$, $|\mathcal{E}| \leq |E|$.

The intuitive idea of the verification process is the following. For any $n \in N'$, we consider a predecessor m of n in $\mathcal{G}$. Thus, we know that $[m..n]$ is an N'-path in the CFG G. If there exist another successor $n' \in N'$ of m such that $n \neq n'$, then $[m..n']$ is another N'-path disjoint from $[m..n]$ and m is an N'-weakly deciding vertex. However, all other successors of m might be from WD instead of N'. Let $succ_{\mathcal{G}}(m)$ and $pred_{\mathcal{G}}(m)$ be the sets of successors and predecessors of m in $\mathcal{G}$. Then, we traverse $\mathcal{G}$ from the nodes in $succ_{\mathcal{G}}(m) \setminus N'$ in the forward direction to find an N'-path from m which is disjoint from $[m..n]$. If it visits a node in N' different from n, then m is an N'-weakly deciding vertex due to having two disjoint N'-paths. Otherwise, we exclude m from WD. Most nodes in WD can be immediately verified by looking into their immediate successors without traversing the whole graph $\mathcal{G}$. Also, the graph $\mathcal{G}$ is usually much smaller than the CFG. Thus, the whole verification process is practically very efficient.

Given the graph $\mathcal{G} = (\mathcal{N}, \mathcal{E})$, Algorithm 3 generates WD_{min} which is the set of minimal N'-weakly deciding vertices. Like Algorithm 2, we use a function $\bar{A}(n)$ to keep track of N'-paths visited from n. Initially, $\bar{A}(n) = \bot$ for all $n \in \mathcal{N} \setminus N'$ and $\bar{A}(n) = n$ otherwise. A boolean function $T(n)$ is set to true if $n \in N'$, and $T(n) = false$ otherwise. Another boolean function $V(n)$, which is initially $false$, is set to $true$ if n is already verified. The procedure $noDisjointNPath(m, \mathcal{G}, R_n, WD_{min}, N')$ used in the algorithm traverses the graph $\mathcal{G}$ from the nodes in R_n in the forward direction visiting each node at most once. If a node in $N' \cup WD_{min}$ different from m is visited, then it returns $true$, otherwise $false$. During this traversal, no successors of a node in $N' \cup WD_{min}$ are visited as an N'-path must end at a node in N'. We skip providing the details of this procedure since it is a simple graph traversal algorithm. Note that $S_n \neq \emptyset$ in step (3). This is because there exists a successor m of n from which n is reached during the backward traversal of the graph $\mathcal{G}$ and $\bar{A}(m) \neq \perp$.

Algorithm 3 (VerifyWDV). *Input:* $\mathcal{G} = (\mathcal{N}, \mathcal{E})$ and N', *Output:* WD_{min}

1. *Initialization :*
   (a) **Forall** $(n \in \mathcal{N} \setminus N')$ **do**
       $\bar{A}(n) = \perp$, $V(n) = false$, and $T(n) = false$
   (b) **Forall** $(n \in N')$ **do**
       $\bar{A}(n) = n$, $V(n) = true$, and $T(n) = true$
   (c) Set the worklist $W = \bigcup_{n \in N'} pred_{\mathcal{G}}(n)$, and set $WD_{min} = \emptyset$
2. **if** *(W is empty)* **then EXIT else** remove n from W and set $V(n) = true$
3. *Compute the following sets:*
$$S_n = \{\bar{A}(m) : m \in succ_{\mathcal{G}}(n), \bar{A}(m) \neq \perp\}$$
$$R_n = \{m : m \in succ_{\mathcal{G}}(n), \bar{A}(m) = \perp\}$$

   Let $m \in S_n$. **if** $(|S_n| > 1)$ **then GOTO** *(a)* **else GOTO** *(b)*
   (a) Set $\bar{A}(n) = n$. **if** $(T(n) = false)$ **then** $WD_{min} = WD_{min} \cup \{n\}$. **GOTO**
       (4)
   (b) **if** $(noDisjointNPath(m, \mathcal{G}, R_n, WD_{min}, N'))$ **then** set $\bar{A}(n) = \bar{A}(m)$
       and **GOTO** *(4)* **else GOTO** *(a)*
4. **Forall** $(n' \in pred_{\mathcal{G}}(n)$ such that $V(n') = false)$ **do**
       $W = W \cup \{n'\}$
   GOTO *(2)*

Theorem 3 below proves that WD_{min} is the minimal weakly control-closed subset of N containing N'.

Theorem 3. *For any WD_{min} computed in Algorithm 3, $WD_G(N') = WD_{min}$.*

Proof. "$\subseteq$": Let $n \in WD_G(N')$. According to Theorem 1, $WD_G(N') \subseteq WD$ and thus $n \in WD$. Suppose $m_1, m_2 \in succ(n)$ since there exist two disjoint N'-paths from n, and also assume that $A(m_i) = n_1^i$ for $i = 1, 2$. Thus, (n, n_1^i) is an edge in $\mathcal{G}$ for $i = 1, 2$. According to Corollary 1, $n_1^i \in N' \cup WD$. If $n_1^i \notin N'$, we can show similarly that there exists a node n_2^i such that (n_1^i, n_2^i) is an edge in $\mathcal{G}$ for some $1 \leq i \leq 2$ and $n_2^i \in N' \cup WD$. Since graph $\mathcal{G}$ and the CFG G are finite, eventually we have the following sequence of edges

$$(n, n_1^1), (n_1^1, n_2^1), \ldots, (n_{k-1}^1, n_k^1) \text{ and } (n, n_1^2), (n_1^2, n_2^2), \ldots, (n_{l-1}^2, n_l^2)$$

such that $n_k^1, n_l^2 \in N'$ for some $k, l \geq 1$. The graph $\mathcal{G}$ is traversed backward from $n_k^i \in N'$ and n will be reached in successive iterations in Algorithm 3. Thus, n is reached by traversing an N'-path $[n..n_k^1]$ backward. Either another N'-path $[n..n_l^2]$ will be discovered immediately during the construction of S_n in step (3) or it will be discovered by calling the procedure $noDisjointNPath$ and we eventually have $n \in WD_{min}$.

"$\supseteq$": Let $n \in WD_{min}$. Thus, there exists a node $m \in N'$ such that n is reached during traversing the graph $\mathcal{G}$ backward and thus $[n..m]$ is an N'-path. Also, there exists a successor $m' \neq m$ of n such that either $m' \in N'$ or $noDisjointNPath$ procedure traverses an N'-path from m_2 which is disjoint from $[n..m]$. Thus, $n \in WD_G(N')$ due to having two disjoint N'-paths.

4.4   Computing Minimal WCC

After obtaining the WD_{min} set containing minimal N'-weakly deciding vertices, computing minimal WCC requires checking the reachability of these nodes from the nodes in N'. Algorithm 4 below provides the complete picture of computing minimal WCC.

Algorithm 4 (minimalWCC). *Input:* $G = (N, E)$ *and* N', *Output:* WCC

1. *Apply Eq. 1 to initialize   A and set $WCC = N'$*
2. *$(A, WD) = OverapproxWD(G, N')$*
3. *Construct $\mathcal{G} = (\mathcal{N}, \mathcal{E})$ according to Definition 9*
4. *$WD_{min} = VerifyWDV(\mathcal{G}, N')$*
5. *Traverse G forward from the nodes in N' visiting each node $n \in N$ at most once and include n to WCC if $n \in WD_{min}$*

Example 4. For the graph $\mathcal{G}$ in Fig. 3 and $N' = \{n_5, n_8\}$, Algorithm 3 generates $WD_{min} = \{n_4, n_6\}$. Algorithm 4 computes $WCC = \{n_4, n_5, n_6, n_8\}$ for the CFG in Fig. 1 and N' as above.

4.5   Worst-Case Time Complexity

Lemma 2. *The worst-case time complexity of Algorithm 2 is $O(|N|^2)$.*

Proof. The worst-case time complexity is dominated by the costs in step (2) of Algorithm 2. Since $|succ(n)| \leq 2$ for any CFG node n, all the operations in steps (2a)-(2c) have constant complexity. However, after removing a node n from W, all the predecessors of n are visited. If the CFG G has no N'-weakly deciding vertices, then Algorithm 2 visits at most $|N|$ nodes and $|E|$ edges after which the operation $y \neq x$ in (2c) is always false, no node will be inserted in W, and thus the cost will be $O(|N| + |E|)$. In order to obtain a vertex in WD, it needs to visit at most $|N|$ nodes and $|E|$ edges and the maximum cost will be $O(|N| + |E|)$. If a node n is included in WD, then we set $A(n) = n$ and n will never be included in W afterwards due to the first conditional instruction in step (2c). Since we can have at most $|N|$ N'-weakly deciding vertices, the total worst-case cost will be $O((|N| + |E|) * |N|)$. Since any CFG node has at most two successors, $O(|E|) = O(|N|)$, and thus the worst-case time complexity is $O(|N|^2)$.

Lemma 3. *The worst-case time complexity of Algorithm 3 is $O(|N|^2)$.*

Proof. The initialization steps in Algorithm 3 have the worst-case cost $O(|\mathcal{N}|)$. The worst-case cost of Algorithm 3 is dominated by the main loop in steps (2)–(4). This main loop iterates at most $|\mathcal{N}|$ times since (i) once an element is removed from W, it is marked as visited and never inserted into W again, and (ii) the loop iterates as long as there are elements in W. Computing the sets $\mathcal{S}_n$ and R_n have constant costs since $|succ_{\mathcal{G}}(n)| \leq 2$. The costs of all other operations in step (3) are also constant except the *noDisjointNPath* procedure which has the

Table 2. Experimental results on selected benchmarks from SPEC CPU 2017 [3]

#	Benchmarks	KLOC	#Proc	T_{wcc}	T_{wccD}	Speedup
1	Mcf	3	40	9.6	56.7	5.9
2	Nab	24	327	55.1	418.6	7.6
3	Xz	33	465	40.5	116.5	2.9
4	X264	96	1449	155.7	896.0	5.8
5	Imagick	259	2586	334.8	2268.9	6.8
6	Perlbench	362	2460	1523.3	32134.8	21.1
7	GCC	1304	17827	26658.1	634413.9	23.8
Average Speedup = 10.6						

worst-case cost of $O(|\mathcal{N}|+|\mathcal{E}|)$ as it is a simple forward graph traversal algorithm visiting each node and edge at most once and other operations have constant cost. Step (4) visits the edges in $\mathcal{E}$ to insert elements in W and cannot visit more than $|\mathcal{E}|$ edges. Thus, the dominating cost of Algorithm 3 is $O((|\mathcal{N}|+|\mathcal{E}|) \times |\mathcal{N}|)$. Since $|\mathcal{N}| \leq N$, $|\mathcal{E}| \leq E$, and $O(|N|) = O(|E|)$, $O(|N|^2)$ is the worst-case time complexity of this algorithm.

Theorem 4. *The worst-case time complexity of Algorithm 4 is $O(|N|^2)$.*

Proof. The worst-case time complexity of Algorithm 4 is dominated by the $VerifyWDV$ and $OverapproxWD$ procedures which have the worst-case time complexity $O(|N|^2)$ according to Lemma 2 and 3.

5   Experimental Evaluation

We implemented ours and the weak control closure algorithms of Danicic et al. [4] in the Clang/LLVM compiler framework [9] and run experiments in an Intel(R) Core(TM) i7-7567U CPU with 3.50 GHz. The experiments are performed on a number of benchmarks consisting of approximately 2081 KLOC written in C language.

Table 2 shows experimental results performed on seven benchmarks selected from the SPEC CPU 2017 [3]. The #Proc column indicates the number of procedures analyzed in the respective benchmarks, T_{wcc} and T_{wccD} columns show total runtime of the algorithms of ours and Danicic et al., and the Speedup column indicates the speedup of our approach over Danicic et al. which is calculated as T_{wccD}/T_{wcc}. Each procedure is analyzed 10 times and the N'-sets are chosen randomly for each run. All times are recorded in microseconds which are converted to milliseconds and the analysis times reported in Table 2 are the average of 10 runs.

Regarding the correctness, both algorithms compute the same weakly control closed sets. As shown in Table 2, we obtain the highest and the lowest speedup of 23.8 and 2.9 from the GCC and the Xz benchmarks, and an average speedup

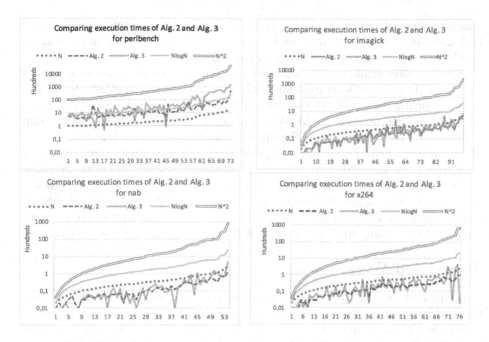

Fig. 4. Comparing execution times of Algorithm 2 and 3. Execution time curves are also compared with the $NlogN$ and N^2 functions where N represents the number of nodes in the CFG. X-axis represents selected CFGs from the respective benchmarks. Y-axis represents either the execution times of the algorithms measured in microseconds or the value of $NlogN$ and N^2. All charts are displayed in the logarithmic scale.

from all benchmarks is 10.6. The Xz benchmark provides the lowest speedup due to the fact that it has fewer procedures than GCC and the sizes of the CFGs for most procedures in this benchmark are very small; the average size of a CFG (i.e. number of CFG nodes) is only 8 per procedure. On the other hand, GCC has 38 times more procedures than Xz and the average size of a CFG per procedure is 20. Also, the greater speedups are obtained in larger CFGs. There are 171 and 55 procedures in GCC with the size of the CFGs greater than 200 and 500 respectively and the maximum CFG size is 15912, whereas the maximum CFG size in Xz is 87. For benchmarks like Mcf and Nab, even though they have fewer procedures than Xz, the average CFG size per procedure in these benchmarks are 21 and 16.

Since Algorithm 2 and 3 dominates the computational complexity of computing WCC, we compare the execution times of these algorithms in Fig. 4. We also plotted the functions $NlogN$ and N^2 to compare the execution curves of the algorithms with these functions. All times are measured in microseconds and an average of 10 runs. If there exist several CFGs with the same size, we keep the execution time of only one of them. As illustrated in the figure, Algorithm 2 performs consistently. However, the performance of Algorithm 3 varies above or below the performance of Algorithm 2. This due to the fact that it shows optimal performance when $noDisjointNPath$ procedure is called minimally. The performance curves of both algorithms are closer to the $NlogN$ curve for perlbench benchmark and closer to the linear curve for other benchmarks depicted in Fig. 4 when the times are measured in microseconds. In the appendix, we provide execution curves of other benchmarks.

We also have evaluated our algorithms by performing the same experiments on a virtual machine (VM) running on the real machine as specified above. The virtual machine uses a 64-bit Ubuntu OS with 10 GB RAM having 2 cores and the real machine runs Mac OS Version 10.15.4 with 16 GB RAM. Due to randomization, the experiments have different N' sets. We obtain a maximum speedup of 12 for *Perlbench* and an average speedup of 5.7 on all benchmarks from the experiments on the VM. Even though we obtain a smaller speedup compared to the speedup on the real machine, our algorithm is still several times faster than the WCC computation of Danicic et al., and we obtain similar performance curves for all benchmarks on VM. Evidently, our algorithm improves the state-of-the-art computation of weak control closure by an order of magnitude.

6 Related Work

Denning and Denning [5] are the pioneers to use dominator-based approach to identify program instructions influenced by the conditional instructions in the context of information-flow security. Weiser [20], the pioneer and prominent author in program slicing, used their approach in program slicing. However, the first formal definition of control dependence is provided by Ferrante et al. [6] in developing the program dependence graph (PDG) which is being used for program slicing and program optimization. This definition became standard afterward and is being used for over two decades.

Podgurski and Clarke [16] provided two control dependence relations called weak and strong syntactic dependence. The strong control dependence corresponds to the standard control dependence relation. The weak control dependence subsumes the strong control dependence relation in the sense that any strong control dependence relation is also a weak control dependence. Moreover, the weak control dependence relation is nontermination sensitive. Bilardi and Pingali [2] provided a generalized framework for the standard and the weak control dependence relation of Podgurski and Clarke by means of the dominance relation parameterized with respect to a set of CFG paths. Different classes of CFG path set provides different control dependence relations.

Ranganath et al. [18,19] considered CFGs possibly having multiple end nodes or no end node. These kinds of CFGs originate from programs containing modern program instructions like exceptions or nonterminating constructs often found in web services or distributed systems. They also considered low-level code such as JVM producing irreducible CFGs, and defined a number of control dependency relations that are nontermination (in)sensitive and conservatively extend the standard control dependency relation. The worst-case time complexity of the algorithms for computing their control dependences is $O(|N|^4 log|N|)$ where $|N|$ is the number of vertices of the CFG.

The control dependence relations defined later are progressively generalized than the earlier definitions, but one may be baffled by the overwhelming number of such definitions, e.g. in [19], to choose the right one. Danicic et al. [4] unified all previously defined control dependence relations and provided the most generalized non-termination insensitive and nontermination sensitive control dependence called weak and strong control-closure. These definitions are based on the weak and strong projections which are the underlying semantics for control dependence developed by the authors. These semantics are opposite to that of Podgurski and Clark in the sense that Danicic et al.'s weak (resp. strong) relation is similar to Podgurski and Clark's strong (resp. weak) relation. The worst-case time complexity of their weak and strong control closure algorithms are $O(|N|^3)$ and $O(|N|^4)$ where $|N|$ is the number of vertices of the CFG. Léchenet et al. [10] provided automated proof of correctness in the Coq proof assistant for the weak control closure algorithm of Danicic et al. and presented an efficient algorithm to compute such control closure. The efficiency of their method is demonstrated by experimental evaluation. However, no complexity analysis of their algorithm is provided.

Khanfar et al. [8] developed an algorithm to compute all direct control dependencies to a particular program statement for using it in demand-driven slicing. Their method only works for programs that must have a unique exit point. Neither the computational complexity nor the practical performance benefits of their algorithm are stated. On the other hand, we compute minimal weak control closure for programs that do not have such restrictions. Our method improves the theoretical computational complexity of computing weak control closure than the state-of-the-art methods, and it is also practically efficient.

7 Conclusion and Future Work

Danicic et al. provided two generalizations called weak and strong control closure (WCC and SCC) that subsume all existing nontermination insensitive and non-termination sensitive control dependency relations. However, their algorithms to compute these relations have cubic and quartic worst-case complexity in terms of the size of the CFG which is not acceptable for client applications of WCC and/or SCC such as program slicing. In this paper, we have developed an efficient and easy to understand method of computing minimal WCC. We provided the theoretical correctness of our method. Our WCC computation method has the quadratic worst-case time complexity in terms of the size of the CFG. We experimentally evaluated the algorithms for computing WCC of ours and Danicic et al. on practical benchmarks and obtained the highest 23.8 and on average 10.6 speedups compared to the state-of-the-art method. The performance of our WCC algorithm for practical applications is closer to either NlogN or linear curve in most cases when time is measured in microseconds. Thus we improve the practical performance of WCC computation by an order of magnitude.

We have applied our algorithms of computing minimal weakly deciding vertices in the computation of strongly control closed sets, implemented ours and the state-of-the-art SCC method in the Clang/LLVM framework, and evaluated these algorithms on practical benchmarks. We also obtained similar speedups in computing SCC. However, we have not included our SCC computation method in this paper due to space limitations.

As regards future work, our algorithm to compute minimal weakly deciding vertices can be applied to compute minimal SSA programs. Recently, Masud and Ciccozzi [12,13] showed that the standard dominance frontier-based SSA construction method increases the size of the SSA program by computing a significant amount of unnecessary ϕ functions. However, they provided complex and expensive algorithms that can generate minimal SSA programs. Our algorithm can be adapted to get an efficient alternative method in computing minimal SSA programs. Another future direction would be to compute WCC and SCC for interprocedural programs.

Acknowledgment. This research is supported by the Knowledge Foundation through the HERO project.

A   Appendix

See Fig. 5.

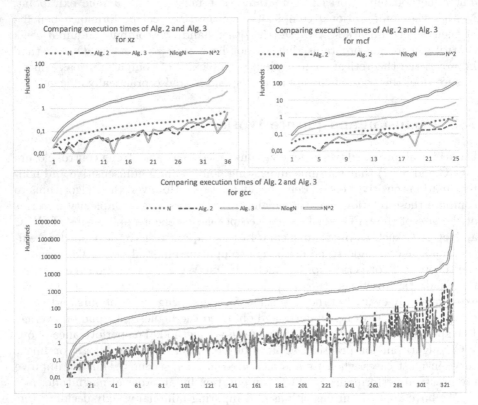

Fig. 5. Comparing execution times of Algorithm 2 and 3. Execution time curves are also compared with the $NlogN$ and N^2 functions where N represents the number of nodes in the CFG. X-axis represents selected CFGs from the respective benchmarks. Y-axis represents either the execution times of the algorithms measured in microseconds or the value of $NlogN$ and N^2. All charts are displayed in the logarithmic scale.

References

1. Amtoft, T.: Correctness of practical slicing for modern program structures. Department of Computing and Information Sciences, Kansas State University, Technical report (2007)
2. Bilardi, G., Pingali, K.: A framework for generalized control dependence. SIGPLAN Not. **31**(5), 291–300 (1996). https://doi.org/10.1145/249069.231435
3. Bucek, J., Lange, K.D., Kistowski, J.V.: Spec cpu2017: next-generation compute benchmark. In: Companion of the 2018 ACM/SPEC International Conference on Performance Engineering, pp. 41–42. ICPE 2018, ACM, New York (2018). https://doi.org/10.1145/3185768.3185771
4. Danicic, S., Barraclough, R., Harman, M., Howroyd, J.D., Kiss, Á., Laurence, M.: A unifying theory of control dependence and its application to arbitrary program structures. Theor. Comput. Sci. **412**(49), 6809–6842 (2011)
5. Denning, D.E., Denning, P.J.: Certification of programs for secure information flow. Commun. ACM **20**(7), 504–513 (1977). https://doi.org/10.1145/359636.359712
6. Ferrante, J., Ottenstein, K.J., Warren, J.D.: The program dependence graph and its use in optimization. ACM Trans. Program. Lang. Syst. **9**(3), 319–349 (1987). https://doi.org/10.1145/24039.24041
7. Khanfar, H., Lisper, B., Masud, A.N.: Static backward program slicing for safety-critical systems. In: de la Puente, J.A., Vardanega, T. (eds.) Ada-Europe 2015. LNCS, vol. 9111, pp. 50–65. Springer, Cham (2015). https://doi.org/10.1007/978-3-319-19584-1_4
8. Khanfar, H., Lisper, B., Mubeen, S.: Demand-driven static backward slicing for unstructured programs. Technical report (May 2019). http://www.es.mdh.se/publications/5511-
9. Lattner, C., Adve, V.: The LLVM Compiler Framework and Infrastructure Tutorial. In: LCPC'04 Mini Workshop on Compiler Research Infrastructures. West Lafayette, Indiana (September 2004)
10. Léchenet, J.-C., Kosmatov, N., Le Gall, P.: Fast computation of arbitrary control dependencies. In: Russo, A., Schürr, A. (eds.) FASE 2018. LNCS, vol. 10802, pp. 207–224. Springer, Cham (2018). https://doi.org/10.1007/978-3-319-89363-1_12
11. Lisper, B., Masud, A.N., Khanfar, H.: Static backward demand-driven slicing. In: Asai, K., Sagonas, K. (eds.) Proceedings of the 2015 Workshop on Partial Evaluation and Program Manipulation, PEPM, Mumbai, India, 15–17 January 2015. pp. 115–126. ACM (2015). https://doi.org/10.1145/2678015.2682538
12. Masud, A.N., Ciccozzi, F.: Towards constructing the SSA form using reaching definitions over dominance frontiers. In: 19th International Working Conference on Source Code Analysis and Manipulation, SCAM 2019, Cleveland, OH, USA, September 30 - October 1, 2019. pp. 23–33. IEEE (2019). https://doi.org/10.1109/SCAM.2019.00012
13. Masud, A.N., Ciccozzi, F.: More precise construction of static single assignment programs using reaching definitions. J. Syst. Softw. **166**, 110590 (2020). https://doi.org/10.1016/j.jss.2020.110590
14. Ottenstein, K.J., Ottenstein, L.M.: The program dependence graph in a software development environment. SIGSOFT Softw. Eng. Notes **9**(3), 177–184 (1984). https://doi.org/10.1145/390010.808263
15. Pingali, K., Bilardi, G.: Optimal control dependence computation and the roman chariots problem. ACM Trans. Program. Lang. Syst. **19**(3), 462–491 (1997)

16. Podgurski, A., Clarke, L.A.: A formal model of program dependences and its implications for software testing, debugging, and maintenance. IEEE Trans. Softw. Eng. **16**(9), 965–979 (1990)
17. Prosser, R.T.: Applications of Boolean matrices to the analysis of flow diagrams. In: Papers Presented at the December 1–3, 1959, Eastern Joint IRE-AIEE-ACM Computer Conference, pp. 133–138. IRE-AIEE-ACM '59 (Eastern), ACM, New York (1959)
18. Ranganath, V.P., Amtoft, T., Banerjee, A., Dwyer, M.B., Hatcliff, J.: A new foundation for control-dependence and slicing for modern program structures. In: Sagiv, M. (ed.) ESOP 2005. LNCS, vol. 3444, pp. 77–93. Springer, Heidelberg (2005). https://doi.org/10.1007/978-3-540-31987-0_7
19. Ranganath, V.P., Amtoft, T., Banerjee, A., Hatcliff, J., Dwyer, M.B.: A new foundation for control dependence and slicing for modern program structures. ACM Trans. Program. Lang. Syst. **29**(5), 27-es (2007)
20. Weiser, M.: Program slicing. In: Proceedings 5th International Conference on Software Engineering, pp. 439–449. ICSE 1981, IEEE Press, Piscataway, NJ, USA (1981). http://dl.acm.org/citation.cfm?id=800078.802557

A Library Modeling Language for the Static Analysis of C Programs

Abdelraouf Ouadjaout[1]($\boxtimes$) and Antoine Miné[1,2]

[1] Sorbonne Université, CNRS, LIP6, 75005 Paris, France
{abdelraouf.ouadjaout,antoine.mine}@lip6.fr
[2] Institut Universitaire de France, 75005 Paris, France

Abstract. We present a specification language aiming at soundly modeling unavailable functions in a static analyzer for C by abstract interpretation. It takes inspiration from Behavioral Interface Specification Languages popular in deductive verification, notably Frama-C's ACSL, as we annotate function prototypes with pre and post-conditions expressed concisely in a first-order logic, but with key differences. Firstly, the specification aims at replacing a function implementation in a safety analysis, not verifying its functional correctness. Secondly, we do not rely on theorem provers; instead, specifications are interpreted at function calls by our abstract interpreter.

We implemented the language into Mopsa, a static analyzer designed to easily reuse abstract domains across widely different languages (such as C and Python). We show how its design helped us support a logic-based language with minimal effort. Notably, it was sufficient to add only a handful transfer functions (including very selective support for quantifiers) to achieve a sound and precise analysis. We modeled a large part of the GNU C library and C execution environment in our language, including the manipulation of unbounded strings, file descriptors, and programs with an unbounded number of symbolic command-line parameters, which allows verifying programs in a realistic setting. We report on the analysis of C programs from the Juliet benchmarks and Coreutils.

1   Introduction

Sound static analysis of real-world C programs is hampered by several difficult challenges. In this work, we address the key problem of analyzing calls to external library functions, when analyzing library code is not an option (e.g., it is unavailable, has unsupported features such as system calls or assembly). More specifically, we target the GNU implementation of the C library [13], a library used in a large number of applications and featuring thousands of functions covering various aspects, such as file management, socket communication, string processing, *etc.* Several approaches have been proposed to analyze programs that depend on such complex libraries:

This work is partially supported by the European Research Council under Consolidator Grant Agreement 681393 — MOPSA.

D. Pichardie and M. Sighireanu (Eds.): SAS 2020, LNCS 12389, pp. 223–247, 2020.
https://doi.org/10.1007/978-3-030-65474-0_11

```
1  size_t strlen(const char* s) {
2    int size;
3    __require_allocated_array(s);
4    size = __get_array_length(s);
5    return size - 1;
6  }
```

(a) Stub of **strlen** in Infer

```
1  /*@ requires: valid_read_string(s);
2    @ assigns \result \from indirect:s[0..];
3    @ ensures: \result == strlen(s);
4    @*/
5  size_t strlen (const char *s);
```

(b) Stub of **strlen** in Frama-C

```
1  /*$
2    * requires: s != NULL ∧ offset(s) ∈ [0, size(s));
3    * requires: ∃i ∈ [0, size(s)-offset(s)): s[i] == 0;
4    * ensures : return ∈ [0, size(s)-offset(s));
5    * ensures : s[return] == 0;
6    * ensures : ∀i ∈ [0, return): s[i] != 0;
7    */
8  size_t strlen(const char s);
```

(c) Stub of **strlen** in Mopsa

```
1  int n = rand()%100;
2  char *p = malloc(n + 1);
3  if (!p) exit (1);
4  for(int i=0;i<n;i++)
5    p[i] = 'x';
6  a[n] = '\0';
7  int m = strlen(p);
```

(d) Example with **strlen**

Fig. 1. Examples of stubs in different analyzers.

Stubs as C Code. A common solution is to provide alternative C implementations of the library functions, called *stubs*. In order to remain sound and be effectively analyzed, stubs are generally simpler and contain calls to special builtins of the analyzer that provide more abstract information than the classic constructs of the language. This approach is adopted by many static analyzers, such as Astrée [4] and Infer [6]. For example, Fig. 1a shows the stub of **strlen** in Infer: it uses builtin functions to check that the argument points to a valid block before returning its allocation size. The approach makes it difficult for the stub programmer to express complex specifications with higher levels of abstractions, as key parts of the semantics are hidden within the builtin implementation. Moreover, writing stubs as C code and hard-coding builtins is acceptable when targeting embedded code [4], that does not rely much on libraries, but is not scalable to programs with more dependencies.

Stubs as Logic Formulas. More adapted specification languages have been proposed to overcome these drawbacks, principally based on formulas written in first-order logic. Some of them exploit the flexibility of the host language in order to define an *embedded domain specific language*, such as CodeContracts checker [11] that can express specifications of C# functions in C# itself. Other solutions propose a dedicated language and specifications are written as comments annotating the function. The most notable examples are JML for Java [18] and ACSL for C [3]. They have been widely used in deductive verification, employing theorem provers that naturally handle logic-based languages, but less in value static analysis by abstract interpretation. We show in Fig. 1b the specification of **strlen** in ACSL, as defined by Frama-C's value analyzer [9]. The syntax is less verbose than the C counterpart. Yet, essential parts of the stub are still computed through builtins. It is worth noting that Frama-C features another, more natural, specification of **strlen**, exploiting the expressiveness of the logic to avoid builtins. But this specification is large (64 lines) and employs quantified formulas that are too complex for the value analysis engine: it is used only by the deductive verification engine.

Abstract Interpretation of Logic Formulas. In this paper, we propose a novel approach based on abstract interpretation [7] that can interpret specifications written in a logic-based language of library functions when they are called. Similarly to CodeContracts checker [11], we do not rely on theorem provers to interpret formulas; instead, specifications are interpreted by abstract domains tailored to this task. The key novelty of our solution is that we consider the logic language as a separate language with its own concrete and abstract semantics, while contracts in cccheck are embedded within the host language as function calls. We believe that this decoupling makes the design more generic and the language is not limited by the semantic nor the syntax of the host language.

We implemented the proposed approach into Mopsa [16], a static analyzer that features a modular architecture that helps reusing abstract domains across different languages. We leverage this modularity and we illustrate how we can improve the analysis by extending C abstract domains to add transfer functions that exploit the expressiveness of formulas and infer better invariants. For example, the stub of `strlen` as defined in Mopsa is shown Fig. 1c. It relies essentially on constraints expressed as formulas instead of specific analyzer builtins. These formulas can be handled by Mopsa, and string lengths can be computed precisely even in the case of dynamically allocated arrays. For instance, at the end of the program shown in Fig. 1d, Mopsa can infer that $m = n$.

Contributions. In summary, we propose the following contributions:

- We present in Sect. 2 a new specification language for C functions and we formalize it with an operational concrete semantic. In addition to standard constructs found in existing languages, it features a resource management system that is general enough to model various objects, such as blocks allocated by `malloc`/`realloc` or file descriptors returned by `open`. Illustrative examples can be found in Appendix A.
- We present in Sect. 3 a generic abstract domain for interpreting the specification language, that is agnostic of the underlying abstraction of C.
- In Sect. 4, we illustrate how a string abstraction can benefit from the expressiveness of the specification language in order to provide better invariants.
- We implemented the analysis in Mopsa and we modeled over 1000 library functions. In Sect. 5, we report on the results of analyzing some Juliet benchmarks and Coreutils programs. More particularly, we show how our analysis combines several symbolic domains in order to analyze C programs with an unbounded number of command-line arguments with arbitrary lengths. To our knowledge, Mopsa is the first static analyzer to perform such an analysis.

Limitations. The following features are not supported by our analysis: recursive functions, longjumps, bitfields, inline assembly, concurrency and multi-dimensional variable length arrays.

$$
\begin{array}{ll}
stub & ::= (stmt \mid case)* \\
case & ::= \textbf{case} \ \{ \ stmt \ * \ \} \\
stmt & ::= effect \mid cond \\
effect & ::= \textbf{alloc} : type \ ident \ = \textbf{new} \ ident; \\
& \mid \quad \textbf{assigns} : expr \ [expr, expr]?; \\
& \mid \quad \textbf{free} : expr; \\[6pt]
cond & ::= \textbf{assumes} : form; \\
& \mid \quad \textbf{requires} : form; \\
& \mid \quad \textbf{ensures} : form; \\[6pt]
ntype & ::= \textbf{char} \mid \textbf{short} \mid \textbf{int} \mid \textbf{long} \mid \textbf{float} \\
stype & ::= ntype \mid \textbf{ptr} \\
type & ::= stype \\
& \mid \quad type\,[n], n \in \mathbb{N} \\
& \mid \quad \textbf{struct} \ \{ \ type \ ident; \ldots \} \\
& \mid \quad \textbf{union} \ \{ \ type \ ident; \ldots \}
\end{array}
$$

$$
\begin{array}{ll}
form & ::= expr \diamond expr, \diamond \in \{ \ \texttt{==}, \texttt{!=}, \ldots \} \\
& \mid \quad expr \in set \\
& \mid \quad \textbf{alive}(expr) \\
& \mid \quad form \wedge form \\
& \mid \quad form \vee form \\
& \mid \quad \neg form \\
& \mid \quad \forall \ ident \in [expr, expr] : form \\
& \mid \quad \exists \ ident \in [expr, expr] : form \\[6pt]
set & ::= [expr, expr] \mid ident \\
expr & ::= c, c \in \mathbb{R} \\
& \mid \quad \texttt{\&}ident \\
& \mid \quad \texttt{*}expr \\
& \mid \quad expr \diamond expr, \diamond \in \{ \ \texttt{+}, \texttt{-}, \ldots \} \\
& \mid \quad \textbf{size}(expr) \\
& \mid \quad \textbf{base}(expr) \\
& \mid \quad \textbf{offset}(expr)
\end{array}
$$

Fig. 2. Syntax of the modeling language.

2   Syntax and Concrete Semantics

We define the syntax and operational concrete semantics of the modeling language. The syntax is inspired from existing specification languages, such as ACSL [3] and JML [18], with the addition of resource management. The semantics expresses a relation between program states before the function call and after.

2.1   Syntax

The syntax is presented in Fig. 2. It features two kinds of statements:

- *Side-effect statements* specify the part of the input state which is modified by the function: assigns specifies that a variable (or an array slice) is modified by the function; alloc creates a fresh resource instance of a specified class (*ident*) and assigns its address to a local variable; conversely, free destroys a previously allocated resource. Any memory portion that is not explicitly mentioned by these statements is implicitly assumed to be unchanged. Resources model dynamic objects, such as memory blocks managed by malloc, realloc and free, or file descriptors managed by open and close. The models of these functions can be found in Appendix A. Assigning a class to resources allows supporting different attributes (e.g., read-only memory blocks) and allocation semantics (e.g., returning the lowest available integer when allocating a descriptor, which is needed to model faithfully the dup function).
- *Condition statements* express pre and post-conditions: requires defines mandatory conditions on the input environment for the function to behave correctly; assumes defines assumptions, and is used for case analysis; ensures expresses conditions on the output environment (the return value, the value of modified variables, and the size and initial state of allocated resources).

Cases. We support a disjunctive construct case (akin to Frama-C's *behaviors*) to describe functions with several possible behaviors. Each case is independently analyzed, after which they are all joined. Statements placed outside cases are common to all cases, which is useful to factor specification. For the sake of clarity, we will focus on the formalization of stubs without cases.

Formulas and Expressions. Formulas are classic first-order, with conjunctions, disjunctions, negations and quantifiers. The atoms are C expressions (without function call nor side-effect), extended with a few built-in functions and predicates: $e \in set$ restricts the range of a numeric value or the class of a resource; alive(e) checks whether a resource has not been freed; given a pointer e, base(e) returns a pointer to the beginning of the memory block containing e, size(e) is the block size, and offset(e) is the byte-offset of e in the block.

2.2 Environments

Concrete memories are defined classically. The memory is decomposed into blocks: $\mathcal{B} \stackrel{\text{def}}{=} \mathcal{V} \cup \mathcal{A}$, which can be either variables in $\mathcal{V}$ or heap addresses in $\mathcal{A}$. Each block is decomposed into scalar elements in $\mathcal{S} \subseteq \mathcal{B} \times \mathbb{N} \times stype$, where $\wr b, o, \tau \wr \in \mathcal{S}$ denotes the memory region in block b starting at offset o and having type τ. A scalar element of type τ can have values in $\mathbb{V}_\tau$, where $\mathbb{V}_\tau$ is $\mathbb{R}$ for numeric types and $\mathbb{V}_{\text{ptr}} \stackrel{\text{def}}{=} \mathcal{B} \times \mathbb{N}$ is a block-offset pair for pointers[1]. The set of all scalar values is $\mathbb{V} \stackrel{\text{def}}{=} \mathbb{R} \cup (\mathcal{B} \times \mathbb{N})$.

Environments, in $\mathcal{E} \stackrel{\text{def}}{=} \mathcal{M} \times \mathcal{R}$, encode the state of the program using: a *memory environment* in $\mathcal{M} \stackrel{\text{def}}{=} \mathcal{S} \rightarrow \mathbb{V}$, mapping scalar elements to values, and a *resource environment* in $\mathcal{R} \stackrel{\text{def}}{=} \mathcal{A} \rightharpoonup (ident \times \mathbb{N} \times \mathbb{B})$, which is a partial map mapping allocated resources to their class, size, and liveness status (as a Boolean).

Example 1. Given the declaration: struct s { int id; char *data; } v, the environment:

$$\left(\begin{array}{ll} \wr v, 0, \text{int} \wr \mapsto 5 & \wr v, 4, \text{ptr} \wr \mapsto (@, 0) \\ \wr @, 0, \text{short} \wr \mapsto 3 & \wr @, 2, \text{short} \wr \mapsto -1 \end{array}, @ \mapsto (\text{malloc}, 4, true) \right)$$

encodes the state where field v.id has value 5 and v.data points to a malloc resource containing two short elements with values 3 and −1 respectively.

2.3 Evaluation

Expressions. The evaluation of expressions, given as $\mathbb{E}[\![\,.\,]\!] \in expr \rightarrow \mathcal{E} \rightarrow \mathcal{P}(\mathbb{V})$, returns the set of possible values to handle possible non-determinism (such as

---

[1] To simplify the presentation, we assume that $\mathcal{S}$ is given (e.g. using block types) and omit NULL and invalid pointers. In practice, our analysis uses the dynamic cell decomposition from [19] to fully handle C pointers, union types, and type-punning.

$\mathbb{E}[\![\,.\,]\!] \in expr \to \mathcal{E} \to \mathcal{P}(\mathbf{V})$

$\mathbb{E}[\![\,\mathtt{size}(e)\,]\!](\rho, \sigma) \stackrel{\text{def}}{=} \{\,\mathtt{sizeof}(b) \mid (b, -) \in \mathbb{E}[\![\,e\,]\!](\rho, \sigma) \wedge b \in \mathcal{V}\,\}$
$\qquad\qquad\qquad\qquad \cup \{\,n \mid (b, -) \in \mathbb{E}[\![\,e\,]\!](\rho, \sigma) \wedge b \in \mathcal{A} \wedge (-, n, -) = \sigma(b)\,\}$

$\mathbb{E}[\![\,\mathtt{base}(e)\,]\!](\rho, \sigma) \stackrel{\text{def}}{=} \{\,b \mid (b, -) \in \mathbb{E}[\![\,e\,]\!](\rho, \sigma)\,\}$

$\mathbb{E}[\![\,\mathtt{offset}(e)\,]\!](\rho, \sigma) \stackrel{\text{def}}{=} \{\,o \mid (-, o) \in \mathbb{E}[\![\,e\,]\!](\rho, \sigma)\,\}$

$\mathbb{E}[\![\,n\,]\!](\rho, \sigma) \stackrel{\text{def}}{=} \{\,n\,\}$

$\mathbb{E}[\![\,\&v\,]\!](\rho, \sigma) \stackrel{\text{def}}{=} \{\,(v, 0)\,\}$

$\mathbb{E}[\![\,{*}e\,]\!](\rho, \sigma) \stackrel{\text{def}}{=} \{\,\rho(\langle b, o, \mathtt{typeof}(*e)\rangle) \mid (b, o) \in \mathbb{E}[\![\,e\,]\!](\rho, \sigma)\,\}$

$\mathbb{E}[\![\,e_1 \diamond e_2\,]\!](\rho, \sigma) \stackrel{\text{def}}{=} \{\,v_1 \diamond v_2 \mid v_1 \in \mathbb{E}[\![\,e_1\,]\!](\rho, \sigma) \wedge v_2 \in \mathbb{E}[\![\,e_2\,]\!](\rho, \sigma)\,\}$

Fig. 3. Concrete semantics of expressions.

$\mathbb{F}[\![\,.\,]\!] \in form \to \mathcal{P}(\mathcal{E})$

$\mathbb{F}[\![\,e \in R\,]\!] \stackrel{\text{def}}{=} \{\,(\rho, \sigma) \mid (b, -) \in \mathbb{E}[\![\,e\,]\!](\rho, \sigma) \wedge b \in \mathcal{A} \wedge \sigma(b) = (R, -, -)\,\}$

$\mathbb{F}[\![\,e \in [a, b]\,]\!] \stackrel{\text{def}}{=} \{\,(\rho, \sigma) \mid$
$\qquad\qquad\qquad n \in \mathbb{E}[\![\,e\,]\!](\rho, \sigma) \wedge l \in \mathbb{E}[\![\,a\,]\!](\rho, \sigma) \wedge u \in \mathbb{E}[\![\,b\,]\!](\rho, \sigma) \wedge n \in [l, u]\,\}$

$\mathbb{F}[\![\,\mathtt{alive}(e)\,]\!] \stackrel{\text{def}}{=} \{\,(\rho, \sigma) \mid (b, -) \in \mathbb{E}[\![\,e\,]\!](\rho, \sigma) \wedge b \in \mathcal{A} \wedge \sigma(b) = (-, -, true)\,\}$

$\mathbb{F}[\![\,e_1 \diamond e_2\,]\!] \stackrel{\text{def}}{=} \{\,(\rho, \sigma) \mid n_1 \in \mathbb{E}[\![\,e_1\,]\!](\rho, \sigma) \wedge n_2 \in \mathbb{E}[\![\,e_2\,]\!](\rho, \sigma) \wedge n_1 \diamond n_2\,\}$

$\mathbb{F}[\![\,\neg f\,]\!] \stackrel{\text{def}}{=} \mathbb{F}[\![\,de\text{-}morgan\text{-}negation(f)\,]\!]$

$\mathbb{F}[\![\,f_1 \wedge f_2\,]\!] \stackrel{\text{def}}{=} \mathbb{F}[\![\,f_1\,]\!] \cap \mathbb{F}[\![\,f_2\,]\!]$

$\mathbb{F}[\![\,f_1 \vee f_2\,]\!] \stackrel{\text{def}}{=} \mathbb{F}[\![\,f_1\,]\!] \cup \mathbb{F}[\![\,f_2\,]\!]$

$\mathbb{F}[\![\,\forall v \in [a, b] : f\,]\!] \stackrel{\text{def}}{=} \{\,(\rho, \sigma) \mid$
$\qquad\qquad l \in \mathbb{E}[\![\,a\,]\!](\rho, \sigma) \wedge u \in \mathbb{E}[\![\,b\,]\!](\rho, \sigma) \wedge (\rho, \sigma) \in \bigcap_{i \in [l, u]} \mathbb{F}[\![\,f[v/i]\,]\!]\,\}$

$\mathbb{F}[\![\,\exists v \in [a, b] : f\,]\!] \stackrel{\text{def}}{=} \{\,(\rho, \sigma) \mid$
$\qquad\qquad l \in \mathbb{E}[\![\,a\,]\!](\rho, \sigma) \wedge u \in \mathbb{E}[\![\,b\,]\!](\rho, \sigma) \wedge (\rho, \sigma) \in \bigcup_{i \in [l, u]} \mathbb{F}[\![\,f[v/i]\,]\!]\,\}$

Fig. 4. Concrete semantics of formulas.

reading random values). It is defined by induction on the syntax, as depicted in Fig. 3. The stub builtin `size` reduces to the C builtin `sizeof` for variables and returns the size stored in the resource map for dynamically allocated blocks. Calls to `base` and `offset` evaluate their pointer argument and extract the first (respectively second) component. To simplify the presentation, we do not give the explicit definition of the C operators, which is complex but standard. Likewise, we omit a precise treatment of invalid and `NULL` pointers (see [19] for a more complete definition). Finally, we omit here reporting of C run-time errors.

Formulas.

The semantics of formulas $\mathbb{F}[\![\,.\,]\!] \in form \to \mathcal{P}(\mathcal{E})$, shown in Fig. 4, returns the set of environments that satisfy it. It is standard, except for built-in predicates: to verify the predicate $e \in R$ (resp. $\mathtt{alive}(e)$), we resolve the instance pointed by e and look up the resource map to check that its class equals R (resp. its liveness flag is *true*).

$$\tilde{\mathbb{E}}[\![\,.\,]\!] \in e\tilde{x}pr \rightarrow \mathcal{E} \times \mathcal{E} \rightarrow \mathcal{P}(\mathbb{V})$$

$$\tilde{\mathbb{E}}[\![\,*e\,]\!]\,\langle\varepsilon,\varepsilon'\rangle \stackrel{\text{def}}{=} \mathbb{E}[\![\,*e\,]\!]\varepsilon$$

$$\tilde{\mathbb{E}}[\![\,(*e)'\,]\!]\,\langle\varepsilon,\varepsilon'\rangle \stackrel{\text{def}}{=} \mathbb{E}[\![\,*e\,]\!]\varepsilon'$$

$$\tilde{\mathbb{E}}[\![\,\texttt{size}(e)\,]\!]\,\langle\varepsilon,\varepsilon'\rangle \stackrel{\text{def}}{=} \mathbb{E}[\![\,\texttt{size}(e)\,]\!]\varepsilon$$

$$\tilde{\mathbb{E}}[\![\,\texttt{size}(e')\,]\!]\,\langle\varepsilon,\varepsilon'\rangle \stackrel{\text{def}}{=} \mathbb{E}[\![\,\texttt{size}(e)\,]\!]\varepsilon'$$

$$\tilde{\mathbb{E}}[\![\,n\,]\!]\,\langle\varepsilon,\varepsilon'\rangle \stackrel{\text{def}}{=} \{\,n\,\}$$

$$\tilde{\mathbb{E}}[\![\,\&v\,]\!]\,\langle\varepsilon,\varepsilon'\rangle \stackrel{\text{def}}{=} \{\,(v,0)\,\}$$

$$\tilde{\mathbb{E}}[\![\,e_1 \diamond e_2\,]\!]\,\langle\varepsilon,\varepsilon'\rangle \stackrel{\text{def}}{=} \{\,v_1 \diamond v_2 \mid v_1 \in \tilde{\mathbb{E}}[\![\,e_1\,]\!]\,\langle\varepsilon,\varepsilon'\rangle \wedge v_2 \in \tilde{\mathbb{E}}[\![\,e_2\,]\!]\,\langle\varepsilon,\varepsilon'\rangle\,\}$$

$$\tilde{\mathbb{E}}[\![\,\texttt{base}(e)\,]\!]\,\langle\varepsilon,\varepsilon'\rangle \stackrel{\text{def}}{=} \{\,b \mid (b,-) \in \tilde{\mathbb{E}}[\![\,e\,]\!]\,\langle\varepsilon,\varepsilon'\rangle\,\}$$

$$\tilde{\mathbb{E}}[\![\,\texttt{offset}(e)\,]\!]\,\langle\varepsilon,\varepsilon'\rangle \stackrel{\text{def}}{=} \{\,o \mid (-,o) \in \tilde{\mathbb{E}}[\![\,e\,]\!]\,\langle\varepsilon,\varepsilon'\rangle\,\}$$

Fig. 5. Concrete semantics of relational expressions.

2.4 Relational Semantics

Statements express some information on pre and post-conditions, that is, on the relation between input and output environments.

Expressions and Formulas. To allow expressions to mention both the input and output state, we use the classic prime notation: e' denotes the value of expression e in the post-state. Denoting $e\tilde{x}pr$ the set of expressions with primes, their semantic on an input-output environment pair is given by $\tilde{\mathbb{E}}[\![\,.\,]\!] \in e\tilde{x}pr \rightarrow \mathcal{E} \times \mathcal{E} \rightarrow \mathcal{P}(\mathbb{V})$. Figure 5 presents the most interesting cases: evaluating a primed dereference $\tilde{\mathbb{E}}[\![\,(*e)'\,]\!]\,\langle\varepsilon,\varepsilon'\rangle$ reduces to the non-relational evaluation $\mathbb{E}[\![\,*e\,]\!]$ on ε', while a non-primed dereference reduces to $\mathbb{E}[\![\,*e\,]\!]$ on ε. The case of $\texttt{size}(e')$ and $\texttt{size}(e)$ is similar. Other cases are analog to non-relational evaluation.

We denote by $f\tilde{o}rm$ formulas with primes, and define their evaluation function $\tilde{\mathbb{F}}[\![\,.\,]\!] \in f\tilde{o}rm \rightarrow \mathcal{P}(\mathcal{E} \times \mathcal{E})$ as returning a relation. As shown in Fig. 6, to evaluate predicates $e \in R$ and $\texttt{alive}(e)$, only input environments are inspected, as the resource class is an immutable property and the liveness flag can be changed only by $\texttt{free}$ statements in previous calls. The remaining definitions are similar to the non-relational case.

Example 2. Consider again variable $\texttt{v}$ shown in Example 1 and the following relational formula: $\texttt{v.data}' == \texttt{v.data} + 1 \wedge *(\texttt{v.data} + \texttt{1})' == 10$. When applied on the previous environment we obtain the relation:

$$\left\langle \begin{array}{l} \left(\begin{array}{ll} \{v,0,\texttt{int}\} \mapsto 5 & \{v,4,\texttt{ptr}\} \mapsto (@,0) \\ \{@,0,\texttt{short}\} \mapsto 3 & \{@,2,\texttt{short}\} \mapsto -1 \end{array}, @ \mapsto (\texttt{malloc},4,\textit{true}) \right) \\ , \\ \left(\begin{array}{ll} \{v,0,\texttt{int}\} \mapsto 5 & \{v,4,\texttt{ptr}\} \mapsto (@,2) \\ \{@,0,\texttt{short}\} \mapsto 3 & \{@,2,\texttt{short}\} \mapsto 10 \end{array}, @ \mapsto (\texttt{malloc},4,\textit{true}) \right) \end{array} \right\rangle$$

Side-effect Statements. We model side-effect statements as relation transformers, $\mathbb{S}_{\text{effect}}[\![\,.\,]\!] \in \textit{effect} \rightarrow \mathcal{P}(\mathcal{E} \times \mathcal{E}) \rightarrow \mathcal{P}(\mathcal{E} \times \mathcal{E})$ shown in Fig. 7. Given an input-output relation as argument, it returns a new relation where the output part is

$$\tilde{\mathbb{F}}[\![\,.\,]\!] \in \widetilde{form} \to \mathcal{P}(\mathcal{E} \times \mathcal{E})$$

$$\tilde{\mathbb{F}}[\![\, e \in R \,]\!] \;\overset{\text{def}}{=}\; \{\, \langle \varepsilon, \varepsilon' \rangle \mid \varepsilon \in \mathbb{F}[\![\, e \in R \,]\!] \,\}$$

$$\tilde{\mathbb{F}}[\![\, e \in [a,b] \,]\!] \;\overset{\text{def}}{=}\; \{\, \langle \varepsilon, \varepsilon' \rangle \mid$$
$$\qquad n \in \tilde{\mathbb{E}}[\![\, e \,]\!]\, \langle \varepsilon, \varepsilon' \rangle \wedge l \in \tilde{\mathbb{E}}[\![\, a \,]\!]\, \langle \varepsilon, \varepsilon' \rangle \wedge u \in \tilde{\mathbb{E}}[\![\, b \,]\!]\, \langle \varepsilon, \varepsilon' \rangle \wedge n \in [l,u] \,\}$$

$$\tilde{\mathbb{F}}[\![\, \texttt{alive}(e) \,]\!] \;\overset{\text{def}}{=}\; \{\, \langle \varepsilon, \varepsilon' \rangle \mid \varepsilon \in \mathbb{F}[\![\, \texttt{alive}(e) \,]\!] \,\}$$

$$\tilde{\mathbb{F}}[\![\, e_1 \diamond e_2 \,]\!] \;\overset{\text{def}}{=}\; \{\, \langle \varepsilon, \varepsilon' \rangle \mid v_1 \in \tilde{\mathbb{E}}[\![\, e_1 \,]\!]\, \langle \varepsilon, \varepsilon' \rangle \wedge v_2 \in \tilde{\mathbb{E}}[\![\, e_2 \,]\!]\, \langle \varepsilon, \varepsilon' \rangle \wedge v_1 \diamond v_2 \,\}$$

$$\tilde{\mathbb{F}}[\![\, \neg f \,]\!] \;\overset{\text{def}}{=}\; \tilde{\mathbb{F}}[\![\, \textit{de-morgan-negation}(f) \,]\!]$$

$$\tilde{\mathbb{F}}[\![\, f_1 \wedge f_2 \,]\!] \;\overset{\text{def}}{=}\; \tilde{\mathbb{F}}[\![\, f_1 \,]\!] \cap \tilde{\mathbb{F}}[\![\, f_2 \,]\!]$$

$$\tilde{\mathbb{F}}[\![\, f_1 \vee f_2 \,]\!] \;\overset{\text{def}}{=}\; \tilde{\mathbb{F}}[\![\, f_1 \,]\!] \cup \tilde{\mathbb{F}}[\![\, f_2 \,]\!]$$

$$\tilde{\mathbb{F}}[\![\, \forall v \in [a,b] : f \,]\!] \;\overset{\text{def}}{=}\; \{\, \langle \varepsilon, \varepsilon' \rangle \mid$$
$$\qquad l \in \tilde{\mathbb{E}}[\![\, a \,]\!]\, \langle \varepsilon, \varepsilon' \rangle \wedge u \in \tilde{\mathbb{E}}[\![\, b \,]\!]\, \langle \varepsilon, \varepsilon' \rangle \wedge \langle \varepsilon, \varepsilon' \rangle \in \bigcap_{i \in [l,u]} \tilde{\mathbb{F}}[\![\, f[v/i] \,]\!] \,\}$$

$$\tilde{\mathbb{F}}[\![\, \exists v \in [a,b] : f \,]\!] \;\overset{\text{def}}{=}\; \{\, \langle \varepsilon, \varepsilon' \rangle \mid$$
$$\qquad l \in \tilde{\mathbb{E}}[\![\, a \,]\!]\, \langle \varepsilon, \varepsilon' \rangle \wedge u \in \tilde{\mathbb{E}}[\![\, b \,]\!]\, \langle \varepsilon, \varepsilon' \rangle \wedge \langle \varepsilon, \varepsilon' \rangle \in \bigcup_{i \in [l,u]} \tilde{\mathbb{F}}[\![\, f[v/i] \,]\!] \,\}$$

Fig. 6. Concrete semantics of relational formulas.

updated to take into account the effect of the statement. Thus, starting from the identity relation, by composing these statements, we can construct a relation mapping each input environment to a corresponding environment with resources allocated or freed, and variables modified. The statement $\texttt{alloc} : \tau * v = \texttt{new } R$ allocates a new instance of resource class R and assigns its address to variable v. The function $\texttt{scalars} \in type \to \mathcal{P}(\mathbb{N} \times stype)$ returns the set of scalar types and their offsets within a given type. We have no information on the block size (except that it is a non-null multiple of the size of τ) nor the block contents; both information can be provided later using an $\texttt{ensures}$ statement. The statement $\texttt{assigns} : e[a,b]$ modifies the memory block pointed by e and fills the elements located between indices a and b with unspecified values. Finally, $\texttt{free} : e$ frees the resource pointed by e by updating its liveness flag. These statements only use non-primed variables, hence, all expressions are evaluated in the input part of the relation, which is left intact by these transformers.

Condition Statements. A condition statement adds a constraint to the initial input-output relation built by the side-effect statements. We define their semantics as a function $\mathbb{S}_{\text{cond}}[\![\,.\,]\!] \in cond \to \mathcal{P}(\mathcal{E} \times \mathcal{E})$. Another role of these statements is to detect specification violation (unsatisfied $\texttt{requires}$). Thus, we enrich the set of output environments with an error state Ω, so that $\langle \varepsilon, \Omega \rangle$ denotes an input environment ε that does not satisfy a pre-condition. The semantics is given in Fig. 7. Both $\texttt{assumes}$ and $\texttt{requires}$ statements use the simple filter $\mathbb{F}[\![\,.\,]\!]$ as they operate on input environments. In contrast, $\texttt{ensures}$ statements express relations between the input and the output and use therefore the relational filter $\tilde{\mathbb{F}}[\![\,.\,]\!]$. Combining two conditions is a little more subtle than intersecting their relations, due to the error state. We define a combination operator $\mathring{,}$ that preserves errors detected by conditions. Due to errors, conditions are not commutative. Indeed $\texttt{assumes} : x > 0; \texttt{requires} : x \neq 0;$ is not equivalent to $\texttt{requires} : x \neq 0; \texttt{assumes} : x > 0$, as the later will report errors when $x \neq 0$.

$\mathbb{S}_{\text{effect}}[\![\,.\,]\!] \in \text{effect} \to \mathcal{P}(\mathcal{E} \times \mathcal{E}) \to \mathcal{P}(\mathcal{E} \times \mathcal{E})$

$\mathbb{S}_{\text{effect}}[\![\,\text{alloc}: \tau* \, x = \text{new } R;\,]\!] X \stackrel{\text{def}}{=}$
$\quad \{\, \langle \varepsilon, (\rho'[x \mapsto (@,0)], c_{1,1} \mapsto v_{1,1}, \ldots, c_{n,m} \mapsto v_{n,m}], \sigma'[@ \mapsto (R, n.\text{sizeof}(\tau), \text{true})]) \rangle \mid$
$\quad\quad \langle \varepsilon, (\rho', \sigma') \rangle \in X \land @ \notin dom(\sigma') \land n \in \mathbb{N}^* \land \{\,(o_1, \tau_1), \ldots, (o_m, \tau_m)\,\} = \text{scalars}(\tau)$
$\quad\quad \land\, \forall i \in [1,n], j \in [1,m] : c_{i,j} = \{@, o_j + (i-1)\text{sizeof}(\tau), \tau_j \int \land v_{i,j} \in \mathbb{V}_{\tau_{i,j}}\,\}$

$\mathbb{S}_{\text{effect}}[\![\,\text{assigns}: e[a,b];\,]\!] X \stackrel{\text{def}}{=}$
$\quad \{\, \langle \varepsilon, (\rho'[c_1 \mapsto v_1, \ldots, c_{u-l+1} \mapsto v_{u-l+1}], \sigma') \rangle \mid \langle \varepsilon, (\rho', \sigma') \rangle \in X$
$\quad\quad \land\, (b,o) \in \mathbb{E}[\![\,e\,]\!](\rho, \sigma) \land l \in \mathbb{E}[\![\,a\,]\!](\rho, \sigma) \land u \in \mathbb{E}[\![\,b\,]\!](\rho, \sigma) \land \tau = \text{typeof}(*e)$
$\quad\quad \land\, \forall k \in [1, l-u+1] : c_k = \{b, o + (k-1)\text{sizeof}(\tau), \tau \int \land v_k \in \mathbb{V}_\tau\,\}$

$\mathbb{S}_{\text{effect}}[\![\,\text{free}: e;\,]\!] X \stackrel{\text{def}}{=}$
$\quad \{\, \langle \varepsilon, (\rho', \sigma'[@ \mapsto (R, n, \text{false})]) \rangle \mid \langle \varepsilon, (\rho', \sigma') \rangle \in X \land (@, -) \in \mathbb{E}[\![\,e\,]\!]\varepsilon\,\}$

$\mathbb{S}_{\text{effect}}[\![\,s_1; s_2;\,]\!] X \stackrel{\text{def}}{=} \mathbb{S}_{\text{effect}}[\![\,s_2\,]\!] \circ \mathbb{S}_{\text{effect}}[\![\,s_1\,]\!] X$

$\mathbb{S}_{\text{cond}}[\![\,.\,]\!] \in \text{cond} \to \mathcal{P}(\mathcal{E} \times \mathcal{E})$

$\mathbb{S}_{\text{cond}}[\![\,\text{assumes}: f;\,]\!] \stackrel{\text{def}}{=} \{\, \langle \varepsilon, \varepsilon' \rangle \mid \varepsilon \in \mathbb{F}[\![\,f\,]\!]\,\}$

$\mathbb{S}_{\text{cond}}[\![\,\text{requires}: f;\,]\!] \stackrel{\text{def}}{=} \{\, \langle \varepsilon, \varepsilon' \rangle \mid \varepsilon \in \mathbb{F}[\![\,f\,]\!]\,\} \cup \{\, \langle \varepsilon, \Omega \rangle \mid \varepsilon \in \mathbb{F}[\![\,\neg f\,]\!]\,\}$

$\mathbb{S}_{\text{cond}}[\![\,\text{ensures}: f;\,]\!] \stackrel{\text{def}}{=} \tilde{\mathbb{F}}[\![\,f\,]\!]$

$\mathbb{S}_{\text{cond}}[\![\,s_1; s_2;\,]\!] \stackrel{\text{def}}{=} \mathbb{S}_{\text{cond}}[\![\,s_1\,]\!] \, \S \, \mathbb{S}_{\text{cond}}[\![\,s_1\,]\!]$

$R_1 \, \S \, R_2 \stackrel{\text{def}}{=} R_1 \cap R_2 \cup \{\, \langle \varepsilon, \Omega \rangle \mid \langle \varepsilon, \Omega \rangle \in R_1\,\} \cup \{\, \langle \varepsilon, \Omega \rangle \mid \langle \varepsilon, \Omega \rangle \in R_2 \land \langle \varepsilon, - \rangle \in R_1\,\}$

Fig. 7. Concrete semantics of statements.

$\mathbb{S}[\![\,.\,]\!] \in \text{stub} \to \mathcal{P}(\mathcal{E}) \to \mathcal{P}(\mathcal{E}) \times \mathcal{P}(\mathcal{E})$

$\mathbb{S}[\![\,\text{body}\,]\!] I \stackrel{\text{def}}{=} \text{let } R_0 = \{\, \langle \varepsilon, \varepsilon \rangle \mid \varepsilon \in I\,\} \text{ in}$
$\quad\quad\quad \text{let } R_1 = \mathbb{S}_{\text{effect}}[\![\,\text{effects}(\text{body})\,]\!] R_0 \text{ in}$
$\quad\quad\quad \text{let } R_2 = R_1 \, \S \, \mathbb{S}_{\text{cond}}[\![\,\text{conditions}(\text{body})\,]\!] \text{ in}$
$\quad\quad\quad \text{let } O = \{\, \varepsilon' \mid \langle -, \varepsilon' \rangle \in R_2 \land \varepsilon' \neq \Omega\,\} \text{ in}$
$\quad\quad\quad \text{let } X = \{\, \varepsilon \mid \langle \varepsilon, \Omega \rangle \in R_2\,\} \text{ in}$
$\quad\quad\quad (O, X)$

Fig. 8. Concrete semantics of the stub.

Iterator. Figure 8 shows the semantic function $\mathbb{S}[\![\,.\,]\!] \in \text{stub} \to \mathcal{P}(\mathcal{E}) \to \mathcal{P}(\mathcal{E}) \times \mathcal{P}(\mathcal{E})$ of a complete stub. It first executes its side-effect statements only $\text{effects}(\text{body})$, then condition statements $\text{conditions}(\text{body})$, and finally applies the resulting relation R_2 to the initial states at function entry I. It returns two sets of environments: the environments O at function exit when pre-conditions are met, and the environments X at function entry that result in a violation of a pre-condition.

3   Generic Abstract Semantics

We show how an existing abstract domain for C can be extended to abstract the concrete semantics of our stubs in a generic way. The next section will focus on specific abstractions exploiting more finely the structure of stub statements.

3.1   Abstract Domain

C Domain. We assume we are given an abstract domain $\mathcal{M}^\sharp$ of memories $\mathcal{P}(\mathcal{M})$ with the standard operators: least element $\perp_\mathcal{M}$, join $\sqcup_\mathcal{M}$, and widening $\triangledown_\mathcal{M}$, as well as a sound abstraction $\mathbb{S}_\mathrm{M}^\sharp [\![.]\!] \in stmt_\mathcal{M} \to \mathcal{M}^\sharp \to \mathcal{M}^\sharp$ for classic memory statement $stmt_\mathcal{M}$, including: $x \leftarrow y$, to model assignments of C expressions; $forget(b, x, y)$, to assign random values to a byte slice $[x, y]$ of a memory block b; $add(b)$, to add a memory block with random values; $remove(b)$ to remove a memory block; and the array sumarization operators $expand(b_1, b_2)$ and $fold(b_1, b_2)$ from [14]. $expand(b_1, b_2)$ creates a *weak copy* b_2 of block b_1, *i.e.* both b_1 and b_2 have the same constraints without being equal. For example, executing $expand(x, z)$ when $x \geq y \wedge x \in [1, 10]$ yields $x \geq y \wedge x \in [1, 10] \wedge z \geq y \wedge z \in [1, 10]$. The converse operation, $fold(b_1, b_2)$, creates a summary in b_1 by keeping only the constraints also implied by b_2, and then removes b_2. We exploit them to abstract unbounded memory allocation and perform weak updates.

Heap Abstraction. We also assume that we are given an abstraction of heap addresses $\mathcal{P}(\mathcal{A})$ into a finite set $\mathcal{A}^\sharp$ of abstract addresses, with least element $\perp_\mathcal{A}$ and join $\sqcup_\mathcal{A}$. Classic examples include call-site abstraction, and the recency abstraction [2] we use in our implementation. An abstract address may represent a single concrete address or a (possibly unbounded) collection of addresses, which is indicated by a cardinality operator $\|.\|_\mathcal{A} \in \mathcal{A}^\sharp \to \{ single, many \}$. Finally, we assume the domain provides an allocation function $\mathbb{A}^\sharp [\![.]\!] \in \mathcal{P}(\mathcal{A}^\sharp) \times \mathcal{M}^\sharp \to \mathcal{A}^\sharp \times \mathcal{M}^\sharp$. As an abstract allocation may cause memory blocks to be expanded or folded, and the pointers to point to different abstract addresses, the function also returns an updated memory environment.

Environments. For each abstract block in $\mathcal{A}^\sharp$, we maintain its byte size in a numeric variable $\mathsf{size}^\sharp \in \mathcal{A}^\sharp \to \mathcal{B}$ in the memory environment, and track its possible resource classes in $\mathcal{P}(\mathcal{C})$, and possible liveness status in the boolean lattice $\mathcal{P}(\{true, false\})$. The abstraction $\mathcal{E}^\sharp$ of environment sets $\mathcal{P}(\mathcal{E})$ is thus:

$$\mathcal{E}^\sharp \stackrel{\mathrm{def}}{=} \mathcal{M}^\sharp \times \mathcal{A}^\sharp \to (\mathcal{P}(\mathcal{C}) \times \mathcal{P}(\{true, false\})) \tag{1}$$

The $\perp_\mathcal{E}$, $\sqcup_\mathcal{E}$, and $\triangledown_\mathcal{E}$ operators are derived naturally from those in $\mathcal{M}^\sharp$ and $\mathcal{A}^\sharp$, and we lift C statements to $\mathbb{S}_\mathrm{C}^\sharp [\![s]\!](\rho^\sharp, \sigma^\sharp) \stackrel{\mathrm{def}}{=} (\mathbb{S}_\mathrm{M}^\sharp [\![s]\!] \rho^\sharp, \sigma^\sharp)$.

3.2   Evaluations

Our abstraction leverages the modular architecture and the communication mechanisms introduced in the Mopsa framework [16]. We will employ notably *symbolic and disjunctive evaluations*, which we recall briefly.

Expressions. In the concrete semantics, expressions are evaluated into values. Abstracting expression evaluation as functions returning abstract values, such as intervals, would limit the analysis to non-relational properties. Instead, domains in Mopsa can evaluate expressions into other expressions: based on the current abstract state, expression parts are simplified into more abstract ones that other domains can process. A common example is relying on abstract variables. For instance, the memory domain will replace a $\texttt{size}(e)$ expression into the variable $\texttt{size}^{\sharp}(b)$ after determining that e points to block b, producing a purely numeric expression. Communicating expressions ensures a low coupling between domains, while preserving relational information (e.g., $\texttt{size}(e) < i$reduces to comparing two numeric variables, $\texttt{size}^{\sharp}(b)$ and i). A domain can also perform a case analysis and transform one expression into a disjunction of several expressions, associated to a partition of the abstract state (e.g., if e can point to several blocks). Formally, a domain $\mathcal{D}^{\sharp}$ implements expression evaluation as a function: $\phi \in expr \rightarrow \mathcal{D}^{\sharp} \rightarrow \mathcal{P}(expr \times \mathcal{D}^{\sharp})$. To express concisely that the rest of the abstract computation should be performed in parallel on each expression and then joined, we define here (and use in our implementation) a monadic bind operator:

$$\text{let}^{\sharp}_{\sqcup} \ (f, Y^{\sharp}) \in \phi[e]X^{\sharp} \ \text{in} \ body \ \overset{\text{def}}{=} \\ \bigsqcup_{(g,Z^{\sharp}) \in \phi[e]X^{\sharp}} body[f/g, Y^{\sharp}/Z^{\sharp}] \tag{2}$$

We illustrate formally abstract expression evaluation $\mathbb{E}^{\sharp}[\![\,.\,]\!]$ on the $\texttt{size}(e)$ expression. First, the pointer domain handles the pointer expression e: $\mathbb{E}^{\sharp}[\![\,e\,]\!]\varepsilon^{\sharp}$ returns a set of triples (b, o, ε') where b is an abstract block, o a numeric offset expression, and ε' the part of ε where e points into block b. Thanks to this disjunction, the abstract semantics of $\texttt{size}(e)$ follows closely the concrete one:

$$\mathbb{E}^{\sharp}[\![\,\texttt{size}(e)\,]\!]\varepsilon^{\sharp} \ \overset{\text{def}}{=} \ \text{let}^{\sharp}_{\sqcup} \ ((b, -), \varepsilon^{\sharp}_1) \in \mathbb{E}^{\sharp}[\![\,e\,]\!] \ \varepsilon^{\sharp} \ \text{in} \\ \text{if} \ b \in \mathcal{V} \ \text{then} \ \{ \ (\texttt{sizeof}(b), \varepsilon^{\sharp}_1) \ \} \\ \text{else} \ \{ \ (\texttt{size}^{\sharp}(b), \varepsilon^{\sharp}_1) \ \} \tag{3}$$

Formulas. Evaluation of formulas is defined by the function $\mathbb{F}^{\sharp}[\![\,.\,]\!] \in formula \rightarrow \mathcal{E}^{\sharp} \rightarrow \mathcal{E}^{\sharp}$, shown in Fig. 9. We focus on the most interesting cases which are the quantified formulas. Existential quantification reduces to assigning to v the interval $[a, b]$ and keeping only environments that satisfy f. Universal quantification are handled very similarly to a loop $\texttt{for(v=a; v<=b; v++) assume(f)}$. We perform an iteration with widening for v from a to b and we over-approximate the sequence of states statisfying f. The overall formula is satisfied for states reaching the end of the sequence. These generic transfer functions can be imprecise in practice. We will show later that specific domains can implement natively more precise transfer functions for selected quantified formulas.

Relations. The concrete semantics requires evaluating expressions and formulas not only on states, by also on relations. To represent relations in the abstract, we simply introduce a family of primed variables: $\texttt{primed}^{\sharp} \in \mathcal{B} \rightarrow \mathcal{B}$ returns the primed version of a block (i.e., the block in the post-state). This classic technique allows lifting any state domain to a relation domain. Combined with relational domains, we can express complex relationships between values in the pre- and the post-state, if needed. The relation abstractions $\tilde{\mathbb{E}}^{\sharp}[\![\ ]\!]$ and $\tilde{\mathbb{F}}^{\sharp}[\![\,.\,]\!]$ of $\mathbb{E}^{\sharp}[\![\,.\,]\!]$ and $\mathbb{F}^{\sharp}[\![\,.\,]\!]$ can be easily expressed in terms of the state abstractions $\mathbb{E}^{\sharp}[\![\,.\,]\!]$ and $\mathbb{F}^{\sharp}[\![\,.\,]\!]$ we already defined. As an example, the evaluation of a primed dereference $(*e)'$

$F^\sharp[\![.]\!] \in form \to \mathcal{E}^\sharp \to \mathcal{E}^\sharp$

$F^\sharp[\![\,\texttt{alive}(e)\,]\!](\rho^\sharp, \sigma^\sharp) \stackrel{\text{def}}{=}$
$\quad \text{let}^\sharp_{\sqcup_\mathcal{E}} \; ((b, -), (\rho^\sharp, \sigma^\sharp)) \in \mathbb{E}^\sharp[\![\,e\,]\!] \,(\rho^\sharp, \sigma^\sharp) \text{ in}$
$\quad \text{if } b \notin \mathcal{A}^\sharp \text{ then } \bot \text{ else}$
$\quad \text{let } (C, f) = \sigma^\sharp(b) \text{ in}$
$\quad \text{if } f = \{\,false\,\} \text{ then } \bot \text{ else}$
$\quad \text{let } f' = \text{if } \|b\|_\mathcal{A} = single \text{ then } \{\,true\,\} \text{ else } f \text{ in}$
$\quad (\rho^\sharp, \sigma^\sharp[b \mapsto (C, f')])$

$F^\sharp[\![\,e \in R\,]\!](\rho^\sharp, \sigma^\sharp) \stackrel{\text{def}}{=}$
$\quad \text{let}^\sharp_{\sqcup_\mathcal{E}} \; ((b, -), (\rho^\sharp, \sigma^\sharp)) \in \mathbb{E}^\sharp[\![\,e\,]\!] \,(\rho^\sharp, \sigma^\sharp) \text{ in}$
$\quad \text{if } b \notin \mathcal{A}^\sharp \text{ then } \bot \text{ else}$
$\quad \text{let } (C, f) = \sigma^\sharp(b) \text{ in}$
$\quad \text{if } R \notin C \text{ then } \bot \text{ else}$
$\quad \text{let } C' = \text{if } \|b\|_\mathcal{A}\| = single \text{ then } \{R\} \text{ else } C \text{ in}$
$\quad (\rho^\sharp, \sigma^\sharp[b \mapsto (C', f)])$

$F^\sharp[\![\,\exists v \in [a, b] : f\,]\!]\varepsilon^\sharp \stackrel{\text{def}}{=} S^\sharp_C[\![\,remove(v)\,]\!] \circ F^\sharp[\![\,f\,]\!] \circ S^\sharp_C[\![\,v \leftarrow [a, b]\,]\!] \circ S^\sharp_C[\![\,add(v)\,]\!]\,\varepsilon^\sharp$

$F^\sharp[\![\,\forall v \in [a, b] : f\,]\!]\varepsilon^\sharp \stackrel{\text{def}}{=}$
$\quad \text{let } \varepsilon^\sharp_0 = F^\sharp[\![\,v \leq b\,]\!] \circ S^\sharp_C[\![\,v \leftarrow a\,]\!] \circ S^\sharp_C[\![\,add(v)\,]\!]\,\varepsilon^\sharp \text{ in}$
$\quad \text{let } \varepsilon^\sharp_1 = \text{lfp}\, \lambda X.\, X \triangledown_\mathcal{E} (\varepsilon^\sharp_0 \sqcup_\mathcal{E} S^\sharp_C[\![\,v \leftarrow v + 1\,]\!] \circ F^\sharp[\![\,f\,]\!] \circ F^\sharp[\![\,v \leq b\,]\!]X) \text{ in}$
$\quad S^\sharp_C[\![\,remove(v)\,]\!] \circ F^\sharp[\![\,v > b\,]\!]\,\varepsilon^\sharp_1$

Fig. 9. Abstract semantics of formulas.

simply evaluates e into a set of memory blocks b and offset expressions o, and outputs a dereference of the primed block $\text{primed}^\sharp(b)$ at the (non-primed) offset expression o, which can be handled by the (relation-unaware) memory domain:

$$\tilde{\mathbb{E}}^\sharp[\![\,(*e)'\,]\!]\varepsilon^\sharp \stackrel{\text{def}}{=} \text{let}^\sharp_\sqcup \; ((b, o), \varepsilon^\sharp_1) \in \tilde{\mathbb{E}}^\sharp[\![\,e\,]\!]\,\varepsilon^\sharp \text{ in} \tag{4}$$
$$\{\,(*(\texttt{typeof}(e))((\texttt{char*})\&\text{primed}^\sharp(b) + o), \varepsilon^\sharp_1)\,\}$$

3.3 Transfer Functions

Side-effect Statements. The effect of a statement is approximated by $S^\sharp_{\text{effect}}[\![\,.\,]\!] \in effect \to \mathcal{E}^\sharp \to \mathcal{E}^\sharp$ defined in Fig. 10. Resource allocation $\texttt{alloc} : v = \texttt{new } R$ first asks the underlying heap abstraction for a new abstract address with $\mathbb{A}^\sharp[\![\,.\,]\!]$, which is bound to a new variable v; a new size variable $\text{size}^\sharp$ is created and the resource map is updated with the class and liveness information. The block is also initialized with random values using *forget*. Assignments $\texttt{assigns} : e[x, y]$ reduces to *forget* on the primed version of the block b e points to (recall that the output value is specified by a later $\texttt{ensures}$). Finally, $\texttt{free} : e$ resets the liveness flag of the primed block.

Condition Statements. The abstract semantics of condition statements is given by $S^\sharp_{\text{cond}}[\![\,.\,]\!] \in cond \to \mathcal{E}^\sharp \to \mathcal{E}^\sharp \times \mathcal{E}^\sharp$, defined in Fig. 10. The function returns a pair of abstract environments: the first one over-approximates the output environments satisfying the condition, while the second one over-approximates the input environments violating mandatory conditions specified with $\texttt{requires}$ statements.

$\mathbb{S}_{effect}^\sharp \llbracket \cdot \rrbracket \in \textit{effect} \to \mathcal{E}^\sharp \to \mathcal{E}^\sharp$

$\mathbb{S}_{effect}^\sharp \llbracket \, \textbf{alloc} : v = \textbf{new } R \, \rrbracket (\rho^\sharp, \sigma^\sharp) \overset{\text{def}}{=}$
  let $(@, \rho_1^\sharp) = \mathbb{A}^\sharp \llbracket \, dom(\sigma^\sharp) \, \rrbracket \, \rho^\sharp$ in
  let $\sigma_2^\sharp = \sigma_1^\sharp [@ \mapsto (\{\, R \,\}, \{\, \textit{true} \,\})]$ in
  let $\varepsilon_2^\sharp = \mathbb{S}_C^\sharp \llbracket v \leftarrow @ \rrbracket \circ \mathbb{S}_C^\sharp \llbracket \, add(v) \, \rrbracket (\rho_1^\sharp, \sigma_2^\sharp)$ in
  let $\varepsilon_3^\sharp = \mathbb{S}_C^\sharp \llbracket \, size^\sharp(@) \geq 0 \, \rrbracket \circ \mathbb{S}_C^\sharp \llbracket \, add(size^\sharp(@)) \, \rrbracket \, \varepsilon_2^\sharp$ in
  $\mathbb{S}_C^\sharp \llbracket \, forget(@, 0, size^\sharp(@) - 1) \, \rrbracket \, \varepsilon_3^\sharp$

$\mathbb{S}_{effect}^\sharp \llbracket \, \textbf{assigns} : e[x, y] \, \rrbracket \varepsilon^\sharp \overset{\text{def}}{=}$
  $let_{\sqcup_\varepsilon}^\sharp \ (b, o), \varepsilon_1^\sharp \in \mathbb{E}^\sharp \llbracket e \rrbracket \, \varepsilon^\sharp$ in
  let $n = \textit{sizeof}(*e)$ in
  $\mathbb{S}_C^\sharp \llbracket \, forget(primed^\sharp(b), o + x \times n), o + y \times n) \, \rrbracket \, \varepsilon_1^\sharp$

$\mathbb{S}_{effect}^\sharp \llbracket \, \textbf{free} : e \, \rrbracket \varepsilon^\sharp \overset{\text{def}}{=}$
  $let_{\sqcup_\varepsilon}^\sharp \ (b, -), (\rho_1^\sharp, \sigma_1^\sharp) \in \mathbb{E}^\sharp \llbracket e \rrbracket \, \varepsilon^\sharp$ in
  if $b \notin \mathcal{A}^\sharp$ then $\perp_\varepsilon$ else
  let $C, f = \sigma_1^\sharp(b)$ in
  if $\|b\|_\mathcal{A} = single$ then $(\rho_1^\sharp, \sigma_1^\sharp[primed^\sharp(b) \mapsto (C, \{\, \textit{false} \,\})])$
  else $(\rho_1^\sharp, \sigma_1^\sharp[primed^\sharp(b) \mapsto (C, f \cup \{\, \textit{false} \,\})])$

$\mathbb{S}_{cond}^\sharp \llbracket \cdot \rrbracket \in \textit{cond} \to \mathcal{E}^\sharp \to \mathcal{E}^\sharp \times \mathcal{E}^\sharp$

$\mathbb{S}_{cond}^\sharp \llbracket \, \textbf{assumes} : f; \, \rrbracket \varepsilon^\sharp \overset{\text{def}}{=}$
  $(\mathbb{F}^\sharp \llbracket f \rrbracket \varepsilon^\sharp, \perp_\varepsilon)$

$\mathbb{S}_{cond}^\sharp \llbracket \, \textbf{requires} : f; \, \rrbracket \varepsilon^\sharp \overset{\text{def}}{=}$
  $(\mathbb{F}^\sharp \llbracket f \rrbracket \varepsilon^\sharp, \mathbb{F}^\sharp \llbracket \neg f \rrbracket \varepsilon^\sharp)$

$\mathbb{S}_{cond}^\sharp \llbracket \, \textbf{ensures} : f; \, \rrbracket \varepsilon^\sharp \overset{\text{def}}{=}$
  $(\mathbb{F}^\sharp \llbracket f \rrbracket \varepsilon^\sharp, \perp_\varepsilon)$

$\mathbb{S}_{cond}^\sharp \llbracket \, s_1; s_2; \, \rrbracket \varepsilon^\sharp \overset{\text{def}}{=}$
  let $(\varepsilon_1^\sharp, \omega_1^\sharp) = \mathbb{S}_{cond}^\sharp \llbracket s_1 \rrbracket \, \varepsilon^\sharp$ in
  let $(\varepsilon_2^\sharp, \omega_2^\sharp) = \mathbb{S}_{cond}^\sharp \llbracket s_2 \rrbracket \, \varepsilon_1^\sharp$ in
  $(\varepsilon_2^\sharp, \omega_1^\sharp \sqcup_\varepsilon \omega_2^\sharp)$

Fig. 10. Abstract semantics of statements.

Iterator. The abstract semantic of a whole stub is defined in Fig. 11. First, the *expand* function is used to construct an identity relation over the input abstract state $\varepsilon_0^\sharp$. To improve efficiency, this is limited to the blocks that are effectively modified by the stub; this set is over-approximated using the `assigned` function, which resolves the pointer expressions occurring in `assigns` statement. Then, side-effect statements are evaluated. Note that, for an `assigns` : $a[x, y]$ statement, while whole blocks pointed by a are duplicated in the output state, only the parts in the $[x, y]$ range are assigned random values. Condition statements are then executed, collecting contract violation and refining the output state. Finally, we remove the unprimed version of primed (i.e., modified) blocks and the primed block into its unprimed version, thus reverting to a state abstraction that models the output state. In case of a primed block b modeling several concrete blocks (i.e., $\|b\|_\mathcal{A} = many$), the primed block is folded into the unprimed version, so as to preserve the values before the call, resulting in a weak update.

4 Specific Abstract Semantics: The Case of C Strings

We now show how we can design a formula-aware abstract domain, with an application to C string analysis. The domain handles precisely selective quantified formula, while reverting in the other cases (as all other domains) to the generic operators.

String Length Domain. Strings in C are arrays of `char` elements containing a delimiting null byte '\0' indicating the end of the string. Many functions in the standard C library take strings as arguments and assume they contain a null byte delimiter. We want to express and check this assumption in the function stubs.

$\mathbb{S}^\sharp[\![.]\!] \in stub \rightarrow \mathcal{E}^\sharp \rightarrow \mathcal{E}^\sharp \times \mathcal{E}^\sharp$

$\mathbb{S}^\sharp[\![body]\!] \varepsilon_0^\sharp \overset{\text{def}}{=}$

    let $(a_1, \ldots, a_n) = \mathbf{assigned}(body)$ in

    $\text{let}_{\sqcup_\varepsilon}^\sharp \, ((b_1, -), \varepsilon_1^\sharp) \in \mathbb{E}^\sharp[\![a_1]\!] \, \varepsilon_0^\sharp$ in

    $\ldots$

    $\text{let}_{\sqcup_\varepsilon}^\sharp \, ((b_n, -), \varepsilon_n^\sharp) \in \mathbb{E}^\sharp[\![a_n]\!] \, \varepsilon_{n-1}^\sharp$ in

    let $\tilde{\varepsilon}_0^\sharp = \mathbb{S}_C^\sharp[\![prime(b_n)]\!] \circ \cdots \circ \mathbb{S}_C^\sharp[\![prime(b_1)]\!] \varepsilon_n^\sharp$ in

    let $\tilde{\varepsilon}_1^\sharp = \mathbb{S}_{\text{effect}}^\sharp[\![\mathbf{effects}(body)]\!] \, \tilde{\varepsilon}_0^\sharp$ in

    let $\tilde{\varepsilon}_2^\sharp, \omega^\sharp = \mathbb{S}_{\text{cond}}^\sharp[\![\mathbf{conditions}(body)]\!] \, \tilde{\varepsilon}_1^\sharp$ in

    let $\varepsilon^\sharp = \mathbb{S}_C^\sharp[\![unprime(b_n)]\!] \circ \cdots \circ \mathbb{S}_C^\sharp[\![unprime(b_1)]\!] \tilde{\varepsilon}_2^\sharp$ in

    $(\varepsilon^\sharp, \omega^\sharp)$

where:

    $prime(b) \overset{\text{def}}{=} expand(b, \mathsf{primed}^\sharp(b))$

    $unprime(b) \overset{\text{def}}{=}$

        if $b \in \mathcal{A}^\sharp \wedge \|b\|_\mathcal{A} = many$ then $fold(\mathsf{primed}^\sharp(b), b)$ else $rename(\mathsf{primed}^\sharp(b), b)$

Fig. 11. Abstract semantics of the stub.

We exploit a classic abstraction already present in Mopsa: the STRINGLENGTH domain [17] that maintains a numeric abstract variable $\mathsf{length}^\sharp \in \mathcal{B} \rightarrow \mathcal{B}$ for arrays to store the offset of the first null byte. It thus infers, for each array a, an invariant of the form:

$$\forall i \in [0, \mathsf{length}^\sharp(a) - 1] : a[i] \neq 0 \wedge a[\mathsf{length}^\sharp(a)] = 0 \tag{5}$$

Example 3. Consider the following example, where n ranges in $[0, 99]$:

```
1  for (int i = 0; i < n; i++) a[i] = 'x';
2  a[n] = '\0';
```

An analysis with the INTERVALS domain will infer that $\mathsf{length}^\sharp(a) \in [0, 99]$. Adding the POLYHEDRA domain, we will moreover infer that $\mathsf{length}^\sharp(a) = n$.

Stub Transfer Functions. Within a stub, a pre-condition stating the validity of a string pointed to by an argument named s is naturally expressed as:

$$\mathtt{requires} : \exists i \in [0, \mathtt{size}(s) - \mathtt{offset}(s) - 1] : s[i] \mathtt{==} 0; \tag{6}$$

Proving this requirement requires checking the emptiness of its negation, which involves a universal quantifier. Using the generic abstraction from last section, it is equivalent to proving emptiness after the loop `for (i = 0; i < size(s)-offset(s); i++) s[i] != 0`. This, in turn, requires an iteration with widening and, unless s has constant length, a relational domain with sufficient precision, which is costly.

To solve these problems, we propose a direct interpretation of both formulas in the string domain, i.e., we add transfer functions for $\mathbb{F}^\sharp[\![\exists i \in [lo, hi] : s[i] \mathtt{==} 0]\!]$ and $\mathbb{F}^\sharp[\![\forall i \in [lo, hi] : s[i] \mathtt{!=} 0]\!]$,[2] as shown in Table. 1. They perform a case analysis: the abstract state $\varepsilon^\sharp$ is split into two cases according to a condition, and

---

[2] We actually support the comparison of $s[i]$ with arbitrary expressions. We limit the description to the case of comparisons with 0 for the sake of clarity.

Table 1. Transfer functions of formulas in the string length domain.

Formula	Case	Condition	State transformer
$\exists i \in [lo, hi] : s[i] == 0$	#1	$\mathsf{length}^\sharp(s) > hi$	$\lambda \epsilon^\sharp . \perp$
	#2	$\mathsf{length}^\sharp(s) \leq hi$	$\lambda \epsilon^\sharp . \epsilon^\sharp$
$\forall i \in [lo, hi] : s[i] \; != 0$	#1	$\mathsf{length}^\sharp(s) \notin [lo, hi]$	$\lambda \epsilon^\sharp . \epsilon^\sharp$
	#2	$\mathsf{length}^\sharp(s) \in [lo, hi]$	$\lambda \epsilon^\sharp . \perp$

we keep all environments in one case ($\lambda \epsilon^\sharp . \epsilon$) and none in the other ($\lambda \epsilon^\sharp . \perp$). For instance, assuming that (5) holds, then Case #1 of $\mathbb{F}^\sharp [\![\exists i \in [lo, hi] : s[i] == 0]\!]$ states that the quantification range $[lo, hi]$ covers only elements before the null byte, so that the formula does not hold. Case #2 states that there is a value in $[lo, hi]$ greater than or equal to the string length, in which case $s[i]$ may be null and the formula may be valid. Similarly, Case #1 of $\mathbb{F}^\sharp [\![\forall i \in [lo, hi] : s[i] \; != 0]\!]$ arises when the null byte is outside the quantification range, so that the formula may be valid. In Case #2, the null byte is in the range, and the formula is definitely invalid. We stress on the fact that all the conditions are interpreted symbolically in the numeric domain; hence, lo and hi are not limited to constants, but can be arbitrary expressions.

Example 4. Let us illustrate how the predicate (6) can be verified on the following abstract environment:

$$\epsilon^\sharp = \begin{pmatrix} \langle s, 0, \mathtt{ptr} \rangle \mapsto \{ (@, 0) \} \\ \mathsf{size}^\sharp(@) \geq 1 \\ \mathsf{length}^\sharp(@) \in [0, \mathsf{size}^\sharp(@) - 1] \end{pmatrix}, @ \mapsto (\{\, \mathtt{malloc} \,\}, true) \quad (7)$$

which represents the case of a variable s pointing to a resource instance @ allocated by $\mathtt{malloc}$ with at least one byte. The string domain indicates that the position of the null byte is between 0 and $\mathsf{size}^\sharp(@) - 1$. When checking the formula $\exists i \in [0, \mathtt{size}(s) - \mathtt{offset}(s) - 1] : s[i] == 0$, the condition for Case #1 never holds since:

$$(\mathtt{size}(s) - \mathtt{offset}(s) - 1 = \mathsf{size}^\sharp(@) - 1) \wedge (\mathsf{length}^\sharp(@) \leq \mathsf{size}^\sharp(@) - 1)$$

When checking its negation, $\forall i \in [0, \mathtt{size}(s) - \mathtt{offset}(s) - 1] : s[i] \; != 0$, Case #1 is also unsatisfiable, for the same reason. As the transformer for Case #2 returns $\perp$, the overall result is $\perp$, proving that Requirement (6) holds: the stub does not raise any alarm.

Genericity of Formulas. An important motivation for using a logic language is to exploit its expressiveness within abstract domains to analyze several stubs with the same transfer functions. We show that this is indeed the case: the transfer function that was used to validate strings in the previous section can be used, without modification, to compute string lengths.

Example 5. Let us go back to the example of the `strlen` function defined as:

```
1  /*$
2   * requires: s != NULL ∧ offset(s) ∈ [0, size(s));
3   * requires: ∃i ∈ [0, size(s)-offset(s)): s[i] == 0;
4   * ensures : return ∈ [0, size(s)-offset(s));
5   * ensures : s[return] == 0;
6   * ensures : ∀i ∈ [0, return): s[i] != 0;
7   */
8  size_t strlen(const char s);
```

and consider again the environment (7). As shown before, the `requires` statements at line 3 validating the string do not raise any alarm. At line 5, the classic transfer functions of the STRINGLENGTH domain [17] infer that:

$$0 \leq \mathsf{length}^{\sharp}(@) \leq \mathtt{return}$$

since $s[\mathtt{return}] = 0$ and $\mathsf{length}^{\sharp}(@)$ is the position of the first null byte. Finally, at line 6, both cases of the second transfer function in Table 1 are valid. Since we keep a non-$\perp$ post-state only for Case #1, we obtain:

$$0 \leq \mathsf{length}^{\sharp}(@) \leq \mathtt{return} \wedge \mathsf{length}^{\sharp}(@) \notin [0, \mathtt{return} - 1]$$
$$\Leftrightarrow 0 \leq \mathsf{length}^{\sharp}(@) \leq \mathtt{return} \wedge \mathsf{length}^{\sharp}(@) > \mathtt{return} - 1$$
$$\Leftrightarrow 0 \leq \mathsf{length}^{\sharp}(@) = \mathtt{return}$$

hence the domain precisely infers that `strlen` returns the length of string @.

5 Experiments

We implemented our analysis in the Mopsa framework [16]. It consists of 29503 lines of OCaml code (excluding parsers). Among them, 16449 lines (56%) are common with analyses of other languages, such as Python. C domains consist of 11342 lines (38%) and the stub abstraction consists of 1712 lines (6%).

We wrote 14191 lines of stub, modeling 1108 functions from 50 headers from the Glibc implementation of the standard C library, version 8.28 [13]. All stubs thoroughly check their arguments (pointers, strings, integers, floats), soundly model their side effects, dynamic memory allocation, open files and descriptors. We refrained form implicit assumptions, such as non-aliasing arguments. At an average of 8 meaningful lines per stub, the language proved to be concise enough. Some examples can be found in Appendix A.

To assess the efficiency and the precision of our implementation, we target two families of programs. We run our analysis on part of NIST Juliet Tests Suite [5], a large collection of small programs with artificially injected errors. These tests are precious to reveal soundness bugs in analyzers, but do not reflect real-world code bases. Hence, we also target more realistic programs from the Coreutils package [12], which are widely used command-line utilities. These programs, while not very large, depend heavily on the C standard library. We run all our tests on an Intel Xeon 3.40 GHz processor running Linux.

Table 2. Analysis results on Juliet. ✔: precise analysis, ⚠: analysis with false alarms.

Code	Title	Tests	Lines	Time (h:m:s)	✔	⚠
CWE121	Stack-based Buffer Overflow	2508	234k	00:59:12	26%	74%
CWE122	Heap-based Buffer Overflow	1556	174k	00:37:12	28%	72%
CWE124	Buffer Underwrite	758	93k	00:18:28	86%	14%
CWE126	Buffer Over-read	600	75k	00:14:45	40%	60%
CWE127	Buffer Under-read	758	89k	00:18:26	87%	13%
CWE190	Integer Overflow	3420	440k	01:24:47	52%	48%
CWE191	Integer Underflow	2622	340k	01:02:27	55%	45%
CWE369	Divide By Zero	497	109k	00:13:17	55%	45%
CWE415	Double Free	190	17k	00:04:21	100%	0%
CWE416	Use After Free	118	14k	00:02:40	99%	1%
CWE469	Illegal Pointer Subtraction	18	1k	00:00:24	100%	0%
CWE476	NULL Pointer Dereference	216	21k	00:04:53	100%	0%

5.1 Juliet

The Juliet Tests Suite [5] is organized using the Common Weakness Enumeration taxonomy [1]. It consists of a large number of tests for each CWE. Each test contains *bad* and *good* functions. Bad functions contain one instance of the CWE, while good functions are safe.

We selected 12 categories from NIST Juliet 1.3 matching the safety violations detected by Mopsa. For each test, we have analyzed the good and the bad functions and measured the analysis time and the number of reported alarms. Three outcomes are possible. The analysis is *precise* if it reports (*i*) exactly one alarm in the bad function that corresponds to the tested CWE, and (*ii*) no alarm in the good function. The analysis is *unsound* if no alarm is reported in the bad function. Otherwise, the analysis is *imprecise*.

The obtained results are summarized in Table 2. From each category, we have excluded tests that contain unsupported features or that do not correspond to runtime errors. As expected, all analyses are sound: Mopsa detects the target CWE in every bad test. However, half of the tests were imprecise. Much of this imprecision comes from the gap between Mopsa's error reporting and the CWE taxonomy. For instance, an invalid string passed to a library function may be reported as a stub violation while Juliet expects a buffer overflow. By considering precise an analysis reporting no alarm in the good function and exactly one alarm in the bad function (without considering its nature), the overall precision increases to 71% (e.g. 89% of CWE121 tests become precise). Other factors also contribute to the imprecisions, such as the lack of disjunctive domains. Finally, many tests use the socket API to introduce non-determinism, and the current file management abstraction was not precise enough to prove the validity of some file descriptors.

5.2   Coreutils

Our second benchmark includes 19 out of 106 programs from Coreutils version 8.30 [12]. Each program consists in a principal C file containing the `main` function, and library functions that are shared among all Coreutils programs. Due to these complex dependencies, it was difficult to extract the number of lines corresponding to individual programs. Instead, we computed the number of atomic statements, consisting of assignments and tests (e.g. in `for`, `while` and `switch` statements), in the functions reached by the analysis. This gives an indication of the size of the program, but the scale is not comparable with line count metrics.

Scenarios. Three scenarios were considered. The first one consists in analyzing the function `main` without any argument. In the second scenario, we call `main` with one symbolic argument with arbitrary size. The last scenario is the most general: `main` is called with a symbolic number of symbolic arguments.

Abstractions. For each scenario, four abstractions were compared. In the first abstraction A_1, we employed the CELLS memory domain [19] over the INTERVALS domain. The second abstraction A_2 enriches A_1 with the STRINGLENGTH domain [17] improved as discussed in Sect. 4. The third abstraction A_3 enriches A_2 with the POLYHEDRA domain [8,15] with a static packing strategy [4]. Finally, A_4 enriches A_3 with a POINTERSENTINEL domain that tracks the position of the first `NULL` pointer in an array of pointers; it is similar to the string length domain and useful to represent a symbolic `argv` and handle functions such as `getopt` (see Appendix A.4).

Limitations. The analysis of recursive calls is not yet implemented in Mopsa. We have found only one recursive function in the analyzed programs, which we replaced with a stub model. The second limitation concerns the `getopt` family of functions. We have not considered the case where these functions modify the `argv` array by rearranging its elements in some specific order, since such modifications make the analysis too imprecise. However, we believe that this kind of operation can be handled by an enhanced POINTERSENTINEL domain. This is left as future work.

Precision. Figure 12a shows the number of alarms for every analysis. The most advanced abstraction A_4 reduces significantly the number of alarms, specially for the fully symbolic scenario. This gain is not due to one specific abstraction, but it comes from the cooperation of several domains, most notably between POLYHEDRA and STRINGLENGTH. This also emphasizes the effectiveness of domain communication mechanisms within Mopsa [16], notably symbolic expression evaluation.

Efficiency. As shown in Fig. 12b, the gain in precision comes at the cost of degraded performances. The most significant decrease corresponds to the introduction of the POLYHEDRA domain. Note that our current packing strategy is naive (assigning for each function one pack holding all its local variables); a more advanced strategy could improve scalability.

Program	Statements	No arg.				One symbolic arg.				Fully symbolic args.			
		A_1	A_2	A_3	A_4	A_1	A_2	A_3	A_4	A_1	A_2	A_3	A_4
cksum	292	53	29	28	36	135	106	106	53	136	107	106	53
dircolors	507	104	54	47	47	185	158	154	100	186	159	154	99
dirname	183	59	14	13	13	120	90	90	22	120	90	90	21
echo	241	16	3	3	3	216	179	175	33	216	179	175	34
false	131	0	0	0	0	89	61	61	13	89	61	61	13
hostid	193	25	9	8	8	91	63	63	16	92	64	63	16
id	193	25	9	8	8	91	63	63	16	92	64	63	16
logname	196	25	8	7	7	93	62	62	15	94	63	62	15
nice	323	16	3	3	3	145	105	104	18	151	111	105	20
nproc	356	81	36	35	35	136	99	99	33	137	100	99	32
printenv	179	70	29	28	28	159	131	130	59	161	133	130	59
pwd	342	81	23	20	20	116	70	68	23	116	70	68	22
sleep	289	25	8	7	7	125	97	97	29	128	99	97	29
stdbuf	546	97	53	52	52	327	269	267	125	329	271	268	127
true	131	0	0	0	0	89	61	61	13	89	61	61	13
uname	251	67	25	24	24	105	72	72	27	106	73	73	33
unexpand	478	149	93	92	92	226	179	179	95	226	179	179	94
unlink	204	25	8	7	7	98	68	68	15	103	71	68	15
whoami	202	27	9	8	8	95	63	63	16	96	64	63	16

(a) Number of reported alarms.

Program	No arg.				One symbolic arg.				Fully symbolic args.			
	A_1	A_2	A_3	A_4	A_1	A_2	A_3	A_4	A_1	A_2	A_3	A_4
cksum	12.62	15.76	46.86	46.32	33.69	39.67	175.92	174.45	34.21	39.3	174.5	193.64
dircolors	70.27	88.49	292.38	228.75	174.46	192.94	514.1	646.22	160.91	198.07	533.13	595.14
dirname	22.56	29.04	97.96	85.65	22.95	30.38	90.99	140.88	24.97	28.89	96.04	119.86
echo	8.73	9.12	13.38	12.48	10.74	13.52	26.03	25.44	11.44	13.24	24.75	156.15
false	8.72	9.17	13.38	13.45	9.33	11.35	19.63	18.9	10.05	11.26	19.54	19.18
hostid	9.87	10.18	21.7	20.63	14.74	16.72	41.13	53.68	14.17	16.61	42.08	53.41
id	9.51	11.53	22.68	20.65	13.66	16.5	43.39	55.37	13.75	18.96	40.51	54.57
logname	9.31	10.75	20.13	19.42	15.97	16.51	39.37	45.06	13.47	17.05	40.69	48.72
nice	9.26	9.08	13.64	12.57	25.42	30.04	113.35	177.38	23.98	30.73	148.1	238.55
nproc	23.1	30.35	103.64	90.52	25.72	32.96	110.4	150.21	25.7	34.17	112.39	128.86
printenv	21.43	27.63	93.83	94.08	22.82	28.34	111.41	206.16	22.52	28.06	131.27	200.63
pwd	23.81	29.34	95.41	84.18	24.1	29.05	88.72	127.68	22.41	29.59	98.15	113.56
sleep	11.48	13.11	26.93	24.77	17.54	19.86	59.62	65.49	16.64	21.42	62.27	71.32
stdbuf	37.23	56.73	214.48	190.39	42.37	63.34	229.52	291.24	42.32	65.75	215.85	255.32
true	8.73	9.13	12.57	12.08	10.89	11.27	18.64	19.4	10.04	11.62	18.95	21.63
uname	21.85	28.46	86.38	81.68	24.19	28.9	85.85	102.31	23.95	30.97	95.13	129.77
unexpand	68.75	137.73	400.55	366.1	65.14	138.18	361.77	525.35	61.9	149.1	378.31	364.11
unlink	11.35	12.88	26.24	27.23	14.74	16.05	40.34	49.04	16.82	18.63	49.03	58.85
whoami	10.51	11.17	21.28	22.17	14.98	16.13	41.89	59.91	14.27	16.69	48.57	61.3

(b) Analysis time in seconds.

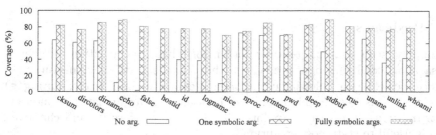

(c) Coverage of abstraction A_4.

Fig. 12. Analysis results on Coreutils programs.

Coverage. We have also measured the ratio of statements reached by the analysis in the three scenarios. While not a formal guarantee of correctness, a high level of coverage provides some reassurance that large parts of the programs are not ignored due to soundness errors in our implementation or our stubs. We discuss only the case of abstraction A_4, as other cases provide similar results. Figure 12c presents the results. In most cases, using one symbolic argument helps covering a significantly larger part of the program compared to analyzing `main` without any argument. Coverage with one or several symbolic arguments is roughly the same, possibly due to the control flow over-approximations caused by even a single symbolic argument. Nevertheless, only the last scenario, covering an unbounded number of arguments, provides a soundness guarantee that all the executions of the program are covered. As far as we know, this is not supported in the static value analyses by Frama-C [10] nor Astrée [4].

6   Conclusion

We presented a static analysis by abstract interpretation of C library functions modeled with a specification language. We defined an operational concrete semantics of the language and proposed a generic abstraction that can be supported by any abstract domain. We also showed how a C string domain could be enriched with specialized transfer functions for specific formulas appearing in stubs, greatly improving the analysis precision. We integrated the proposed solution into the Mopsa static analyzer and experimented it on Juliet benchmarks and Coreutils programs. In the future, we plan to extend our coverage of the standard C library, provide models for other well-known libraries, such as OpenSSL, and experiment on larger program analyses. In addition, we envisage to upgrade our specification language to support more expressive logic. Finally, we want to improve the quality of our results by adding more precise abstractions, such as trace partitioning, or more efficient modular iterators.

A   Stub Examples

This appendix presents additional representative examples of the stubs we developed for the GNU C library.

A.1   Predicates

To simplify stub coding, following other logic-base specification languages, Mopsa allows defining logic predicates, that can be then used in stubs. For instance, we define the following useful predicates on C strings: `valid_string(s)` states that s is zero-terminated, and is useful as argument precondition; `in_string(x,s)` states that x points within string s before its null character, which is useful to state post-conditions.

```
1   /*$
2    * predicate valid_string(s):
3    *    s != NULL ∧ offset(s) ∈ [0, size(s) - 1]
4    *    ∧ ∃ k ∈ [0, size(s) - offset(s) - 1]: s[k] == 0;
5    */
6
7   /*$
8    * predicate in_string(x,s):
9    *    ∃ k ∈ [0, size(s) - offset(s) - 1]:
10   *     ( x == s + k
11   *        ∧ ∀ l ∈ [0, k - 1]: s[l] != 0 );
12   */
```

A.2   Memory Management

Memory allocation functions show examples of resource allocation, and the use of cases to simplify the specification of functions with several behaviors.

```
1   /*$
2    * case {
3    *    alloc:    void* r = new malloc;
4    *    ensures:  size(r) == __size;
5    *    ensures:  return == r;
6    * }
7    *
8    * case {
9    *    assigns: _errno;
10   *    ensures: return == NULL;
11   * }
12   *
13   * case {
14   *    assumes: __size == 0;
15   *    ensures: return == NULL;
16   * }
17   */
18  void *malloc (size_t __size);
1   /*$
2    * case {
3    *    assumes:  __ptr == NULL;
4    * }
5    *
6    * case {
7    *    assumes:  __ptr != NULL;
8    *    requires: __ptr ∈ malloc;
9    *    requires: alive(__ptr);
10   *    requires: offset(__ptr) == 0;
11   *    free:     __ptr;
12   * }
13   */
14  void free (void *__ptr);
```

```
 1  /*$
 2   * case {
 3   *    assumes:  __ptr == NULL;
 4   *    assumes:  __size == 0;
 5   *    ensures: return == NULL;
 6   * }
 7   *
 8   * case {
 9   *    assumes:  __ptr == NULL;
10   *    alloc:    void* r = new malloc;
11   *    ensures:  size(r) == __size;
12   *    ensures: return == r;
13   * }
14   *
15   * case {
16   *    assumes:  __ptr != NULL;
17   *    assumes:  __size == 0;
18   *    requires: __ptr ∈ malloc;
19   *    free:     __ptr;
20   *    ensures: return == NULL;
21   * }
22   *
23   * case {
24   *    assumes:  __ptr != NULL;
25   *    requires: __ptr ∈ malloc;
26   *    local:    void* r = new malloc;
27   *    ensures:  size(r) == __size;
28   *    ensures:  size(__ptr) >= __size ⇒
29   *              ∀ i ∈ [0, __size):
30   *                 ((unsigned char*)r)[i] == ((unsigned char*)__ptr)[i];
31   *    ensures:  size(__ptr) <= __size ⇒
32   *              ∀ i ∈ [0, size(__ptr)):
33   *                 ((unsigned char*)r)[i] == ((unsigned char*)__ptr)[i];
34   *    free:     __ptr;
35   *    ensures: return == r;
36   * }
37   *
38   * case {
39   *    assigns: _errno;
40   *    ensures: return == NULL;
41   * }
42   */
43  void *realloc (void *__ptr, size_t __size);
```

A.3 File Descriptors

File descriptors are another example of resource allocation, but use a specific class that the analyzer can track to allocate integer file descriptors according to the C library policy: the least unused integer is picked. This allows modeling precisely patterns such as close(0); int f = open("...");. read reads non-deterministic values, after checking that the file has been opened and not closed.

```
 1   /*$
 2    * requires: valid_string(__file);
 3    *
 4    * case {
 5    *    alloc:   int fd = new FileDescriptor;
 6    *    ensures: return == fd;
 7    * }
 8    *
 9    * case {
10    *    assigns: _errno;
11    *    ensures: return == -1;
12    * }
13    */
14   int open (const char *__file, int __oflag, ...);
 1   /*$
 2    * requires: __fd ∈ FileDescriptor;
 3    * requires: alive(__fp as FileDescriptor);
 4    * requires: size(__buf) >= offset(__buf) + __nbytes;
 5    *
 6    * case {
 7    *    assigns: ((char*)__buf)[0, __nbytes);
 8    *    ensures: return ∈ [0, __nbytes];
 9    * }
10    *
11    * case {
12    *    assigns: _errno;
13    *    ensures: return == -1;
14    * }
15    */
16   ssize_t read (int __fd, void *__buf, size_t __nbytes);
 1   /*$
 2    * requires: __fd ∈ FileDescriptor;
 3    * requires: alive(__fp as FileDescriptor);
 4    *
 5    * case {
 6    *    free:    __fd as FileDescriptor;
 7    *    ensures: return == 0;
 8    * }
 9    *
10    * case {
11    *    assigns: _errno;
12    *    ensures: return == -1;
13    * }
14    */
15   int close (int __fd);
```

A.4   Command-Line Arguments

We provide the simplified model of the getopt function we used in Coreutil analyses.

```
 1  /*$
 2   * requires: ___argc > 0;
 3   * requires: optind ∈ [0, ___argc];
 4   * requires: valid_string(__shortopts);
 5   * requires: ∀ i ∈ [0, ___argc - 1]: valid_string(___argv[i]);
 6   * assigns: optind;
 7   * assigns: opterr;
 8   * assigns: optopt;
 9   * assigns: optarg;
10   * ensures: optind'∈[1, ___argc];
11   * ensures: optarg' != NULL ⇒ ∃ i ∈ [0, ___argc - 1]:
12   *              in_string(optarg', ___argv[i]);
13   * ensures: return ∈ [-1, 255];
14   * case {
15   *    assigns: ___argv[0, ___argc - 1];
16   *    ensures: ∀ i ∈ [0, ___argc - 1]: ∃ j ∈ [0, ___argc - 1]:
17   *       (___argv[i])' == ___argv[j];
18   * }
19   */
20  int getopt (int ___argc, char *const *___argv, const char *__shortopts);
```

References

1. Common weakness enumeration: A community-developed list of software weakness types. https://cwe.mitre.org/. Accessed 24 May 2020
2. Balakrishnan, G., Reps, T.: Recency-abstraction for heap-allocated storage. In: Yi, K. (ed.) SAS 2006. LNCS, vol. 4134, pp. 221–239. Springer, Heidelberg (2006). https://doi.org/10.1007/11823230_15
3. Baudin, P., Cuoq, P., Fillâtre, J., Marché, C., Monate, B., Moy, Y., Prevosto, V.: ACSL:ANSI/ISO C Specification Language. http://frama-c.com/acsl.html
4. Bertrane, J., Cousot, P., Cousot, R., Feret, J., Mauborgne, L., Miné, A., Rival, X.: Static analysis and verification of aerospace software by abstract interpretation. In: AIAA Infotech@Aerospace, pp. 1–38. No. 2010–3385, AIAA, April 2010
5. Black, P.E.: Juliet 1.3 test suite: changes from 1.2. Tech. Rep. NIST TN - 1995, NIST, June 2018
6. Calcagno, C., et al.: Moving fast with software verification. In: NFM, pp. 3–11. Springer, Heidelberg (2015)
7. Cousot, P., Cousot, R.: Abstract interpretation: a unified lattice model for static analysis of programs by construction or approximation of fixpoints. In: Proceedings of POPL 1977, pp. 238–252. ACM, January 1977
8. Cousot, P., Halbwachs, N.: Automatic discovery of linear restraints among variables of a program. In: Conference Record of the 5th Annual ACM SIGPLAN/SIGACT Symposium on Principles of Programming Languages (POPL 1978), pp. 84–97. ACM (1978)
9. Kirchner, F., Kosmatov, N., Prevosto, V., Signoles, J., Yakobowski, B.: Frama-C: a software analysis perspective. Formal Aspects Comput. 27(3), 573–609 (2015). https://doi.org/10.1007/s00165-014-0326-7

10. Bühler, P.C., Yakobowski, B.: Eva: The evolved value analysis plug-in
11. Fähndrich, M.: Static verification for code contracts. In: Cousot, R., Martel, M. (eds.) SAS 2010. LNCS, vol. 6337, pp. 2–5. Springer, Heidelberg (2010). https://doi.org/10.1007/978-3-642-15769-1_2
12. GNU: Coreutils: GNU core utilities. https://www.gnu.org/software/coreutils/
13. GNU: The GNU C library. https://www.gnu.org/software/libc/
14. Gopan, D., DiMaio, F., Dor, N., Reps, T., Sagiv, M.: Numeric domains with summarized dimensions. In: Jensen, K., Podelski, A. (eds.) TACAS 2004. LNCS, vol. 2988, pp. 512–529. Springer, Heidelberg (2004). https://doi.org/10.1007/978-3-540-24730-2_38
15. Jeannet, B., Miné, A.: Apron: a library of numerical abstract domains for static analysis. In: Proceedings of the 21st International Conference on Computer Aided Verification, pp. 661–667. CAV 2009, Springer, Heidelberg (2009)
16. Journault, M., Miné, A., Monat, M., Ouadjaout, A.: Combinations of reusable abstract domains for a multilingual static analyzer. In: Proceedings of VSTTE 2019, pp. 1–17 (2019)
17. Journault, M., Ouadjaout, A., Miné, A.: Modular static analysis of string manipulations in C programs. In: Proceedings of SAS 2018. LNCS (2018)
18. Leavens, G., Ruby, C., Leino, K.R.M., Poll, E., Jacobs, B.: JML: Notations and tools supporting detailed design in Java. In: Proceedings of OOPSLA 2018, pp. 105–106 (2000)
19. Miné, A.: Field-sensitive value analysis of embedded C programs with union types and pointer arithmetics. In: Proceedings of LCTES 2006, pp. 54–63. ACM, June 2006

Interprocedural Shape Analysis Using Separation Logic-Based Transformer Summaries

Hugo Illous[1,2], Matthieu Lemerre[1], and Xavier Rival[2(✉)]

[1] Université Paris -Saclay, CEA, List, F-91120 Palaiseau, France
`matthieu.lemerre@cea.fr`
[2] INRIA Paris/CNRS/École Normale Supérieure/PSL Research University,
Paris, France
`xavier.rival@inria.fr`

Abstract. Shape analyses aim at inferring semantic invariants related to the data-structures that programs manipulate. To achieve that, they typically abstract the set of reachable states. By contrast, abstractions for transformation relations between input states and output states not only provide a finer description of program executions but also enable the composition of the effect of program fragments so as to make the analysis modular. However, few logics can efficiently capture such transformation relations. In this paper, we propose to use connectors inspired by separation logic to describe memory state transformations and to represent procedure summaries. Based on this abstraction, we design a top-down interprocedural analysis using shape transformation relations as procedure summaries. Finally, we report on implementation and evaluation.

1 Introduction

Static analyses based on abstractions of sets of states (or for short, *state analyses*) compute an over-approximation of the states that a program may reach, so as to answer questions related, e.g., to safety (absence of errors or structural invariant violations). By contrast, one may also design static analyses that discover relations between program initial states and output states. In this paper, we refer to such static analyses as *transformation analyses*. A transformation relation between the initial state and the output state of a given execution can provide an answer to questions related to the functional correctness of a program (i.e., does it compute a correct result when it does not crash and terminates). Another application of such a transformation relation is to let the analysis reuse multiple times the result obtained for a given code fragment (e.g., a procedure), provided the analysis can compose transformation relations. The great advantage of this approach is to reduce the analysis cost, by avoiding to recalculate the effect, e.g., of a procedure in multiple calling contexts. This is known as the relational approach to interprocedural analysis [35].

However, a major difficulty is to find an accurate and lightweight representation of the input-output transformation relation of each procedure. A first

D. Pichardie and M. Sighireanu (Eds.): SAS 2020, LNCS 12389, pp. 248–273, 2020.
https://doi.org/10.1007/978-3-030-65474-0_12

solution is to resort to tables of abstract pre- and post-conditions that are all expressed in a given state abstract domain [2,10,15,22]. However, this generally makes composition imprecise unless very large tables can be computed. A second solution is to build upon a *relational abstract domain*, namely, an abstract domain that can capture relations across distinct program variables. The transformation between states is then expressed using "primed" and "non-primed" variables where the former describe the input state and the latter the output state [24,26,27]. As an example, we consider a procedure that computes the absolute value of input x and stores it into y (for the sake of simplicity we assume mathematical integers):

- Using the intervals abstract domain [9], we can provide the table $[((x \in [-5,-1], y \in]-\infty,+\infty[) \mapsto (x \in [-5,-1], y \in [1,5]));((x \in [-1,10], y \in]-\infty,+\infty[) \mapsto (x \in [-1,10], y \in [0,10]))]$ (this table is obviously not unique);
- Using the relational abstract domain of polyhedra [11], we can construct the transformation relation $(x' = x \wedge y' \geq x \wedge y' \geq -x)$.

We note that, while the expressiveness of the two is not comparable, the latter option is more adapted to compositional reasoning. For instance, given precondition $-10 \leq x \leq -5$, the analysis based on a table either returns a very imprecise answer or requires enriching the table whereas the analysis with a relational domain can immediately derive $x' = x \in [-10,-5]$ (x has not changed) and $y' \geq 5$.

Such reasoning becomes more complex when considering non-numerical facts, such as memory shape properties. Many works rely on the tabulation approach, using a conventional shape state abstraction [2,15,22]. In general, the tabulation approach restricts the ability to precisely relate procedure input and output states and may require large tables of pairs of formulas for a good level of precision. The approach based on a relational domain with primed and non-primed variables has been implemented by [18,19] in the TVLA shape analysis framework [33]. However, it is more difficult to extend shape analyses that are based on separation logic [28] since a separation logic formula describes a region of a given heap; thus, it does not naturally constrain fragments of two different states. To solve this issue, a first approach is to modify the semantics of separation logic connectors to pairs of states [34]. A more radical solution is to construct novel logical connectors over state transformation relations that are inspired by separation logic [17]. These transformations can describe the effect of a program and express facts such as "memory region A is left untouched whereas a single element is inserted into the list stored inside memory region B and the rest of that list is not modified". The analysis of [17] is designed as a forward abstract interpretation which produces abstract transformation relations. Therefore, it can describe tranformations precisely using separation logic predicates and without accumulating tables of input and output abstract states.

However, this analysis still lacks several important components to actually make interprocedural analysis modular. In particular, it lacks a *composition* algorithm over abstract transformation relations. Modular interprocedural analysis also needs to synchronize two distinct processes that respectively aim at *computing procedure summaries* and at *instantiating* them at a call-site. In this

```
1  typedef struct list { struct list * n; /* ... */ } list;
2  void append( list *l0, list *l1 ){
3     assume(l0 != NULL); list *c = l0;
4     while( c->n != NULL ){ c = c->n; }
5     c->n = l1;
6  }
7  void double_append( list *k0, list *k1; list *k2 ){
8     assume(k0 != NULL); append( k0, k1 ); append( k0, k2 );
9  }
```

Fig. 1. Simple and double list append procedures.

paper, we propose a top-down analysis based on shape summaries and make the following contributions:

- in Sect. 2, we demonstrate the use of abstract shape transformations;
- in Sect. 3 and Sect. 4, we formalize transformation summaries based on separation logic (intraprocedural analysis is presented in Sect. 5);
- in Sect. 6, we build a composition algorithm over transformation summaries;
- in Sect. 7, we formalize a modular interprocedural analysis;
- in Sect. 8, we report on implementation and evaluation.

2   Overview

In this section, we study a restricted example to highlight some issues in interprocedural analysis. We consider a recursive implementation of C linked lists, with a couple of procedures shown in Fig. 1. The function append takes two lists as arguments and assumes the first one non-empty, it traverses the first list, and mutates the pointer field of the last element. The function double_append takes three lists as arguments (the first one is assumed non-empty) and concatenates all three by calling append. The topic of our discussion is only the invariants underlying this code and their discovery, not the efficiency of the code itself.

State Abstraction and Analysis. We consider an abstraction based on separation logic [28], as shown, e.g., in [6,13]. To describe sets of states, we assume a predicate $\mathbf{lseg}(\alpha_0, \alpha_1)$ that represents heap regions that consist of a list segment starting at some address represented by the symbolic variable α_0 and such that the last element points to some address represented by α_1. Such a segment may be empty. For short, we note $\mathbf{list}(\alpha)$ for the instance $\mathbf{lseg}(\alpha, \mathbf{0x0})$, which denotes a complete singly-linked list (as the last element contains a null next link). A single list element writes down $\alpha_0 \cdot \underline{\mathbf{n}} \mapsto \alpha_1$ where $\underline{\mathbf{n}}$ denotes the next field offset (we elide other fields). More generally, $\alpha_0 \mapsto \alpha_1$ denotes a single memory cell of address α_0 and content α_1. Thus $\&\mathbf{x} \mapsto \alpha$ expresses that variable x stores a value α (which may be either a base value or the address of a memory cell). Predicates $\mathbf{lseg}$ and $\mathbf{list}$ are *summary* predicates as they describe unbounded memory regions; their denotation is naturally defined by induction. As usual, separating conjunction $*$ conjoins predicates over *disjoint* heap regions.

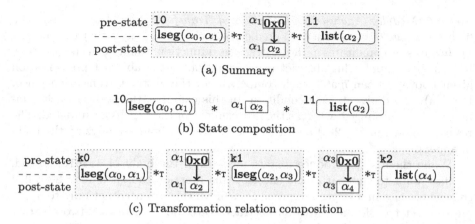

(a) Summary

(b) State composition

(c) Transformation relation composition

Fig. 2. A shape transformation procedure summary and composition.

Assuming the abstract precondition $\&10 \mapsto \alpha_0 p \mathbf{lseg}(\alpha_0, \alpha_1) * \alpha_1 \cdot \underline{\mathbf{n}} \mapsto$ $\mathbf{0x0} * \&11 \mapsto \alpha_2 * \mathbf{list}(\alpha_2)$, existing state shape analyses [6,13] can derive the post-condition $\&10 \mapsto \alpha_0 * \mathbf{lseg}(\alpha_0, \alpha_1) * \alpha_1 \cdot \underline{\mathbf{n}} \mapsto \alpha_2 * \&11 \mapsto \alpha_2 *$ $\mathbf{list}(\alpha_2)$ by a standard forward abstract interpretation [9] of the body of append. The analysis proceeds by abstract interpretation of basic statements, unfolds summaries when analyzing reads or writes into the regions that they represent, and folds basic predicates into summaries at loop heads. The convergence of the loop analysis takes a few iterations and involves widening which is often a rather costly operation.

The analysis of double_append by inlining follows similar steps. One important note though is that it analyses the body of append twice, namely once per calling context, and thus also the loop inside append. In turn, if double_append is called in several contexts in a larger program, or inside a loop, its body will also be analyzed multiple times, which increases even more the overall analysis cost.

Transformation Analysis. Unlike state analyses, transformation analyses compute abstractions of the input-output relation of a program fragment. As an example, given the above abstract pre-condition, the analysis of [17] infers relations as shown in Fig. 2(a).   This graphical view states that the procedure append keeps both summary predicates unchanged and only modifies the middle list element so as to append the two lists. This transformation is formally represented using three basic kinds of relational predicates that respectively state that one region is preserved, that one region is "transformed" into another one, and that two transformations are conjoined at the transformation level. To stress the difference, we write $*_T$ for the latter, instead of just $*$. Although it uses transformation predicates, the analysis follows similar abstract interpretation steps as [6,13].

Towards Modular Analysis: Composition of Transformation Abstractions. The first advantage of transformation predicates such as Fig. 2(a) is that they can be *applied* to state predicates in the abstract, as a function would be in the concrete. Indeed, if we apply this abstract transformation to the abstract pre-condition given above, we can match each component of the abstract transformation of Fig. 2(a), and derive its post-condition. In this example, the body of each summary is left unchanged, whereas the last element of the first list is updated. The result is shown in Fig. 2(b) and it can be derived without reanalyzing the body of append.

While these steps produce a state analysis of the body of double_append, we may want to summarize the effect of this function too, as it may be called somewhere else in a larger program. To achieve this, we need not only to apply an abstract transformation to an abstract state, but to *compose* two abstract transformations together. Intuitively, this composition should proceed in a similar way as the application that we sketc.hed above. In the case of double_append, the analysis requires case splits depending on whether k1 is empty or not. For brevity, we show only the case where this list is non-empty in Fig. 2(c). In general, the composition of two transformations requires to match the post-condition of the first and the pre-condition of the second, and to refine them, using some kind of intersection as shown in Sect. 6. Another important issue is the summary computation process. Bottom-up analyses strive for general summaries whatever the calling context. However, a procedure may behave differently when applied to other structures (e.g., a binary tree or a doubly linked list), thus the top-down approach which provides information about the calling contexts before they are analyzed seems more natural. However, this means that the analysis should infer summaries and apply them simultaneously, and that the discovery of new calling contexts may require for more general summaries. We describe this in Sect. 7.

3   Abstraction of Sets of States and State Transformations

In the following sections, we restrict ourselves to a small imperative language that is sufficient to study procedure transformation summaries, although our implementation described in Sect. 8 supports a larger fragment of C. We also only consider basic singly linked lists in the formalization although the implementation supports a large range of list or tree-like inductive data-structures.

Concrete States, Programs, and Semantics. We write $\mathbb{X}$ for the set of program variables and $\mathbb{V}$ for the set of values, which include memory addresses. The address of a variable x is assumed fixed and noted &x. Structure fields are viewed both as names and as offsets; they include the null offset (basic pointer) and $\underline{n}$, the "next" field of a list element. We let a memory state $\sigma \in \mathbb{M}$ be a partial function from variable addresses and heap addresses to values. We write $\mathbf{dom}(\sigma)$ for the domain of σ, that is the set of elements for which it is defined. Additionally, if σ_0, σ_1 are such that $\mathbf{dom}(\sigma_0) \cap \mathbf{dom}(\sigma_1) = \emptyset$, we let $\sigma_0 \circledast \sigma_1$ be the memory state obtained by appending σ_1 to σ_0 (its domain is $\mathbf{dom}(\sigma_0) \cup \mathbf{dom}(\sigma_1)$). If a is an address and v a value, we write $[a \mapsto v]$ for the memory state σ such

$$C ::= x = y \mid x = v \mid x \text{ -> } \underline{n} = y \mid x = y \text{ -> } \underline{n} \mid C; C \mid \textbf{while}(x \neq \textbf{0x0})\{C\}$$
$$\mid \textbf{decl}\, x; \mid f(x_0, \ldots, x_k)$$
$$P ::= \textbf{proc}\, f(p_0, \ldots, p_k)\{C\} \qquad R ::= P_0 \; \ldots \; P_l \; \textbf{proc}\, \text{main}()\{C\}$$

$$n(\in \mathbb{N}) ::= \alpha \quad (\alpha \in \mathbb{A}) \mid \&x \quad (x \in \mathbb{X}) \qquad c^\# ::= n \odot \textbf{0x0} \quad (\odot \in \{=, \neq\}) \mid n = n'$$
$$h^\#(\in \mathbb{H}) ::= \textbf{emp} \mid n \cdot \underline{f} \mapsto n' \mid \textbf{lseg}(\alpha, \alpha') \mid \textbf{list}(\alpha) \mid h^\# *_s h^\# \mid h^\# \wedge c^\#$$

(a) Abstract states syntax

$$\gamma_H(n \cdot \underline{f} \mapsto n') = \{([\nu(n) + \underline{f} \mapsto \nu(n')], \nu)\} \qquad \gamma_H(\textbf{emp}) = \{([], \nu)\}$$
$$\gamma_H(h_0^\# *_s h_1^\#) = \{(\sigma_0 \circledast \sigma_1, \nu) \mid (\sigma_0, \nu) \in \gamma_H(h_0^\#) \wedge (\sigma_1, \nu) \in \gamma_H(h_1^\#)\}$$
$$\gamma_H(h^\# \wedge c^\#) = \{(\sigma, \nu) \mid (\sigma, \nu) \in \gamma_H(h^\#) \wedge \nu \in \gamma_c(c^\#)\}$$

(b) Concretization of abstract states

Fig. 3. Syntax and concretization of the abstract states.

that $\textbf{dom}(\sigma) = \{a\}$ and $\sigma(a) = v$. A command C is either an assignment, a local variable declaration or a loop (we omit tests and memory allocation out as our procedure summary analysis handles them in a very standard way). A procedure P is defined by a list of arguments and a body (we let function returns be encoded via parameter passing by reference). A program is made of a series of procedures including a main. All variables are local. The syntax of programs is defined by the grammar below:

$$C ::= x = y \mid x = v \mid x \text{ -> } \underline{n} = y \mid x = y \text{ -> } \underline{n} \mid C; C \mid \textbf{while}(x \neq \textbf{0x0})\{C\}$$
$$\mid \textbf{decl}\, x; \mid f(x_0, \ldots, x_k)$$
$$P ::= \textbf{proc}\, f(p_0, \ldots, p_k)\{C\} \qquad R ::= P_0 \; \ldots \; P_l \; \textbf{proc}\, \text{main}()\{C\}$$

We let the semantics of a command C be a function $[\![C]\!]_T : \mathcal{P}(\mathbb{M}) \to \mathcal{P}(\mathbb{M})$ that maps a set of input states into a set of output states. We do not detail the definition of this semantics as it is standard. In the following, require for more general summaries, that respectively describe sets of states and relations over states.

Abstract States and Transformations. The syntax of abstract heaps $h^\# \in \mathbb{H}$ is shown in Fig. 3(a). We let $\mathbb{A} = \{\alpha, \alpha', \ldots\}$ denote a set of *symbolic variables* that abstract heap addresses and values. A *symbolic name* $n \in \mathbb{N}$ is either a variable address $\&x$ or a symbolic value α. Numerical constraints $c^\#$ describe predicates over symbolic names. An abstract heap (or state) $h^\# \in \mathbb{H}$ is the (possibly) separating conjunction of region predicates that abstract *separate* regions [28], which consist either of an empty region **emp**, or of a basic memory block (described by a points-to predicate $n \cdot \underline{f} \mapsto n'$), or inductive summaries, and may include some numerical constraints (that do not represent any memory region and only constrain symbolic names). We note $*_s$ for separating conjunction over states. The abstract states defined in Fig. 3(a) are of a comparable level of expressiveness as the abstractions used in common shape analysis tools such as [2,6,13,14] to verify properties such as the absence of memory errors or the preservation of structural invariants.

$$\&l0 \mapsto \alpha_0 *_S \&l1 \mapsto \alpha_2 *_S \alpha_0 \cdot \underline{n} \mapsto \alpha_1 *_S \alpha_1 \cdot \underline{n} \mapsto \alpha_2 *_S \alpha_2 \cdot \underline{n} \mapsto \alpha_3 \wedge \alpha_3 = 0$$

$$t^\sharp (\in \mathbb{T}) ::= \mathtt{Id}(h^\sharp) \mid [h_i^\sharp \dashrightarrow h^\sharp] \mid t^\sharp *_T t^\sharp \mid t^\sharp \wedge c^\sharp$$

(a) Abstract transformations syntax

$$\gamma_T(\mathtt{Id}(h^\sharp)) = \{(\sigma, \sigma, \nu) \mid (\sigma, \nu) \in \gamma_H(h^\sharp)\}$$
$$\gamma_T([h_i^\sharp \dashrightarrow h_o^\sharp]) = \{(\sigma_i, \sigma_o, \nu) \mid (\sigma_i, \nu) \in \gamma_H(h_i^\sharp) \wedge (\sigma_o, \nu) \in \gamma_H(h_o^\sharp)\}$$
$$\gamma_T(t_0^\sharp *_T t_1^\sharp) = \{(\sigma_{0,i} \circledast \sigma_{1,i}, \sigma_{0,o} \circledast \sigma_{1,o}, \nu) \mid$$
$$(\sigma_{0,i}, \sigma_{0,o}, \nu) \in \gamma_T(t_0^\sharp) \wedge \mathbf{dom}(\sigma_{0,i}) \cap \mathbf{dom}(\sigma_{1,o}) = \emptyset$$
$$\wedge (\sigma_{1,i}, \sigma_{1,o}, \nu) \in \gamma_T(t_1^\sharp) \wedge \mathbf{dom}(\sigma_{1,i}) \cap \mathbf{dom}(\sigma_{0,o}) = \emptyset\}$$
$$\gamma_T(t^\sharp \wedge c^\sharp) = \{(\sigma_i, \sigma_o, \nu) \in \gamma_T(t^\sharp) \mid \nu \in \gamma_C(c^\sharp)\}$$

(b) Concretization of abstract transformations

Fig. 4. Syntax and concretization of abstract transformations.

The concretization of abstract states is shown in Fig. 3(b). It uses valuations to tie the abstract names and the value they denote. A valuation consists of a function $\nu : \mathbb{N} \to \mathbb{V}$. We assume the concretization $\gamma_C(c^\sharp)$ of a numeric constraint $c^\sharp$ returns the set of valuations that meet this constraint. Abstract heaps are concretized into sets of pairs made of a heap and of the valuation that realizes this heap. The concretization of summary predicates **list** and **lseg** is defined recursively, by unfolding. Indeed, we let $\gamma_H(h_0^\sharp) = \bigcup\{\gamma_H(h_1^\sharp) \mid h_0^\sharp \to_\mathfrak{u} h_1^\sharp\}$, where $\to_\mathfrak{u}$ is defined by (cases for **list** are similar):

$$\mathbf{lseg}(\alpha_0, \alpha_1) \to_\mathfrak{u} \mathbf{emp} \wedge \alpha_0 = \alpha_1$$
$$\mathbf{lseg}(\alpha_0, \alpha_1) \to_\mathfrak{u} \alpha_0 \cdot \underline{n} \mapsto \alpha_2 *_S \mathbf{lseg}(\alpha_2, \alpha_1) \wedge \alpha_0 \neq \alpha_1$$

Example 1 (Abstract state). The abstract state in Fig. 2(b) writes down as:

$$\&l0 \mapsto \alpha_0 *_S \&l1 \mapsto \alpha_2 *_S \mathbf{lseg}(\alpha_0, \alpha_1) *_S \alpha_1 \cdot \underline{n} \mapsto \alpha_2 *_S \mathbf{list}(\alpha_2)$$

Assuming both $\mathbf{lseg}(\alpha_0, \alpha_1)$ and $\mathbf{list}(\alpha_2)$ unfold to structures of length one, it concretizes in the same way as:

$$\&l0 \mapsto \alpha_0 *_S \&l1 \mapsto \alpha_2 *_S \alpha_0 \cdot \underline{n} \mapsto \alpha_1 *_S \alpha_1 \cdot \underline{n} \mapsto \alpha_2 *_S \alpha_2 \cdot \underline{n} \mapsto \alpha_3 \wedge \alpha_3 = 0$$

Abstract Transformations. Abstract transformations are defined on top of abstract states and rely on specific logical connectors. Their syntax is defined in Fig. 4(a). A heap transformation is either the identity $\mathtt{Id}(h^\sharp)$, which denotes physical equality over pairs of states that are both described by $h^\sharp$, a state transformation $[h_i^\sharp \dashrightarrow h_o^\sharp]$ which captures input/output pairs of states respectively defined by $h_i^\sharp$ and by $h_o^\sharp$, or a separating conjunction of transformations $t_0^\sharp *_T t_1^\sharp$ (we write $*_T$ to stress the distinction with the state separating conjunction $*_S$). The concretization of transformations is shown in Fig. 4(b). It is built upon the previously defined γ_H and also utilizes valuations. The most interesting case is that of $*_T$: this connector imposes disjointness not only of the sub-heaps in both the pre- and post-state, but also across them. In this paper, we study only a basic form of the transformation predicate $*_T$ although it may be strengthened with additional constraints [16], e.g., to assert that the footprint has not changed or that only specific fields may have been modified. We leave out such constraints as their goal is orthogonal to the focus of this paper. Finally, the analysis uses finite disjunctions of transformations.

Example 2 (Abstract transformation). The transformation informally described in Fig. 2(a) is captured by the abstract transformation below:

$$t^\sharp = \mathtt{Id}\,(\&10 \mapsto \alpha_0 *_\mathtt{S} \&11 \mapsto \alpha_2 *_\mathtt{S} \mathbf{lseg}(\alpha_0, \alpha_1) *_\mathtt{S} \mathbf{list}(\alpha_2))$$
$$*_T\,[(\alpha_1 \cdot \underline{\mathtt{n}} \mapsto \mathtt{0x0}) \dashrightarrow (\alpha_1 \cdot \underline{\mathtt{n}} \mapsto \alpha_2)]$$

In the following, we write $h_0^\sharp \to_\mathfrak{u} h_1^\sharp$ when $h_0^\sharp$ may be rewritten into $h_1^\sharp$ by applying $\to_\mathfrak{u}$ to any of its sub-terms. We use this notation for both heaps and transformations. Last, we let $\to_{\mathfrak{u}[\alpha]}$ denote unfolding of a $\mathbf{list}(\alpha)$ or $\mathbf{lseg}(\alpha, \ldots)$ predicate.

4   Procedure Summarization

The semantics of a procedure boils down to a relation between its input states and its output states, thus our first attempt at summaries over-approximates the input-output relation of the procedure. To express this, we introduce the following notation. If $f : \mathcal{P}(A) \to \mathcal{P}(B)$ is a function and $R \subseteq A \times B$ is a relation, we note $f \Subset R$ if and only if $\forall X \subseteq A$, $X \times f(X) \subseteq R$.

Definition 1 (Global transformation summary). *A sound global transformation summary (or, for short, global summary) of procedure* **proc** $f(\ldots)\{C\}$ *is an abstract transformation* $t^\sharp$ *that over-approximates* $[\![C]\!]_T$ *in the sense that:*

$$[\![C]\!]_T \Subset \{(\sigma_\mathrm{i}, \sigma_\mathrm{o}) \mid \exists \nu,\ (\sigma_\mathrm{i}, \sigma_\mathrm{o}, \nu) \in \gamma_\mathbb{T}(t^\sharp)\}$$

For example, function **append** (Fig. 1) can be described using a global procedure summary (noted $t^\sharp$ in Example 2). While this notion of summary may account for the effect of a procedure, it is not adequate to describe intermediate analysis results. As an example, a procedure f is likely to be called in multiple contexts. In that case, when the analysis reaches a first context, it computes a summary $t^\sharp$, that accounts for the effect of the procedure in that context, for a given set of procedure input states. When it reaches a second context, it should be able to decide whether $t^\sharp$ also covers the states that reach the procedure in that second context. Observe that the pre-state of $t^\sharp$ does not suffice since $t^\sharp$ may have been computed for some very specific context. Moreover, the left projection of $t^\sharp$ may not account for some call states encountered so far when these lead to non-termination or to an error in the body of f. To overcome this issue, an over-approximation of the procedure input states observed so far should be adjoined to the global summary:

Definition 2 (Context transformation summary). *A* sound context transformation summary *(or, for short,* context summary*) of procedure* **proc** $f(\ldots)\{C\}$ *is a pair* $(h_f^\sharp, t_f^\sharp)$ *such that the following holds:*

$$(\lambda(M \subseteq \{\sigma \mid \exists \nu, (\sigma, \nu) \in \gamma_H(h_f^\sharp)\}) \cdot [\![C]\!]_T(M)) \Subset \{(\sigma_i, \sigma_o) \mid \exists \nu, (\sigma_i, \sigma_o, \nu) \in \gamma_T(t_f^\sharp)\}$$

Intuitively, Definition 2 asserts that $(h_f^\sharp, t_f^\sharp)$ captures all the functions such that their restriction to states in $h_f^\sharp$ can be over-approximated by relation $t_f^\sharp$. Although we do not follow this approach here, the $h_f^\sharp$ component may be used in order to augment summaries with context sensitivity. We note that $h_f^\sharp$ accounts for all states found to enter the body of f so far, even though they may lead to no output state in $t_f^\sharp$ (e.g., if the evaluation of the body of f from them does not terminate or fails due to an error, as shown in Example 4).

Example 3 (Context summary). We let $h^\sharp = \&10 \mapsto \alpha_0 \ast_S \mathbf{lseg}(\alpha_0, \alpha_1) \ast_S \alpha_1 \cdot \underline{n} \mapsto 0x0 \ast_S \&11 \mapsto \alpha_2 \ast_S \mathbf{list}(\alpha_2)$ and assume that $t^\sharp$ is defined as in Example 2. Then, $(h^\sharp, t^\sharp)$ defines a valid context summary for append (Fig. 1).

Example 4 (Role of the pre-condition approximation in context summaries). We consider the function below and assume it is always called in a state where 10 is a valid pointer and 11 points to a well-formed, but possibly empty, singly-linked list:

```
1  void getnext( list **10, list *11 ){ *10 = 11->n; }
```

Obviously, this function will crash when the list is empty, i.e., when 10 is the null pointer. However, the pair $(h_f^\sharp, t_f^\sharp)$ below defines a valid transformation summary for this procedure:

$$h_f^\sharp = \&10 \mapsto \alpha_0 \ast_S \alpha_0 \mapsto \alpha_1 \ast_S \&11 \mapsto \alpha_2 \ast_S \mathbf{list}(\alpha_2)$$
$$t_f^\sharp = \mathbf{Id}(\&10 \mapsto \alpha_0 \ast_S \&11 \mapsto \alpha_2 \ast_S \alpha_2 \cdot \underline{n} \mapsto \alpha_3 \ast_S \mathbf{list}(\alpha_3))$$
$$\ast_T [\alpha_0 \mapsto \alpha_1 \dashrightarrow \alpha_0 \mapsto \alpha_3]$$

We observe that the $h_f^\sharp$ component describes not only states for which the procedure returns but also states for which it crashes since the list pointer c11 is null. The former are not part of the concretization of the transformation component $h_f^\sharp$.

The above example shows the importance of the first component of the transformation summary: it conveys the fact that a set of states have been considered by the analysis as a pre-condition for a program fragment, even when the program fragment may not produce any post-condition for these states hereby they can be omitted from the transformation part.

5   Intraprocedural Analysis

The analysis performs a forward abstract interpretation [9] over abstract transformations (rather than on abstract states). More precisely, the abstract semantics $[\![C]\!]_T^\sharp$ of a command C inputs a transformation describing the entire computation so far, before executing C, and outputs a new transformation that reflects the effect of C on top of that computation. Intuitively, the input of $[\![C]\!]_T^\sharp$ may be viewed the dual of a continuation. Formally, the analysis is designed so as to meet the following soundness statement, for any transformation $t^\sharp$:

$$\forall(\sigma_0,\sigma_1,\nu) \in \gamma_T(t^\sharp), \sigma_2 \in \mathbb{M}, \ (\sigma_1,\sigma_2) \in [\![C]\!]_T \implies (\sigma_0,\sigma_2,\nu) \in \gamma_T([\![C]\!]_T^\sharp(t^\sharp)) \quad (1)$$

The analysis of assignments and loops follows from [17]. It may require finite disjunctions of transformations although we do not formalize this aspect since it is orthogonal to the goal of this paper. We recall the main aspects of their algorithms in this section and refer the reader to [17] for a full description.

Post-conditions for Assignment. We consider an assignment command $x\text{->}\underline{n} = y$ (the analysis of other kinds of commands is similar), and a pre-transformation $t^\sharp$, and we discuss the computation of $[\![x \text{->} \underline{n} = y]\!]_T^\sharp(t^\sharp)$. To do this, the analysis should first localize both $x\text{->}\underline{n}$ and y in the post-state of $t^\sharp$, by rewriting $t^\sharp$ into an expression of the form $\mathrm{Id}(\&x \mapsto \alpha_0 *_S \&y \mapsto \alpha_1) *_T t_0^\sharp$ or $[(\ldots) \dashrightarrow (\&x \mapsto \alpha_0 *_S \&y \mapsto \alpha_1)] *_T t_0^\sharp$, and searching for α_0 in $t_0^\sharp$. Two main cases may arise:

- if $t_0^\sharp$ contains a term of the form $\mathrm{Id}(\alpha_0 \cdot \underline{n} \mapsto \alpha_2)$ or $[(\ldots) \dashrightarrow (\alpha_0 \cdot \underline{n} \mapsto \alpha_2)]$, the post-transformation is derived by a *mutation* over the pointer cell, which produces a term of the form $[(\ldots) \dashrightarrow (\alpha_0 \cdot \underline{n} \mapsto \alpha_1)]$;
- if $t_0^\sharp$ contains a term $\mathrm{Id}(h_0^\sharp)$ or $[(\ldots) \dashrightarrow h_0^\sharp]$ where $h_0^\sharp$ is either $\mathsf{list}(\alpha_0)$ or $\mathsf{lseg}(\alpha_0,\ldots)$, the summary should be unfolded so that the modified cell can be resolved as in the previous case; this step relies on relation $\rightarrow_\mathfrak{u}$ (Sect. 3).

It is also possible that the localization of $x \text{->} \underline{n}$ fails, which typically indicates that the program being analyzed may dereference an invalid pointer. Besides assignment, the analysis also supports other such operations; for instance, we write $\mathbf{newV}_T^\sharp[x_0,\ldots,x_n]$ (resp., $\mathbf{delV}_T^\sharp[x_0,\ldots,x_n]$) for the operation that adds (resp., removes) variables $x_0,\ldots,x_n$ to the output state of the current transformation. They over-approximate concrete operations noted $\mathbf{newV}$ and $\mathbf{delV}$.

Weakening. The analysis of loop statements proceeds by abstract iteration over the loop body with widening. Intuitively, the widening $t_0^\sharp \triangledown_T t_1^\sharp$ of transformations $t_0^\sharp, t_1^\sharp$ returns a new transformation $t^\sharp$, such that $\gamma_T(t_i^\sharp) \subseteq \gamma_T(t^\sharp)$ for all $i \in \{0,1\}$. In the state level, widening replaces basic blocks with summaries (effectively inversing $\rightarrow_\mathfrak{u}$). In the transformation level, widening commutes with Id and $*_T$ whenever their arguments can be widened as above, and weakens them into $[\dashrightarrow]$ transformations otherwise. Furthermore, this transformation introduces summary predicates so as to ensure termination of all widening sequences [17]. Similarly, $t_0^\sharp \sqsubseteq_T t_1^\sharp$ conservatively decides inclusion test (if $t_0^\sharp \sqsubseteq_T t_1^\sharp$ holds, then $\gamma_T(t_0^\sharp) \subseteq \gamma_T(t_1^\sharp)$).

Example 5 (Analysis of the loop of append). In this example, we consider the loop at line 4 in the **append** function (Fig. 1) and only present the part of the memory reachable from c. The analysis of the loop starts with the transformation $\mathrm{Id}(\&10 \mapsto \alpha *_S \&c \mapsto \alpha *_S \mathsf{list}(\alpha)) \wedge \alpha \neq 0$. The analysis of the assignment inside the loop body forces the unfolding of **list**, and produces $\mathrm{Id}(\&\mathrm{l0} \mapsto \alpha *_\mathrm{s}$ $\alpha \cdot \underline{\mathrm{n}} \mapsto \alpha' *_\mathrm{s} \mathbf{list}(\alpha')) *_\mathrm{T} [(\&\mathrm{c} \mapsto \alpha) \dashrightarrow (\&\mathrm{c} \mapsto \alpha')] \wedge \alpha \neq 0$. The widening of these two transformations produces $\mathrm{Id}(\&\mathrm{l0} \mapsto \alpha *_\mathrm{s} \mathbf{lseg}(\alpha, \alpha') *_\mathrm{s} \mathbf{list}(\alpha')) *_\mathrm{T}$ $[(\&\mathrm{c} \mapsto \alpha) \dashrightarrow (\&\mathrm{c} \mapsto \alpha')] \wedge \alpha \neq 0$, which also turns out to be the loop invariant.

6 Abstract Composition

In this section, we set up the abstract operations that are required to rely on transformations for modular analysis. In Sect. 2, we mentioned *application* and *composition*. We remark that the application of a transformation $\mathrm{t}^\sharp$ to an abstract state $\mathrm{h}^\sharp$ boils down to the abstract composition of $\mathrm{t}^\sharp$ with $\mathrm{Id}(\mathrm{h}^\sharp)$, since the latter represents exactly the set of pairs (σ, σ) where σ is described by $\mathrm{h}^\sharp$. Moreover, we observed in Sect. 2 that composition requires to reason over intersection of abstract states. Thus, we only define intersection and composition in this section.

Abstract Intersection. In this paragraph, we set up an abstract operator $\mathbf{inter}^\sharp$, which inputs two abstract states and returns a disjunctive abstract state that over-approximates their intersection. The computation over abstract heaps is guided by a set of rewriting rules that are shown in Fig. 5. The predicate $\mathrm{h}_0^\sharp \sqcap \mathrm{h}_1^\sharp \rightsquigarrow_\sqcap H$ means that the computation of the intersection of $\mathrm{h}_0^\sharp$ and $\mathrm{h}_1^\sharp$ may produce the disjunction of abstract heaps H (there may exist several solutions for a given pair of arguments). We remark that the definition of γ_H lets symbolic variables be existentially quantified, thus they may be renamed without changing the concretization, following usual α-equivalence. Therefore, the rules of Fig. 5 assume that both arguments follow a consistent naming, although the implementation should perform α-equivalence whenever needed and maintain a correspondence of symbolic variables [5]. Rule $\sqcap_{*_\mathrm{s}}$ states that intersection can be computed locally. Rule $\sqcap_=$ expresses that intersection behaves like identity

$$\frac{\mathrm{h}_{0,0}^\sharp \sqcap \mathrm{h}_{1,0}^\sharp \rightsquigarrow_\sqcap H_0 \qquad \mathrm{h}_{0,1}^\sharp \sqcap \mathrm{h}_{1,1}^\sharp \rightsquigarrow_\sqcap H_1}{(\mathrm{h}_{0,0}^\sharp *_\mathrm{s} \mathrm{h}_{0,1}^\sharp) \sqcap (\mathrm{h}_{1,0}^\sharp *_\mathrm{s} \mathrm{h}_{1,1}^\sharp) \rightsquigarrow_\sqcap \{\mathrm{h}_0^\sharp *_\mathrm{s} \mathrm{h}_1^\sharp \mid \mathrm{h}_0^\sharp \in H_0 \wedge \mathrm{h}_1^\sharp \in H_1\}} \; \sqcap_{*_\mathrm{s}}$$

$$\frac{\mathrm{h}^\sharp \text{ is either } \mathbf{emp}, \text{ or } \mathrm{n} \cdot \underline{\mathrm{f}} \mapsto \mathrm{n}', \text{ or } \mathbf{list}(\alpha), \text{ or } \mathbf{lseg}(\alpha, \alpha')}{\mathrm{h}^\sharp \sqcap \mathrm{h}^\sharp \rightsquigarrow_\sqcap \{\mathrm{h}^\sharp\}} \; \sqcap_=$$

$$\frac{\mathbf{list}(\alpha_1) \sqcap \mathrm{h}_1^\sharp \rightsquigarrow_\sqcap H}{\mathbf{list}(\alpha_0) \sqcap (\mathbf{lseg}(\alpha_0, \alpha_1) *_\mathrm{s} \mathrm{h}_1^\sharp) \rightsquigarrow_\sqcap \{\mathbf{lseg}(\alpha_0, \alpha_1) *_\mathrm{s} \mathrm{h}^\sharp \mid \mathrm{h}^\sharp \in H\}} \; \sqcap[l, s]$$

$$\frac{\mathbf{lseg}(\alpha_1, \alpha_2) \sqcap \mathrm{h}_1^\sharp \rightsquigarrow_\sqcap H \qquad \alpha_2 \neq \alpha_1}{\mathbf{lseg}(\alpha_0, \alpha_2) \sqcap (\mathbf{lseg}(\alpha_0, \alpha_1) *_\mathrm{s} \mathrm{h}_1^\sharp) \rightsquigarrow_\sqcap \{\mathbf{lseg}(\alpha_0, \alpha_1) *_\mathrm{s} \mathrm{h}^\sharp \mid \mathrm{h}^\sharp \in H\}} \; \sqcap[s, s]$$

$$\frac{\mathrm{h}_0^\sharp \text{ contains a } \mathbf{list}(\alpha_0) \text{ or } \mathbf{lseg}(\alpha_0, \alpha_1) \text{ term} \qquad \alpha_0 \text{ carries no summary in } \mathrm{h}_1^\sharp}{\mathrm{h}_0^\sharp \sqcap \mathrm{h}_1^\sharp \rightsquigarrow_\sqcap \{\mathrm{h}^\sharp \mid \exists \mathrm{h}_{0,u}^\sharp, H, (\mathrm{h}_0^\sharp \rightarrow_{\mathfrak{u}[\alpha_0]} \mathrm{h}_{0,u}^\sharp) \wedge (\mathrm{h}_{0,u}^\sharp \sqcap \mathrm{h}_1^\sharp \rightsquigarrow_\sqcap H) \wedge \mathrm{h}^\sharp \in H\}} \; \sqcap_u$$

Fig. 5. Abstract intersection rewriting rules.

$$\frac{t_{0,0}^\sharp \,\mathring{,}\, t_{1,0}^\sharp \rightsquigarrow_\mathring{,} T_0 \qquad t_{0,1}^\sharp \,\mathring{,}\, t_{1,1}^\sharp \rightsquigarrow_\mathring{,} T_1}{(t_{0,0}^\sharp *_\mathrm{T} t_{0,1}^\sharp) \,\mathring{,}\, (t_{1,0}^\sharp *_\mathrm{T} t_{1,1}^\sharp) \rightsquigarrow_\mathring{,} \{t_0^\sharp *_\mathrm{T} t_1^\sharp \mid t_0^\sharp \in T_0 \wedge t_1^\sharp \in T_1\}} \; {}^\mathring{,}*_\mathrm{T}$$

$$\frac{h_0^\sharp \sqcap h_1^\sharp \rightsquigarrow_\sqcap H}{\mathbf{Id}(h_0^\sharp) \,\mathring{,}\, \mathbf{Id}(h_1^\sharp) \rightsquigarrow_\mathring{,} \{\mathbf{Id}(h^\sharp) \mid h^\sharp \in H\}} \; {}^\mathring{,}\mathrm{Id}$$

$$\frac{h_{0,o}^\sharp \sqcap h_{1,i}^\sharp \rightsquigarrow_\sqcap H \qquad H \neq \emptyset}{[h_{0,i}^\sharp \dashrightarrow h_{0,o}^\sharp] \,\mathring{,}\, [h_{1,i}^\sharp \dashrightarrow h_{1,o}^\sharp] \rightsquigarrow_\mathring{,} [h_{0,i}^\sharp \dashrightarrow h_{1,o}^\sharp]} \; {}^\mathring{,}\dashrightarrow$$

$$\frac{h_0^\sharp \sqcap h_{1,i}^\sharp \rightsquigarrow_\sqcap H}{\mathbf{Id}(h_0^\sharp) \,\mathring{,}\, [h_{1,i}^\sharp \dashrightarrow h_{1,o}^\sharp] \rightsquigarrow_\mathring{,} \{[h_i^\sharp \dashrightarrow h_{1,o}^\sharp] \mid h_i^\sharp \in H\}} \; {}^\mathring{,}\mathrm{Id},\dashrightarrow,l$$

$$\frac{[(h_0^\sharp *_\mathrm{s} h_{0,i}^\sharp) \dashrightarrow (h_0^\sharp *_\mathrm{s} h_{0,o}^\sharp)] \,\mathring{,}\, t_1^\sharp \rightsquigarrow_\mathring{,} T}{(\mathbf{Id}(h_0^\sharp) *_\mathrm{T} [h_{0,i}^\sharp \dashrightarrow h_{0,o}^\sharp]) \,\mathring{,}\, t_1^\sharp \rightsquigarrow_\mathring{,} T} \; {}^\mathring{,}\mathrm{weak},\mathrm{Id},l$$

$$\frac{([(h_{0,i}^\sharp *_\mathrm{s} h_{1,i}^\sharp) \dashrightarrow (h_{0,o}^\sharp *_\mathrm{s} h_{1,o}^\sharp)] *_\mathrm{T} t_2^\sharp) \,\mathring{,}\, t_3^\sharp \rightsquigarrow_\mathring{,} T}{([h_{0,i}^\sharp \dashrightarrow h_{0,o}^\sharp] *_\mathrm{T} [h_{1,i}^\sharp \dashrightarrow h_{1,o}^\sharp] *_\mathrm{T} t_2^\sharp) \,\mathring{,}\, t_3^\sharp \rightsquigarrow_\mathring{,} T} \; {}^\mathring{,}\mathrm{weak},*_\mathrm{T},l$$

$$\frac{t_0^\sharp \text{ contains an } \mathbf{list}(\alpha_0) \text{ or } \mathbf{lseg}(\alpha_0,\alpha_1) \text{ term}}{t_0^\sharp \,\mathring{,}\, t_1^\sharp \rightsquigarrow_\mathring{,} \{t^\sharp \mid \exists t_{0,u}^\sharp, (t_0^\sharp \rightarrow_{\mathfrak{U}[\alpha_0]} t_{0,u}^\sharp) \wedge (t_{0,u}^\sharp \,\mathring{,}\, t_1^\sharp \rightsquigarrow_\mathring{,} T) \wedge t^\sharp \in T\}} \; {}^\mathring{,}\mathrm{unf},l$$

Fig. 6. Abstract composition rewriting rules (rules ${}^\mathring{,}\mathrm{Id},\dashrightarrow,r$, ${}^\mathring{,}\mathrm{weak},\mathrm{Id},r$, ${}^\mathring{,}\mathrm{weak},*_\mathrm{T},r$, and ${}^\mathring{,}\mathrm{unf},r$ which are right versions of rules ${}^\mathring{,}\mathrm{Id},\dashrightarrow,l$, ${}^\mathring{,}\mathrm{weak},\mathrm{Id},l$, ${}^\mathring{,}\mathrm{weak},*_\mathrm{T},l$, and ${}^\mathring{,}\mathrm{unf},l$, can be systematically derived by symmetry, and are omitted for the sake of brevity).

when both of its arguments are the same basic term. Rules $\sqcap[l,s]$ and $\sqcap[s,s]$ implement structural reasoning over summaries. Finally, rule $\sqcap_u$ unfolds one argument so as to consider all subsequent cases. The result may differ depending on the order of application or even on the way each rule is applied. As an example, $\sqcap_{*_\mathrm{s}}$ may produce different results depending on the way both arguments are split into $h_{i,0}^\sharp$ and $h_{i,1}^\sharp$, which may affect precision. Therefore, our implementation follows a carefully designed application strategy that attempts to maximize the use of $\sqcap_=$. We omit the numerical predicate intersection (handled by a numerical domain intersection operator). Given two abstract heaps $h_0^\sharp, h_1^\sharp$, the computation of $\mathbf{inter}^\sharp(h_0^\sharp, h_1^\sharp)$ proceeds by proof search following the rules of Fig. 5 up-to commutativity (standard rule, not shown). In case this system fails to infer a solution, returning either argument provides a sound result.

Definition 3 (Abstract intersection algorithm). *The operator* $\mathbf{inter}^\sharp$ *is a partial function that inputs two abstract heaps* $h_0^\sharp, h_1^\sharp$ *and returns a disjunction of abstract heaps* H *such that* $h_0^\sharp \sqcap h_1^\sharp \rightsquigarrow_\sqcap H$ *following Fig. 5.*

Theorem 1 (Soundness of abstract intersection). *Abstract intersection is sound in the sense that, for all* $h_0^\sharp, h_1^\sharp$, $\gamma_\mathsf{H}(h_0^\sharp) \cap \gamma_\mathsf{H}(h_1^\sharp) \subseteq \gamma_\mathsf{H}(\mathbf{inter}^\sharp(h_0^\sharp, h_1^\sharp))$.

Example 6 (Abstract intersection). Let us consider:

- $h_0^\sharp = \&x \mapsto \alpha_0 *_S \&y \mapsto \alpha_2 *_S \mathbf{lseg}(\alpha_0, \alpha_2) *_S \alpha_2 \cdot \underline{n} \mapsto \alpha_3 *_S \mathbf{list}(\alpha_3)$ and
- $h_1^\sharp = \&x \mapsto \alpha_0 *_S \&y \mapsto \alpha_2 *_S \mathbf{lseg}(\alpha_0, \alpha_1) *_S \alpha_1 \cdot \underline{n} \mapsto \alpha_2 *_S \mathbf{list}(\alpha_2)$.

Then, $\mathbf{inter}^\sharp(h_0^\sharp, h_1^\sharp)$ returns $\&x \mapsto \alpha_0 *_S \&y \mapsto \alpha_2 *_S \mathbf{lseg}(\alpha_0, \alpha_1) *_S \alpha_1 \cdot \underline{n} \mapsto \alpha_2 *_S \alpha_2 \cdot \underline{n} \mapsto \alpha_3 *_S \mathbf{list}(\alpha_3)$. Note that the computation involves the structural rule $\sqcap[s, s]$ and the unfolding rule to derive this result, where both the segment between x and y and the list pointed to by y are non-empty. This result is exact (no precision is lost) and the result is effectively more precise than both arguments.

Composition of Abstract Transformations. We now study the composition of abstract transformations. Again, the computation is based on a rewriting system, that gradually processes two input transformations into an abstraction of their composition. The rules are provided in Fig. 6. The predicate $t_0^\sharp \,\mathbin{\S}\, t_1^\sharp \leadsto_\S T$ means that the effect of applying transformation $t_0^\sharp$ and then transformation $t_1^\sharp$ can be described by the union of the transformations in T. Rule $\S_{*_T}$ enables local reasoning over composition, at the transformation level. Rules $\S_{\mathbf{Id}}$ and $\S_{---\rightarrow}$ respectively compose matching identity transformations and matching modifying transformations. Similarly, $\S_{\mathbf{Id},---\rightarrow,l}$ composes an identity followed by a modifying transformation with a consistent support (this rule, as the following, has a corresponding right version that we omit for the sake of brevity). Rule $\S_{\mathbf{weak},\mathbf{Id},l}$ implements a weakening based on the inclusion $\gamma_\mathbb{T}(\mathbf{Id}(t^\sharp)) \subseteq \gamma_\mathbb{T}([t^\sharp ---\rightarrow t^\sharp])$ (the inclusion is proved in [17]). Similarly, rule $\S_{\mathbf{weak},*_T,l}$ weakens $[h_{0,i}^\sharp ---\rightarrow h_{0,o}^\sharp] *_T [h_{1,i}^\sharp ---\rightarrow h_{1,o}^\sharp]$ into $[(h_{0,i}^\sharp *_S h_{1,i}^\sharp) ---\rightarrow (h_{0,o}^\sharp *_S h_{1,o}^\sharp)]$. Finally, rule $\S_{\mathbf{unf},l}$ unfolds a summary to enable composition. The abstract composition operation performs a proof search. Just as for intersection, the composition operator may produce different results depending on the application order; our implementation relies on a strategy designed to improve precision by maximizing the use of $\S_{\mathbf{Id}}$.

Definition 4 (Abstract composition algorithm). *The operator* $\mathbf{comp}^\sharp$ *is a partial function that inputs two abstract transformations* $t_0^\sharp, t_1^\sharp$ *and returns a set of abstract transformations* T *such that* $t_0^\sharp \,\mathbin{\S}\, t_1^\sharp \leadsto_\S T$ *following Fig. 6.*

Theorem 2 (Soundness of abstract composition). *Let* $t_0^\sharp, t_1^\sharp$ *be two transformations,* $h_0^\sharp, h_1^\sharp, h_2^\sharp$ *be abstract heaps and* ν *be a valuation. We assume that* $\mathbf{comp}^\sharp(t_0^\sharp, t_1^\sharp)$ *evaluates to the set of transformations* T. *Then:*

$$(\sigma_0, \sigma_1, \nu) \in \gamma_\mathbb{T}(t_0^\sharp) \wedge (\sigma_1, \sigma_2, \nu) \in \gamma_\mathbb{T}(t_1^\sharp) \implies \exists t^\sharp \in T, (\sigma_0, \sigma_2, \nu) \in \gamma_\mathbb{T}(t^\sharp)$$

Example 7 Abstract composition and analysis compositionality). In this example, we study the classical case of an in-place list reverse code snippet:

```
1  // l points to a list
2  list *c = l; list *x = 0;
3  while( l != NULL ){ c = l->n; l->n = x; x = l; l = c; }
```

The effects of $c = 1->n$ and of $1->n = x$ can be described by the abstract transformations $t_0^\sharp$ and $t_1^\sharp$:

$$t_0^\sharp = \text{Id}(\&1 \mapsto \alpha_0 *_s \alpha_0 \cdot \underline{n} \mapsto \alpha_1 *_s \&x \mapsto \alpha_2 *_s \text{list}(\alpha_1) *_s \text{list}(\alpha_2))$$
$$*_T \, [(\&c \mapsto \alpha_3) \dashrightarrow (\&c \mapsto \alpha_1)]$$
$$t_1^\sharp = \text{Id}(\&1 \mapsto \alpha_0 *_s \&x \mapsto \alpha_2 *_s \&c \mapsto \alpha_1 *_s \text{list}(\alpha_1) *_s \text{list}(\alpha_2))$$
$$*_T \, [(\alpha_0 \cdot \underline{n} \mapsto \alpha_1) \dashrightarrow (\alpha_0 \cdot \underline{n} \mapsto \alpha_2)]$$

The composition of these two transformations needs to apply the weakening rules to match terms that are under the Id constructors. The result is the following transformation $t_0^\sharp \, \mathring{,} \, t_1^\sharp$:

$$\text{Id}(\&1 \mapsto \alpha_0 *_s \&x \mapsto \alpha_2 *_s \text{list}(\alpha_1) *_s \text{list}(\alpha_2))$$
$$*_T \, [(\&c \mapsto \alpha_3) \dashrightarrow (\&c \mapsto \alpha_1)] *_T [(\alpha_0 \cdot \underline{n} \mapsto \alpha_1) \dashrightarrow (\alpha_0 \cdot \underline{n} \mapsto \alpha_2)]$$

This description is actually a very precise account for the effect of the sequence of these two assignment commands. This example shows that composition may be used not only for interprocedural analysis (as we show in the next section), but also to supersede some operations of the intraprocedural analysis of Sect. 5.

Example 8 (Abstract application). As observed at the beginning of the section, composition may also be used as a means to analyze the application of a transformation to an abstract state. We consider the composition of the transformation $t^\sharp$ corresponding to function **append** (shown in Example 2 and Fig. 1) and the abstract pre-state $h^\sharp = \&10 \mapsto \alpha_0 *_s \&11 \mapsto \alpha_2 *_s \text{lseg}(\alpha_0, \alpha_1) *_s \alpha_1 \cdot \underline{n} \mapsto \alpha_3 *_s \text{list}(\alpha_2) \wedge \alpha_3 = \text{0x0}$. Then, the composition $\text{Id}(h^\sharp) \, \mathring{,} \, t^\sharp$ returns:

$$\&10 \mapsto \alpha_0 *_s \&11 \mapsto \alpha_2 *_s \text{lseg}(\alpha_0, \alpha_1) *_s \alpha_1 \cdot \underline{n} \mapsto \alpha_2 *_s \text{list}(\alpha_2)$$

7   Interprocedural Analysis Based on Function Summaries

In this section, we study two mutually dependent aspects: the application of summaries at call-sites and their inference by static analysis in a top down manner. We first focus on non-recursive calls and discuss recursive calls at the end of the section. The analysis maintains a context summary $(h_f^\sharp, t_f^\sharp)$ for each procedure f. Initially, this context summary is set to $(\bot, \bot)$. When the analysis reaches a call to procedure f it should attempt to utilize the existing summary (Sect. 7.1). When the existing summary does not account for all the states that may reach the current context, a new summary needs to be computed first (Sect. 7.2).

7.1   Analysis of a Call Site Using an Existing Summary

We assume a procedure **proc** $f(p_0, \ldots, p_k)\{C\}$ and a sound context summary $(h_f^\sharp, t_f^\sharp)$. We consider the analysis $[\![f(x_0, \ldots, x_k)]\!]_T^\sharp$ of a call to this procedure, with transformation $t_{\text{pre}}^\sharp$ as a pre-transformation. To analyze the call, the analysis should (1) process parameter passing, (2) detect which part of $t_{\text{pre}}^\sharp$ may be modified by f, (3) check whether the context summary covers this context, and (4) apply the summary, if (3) succeeds (the case where it fails is studied in Sect. 7.2).

Parameter Passing. Parameter passing boils down to creating the variables $p_0, \ldots, p_k$ using transfer function $\mathbf{newV_T}^{\sharp}$ and then to analyzing assignment statements $p_0 = x_0, \ldots, p_k = x_k$. These operations can all be done using the transfer functions defined in Sect. 5:

$$t^{\sharp}_{\mathrm{pars}} = ([\![p_k = x_k]\!]^{\sharp}_{\mathsf{T}} \circ \ldots \circ [\![p_0 = x_0]\!]^{\sharp}_{\mathsf{T}} \circ \mathbf{newV_T}^{\sharp}[p_0, \ldots, p_k])(t^{\sharp}_{\mathrm{pre}})$$

Procedure Footprint. To identify the fragment of the abstract heap that f can view and may modify, the analysis should first extract from $t^{\sharp}_{\mathrm{pars}}$ an abstraction of the set of states that enter the body of f. This is the goal of function $\mathcal{O} : \mathbb{T} \to \mathbb{H}$:

$$\mathcal{O}(\mathrm{Id}(h^{\sharp})) = h^{\sharp} \qquad\qquad \mathcal{O}(t^{\sharp}_0 *_{\mathsf{T}} t^{\sharp}_1) = \mathcal{O}(t^{\sharp}_0) *_{\mathsf{S}} \mathcal{O}(t^{\sharp}_1)$$
$$\mathcal{O}([h^{\sharp}_0 \dashrightarrow h^{\sharp}_1]) = h^{\sharp}_1 \qquad\qquad \mathcal{O}(t^{\sharp} \wedge c^{\sharp}) = \mathcal{O}(t^{\sharp}) \wedge c^{\sharp}$$

Intuitively, $\mathcal{O}$ projects the "output" part of a transformation. Thus $\mathcal{O}(t^{\sharp}_{\mathrm{pars}})$ over-approximates the set of states that enter C. However, only the fragment of $\mathcal{O}(t^{\sharp}_{\mathrm{pars}})$ that is reachable from the parameters of f is relevant. Given an abstract heap $h^{\sharp}$, we can compute the set of symbolic names $R[h^{\sharp}]$ that are relevant based on the following rules:

$$\frac{}{(\&p_i) \in R[h^{\sharp}]} \qquad\qquad \frac{n \in R[h^{\sharp}] \qquad h^{\sharp} \text{ contains a term } n \cdot \underline{f} \mapsto n' \text{ or } \mathbf{lseg}(n, n')}{n' \in R[h^{\sharp}]}$$

The slice $\mathcal{R}[p_0, \ldots, p_k](h^{\sharp})$ of $h^{\sharp}$ with respect to $p_0, \ldots, p_k$ retains only the terms of $h^{\sharp}$ that contain only names in $R[h^{\sharp}]$ defined as the least solution of the above rules. Similarly, we let $\mathcal{I}[p_0, \ldots, p_k](h^{\sharp})$ be the abstract heap made of the remaining terms. Therefore, we have the equality $h^{\sharp} = \mathcal{R}[p_0, \ldots, p_k](h^{\sharp}) *_{\mathsf{S}} \mathcal{I}[p_0, \ldots, p_k](h^{\sharp})$.

Context Summary Coverage Test. Based on the above, the set of states that reach the body of f under the calling context defined by $t^{\sharp}_{\mathrm{pre}}$ can be over-approximated by $h^{\sharp}_{\mathrm{in,f}} = \mathcal{R}[p_0, \ldots, p_k](\mathcal{O}(t^{\sharp}_{\mathrm{pars}}))$. We let $h^{\sharp}_{\mathrm{rem}} = \mathcal{I}[p_0, \ldots, p_k](\mathcal{O}(t^{\sharp}_{\mathrm{pars}}))$ be the remainder part. The context summary $(h^{\sharp}_f, t^{\sharp}_f)$ covers $h^{\sharp}_{\mathrm{in,f}}$ if and only if $h^{\sharp}_{\mathrm{in,f}} \sqsubseteq_{\mathbb{H}} h^{\sharp}_f$ holds where $\sqsubseteq_{\mathbb{H}}$ is a sound abstract state inclusion test as defined in, e.g., [6, 13]. When this condition does not hold, the context summary should be re-computed with a more general pre-condition (this point is discussed in Sect. 7.2).

Summary Application. Given the above notation, the effect of the procedure (described by $t^{\sharp}_f$) should be applied to $h^{\sharp}_{\mathrm{in,f}}$ whereas $h^{\sharp}_{\mathrm{rem}}$ should be preserved. To do this, the following transformation should be composed with the abstract transformation $t^{\sharp}_f *_{\mathsf{T}} \mathrm{Id}(h^{\sharp}_{\mathrm{rem}})$ (note that the identity part is applied to the part of the pre-transformation that is not relevant to the execution of the body of f).

Data: Existing context summary $(h_f^\sharp, t_f^\sharp)$ for **proc** $f(p_0, \ldots, p_k)\{C\}$
Data: Input transformation $t_{pre}^\sharp$ (computation before the call)
Result: Output transformation $t_{post}^\sharp$ (computation before the call + body of f)
Result: Update of the context summary if it does not cover the context of $t_{pre}^\sharp$

1 $t_{pars}^\sharp \leftarrow [\![p_k = x_k]\!]_T^\sharp \circ \ldots \circ [\![p_0 = x_0]\!]_T^\sharp \circ \mathbf{newV}_T^\sharp[p_0, \ldots, p_k](t_{pre}^\sharp)$;
2 $h_{in,f}^\sharp = \mathcal{R}[p_0, \ldots, p_k](\mathcal{O}(t_{pars}^\sharp))$;
3 $h_{rem}^\sharp = \mathcal{I}[p_0, \ldots, p_k](\mathcal{O}(t_{pars}^\sharp))$;
4 **if** $\neg(h_{in,f}^\sharp \sqsubseteq_H h_f^\sharp)$ **then**
5 $\quad$ $h_f^\sharp \leftarrow h_f^\sharp \triangledown_H h_{in,f}^\sharp$;
6 $\quad$ $t_f^\sharp \leftarrow [\![C]\!]_T^\sharp(\mathrm{Id}(h_f^\sharp))$
7 **end**
8 $t_{post}^\sharp \leftarrow \mathbf{delV}_T^\sharp[p_0, \ldots p_k](\mathbf{comp}^\sharp(t_{pars}^\sharp, t_f^\sharp *_T \mathrm{Id}(h_{rem}^\sharp)))$

Fig. 7. Interprocedural analysis: algorithm for the analysis of a procedure call.

Thus, the transformation that accounts for the computation from the program entry point till the return point of f is:

$$\mathbf{delV}_T^\sharp[p_0, \ldots p_k](\mathbf{comp}^\sharp(t_{pars}^\sharp, t_f^\sharp *_T \mathrm{Id}(h_{rem}^\sharp)))$$

Example 9 (Context summary coverage and application). In this example, we assume the context summary defined in Example 3 for procedure **append**:

- $h^\sharp = \&10 \mapsto \alpha_0 *_S \mathbf{lseg}(\alpha_0, \alpha_1) *_S \alpha_1 \cdot \underline{n} \mapsto 0x0 *_S \&11 \mapsto \alpha_2 *_S \mathbf{list}(\alpha_2)$;
- $t^\sharp = \mathrm{Id}(\&10 \mapsto \alpha_0 *_S \mathbf{lseg}(\alpha_0, \alpha_1)) *_T [(\alpha_1 \cdot \underline{n} \mapsto 0x0) \dashrightarrow (\alpha_1 \cdot \underline{n} \mapsto \alpha_2)] *_T \mathrm{Id}(\&11 \mapsto \alpha_2 *_S \mathbf{list}(\alpha_2))$

Moreover, we consider the call **append(a,b)** with the abstract transformation below as a pre-condition (note that variable c is not accessed by **append**):

$$\mathrm{Id}(\&a \mapsto \alpha_0 *_S \alpha_0 \cdot \underline{n} \mapsto 0x0 *_S \&b \mapsto \alpha_1 *_S \alpha_1 \cdot \underline{n} \mapsto 0x0 *_S \&c \mapsto \alpha_3)$$

After parameter passing, computation of the heap fragment f may view, and projection of the output, we obtain the abstract state $\&10 \mapsto \alpha_0 *_S \alpha_0 \cdot \underline{n} \mapsto 0x0 *_S \&11 \mapsto \alpha_1 *_S \alpha_1 \cdot \underline{n} \mapsto 0x0$, which is obviously included in $h^\sharp$. The composition with the summary of the procedure produces the abstract transformation below:

$$\mathrm{Id}(\&a \mapsto \alpha_0) *_T [(\alpha_0 \cdot \underline{n} \mapsto 0x0) \dashrightarrow (\alpha_0 \cdot \underline{n} \mapsto \alpha_1)]$$
$$*_T \mathrm{Id}(\&b \mapsto \alpha_1 *_S \alpha_1 \cdot \underline{n} \mapsto 0x0 *_S \&c \mapsto \alpha_3)$$

The whole algorithm is shown in Fig. 7. It implements the steps described above and in Sect. 7.2. The case considered in this subsection (when $h_{in,f}^\sharp \sqsubseteq_H h_f^\sharp$ holds) corresponds to the case where the if branch at lines 5–6 is not taken.

7.2   Inference of a New Context Summary

We now discuss the case where the previously existing context summary of f does not cover the executions corresponding to $t^\sharp$. As mentioned above, this corresponds to the case where the abstract inclusion $h^\sharp_{\mathrm{in},f} \sqsubseteq_\mathbb{H} h^\sharp_f$ does not hold.

Summary Computation. The computation of a new context summary should take into account a context that is general enough to encompass both $h^\sharp_f$ and $h^\sharp_{\mathrm{in},f}$:

- the new abstract context is $h^\sharp_f \triangledown_\mathbb{H} h^\sharp_{\mathrm{in},f}$ using abstract state widening $\triangledown_\mathbb{H}$ [6];
- the new summary related to this abstract context is derived by analysis of the body of f, thus by updating $t^\sharp_f$ with $[\![C]\!]^\sharp_\mathbb{T}(\mathrm{Id}(h^\sharp_f \triangledown_\mathbb{T} h^\sharp_{\mathrm{in},f}))$.

Then, the context summary for f is updated with this new context summary.

Application. Once a new summary has been computed, by definition, it satisfies the inclusion $h^\sharp_{\mathrm{in},f} \sqsubseteq_\mathbb{H} h^\sharp_f$, thus it can be applied so as to compute an abstract transformation after the call to f as shown in Sect. 7.1.

The overall procedure call analysis algorithm is displayed in Fig. 7. The case examined in this subsection corresponds to the case where the **if** branch at lines 5–6 is taken. We observe that it necessarily occurs whenever a procedure is analyzed for the first time, as context summaries are initially set to $(\bot, \bot)$. Moreover, we note that the application of the summary after its update is done as in Sect. 7.1.

The following result formalizes the soundness of Fig. 7, under the assumption that there is no recursive call.

Theorem 3 (Soundness of the analysis of a procedure call using a context summary). *We consider the call to f with the abstract transformation $t^\sharp_{\mathrm{pre}}$ as input, and the post-condition $t^\sharp_{\mathrm{post}}$ returned by the algorithm of Fig. 7. We denote by $(h^\sharp_f, t^\sharp_f)$ the context summary for f after the analysis of the call. We let $(\sigma_0, \sigma_1, \nu) \in \gamma_\mathbb{T}(t^\sharp_{\mathrm{pre}})$, $\sigma'_1 \in [\![p_0 = x_0]\!]_\mathbb{T} \circ \ldots \circ [\![p_k = x_k]\!]_\mathbb{T} \circ \mathbf{newV}[p_0, \ldots p_k](\{\sigma_1\})$, $\sigma'_2 \in [\![C]\!]_\mathbb{T}(\{\sigma'_1\})$, and $\sigma_2 \in \mathbf{delV}[p_0, \ldots, p_k](\{\sigma'_2\})$ (i.e., $\sigma_2 \in [\![f(x_0, \ldots, x_k)]\!]_\mathbb{T}(\{\sigma_1\}))$. Then, the following property holds:*

$$(\sigma_0, \sigma_2, \nu) \in \gamma_\mathbb{T}(t^\sharp_{\mathrm{post}}) \wedge (\sigma'_1, \nu) \in \gamma_\mathbb{H}(h^\sharp_f) \wedge (\sigma'_1, \sigma'_2, \nu) \in \gamma_\mathbb{T}(t^\sharp_f)$$

This result means that not only the transformation $t^\sharp_{\mathrm{post}}$ over-approximates the state after the call, but also the new context summary accounts for this call. This entails that context summaries account for all the calls that are encountered in the analysis of a complete interprocedural program. Moreover, Theorem 3 entails Eq. 1 for procedure calls.

Example 10 (Context summary computation). In this example, we consider the function **append** again, but assume that the analysis starts with the $(\bot, \bot)$ context summary for it. We study the code **append(a, b); append(a, c);** where a, b, and c are initially lists of length 1. Then:

- the first call results in the update of the summary with a context summary $(h^\sharp, t^\sharp)$ where $h^\sharp$ assumes that the first argument is a single list element, i.e., is of the form $\&10 \mapsto \alpha_0 *_s \alpha_0 \cdot \underline{n} \mapsto 0x0 *_s \&11 \mapsto \alpha_1 *_s \ldots;$
- when the second call is encountered this first summary does not cover the second context (at this point, the argument a has length 2), thus a new context summary needs to be calculated; this new summary $(h^\sharp, t^\sharp)$ is such that $h^\sharp$ only assumes that the first argument may be a list of any length (as derived by widening), i.e., it is of the form $\&10 \mapsto \alpha_0 *_s \mathbf{lseg}(\alpha_0, \alpha_1) *_s \alpha_1 \cdot \underline{n} \mapsto 0x0 *_s \&11 \mapsto \alpha_1 *_s \ldots$.

This last summary may still not be as general as the summary shown in Example 9, and may thus be generalized even more at subsequent call points.

Analysis of Recursive Calls. So far, we have focused on the case where there are no recursive calls. Actually, the presence of recursive calls changes relatively little to the principle of our analysis (although the formalization would be significantly heavier and is left out). Indeed, it only requires to extend the algorithm of Fig. 7 with a fixpoint computation over context summaries, so as to determine an over-approximation of both components of the procedure context summary.

- when a recursive call is encountered and when the calling context is not accounted for in the current context summary (Fig. 7, condition at line 4 evaluated to false), the $h_f^\sharp$ component should be widened and the current $t_f^\sharp$ should be used directly;
- at the end of the analysis of the procedure body, the $t_f^\sharp$ component should be widened with the previously known transformation, and the analysis of the procedure body iterated until this transformation stabilizes.

Convergence is ensured by widening both on abstract states and transformations.

8 Experimental Evaluation

In this section, we report on the evaluation of the interprocedural analysis based on function summaries, with respect to the following questions:

1. Is it able to infer precise invariants?
2. Does it scale better than a classical call-string-based analysis?
3. How effective are context summaries, i.e., do they often have to be recomputed?

We have implemented the interprocedural analysis based on context summaries for a large fragment of the C language. Our tool is a plugin for Frama-C [20]. It supports conventional control flow structures of C and can be parameterized by the inductive definition of the structure to consider, as in [5]. However, it leaves out non recursive structures and data-types that are not immediately related to the analysis principle (strings, arrays, numeric types). Furthermore, we have

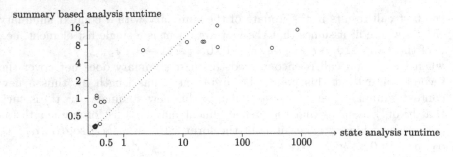

Fig. 8. Per-function comparison of analysis runtime (times in seconds)

also implemented as another extension of Frama-C an analysis relying on the call-string approach, i.e., that inlines procedures at call sites.

Experiments and Raw Data. We did two experiments. First, we ran the two analyses on a fragment of the GNU Emacs 25.3 editor. This fragment comprises 22 functions of the Fx_show_tip feature and is implemented in C. It manipulates descriptions of Lisp objects including lists built as Cons pairs. The analyzed code corresponds to about 3 kLOC. Analyses were ran on an Intel Core i7 laptop at 2.3 GHz with 16 Gb of RAM. The raw data are provided in Appendix A and the following paragraphs discuss the main points related to the above questions. Second, we analyzed a set of basic recursive functions on trees and lists to validate the recursive call analysis.

Precision. We compared the result of the analysis of the body of each procedure. More precisely, we checked whether the transformation computed for the whole procedure body for its entry abstract state (the first component of context summaries) is at least as precise as the post-condition produced by the state analysis. For 15 functions, the body contains nested calls and the result is as precise. The remaining 7 functions do not contain any call, thus are not relevant to validate the absence of precision loss at call sites.

Scalability. The total measured analysis time was 14.20 s for the transformation-based analysis against 877.12 s for the state analysis, which shows a high overall speedup. Secondly, we show the average analysis time of the body of each function in Fig. 8 (these values are average analysis times, and not total time spent analyzing each function, as the effectiveness of summary reuse is the topic of the next paragraph). We observe that for some functions the speedup is low or even negative. These functions mostly correspond to low analysis times. Upon inspection, they all occupy a low position in the call tree: they call few functions, and the transformation analysis overhead is not compensated by a high gain from many summary applications to avoid the analysis of down calls. Conversely functions at the top of the call graph (such as the entry point) show a very high gain.

Effectiveness. Finally, we assessed the effectiveness of the summary reuse, which depends not only on the call graph shape (functions that are called at a single site offer no gain opportunity) but also on the function behavior and the analysis (depending on the contexts that are encountered, some procedure may need to be reanalyzed multiple times or not). We observed that only one procedure needed to be reanalyzed (Fcons was reanalyzed 3 times). All other summaries were computed only once (i.e., the branch at lines 4–6 in Fig. 7 is taken only once). For functions called at a single point (11 of the total) summaries could not be reused, but for 8 functions, summaries were reused multiple times (3 to 44 times). By contrast, the state analysis had to reanalyze most functions several times: in particular 11 functions were reanalyzed 15 times or more (up to 296 times). Therefore, the summary-based analysis provides significant gain even for small functions.

Recursive Calls. We ran the analysis on a series of recursive implementations of classical functions on lists and binary trees, including size, allocation, deallocation, insertion, search and deep copy, and also list concatenation and filter. For all these functions, the expected invariants could be inferred in under 5 ms (Appendix A).

9 Related Works and Conclusion

Since Sharir and Pnueli's seminal paper [35], many works have studied approaches to interprocedural analyses. The relational approach strives for modularity, which has been a concern in static analysis even beyond interprocedural code [8, 10]. A major advantage of modular approaches is to avoid the reanalysis of program fragments that are called repeatedly. However, it is generally difficult to apply as it requires an accurate and efficient representation for summaries. While relational numerical abstract domains [11] naturally provide a way to capture numerical input/output relations [26,27], this is harder to achieve when considering memory abstractions. The TVLA framework [33] supports such relation using the classical "primed variables" technique [18,19] where input and output variables are distinguished using prime symbols. Some pointer analyses such as [12] rely on specific classes of procedure summaries to enable modular analysis. However, separation logic [28] does not naturally support this since formulas describe regions of a given heap. The classical solution involves the tabulation of pairs of separation logic formulas [2,15,22], but this approach does not allow to relate the description of heap regions in a fine manner. To circumvent this, we use transformations introduced in [17], which are built on connectors inspired by separation logic. The advantage is twofold: it enables not only a more concise representation of transformations (since tables of pairs may need to grow large to precisely characterize the effect of procedures) but also a more local description of the relation between procedure input and output states. Our graph representation of abstract states and transformations opens the way to a resolution of the frame problem [29,30] using intersection operation. The results of our top-down, context summary-based analysis confirm that this approach brings a gain in analysis scalability once the upfront cost of summaries is amortized.

Many pointer analyses and weak forms of shape analyses have introduced specific techniques in order to construct and compute procedure summaries [21,23,25]. These works typically rely on some notion of graph that describes both knowledge about memory entities and procedure calls, therefore the interprocedural analysis reduces to graph algorithms. Moreover, context sensitivity information may be embedded into these graphs. Our approach differs in that it relies on a specific algebra of summaries, although we may also augment our summaries with context information. Another difference is that the summary predicates our abstract domain is based on allow a very high level of precision and that the abstract procedure call analysis algorithm (with intersection and composition) aims at preserving this precision. We believe that two interesting avenues for future works would consider the combination of various levels of context sensitivity and of less less expressive summaries with our analysis framework.

A very wide range of techniques have been developed to better cope with interprocedural analysis, many of which could be combined with context summaries. First, we do not consider tabulation of procedure summaries [10], however, we could introduce this technique together with some amount of context sensitivity [1]. Indeed, while relations reduce the need for tables of abstract pre- and post-conditions, combining context summaries and finer context abstraction may result in increased precision [7]. Bi-abduction [3] has been proposed as a technique to infer relevant abstract pre-conditions of procedures. In [3], this process was implemented on a state abstract domain, but the core principle of the technique is orthogonal to that choice, thus bi-abduction could also be applied to abstract transformations. Moreover, while our analysis proceeds top-down, it would be interesting to consider the combination with a bottom-up inference of summaries for some procedures [4]. Last, many works have considered the abstraction of the stack-frame and of the relations between the stack frame structure and the heap structures manipulated by procedures [31,32]. The notion of cut-points has been proposed in [29,30] to describe structures tightly intertwined with the stack. An advantage of our technique is that the use of an abstraction based on transformations which can express that a region of the heap is preserved reduces the need to reason over cutpoints.

Acknowledgments. We would like to thank the anonymous reviewers for their suggestions that helped greatly improve the quality of this paper. This work has received support from the French ANR as part of the VeriAMOS grant.

A   Raw Experimental Data

Analysis of Fx_show_tip. The table below lists the per call average analysis times of each procedure, whether the summary analysis is as precise as the state analysis ("as precise" means the results are at least as precise; "irrel." means the measure is irrelevant as the function body does not contain any call) and the depth in the call graph.

Function name	State time (s)	Summary time (s)	Precision	Depth
Fcons	0.33	0.34	irrel.	8
list2	0.32	0.32	as precise	7
list4	0.33	0.32	as precise	7
Fassq	2.16	6.46	irrel.	6
Fcar	0.32	0.33	irrel.	3
Fcdr	0.33	0.33	irrel.	2
Fnthcdr	0.33	0.34	irrel.	3
Fnth	0.34	0.34	as precise	2
make_monitor_attribute_list	0.33	0.74	as precise	6
check_x_display_info	0.33	0.33	irrel.	3
Fx_display_monitor_attributes_list	0.41	0.86	as precise	2
x_get_monitor_for_frame	0.40	0.37	irrel.	6
x_make_monitor_attribute_list	0.47	0.87	as precise	5
x_get_monitor_attributes_fallback	0.35	1.01	as precise	4
x_get_monitor_attributes	0.35	1.11	as precise	3
x_get_arg	11.82	8.76	as precise	5
x_frame_get_arg	21.75	8.87	as precise	4
x_default_parameter	23.00	8.91	as precise	3
compute_tip_xy	38.24	16.80	as precise	1
x_default_font_parameter	39.06	7.17	as precise	2
x_create_tip_frame	321.77	6.96	as precise	1
Fx_show_tip	877.12	14.20	as precise	0

The table below lists the number of times the body of a procedure is reanalyzed:

– column #state counts reanalyses by the state analysis;
– column #total counts the number of times a call site to this procedure is encountered by the summary analysis;
– column #recomp counts the number of times the summary based analysis needs to reanalyze the body of this procedure to come up with more general summary;
– column #reuse counts the number of times a summary is reused without recomputation.

Function name	#state	#total	#recomp	#reuse
Fcons	296	47	3	44
list2	12	2	1	1
list4	24	4	1	3
Fassq	64	16	1	15
Fcar	24	1	1	0
Fcdr	12	4	1	3
Fnthcdr	24	1	1	0
Fnth	24	8	1	7
make_monitor_attribute_list	6	2	1	1
check_x_display_info	3	1	1	0
Fx_display_monitor_attributes_list	3	1	1	0
x_get_monitor_for_frame	6	2	1	1
x_make_monitor_attribute_list	3	1	1	0
x_get_monitor_attributes_fallback	3	1	1	0
x_get_monitor_attributes	3	1	1	0
x_get_arg	19	5	1	4
x_frame_get_arg	15	1	1	0
x_default_parameter	15	15	1	14
compute_tip_xy	3	3	1	2
x_default_font_parameter	1	1	1	0
x_create_tip_frame	1	1	1	0
Fx_show_tip	1	1	1	0

Analysis of recursive list and tree classical algorithms. The table below lists the analysis times of a series of classical functions over lists and trees.

Structure	function	time (ms)
List	length	1.256
List	get_n	2.179
List	alloc	1.139
List	dealloc	0.842
List	concat	1.833
List	map	0.904
List	deep_copy	1.540
List	filter	3.357
Tree	visit	1.078
Tree	size	1.951
Tree	search	3.818
Tree	dealloc	1.391
Tree	insert	5.083
Tree	deep_copy	2.603

References

1. Bourdoncle, F.: Abstract interpretation by dynamic partitioning. J. Funct. Program **2**(4), 407–423 (1992)
2. Calcagno, C., Distefano, D., O'Hearn, P.W., Yang, H.: Footprint analysis: a shape analysis that discovers preconditions. In: Nielson, H.R., Filé, G. (eds.) SAS 2007. LNCS, vol. 4634, pp. 402–418. Springer, Heidelberg (2007). https://doi.org/10.1007/978-3-540-74061-2_25
3. Calcagno, C., Distefano, D., O'Hearn, P., Yang, H.: Compositional shape analysis by means of bi-abduction. In: Symposium on Principles of Programming Languages (POPL), pp. 289–300. ACM (2009)
4. Castelnuovo, G., Naik, M., Rinetzky, N., Sagiv, M., Yang, H.: Modularity in lattices: a case study on the correspondence between top-down and bottom-up analysis. In: Blazy, S., Jensen, T. (eds.) SAS 2015. LNCS, vol. 9291, pp. 252–274. Springer, Heidelberg (2015). https://doi.org/10.1007/978-3-662-48288-9_15
5. Chang, B.Y.E., Rival, X.: Relational inductive shape analysis. In Symposium on Principles of Programming Languages (POPL), pp. 247–260. ACM (2008)
6. Chang, B.-Y.E., Rival, X., Necula, G.C.: Shape analysis with structural invariant checkers. In: Nielson, H.R., Filé, G. (eds.) SAS 2007. LNCS, vol. 4634, pp. 384–401. Springer, Heidelberg (2007). https://doi.org/10.1007/978-3-540-74061-2_24
7. Chatterjee, R., Ryder, B.G., Landi, W.A.: Relevant context inference. In: Symposium on Principles of Programming Languages (POPL), pp. 133–146. ACM (1999)
8. Codish, M., Debray, S.K., Giacobazzi, R.: Compositional analysis of modular logic programs. In: Symposium on Principles of Programming Languages (POPL), pp. 451–464. ACM (1993)
9. Cousot, P., Cousot, R.: Abstract interpretation: a unified lattice model for static analysis of programs by construction or approximation of fixpoints. In: Symposium on Principles of Programming Languages (POPL), ACM (1977)
10. Cousot, P., Cousot, R.: Modular static program analysis. In: Horspool, R.N. (ed.) CC 2002. LNCS, vol. 2304, pp. 159–179. Springer, Heidelberg (2002). https://doi.org/10.1007/3-540-45937-5_13
11. Cousot, P., Halbwachs, N.: Automatic discovery of linear restraints among variables of a program. In: Symposium on Principles of Programming Languages (POPL), pp. 84–97. ACM (1978)
12. Dillig, I., Dillig, T., Aiken, A. and Sagiv, M.: Precise and compact modular procedure summaries for heap manipulating programs. In: Hall, M.W., Padua, D.A. (eds.) Conference on Programming Languages Design and Implementation (PLDI), pp. 567–577. ACM (2011)
13. Distefano, D., O'Hearn, P.W., Yang, H.: A local shape analysis based on separation logic. In: Hermanns, H., Palsberg, J. (eds.) TACAS 2006. LNCS, vol. 3920, pp. 287–302. Springer, Heidelberg (2006). https://doi.org/10.1007/11691372_19
14. Dudka, K., Peringer, P., Vojnar, T.: Predator: a practical tool for checking manipulation of dynamic data structures using separation logic. In: Gopalakrishnan, G., Qadeer, S. (eds.) CAV 2011. LNCS, vol. 6806, pp. 372–378. Springer, Heidelberg (2011). https://doi.org/10.1007/978-3-642-22110-1_29
15. Gulavani, B.S., Chakraborty, S., Ramalingam, G., Nori, A.V.: Bottom-up shape analysis. In: Palsberg, J., Su, Z. (eds.) SAS 2009. LNCS, vol. 5673, pp. 188–204. Springer, Heidelberg (2009). https://doi.org/10.1007/978-3-642-03237-0_14
16. Illous, H.: Abstract Heap Relations for a Compositional Shape Analysis. PhD thesis, École Normale Supérieure (2018)

17. Illous, H., Lemerre, M., Rival, X.: A relational shape abstract domain. In: Barrett, C., Davies, M., Kahsai, T. (eds.) NFM 2017. LNCS, vol. 10227, pp. 212–229. Springer, Cham (2017). https://doi.org/10.1007/978-3-319-57288-8_15

18. Jeannet, B., Loginov, A., Reps, T., Sagiv, M.: A relational approach to interprocedural shape analysis. ACM Trans. Program. Lang. Syst. (TOPLAS) 32(2), 5 (2010)

19. Jeannet, B., Loginov, A., Reps, T.W., Sagiv, S.: A relational approach to interprocedural shape analysis. In: Static Analysis Symposium (SAS), pp. 246–264 (2004)

20. Kirchner, F., Kosmatov, N., Prevosto, V., Signoles, J., Yakobowski, B.: Frama-c: a software analysis perspective. Formal Aspects Comput. 27(3), 573–609 (2015)

21. Lattner, C., Lenharth, A., Adve, V.: Making context-sensitive points-to analysis with heap cloning practical for the real world. In: Ferrante, J., McKinley, K.S. (eds), Conference on Programming Languages Design and Implementation (PLDI), pp. 278–289. ACM (2007)

22. Le, Q.L., Gherghina, C., Qin, S., Chin, W.-N.: Shape analysis via second-order biabduction. In: Biere, A., Bloem, R. (eds.) CAV 2014. LNCS, vol. 8559, pp. 52–68. Springer, Cham (2014). https://doi.org/10.1007/978-3-319-08867-9_4

23. Lei, Y., Sui, Y.: Fast and precise handling of positive weight cycles for field-sensitive pointer analysis. In: Chang, B.-Y.E. (ed.) SAS 2019. LNCS, vol. 11822, pp. 27–47. Springer, Cham (2019). https://doi.org/10.1007/978-3-030-32304-2_3

24. Manna, Z., Pnueli, A.: Axiomatic approach to total correctness of programs. Acta Informatica 3, 243–263 (1974)

25. Marron, M., Hermenegildo, M., Kapur, D., Stefanovic, D.: Efficient context-sensitive shape analysis with graph based heap models. In: Hendren, L. (ed.) CC 2008. LNCS, vol. 4959, pp. 245–259. Springer, Heidelberg (2008). https://doi.org/10.1007/978-3-540-78791-4_17

26. Müller-Olm, M., Seidl, H.: Precise interprocedural analysis through linear algebra. In: Symposium on Principles of Programming Languages (POPL), pp. 330–341. ACM (2004)

27. Popeea, C., Chin, W.-N.: Inferring disjunctive postconditions. In: Okada, M., Satoh, I. (eds.) ASIAN 2006. LNCS, vol. 4435, pp. 331–345. Springer, Heidelberg (2007). https://doi.org/10.1007/978-3-540-77505-8_26

28. Reynolds, J.: Separation logic: a logic for shared mutable data structures. In: Symposium on Logics In Computer Science (LICS), pp. 55–74. IEEE (2002)

29. Rinetzky, N., Bauer, J., Reps, T., Sagiv, M., Wilhelm, R.: A semantics for procedure local heaps and its abstractions. In: Symposium on Principles of Programming Languages (POPL), pp. 296–309 (2005)

30. Noam Rinetzky, Mooly Sagiv, and Eran Yahav. Interprocedural shape analysis for cutpoint-free programs. In: Hankin, C., Siveroni, I. (eds.) Static Analysis Symposium (SAS), Springer, Berlin, pp. 284–302 (2005) https://doi.org/10.1007/11547662_20

31. Rinetzky, N., Sagiv, M.: Interprocedural shape analysis for recursive programs. In: Wilhelm, R. (ed.) CC 2001. LNCS, vol. 2027, pp. 133–149. Springer, Heidelberg (2001). https://doi.org/10.1007/3-540-45306-7_10

32. Rival, X., Chang, B.Y.E.: Calling context abstraction with shapes. In: Symposium on Principles of Programming Languages (POPL), pp. 173–186. ACM (2011)

33. Sagiv, M., Reps, T., Whilhelm, R.: Solving shape-analysis problems in languages with destructive updating. ACM Trans. Program. Lang. Syst. (TOPLAS) 20(1), 50 (1998)

34. Schaefer, I., Podelski, A.: Local reasoning for termination. In: COSMICAH 2005: Workshop on Verification of COncurrent Systems with dynaMIC Allocated Heaps, pp. 16–30 (2005)
35. Sharir, M., Pnueli, A.: Two approaches to interprocedural data flow analysis. In: Program Flow Analysis: Theory and Applications, chapter 7. Prentice-Hall Inc, Englewood Cliffs, New Jersey (1981)

Probabilistic Lipschitz Analysis of Neural Networks

Ravi Mangal[1]([⊠]), Kartik Sarangmath[1], Aditya V. Nori[2], and Alessandro Orso[1]

[1] Georgia Institute of Technology, Atlanta, GA 30332, USA
{rmangal3,kartiksarangmath,orso}@gatech.edu
[2] Microsoft Research, Cambridge CB1 2FB, UK
Aditya.Nori@microsoft.com

Abstract. We are interested in algorithmically proving the robustness of neural networks. Notions of robustness have been discussed in the literature; we are interested in probabilistic notions of robustness that assume it feasible to construct a statistical model of the process generating the inputs of a neural network. We find this a reasonable assumption given the rapid advances in algorithms for learning generative models of data. A neural network f is then defined to be probabilistically robust if, for a randomly generated pair of inputs, f is likely to demonstrate k-Lipschitzness, i.e., the distance between the outputs computed by f is upper-bounded by the kth multiple of the distance between the pair of inputs. We name this property, *probabilistic Lipschitzness*.

We model generative models and neural networks, together, as programs in a simple, first-order, imperative, probabilistic programming language, *pcat*. Inspired by a large body of existing literature, we define a denotational semantics for this language. Then we develop a sound *local Lipschitzness* analysis for *cat*, a non-probabilistic sublanguage of *pcat*. This analysis can compute an upper bound of the "Lipschitzness" of a neural network in a bounded region of the input set. We next present a provably correct algorithm, PROLIP, that analyzes the behavior of a neural network in a user-specified box-shaped input region and computes - (i) lower bounds on the probabilistic mass of such a region with respect to the generative model, (ii) upper bounds on the Lipschitz constant of the neural network in this region, with the help of the local Lipschitzness analysis. Finally, we present a sketch of a proof-search algorithm that uses PROLIP as a primitive for finding proofs of probabilistic Lipschitzness. We implement the PROLIP algorithm and empirically evaluate the computational complexity of PROLIP.

1 Introduction

Neural networks (NNs) are useful for modeling a variety of computational tasks that are beyond the reach of manually written programs. We like to think of NNs as programs in a first-order programming language specialized to operate over vectors from high-dimensional Euclidean spaces. However, NNs are algorithmically learned from observational data about the task being modeled. These tasks

D. Pichardie and M. Sighireanu (Eds.): SAS 2020, LNCS 12389, pp. 274–309, 2020.
https://doi.org/10.1007/978-3-030-65474-0_13

typically represent natural processes for which we have large amounts of data but limited mathematical understanding. For example, NNs have been successful at image recognition [40] - assigning descriptive labels to images. In this case, the underlying natural process that we want to mimic computationally is image recognition as it happens in the human brain. However, insufficient mathematical theory about this task makes it hard to develop a hand-crafted algorithm.

Given that NNs are discovered algorithmically, it is important to ensure that a learned NN actually models the computational task of interest. With the perspective of NNs as programs, this reduces to proving that the NN behaves in accordance with the formal specification of the task at hand. Unfortunately, limited mathematical understanding of the tasks implies that, in general, we are unable to even state the formal specification. In fact, it is precisely in situations where we are neither able to manually design an algorithm nor able to provide formal specifications in which NNs tend to be deployed. This inability to verify or make sense of the computation represented by a NN is one of the primary challenges to the widespread adoption of NNs, particularly for safety critical applications. In practice, NNs are tested on a limited number of manually provided tests (referred to as test data) before deploying. However, a natural question is, what formal correctness guarantees, if any, can we provide about NNs?

A hint towards a useful notion of correctness comes from an important observation about the behavior of NNs, first made by [51]. They noticed that state-of-the-art NNs that had been learned to perform the image recognition task were unstable - small changes in the inputs caused the learned NNs to produce large, unexpected, and undesirable changes in the outputs. In the context of the image recognition task, this meant that small changes to the images, imperceptible to humans, caused the NN to produce very different labels. The same phenomenon has been observed by others, and in the context of very different tasks, like natural language processing [2,35] and speech recognition [13,14,45]. This phenomenon, commonly referred to as lack of *robustness*, is widespread and undesirable. This has motivated a large body of work (see [43,59,62] for broad but non-exhaustive surveys) on algorithmically proving NNs robust. These approaches differ not only in the algorithms employed but also in the formal notions of robustness that they prove.

An majority of the existing literature has focused on local notions of robustness. Informally, a NN is *locally robust* at a specific input, x_0, if it behaves robustly in a bounded, local region of the input Euclidean space centered at x_0. There are multiple ways of formalizing this seemingly intuitive property. A common approach is to formalize this property as, $\forall x.(\|x - x_0\| \leqslant r) \rightarrow \phi((fx), (fx_0))$, where f is the NN to be proven locally robust at x_0, (fx) represents the result of applying the NN f on input x, $\phi((fx), (fx_0))$ represents a set of linear constraints imposed on (fx), and $\|\cdot\|$ represents the norm or distance metric used for measuring distances in the input and output Euclidean spaces (typically, an l_p norm is used with $p \in \{1, 2, \infty\}$). An alternate, less popular, formulation of local robustness, referred to as *local Lipschitzness* at a point, requires that $\forall x, x'.(\|x - x_0\| \leqslant r) \wedge (\|x' - x_0\| \leqslant r) \rightarrow (\|fx - fx'\| \leqslant k * \|x - x'\|)$. Local

Lipschitzness ensures that in a ball of radius r centered at x_0, changes in the input only lead to bounded changes in the output. One can derive other forms of local robustness from local Lipschitzness. (see Theorem 3.2 in [58]). We also find local Lipschitzness to be an aesthetically more pleasing and natural property of a function. But, local Lipschitzness is a relational property [6,12]/hyperproperty [18] unlike the first formulation, which is a safety property [41]. Algorithms for proving safety properties of programs have been more widely studied and there are a number of mature approaches to build upon, which may explain the prevalence of techniques for proving the former notion of local robustness. For instance, [28,49] are based on variants of polyhedral abstract interpretation [10,21,37,38] encode the local robustness verification problem as an SMT constraint.

Local robustness (including local Lipschitzness) is a useful but limited guarantee. For inputs where the NN has not been proven to be locally robust, no guarantees can be given. Consequently, a global notion of robustness is desirable. Local Lipschitzness can be extended to a global property - a NN f is *globally Lipschitz* or *k-Lipschitz* if, $\forall x, x'.(\|fx - fx'\| \leqslant k * \|x - x'\|)$. Algorithms have been proposed in programming languages and machine learning literature for computing Lipschitz constant upper bounds. Global robustness is guaranteed if the computed upper bound is $\leqslant k$.

Given the desirability of global robustness over local robustness, the focus on local robustness in the existing literature may seem surprising. There are two orthogonal reasons that, we believe, explain this state of affairs - (i) proving global Lipschitzness, particularly with a tight upper bound on the Lipschitz constant, is more technically and computationally challenging than proving local Lipschitzness, which is itself hard to prove due its relational nature; (ii) requiring NNs to be globally Lipschitz with some low constant k can be an excessively stringent specification, unlikely to be met by most NNs in practice. NNs, unlike typical programs, are algorithmically learnt from data. Unless the learning algorithm enforces the global robustness constraint, it is unlikely for a learned NN to exhibit this "strong" property. Unfortunately, learning algorithms are ill-suited for imposing such logical constraints. These algorithms search over a set of NNs (referred to as the hypothesis class) for the NN minimizing a cost function (referred to as loss function) that measures the "goodness" of a NN for modeling the computational task at hand. These algorithms are greedy and iterative, following the gradient of the loss function. Modifying the loss function in order to impose the desired logical constraints significantly complicates the function structure and makes the gradient-based, greedy learning algorithms ineffective.[1]

Consequently, in this work, we focus on a probabilistic notion of global robustness. This formulation, adopted from [44], introduces a new mathematical object to the NN verification story, namely, a probability measure over the inputs to the NN under analysis. One assumes it feasible to construct a statistical model of the process generating the inputs of a NN. We find this a reasonable assumption given the rapid advances in algorithms for learning generative models of data [32,39]. Such a statistical model yields a distribution D over the inputs of the

---

[1] Recent work has tried to combine loss functions with logical constraints [27].

NN. Given distribution D and a NN f, this notion of robustness, that we refer to as *probabilistic Lipschitzness*, is formally stated as,

$$\Pr_{x,x' \sim D} \left(\|fx - fx'\| \leqslant k * \|x - x'\| \mid \|x - x'\| \leqslant r \right) \geqslant 1 - \epsilon$$

This says that if we randomly draw two samples, x and x' from the distribution D, then, under the condition that x and x' are r-close, there is a high probability $(\geqslant (1-\epsilon))$ that NN f behaves stably for these inputs. If the parameter $\epsilon = 0$ and $r = \infty$, then we recover the standard notion of k-Lipschitzness. Conditioning on the event of x and x' being r-close reflects the fact that we are primarily concerned with the behavior of the NN on pairs of inputs that are close.

To algorithmically search for proofs of probabilistic Lipschitzness, we model generative models and NNs together as programs in a simple, first-order, imperative, probabilistic programming language, *pcat*. First-order probabilistic programming languages with a `sample` construct, like *pcat*, have been well-studied.[2] Programs in *pcat* denote transformers from Euclidean spaces to probability measures over Euclidean spaces. *pcat*, inspired by the non-probabilistic language *cat* [28], is explicitly designed to model NNs, with vectors in $\mathbb{R}^n$ as the basic datatype. The suitability of *pcat* for representing generative models stems from the fact that popular classes of generative models (for instance, the generative network of generative adversarial networks [32] and the decoder network of variational autoencoders [39]) are represented by NNs. Samples from the input distribution D are obtained by drawing a sample from a standard distribution (typically a normal distribution) and running this sample through generative or decoder networks. In *pcat*, this can be represented as the program, $z \hookleftarrow N(0,1); g$, where the first statement represents the sampling operation (referred to as sampling from the latent space, with z as the latent variable) and g is the generative or decoder NN. If the NN to be analyzed is f, then we can construct the program, $z \hookleftarrow N(0,1); g; f$, in *pcat*, and subject it to our analysis.

Adapting a language-theoretic perspective allows us to study the problem in a principled, general manner and utilize existing program analysis and verification literature. In particular, we are interested in sound algorithms that can verify properties of probabilistic programs without needing manual intervention. Thus approaches based on interactive proofs [8,9], requiring manually-provided annotations and complex side-conditions [7,15,36] or only providing statistical guarantees [11,46] are precluded. Frameworks based on abstract interpretation [22,54] are helpful for thinking about analysis of probabilistic programs but we focus on a class of completely automated proof-search algorithms [1,29,47] that only consider probabilistic programs where all randomness introducing statements (i.e., `sample` statements) are independent of program inputs, i.e. samples are drawn from fixed, standard probability distributions, similar to our setting. These algorithms analyze the program to generate symbolic constraints (i.e., sentences in first-order logic with theories supported by SMT solvers) and then compute the probability mass or "volume", with respect to a fixed probability

---

[2] *pcat* has no `observe` or `score` construct and cannot be used for Bayesian reasoning.

278 R. Mangal et al.

measure, of the set of values satisfying these constraints. These algorithms are unsuitable for parametric probability measures but suffice for our problem. Both generating symbolic constraints and computing volumes can be computationally expensive (and even intractable for large programs), so a typical strategy is to break down the task into simpler sub-goals. This is usually achieved by defining the notion of "program path" and analyzing each path separately. This per path strategy is unsuitable for NNs, with their highly-branched program structure. We propose partitioning the program input space (i.e., the latent space in our case) into box-shaped regions, and analyzing the program behavior separately on each box. The box partitioning strategy offers two important advantages - (i) by not relying explicitly on program structure to guide partitioning strategy, we have more flexibility to balance analysis efficiency and precision; (ii) computing the volume of boxes is easier than computing the same for sets with arbitrary or even convex structure.

For the class of probabilistic programs we are interested in (with structure, $z \leftsquigarrow N(0, 1); g; f$), the box-partitioning strategy implies repeatedly analyzing the program $g; f$ while restricting z to from box shaped regions. In every run, the analysis of $g; f$ involves computing a box-shaped overapproximation, x_B, of the outputs computed by g when z is restricted to some specific box z_B and computing an upper bound on the local Lipschitz constant of f in the box-shaped region x_B. We package these computations, performed in each iteration of the proof-search algorithm, in an algorithmic primitive, PROLIP. For example, consider the scenario where f represents a classifier, trained on the MNIST dataset, for recognizing hand-written digits, and g represents a generative NN modeling the distribution of the MNIST dataset. In order to prove probabilistic Lipschitzness of f with respect to the distribution D represented by the generative model $z \leftsquigarrow N(0, 1); g$, we iteratively consider box-shaped regions in the latent space (i.e., in the input space of g). For each such box-shaped region σ^B in the input space of g, we first compute an overapproximation $\tilde{\sigma}^B$ of the corresponding box-shaped region in the output space of g. Since the output of g is the input of f, we next compute an upper bound on the local Lipschitz constant of f in the region $\tilde{\sigma}^B$. If the computed upper bound is less than the required bound, we add the probabilistic mass of region σ^B to an accumulator maintaining the probability of f being Lipschitz with respect to the distribution D.

For computing upper bounds on local Lipschitz constants, we draw inspiration from existing literature on Lipschitz analysis of programs [16] and NNs [19, 26, 33, 42, 51–53, 57, 61]. In particular, we build on the algorithms presented in [57, 61]. We translate these algorithms in to our language-theoretic setting and present the local Lipschitzness analysis in the form of an abstract semantics for the *cat* language, which is a non-probabilistic sublanguage of *pcat*. In the process, we also simplify and generalize the original algorithms.

To summarize, our primary contributions in this work are - (i) we present a provably sound algorithmic primitive PROLIP and a sketch of a proof-search algorithm for probabilistic Lipschitzness of NNs, (ii) we develop a simplified and generalized version of the local Lipschitzness analysis in [57], capable of comput-

$$\begin{aligned}
\text{(variables)} \quad & x, y \in V \\
\text{(naturals)} \quad & m, n \in \mathbb{N} \\
\text{(weights)} \quad & w \in \bigcup_{m,n \in \mathbb{N}} \mathbb{R}^{m \times n} \\
\text{(biases)} \quad & \beta \in \bigcup_{n \in \mathbb{N}} \mathbb{R}^{n}
\end{aligned}$$

$$
\begin{aligned}
s &::= \textbf{skip} \mid y \leftarrow w \cdot x + \beta \mid y \leftsquigarrow N(0,1) \mid s;s \mid \textbf{if } b \textbf{ then } s \textbf{ else } s \\
s^{-} &::= \textbf{skip} \mid y \leftarrow w \cdot x + \beta \mid s^{-};s^{-} \mid \textbf{if } b \textbf{ then } s^{-} \textbf{ else } s^{-} \\
b &::= \pi(x,m) \geqslant \pi(y,n) \mid \pi(x,n) \geqslant 0 \mid \pi(x,n) < 0 \mid b \wedge b \mid \neg b \\
e &::= \pi(x,n) \mid w \cdot x + \beta
\end{aligned}
$$

Fig. 1. *pcat* syntax

ing an upper bound on the local Lipschitz constant of box-shaped input regions for any program in the *cat* language, (iii) we develop a strategy for computing proofs of probabilistic programs that limits probabilistic reasoning to volume computation of regularly shaped sets with respect to standard distributions, (iv) we implement the PROLIP algorithm, and evaluate its computational complexity.

2 Language Definition

2.1 Language Syntax

pcat (probabilistic conditional affine transformations) is a first-order, imperative probabilistic programming language, inspired by the *cat* language [28]. *pcat* describes always terminating computations on data with a base type of vectors over the field of reals (i.e., of type $\bigcup_{n \in \mathbb{N}} \mathbb{R}^{n}$). *pcat* is not meant to be a practical language for programming, but serves as a simple, analyzable, toy language that captures the essence of programs structured like NNs. We emphasize that *pcat* does not capture the learning component of NNs. We think of *pcat* programs as objects learnt by a learning algorithm (commonly stochastic gradient descent with symbolic gradient computation). We want to analyze these learned programs and prove that they satisfy the probabilistic Lipschitzness property.

pcat can express a variety of popular NN architectures and generative models. For instance, *pcat* can express ReLU, convolution, maxpool, batchnorm, transposed convolution, and other structures that form the building blocks of popular NN architectures. We describe the encodings of these structures in Appendix F. The probabilistic nature of *pcat* further allows us to express a variety of generative models, including different generative adversarial networks (GANs) [32] and variational autoencoders (VAEs) [39].

pcat syntax is defined in Fig. 1. *pcat* variable names are drawn from a set V and refer to vector of reals. Constant matrices and vectors appear frequently in *pcat* programs, playing the role of learned weights and biases of NNs, and are typically represented by w and β, respectively. Programs in *pcat* are composed of basic statements for performing linear transformations of vectors ($y \leftarrow w \cdot x + \beta$) and sampling vectors from normal distributions ($y \leftsquigarrow N(0,1)$). Sampling from parametric distributions is not allowed. Programs can be composed sequentially

$$\Sigma \triangleq V \to \bigcup_{n \in \mathbb{N}} \mathbb{R}^n$$
$$[\![e]\!] \ : \ \Sigma \to \bigcup_{n \in \mathbb{N}} \mathbb{R}^n$$
$$[\![\pi(x,n)]\!](\sigma) = \sigma(x)_n$$
$$[\![w \cdot x + \beta]\!](\sigma) = w \cdot \sigma(x) + \beta$$

$$[\![b]\!] \ : \ \Sigma \to \{\mathbf{tt}, \mathbf{ff}\}$$
$$[\![\pi(x,m) \geqslant \pi(y,n)]\!](\sigma) = \mathbf{if} \ ([\![\pi(x,m)]\!](\sigma) \geqslant [\![\pi(y,n)]\!](\sigma)) \ \mathbf{then} \ \mathbf{tt} \ \mathbf{else} \ \mathbf{ff}$$
$$[\![\pi(x,m) \geqslant 0]\!](\sigma) = \mathbf{if} \ ([\![\pi(x,m) \geqslant 0]\!](\sigma)) \ \mathbf{then} \ \mathbf{tt} \ \mathbf{else} \ \mathbf{ff}$$
$$[\![\pi(x,m) < 0]\!](\sigma) = \mathbf{if} \ ([\![\pi(x,m)]\!](\sigma) < 0) \ \mathbf{then} \ \mathbf{tt} \mathbf{else} \ \mathbf{ff}$$
$$[\![b_1 \wedge b_2]\!](\sigma) = [\![b_1]\!](\sigma) \wedge [\![b_2]\!](\sigma)$$
$$[\![\neg b]\!](\sigma) = \mathbf{if} \ ([\![b]\!] = \mathbf{tt}) \ \mathbf{then} \ \mathbf{ff} \ \mathbf{else} \ \mathbf{tt}$$

$$[\![s]\!] \ : \ \Sigma \to P(\Sigma)$$
$$[\![\mathbf{skip}]\!](\sigma) = \delta_\sigma$$
$$[\![y \leftarrow w \cdot x + \beta]\!](\sigma) = \delta_{\sigma[y \mapsto [\![w \cdot x + \beta]\!](\sigma)]}$$
$$[\![y \rightsquigarrow N(0,1)]\!](\sigma) = \mathbb{E}_{a \sim N(0,1)}[\lambda \nu. \delta_{\sigma[y \mapsto \nu]}]$$
$$[\![s_1; s_2]\!](\sigma) = \mathbb{E}_{\tilde{\sigma} \sim [\![s_1]\!](\sigma)}[[\![s_2]\!]]$$
$$[\![\mathbf{if} \ b \ \mathbf{then} \ s_1 \ \mathbf{else} \ s_2]\!](\sigma) = \mathbf{if} \ ([\![b]\!](\sigma)) \ \mathbf{then} \ [\![s_1]\!](\sigma) \ \mathbf{else} \ [\![s_2]\!](\sigma)$$

$$\widehat{[\![s]\!]} \ : \ P(\Sigma) \to P(\Sigma)$$
$$\widehat{[\![s]\!]}(\mu) = \mathbb{E}_{\sigma \sim \mu}[[\![s]\!]]$$

$$\widetilde{[\![s^-]\!]} \ : \ \Sigma \to \Sigma$$
$$\widetilde{[\![\mathbf{skip}]\!]}(\sigma) = \sigma$$
$$\widetilde{[\![y \leftarrow w \cdot x + \beta]\!]}(\sigma) = \sigma[y \mapsto [\![w \cdot x + \beta]\!](\sigma)]$$
$$\widetilde{[\![s_1; s_2]\!]}(\sigma) = \widetilde{[\![s_2]\!]}(\widetilde{[\![s_1]\!]}(\sigma))$$
$$\widetilde{[\![\mathbf{if} \ b \ \mathbf{then} \ s_1 \ \mathbf{else} \ s_2]\!]}(\sigma) = \mathbf{if} \ ([\![b]\!](\sigma)) \ \mathbf{then} \ \widetilde{[\![s_1]\!]}(\sigma) \ \mathbf{else} \ \widetilde{[\![s_2]\!]}(\sigma)$$

Fig. 2. *pcat* denotational semantics

($s; s$) or conditionally (**if** b **then** s **else** s). *pcat* does not have a loop construct, acceptable as many NN architectures do not contain loops. *pcat* provides a projection operator $\pi(x,n)$ that reads the nth element of the vector referred by x. For *pcat* programs to be well-formed, all the matrix and vector dimensions need to fit together. Static analyses [31,50] can ensure correct dimensions. In the rest of the paper, we assume that the programs are well-formed.

2.2 Language Semantics

We define the denotational semantics of *pcat* in Fig. 2, closely following those presented in [8]. We present definitions required to understand these semantics.

Definition 1. *A $\sigma-$algebra on a set X is a set Σ of subsets of X such that it contains X, is closed under complements and countable unions. A set with a $\sigma-$algebra is a measurable space and the subsets in Σ are measurable.*

A measure on a measurable space (X, Σ) *is a function* $\mu : \Sigma \to [0, \infty]$ *such that* $\mu(\varnothing) = 0$ *and* $\mu(\bigcup_{i \in \mathbb{N}} B_i) = \sum_{i \in \mathbb{N}} \mu(B_i)$ *such that* B_i *is a countable family of disjoint measurable sets. A probability measure or probability distribution is a measure* μ *with* $\mu(X) = 1$.

Given set X, we use $P(X)$ to denote the set of all probability measures over X. A *Dirac distribution* centered on x, written δ_x, maps x to 1 and all other elements of the underlying set to 0. Note that when giving semantics to probabilistic programming languages, it is typical to consider sub-distributions (measures such that $\mu(X) \leqslant 1$ for a measurable space (X, Σ)), as all programs in *pcat* terminate, we do not describe the semantics in terms of sub-distributions. Next, following [8], we give a monadic structure to probability distributions.

Definition 2. *Let* $\mu \in P(A)$ *and* $f : A \to P(B)$. *Then,* $\mathbb{E}_{a \sim \mu}[f] \in P(B)$ *is defined as,* $\mathbb{E}_{a \sim \mu}[f] \triangleq \lambda \nu. \int_A f(a)(\nu) \, d\mu(a)$

Note that in the rest of the paper, we write expressions of the form $\int_A f(a) \, d\mu(a)$ as $\int_{a \in A} \mu(a) \cdot f(a)$ for notational convenience. The metalanguage used in Fig. 2 and the rest of the paper is standard first-order logic with ZFC set theory, but we borrow notation from a variety of sources including languages like C and ML as well as standard set-theoretic notation. As needed, we provide notational clarification.

We define the semantics of *pcat* with respect to the set Σ of states. A state σ is a map from variables V to vectors of reals of any finite dimension. The choice of real vectors as the basic type of values is motivated by the goal of *pcat* to model NN computations. The set $P(\Sigma)$ is the set of probability measures over Σ. A *pcat* statement transforms a distribution over Σ to a new distribution over the same set. $\llbracket e \rrbracket$ and $\llbracket b \rrbracket$ denote the semantics of expressions and conditional checks, respectively. Expressions map states to vectors of reals while conditional checks map states to boolean values.

The semantics of statements are defined in two steps. We first define the standard semantics $\llbracket s \rrbracket$ where statements map incoming states to probability distributions. Next, the lifted semantics, $\widehat{\llbracket s \rrbracket}$, transform a probability distribution over the states, say μ, to a new probability distribution. The lifted semantics ($\widehat{\llbracket s \rrbracket}$) are obtained from the standard semantics ($\llbracket s \rrbracket$) using the monadic construction of Definition 2. Finally, we also defined a lowered semantics ($\widetilde{\llbracket s^- \rrbracket}$) for the *cat* sublanguage of *pcat*. As per these lowered semantics, statements are maps from states to states. Moreover, the lowered semantics of *cat* programs is tightly related to their standard semantics, as described by the following lemma.

Lemma 3. *(Equivalence of semantics)*
$\forall p \in s^-, \sigma \in \Sigma. \; \llbracket p \rrbracket(\sigma) = \delta_{\widetilde{\llbracket p \rrbracket}(\sigma)}$

Proof. Appendix A   ∎

The lemma states that one can obtain the standard probabilistic semantics for a program p in *cat*, given an initial state σ, by a Dirac delta distribution centered at $\widetilde{\llbracket p \rrbracket}(\sigma)$. Using this lemma, one can prove the following useful corollary.

Corollary 4. $\forall p \in s^-, \sigma \in \Sigma, \mu \in P(\sigma). \widehat{[\![p]\!]}(\mu)(\widetilde{[\![p]\!]}(\sigma)) \geqslant \mu(\sigma)$

Proof. Appendix B ∎

3 Lipschitz Analysis

A function f is locally Lipschitz in a bounded set S if, $\forall x, x' \in S. \|fx - fx'\| \leqslant k \cdot \|x - x'\|$, where $\|\cdot\|$ can be any l_p norm. Quickly computing tight upper bounds on the local Lipschitzness constant (k) is an important requirement of our proof-search algorithm for probabilistic Lipschitzness of *pcat* programs. However, as mentioned previously, local Lipschitzness is a relational property (hyperproperty) and computing upper bounds on k can get expensive.

The problem can be made tractable by exploiting a known relationship between Lipschitz constants and directional directives of a function. Let f be a function of type $\mathbb{R}^m \rightarrow \mathbb{R}^n$, and let $S \subset \mathbb{R}^m$ be a convex bounded set. From [58] we know that the local Lipschitz constant of f in the region S can be upper bounded by the maximum value of the norm of the directional directives of f in S, where the directional directive, informally, is the derivative of f in the direction of some vector v. Since f is a vector-valued function (i.e., mapping vectors to vectors), the derivative (including directional derivative) of f appears as a matrix of the form, $\mathbf{J} = \begin{bmatrix} \frac{\partial y_1}{\partial x_1} & \cdots & \frac{\partial y_1}{\partial x_m} \\ \cdots & & \cdots \\ \frac{\partial y_n}{\partial x_1} & \cdots & \frac{\partial y_n}{\partial x_m} \end{bmatrix}$, referred to as the Jacobian matrix of f (with x and y referring to the input and output of f). Moreover, to compute the norm of $\mathbf{J}$, i.e. $\|\mathbf{J}\|$, we use the operator norm, $\|\mathbf{J}\| = \inf\{c \geqslant 0 \mid \|\mathbf{J}v\| \leqslant c\|v\|$ for all $v \in \mathbb{R}^m\}$. Intuitively, thinking of a matrix M as a linear operator mapping between two vector spaces, the operator norm of M measures the maximum amount by which a vector gets "stretched" when mapped using M.

For piecewise linear functions with a finite number of "pieces"(i.e., the type of functions that can be computed by *cat*), using lemma 3.3 from [58], we can compute an upper bound on the Lipschitz constant by computing the operator norm of the Jacobian of each linear piece, and picking the maximum value. Since each piece of the function is linear, computing the Jacobian for a piece is straightforward. But the number of pieces in piecewise linear functions represented by NNs (or *cat* programs) can be exponential in the number of layers in the NN, even in a bounded region S. Instead of computing the Jacobian for each piece, we instead define a static analysis inspired by the Fast-Lip algorithm presented in [57] that computes lower and upper bounds of each element (i.e., each partial derivative) appearing in the Jacobian. Since our analysis is sound, such an interval includes all the possible values of the partial derivative in a given convex region S. We describe this Jacobian analysis in the rest of the section.

3.1 Instrumented *cat* Semantics

We define an instrumented denotational semantics for *cat* (the non-probabilistic sublanguage of *pcat*) in Fig. 3 that computes Jacobians for a particular program

$$\Sigma^D \triangleq \Sigma \times (V \to ((\bigcup_{m,n\in\mathbb{N}}(\mathbb{R})^{m\times n}) \times V)$$
$$\widetilde{[\![e]\!]}_D : \Sigma^D \to \bigcup_{n\in\mathbb{N}}\mathbb{R}^n \times (V \to ((\bigcup_{m,n\in\mathbb{N}}(\mathbb{R})^{m\times n}))$$
$$\widetilde{[\![w\cdot x+\beta]\!]}_D(\sigma^D) = \text{let } l = \mathbf{dim}(w)_1 \text{ in}$$
$$\text{let } m = \mathbf{dim}(w)_2 \text{ in}$$
$$\text{let } n = \mathbf{dim}(\sigma_2^D(x)_1)_2 \text{ in}$$
$$\text{let } a = [\![w\cdot x+\beta]\!](\sigma_1^D) \text{ in}$$
$$\text{let } b =$$
$$\left[\sum_{i=1}^m w_{j,i}\cdot(((\sigma_2^D(x))_1)_{i,k}) \,\Big|\, j\in\{1,..,l\},\ k\in\{1,...,n\}\right] \text{ in}$$
$$(a,b)$$

$$\widetilde{[\![b]\!]}_D : \Sigma^D \to \{\mathbf{tt},\mathbf{ff}\}$$
$$\widetilde{[\![b]\!]}_D(\sigma^D) = [\![b]\!](\sigma_1^D)$$

$$\widetilde{[\![s]\!]}_D : \Sigma^D \to \Sigma^D$$
$$\widetilde{[\![\mathbf{skip}]\!]}_D(\sigma^D) = \sigma^D$$
$$\widetilde{[\![y \leftarrow w\cdot x+\beta]\!]}_D(\sigma^D) = (\sigma_1^D[y \mapsto (\widetilde{[\![w\cdot x+\beta]\!]}_D(\sigma^D))_1], \sigma_2^D[y \mapsto ((\widetilde{[\![w\cdot x+\beta]\!]}_D(\sigma^D))_2, \sigma_2^D(x)_2)])$$
$$\widetilde{[\![s_1;s_2]\!]}_D(\sigma^D) = \widetilde{[\![s_2]\!]}_D(\widetilde{[\![s_1]\!]}_D(\sigma^D))$$
$$\widetilde{[\![\mathbf{if}\ b\ \mathbf{then}\ s_1\ \mathbf{else}\ s_2]\!]}_D(\sigma^D) = \mathbf{if}\ (\widetilde{[\![b]\!]}_D(\sigma^D) = \mathbf{tt})\ \mathbf{then}\ \widetilde{[\![s_1]\!]}_D(\sigma^D)\ \mathbf{else}\ \widetilde{[\![s_2]\!]}_D(\sigma^D)$$

Fig. 3. *cat* denotational semantics instrumented with Jacobians

path, in addition to the standard meaning of the program (as defined in Fig. 2). The semantics are notated by $\widetilde{[\![\cdot]\!]}_D$ (notice the subscript D). Program states, Σ^D, are pairs of maps such that the first element of each pair belongs to the previously defined set Σ of states, while the second element of each pair is a map that records the Jacobians. The second map is of type $V \to ((\bigcup_{m,n\in\mathbb{N}}(\mathbb{R})^{m\times n}) \times V)$, mapping each variable in V to a pair of values, namely, a Jacobian which is matrix of reals, and a variable in V. A *cat* program can map multiple input vectors to multiple output vectors, so one can compute a Jacobian of the *cat* program for each output vector with respect to each input vector. This explains the type of the second map in Σ^D - for each variable, the map records the corresponding Jacobian of the *cat* program computed with respect to the input variable that forms the second element of the pair.

Before explaining the semantics in Fig. 3, we clarify the notation used in the figure. We use subscript indices, starting from 1, to refer to elements in a pair or a tuple. For instance, we can read $((\sigma_2^D(x))_1)_{i,k}$ in the definition of $\widetilde{[\![w\cdot x+\beta]\!]}_D$ as follows - σ_2^D refers to the second map of the σ^D pair, $\sigma_2^D(x)_1$ extracts the first element (i.e., the Jacobian matrix) of the pair mapped to variable x, and then finally, we extract the element at location (i,k) in the Jacobian matrix. Also, we use let expressions in a manner similar to ML, and list comprehensions similar to Haskell (though we extend the notation to handle matrices). **dim** is polymorphic and returns the dimensions of vectors and matrices.

The only interesting semantic definitions are the ones associated with the expression $w \cdot x + \beta$ and the statement $y \leftarrow w \cdot x + \beta$. The value associated with any variable in a *cat* program is always of the form, $w_n(w_{n-1}(...(w_2(w_1 \cdot x + \beta_1) + \beta_2)...) + \beta_{n-1}) + \beta_n = w_n \cdot w_{n-1} \cdot ... \cdot w_2 \cdot w_1 \cdot x + w_n \cdot w_{n-1} \cdot ... \cdot$

$w_2 \cdot \beta_1 + w_n \cdot w_{n-1} \cdot ... \cdot w_3 \cdot \beta_2 + ... + \beta_n$. The derivative (the Jacobian) of this term with respect to x is $w_n \cdot w_{n-1} \cdot ... \cdot w_2 \cdot w_1$. Thus, calculating the Jacobian of a *cat* program for a particular output variable with respect to a particular input variable only requires multiplying the relevant weight matrices together and the bias terms can be ignored. This is exactly how we define the semantics of $w \cdot x + \beta$.

$$\Sigma^B \triangleq V \to \bigcup_{n \in \mathbb{N}} (\mathbb{R} \times \mathbb{R})^n$$
$$\Sigma^L \triangleq \Sigma^B \times (V \to ((\bigcup_{m,n \in \mathbb{N}} (\mathbb{R} \times \mathbb{R})^{m \times n}) \times (V \cup \{\bot, \top\})))$$
$$[\![e]\!]_L : \Sigma^L \to ((\bigcup_{n \in \mathbb{N}} (\mathbb{R} \times \mathbb{R})^n) \times (\bigcup_{m,n \in \mathbb{N}} (\mathbb{R} \times \mathbb{R})^{m \times n}))$$
$$[\![w \cdot x + \beta]\!]_L (\sigma^L) = \textbf{let } l = \textbf{dim}(w)_1 \textbf{ in}$$
$$\textbf{let } m = \textbf{dim}(w)_2 \textbf{ in}$$
$$\textbf{let } n = \textbf{dim}(\sigma_2^L(x)_1)_2 \textbf{ in}$$
$$\textbf{let } a = [\![w \cdot x + \beta]\!]_B (\sigma_1^L) \textbf{ in}$$
$$\textbf{let } b =$$

$$\left[\left. \begin{matrix} ((\sum_{i=1 \land w_{j,i} \geq 0}^{m} w_{j,i} \cdot (((\sigma_2^L(x))_1)_{i,k})_1 + \\ \sum_{i=1 \land w_{j,i} < 0}^{m} w_{j,i} \cdot (((\sigma_2^L(x))_1)_{i,k})_2) \\ (\sum_{i=1 \land w_{j,i} \geq 0}^{m} w_{j,i} \cdot (((\sigma_2^L(x))_1)_{i,k})_2 + \\ \sum_{i=1 \land w_{j,i} < 0}^{m} w_{j,i} \cdot (((\sigma_2^L(x))_1)_{i,k})_1)) \end{matrix} \right| j \in \{1,..,l\}, \; k \in \{1,...,n\} \right] \textbf{ in}$$
$$(a, b)$$

$$\bigsqcup_L : \Sigma^L \times \Sigma^L \to \Sigma^L$$
$$\sigma^L \bigsqcup_L \tilde{\sigma}^L = ((\sigma_1^L \bigsqcup_B \sigma_2^L),$$
$$(\lambda v. \; \textbf{let } (m, n) = \textbf{dim}(\sigma_2^L(v)) \textbf{ in}$$
$$\textbf{if } (\sigma_2^L(v)_2 = \tilde{\sigma}_2^L(v)_2) \textbf{ then}$$
$$([[\min\{(\sigma_2^L(v)_1)_{i,j}, (\tilde{\sigma}_2^L(v)_1)_{i,j}\}, \max\{(\sigma_2^L(v)_1)_{i,j}, (\tilde{\sigma}_2^L(v)_1)_{i,j}\}\} \mid$$
$$i \in \{1,...,m\}, \; j \in \{1,...,n\}], \sigma_2^L(v)_2)$$
$$\textbf{else } ([[(-\infty, \infty) \mid i \in \{1,...,m\}, \; j \in \{1,...,n\}], \top)$$

$$[\![b]\!]_L : \Sigma^L \to \{\textbf{tt}, \textbf{ff}, \top\}$$
$$[\![b]\!]_L (\sigma^L) = [\![b]\!]_B (\sigma_1^L)$$

$$[\![s^-]\!]_L : \Sigma^L \to \Sigma^L$$
$$[\![\textbf{skip}]\!]_L (\sigma^L) = \sigma^L$$
$$[\![\textbf{assert } b]\!]_L (\sigma^L) = (([\![\textbf{assert } b]\!]_B (\sigma_1^L)), \sigma_2^L)$$
$$[\![y \leftarrow w \cdot x + \beta]\!]_L (\sigma^L) = (\sigma_1^L [y \mapsto ([\![w \cdot x + \beta]\!]_L (\sigma^L))_1], \sigma_2^L [y \mapsto (([\![w \cdot x + \beta]\!]_L (\sigma^L))_2, \sigma_2^L(x)_2)])$$
$$[\![s_1; s_2]\!]_L (\sigma^L) = [\![s_2]\!]_L ([\![s_1]\!]_L (\sigma^L))$$
$$[\![\textbf{if } b \textbf{ then } s_1 \textbf{ else } s_2]\!]_L (\sigma^L) = \textbf{if} \quad ([\![b]\!]_L (\sigma^L) = \textbf{tt}) \textbf{ then } [\![s_1]\!]_L (\sigma^L)$$
$$\textbf{else if } ([\![b]\!]_L (\sigma^L) = \textbf{ff}) \textbf{ then } [\![s_2]\!]_L (\sigma^L)$$
$$\textbf{else} \quad [\![s_1]\!]_L ([\![\textbf{assert } b]\!]_L (\sigma^L)) \bigsqcup_L [\![s_2]\!]_L ([\![\textbf{assert } \neg b]\!]_L (\sigma^L))$$

Fig. 4. *cat* abstract semantics for Jacobian analysis

3.2   Jacobian Analysis

The abstract version of the instrumented denotational semantics of *cat* is defined in Fig. 4. The semantics are notated by $[\![\cdot]\!]_L$ (notice the subscript L). The analysis computes box-shaped overapproximations of all the possible outcomes of a *cat* program when executed on inputs from a box-shaped bounded set. This is similar to standard interval analysis except that *cat* operates on data of base type of real vectors. The analysis maintains bounds on real vectors by computing intervals for every element of a vector. In addition, this analysis also computes an overapproximation of all the possible Jacobian matrices. Note that the Jacobian matrices computed by the instrumented semantics of *cat* only depend on the path through the program, i.e. the entries in the computed Jacobian are control-dependent on the program inputs but not data-dependent. Consequently, for precision, it is essential that our analysis exhibit some notion of path-sensitivity. We achieve this by evaluating the branch conditions using the computed intervals and abstractly interpreting both the branches of an **if then else** statement only if the branch direction cannot be resolved.

An abstract program state, $\sigma^L \in \Sigma^L$, is a pair of maps. The first map in an abstract state maps variables in V to abstract vectors representing a box-shaped set of vectors. Each element of an abstract vector is pair of reals representing a lower bound and an upper bound on the possible values (first element of the pair is the lower bound and second element is the upper bound). The second map in an abstract state maps variables in V to pairs of abstract Jacobian matrices and elements in V extended with a top and a bottom element. Like abstract vectors, each element of an abstract Jacobian matrix is a pair of reals representing lower and upper bounds of the corresponding partial derivative.

The definition of the abstract semantics is straightforward but we describe the abstract semantics for affine expressions and for conditional statements. First, we discuss affine expressions. As a quick reminder of the notation, a term of the form $(((\sigma_2^L(x))_1)_{i,k})_1$ represents the lower bound of the element at location (i,k) in the abstract Jacobian associated with variable x. Now, recall that the instrumented semantics computes Jacobians simply by multiplying the weight matrices. In the abstract semantics, we multiply abstract Jacobians such that the bounds on each abstract element in the output abstract Jacobian reflect the minimum and maximum possible values that the element could take given the input abstract Jacobians. The abstract vectors for the first map are computed using the abstract box semantics (notated by $[\![\cdot]\!]_B$), defined in Appendix G. For conditional statements, as mentioned previously, we first evaluate the branch condition using the abstract state. If this evaluation returns $\top$, meaning that the analysis was unable to discern the branch to be taken, we abstractly interpret both the branches and then join the computed abstract states. Note that before abstractly interpreting both branches, we update the abstract state to reflect that the branch condition should hold before executing s_1 and should not hold before executing s_2. However, the **assert** b statement is not a part of the *cat* language, and only used for defining the abstract semantics. The join operation $(\bigcup_L)$ is as expected, except for one detail that we want to highlight - in case the Jacobians along different branches are computed with respect to different input variables we make the most conservative choice when joining the abstract Jacobians, bounding each element with $(-\infty, \infty)$ as well as recording $\top$ for the input variable.

Next, we define the concretization function (γ_L) for the abstract program states that maps elements in Σ^L to sets of elements in Σ^D and then state the soundness theorem for our analysis.

Definition 5. *(Concretization function for Jacobian analysis)*
$\gamma_L(\sigma^L) = \{\sigma^D \mid (\bigwedge_{v \in V} .\sigma_1^L(v)_1 \leqslant \sigma_1^D(v) \leqslant \sigma_1^L(v)_2) \wedge (\bigwedge_{v \in V} .(\sigma_2^L(v)_1)_1 \leqslant \sigma_2^D(v)_1 \leqslant (\sigma_2^L(v)_1)_2) \wedge \sigma_2^D(v)_2 \in \gamma_V(\sigma_2^L(v)_2)\}$ where $\gamma_V(v) = v$ and $\gamma_V(\top) = V$

Theorem 6. *(Soundness of Jacobian analysis)*
$\forall p \in s^-, \sigma^L \in \Sigma^L. \{\widetilde{[\![p]\!]}_D(\sigma^D) \mid \sigma^D \in \gamma_L(\sigma^L)\} \subseteq \gamma_L([\![p]\!]_L(\sigma^L))$

Proof. Appendix C   ∎

We next define the notion of operator norm of an abstract Jacobian. This definition is useful for stating Corollary 8. Given an abstract Jacobian, we construct a matrix J such that every element of J is the maximum of the absolute values of the corresponding lower and upper bound in the abstract Jacobian.

Definition 7. *(Operator norm of abstract Jacobian)*
If $J = \sigma_2^L(v)_1$ for some σ^L and v, and $(m,n) = \dim(J)$ then $\|J\|_L$ is defined as,
$\|J\|_L = \|[\max\{|(J_{k,l})_1|, |(J_{k,l})_2|\} \mid k \in \{1,...,m\}, l \in \{1,...,n\}]\|$

Corollary 8 shows that the operator norm of the abstract Jacobian computed by the analysis for some variable v is an upper bound of the operator norms of all the Jacobians possible for v when a program p is executed on the set of inputs represented by $\gamma_L(\sigma^L)$, for any program p and any abstract state σ^L.

Corollary 8. *(Upper bound of Jacobian operator norm)*
$\forall p \in s^-, \sigma^L \in \Sigma^L, v \in V.$
$\max\{\left\|((\widetilde{[\![p]\!]}_D(\sigma^D))_2)(v)_1\right\| \mid \sigma^D \in \gamma_L(\sigma^L)\} \leqslant \|(([\![p]\!]_L(\sigma^L))_2(v))_1\|_L$

Proof. Appendix D   ∎

3.3 Box Analysis

The box analysis abstracts the lowered *cat* semantics instead of the instrumented semantics. Given a box-shaped set of input states, it computes box-shaped over-approximations of the program output in a manner similar to the Jacobian analysis. In fact, the box analysis only differs from the Jacobian analysis in not computing abstract Jacobians. We define a separate box analysis to avoid computing abstract Jacobians when not needed. The concretization function (γ_B) for the box analysis and the soundness theorem are stated below. However, we do not provide a separate proof of soundness for the box analysis since such a proof is straightforward given the soundness proof for the Jacobian analysis. Details of the box analysis are available in Appendix G.

Definition 9. *(Concretization function for box analysis)*
$\gamma_B(\sigma^B) = \{\sigma \mid \bigwedge_{v \in V} .\sigma^B(v)_1 \leqslant \sigma(v) \leqslant \sigma^B(v)_2\}$

Theorem 10. *(Soundness of box analysis)*
$\forall p \in s^-, \sigma^B \in \Sigma^B. \{\widetilde{[\![p]\!]}(\sigma) \mid \sigma \in \gamma_B(\sigma^B)\} \subseteq \gamma_B([\![p]\!]_B(\sigma^B))$

4 Algorithms

We now describe our proof-search algorithms for probabilistic Lipschitzness of
NNs. The PROLIP algorithm (Sect. 4.1) is an algorithmic primitive that can be
used by a proof-search algorithm for probabilistic Lipschitzness. We provide the
sketch of such an algorithm using PROLIP in Sect. 4.2.

4.1 PROLIP Algorithmic Primitive

The PROLIP algorithm expects a *pcat* program p of the form $z \hookleftarrow N(0,1); g; f$ as
input, where g and f are *cat* programs. $z \hookleftarrow N(0,1); g$ represents the generative
model and f represents the NN under analysis. Other inputs expected by PROLIP
are a box-shaped region z_B in z and the input variable as well as the output
variable of f (**in** and **out** respectively). Typically, NNs consume a single input
and produce a single output. The outputs produced by PROLIP are (i) k_U, an
upper bound on the local Lipschitzness constant of f in a box-shaped region of **in**
(say in_B) that overapproximates the set of **in** values in the image of z_B under g,
(ii) d, the maximum distance between **in** values in in_B, (iii) *vol*, the probabilistic
volume of the region $z_B \times z_B$ with respect to the distribution $N(0,1) \times N(0,1)$.

Algorithm 1: PROLIP algorithmic primitive

Input:
  p: *pcat* program.
  z_B: Box in z.
  in: Input variable of f.
  out: Output variable of f.
Output:
  k_U: Lipschitz constant.
  d: Max **in** distance.
  vol: Mass of $z_B \times z_B$.

1 $\sigma^B := \lambda v.(-\infty, \infty)$;
2 $\tilde{\sigma}^B := [\![g]\!]_B(\sigma^B[z \mapsto z_B])$;
3 $\sigma^L := (\tilde{\sigma}^B, \lambda v.(I, v))$;
4 $\tilde{\sigma}^L := [\![f]\!]_L(\sigma^L)$;
5 **if** $(\tilde{\sigma}_2^L(\textbf{out})_2 = \textbf{in})$ **then**
6 $\quad J := \tilde{\sigma}_2^L(\textbf{out})_1$;
7 $\quad k_U := \|J\|_L$;
8 **else**
9 $\quad k_U := \infty$;
10 $d := \text{DIAG\_LEN}(\tilde{\sigma}^B(\textbf{in}))$;
11 $vol := \text{VOL}(N \times N, z_B \times z_B)$;
12 **return** (k_U, d, vol);

PROLIP starts by constructing an initial abstract program state (σ^B) suitable
for the box analysis (line 1). σ^B maps
every variable in V to abstract vectors
with elements in the interval $(-\infty, \infty)$. We
assume that for the variables accessed in
p, the length of the abstract vectors is
known, and for the remaining variables we
just assume vectors of length one in this
initial state. Next, the initial entry in σ^B
for z is replaced by z_B, and this updated
abstract state is used to perform box analysis of g, producing $\tilde{\sigma}^B$ as the result (line
2). Next, $\tilde{\sigma}^B$ is used to create the initial
abstract state σ^L for the Jacobian analysis of f (line 3). Initially, every variable is
mapped to an identity matrix as the Jacobian and itself as the variable with respect
to which the Jacobian is computed. The
initial Jacobian is a square matrix with
side length same as that of the abstract
vector associated with the variable being
mapped. Next, we use σ^L to perform Jacobian analysis of f producing $\tilde{\sigma}^L$ as the
result (line 4). If the abstract Jacobian
mapped to **out** in $\tilde{\sigma}^L$ is computed with
respect to **in** (line 5), we proceed down

288   R. Mangal et al.

the true branch else we assume that nothing is known about the required Jacobian and set k_U to ∞ (line 9). In the true branch, we first extract the abstract Jacobian and store it in J (line 6). Next, we compute the operator norm of the abstract Jacobian J using Definition 7, giving us the required upper bound on the Lipschitz constant (line 7). We then compute the maximum distance between **in** values in the box described by $\tilde{\sigma}^B(\mathbf{in})$ using the procedure DIAG_LEN that just computes the length of the diagonal of the hyperrectangle represented by $\tilde{\sigma}^B(\mathbf{in})$ (line 10). We also compute the probabilistic mass of region $z_B \times z_B$ with respect to the distribution $N(0,1) \times N(0,1)$ (line 11). This is an easy computation since we can form an analytical expression and just plug in the boundaries of z_B. Finally, we return the tuple (k_U, d, vol) (line 12). This PROLIP algorithm is correct as stated by the following theorem.

Theorem 11. *(Soundness of PROLIP)*
Let $p = z \leftsquigarrow N(0,1); g; f$ *where* $g, f \in s^-$, $(k_U, d, vol) = $ PROLIP(p, z_B), $z \notin$ **outv**(g), $z \notin$ **outv**(f), $x \in$ **inv**(f), *and* $y \in$ **outv**(f) *then,* $\forall \sigma_0 \in \Sigma$.
$$\Pr_{\sigma,\sigma' \sim [\![p]\!](\sigma_0)} ((\|\sigma(y) - \sigma'(y)\| \leqslant k_U \cdot \|\sigma(x) - \sigma'(x)\|) \wedge (\sigma(z), \sigma'(z) \in \gamma(z_B))) \geqslant vol$$

Proof. Appendix E ∎

This theorem is applicable for any program p in the required form, such that g and f are *cat* programs, variable z is not written to by g and f (**outv**$(\cdot)$ gives the set of variables that a program writes to, **inv**$(\cdot)$ gives the set of live variables at the start of a program). It states that the result (k_U, d, vol) of invoking PROLIP on p with box z_B is safe, i.e., with probability at least vol, any pair of program states (σ, σ'), randomly sampled from the distribution denoted by $[\![p]\!](\sigma_0)$, where σ_0 is any initial state, satisfies the Lipschitzness property (with constant k_U) and has z variables mapped to vectors in the box z_B.

4.2 Sketch of Proof-Search Algorithm

We give a sketch of a proof-search algorithm that uses the PROLIP algorithm as a primitive. The inputs to such an algorithm are a *pcat* program p in the appropriate form, the constants r, ϵ, and k that appear in the formulation of probabilistic Lipschitzness, and a resource bound gas that limits the number of times PROLIP is invoked. This algorithm either finds a proof or runs out of gas. Before describing the algorithm, we recall the property we are trying to prove, stated as follows,
$$\Pr_{\sigma,\sigma' \sim [\![p]\!](\sigma_0)} (\|\sigma(y) - \sigma'(y)\| \leqslant k * \|\sigma(x) - \sigma'(x)\| \mid \|\sigma(x) - \sigma'(x)\| \leqslant r) \geqslant 1 - \epsilon$$
The conditional nature of this probabilistic property complicates the design of the proof-search algorithm, and we use the fact that $Pr(A \mid B) = Pr(A \wedge B)/Pr(B)$ for computing conditional probabilities. Accordingly, the algorithm maintains three different probability counters, namely, pr_l, pr_r, and pr_f, which are all initialized to zero as the first step (line 1).

Algorithm 2: Checking Probabilistic Robustness.

Input:
- p: *pcat* program.
- r: Input closeness bound.
- ϵ: Probabilistic bound.
- k: Lipschitz constant.
- **gas**: Iteration bound.

Output: $\{tt, ?\}$

1   $pr_l := 0;\ pr_r := 0;\ pr_f := 0;$
2   $\alpha := \text{INIT\_AGENT}(\mathbf{dim}(z), r, \epsilon, k);$
3   **while** $(pr_l < (1 - \epsilon)) \wedge (\mathbf{gas} \neq 0)$ **do**
4     $\mathbf{gas} := \mathbf{gas} - 1;$
5     $z_B := \text{CHOOSE}(\alpha);$
6     $(k_U, d, vol) :=$ $\text{PROLIP}(p, z_B, x, y);$
7     $\text{UPDATE\_AGENT}(\alpha, k_U, d, vol);$
8   **if** $d \leq r$ **then**
9       $pr_r := pr_r + vol;$
10   **if** $k_U \leq k$ **then**
11         $pr_l := pr_l + vol;$
12         $pr_f := pr_f / pr_r;$
13
14
15 **end while**
16 **if gas** $= 0$ **then**
17   **return** ? ;
18 **else**
19   **return tt** ;
20

pr_l records the probability that a randomly sampled pair of program states (σ, σ') satisfies the Lipschitzness and closeness property (i.e., $(\|\sigma(y) - \sigma'(y)\| \leq k * \|\sigma(x) - \sigma'(x)\|) \wedge (\|\sigma(x) - \sigma'(x)\| \leq r))$. pr_r records the probability that a randomly sampled pair of program states satisfies the closeness property (i.e., $\|\sigma(x) - \sigma'(x)\| \leq r$). pr_f tracks the conditional probability which is equal to pr_l/pr_r. After initializing the probability counters, the algorithm initializes an "agent" (line 2), which we think of as black-box capable of deciding which box-shaped regions in z should be explored. Ideally, we want to pick a box such that - (i) it has a high probability mass, (ii) it satisfies, both, Lipschitzness and closeness. Of course, we do not know a priori if Lipschitzness and closeness will hold for a particular box in z, the crux of the challenge in designing a proof-search algorithm. Here, we leave the algorithm driving the agent's decisions unspecified (and hence, refer to the proof-search algorithm as a sketch). After initializing the agent, the algorithm enters a loop (lines 3–13) that continues till we have no **gas** left or we have found a proof. Notice that if $(pr_l \geq (1 - \epsilon))$, the probabilistic Lipschitzness property is certainly true, but this is an overly strong condition that maybe false even when probabilistic Lipschitzness holds. For instance, if ϵ was 0.1 and the ground-truth value of pr_r for the program p was 0.2, then pr_l could never be ≥ 0.9, even if probabilistic Lipschitzness holds. However, continuing with our algorithm description, after decrementing **gas** (line 4), the algorithm queries the agent for a box in z (line 5), and runs PROLIP with this box, assuming x as the input variable of f and y as the output (line 6). Next, the agent is updated with the result of calling PROLIP, allowing the agent to update it's internal state (line 7). Next, we check if for the currently considered box (z_B), the maximum distance between the inputs to f is less than r (line 8), and if so, we update the closeness probability counter pr_r (line 9). We also check if the upper bound of the local Lipschitzness constant returned by PROLIP is less than

k (line 10), and if so, update pr_l (line 11) and pr_f (line 12). Finally, if we have exhausted the `gas`, we were unable to prove the property, otherwise we have a proof of probabilistic Lipschitzness.

4.3   Discussion

Informally, we can think of the Jacobian analysis as computing two different kinds of "information" about a neural network: (i) an overapproximation of the outputs, given a set of inputs σ^B, using the box analysis; (ii) an upper bound on the local Lipschitz constant of the neural network for inputs in σ^B. The results of the box analysis are used to overapproximate the set of "program paths" in the neural network exercised by inputs in σ^B, safely allowing the Jacobian computation to be restricted to this set of paths. Consequently, it is possible to replace the use of box domain in (i) with other abstract domains like zonotopes [30] or DeepPoly [49] for greater precision in overapproximating the set of paths. In contrast, one needs to be very careful with the abstract domain used for the analysis of the generative model g in Algorithm 1, since the choice of the abstract domain has a dramatic effect on the complexity of the volume computation algorithm `VOL` invoked by the `PROLIP` algorithm. While Gaussian volume computation of boxes is easy, it is hard for general convex bodies [4, 23, 25] unless one uses randomized algorithms for volume computation [20, 24]. Finally, note that the design of a suitable agent for iteratively selecting the input regions to analyze in Algorithm 2 remains an open problem.

5   Empirical Evaluation

We aim to empirically evaluate the computational complexity of `PROLIP`. We ask the following questions: **(RQ1)** Given a program, is the run time of `PROLIP` affected by the size and location of the box in z? **(RQ2)** What is the run time of `PROLIP` on popular generative models and `NN`s?

5.1   Experimental Setup

We implement `PROLIP` in Python, using Pytorch, Numpy, and SciPy for the core functionalities, and Numba for program optimization and parallelization. We run `PROLIP` on three *pcat* programs corresponding to two datasets: the MNIST dataset and the CIFAR-10 dataset. Each program has a generator network g and a classifier network f. The g networks in each program consist of five convolution transpose layers, four batch norm layers, four ReLU layers, and a tanh layer. The full generator architectures and parameter weights can be seen in [48]. The f network for the MNIST program consists of three fully connected layers and two ReLU layers. For the CIFAR-10 dataset, we create two different *pcat* programs: one with a large classifier architecture and one with a small classifier architecture. The f network for the large CIFAR-10 program consists of seven convolution layers, seven batch norm layers, seven ReLU layers, four maxpool layers, and one fully connected layer. The f network for the small CIFAR-10 program consists of two convolution layers, two maxpool layers, two ReLU layers, and three fully connected layers. The full classifier architectures and parameter weights for the MNIST and large CIFAR-10 program can be seen in [17].

In our experiments, each generative model has a latent space dimension of 100, meaning that the model samples a vector of length 100 from a multi-dimensional normal distribution, which is then used by the generator network. We create five random vectors of length 100 by randomly sampling each element of the vectors from a normal distribution. For each vector, we create three different sized square boxes by adding and subtracting a constant from each element in the vector. This forms an upper and lower bound for the randomly-centered box. The constants we chose to form these boxes are 0.00001, 0.001, and 0.1. In total, 15 different data points are collected for each program. We ran these experiments on a Linux machine with 32 vCPU's, 204 GB of RAM, and no GPU.

5.2   Results

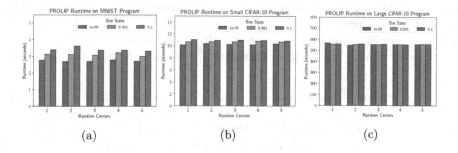

Fig. 5. PROLIP run times

RQ1. As seen in Figs. 5a and 5b, there is a positive correlation between box size and run time of PROLIP on the MNIST and small CIFAR-10 programs. This is likely because as the z input box size increases, more branches in the program stay unresolved, forcing the analysis to reason about more of the program. However, z box size does not seem to impact PROLIP run time on the large CIFAR-10 program (Fig. 5c) as the time spent in analyzing convolution layers completely dominates any effect on run time of the increase in z box size.

RQ2. There is a significant increase in the run time of PROLIP for the large CIFAR-10 program compared to the MNIST and small CIFAR-10 programs, and this is due to the architectures of their classifiers. When calculating the abstract Jacobian matrix for an affine assignment statement $(y \leftarrow w \cdot x + \beta)$, we multiply the weight matrix with the incoming abstract Jacobian matrix. The dimensions of a weight matrix for a fully connected layer is $N_{in} \times N_{out}$ where N_{in}

is the number of input neurons and N_{out} is the number of output neurons. The dimensions of a weight matrix for a convolution layer are $C_{out} \cdot H_{out} \cdot W_{out} \times C_{in} \cdot H_{in} \cdot W_{in}$ where C_{in}, H_{in}, and W_{in} are the input's channel, height, and width dimensions and C_{out}, H_{out}, and W_{out} are the output's channel, height, and width dimensions. For our MNIST and small CIFAR-10 classifiers, the largest weight matrices formed had dimensions of 784×256 and 4704×3072 respectively. In comparison, the largest weight matrix calculated in the large CIFAR-10 classifier had a dimension of 131072×131072. Propagating the Jacobian matrix for the large CIFAR-10 program requires first creating a weight matrix of that size, which is memory intensive, and second, multiplying the matrix with the incoming abstract Jacobian matrix, which is computationally expensive. The increase in run time of the PROLIP algorithm can be attributed to the massive size blow-up in the weight matrices computed for convolution layers.

Other Results. Table 1 shows the upper bounds on local Lipschitz constant computed by the PROLIP algorithm for every combination of box size and *pcat* program considered in our experiments. The computed upper bounds are comparable to those computed by the Fast-Lip algorithm from [57] as well as other state-of-the-art approaches for computing Lipschitz constants of neural networks. A phenomenon observed in our experiments is the convergence of local Lipschitz constants to an upper bound, as the z box size increases. This occurs because beyond a certain z box size, for every box in z, the output bounds of g represent the entire input space for f. Therefore any increase in the z box size, past

Table 1. Local Lipschitz constants discovered by PROLIP

Box size	MNIST lip constant	Large CIFAR lip constant	Small CIFAR lip constant
1e−05	1.683e1	5.885e14	3.252e5
0.001	1.154e2	8.070e14	4.218e5
0.1	1.154e2	8.070e14	4.218e5
1e−05	1.072e1	5.331e14	1.814e5
0.001	1.154e2	8.070e14	4.218e5
0.1	1.154e2	8.070e14	4.218e5
1e−05	1.460e1	6.740e14	2.719e5
0.001	1.154e2	8.070e14	4.218e5
0.1	1.154e2	8.070e14	4.218e5
1e−05	1.754e1	6.571e14	2.868e5
0.001	1.154e2	8.070e14	4.218e5
0.1	1.154e2	8.070e14	4.218e5
1e−05	1.312e1	5.647e14	2.884e5
0.001	1.154e2	8.070e14	4.218e5
0.1	1.154e2	8.070e14	4.218e5

the tipping point, results in computing an upper bound on the global Lipschitz constant of f.

The run time of the PROLIP algorithm can be improved by utilizing a GPU for matrix multiplication. The multiplication of massive matrices computed in the Jacobian propagation of convolution layers or large fully connected layers accounts for a significant portion of the run time of PROLIP, and the run time can benefit from GPU-based parallelization of matrix multiplication. Another factor that slows down our current implementation of PROLIP algorithm is the creation of the weight matrix for a convolution layer. These weight matrices are quite sparse, and constructing sparse matrices that hold '0' values implicitly can be much faster than explicitly constructing the entire matrix in memory, which is what our current implementation does.

6   Related Work

Our work draws from different bodies of literature, particularly literature on *verification of NNs, Lipschitz analysis of programs and NNs*, and *semantics and verification of probabilistic programs*. These connections and influences have been described in detail in Sect. 1. Here, we focus on describing connections with existing work on proving probabilistic/statistical properties of NNs.

[44] is the source of the probabilistic Lipschitzness property that we consider. They propose a proof-search algorithm that (i) constructs a product program [5], (ii) uses an abstract interpreter with a powerset polyhedral domain to compute input pre-conditions that guarantee the satisfaction of the Lipschitzness property, (iii) computes approximate volumes of these input regions via sampling. They do not implement this algorithm. If one encodes the Lipschitzness property as disjunction of polyhedra, the number of disjuncts is exponential in the number of dimensions of the output vector. There is a further blow-up in the number of disjuncts as we propagate the abstract state backwards.

Other works on probabilistic properties of NNs [55,56] focus on local robustness. Given an input x_0, and an input distribution, they compute the probability that a random sample x' drawn from a ball centered at x_0 causes non-robust behavior of the NN at x' compared with x_0. [55] computes these probabilities via sampling while [56] constructs analytical expressions for computing upper and lower bounds of such probabilities. Finally, [3] presents a model-counting based approach for proving quantitative properties of NNs. They translate the NN as well as the property of interest into SAT constraints, and then invoke an approximate model-counting algorithm to estimate the number of satisfying solutions. We believe that their framework may be general enough to encode our problem but the scalability of such an approach remains to be explored. We also note that the guarantees produced by [3] are statistical, so one is unable to claim with certainty if probabilistic Lipschitzness is satisfied or violated.

7   Conclusion

We study the problem of algorithmically proving probabilistic Lipschitzness of NNs with respect to generative models representing input distributions. We employ a language-theoretic lens, thinking of the generative model and NN, together, as programs of the form $z \leftsquigarrow N(0,1); g; f$ in a first-order, imperative, probabilistic programming language *pcat*. We develop a sound local Lipschitzness analysis for *cat*, a non-probabilistic sublanguage of *pcat* that performs a Jacobian analysis under the hood. We then present PROLIP, a provably correct algorithmic primitive that takes in a box-shaped region in the latent space of the generative model as an input, and returns a lower bound on the volume of this region as well as an upper bound on a local Lipschitz constant of f. Finally, we sketch a proof-search algorithm that uses PROLIP and avoids expensive volume computation operations in the process of proving theorems about probabilistic programs. Empirical evaluation of the computational complexity of PROLIP suggests its feasibility as an algorithmic primitive, although convolution-style operations can be expensive and warrant further investigation.

A   Proof of Lemma 3

Lemma 3. *(Equivalence of semantics)*
$\forall p \in s^{-}, \sigma \in \Sigma. \ [\![p]\!](\sigma) = \delta_{\widetilde{[\![p]\!](\sigma)}}$

Proof. We prove this by induction on the structure of statements in s^{-}.
We first consider the base cases:

(i) **skip**
By definition, for any state σ,
$[\![\mathbf{skip}]\!](\sigma) = \delta_{\sigma} = \delta_{\widetilde{[\![\mathbf{skip}]\!](\sigma)}}$

(ii) $y \leftarrow w \cdot x + \beta$
Again, by definition, for any state σ,
$[\![y \leftarrow w \cdot x + \beta]\!](\sigma) = \delta_{\sigma[y \mapsto [\![w \cdot x + \beta]\!](\sigma)]} = \delta_{\widetilde{[\![y \leftarrow w \cdot x + \beta]\!](\sigma)}}$

Next, we consider the inductive cases:

(iii) $s_1^{-}; s_2^{-}$

$$
\begin{aligned}
[\![s_1^{-}; s_2^{-}]\!](\sigma) &= \mathbb{E}_{\tilde{\sigma} \sim [\![s_1^{-}]\!](\sigma)}[[\![s_2^{-}]\!]] \\
&= \lambda \nu. \int_{\tilde{\sigma} \in \Sigma} [\![s_1^{-}]\!](\sigma)(\tilde{\sigma}) \cdot [\![s_2^{-}]\!](\tilde{\sigma})(\nu) \\
&= \lambda \nu. \int_{\tilde{\sigma} \in \Sigma} \delta_{\widetilde{[\![s_1^{-}]\!](\sigma)}}(\tilde{\sigma}) \cdot \delta_{\widetilde{[\![s_2^{-}]\!](\tilde{\sigma})}}(\nu) \quad \text{(using inductive hypothesis)} \\
&= \lambda \nu. \delta_{\widetilde{[\![s_2^{-}]\!](\widetilde{[\![s_1^{-}]\!](\sigma)})}}(\nu) \\
&= \delta_{\widetilde{[\![s_2^{-}]\!](\widetilde{[\![s_1^{-}]\!](\sigma)})}} \\
&= \delta_{\widetilde{[\![s_1^{-}; s_2^{-}]\!](\sigma)}}
\end{aligned}
$$

(iv) **if** b **then** s_1^- **else** s_2^-

$$[\![\text{if } b \text{ then } s_1^- \text{ else } s_2^-]\!](\sigma) = \text{if } ([\![b]\!](\sigma)) \text{ then } [\![s_1^-]\!](\sigma) \text{ else } [\![s_2^-]\!](\sigma)$$
$$= \text{if } ([\![b]\!](\sigma)) \text{ then } \delta_{\widetilde{[\![s_1^-]\!](\sigma)}} \text{ else } \delta_{\widetilde{[\![s_2^-]\!](\sigma)}}$$
$$\text{(using inductive hypothesis)}$$
$$= \delta_{\text{if } ([\![b]\!](\sigma)) \text{ then } \widetilde{[\![s_1^-]\!]}(\sigma) \text{ else } \widetilde{[\![s_2^-]\!]}(\sigma)}$$
$$= \delta_{\widetilde{[\![\text{if } ([\![b]\!](\sigma)) \text{ then } s_1^- \text{ else } s_2^-]\!](\sigma)}}$$

∎

B   Proof of Corollary 4

Corollary 4. $\forall p \in s^-, \sigma \in \Sigma, \mu \in P(\Sigma).\ \widehat{[\![p]\!]}(\mu)(\widetilde{[\![p]\!]}(\sigma)) \geqslant \mu(\sigma)$

Proof. By definition,

$$\widehat{[\![p]\!]}(\mu) = \mathbb{E}_{\sigma \sim \mu}[\widetilde{[\![p]\!]}]$$
$$= \lambda\nu.\int_{\sigma \in \Sigma} \mu(\sigma) \cdot \widetilde{[\![p]\!]}(\sigma)(\nu)$$
$$= \lambda\nu.\int_{\sigma \in \Sigma} \mu(\sigma) \cdot \delta_{\widetilde{[\![p]\!]}(\sigma)}(\nu) \quad \text{(using previous lemma)}$$

Now suppose, $\nu = \widetilde{[\![p]\!]}(\tilde\sigma)$. Then, continuing from above,

$$\widehat{[\![p]\!]}(\mu)(\widetilde{[\![p]\!]}(\tilde\sigma)) = \int_{\sigma \in \Sigma} \mu(\sigma) \cdot \delta_{\widetilde{[\![p]\!]}(\sigma)}(\widetilde{[\![p]\!]}(\tilde\sigma))$$
$$\geqslant \mu(\tilde\sigma)$$

∎

C   Proof of Theorem 6

We first prove a lemma needed for the proof.

Lemma 12. *(Soundness of abstract conditional checks)*
$\forall c \in b, \sigma^L \in \Sigma^L.\ \{[\![\widetilde{c}]\!]_D (\sigma^D) \mid \sigma^D \in \gamma_L(\sigma^L)\} \subseteq \gamma_C([\![c]\!]_L (\sigma^L))$ *where*
$\gamma_C(\text{tt}) = \{\text{tt}\},\ \gamma_C(\text{ff}) = \{\text{ff}\},\ \gamma_C(\top) = \{\text{tt}, \text{ff}\}$

Proof. We prove this by induction on the structure of the boolean expressions in b.
We first consider the base cases:

(i) $\pi(x, m) \geqslant \pi(y, n)$
By definition, $[\![\pi(x, m) \geqslant \pi(y, n)]\!]_L (\sigma^L) = [\![\pi(x, m) \geqslant \pi(y, n)]\!]_B (\sigma_1^L)$

Consider the case where, $[\![\pi(x, m) \geqslant \pi(y, n)]\!]_B (\sigma_1^L) = \text{tt}$, then, by the semantics described in Fig. 6, we know that,

$$\sigma_1^L(x)_m)_1 \geqslant (\sigma_1^L(y)_n)_2) \tag{1}$$

By the definition of γ_L (Definition 5), we also know that,

$$\forall \sigma^D \in \gamma_L. \ (\sigma_1^L(x)_1 \leqslant \sigma_1^D(x) \leqslant \sigma_1^L(x)_2) \wedge (\sigma_1^L(y)_1 \leqslant \sigma_1^D(y) \leqslant \sigma_1^L(y)_2) \qquad (2)$$

where the comparisons are performed pointwise for every element in the vector.

From 1 and 2, we can conclude that,

$$\forall \sigma^D \in \gamma_L(\sigma^L). \ \sigma_1^D(y)_n \leqslant (\sigma_1^L(y)_n)_2 \leqslant (\sigma_1^L(x)_m)_1 \leqslant \sigma_1^D(x)_m \qquad (3)$$

Now,

$$\begin{aligned}
\llbracket \widetilde{\boldsymbol{\pi}(x,m) \geqslant \boldsymbol{\pi}(y,n)} \rrbracket_D (\sigma^D) = \llbracket \boldsymbol{\pi}(x,m) \geqslant \boldsymbol{\pi}(y,n) \rrbracket (\sigma_1^D) = \\
\text{if } \sigma_1^D(x)_m \geqslant \sigma_1^D(y)_n \text{ then tt else ff}
\end{aligned} \qquad (4)$$

From 3 and 4, we can conclude that,
$\forall \sigma^D \in \gamma_L(\sigma^L). \ \llbracket \widetilde{\boldsymbol{\pi}(x,m) \geqslant \boldsymbol{\pi}(y,n)} \rrbracket_D (\sigma^D) = \mathbf{tt}$, or in other words,
$\{ \llbracket \widetilde{\boldsymbol{\pi}(x,m) \geqslant \boldsymbol{\pi}(y,n)} \rrbracket_D (\sigma^D) \mid \sigma^D \in \gamma_L(\sigma^L) \} \subseteq \gamma_C (\llbracket \widetilde{\boldsymbol{\pi}(x,m) \geqslant \boldsymbol{\pi}(y,n)} \rrbracket_L (\sigma^L))$
when the analysis returns $\mathbf{tt}$.
We can similarly prove the case when the analysis returns $\mathbf{ff}$. In case, the analysis returns $\top$, the required subset containment is trivially true since $\gamma_C(\top) = \{\mathbf{tt}, \mathbf{ff}\}$.

(ii) $\boldsymbol{\pi}(x,m) \geqslant 0$
The proof is very similar to the first case, and we skip the details.

(iii) $\boldsymbol{\pi}(x,m) < 0$
The proof is very similar to the first case, and we skip the details.

We next consider the inductive cases:

(iv) $b_1 \wedge b_2$
By the inductive hypothesis, we know that,
$\{ \llbracket \widetilde{b_1} \rrbracket_D (\sigma^D) \mid \sigma^D \in \gamma_L(\sigma^L) \} \subseteq \gamma_C (\llbracket b_1 \rrbracket_L (\sigma^L))$
$\{ \llbracket \widetilde{b_2} \rrbracket_D (\sigma^D) \mid \sigma^D \in \gamma_L(\sigma^L) \} \subseteq \gamma_C (\llbracket b_2 \rrbracket_L (\sigma^L))$
If $\llbracket b_1 \rrbracket_L (\sigma^L) = \top \vee \llbracket b_2 \rrbracket_L (\sigma^L) = \top$, then, as per the semantics in Fig. 6, $\llbracket b_1 \wedge b_2 \rrbracket_L (\sigma^L) = \top$, and the desired property trivially holds.
However, if $\llbracket b_1 \rrbracket_L (\sigma^L) \neq \top \wedge \llbracket b_2 \rrbracket_L (\sigma^L) \neq \top$, then using the inductive hypotheses, we know that for all $\sigma^D \in \gamma_L(\sigma^L)$, $\llbracket \widetilde{b_1} \rrbracket_D (\sigma^D)$ evaluates to the same boolean value as $\llbracket b_1 \rrbracket_L (\sigma^L)$. We can make the same deduction for b_2. So, evaluating $\llbracket \widetilde{b_1 \wedge b_2} \rrbracket_D$ also yields the same boolean value for all $\sigma^D \in \gamma_L(\sigma^L)$, and this value is equal to $\llbracket b_1 \wedge b_2 \rrbracket_L (\sigma^L)$.

(v) $\neg b$
By the inductive hypothesis, we know that,
$\{ \llbracket \widetilde{b} \rrbracket_D (\sigma^D) \mid \sigma^D \in \gamma_L(\sigma^L) \} \subseteq \gamma_C (\llbracket b \rrbracket_L (\upsilon^L))$

If $[\![b]\!]_L(\sigma^L) = \mathbf{tt}$, then $\forall \sigma^D \in \gamma_L(\sigma^L)$. $\widetilde{[\![b]\!]}_D(\sigma^D) = \mathbf{tt}$.

So, $\forall \sigma^D \in \gamma_L(\sigma^L)$. $\widetilde{[\![\neg b]\!]}_D(\sigma^D) = \mathbf{ff}$, and we can conclude that,

$\{\widetilde{[\![\neg b]\!]}_D(\sigma^D) \mid \sigma^D \in \gamma_L(\sigma^L)\} \subseteq \gamma_C([\![\neg b]\!]_L(\sigma^L)) = \{\mathbf{ff}\}$.

We can similarly argue about the case when $[\![b]\!]_L(\sigma^L) = \mathbf{ff}$, and as stated previously, the case with, $[\![b]\!]_L(\sigma^L) = \top$ trivially holds. ∎

Theorem 13. *(Soundness of Jacobian analysis)*

$\forall p \in s^-, \sigma^L \in \Sigma^L . \{\widetilde{[\![p]\!]}_D(\sigma^D) \mid \sigma^D \in \gamma_L(\sigma^L)\} \subseteq \gamma_L([\![p]\!]_L(\sigma^L))$

Proof. We prove this by induction on the structure of statements in s^-. We first consider the base cases:

(i) **skip**

By definition, for any state σ^L,

$$[\![\mathbf{skip}]\!]_L(\sigma^L) = \sigma^L \tag{5}$$

$$\{\widetilde{[\![\mathbf{skip}]\!]}_D(\sigma^D) \mid \sigma^D \in \gamma_L(\sigma^L)\} = \{\sigma^D \mid \sigma^D \in \gamma_L(\sigma^L)\} = \gamma_L(\sigma^L) \tag{6}$$

From Eqs. 5 and 6,

$$\{\widetilde{[\![\mathbf{skip}]\!]}_D(\sigma^D) \mid \sigma^D \in \gamma_L(\sigma^L)\} \subseteq \gamma_L([\![\mathbf{skip}]\!]_L(\sigma^L)) \tag{7}$$

(ii) $y \leftarrow w \cdot x + \beta$

We first observe that when multiplying an interval (l, u) with a constant c, if $c \geqslant 0$, then the result is simply given by the interval $(c \cdot l, c \cdot u)$. But if $c < 0$, then the result is in the interval $(c \cdot u, c \cdot l)$, i.e., the use of the lower bounds and upper bounds gets flipped. Similarly, when computing the dot product of an abstract vector v with a constant vector w, for each multiplication operation $v_i \cdot w_i$, we use the same reasoning as above. Then, the lower bound and upper bound of the dot product result are given by,

$(\sum_{i=1 \wedge w_i \geqslant 0}^{n} w_i \cdot (v_i)_1 + \sum_{i=1 \wedge w_i < 0}^{n} w_i \cdot (v_i)_2, \quad \sum_{i=1 \wedge w_i \geqslant 0}^{n} w_i \cdot (v_i)_2 + \sum_{i=1 \wedge w_i < 0}^{n} w_i \cdot (v_i)_1)$

where $(v_i)_1$ represents the lower bound of the ith element of v and $(v_i)_2$ represents the lower bound of the ith element of v, and we assume $\mathbf{dim}(w) = \mathbf{dim}(v) = n$.

We do not provide the rest of the formal proof for this case since it just involves using the definitions.

Next, we consider the inductive cases:

(iii) $s_1^- ; s_2^-$

From the inductive hypothesis, we know,

$$L_1 = \{\widetilde{[\![s_1^-]\!]}_D(\sigma^D) \mid \sigma^D \in \gamma_L(\sigma^L)\} \subseteq \gamma_L([\![s_1^-]\!]_L(\sigma^L)) \tag{8}$$

$$L_2 = \{\widetilde{[\![s_2^-]\!]}_D(\sigma^D) \mid \sigma^D \in \gamma_L([\![s_1^-]\!]_L(\sigma^L))\} \subseteq \gamma_L([\![s_2^-]\!]_L([\![s_1^-]\!]_L(\sigma^L))) \quad (9)$$

From Eqs. 8 and 9, we conclude,

$$\{\widetilde{[\![s_2^-]\!]}_D(\sigma^D) \mid \sigma^D \in L_1\} \subseteq L_2 \subseteq \gamma_L([\![s_2^-]\!]_L([\![s_1^-]\!]_L(\sigma^L))) \quad (10)$$

Rewriting, we get,

$$\{\widetilde{[\![s_2^-]\!]}_D(\widetilde{[\![s_1^-]\!]}_D(\sigma^D)) \mid \sigma^D \in \gamma_L(\sigma^L)\} \subseteq \gamma_L([\![s_2^-]\!]_L([\![s_1^-]\!]_L(\sigma^L))) \quad (11)$$

and this can be simplified further as,

$$\{\widetilde{[\![s_1^-; s_2^-]\!]}_D(\sigma^D) \mid \sigma^D \in \gamma_L(\sigma^L)\} \subseteq \gamma_L([\![s_1^-; s_2^-]\!]_L(\sigma^L)) \quad (12)$$

(iv) **if** b **then** s_1^- **else** s_2^-

From the inductive hypothesis, we know,

$$\{\widetilde{[\![s_1^-]\!]}_D(\sigma^D) \mid \sigma^D \in \gamma_L(\sigma^L)\} \subseteq \gamma_L([\![s_1^-]\!]_L(\sigma^L)) \quad (13)$$

$$\{\widetilde{[\![s_2^-]\!]}_D(\sigma^D) \mid \sigma^D \in \gamma_L(\sigma^L)\} \subseteq \gamma_L([\![s_2^-]\!]_L(\sigma^L)) \quad (14)$$

The conditional check can result in three different outcomes while performing the analysis - **tt**, **ff**, or ⊤. From Lemma 12, we know that the abstract boolean checks are sound. We analyze each of the three cases separately.

(a) **tt**

Since we only consider the true case, we can write,

$$[\![\text{if } b \text{ then } s_1^- \text{ else } s_2^-]\!]_L(\sigma^L) = [\![s_1^-]\!]_L(\sigma^L) \quad (15)$$

Also, from Lemma 12,

$$\{\widetilde{[\![\text{if } b \text{ then } s_1^- \text{ else } s_2^-]\!]}_D(\sigma^D) \mid \sigma^D \in \gamma_L(\sigma^L)\} = \{\widetilde{[\![s_1^-]\!]}_D(\sigma^D) \mid \sigma^D \in \gamma_L(\sigma^L)\} \quad (16)$$

From 13, 15, and 16,

$$\{\widetilde{[\![\text{if } b \text{ then } s_1^- \text{ else } s_2^-]\!]}_D(\sigma^D) \mid \sigma^D \in \gamma_L(\sigma^L)\} \subseteq \gamma_L([\![\text{if } b \text{ then } s_1^- \text{ else } s_2^-]\!]_L(\sigma^L)) \quad (17)$$

(b) **ff**

Similar to the **tt** case, for the **ff** case, we can show,

$$\{\widetilde{[\![\text{if } b \text{ then } s_1^- \text{ else } s_2^-]\!]}_D(\sigma^D) \mid \sigma^D \in \gamma_L(\sigma^L)\} \subseteq \gamma_L([\![\text{if } b \text{ then } s_1^- \text{ else } s_2^-]\!]_L(\sigma^L)) \quad (18)$$

(c) $\top$

We first prove the following about the join ($\bigsqcup_L$) operation,

$$\gamma_L(\sigma^L) \cup \gamma_L(\tilde{\sigma}^L) \subseteq \gamma_L(\sigma^L \sqcup_L \tilde{\sigma}^L) \tag{19}$$

By definition of γ_L,

$$\gamma_L(\sigma^L) = \{\sigma^D \mid (\bigwedge_{v \in V} .\sigma_1^L(v)_1 \leqslant \sigma_1^D(v) \leqslant \sigma_1^L(v)_2) \wedge$$

$$(\bigwedge_{v \in V} .(\sigma_2^L(v)_1)_1 \leqslant \sigma_2^D(v)_1 \leqslant (\sigma_2^L(v)_1)_2) \wedge \tag{20}$$

$$\sigma_2^D(v)_2 \in \gamma_V(\sigma_2^L(v)_2)\}$$

$\gamma_L(\tilde{\sigma}^L)$ can be defined similarly.

The join operation combines corresponding intervals in the abstract states by taking the smaller of the two lower bounds and larger of the two upper bounds. We do not prove the following formally, but from the definition of γ_L and $\bigsqcup_L$, one can see that the intended property holds.

Next, we consider the **assert** statements that appear in the abstract denotational semantics for the $\top$ case.

Let us call, $\sigma_1^L = [\![\textbf{assert } b]\!]_L(\sigma^L)$ and $\sigma_2^L = [\![\textbf{assert } \neg b]\!]_L(\sigma^L)$.

From inductive hypothesis (13 and 14) we know,

$$L_1 = \{\widetilde{[\![s_1^-]\!]}_D(\sigma^D) \mid \sigma^D \in \gamma_L(\sigma_1^L)\} \subseteq \gamma_L([\![s_1^-]\!]_L(\sigma_1^L)) \tag{21}$$

$$L_2 = \{\widetilde{[\![s_2^-]\!]}_D(\sigma^D) \mid \sigma^D \in \gamma_L(\sigma_2^L)\} \subseteq \gamma_L([\![s_2^-]\!]_L(\sigma_2^L)) \tag{22}$$

From 19, 21, and 22,

$$L_1 \cup L_2 \subseteq \gamma_L([\![s_1^-]\!]_L(\sigma_1^L)) \cup \gamma_L([\![s_2^-]\!]_L(\sigma_2^L)) \subseteq \gamma_L([\![s_1^-]\!]_L(\sigma_1^L) \sqcup [\![s_2^-]\!]_L(\sigma_2^L)) \tag{23}$$

Then, if we can show that,

$$\{\sigma^D \mid \sigma^D \in \gamma_L(\sigma^L) \wedge [\![b]\!](\sigma^D) = \textbf{tt}\} \subseteq \gamma_L(\sigma_1^L) \tag{24}$$

$$\{\sigma^D \mid \sigma^D \in \gamma_L(\sigma^L) \wedge [\![b]\!](\sigma^D) = \textbf{ff}\} \subseteq \gamma_L(\sigma_2^L) \tag{25}$$

then, from 21, 22, 23, 24, 25, and the semantics of **if** b **then** s_1^- **else** s_2^-, we can say,

$$\{\widetilde{[\![\textbf{if } b \textbf{ then } s_1^- \textbf{ else } s_2^-]\!]}_D(\sigma^D) \mid \sigma^D \in \gamma_L(\sigma^L)\} \subseteq \gamma_L([\![\textbf{if } b \textbf{ then } s_1^- \textbf{ else } s_2^-]\!]_L(\sigma^L)) \tag{26}$$

Now, we need to show that 24 and 25 are true. The **assert** statements either behave as identity or produce a modified abstract state (see Fig. 6). When **assert** behaves as identity, 24 and 25 are obviously true. We skip the proof of the case when **assert** produces a modified abstract state.

■

D   Proof of Corollary 8

Corollary 8. *(Upper bound of Jacobian operator norm)*
$\forall p \in s^-, \sigma^L \in \Sigma^L, v \in V.$
$\mathbf{max}\{\left\| (([\![\widetilde{p}]\!]_D(\sigma^D))_2)(v)_1 \right\| \mid \sigma^D \in \gamma_L(\sigma^L)\} \leqslant \left\| (([\![p]\!]_L(\sigma^L))_2(v))_1 \right\|_L$

Proof. From Theorem 6, we know that for any $p \in s^-, \sigma^L \in \Sigma^L$,

$$\{[\![\widetilde{p}]\!]_D(\sigma^D) \mid \sigma^D \in \gamma_L(\sigma^L)\} \subseteq \gamma_L([\![p]\!]_L(\sigma^L)) \tag{1}$$

Let us define, $D_V = \{(([\![\widetilde{p}]\!]_D(\sigma^D))_2(v))_1 \mid \sigma^D \in \gamma_L(\sigma^L)\}$. This is the set of all Jacobian matrices associated with the variable v after executing p on the set of input states, $\gamma_L(\sigma^L)$. Note that the set D_V does not distinguish the Jacobians on the basis of the input that we are differentiating with respect to.
Let $D_V^L = \{(\tilde{\sigma}_2^D(v))_1 \mid \tilde{\sigma}^D \in \gamma_L([\![p]\!]_L(\sigma^L))\}$, and $J = (([\![p]\!]_L(\sigma^L))_2(v))_1$.
Using Definition 5 of γ_L, we can show,

$$\forall d \in D_V^L. \ J_1 \leqslant d \leqslant J_2 \tag{2}$$

where $\leqslant$ is defined pointwise on the matrices, and $J_1(J_2)$ refers to the matrix of lower(upper) bounds.
Then, from 1 and definitions of D_V and D_V^L, we can deduce that,

$$D_V \subseteq D_V^L \tag{3}$$

From 2 and 3,
$$\forall d \in D_V. \ J_1 \leqslant d \leqslant J_2 \tag{4}$$

Let $J' = [\mathbf{max}\{|(J_{k,l})_1|, |(J_{k,l})_2|\} \mid k \in \{1, ..., m\}, l \in \{1, ..., n\}]$. Then,

$$\forall d \in D_V. \ |d| \leqslant J' \tag{5}$$

where $|\cdot|$ applies pointwise on matrices d.
Using definition of operator norm, one can show that,

$$M_1 \leqslant M_2 \implies \|M_1\| \leqslant \|M_2\| \tag{6}$$

where M_1 and M_2 are matrices with $\leqslant$ applied pointwise.
Finally, from 5 and 6, we conclude,

$$\forall d \in D_V. \ \|d\| \leqslant \|J'\| = \|J\| \tag{7}$$

Unrolling the definitions,

$$\mathbf{max}\{\left\| (([\![\widetilde{p}]\!]_L(\sigma^D))_2)(v)_1 \right\| \mid \sigma^D \in \gamma(\sigma^L)\} \leqslant \left\| (([\![p]\!]_L(\sigma^L))_2(v))_1 \right\|_L \tag{8}$$

∎

E   Proof of Theorem 11

Theorem 11. *(Soundness of* PROLIP*)*
Let $p = z \leftsquigarrow N(0,1); g; f$ *where* $g, f \in s^-$, $(k_U, d, vol) = $ PROLIP(p, z_B), $z \notin$
outv(g), $z \notin$ **outv**(f), $x \in$ **inv**(f), *and* $y \in$ **outv**(f) *then,* $\forall \sigma_0 \in \Sigma$.
$$\Pr_{\sigma,\sigma' \sim [\![p]\!](\sigma_0)} ((\|\sigma(y) - \sigma'(y)\| \leqslant k_U \cdot \|\sigma(x) - \sigma'(x)\|) \wedge (\sigma(z), \sigma'(z) \in \gamma(z_B))) \geqslant vol$$

Proof. We prove this theorem in two parts.

First, let us define set Σ_P as, $\Sigma_P = \{\sigma \mid \sigma \in \gamma_B([\![f]\!]_L([\![g]\!]_B(\sigma^B[z \mapsto z_B])))_1)\}$
In words, Σ_P is the concretization of the abstract box produced by abstractly
"interpreting" $g; f$ on the input box z_B. Assuming that z is not written to by
g or f, it is easy to see from the definitions of the abstract semantics in Figs. 6
and 4 that, $([\![f]\!]_L([\![g]\!]_B(\sigma^B[z \mapsto z_B])))_1(z) = z_B$, i.e., the final abstract value
of z is the same as the initial value z_B. Moreover, from Theorem 8, we know
that the operator norm of the abstract Jacobian matrix, $\|J\|_L$ upper bounds the
operator norm of every Jacobian of f for variable y with respect to x (since
$x \in$ **inv**$(f), y \in$ **outv**(f)) for every input in $\gamma_B([\![g]\!]_B(\sigma^B[z \mapsto z_B]))$, which itself
is an upper bound on the local Lipschitz constant in the same region.
In other words, we can say that,
$$\forall \sigma, \sigma' \in \Sigma_P. \sigma(z), \sigma'(z) \in \gamma(z_B) \wedge \|\sigma(y) - \sigma'(y)\| \leqslant k_U \cdot \|\sigma(x) - \sigma'(x)\|.$$

To complete the proof, we need to show that, $\Pr_{\sigma,\sigma' \sim [\![p]\!](\sigma_0)} (\sigma, \sigma' \in \Sigma_P) \geqslant vol$. We
show this in the second part of this proof.
Using the semantic definition of *pcat* (Fig. 2), we know that,
$[\![p]\!](\sigma_0) = \widehat{[\![f]\!]}(\widehat{[\![g]\!]}([\![z \leftsquigarrow N(0,1)]\!](\sigma_0)))$
We first analyze $[\![z \leftsquigarrow N(0,1)]\!](\sigma_0)$. Again using the semantic definition of *pcat*,
we write,

$$
\begin{aligned}
[\![z \leftsquigarrow N(0,1)]\!](\sigma_0) &= \mathbb{E}_{z \sim N(0,1)}[\lambda\nu.\delta_{\sigma_0[z \mapsto \nu]}] \\
&= \lambda\nu'. \int_a N(a) \cdot \delta_{\sigma_0[z \mapsto a]}(\nu') \\
&= \lambda\nu'.1_{\nu'=\sigma_0[z \mapsto a]} \cdot N(a)
\end{aligned}
\tag{1}
$$

We are interested in the volume of the set Σ_z, defined as, $\Sigma_z = \{\sigma \mid \sigma(z) \in z_B\}$.
Using the expression for $[\![z \leftsquigarrow N(0,1)]\!](\sigma_0)$ from above, we can now compute
the required probability as follows,

$$
\begin{aligned}
\Pr_{\sigma \sim [\![z \leftsquigarrow N(0,1)]\!](\sigma_0)} (\sigma \in \Sigma_z) &= \int_{\sigma \in \Sigma}([\![z \leftsquigarrow N(0,1)]\!](\sigma_0))(\sigma) \cdot 1_{\sigma \in \Sigma_z} \\
&= \int_{\sigma \in \Sigma}(1_{\sigma = \sigma_0[z \mapsto a]} \cdot N(a)) \cdot 1_{\sigma \in \Sigma_z} \\
&= \int_{\sigma \in \Sigma_z}(1_{\sigma = \sigma_0[z \mapsto a]} \cdot N(a)) \\
&= \int_{a \in z_B} N(a) \quad \text{(by uniqueness of } \sigma_0[z \mapsto a]) \\
&= vol'
\end{aligned}
\tag{2}
$$

This shows that starting from any $\sigma_0 \in \Sigma$, after executing the first statement of
p, the probability that the value stored at z lies in the box z_B is vol'.

Next, we analyze $[\![z \rightsquigarrow N(0,1)]\!](\sigma_0)$. In particular, we are interested in the volume of the set, $\widetilde{[\![g]\!]}(\Sigma_z)$ (which is notational abuse for the set $\{\widetilde{[\![g]\!]}(\sigma) \mid \sigma \in \Sigma_z\}$). We can lower bound this volume as follows,

$$\Pr_{\sigma \sim \widehat{[\![g]\!]}([\![z \rightsquigarrow N(0,1)]\!](\sigma_0))} (\sigma \in \widetilde{[\![g]\!]}(\Sigma_z)) = \int_{\sigma \in \Sigma} (\widehat{[\![g]\!]}([\![z \rightsquigarrow N(0,1)]\!](\sigma_0)))(\sigma) \cdot 1_{\sigma \in \widetilde{[\![g]\!]}(\Sigma_z)}$$

$$= \int_{\sigma \in \widetilde{[\![g]\!]}(\Sigma_z)} \widehat{[\![g]\!]}([\![z \rightsquigarrow N(0,1)]\!](\sigma_0))(\sigma) \quad (3)$$
$$\geq \int_{\sigma \in \Sigma_z} [\![z \rightsquigarrow N(0,1)]\!](\sigma_0))(\sigma) \text{ (from Corollary 4)}$$
$$= vol' \quad \text{(from 2)}$$

We can similarly show that,

$$\Pr_{\sigma \sim \widehat{[\![f]\!]}(\widehat{[\![g]\!]}([\![z \rightsquigarrow N(0,1)]\!](\sigma_0)))} (\sigma \in \widetilde{[\![f]\!]}(\widetilde{[\![g]\!]}(\Sigma_z))) \geq vol' \quad (4)$$

Now, $\sigma^B[z \mapsto z_B]$ defined on line 2 of Algorithm 1 is such that $\gamma(\sigma^B[z \mapsto z_B]) = \Sigma_z$. From Theorem 10, we can conclude that,

$$\widetilde{[\![g]\!]}(\Sigma_z) \subseteq \gamma([\![g]\!]_B(\sigma^B[z \mapsto z_B])) \quad (5)$$

Similarly, from Theorem 6, we can conclude that,

$$\widetilde{[\![f]\!]}(\widetilde{[\![g]\!]}(\Sigma_z)) \subseteq \gamma([\![f]\!]_L([\![g]\!]_B(\sigma^B[z \mapsto z_B]))_1) \quad (6)$$

From 4 and 6, we conclude that,

$$\Pr_{\sigma \sim [\![p]\!](\sigma_0)} (\sigma \in \gamma([\![f]\!]_L([\![g]\!]_B(\sigma^B[z \mapsto z_B])))_1) \geq vol' \quad (7)$$

Consequently,

$$\Pr_{\sigma, \sigma' \sim [\![p]\!](\sigma_0)} (\sigma, \sigma' \in \gamma([\![f]\!]_L([\![g]\!]_B(\sigma^B[z \mapsto z_B])))_1) \geq vol' \times vol' = vol \quad (8)$$

since each act of sampling is independent.   ∎

F   Translating Neural Networks into *pcat*

NNs are often described as a sequential composition of "layers", with each layer describing the computation to be performed on an incoming vector. Many commonly used layers can be expressed in the *pcat* language. For instance, [28] describes the translation of maxpool, convolution, ReLU, and fully connected layers into the *cat* language. Here, we describe the translation of two other common layers, namely, the batchnorm layer [34] and the transposed convolution layer (also referred to as the deconvolution layer) [60].

Batchnorm Layer. A batchnorm layer typically typically expects an input $x \in \mathbb{R}^{C \times H \times W}$ which we flatten, using a row-major form in to $x' \in \mathbb{R}^{C \cdot H \cdot W}$ where, historically, C denotes the number of channels in the input, H denotes the height, and W denotes the width. For instance, given an RGB image of dimensions 28×28 pixels, $H = 28$, $W = 28$, and $C = 3$.

A batchnorm layer is associated with vectors m and v such that $\mathbf{dim}(m) = \mathbf{dim}(v) = C$ where $\mathbf{dim}(\cdot)$ returns the dimension of a vector. m and v represent the running-mean and running-variance of the values in each channel observed during the training time of the NN. A batchnorm layer is also associated with a scaling vector s^1 and a shift vector s^2, both also of dimension c. For a particular element $x_{i,j,k}$ in the input, the corresponding output element is $s_i^1 \cdot (\frac{x_{i,j,k} - m_i}{\sqrt{v_i + \epsilon}}) + s_i^2$ where ϵ is a constant that is added for numerical stability (commonly set to $1e^{-5}$). Note that the batchnorm operation produces an output of the same dimensions as the input. We can represent the batchnorm operation by the statement, $y \leftarrow w \cdot x' + \beta$, where x' is the flattened input, w is a weight matrix of dimension $C \cdot H \cdot W \times C \cdot H \cdot W$ and β is a bias vector of dimension $C \cdot H \cdot W$, such that,

$$w = I \cdot [\frac{s_{\lfloor i/H \cdot W \rfloor}^1}{\sqrt{v_{\lfloor i/H \cdot W \rfloor} + \epsilon}} \mid i \in \{1, ..., C \cdot H \cdot W\}]$$

$$\beta = [-\frac{s_{\lfloor i/H \cdot W \rfloor}^1 \cdot m_{\lfloor i/H \cdot W \rfloor}}{\sqrt{v_{\lfloor i/H \cdot W \rfloor} + \epsilon}} + s_{\lfloor i/H \cdot W \rfloor}^2 \mid i \in \{1, ..., C \cdot H \cdot W\}]$$

where I is the identity matrix with dimension $(C \cdot H \cdot W, C \cdot H \cdot W)$, $\lfloor \cdot \rfloor$ is the floor operation that rounds down to an integer, and $[\,|\,]$ is the list builder/comprehension notation.

Transposed Convolution Layer. A convolution layer applies a kernel or a filter on the input vector and typically, compresses this vector so that the output vector is of a smaller dimension. A deconvolution or transposed convolution layer does the opposite - it applies the kernel in a manner that produces a larger output vector. A transposed convolution layer expects an input $x \in \mathbb{R}^{C_{in} \times H_{in} \times W_{in}}$ and applies a kernel $k \in \mathbb{R}^{C_{out} \times C_{in} \times K_h \times K_w}$ using a stride S. For simplicity of presentation, we assume that $K_h = K_w = K$ and $W_{in} = H_{in}$. In $pcat$, the transposed convolution layer can be expressed by the statement, $y \leftarrow w \cdot x'$, where x' is the flattened version of input x, w is a weight matrix that we derive from the parameters associated with the transposed convolution layer, and the bias vector, β, is a zero vector in this case. To compute the dimensions of the weight matrix, we first calculate the height (H_{out}) and width (W_{out}) of each channel in the output using formulae, $H_{out} = H_{in} \cdot S + K$, and $W_{out} = W_{in} \cdot S + K$. Since we assume $W_{in} = H_{in}$, we have $W_{out} = H_{out}$ here. Then, the dimension of w is $C_{out} \cdot H_{out} \cdot W_{out} \times C_{in} \cdot H_{in} \cdot W_{in}$, and the definition of w is as follows,

$$w = \left[\begin{array}{ll} \textbf{let } x = \lceil i/C_{out} \rceil & \text{in} \\ \textbf{let } y = \lceil j/C_{in} \rceil & \text{in} \\ \textbf{let } h = 1 + \lfloor ((i \bmod C_{out}) - (\lfloor ((j \bmod C_{in}) - 1)/H_{in} \rfloor \cdot & \\ \quad H_{out} \cdot S + 1 + (((j \bmod C_{in}) - 1) \bmod H_{in}) \cdot S))/H_{out} \rfloor & \text{in} \\ \textbf{let } w = 1 + ((i \bmod C_{out}) - (\lfloor ((j \bmod C_{in}) - 1)/H_{in} \rfloor \cdot & \\ \quad H_{out} \cdot S + 1 + (((j \bmod C_{in}) - 1) \bmod H_{in}) \cdot S)) \bmod H_{out} & \text{in} \\ \textbf{if } h, w \in [1...K] \textbf{ then } k_{x,y,h,w} \textbf{ else } 0 \end{array} \right]_{\substack{i \in I, \\ j \in J}}$$

where $I = \{1, ..., C_{out} \cdot H_{out} \cdot W_{out}\}$ and $J = \{1, ..., C_{in} \cdot H_{in} \cdot W_{in}\}$

G   Details of Box Analysis

$$\Sigma^B \triangleq V \to \bigcup_{n \in \mathbb{N}} (\mathbb{R} \times \mathbb{R})^n$$

$$[\![e]\!]_B : \Sigma^B \to \bigcup_{n \in \mathbb{N}} (\mathbb{R} \times \mathbb{R})^n$$

$$[\![\pi(x,n)]\!]_B (\sigma^B) = \sigma^B (x)_n$$

$$[\![w \cdot x + \beta]\!]_B (\sigma^B) = \mathbf{let}\ m = \mathbf{dim}(w)_1\ \mathbf{in}$$

$$\mathbf{let}\ n = \mathbf{dim}(\sigma^B (x))\ \mathbf{in}$$

$$[((\sum_{j=1 \wedge w_{i,j} \geqslant 0}^{n} w_{i,j} \cdot (\sigma^B (x)_i)_1 +$$

$$\sum_{j=1 \wedge w_{i,j} < 0}^{n} w_{i,j} \cdot (\sigma^B (x)_i)_2 + \beta_i),$$

$$(\sum_{j=1 \wedge w_{i,j} \geqslant 0}^{n} w_{i,j} \cdot (\sigma^B (x)_i)_2 +$$

$$\sum_{j=1 \wedge w_{i,j} < 0}^{n} w_{i,j} \cdot (\sigma^B (x)_i)_1 + \beta_i)) \mid i \in \{1, ..., m\}]$$

$$[\![b]\!]_B : \Sigma^B \to \{\mathbf{tt}, \mathbf{ff}, \top\}$$

$$[\![\pi(x,m) \geqslant \pi(y,n)]\!]_B (\sigma^B) = \mathbf{if}\quad ((\sigma^B (x)_m)_1 \geqslant (\sigma^B (y)_n)_2)\ \mathbf{then}\ \mathbf{tt}$$

$$\mathbf{else\ if}\ ((\sigma^B (x)_m)_2 < (\sigma^B (y)_n)_1)\ \mathbf{then}\ \mathbf{ff}$$

$$\mathbf{else}\quad \top$$

$$[\![\pi(x,m) \geqslant 0]\!]_B (\sigma^B) = \mathbf{if}\quad ((\sigma^B (x)_m)_1 \geqslant 0)\ \mathbf{then}\ \mathbf{tt}$$

$$\mathbf{else\ if}\ ((\sigma^B (x)_m)_2 < 0)\ \mathbf{then}\ \mathbf{ff}$$

$$\mathbf{else}\quad \top$$

$$[\![\pi(x,m) < 0]\!]_B (\sigma^B) = \mathbf{if}\quad ((\sigma^B (x)_m)_2 < 0)\ \mathbf{then}\ \mathbf{tt}$$

$$\mathbf{else\ if}\ ((\sigma^B (x)_m)_1 \geqslant 0)\ \mathbf{then}\ \mathbf{ff}$$

$$\mathbf{else}\quad \top$$

$$[\![b_1 \wedge b_2]\!]_B (\sigma^B) = \mathbf{if}\quad ([\![b_1]\!]_B (\sigma^B) = \top \vee [\![b_2]\!]_B (\sigma^B) = \top)\ \mathbf{then}\ \top$$

$$\mathbf{else}\ [\![b_1]\!]_B (\sigma^B) \wedge [\![b_2]\!]_B (\sigma^B)$$

$$[\![\neg b]\!]_B (\sigma^B) = \mathbf{if}\quad ([\![b]\!]_B (\sigma^B) = \mathbf{tt})\ \mathbf{then}\ \mathbf{ff}$$

$$\mathbf{else\ if}\ ([\![b]\!]_B (\sigma^B) = \mathbf{ff})\ \mathbf{then}\ \mathbf{tt}$$

$$\mathbf{else}\ \top$$

$$\bigsqcup_B : \Sigma^B \times \Sigma^B \to \Sigma^B$$

$$\sigma^B \bigsqcup_B \tilde{\sigma}^B = \lambda v.\ [(\mathbf{min}\{(\sigma^B (v)_i)_1, (\tilde{\sigma}^B (v)_i)_1\}, \mathbf{max}\{(\sigma^B (v)_i)_2, (\tilde{\sigma}^B (v)_i)_2\}) \mid$$

$$i \in \{1, ..., \mathbf{dim}(\sigma^B (v))\}]$$

$$[\![s^-]\!]_B : \Sigma^B \to \Sigma^B$$

$$[\![\mathbf{skip}]\!]_B (\sigma^B) = \sigma^B$$

$$[\![\mathbf{assert}\ \pi(x,m) \geqslant 0]\!]_B (\sigma^B) = \sigma^B [x_m \mapsto (0, \mathbf{max}\{(\sigma^B (x)_m)_2, 0\})]$$

$$[\![\mathbf{assert}\ \pi(x,m) < 0]\!]_B (\sigma^B) = \sigma^B [x_m \mapsto (\mathbf{min}\{(\sigma^B (x)_m)_1, 0\}, 0)]$$

$$[\![\mathbf{assert}\ \neg(\pi(x,m) \geqslant 0)]\!]_B (\sigma^B) = [\![\mathbf{assert}\ \pi(x,m) < 0]\!]_B (\sigma^B)$$

$$[\![\mathbf{assert}\ \neg(\pi(x,m) < 0)]\!]_B (\sigma^B) = [\![\mathbf{assert}\ \pi(x,m) \geqslant 0]\!]_B (\sigma^B)$$

$$[\![\mathbf{assert}\ \hat{b}]\!]_B (\sigma^B) = \sigma^B\ (\text{where}\ \hat{b}\ \text{refers to all other boolean expressions})$$

$$[\![y \leftarrow w \cdot x + \beta]\!]_B (\sigma^B) = \sigma^B [y \mapsto [\![w \cdot x + \beta]\!]_B (\sigma^B)]$$

$$[\![s_1; s_2]\!]_B (\sigma^B) = [\![s_2]\!]_B ([\![s_1]\!]_B (\sigma^B))$$

$$[\![\mathbf{if}\ b\ \mathbf{then}\ s_1\ \mathbf{else}\ s_2]\!]_B (\sigma^B) = \mathbf{if}\quad ([\![b]\!]_B (\sigma^B) = \mathbf{tt})\ \mathbf{then}\ [\![s_1]\!]_B (\sigma^B)$$

$$\mathbf{else\ if}\ ([\![b]\!]_B (\sigma^B) = \mathbf{ff})\ \mathbf{then}\ [\![s_2]\!]_B (\sigma^B)$$

$$\mathbf{else}\quad [\![s_1]\!]_B ([\![\mathbf{assert}\ b]\!]_B (\sigma^B)) \bigsqcup_B [\![s_2]\!]_B ([\![\mathbf{assert}\ \neg b]\!]_B (\sigma^B))$$

Fig. 6. *cat* abstract semantics for box analysis

References

1. Albarghouthi, A., D'Antoni, L., Drews, S., Nori, A.V.: FairSquare: probabilistic verification of program fairness. Proc. ACM Program. Lang. **1**(OOPSLA), 80:1–80:30 (2017)
2. Alzantot, M., Sharma, Y., Elgohary, A., Ho, B.J., Srivastava, M., Chang, K.W.: Generating natural language adversarial examples. In: Proceedings of the 2018 Conference on Empirical Methods in Natural Language Processing, pp. 2890–2896. Association for Computational Linguistics, Brussels (October 2018)
3. Baluta, T., Shen, S., Shinde, S., Meel, K.S., Saxena, P.: Quantitative verification of neural networks and its security applications. In: Proceedings of the 2019 ACM SIGSAC Conference on Computer and Communications Security, CCS 2019, pp. 1249–1264. Association for Computing Machinery, London (November 2019)
4. Bárány, I., Füredi, Z.: Computing the volume is difficult. Discret. Comput. Geom. **2**(4), 319–326 (1987)
5. Barthe, G., D'Argenio, P., Rezk, T.: Secure information flow by self-composition. In: Proceedings of 17th IEEE Computer Security Foundations Workshop, 2004, pp. 100–114 (June 2004)
6. Barthe, G., Crespo, J.M., Kunz, C.: Relational verification using product programs. In: Butler, M., Schulte, W. (eds.) FM 2011. LNCS, vol. 6664, pp. 200–214. Springer, Heidelberg (2011). https://doi.org/10.1007/978-3-642-21437-0_17
7. Barthe, G., Espitau, T., Ferrer Fioriti, L.M., Hsu, J.: Synthesizing probabilistic invariants via Doob's decomposition. In: Chaudhuri, S., Farzan, A. (eds.) CAV 2016. LNCS, vol. 9779, pp. 43–61. Springer, Cham (2016). https://doi.org/10.1007/978-3-319-41528-4_3
8. Barthe, G., Espitau, T., Gaboardi, M., Grégoire, B., Hsu, J., Strub, P.-Y.: An assertion-based program logic for probabilistic programs. In: Ahmed, A. (ed.) ESOP 2018. LNCS, vol. 10801, pp. 117–144. Springer, Cham (2018). https://doi.org/10.1007/978-3-319-89884-1_5
9. Barthe, G., Espitau, T., Grégoire, B., Hsu, J., Strub, P.Y.: Proving expected sensitivity of probabilistic programs. Proc. ACM Program. Lang. **2**(POPL), 57:1–57:29 (2017)
10. Bastani, O., Ioannou, Y., Lampropoulos, L., Vytiniotis, D., Nori, A., Criminisi, A.: Measuring neural net robustness with constraints. In: Lee, D.D., Sugiyama, M., Luxburg, U.V., Guyon, I., Garnett, R. (eds.) Advances in Neural Information Processing Systems, vol. 29, pp. 2613–2621. Curran Associates, Inc. (2016). http://papers.nips.cc/paper/6339-measuring-neural-net-robustness-with-constraints.pdf
11. Bastani, O., Zhang, X., Solar-Lezama, A.: Probabilistic verification of fairness properties via concentration. Proc. ACM Program. Lang. **3**(OOPSLA), 118:1–118:27 (2019)
12. Benton, N.: Simple relational correctness proofs for static analyses and program transformations. In: Proceedings of the 31st ACM SIGPLAN-SIGACT Symposium on Principles of Programming Languages, POPL 2004, pp. 14–25. Association for Computing Machinery, Venice (January 2004)
13. Carlini, N., et al.: Hidden voice commands. In: 25th USENIX Security Symposium (USENIX Security 16), pp. 513–530 (2016). https://www.usenix.org/conference/usenixsecurity16/technical-sessions/presentation/carlini
14. Carlini, N., Wagner, D.: Audio adversarial examples: targeted attacks on speech-to-text. In: 2018 IEEE Security and Privacy Workshops (SPW), pp. 1–7 (May 2018)

15. Chakarov, A., Sankaranarayanan, S.: Probabilistic program analysis with martingales. In: Sharygina, N., Veith, H. (eds.) CAV 2013. LNCS, vol. 8044, pp. 511–526. Springer, Heidelberg (2013). https://doi.org/10.1007/978-3-642-39799-8_34

16. Chaudhuri, S., Gulwani, S., Lublinerman, R., Navidpour, S.: Proving programs robust. In: Proceedings of the 19th ACM SIGSOFT Symposium and the 13th European Conference on Foundations of Software Engineering, ESEC/FSE 2011, pp. 102–112. Association for Computing Machinery, Szeged (September 2011)

17. Chen, A.: Aaron-xichen/pytorch-playground (May 2020). https://github.com/aaron-xichen/pytorch-playground

18. Clarkson, M.R., Schneider, F.B.: Hyperproperties. In: 2008 21st IEEE Computer Security Foundations Symposium, pp. 51–65 (June 2008)

19. Combettes, P.L., Pesquet, J.C.: Lipschitz certificates for neural network structures driven by averaged activation operators. arXiv:1903.01014 (2019)

20. Cousins, B., Vempala, S.: Gaussian cooling and $O^*(n^3)$ algorithms for volume and Gaussian volume. SIAM J. Comput. **47**(3), 1237–1273 (2018)

21. Cousot, P., Halbwachs, N.: Automatic discovery of linear restraints among variables of a program. In: Proceedings of the 5th ACM SIGACT-SIGPLAN Symposium on Principles of Programming Languages, POPL 1978, pp. 84–96. Association for Computing Machinery, Tucson (January 1978)

22. Cousot, P., Monerau, M.: Probabilistic abstract interpretation. In: Seidl, H. (ed.) ESOP 2012. LNCS, vol. 7211, pp. 169–193. Springer, Heidelberg (2012). https://doi.org/10.1007/978-3-642-28869-2_9

23. Dyer, M.E., Frieze, A.M.: On the complexity of computing the volume of a polyhedron. SIAM J. Comput. **17**(5), 967–974 (1988)

24. Dyer, M., Frieze, A., Kannan, R.: A random polynomial-time algorithm for approximating the volume of convex bodies. J. ACM **38**(1), 1–17 (1991)

25. Elekes, G.: A geometric inequality and the complexity of computing volume. Discret. Comput. Geom. **1**(4), 289–292 (1986)

26. Fazlyab, M., Robey, A., Hassani, H., Morari, M., Pappas, G.: Efficient and accurate estimation of lipschitz constants for deep neural networks. In: Wallach, H., Larochelle, H., Beygelzimer, A., Alché-Buc, F., Fox, E., Garnett, R. (eds.) Advances in Neural Information Processing Systems, vol. 32, pp. 11427–11438. Curran Associates, Inc. (2019). http://papers.nips.cc/paper/9319-efficient-and-accurate-estimation-of-lipschitz-constants-for-deep-neural-networks.pdf

27. Fischer, M., Balunovic, M., Drachsler-Cohen, D., Gehr, T., Zhang, C., Vechev, M.: DL2: training and querying neural networks with logic. In: International Conference on Machine Learning, pp. 1931–1941 (May 2019). http://proceedings.mlr.press/v97/fischer19a.html

28. Gehr, T., Mirman, M., Drachsler-Cohen, D., Tsankov, P., Chaudhuri, S., Vechev, M.: AI2: safety and robustness certification of neural networks with abstract interpretation. In: 2018 IEEE Symposium on Security and Privacy (SP), pp. 3–18 (May 2018)

29. Geldenhuys, J., Dwyer, M.B., Visser, W.: Probabilistic symbolic execution. In: Proceedings of the 2012 International Symposium on Software Testing and Analysis, ISSTA 2012, pp. 166–176. Association for Computing Machinery, Minneapolis (July 2012)

30. Ghorbal, K., Goubault, E., Putot, S.: The zonotope abstract domain Taylor1+. In: Bouajjani, A., Maler, O. (eds.) CAV 2009. LNCS, vol. 5643, pp. 627–633. Springer, Heidelberg (2009). https://doi.org/10.1007/978-3-642-02658-4_47

31. Gibbons, J.: APLicative programming with Naperian functors. In: Yang, H. (ed.) ESOP 2017. LNCS, vol. 10201, pp. 556–583. Springer, Heidelberg (2017). https://doi.org/10.1007/978-3-662-54434-1_21

32. Goodfellow, I., et al.: Generative adversarial nets. In: Ghahramani, Z., Welling, M., Cortes, C., Lawrence, N.D., Weinberger, K.Q. (eds.) Advances in Neural Information Processing Systems, vol. 27, pp. 2672–2680. Curran Associates, Inc. (2014). http://papers.nips.cc/paper/5423-generative-adversarial-nets.pdf

33. Gouk, H., Frank, E., Pfahringer, B., Cree, M.: Regularisation of neural networks by enforcing lipschitz continuity. arXiv:1804.04368 (September 2018). http://arxiv.org/abs/1804.04368

34. Ioffe, S., Szegedy, C.: Batch normalization: accelerating deep network training by reducing internal covariate shift. In: Proceedings of the 32nd International Conference on International Conference on Machine Learning, ICML 2015, vol. 37, pp. 448–456. JMLR.org, Lille (July 2015)

35. Jia, R., Liang, P.: Adversarial examples for evaluating reading comprehension systems. In: Proceedings of the 2017 Conference on Empirical Methods in Natural Language Processing, pp. 2021–2031. Association for Computational Linguistics, Copenhagen (September 2017)

36. Katoen, J.-P., McIver, A.K., Meinicke, L.A., Morgan, C.C.: Linear-invariant generation for probabilistic programs. In: Cousot, R., Martel, M. (eds.) SAS 2010. LNCS, vol. 6337, pp. 390–406. Springer, Heidelberg (2010). https://doi.org/10.1007/978-3-642-15769-1_24

37. Katz, G., Barrett, C., Dill, D.L., Julian, K., Kochenderfer, M.J.: Reluplex: an efficient SMT solver for verifying deep neural networks. In: Majumdar, R., Kunčak, V. (eds.) Computer Aided Verification, CAV 2017. Lecture Notes in Computer Science, vol. 10426. Springer, Cham (2017). https://doi.org/10.1007/978-3-319-63387-9_5

38. Katz, G., et al.: The Marabou framework for verification and analysis of deep neural networks. In: Dillig, I., Tasiran, S. (eds.) CAV 2019. LNCS, vol. 11561, pp. 443–452. Springer, Cham (2019). https://doi.org/10.1007/978-3-030-25540-4_26

39. Kingma, D.P., Welling, M.: Auto-encoding variational Bayes. arXiv:1312.6114 (May 2014). http://arxiv.org/abs/1312.6114

40. Krizhevsky, A., Sutskever, I., Hinton, G.E.: ImageNet classification with deep convolutional neural networks. In: Pereira, F., Burges, C.J.C., Bottou, L., Weinberger, K.Q. (eds.) Advances in Neural Information Processing Systems, vol. 25, pp. 1097–1105. Curran Associates, Inc. (2012). http://papers.nips.cc/paper/4824-imagenet-classification-with-deep-convolutional-neural-networks.pdf

41. Lamport, L.: Proving the correctness of multiprocess programs. IEEE Trans. Softw. Eng. 3(2), 125–143 (1977)

42. Latorre, F., Rolland, P., Cevher, V.: Lipschitz constant estimation of neural networks via sparse polynomial optimization. arXiv:2004.08688 (April 2020). http://arxiv.org/abs/2004.08688

43. Liu, C., Arnon, T., Lazarus, C., Barrett, C., Kochenderfer, M.J.: Algorithms for verifying deep neural networks. arXiv:1903.06758 (March 2019). http://arxiv.org/abs/1903.06758

44. Mangal, R., Nori, A.V., Orso, A.: Robustness of neural networks: a probabilistic and practical approach. In: Proceedings of the 41st International Conference on Software Engineering: New Ideas and Emerging Results, ICSE NIER 2019, pp. 93–96. IEEE Press, Montreal (May 2019)

45. Qin, Y., Carlini, N., Cottrell, G., Goodfellow, I., Raffel, C.: Imperceptible, robust, and targeted adversarial examples for automatic speech recognition. In: International Conference on Machine Learning, pp. 5231–5240 (May 2019). http://proceedings.mlr.press/v97/qin19a.html

46. Sampson, A., Panchekha, P., Mytkowicz, T., McKinley, K.S., Grossman, D., Ceze, L.: Expressing and verifying probabilistic assertions. In: Proceedings of the 35th ACM SIGPLAN Conference on Programming Language Design and Implementation, PLDI 2014, pp. 112–122. Association for Computing Machinery, Edinburgh (June 2014)

47. Sankaranarayanan, S., Chakarov, A., Gulwani, S.: Static analysis for probabilistic programs: inferring whole program properties from finitely many paths. In: Proceedings of the 34th ACM SIGPLAN Conference on Programming Language Design and Implementation, PLDI 2013, pp. 447–458. Association for Computing Machinery, Seattle (June 2013)

48. Singh, C.: Csinva/gan-vae-pretrained-pytorch (May 2020). https://github.com/csinva/gan-vae-pretrained-pytorch

49. Singh, G., Gehr, T., Püschel, M., Vechev, M.: An abstract domain for certifying neural networks. Proc. ACM Program. Lang. 3(POPL), 41:1–41:30 (2019)

50. Slepak, J., Shivers, O., Manolios, P.: An array-oriented language with static rank polymorphism. In: Shao, Z. (ed.) ESOP 2014. LNCS, vol. 8410, pp. 27–46. Springer, Heidelberg (2014). https://doi.org/10.1007/978-3-642-54833-8_3

51. Szegedy, C., et al.: Intriguing properties of neural networks. In: International Conference on Learning Representations (2014). http://arxiv.org/abs/1312.6199

52. Tsuzuku, Y., Sato, I., Sugiyama, M.: Lipschitz-margin training: scalable certification of perturbation invariance for deep neural networks. In: Proceedings of the 32nd International Conference on Neural Information Processing Systems, NIPS 2018, pp. 6542–6551. Curran Associates Inc., Montréal (December 2018)

53. Virmaux, A., Scaman, K.: Lipschitz regularity of deep neural networks: analysis and efficient estimation. In: Bengio, S., Wallach, H., Larochelle, H., Grauman, K., Cesa-Bianchi, N., Garnett, R. (eds.) Advances in Neural Information Processing Systems, vol. 31, pp. 3835–3844. Curran Associates, Inc. (2018). http://papers.nips.cc/paper/7640-lipschitz-regularity-of-deep-neural-networks-analysis-and-efficient-estimation.pdf

54. Wang, D., Hoffmann, J., Reps, T.: PMAF: an algebraic framework for static analysis of probabilistic programs. In: Proceedings of the 39th ACM SIGPLAN Conference on Programming Language Design and Implementation, PLDI 2018, pp. 513–528. Association for Computing Machinery, Philadelphia (June 2018)

55. Webb, S., Rainforth, T., Teh, Y.W., Kumar, M.P.: A statistical approach to assessing neural network robustness. In: International Conference on Learning Representations (September 2018). https://openreview.net/forum?id=S1xcx3C5FX

56. Weng, L., et al.: PROVEN: verifying robustness of neural networks with a probabilistic approach. In: International Conference on Machine Learning, pp. 6727–6736 (May 2019). http://proceedings.mlr.press/v97/weng19a.html

57. Weng, L., et al.: Towards fast computation of certified robustness for ReLU networks. In: International Conference on Machine Learning, pp. 5276–5285 (July 2018). http://proceedings.mlr.press/v80/weng18a.html

58. Weng, T.W., et al.: Evaluating the robustness of neural networks: an extreme value theory approach. In: International Conference on Learning Representations (February 2018). https://openreview.net/forum?id=BkUHlMZ0b

59. Yuan, X., He, P., Zhu, Q., Li, X.: Adversarial examples: attacks and defenses for deep learning. arXiv:1712.07107 (July 2018). http://arxiv.org/abs/1712.07107

60. Zeiler, M.D., Krishnan, D., Taylor, G.W., Fergus, R.: Deconvolutional networks. In: 2010 IEEE Computer Society Conference on Computer Vision and Pattern Recognition, pp. 2528–2535 (June 2010)
61. Zhang, H., Zhang, P., Hsieh, C.J.: RecurJac: an efficient recursive algorithm for bounding Jacobian matrix of neural networks and its applications. In: Proceedings of the AAAI Conference on Artificial Intelligence, vol. 33, no. 01, pp. 5757–5764 (2019)
62. Zhang, J.M., Harman, M., Ma, L., Liu, Y.: Machine learning testing: survey, landscapes and horizons. IEEE Trans. Softw. Eng. 1 (2020)

On Multi-language Abstraction
Towards a Static Analysis of Multi-language Programs

Samuele Buro[1]([✉]), Roy L. Crole[2], and Isabella Mastroeni[1]

[1] Department of Computer Science, University of Verona,
Strada le Grazie 15, 37134 Verona, Italy
{samuele.buro,isabella.mastroeni}@univr.it
[2] Department of Computer Science, University of Leicester, University Road,
Leicester LE1 7RH, UK
rlc3@le.ac.uk

Abstract. Modern software development rarely takes place within a single programming language. Often, programmers appeal to *cross-language interoperability*. Examples are exploitation of novel features of one language within another, and cross-language code reuse. Previous works developed a theory of so-called *multi-languages*, which arise by *combining existing languages*, defining a precise notion of (*algebraic*) multi-language semantics. As regards static analysis, the heterogeneity of the multi-language context opens up new and unexplored scenarios. In this paper, we provide a general theory for the *combination of abstract interpretations* of existing languages, regardless of their inherent nature, in order to gain an abstract semantics of *multi-language programs*. As a part of this general theory, we show that formal properties of interest of multi-language abstractions (*e.g.*, *soundness* and *completeness*) boil down to the features of the interoperability mechanism that binds the underlying languages together. We extend many of the standard concepts of abstract interpretation to the framework of multi-languages.

Keywords: Multi-languages · Abstract interpretation · Interoperability · Algebraic semantics

1 Introduction

There is currently a myriad of programming languages, many of which have extensive library support. With programs becoming larger and increasingly complex, *interoperability mechanisms* streamline program development by enabling the interplay between pieces of code written in different languages. Examples are *embedded interpreters* [39], consisting of a runtime engine implemented in the host language (such as Jython [28] that lets Java interoperate with Python), or the *foreign function interface* system that allows one language to call routines

Supported by *Progetto ricerca di base 2017 (prot. RBVR1772AA)*, funded by University of Verona.

D. Pichardie and M. Sighireanu (Eds.): SAS 2020, LNCS 12389, pp. 310–332, 2020.
https://doi.org/10.1007/978-3-030-65474-0_14

written in another (*e.g.*, the Java Native Interface [31] enables Java code to call C++ functions). On one hand these mechanisms are essential tools, but on the other hand they hamper our understanding of the resulting programs.

The *multi-language* framework of [7] provides a theoretical model to formalise cross-language interoperability from an abstract standpoint. Multi-languages arise from the combination of already existing languages [1, 11, 18, 25, 33, 37, 38]. Intuitively, terms of multi-languages are obtained by performing cross-language substitutions (*e.g.*, the multi-language designed in [33] allows programmers to replace ML expressions with Scheme expressions and vice versa) and the semantics is determined by new constructs able to regulate the flow of values between the underlying languages, the so-called *boundary functions* [33].

The Problem. Despite the wide range of frameworks for interoperability, there is a lack of techniques for combining *static analyses* of different languages. Static analysis consists of a range of well-established and widely used techniques for automatically extracting dynamic (*i.e.*, runtime) behaviours statically (i.e., without executing the code). When it comes to multi-languages, two new challenges need to be tackled. Firstly, single-language analysers are not conceived for inspecting external code, and secondly the combination of analyses is not straightforward, since the interoperability mechanism that blends the underlying languages adds a new semantic layer. For instance, consider the following Java code snippet analysed with SonarQube Scanner [10]:[1]

```
String hello = null;
String helloWorld = hello.concat(" World!"); // NullPointerException: hello is null
```

The analyser raises a warning of a null pointer exception at the second line. Instead, if we run the analyser on the next semantically equivalent but multi-language code the runtime exception goes unnoticed.

```
String hello = (String) js.eval("null"); // Evaluate "null" in JS and convert it back
String helloWorld = hello.concat(" World!"); // NullPointerException: hello is null
```

The method `eval` evaluates the JavaScript code `null` via the Nashorn engine (a JavaScript interpreter developed by Oracle and included in Java 8) and returns the equivalent Java value `null`. This trivial example underlines how easy it is to deceive an analysis when writing multi-language programs.

Of course, nothing prevents us from redesigning the abstract semantics of the multi-language from scratch and to implement the corresponding analyser. However, besides the obvious time-consuming task, we will end up without any theoretical properties of the abstraction (*e.g.*, soundness or completeness). In fact, what we would like to achieve is a framework that takes advantage, as far as possible, of the already existing abstractions of the underlying languages and at the same time provides theoretical results.

---

[1] A commercial static code analyser for Java (version 3.2.0.1227 for Linux 64 bit).

A General Solution. Abstract interpretation [14] has allowed a disparate collection of (practical) methods and algorithms proposed along the years for static analysis to evolve into a mature discipline, founded on a robust theoretical framework. This provides a good environment for designing static analysis methods within a language, semantics, and approximation independent way [15]. It has broad scope and wide applicability. Our aim is to retain such broad scope, but to work with multi-language programs: Instead of fixing two programming languages and combining their respective analyses, we model abstract interpretation itself, within the algebraic framework of multi-language semantics [7]. Such an approach allows us to lay down the first steps of a general technique for designing static analyses of multi-language programs, in a way that (1) is independent of both underlying languages and analyses and (2) preserves the design and properties of the single-language abstract semantics.

Contributions and Paper Structure. Our main contribution is a general technique for abstracting multi-language semantics given the interoperation of the underlying languages and of their abstract semantics. We exploit abstract interpretation theory [14] for retaining independency from the underlying analyses, and the algebraic framework of multi-languages [7] for generality of the blended languages. In Sect. 2, we provide background definitions for multi-languages. In Sect. 3, we give a general, algebraic, and fixpoint construction of the *collecting semantics*, namely the reference semantics for defining and proving the correctness of approximated properties. In Sect. 4, we instantiate the abstract interpretation-based semantics approximation in the algebraic framework, in order to fill the gap between the algebraic approach to program semantics and static analysis. Finally, in Sect. 5, we combine all these concepts, obtaining an algebraic framework for modeling *abstract interpretation of multi-language programs*. We assume familiarity with abstract interpretation theory.

Running Example. The whole paper is accompanied by a *running example* inspired by a common scenario in the interoperability field: The *language binding*, an Application Program Interface (API) that allows one language to call library functions implemented in another language. Major examples include openGL library, which is interoperable with Java through the Java OpenGL (JOGL) wrapper library or from Python via PyOpenGL, and GNU Octave language that has interoperability with Ruby and Python (*e.g.*, see octave-ruby and oct2py libraries). Our running example mimics such an interoperability mechanism: We present the core of an imperative language Imp, and we let it interoperate with a very simple mathematical language Num (in the spirit of Octave). We refer to such a multi-language as NImp. We then show how to build multi-language abstractions of NImp by combining the abstract semantics of Imp and Num.

2   The Multi-language Framework

We summarise the framework of multi-languages [7] based on the theory of order-sorted algebras [22]. Intuitively, multi-languages result from the combination of

$$\text{(Const)} \ \frac{}{k:s} \ (k:s) \quad \text{(Fun)} \ \frac{(\forall 1 \le i \le n) \ t_i : s_i}{f(t_1, \ldots, t_n) : s} \ (f: s_1, \ldots, s_n \to s) \quad \text{(Sub)} \ \frac{t:s}{t:r} \ (s \le r)$$

Fig. 1. Well-formed terms generated by an order-sorted signature Sg.

two order-sorted specifications defining syntax and semantics of the underlying languages. Order-sorted algebras provide a simple and yet powerful framework for modelling formal systems as algebraic structure, and have been widely used for specifying and prototyping programming languages (see [21] for survey).

Sorted Sets and Functions. Let S be a **set of sorts**. An **S-sorted set** is a family of sets $A \triangleq (A_s \mid s \in S)$. Given two S-sorted sets A and B, an **S-sorted function** $h: A \to B$ is a family $(h_s: A_s \to B_s \mid s \in S)$ of set-theoretic functions. If $f: A \to B$ and $g: B \to C$ are two S-sorted functions, clearly their composition $g \circ f \triangleq ((g \circ f)_s \triangleq g_s \circ f_s \mid s \in S)$ is an S-sorted function from A to C. We extend set-theoretic operators and predicates componentwise. For instance, if A and B are two S-sorted sets, $A \subseteq B$ if $A_s \subseteq B_s$ for each $s \in S$, and we define the cartesian product $A \times B$ by taking each component $(A \times B)_s \triangleq A_s \times B_s$. If A is an S-sorted set and $w \triangleq s_1 \ldots s_n \in S^*$, we denote by A_w the cartesian product $A_{s_1} \times \cdots \times A_{s_n}$ (when $w \triangleq \varepsilon$, then $A_w \triangleq \{\bullet\}$ is the one-point domain). Likewise, if f is an S-sorted function and $a_i \in A_{s_i}$ for $i \triangleq 1, \ldots, n$, then the function $f_w: A_w \to B_w$ is defined by $f_w(a_1, \ldots, a_n) \triangleq (f_{s_1}(a_1), \ldots, f_{s_n}(a_n))$. Moreover, if S is partially ordered by $\le$, then S^* inherits the pointwise order. Finally, we introduce the product operator $\times$ used in Sect. 3. Let A be a family of sets indexed by I. The product operator $\times: \prod_{i \in I} \wp(A_i) \to \wp(\prod_{i \in I} A_i)$ defines the mapping $(X_1, \ldots, X_n) \mapsto X_1 \times \cdots \times X_n$.

2.1 Order-Sorted Algebras

A *signature* defines the symbols of the language (that is, the syntax), and an *algebra* provides them with a meaning.

Definition 1 (Order-Sorted Signature). *An **order-sorted signature** Sg is specified by*

- *a poset $\langle S, \le \rangle$ of **sorts**;*
- *a set of **function symbols** $f: s_1, \ldots, s_n \to s$ each with **arity** $n \ge 1$ and $(w, s) \in S^* \times S$ the **rank** of f where $w \triangleq s_1 \ldots s_n$;*
- *a set of **constants** $k: s$, each of a unique **rank** s (just a single sort); and*
- *a **monotonicity requirement** that whenever $f: w_1 \to s$ and $f: w_2 \to r$ with $w_1 \le w_2$, then $s \le r$.*

*By an **operator** we mean either a function symbol or a constant.*

Well-formed (ground) **terms** generated by a signature Sg are defined by the inference rules depicted in Fig. 1. A judgement of the form $t: s$ means that t is a well-formed term of sort s built out of Sg. Note that a term t may have more than one sort, and we call t **polymorphic**; see [22] for details on polymorphism in order-sorted algebras and [7] for the role of polymorphism in multi-languages.

Definition 2 (Order-Sorted Algebra). *Given an order-sorted signature* Sg, *an* Sg-*algebra* $\mathscr{C}$ *is specified by*

- *a* **carrier set** $[\![s]\!]_{\mathscr{C}}$ *for each sort* s *and a set* $[\![w]\!]_{\mathscr{C}} \triangleq [\![s_1]\!]_{\mathscr{C}} \times \cdots \times [\![s_n]\!]_{\mathscr{C}}$ *for each* $w \triangleq s_1 \ldots s_n \in S^*$;
- *a function* $[\![f: w \to s]\!]_{\mathscr{C}} : [\![w]\!]_{\mathscr{C}} \to [\![s]\!]_{\mathscr{C}}$ *for each* $f: w \to s$ *and an element* $[\![k]\!]_{\mathscr{C}} \in [\![s]\!]_{\mathscr{C}}$ *for each constant* $k: s$

such that if $s \leq r$ *then* $[\![s]\!]_{\mathscr{C}} \subseteq [\![r]\!]_{\mathscr{C}}$, *and if the function symbol* f *appears with more than one rank* $f: w_1 \to s$ *and* $f: w_2 \to r$ *in* Sg *with* $w_1 \leq w_2$, *then* $[\![f: w_1 \to s]\!]_{\mathscr{C}}(x) = [\![f: w_2 \to r]\!]_{\mathscr{C}}(x)$ *for each* $x \in [\![w_1]\!]_{\mathscr{C}}$.

We often refer to the **carrier set** of an Sg-algebra $\mathscr{C}$, meaning the S-sorted family of carrier sets $C \triangleq (C_s \triangleq [\![s]\!]_{\mathscr{C}} \mid s \in S)$, where S is the set of sorts in Sg.

Example 1. If Sg is the signature of an imperative language, then the *loop* and *skip* operators are likely to be sorted as *loop*: *exp*, *com* $\to$ *com* and *skip*: *com*. Their denotational semantics may be defined by an algebra $\mathscr{D}$, where $[\![skip]\!]_{\mathscr{D}} \triangleq \rho \mapsto \rho$ and $[\![loop]\!]_{\mathscr{D}}(e, c) \triangleq \mathrm{lfp} F_{e,c}$ (assume ρ to be an environment and F the usual continuous operator [43]).

The *term algebra* $\mathscr{T}_{\mathsf{Sg}}$ has carrier sets each consisting of terms of a given sort:

Definition 3 (Order-Sorted Term Algebra). *The* **term** Sg-*algebra* $\mathscr{T}_{\mathsf{Sg}}$ *is defined by taking* $[\![s]\!]_{\mathscr{T}_{\mathsf{Sg}}} \triangleq \{\, t \mid t: s \text{ in } \mathsf{Sg} \,\}$ *and by syntactically interpreting each operator, i.e.,* $[\![k]\!]_{\mathscr{T}_{\mathsf{Sg}}} \triangleq k$ *for each* $k: s$ *and* $[\![f: w \to s]\!]_{\mathscr{T}_{\mathsf{Sg}}}(t_1, \ldots, t_n) \triangleq f(t_1, \ldots, t_n)$ *for each* $f: w \to s$, *where* $w \triangleq s_1 \ldots s_n$ *and* $t_i \in [\![s_i]\!]_{\mathscr{T}_{\mathsf{Sg}}}$.

Homomorpisms between algebras are sorted functions between carrier sets that preserve the meaning of the operators:

Definition 4 (Order-Sorted Homomorpism). *Let* $\mathscr{C}$ *and* $\mathscr{D}$ *be two order-sorted* Sg-*algebras. An* **order-sorted** Sg-*homomorphism* $h: \mathscr{C} \to \mathscr{D}$ *is an* S-*sorted function* $h: C \to D$ *between their carrier sets satisfying the following:*

- $h_s([\![k]\!]_{\mathscr{C}}) = [\![k]\!]_{\mathscr{D}}$ *for each* $k: s$ *and* $h_s \circ [\![f: w \to s]\!]_{\mathscr{C}} = [\![f: w \to s]\!]_{\mathscr{D}} \circ h_w$ *for each* $f: w \to s$ *(recall the sorted function notation); and*
- *if* $s \leq r$, *then* $h_s(x) = h_r(x)$ *for each* $x \in [\![s]\!]_{\mathscr{C}}$.

When the source of a homomorphism $h: \mathscr{T}_{\mathsf{Sg}} \to \mathscr{C}$ is the term algebra, it provides terms of Sg with a meaning in the carrier set C of $\mathscr{C}$. The class of Sg-algebras and Sg-homomorphisms form a category denoted by **Alg(Sg)**. If the signature Sg is *regular* (intuitively, regularity is a natural condition on the signature which allows each term to have a unique least sort) there is a unique homomorphism $h: \mathscr{T}_{\mathsf{Sg}} \to C$ for each Sg-algebra $\mathscr{C}$:

(i)	$\langle exp_1 \rangle ::= i$	integers $(i \in \mathbb{Z}_\perp)$
(x)	$\langle exp_1 \rangle ::= x$	variables $(x \in \mathbb{X})$
$(bop_\odot)$	$\langle exp_1 \rangle ::= \langle exp_1 \rangle \odot \langle exp_1 \rangle$	binary operations
$(skip)$	$\langle com_1 \rangle ::= \text{skip}$	do-nothing
$(assign_x)$	$\langle com_1 \rangle ::= \text{x} = \langle exp_1 \rangle$	assignment
$(cond)$	$\langle com_1 \rangle ::= \text{if } \langle exp_1 \rangle \text{ then } \langle com_1 \rangle \text{ else } \langle com_1 \rangle$	conditional
$(loop)$	$\langle com_1 \rangle ::= \text{while} \langle exp_1 \rangle \text{ do} \langle com_1 \rangle$	loop statement
(seq)	$\langle com_1 \rangle ::= \langle com_1 \rangle; \langle com_1 \rangle$	composition

Fig. 2. Syntax of the imperative language Imp.

Definition 5 (Regularity [22]). *An order-sorted signature* Sg *is* **regular** *if for each* $f \colon w \to s$ *and for each lower bound* $w_l \leq w$ *the set* $\{ (w', s') \mid f \colon w' \to s' \wedge w_l \leq w' \} \subseteq S^n \times S$ *has a minimum.*

Theorem 1 [22]. *If* Sg *is regular, the term algebra* $\mathscr{T}_{\text{Sg}}$ *is initial in* $\mathbf{Alg}(\text{Sg})$, *that is, for every algebra* $\mathscr{C}$ *there is a unique homomorphism* $h \colon \mathscr{T}_{\text{Sg}} \to \mathscr{C}$.

We refer to any such $h \colon \mathscr{T}_{\text{Sg}} \to \mathscr{C}$ as a **semantic function**. In the following, we write $[\![t]\!]_\mathscr{C} \triangleq h_{ls(t)}(t)$ where $ls(t)$ is the least sort of t, which exists by regularity [22, Prop. 2.10].

We conclude the section by illustrating two simple programming languages. We provide their order-sorted signatures and algebras. The semantics of the resulting programs follows by the previous theorem.

Running Example 1. Let Imp be (the syntax of) the imperative programming language in Fig. 2. Variables $x \in \mathbb{X}$ and values $i \in \mathbb{Z}_\perp$ (where $\mathbb{Z}_\perp \triangleq \mathbb{Z} \cup \{\perp\}$) occur in the language as terminal symbols, and for each production defining the syntax of Imp (on the right), we introduce a corresponding algebraic operator (on the left), or a family of operators when they are parametric on a subscript. The rank of each algebraic operator can be inferred by the non-terminals appearing in the production rules; for instance, the operator $cond$ is sorted as $cond \colon exp_1, com_1, com_1 \to com_1$, where com_1 and exp_1 denote the sort of commands and expressions of Imp. We assume a denotational semantics $[\![-]\!]_{\mathscr{D}_1}$ provided by an Imp-algebra $\mathscr{D}_1$ (see, for instance, [43]). As usual, we let $\mathbb{Env}_1 \triangleq \mathbb{X} \to \mathbb{Z}_\perp$ be the set of environments of Imp, and we set $\mathbb{Env}_1^\perp \triangleq \mathbb{Env}_1 \cup \{\perp\}$. The carrier sets of commands and expressions are $[\![com_1]\!]_{\mathscr{D}_1} \triangleq \mathbb{Env}_1^\perp \to \mathbb{Env}_1^\perp$ and $[\![exp_1]\!]_{\mathscr{D}_1} \triangleq \mathbb{Env}_1 \to \mathbb{Z}_\perp$. Moreover, we assume that Imp provides users with very basic operators, *i.e.*, $\odot \in \{+, -, <, >, ==, !=\}$.

We let Num be a mathematical language with more advanced numerical functions, such as modulo and bitwise operators, rational numbers, trigonometric functions, *etc.* Its syntax is depicted in Fig. 3. We consider variables $x \in \mathbb{X}$ and values $q \in \mathbb{Q}_\perp \triangleq \mathbb{Q} \cup \{\perp\}$ as terminal symbols. We denote by f_n mathematical functions of the language with arity n, such as the modulo binary operator %, the unary sin function, etc. Here too we assume a denotational semantics

(q)	$\langle exp_2\rangle ::= q$	rationals ($q \in \mathbb{Q}_\bot$)
(x)	$\langle exp_2\rangle ::= x$	variables ($x \in \mathbb{X}$)
(f_n)	$\langle exp_2\rangle ::= f_n(\,\langle exp_2\rangle_1,\ldots,\langle exp_2\rangle_n\,)$	n-ary operations
$(?)$	$\langle exp_2\rangle ::= \langle exp_2\rangle\ ?\ \langle exp_2\rangle : \langle exp_2\rangle$	ternary operator
(let_x)	$\langle com_2\rangle ::= \mathsf{x} = \langle com_2\rangle$	assignment
$(block)$	$\langle com_2\rangle ::= \{\ \langle com_2\rangle_1;\ldots;\ \langle com_2\rangle_n\ \}$	statements block

Fig. 3. Syntax of the mathematical language Num.

$[\![-]\!]_{\mathscr{D}_2}$ induced by the Num-algebra $\mathscr{D}_2$, where $[\![exp_2]\!]_{\mathscr{D}_2} \triangleq \mathbb{E}\mathsf{nv}_2 \to \mathbb{Q}_\bot$ and $[\![com_2]\!]_{\mathscr{D}_2} \triangleq \mathbb{E}\mathsf{nv}_2 \to \mathbb{E}\mathsf{nv}_2$ with $\mathbb{E}\mathsf{nv}_2 \triangleq \mathbb{X} \to \mathbb{Q}_\bot$.

The reader may want to check Appendix A for the thorough formalisation of the algebraic semantics provided by $\mathscr{D}_1$ and $\mathscr{D}_2$.

2.2   Multi-languages and Their Algebras

We next provide an analogue of the previous section for multi-languages. A *multi-language* signature, defining a *multi-language*, is specified by two order-sorted signatures together with an *interoperability relation* on sorts:

Definition 6 (Multi-language Signature).   *A **multi-language signature** $\mathsf{SG} \triangleq (\mathsf{Sg}_1, \mathsf{Sg}_2, \ltimes)$ is specified by*

- *a pair of order-sorted signatures Sg_1 and Sg_2 with posets of sorts $\langle S_1, \leq_1\rangle$ and $\langle S_2, \leq_2\rangle$, respectively; and*
- *an **interoperability (binary) relation** $\ltimes$ over $S_1 \cup S_2$ such that $s \ltimes s'$ implies $s \in S_i$ and $s' \in S_j$ with $i,j \in \{1,2\}$ and $i \neq j$.*

We suppose that S_1 and S_2 are two disjoint sets (note that such an hypothesis is non-restrictive: We can always construct a disjoint union).

We shall see that an interoperability constraint $s \ltimes s'$ enables the use of Sg_i-terms of sort s in place of Sg_j-terms of sort s' (as in [33], "ML code can be used in place of Scheme code"). The **multi-language terms** are inductively defined by the rules in Fig. 4. Note that single-language operators, k or f, of Sg_i are tagged as k_i and f_i in multi-language terms, precisely for avoiding the introduction of unintended polymorphism (Sg_1 and Sg_2 may share operators with the same name). And also note the role of **conversion operators** $\hookrightarrow_{s,s'}$ that move terms t of sort s to terms $\hookrightarrow_{s,s'}(t)$ of sort s', for each $s \ltimes s'$. Henceforth, when we write an order-sorted signature Sg_i, we understand its poset of sorts to be denoted by $\langle S_i, \leq_i\rangle$, and for each $s \ltimes s'$ we tacitly assume that s in Sg_i and s' in Sg_j with $i,j \in \{1,2\}$ and $i \neq j$.

A multi-language SG-algebra is a pair of order-sorted algebras together with a family of *boundary functions*.

$$\text{(CONST)} \ \frac{-}{k_i \colon s} \ (k \colon s \text{ in } \mathbf{Sg}_i) \qquad \text{(FUN)} \ \frac{(\forall 1 \leq j \leq n) \ t_j \colon s_j}{f_i(t_1, \ldots, t_n) \colon s} \ (f \colon s_1, \ldots, s_n \to s \text{ in } \mathbf{Sg}_i)$$

$$\text{(SUB)} \ \frac{t \colon s}{t \colon r} \ (s \leq_i r \text{ in } \mathbf{Sg}_i) \qquad \text{(CONV)} \ \frac{t \colon s}{\hookrightarrow_{s,s'}(t) \colon s'} \ (s \bowtie s' \text{ in } \mathbf{SG})$$

Fig. 4. Multi-language terms generated by $\mathsf{SG} \triangleq (\mathbf{Sg}_1, \mathbf{Sg}_2, \bowtie)$.

Definition 7 (Multi-language Algebra). *Let* $\mathsf{SG} \triangleq (\mathbf{Sg}_1, \mathbf{Sg}_2, \bowtie)$ *be a multi-language signature. An* SG*-**algebra** $\mathscr{C}$ is given by*

- *a pair of order-sorted algebras* $\mathscr{C}_1$ *and* $\mathscr{C}_2$ *on* $\mathbf{Sg}_1$ *and* $\mathbf{Sg}_2$*, respectively; and*
- *a* **boundary function** $[\![s \bowtie s']\!]_\mathscr{C} \colon [\![s]\!]_{\mathscr{C}_i} \to [\![s']\!]_{\mathscr{C}_j}$ *for each constraint* $s \bowtie s'$.

Boundary functions are understood as the semantics of conversion operators, that is they specify *how* the underlying languages interoperate.

The multi-language term algebra is defined in a similar way to the order-sorted one in order to carry multi-language terms.

Definition 8 (Multi-language Term Algebra). *Let* $\mathscr{T}_\mathsf{SG}$ *denote the multi-language term* SG*-algebra. The underlying* $\mathbf{Sg}_i$*-algebras* $(\mathscr{T}_\mathsf{SG})_i$ *are defined by taking* $[\![s]\!]_{(\mathscr{T}_\mathsf{SG})_i} \triangleq \{\, t \mid t \colon s \text{ in } \mathsf{SG} \,\}$ *for each sort* s *in* $\mathbf{Sg}_i$ *and by defining* $[\![k]\!]_{(\mathscr{T}_\mathsf{SG})_i} \triangleq k_i$ *for each* $k \colon s$ *in* $\mathbf{Sg}_i$ *and* $[\![f \colon w \to s]\!]_{(\mathscr{T}_\mathsf{SG})_i}(t_1, \ldots, t_n) \triangleq f_i(t_1, \ldots, t_n)$ *for each* $f \colon s_1, \ldots, s_n \to s$ *in* $\mathbf{Sg}_i$*, where* $t_j \in [\![s_j]\!]_{(\mathscr{T}_\mathsf{SG})_i}$*. Boundary functions of* $\mathscr{T}_\mathsf{SG}$ *are defined as* $[\![s \bowtie s']\!]_{\mathscr{T}_\mathsf{SG}}(t) \triangleq \hookrightarrow_{s,s'}(t)$*, for each* $s \bowtie s'$ *and* $t \in [\![s]\!]_{(\mathscr{T}_\mathsf{SG})_i}$*.*

Definition 9 (Multi-language Homomorphism). *Let* $\mathsf{SG} \triangleq (\mathbf{Sg}_1, \mathbf{Sg}_2, \bowtie)$ *be a multi-language signature, and let* $\mathscr{C}$ *and* $\mathscr{D}$ *be two* SG*-algebras. An* SG*-**homomorphism** $h \colon \mathscr{C} \to \mathscr{D}$ is given by a pair of order-sorted homomorphisms* $h_1 \colon \mathscr{C}_1 \to \mathscr{D}_1$ *and* $h_2 \colon \mathscr{C}_2 \to \mathscr{D}_2$ *such that they commute with boundary functions, namely, if* $s \bowtie s'$*, then* $(h_j)_{s'} \circ [\![s \bowtie s']\!]_\mathscr{C} = [\![s \bowtie s']\!]_\mathscr{D} \circ (h_i)_s$*.*

Given a multi-language algebra $\mathscr{C}$, we can define an S-sorted set C by setting $C_{s_i} \triangleq [\![s]\!]_{\mathscr{C}_i}$; and given any homomorphism $h \colon \mathscr{C} \to \mathscr{D}$, there is an S-sorted homomorphism $\overline{h} \colon C \to D$ given by $\overline{h}_{s_i} \triangleq (h_i)_s \colon C_{s_i} \to D_{s_i}$. Note that we will usually write h for $\overline{h}$, thus identifying the two concepts, and regard $h \colon \mathscr{C} \to \mathscr{D}$ and $h \colon C \to D$ as inter-changeable throughout the paper.

SG-algebras and SG-homomorphisms form a category denoted by $\mathbf{Alg}(\mathsf{SG})$. [7] provides the multi-language version of Theorem 1, so that for every multi-language algebra $\mathscr{C}$, there is a unique SG-homomorphism $h \colon \mathscr{T}_\mathsf{SG} \to \mathscr{C}$ providing multi-language terms with a meaning, and we use the same notation $[\![t]\!]_\mathscr{C}$ for denoting its semantics.

We now apply the theory of multi-languages to combine the languages introduced in Example 1.

Running Example 2. Num provides users with more advanced binary operators and values than those of Imp. However, the purpose of Num is limited to define handy mathematical functions (indeed, it is not even Turing-complete). We can take advantage of such mathematical expressiveness without sacrificing computational power by allowing the use of Num-expressions (that is, terms with sort exp_2) into Imp-programs, in place of Imp-expression of sort exp_1. Therefore, the interoperability relation shall simply specify $exp_2 \ltimes exp_1$, and we let NImp to be formally defined as NImp $\triangleq$ (Imp, Num, $\ltimes$). As a result, programmers may write programs such as the one in Fig. 5, where terms in magenta are Num-expressions used in place of Imp-expressions (*i.e.*, we use colours rather than applying the conversion operator $\hookrightarrow_{exp_2,exp_1}$ for clarity reasons).

```res = 1;```
```while n > 0 do```
``` if n & 1 then // true iff n is odd```
```   res = res * a;```
``` a = a * a;```
``` n = n >> 1 // division by 2```
	The multi-language program on the right implements the exponentiation by squaring [12] for efficiently computing the powers of an integer number: It stores in res the n-th power of a. The binary operator & is the bitwise and operator and >> is the right shift operation.

Fig. 5. Multi-language exponentiation by squaring algorithm.

We denote by $\mathscr{D}$ the multi-language NImp-algebra defined by coupling $\mathscr{D}_1$ and $\mathscr{D}_2$ with the boundary function $[\![exp_2 \ltimes exp_1]\!]_\mathscr{D}$ defined below (recall Definition 7). Note that values of Num-expressions range over the set of rational numbers $\mathbb{Q}$, whereas Imp only handles integer values in $\mathbb{Z}$. A natural choice for the boundary function $[\![exp_2 \ltimes exp_1]\!]_\mathscr{D}$ of NImp that converts Num-expressions to Imp-expressions is to *truncate* the value of Num-expression to their nearest integer value. Since expressions only have values with respect to an environment, we shall specify a conversion from $\mathbb{E}nv_2 \to \mathbb{Q}_\perp$ to $\mathbb{E}nv_1 \to \mathbb{Z}_\perp$ (we use ρ_1 and ρ_2 as metavariables for $\mathbb{E}nv_1$ and $\mathbb{E}nv_2$, respectively):

$$[\![exp_2 \ltimes exp_1]\!]_\mathscr{D}(e \in \mathbb{E}nv_2 \to \mathbb{Q}_\perp) \triangleq \rho_1 \in \mathbb{E}nv_1 \mapsto \psi(e(\phi(\rho_1))) \in \mathbb{Z}_\perp$$

where $\phi \colon \mathbb{E}nv_1 \to \mathbb{E}nv_2$ is the inclusion function and $\psi \colon \mathbb{Q}_\perp \to \mathbb{Z}_\perp$ truncates rational values, *i.e.*, $\psi(q) \triangleq$ truncate(q) if $q \neq \perp$ and $\psi(\perp) \triangleq \perp$. For instance, the semantics of the Num-expression $[\![n \ / \ 2]\!]_{\mathscr{D}_2} = \rho_2 \mapsto \rho_2(n) \ / \ 2$ is mapped by $[\![exp_2 \ltimes exp_1]\!]_\mathscr{D}$ to the function $\rho_1 \mapsto \rho_1(n) /_z 2$, where $/_z$ is the integer division.[2]

3 Algebraic Perspective on Collecting Semantics

We now give a general construction of *collecting semantics*. First we set up notation. We let Sg be a regular order-sorted signature and $\mathscr{C}$ an Sg-algebra. Theorem 1 guarantees the existence of a homomorphism $[\![-]\!]_\mathscr{C} \colon \mathscr{T}_{Sg} \to \mathscr{C}$ providing Sg-terms P, called **programs**, with a meaning $[\![P]\!]_\mathscr{C}$.

---

[2] We ignore the case where $\rho_2(n) = \perp$, as it is clearly trivial.

Remark 1. Signatures are of course completely general. Sg might specify an enriched lambda-calculus with $[\![-]\!]_{\mathscr{C}}$ its denotational semantics, as in [23, Sect. 3.2], or Sg might specify the syntax of an imperative language with $[\![-]\!]_{\mathscr{C}}$ its small-step operational semantics.

A property of a set is any subset. By *semantic* properties of programs, we mean properties of the (components of) the carrier set C of an algebra $\mathscr{C}$. In this section, we provide a systematic construction of an algebra $\mathscr{C}^*$ able to compute the **strongest property of programs**, that is $[\![P]\!]_{\mathscr{C}^*} = \{[\![P]\!]_{\mathscr{C}}\}$ for each program P (Proposition 1). The induced semantic function $[\![-]\!]_{\mathscr{C}^*}$ is usually called the **(standard) collecting semantics** [16]. Henceforth, we distinguish the semantics $[\![-]\!]_{\mathscr{C}}$ from the collecting semantics $[\![-]\!]_{\mathscr{C}^*}$ by referring to the former as the **standard semantics**, and we shall link them algebraically in the category of algebras **Alg(Sg)** via Proposition 2. We conclude this section by providing a general fixpoint calculation of $[\![-]\!]_{\mathscr{C}^*}$ whenever $[\![-]\!]_{\mathscr{C}}$ is a fixpoint semantics (Theorem 3).

Definition 10 (Collecting Semantics). *Let $\mathscr{C}$ be an Sg-algebra. The collecting semantics $\mathscr{C}^*$ over $\mathscr{C}$ is defined as follows:*

- *the carrier sets are $[\![s]\!]_{\mathscr{C}^*} \triangleq \wp[\![s]\!]_{\mathscr{C}}$ for each sort s; and*
- *the semantics of the operators is $[\![k]\!]_{\mathscr{C}^*} \triangleq \{[\![k]\!]_{\mathscr{C}}\}$ for each constant k: s, and $[\![f\colon w \to s]\!]_{\mathscr{C}^*} \triangleq \wp[\![f\colon w \to s]\!]_{\mathscr{C}} \circ \times$ (see Sect. 2 for the definition of $\times$) for each function symbol $f\colon w \to s$, where for any function $\theta\colon A \to B$ the function $\wp(\theta)\colon \wp(A) \to \wp(B)$ computes the image of θ.*

The homomorphism $[\![-]\!]_{\mathscr{C}^*}\colon \mathscr{T}_{\mathsf{Sg}} \to \mathscr{C}^*$ induced by $\mathscr{C}^*$ maps programs to their most precise semantic property, justifying the name of collecting semantics:

Proposition 1. $[\![-]\!]_{\mathscr{C}^*}\colon \mathscr{T}_{\mathsf{Sg}} \to \mathscr{C}^*$ *computes the strongest program property for each program P generated from* Sg, *that is $[\![P]\!]_{\mathscr{C}^*} = \{[\![P]\!]_{\mathscr{C}}\}$.*

Remark 2. Other forms of collecting semantics found in literature are abstractions of the collecting semantics provided here. For instance, [2] defines a collecting semantics for functional programs interpreted on $D_\perp \to D_\perp$ by taking $f\colon D_\perp \to D_\perp$ to $\wp(f)$ on the lifted domain $\wp(D_\perp) \to_{\mathsf{cjm}} \wp(D_\perp)$ of *complete-join morphisms* (cjm). Such a collecting semantics computes all the possible results of a functional program with respect to a set of input values, and it can be obtained as an abstraction of the standard collecting semantics:[3]

$$\alpha\big(S \in \wp(D_\perp \to D_\perp)\big) \triangleq X \in \wp(D_\perp) \mapsto \{ f(x) \in D_\perp \mid x \in X \wedge f \in S \}$$

$$\gamma\big(F \in \wp(D_\perp) \to_{\mathsf{cjm}} \wp(D_\perp)\big) \triangleq \{ x \in D_\perp \mapsto f(x) \in D_\perp \mid f(x) \in F(\{x\}) \}$$

The *(forward) reachability semantics* is widely used for invariance analyses or, in general, for discovering state properties of programs [6,29,41]. For each

---

[3] One can check that $\alpha(S)$ is a cjm and (α, γ) form a Galois connection.

program P, it collects the set of states that are reachable by running P from a set of initial states. It can be shown that it is an abstraction of the standard collecting semantics over, for instance, a *trace semantics*.

Standard and collecting semantics are related by the property established in Proposition 1. Moreover, the singleton function $\{-\}\colon C \to \wp(C)$ that maps standard semantics $[\![P]\!]_{\mathscr{C}}$ of programs to their strongest property $\{[\![P]\!]_{\mathscr{C}}\}$ is an Sg-homomorphism $\{-\}\colon \mathscr{C} \to \mathscr{C}^*$. From the abstract interpretation perspective, it means that $\{-\}$ acts as a *complete abstraction*, hence with no loss of precision [19].

Proposition 2. *The singleton function* $\{-\}\colon C \to \wp(C)$ *defined by* $c \mapsto \{c\}$ *is an Sg-homomorphism* $\{-\}\colon \mathscr{C} \to \mathscr{C}^*$, *and therefore* $\{-\} \circ [\![-]\!]_{\mathscr{C}} = [\![-]\!]_{\mathscr{C}^*}$.

Remark 3. Readers familiar with category theory may notice that $\{-\}$ is the unit of the *powerset monad* on **Alg(Sg)**. However, we do not pursue this here.

3.1 Fixpoint Calculation of Collecting Semantics

Preliminary Notions. We call $[\![-]\!]_{\mathscr{C}}$ a **fixpoint semantics** if $[\![P]\!]_{\mathscr{C}} \triangleq \mathrm{lfp}_{\perp}^{\preccurlyeq} F$ for some *semantic transformer* $F\colon C \to C$ (depending on Sg) on a *semantic domain* $\langle C, \preccurlyeq, \perp, \Upsilon \rangle$. More precisely, we follow [13] and we assume the following:

- The **semantic domain** $\langle C, \preccurlyeq, \perp, \Upsilon \rangle$ is a poset $\langle C, \preccurlyeq \rangle$ with a smallest element $\perp$ and a *partially* defined least upper bound (lub) operator Υ.
- The **semantic transformer** $F\colon C \to C$ is a monotone function such that its *transfinite iterates* $F^0 \triangleq \perp$, $F^{\delta+1} \triangleq F(F^\delta)$ for successor ordinals $\delta + 1$, and $F^\lambda \triangleq \Upsilon_{\delta < \lambda} F^\delta$ for limit ordinals λ are well-defined.

Under these assumptions, the fixpoint semantics is exactly $[\![P]\!]_{\mathscr{C}} \triangleq \mathrm{lfp}_{\perp}^{\preccurlyeq} F = F^\epsilon$, where ϵ is the least ordinal such that $F(F^\epsilon) = F^\epsilon$.

The goal of this section is to provide a fixpoint calculation of the collecting semantics. We assume the standard semantics $[\![P]\!]_{\mathscr{C}} \triangleq \mathrm{lfp}_{\perp}^{\preccurlyeq} F$ to be a fixpoint semantics over a generic semantic domain $\langle C, \preccurlyeq, \perp, \Upsilon \rangle$, and we define a new *computational order* $\preccurlyeq^*$ on $\wp(C)$ that makes the collecting semantics $[\![P]\!]_{\mathscr{C}^*}$ the least fixpoint of $F^* \triangleq \wp(F)$ (Theorem 3).

Remark 4. The problem of finding the right partial order $\preccurlyeq^*$ on $\wp(C)$ for achieving such a fixpoint definition of the collecting semantics has been recently addressed in [16, Sect. 7.2], by considering a preorder on $\wp(C)$ that is partial *only* along the iterates.[4] Here, we show that it can be extended to a fully-fledged partial order $\preccurlyeq^*$ over the whole set $\wp(C)$.

Definition 11 (Collecting Semantics Domain). *Let* $\langle C, \preccurlyeq, \perp, \Upsilon \rangle$ *be a (non-trivial) semantic domain. The **collecting semantics domain** $\langle \wp(C), \preccurlyeq^*, \perp^*, \Upsilon^* \rangle$ with respect to $\langle C, \preccurlyeq, \perp, \Upsilon \rangle$ is defined as follows:*

---

[4] A similar approach has been previously taken in [32] and in the thesis of Pasqua [36].

– *Let $X, Y \in \wp(C)$. Then,*

$$X \preccurlyeq^* Y \text{ iff } \begin{cases} X = \{x\} \wedge Y = \{y\} \wedge x \preccurlyeq y \text{ for some } x, y \in C & (1) \\ X = Y & (2) \\ X = \{x\} \wedge Y \neq \{y\} \text{ for some } x \in C \text{ and for all } y \in C & (3) \end{cases}$$

Example 2. Let $C \triangleq \mathbb{N}$ and $\preccurlyeq \; \triangleq \; \leq$. Then, $\langle \wp(\mathbb{N}), \leq^* \rangle$ is

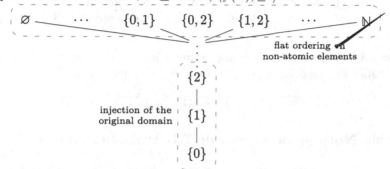

The smallest element of $\langle \wp(C), \preccurlyeq^* \rangle$ is $\bot^* = \{\bot\}$ and the following lemma characterises the lub operator $\curlyvee^*$ on chains of atoms (*i.e.*, singletons):

Lemma 1. *Let $\mathcal{D} \subseteq \wp(C)$ be a non-empty set of atoms of the form $\{x\}$ for some $x \in C$. Then, $\curlyvee^* \mathcal{D}$ exists if and only if $\curlyvee \cup \mathcal{D}$ exists, and when either one exists $\curlyvee^* \mathcal{D} = \{\curlyvee \cup \mathcal{D}\}$.*

Let us recall that $F^* \triangleq \wp(F) \triangleq X \in \wp(C) \mapsto \{F(x) \in C \mid x \in X\}$. F^* is trivially monotone, and we shall now prove that its transfinite iterates exist:

Proposition 3. *For each ordinal δ, $(F^*)^\delta = \{F^\delta\}$.*

Proof. By transfinite induction:

– Let $\delta \triangleq 0$. Then, $(F^*)^0 = \bot^* = \{\bot\} = \{F^0\}$.
– Let $\delta + 1$ be a successor ordinal. Then, $(F^*)^{\delta+1} = F^*((F^*)^\delta) \overset{\text{IH}}{=} F^*(\{F^\delta\}) = \{F(F^\delta)\} = \{F^{\delta+1}\}$.
– Let λ be a limit ordinal. Then, $(F^*)^\lambda = \curlyvee^*_{\delta < \lambda} (F^*)^\delta \overset{\text{IH}}{=} \curlyvee^*_{\delta < \lambda} \{F^\delta\}$. Since $(\{F^\delta\} \mid \delta < \lambda)$ is a set of atoms, by Lemma 1 we conclude

$$(F^*)^\lambda = \curlyvee^*_{\delta < \lambda} \{F^\delta\} = \{\curlyvee \bigcup_{\delta < \lambda} \{F^\delta\}\} = \{\curlyvee_{\delta < \lambda} F^\delta\} = \{F^\lambda\}$$

By Proposition 3, F^* is a proper semantic transformer over the previously defined collecting semantics domain. The fixpoint definition of the collecting semantics now follows from the application of the Kleenian fixpoint transfer theorem in its most general formulation (that we now recall).

Theorem 2 (Kleenian Fixpoint Transfer Theorem [13]). *Let $(D, \leq, \bot, \vee)$ and $(D^\natural, \leq^\natural, \bot^\natural, \vee^\natural)$ be two semantic domains and $F\colon D \to D$ and $F^\natural\colon D^\natural \to D^\natural$ two semantic transformer over them. Let $\alpha\colon D \to D^\natural$ be a function such that (i) $\alpha(\bot) = \bot^\natural$, (ii) $F^\natural \circ \alpha = \alpha \circ F$, and (iii) α preserves the lub of the iterates, that is $\alpha(\vee_{\delta < \lambda} F^\delta) = \vee^\natural_{\delta < \lambda} \alpha(F^\delta)$ for each limit ordinal λ. Then, $\alpha(\mathrm{lfp}^\leq_\bot F) = \mathrm{lfp}^{\leq^\natural}_{\bot^\natural} F^\natural$.*

The singleton function $\{-\}\colon C \to \wp(C)$ introduced in Proposition 2 satisfies the hypotheses for α in Theorem 2 for domains $\langle C, \preccurlyeq, \bot, \curlyvee \rangle$ and $\langle \wp(C), \preccurlyeq^*, \bot^*, \curlyvee^* \rangle$ and transformers F and F^*, respectively. Therefore, given the above,

Theorem 3 (Fixpoint Collecting Semantics). *The function $\{-\}\colon C \to \wp(C)$ satisfies the hypotheses (i), (ii), and (iii) of Theorem 2, hence*

$$\llbracket \mathsf{P} \rrbracket_{\mathscr{C}^*} \overset{\text{Proposition 1}}{=} \{\llbracket \mathsf{P} \rrbracket_\mathscr{C}\} \overset{\text{Hypo.}}{=} \{\mathrm{lfp}^\preccurlyeq_\bot F\} \overset{\text{Theorem 2}}{=} \mathrm{lfp}^{\preccurlyeq^*}_{\bot^*} F^*$$

4   Basic Notions of Algebraic Abstract Semantics

We proceed to characterise *abstract interpretations* of the standard collecting semantics in the algebraic setting. There are several frameworks in which to design sound approximations of program semantics [15]. Here, we study both the ideal case in which a *Galois connection* (gc) ties the concrete and the abstract domain, and the more general scenario characterised by the absence of a best approximation function. Although it is not the most general abstract interpretation framework to work with, it meets the usual setting in which static analyses are designed [40].

We still denote by $\mathscr{C}$ the Sg-algebra inducing the standard semantics of the language. We recall that C is the carrier set of $\mathscr{C}$ and $\wp(C)$ the carrier set of the collecting semantics $\mathscr{C}^*$. An Sg-algebra $\mathscr{A}$ is said to be **abstract** with respect to $\mathscr{C}$ if (1) its carrier set A is a poset $\langle A, \sqsubseteq \rangle$ and (2) it is equipped with a monotone **concretisation function** $\gamma\colon \langle A, \sqsubseteq \rangle \to \langle \wp(C), \subseteq \rangle$ that maps abstract elements to concrete properties. We refer to the carrier set A as an **abstract domain** and we call the induced semantic function $\llbracket - \rrbracket_\mathscr{A}$ the **abstract semantics**.

Definition 12 (Soundness). *Let $\mathscr{A}$ be an abstract Sg-algebra (with carrier set A) and $\gamma\colon A \to \wp(C)$ a monotone concretisation function. The algebra $\mathscr{A}$ is **sound** if its operators soundly approximate the concrete ones, i.e.,*

- *$\llbracket f\colon w \to s \rrbracket_{\mathscr{C}^*} \circ \gamma \subseteq \gamma \circ \llbracket f\colon w \to s \rrbracket_\mathscr{A}$ for each $f\colon w \to s$; and*
- *$\llbracket k \rrbracket_{\mathscr{C}^*} \subseteq \gamma \llbracket k \rrbracket_\mathscr{A}$ for each constant $k\colon s$.*

A straightforward consequence of this definition is that sound algebras induce sound abstract semantic functions:

Proposition 4. *If $\mathscr{A}$ is sound, then $\llbracket \mathsf{P} \rrbracket_{\mathscr{C}^*} \subseteq \gamma \llbracket \mathsf{P} \rrbracket_\mathscr{A}$ for each program P.*

If $\langle \wp(C), \subseteq \rangle \xleftrightarrow[\alpha]{\gamma} \langle A, \sqsubseteq \rangle$ is a gc between the concrete and the abstract domain, we can define the *most precise (abstract)* Sg-algebra $\mathscr{A}^\diamond$ out of the *best correct approximation* provided by (α, γ).

Definition 13 (Most Precise Algebra). *Let* $\langle \wp(C), \subseteq \rangle \xrightleftharpoons[\alpha]{\gamma} \langle A, \sqsubseteq \rangle$ *be a gc between the concrete and the abstract domain. The **most precise algebra** $\mathscr{A}^\circ$ approximating $\mathscr{C}$ with respect to (α, γ) is defined as follows:*

- *carrier sets are* $[\![s]\!]_{\mathscr{A}^\circ} \triangleq A_s$ *(recall the notation for sorted sets); and*
- *the semantics of the operators is* $[\![k]\!]_{\mathscr{A}^\circ} \triangleq \alpha [\![k]\!]_{\mathscr{C}^*}$ *for each constant* $k\colon s$, $[\![f\colon w \to s]\!]_{\mathscr{A}^\circ} \triangleq \alpha \circ [\![f\colon w \to s]\!]_{\mathscr{C}^*} \circ \gamma$ *for each function symbol* $f\colon w \to s$.

The abstract semantics $[\![-]\!]_{\mathscr{A}^\circ}$ induced by $\mathscr{A}^\circ$ enjoys the soundness property (the reader may want to check that $\mathscr{A}^\circ$ is a proper Sg-algebra), and it is the most precise among all the sound algebras, in the following sense:

Proposition 5. $\mathscr{A}^\circ$ *soundly approximates the concrete semantics. Moreover,* $\mathscr{A}^\circ$ *is the most precise abstraction with respect to* (α, γ), *that is, for any other sound algebra* $\mathscr{A}$, $\gamma \circ [\![f\colon w \to s]\!]_{\mathscr{A}^\circ} \subseteq \gamma \circ [\![f\colon w \to s]\!]_{\mathscr{A}}$ *and* $\gamma [\![k]\!]_{\mathscr{A}^\circ} \subseteq \gamma [\![k]\!]_{\mathscr{A}}$ *for each operator in* Sg. *Therefore, by Proposition 4,* $\gamma [\![P]\!]_{\mathscr{A}^\circ} \subseteq \gamma [\![P]\!]_{\mathscr{A}}$ *for each program* P.

In general, abstraction and concretisation functions α and γ are not homomorphisms between $\mathscr{A}$ and $\mathscr{C}^*$. However, if they are homomorphisms, then $\mathscr{A}$ is *backward* and *forward complete*, respectively (Propositions 6 and 7).

Definition 14 ((Backward) Completeness). *Let* $\mathscr{A}$ *be an* Sg*-algebra and* $\langle \wp(C), \subseteq \rangle \xrightleftharpoons[\alpha]{\gamma} \langle A, \sqsubseteq \rangle$ *a gc. The left adjoint* α *encodes concrete properties in the abstract domain. The algebra* $\mathscr{A}$ *is **complete** with respect to*

- *a function symbol* $f\colon w \to s$ *if* $\alpha \circ [\![f\colon w \to s]\!]_{\mathscr{C}^*} = [\![f\colon w \to s]\!]_{\mathscr{A}} \circ \alpha$; *and*
- *a constant* $k\colon s$ *if* $\alpha [\![k]\!]_{\mathscr{C}^*} = [\![k]\!]_{\mathscr{A}}$.

Proposition 6. *Let* $\alpha\colon \mathscr{C}^* \to \mathscr{A}$ *be an* Sg*-homomorphism. Then,* $\mathscr{A}$ *is complete with respect to each operator in* Sg, *and therefore* $\alpha [\![P]\!]_{\mathscr{C}^*} = [\![P]\!]_{\mathscr{A}}$ *for each program* P.

Note that, in general, the existence of a best abstract approximation is not guaranteed (*e.g.*, for convex polyhedra [17] or the final state automata domain [3]). In such cases, a dual notion of completeness (*forward completeness* [20]) with respect to the concretisation function is investigated.

Definition 15 (Forward Completeness). *Let* $\mathscr{A}$ *be an algebra over* Sg *and* $\gamma\colon A \to \wp(C)$ *a monotone concretisation function. The algebra* $\mathscr{A}$ *is **forward complete** with respect to*

- *a function symbol* $f\colon w \to s$ *if* $[\![f\colon w \to s]\!]_{\mathscr{C}^*} \circ \gamma = \gamma \circ [\![f\colon w \to s]\!]_{\mathscr{A}}$; *and*
- *a constant* $k\colon s$ *if* $[\![k]\!]_{\mathscr{C}^*} = \gamma [\![k]\!]_{\mathscr{A}}$.

Proposition 7. *Let* $\gamma\colon \mathscr{A} \to \mathscr{C}^*$ *be an* Sg*-homomorphism. Then,* $\mathscr{A}$ *is forward complete with respect to each operator in* Sg, *and therefore* $[\![P]\!]_{\mathscr{C}^*} = \gamma [\![P]\!]_{\mathscr{A}}$ *for each program* P.

5   The Multi-language Abstraction

Our aim in this section is to define *abstractions of the multi-language semantics* by relying on the *abstractions of the single-languages*. In the next paragraph we recall the multi-language construction [7] and we set up the notation. In Sect. 5.1 we define the combination of abstract interpretations of different languages, a key contribution of our work. By example we apply our theory to two different sign abstract semantics of Imp and Num, and we show how to derive the sign semantics for the multi-language NImp obtained by blending Imp and Num.

The Multi-language Construction. Throughout this section, we let Sg_1 and Sg_2 be two order-sorted signatures defining the syntax of two languages, and let $i \triangleq 1, 2$. We denote by $\mathscr{C}_i$ the order-sorted Sg_i-algebra inducing the semantics $[\![-]\!]_{\mathscr{C}_i}$ of the language. Recall (Definition 6) that the signature of a multi-language, which we shall refer to as SG, is specified by blending the order-sorted signatures Sg_1 and Sg_2 of the single-languages through an *interoperability relation* $\ltimes$ on sorts. In particular, an interoperability constraint $s \ltimes s'$ implies that Sg_i-terms of sort s can be used in place of Sg_j-terms of sort s' (with $i, j \in \{1, 2\}$ and $i \neq j$). This determines the terms of the multi-language $SG \triangleq (Sg_1, Sg_2, \ltimes)$. The multi-language SG-semantics $\mathscr{C}$ is then obtained by pairing the single-language algebras $\mathscr{C}_1$ and $\mathscr{C}_2$ with boundary functions $[\![s \ltimes s']\!]_{\mathscr{C}} : [\![s]\!]_{\mathscr{C}_i} \to [\![s']\!]_{\mathscr{C}_j}$ that specify how terms of sort s in Sg_i can be interpreted as terms of sort s' in Sg_j. In other words, boundary functions regulate the flow of values between the underlying languages [33]. For instance, they can act as a bridge between different type representations in the underlying languages (*e.g.*, to enable the interoperability of Java and JavaScript in Nashorn [35] or the interoperability of Java and Kotlin [27]), or deal between different machine-integers implementation (*e.g.*, the mapping between Java primitive types and C types in JNI [34]), etc. An interesting example on object passing between a weakly and a strongly typed language can be observed in Nashorn: JavaScript objects that need to flow to Java are encapsulated into the (Java) `ScriptObjectMirror` class which provides a Java representation of the underlying JavaScript object.

5.1   Combining Abstractions of Different Languages

The first step towards an abstract interpretation theory for multi-languages is to find a suitable notion of *multi-language collecting semantics*.

Definition 16 (Multi-language Collecting Semantics). *Let $\mathscr{C}$ be a multi-language SG-algebra over the multi-language signature $SG \triangleq (Sg_1, Sg_2, \ltimes)$. The* **multi-language collecting semantics** $\mathscr{C}^*$ *over $\mathscr{C}$ is specified by:*

- *the collecting Sg_i-semantics $\mathscr{C}_i^*$ over $\mathscr{C}_i$, for $i = 1, 2$; and*
- *boundary functions $[\![s \ltimes s']\!]_{\mathscr{C}^*} \triangleq \wp[\![s \ltimes s']\!]_{\mathscr{C}}$ for each $s \ltimes s'$.*

We can then lift Proposition 1 and 2 to the multi-language world in order to show that $\mathscr{C}^*$ has the desired properties:

Proposition 8. *Let $\mathscr{C}$ be a multi-language SG-algebra. The collecting semantics $[\![-]\!]_{\mathscr{C}^*}$ induced by $\mathscr{C}^*$ computes the strongest program property for each multi-language program* P *generated by* SG, *that is* $[\![P]\!]_{\mathscr{C}^*} = \{[\![P]\!]_{\mathscr{C}}\}$. *Moreover, the singleton function* $\{-\} \colon \mathscr{C} \to \mathscr{C}^*$ *is a multi-language SG-homomorphism.*

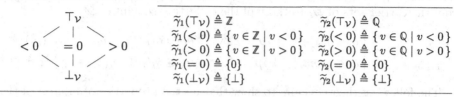

$$
\begin{aligned}
\widetilde{\gamma}_1(\top_\mathcal{V}) &\triangleq \mathbb{Z} & \widetilde{\gamma}_2(\top_\mathcal{V}) &\triangleq \mathbb{Q} \\
\widetilde{\gamma}_1(< 0) &\triangleq \{v \in \mathbb{Z} \mid v < 0\} & \widetilde{\gamma}_2(< 0) &\triangleq \{v \in \mathbb{Q} \mid v < 0\} \\
\widetilde{\gamma}_1(> 0) &\triangleq \{v \in \mathbb{Z} \mid v > 0\} & \widetilde{\gamma}_2(> 0) &\triangleq \{v \in \mathbb{Q} \mid v > 0\} \\
\widetilde{\gamma}_1(= 0) &\triangleq \{0\} & \widetilde{\gamma}_2(= 0) &\triangleq \{0\} \\
\widetilde{\gamma}_1(\bot_\mathcal{V}) &\triangleq \{\bot\} & \widetilde{\gamma}_2(\bot_\mathcal{V}) &\triangleq \{\bot\}
\end{aligned}
$$

Fig. 6. Sign abstract domain.

Fig. 7. Concretisation functions $\widetilde{\gamma}_i \colon A_\mathcal{V} \to \wp(\mathbb{V}_i)$.

We are now interested in whether we can obtain a fixpoint definition of the multi-language collecting semantics $[\![-]\!]_{\mathscr{C}^*}$ induced by $\mathscr{C}^*$. At a minimum, a fixpoint definition of the two underlying language semantics is needed, since every single-language program is also a multi-language one. However, the semantics of the multi-language does not only depend on these specifications (that is, it is not a *universal property* of the underlying semantics) but is determined up to a family of boundary functions defining the interoperability of Sg_1 and Sg_2.

Theorem 4. *Let $\mathscr{C}$ be a multi-language SG-algebra whose boundary functions admit a constructive definition, that is $[\![s \ltimes s']\!]_{\mathscr{C}} \triangleq \mathrm{lfp}F_{s \ltimes s'}$ for each $s \ltimes s'$ in* SG *and for some $F_{s \ltimes s'} \colon ([\![s]\!]_{\mathscr{C}_i} \to [\![s']\!]_{\mathscr{C}_j}) \to ([\![s]\!]_{\mathscr{C}_i} \to [\![s']\!]_{\mathscr{C}_j})$. Then, the multi-language collecting semantics $[\![-]\!]_{\mathscr{C}^*}$ induced by $\mathscr{C}^*$ admits a fixpoint computation if and only if $\mathscr{C}_1$ and $\mathscr{C}_2$ does.*

Proof (Sketch). Each operator in SG admits a fixpoint definition.

The second step is to combine the already existing abstractions of the underlying languages. Let $\mathscr{A}_1$ and $\mathscr{A}_2$ be the Sg_i-algebras providing the abstract semantics of Sg_i, with $i \triangleq 1, 2$, and $\gamma_i \colon A_i \to \wp(D_i)$ their concretisation functions, respectively. We can blend $\mathscr{A}_1$ and $\mathscr{A}_2$ into the multi-language SG-algebra $\mathscr{A}$ by defining an abstract semantics of the conversion operators $[\![s \ltimes s']\!]_{\mathscr{A}}$, for each $s \ltimes s'$. We call such an $\mathscr{A}$ an **abstract** multi-language algebra.

Running Example 3. Let $\langle A_\mathcal{V}, \sqsubseteq_\mathcal{V}, \sqcup_\mathcal{V}, \sqcap_\mathcal{V}, \bot_\mathcal{V}, \top_\mathcal{V} \rangle$ be the standard sign domain (Fig. 6) and $\widetilde{\gamma}_i \colon A_\mathcal{V} \to \wp(\mathbb{V}_i)$ (where $\mathbb{V}_1 \triangleq \mathbb{Z}_\bot$ and $\mathbb{V}_2 \triangleq \mathbb{Q}_\bot$) the corresponding concretisation function (Fig. 7). We let $\mathscr{A}_1$ and $\mathscr{A}_2$ be the abstract algebras defining a sign analysis for languages Imp and Num, respectively (that is, the computation induced by $\mathscr{A}_i$ is carried out using abstract values in $A_\mathcal{V}$ instead of concrete ones in $\mathbb{V}_i$). The abstract semantics $\mathscr{A}_i$ is the standard one (see, for instance, [40]), and it is reported in Appendix A for completeness.

The concretisation of abstract environments $\mathbb{E}\text{nv}^{\natural} \triangleq \mathbb{X} \to A_{\mathcal{V}}$ is defined by $\mathring{\gamma}_i(\rho^{\natural} \in \mathbb{E}\text{nv}^{\natural}) \triangleq \{\, \rho_i \in \mathbb{E}\text{nv}_i \mid \forall x \in \mathbb{X} \,.\, \rho_i(x) \in \widetilde{\gamma}_i(\rho^{\natural}(x)) \,\}$. The abstract interpretation of an expression E in Imp or Num is a function $e^{\natural} \in [\![exp_i]\!]_{\mathscr{A}_i} \triangleq \mathbb{E}\text{nv}^{\natural} \to A_{\mathcal{V}}$ that takes abstract environments to abstract values. Similarly, the abstract interpretation $c^{\natural} \in [\![com_i]\!]_{\mathscr{A}_i} \triangleq \mathbb{E}\text{nv}^{\natural} \to \mathbb{E}\text{nv}^{\natural}$ of a command C is a transformation of abstract environments. The concretisations of $e^{\natural}$ and $c^{\natural}$ are therefore (sorted) functions $(\gamma_i)_{exp_i} \colon [\![exp_i]\!]_{\mathscr{A}_i} \to [\![exp_i]\!]_{\mathscr{D}_i^*}$ and $(\gamma_i)_{com_i} \colon [\![com_i]\!]_{\mathscr{A}_i} \to [\![com_i]\!]_{\mathscr{D}_i^*}$ from the carrier sets of $\mathscr{A}_i$ to those of the collecting semantics $\mathscr{D}_i^*$:

$$(\gamma_i)_{exp_i}(e^{\natural}) \triangleq \{\, e_i \in [\![exp_i]\!]_{\mathscr{D}_i} \mid \forall \rho^{\natural} \in \mathbb{E}\text{nv}^{\natural} \,.\, \forall \rho_i \in \mathring{\gamma}_i(\rho^{\natural}) \,.\, e_i(\rho_i) \in \widetilde{\gamma}_i(e^{\natural}(\rho^{\natural})) \,\}$$

$$(\gamma_i)_{com_i}(c^{\natural}) \triangleq \{\, c_i \in [\![com_i]\!]_{\mathscr{D}_i} \mid \forall \rho^{\natural} \in \mathbb{E}\text{nv}^{\natural} \,.\, \forall \rho_i \in \mathring{\gamma}_i(\rho^{\natural}) \,.\, c_i(\rho_i) \in \mathring{\gamma}_i(c^{\natural}(\rho^{\natural})) \,\}$$

The following theorems aim to show that all the properties of interest of the resulting multi-language abstraction rely entirely on the abstract semantics of the boundary functions. We recall that when we write $s \ltimes s'$ we implicitly assume that s is a sort of Sg_i and s' one of Sg_j for $i, j \in \{1, 2\}$ and $i \neq j$.

Theorem 5 (Soundness). *Let $\mathscr{A}_1$ and $\mathscr{A}_2$ be sound Sg_i-algebras with concretisation functions $\gamma_i \colon A_i \to \wp(C_i)$, for $i \triangleq 1, 2$. If $[\![s \ltimes s']\!]_{\mathscr{C}^*} \circ \gamma_i \subseteq \gamma_j \circ [\![s \ltimes s']\!]_{\mathscr{A}}$ for each $s \ltimes s'$, then the multi-language abstract semantics $\mathscr{A}$ is sound, that is $[\![\mathsf{P}]\!]_{\mathscr{C}^*} \subseteq \gamma [\![\mathsf{P}]\!]_{\mathscr{A}}$ for each multi-language program P generated by SG.*

The derived abstraction $\mathscr{A}$ of the multi-language semantics preserves the completeness of single-language operators.

Theorem 6 (Completeness). *Let $\mathscr{A}$ be the multi-language abstract semantics. If the order-sorted Sg_i-algebra $\mathscr{A}_i$ is forward (resp., backward) complete with respect to $k \colon s$ and $f \colon w \to s$ in Sg_i, then $\mathscr{A}$ is forward (resp., backward) complete with respect to $k_i \colon s$ and $f_i \colon w \to s$ in SG, respectively.*

Then, complete boundary functions do not alter the completeness of complete programs as a corollary:

Corollary 1. *Let $\mathscr{A}$ be the multi-language abstract semantics and $[\![s \ltimes s']\!]_{\mathscr{A}}$ a forward (resp., backward) complete boundary functions. For each multi-language program P sorted by s, if P is forward (resp., backward) complete, then so too is the program $\hookrightarrow_{s \ltimes s'}(\mathsf{P})$.*

Equivalent multi-language versions of Propositions 6 and 7 also apply. The proof boils down to the fact that multi-language homomorphisms are pair of order-sorted homomorphisms that also commute with boundary functions.

Running Example 4. The multi-language abstract algebra $\mathscr{A}$ is obtained by coupling $\mathscr{A}_1$ and $\mathscr{A}_2$ with an abstraction of the boundary function $[\![exp_2 \ltimes exp_1]\!]_{\mathscr{D}}$ defined in Example 2. Since the underlying algebras share the same abstract domain for expressions, that is $[\![exp_1]\!]_{\mathscr{A}_1} = [\![exp_2]\!]_{\mathscr{A}_2}$, there is no need to convert abstract values between two identical domains, therefore we set $[\![exp_2 \ltimes exp_1]\!]_{\mathscr{A}} = id$.

Let us show the computation of the abstract semantics of the multi-language program in Fig. 5, starting from the set of initial states in which both a and n are greater than 0. The abstract precondition before entering the loop is given by the abstract environment $\{a \mapsto (>0), n \mapsto (>0), res \mapsto (>0)\}$, where res is positive due to the assignment on line 1. The abstract iterates of the loop converge in three steps, as shown in Fig. 8. Since the example trivially satisfies the hypotheses of Theorem 5, the result is sound.

Step	0	1	2
res	(>0)	(>0)	(>0)
a	(>0)	(>0)	(>0)
n	(>0)	$\top_{\mathcal{V}}$	$\top_{\mathcal{V}}$

The abstract interpretation of the program in Fig. 5 guarantees the result of a^n, with $a, n > 0$, to be positive. The imprecision on the final abstract value of the variable n is due to poor choice of the abstract domain.

Fig. 8. The abstract iterates of the loop in Fig. 5.

6   Related Works

Cross-language interoperability is a popular field of research which has been driven more by practical needs than by theoretical questions. Several works focus on the implementation of runtime mechanisms for interoperability. Non-exhaustive examples are [24], defining a type system for the Microsoft Intermediate Language (IL) employed by the .NET to interoperate underlying languages (*e.g.*, C#, Visual Basic, VBScript, *etc.*). [26] designs a virtual machine able to interoperate with dynamically typed programming languages (Ruby and JavaScript) with a statically typed one (C). [4] describes a multi-language runtime mechanism obtained by blending single-language interpreters of Python and Prolog. More examples can be found in [33]. On the other hand, various works [5,25,37,39] focus on specific theoretical problems arising from language interoperability, such as typing issues and value exchanging techniques. To the best of our knowledge, the first paper addressing the problem of formal reasoning in a multi-language context has been [33]. The authors introduced the notion of *boundary functions* as language constructs that move values between the underlying languages (ML and Scheme), ensuring their interoperability. Buro and Mastroeni [7–9] generalises such an approach in a language independent way, extending the construction to the broader class of order-sorted algebras. Finally, a few works concentrated on analysis-related aspects in a multi-language scenario. In the Java Native Interface context, [42] proposes a specification language which extends the Java Virtual Machine Language with primitives that approximate C code that cannot be compiled into Java. [30] introduces Pungi, a system that transforms Python/C interface code to affine programs with the aim of correctly handling Python's heap when it interoperates with C++.

7 Discussion and Concluding Remarks

The lack of static analysis techniques for verifying multi-language programs is a major issue so long as modern software relies on heterogenous code. Current state of the art sees relatively few works [30,42] that solve context-specific tasks in the cross-language interoperability field. However, none of these works address the problem from a general, theoretical point of view.

In this paper, we applied abstract interpretation theory to the algebraic framework of multi-languages, providing a general technique for defining the abstract semantics of the combined language. The taken approach has the advantage of being independent both from the underlying languages and analyses, and, at the same time, guarantees theoretical properties of interest, *e.g.*, soundness and completeness of the abstraction. Moreover, we have shown that such properties rely crucially on the definition of the boundary functions, thus providing guidelines for defining their abstract semantics.

$$[\![exp_1]\!]_{\mathscr{D}_1} \triangleq \mathsf{Env}_1 \to \mathbb{Z}_\bot \qquad\qquad [\![exp_1]\!]_{\mathscr{A}_1} \triangleq \mathsf{Env}^\natural \to A_\mathcal{V}$$

$$[\![i]\!]_{\mathscr{D}_1} \triangleq \rho_1 \mapsto i \qquad\qquad\qquad [\![i]\!]_{\mathscr{A}_1} \triangleq \rho^\natural \mapsto \tilde{\alpha}_1(\{i\})$$

$$[\![x]\!]_{\mathscr{D}_1} \triangleq \rho_1 \mapsto \rho_1(x) \qquad\qquad [\![x]\!]_{\mathscr{A}_1} \triangleq \rho^\natural \mapsto \rho^\natural(x)$$

$$[\![bop_\odot]\!]_{\mathscr{D}_1}(e_1,e_2) \triangleq \rho_1 \mapsto e_1(\rho_1) \odot e_2(\rho_1) \quad [\![bop_\odot]\!]_{\mathscr{A}_1}(e_1^\natural,e_2^\natural) \triangleq \rho^\natural \mapsto e_1^\natural(\rho^\natural) \odot^\natural e_2^\natural(\rho^\natural)$$

Fig. 9. Denotational and sign semantics of Imp expressions.

Further research should consider the *asymmetrical* lifting of a single-language analysis to a multi-language. In the previous section, we assumed the existence of two algebras, $\mathscr{A}_1$ and $\mathscr{A}_2$, providing the abstract semantics of the underlying languages. Then, the abstract semantics of boundary functions defines the flow of abstract values during the abstract computations. Even though our framework is general enough to allow such algebras to be different (*e.g.*, $\mathscr{A}_1$ may define a sign semantics whereas $\mathscr{A}_2$ provides an interval analysis), we do not discuss the case in which there exists only one anlaysis. It may be fruitful to investigate this asymmetrical situation, for instance in the case where one of the underlying languages cannot alter the values flowing from the other (see the *lump embedding* construction of [33]).

In addition, future studies must focus on practical aspects of implementation. The proof of Thm. 2 in [7] provides a recursive definition of homomorphisms out of the multi-language term algebra, *i.e.*, semantic functions, that suggests there is a straightforward implementation of the multi-language abstract interpreter.

A   Concrete and Abstract Semantics of Imp and Num

We define the denotational semantics $\mathscr{D}_i$ and the sign semantics $\mathscr{A}_i$ for both languages Imp and Num (we omit the concrete semantics of commands since it is the standard one).

Concrete and Abstract Semantics of Expressions Denotational and sign semantics of expressions are defined in Figs. 9 and 10. The carrier sets on which they are defined are $[\![exp_i]\!]_{\mathscr{D}_i} \triangleq \mathsf{Env}_i \to \mathbb{V}_i$ and $[\![exp_i]\!]_{\mathscr{A}_i} \triangleq \mathsf{Env}^\natural \to A_\mathcal{V}$, respectively. Note that there is an obvious abstraction function $\widetilde{\alpha}_i \colon \wp(\mathbb{V}_i) \to A_\mathcal{V}$ left adjoint to $\widetilde{\gamma}_i$ (Fig. 7) providing $\langle \wp(\mathbb{V}_i), \subseteq \rangle \xleftrightarrow[\widetilde{\alpha}_i]{\widetilde{\gamma}_i} \langle A_\mathcal{V}, \sqsubseteq_\mathcal{V} \rangle$; and also note that we abuse notation and assume that $\odot$ and f_n are both syntactical symbols and functions over values, that is $\odot \colon \mathbb{Z}_\perp^2 \to \mathbb{Z}_\perp$ and $f_n \colon \mathbb{Q}_\perp^n \to \mathbb{Q}_\perp$. We denote by $\odot^\natural \colon A_\mathcal{V}^2 \to A_\mathcal{V}$ and $f_n^\natural \colon A_\mathcal{V}^n \to A_\mathcal{V}$ the sign semantics of $\odot$ and f_n, respectively.

$$[\![exp_2]\!]_{\mathscr{D}_2} \triangleq \mathsf{Env}_2 \to \mathbb{Q}_\perp \qquad\qquad [\![exp_2]\!]_{\mathscr{A}_2} \triangleq \mathsf{Env}^\natural \to A_\mathcal{V}$$

$$[\![q]\!]_{\mathscr{D}_2} \triangleq \rho_2 \mapsto q \qquad\qquad [\![q]\!]_{\mathscr{A}_2} \triangleq \rho^\natural \mapsto \widetilde{\alpha}_2(\{q\})$$

$$[\![x]\!]_{\mathscr{D}_2} \triangleq \rho_2 \mapsto \rho_2(x) \qquad\qquad [\![x]\!]_{\mathscr{A}_2} \triangleq \rho^\natural \mapsto \rho^\natural(x)$$

$$[\![f_n]\!]_{\mathscr{D}_2}(e_1, e_2) \triangleq \rho_2 \mapsto f_n(e_1(\rho_2), e_2(\rho_2)) \quad [\![f_n]\!]_{\mathscr{A}_2}(e_1^\natural, e_2^\natural) \triangleq \rho^\natural \mapsto f_n^\natural(e_1^\natural(\rho^\natural), e_2^\natural(\rho^\natural))$$

$$[\![?]\!]_{\mathscr{D}_2}(e_1, e_2, e_3) \triangleq \rho_2 \mapsto \begin{cases} \perp & e_1(\rho_2) = \perp \\ e_2(\rho_2) & e_1(\rho_2) \neq 0 \\ e_3(\rho_2) & e_1(\rho_2) = 0 \end{cases}$$

$$[\![?]\!]_{\mathscr{A}_2}(e_1^\natural, e_2^\natural, e_3^\natural) \triangleq \rho^\natural \mapsto \begin{cases} \perp_\mathcal{V} & e_1^\natural(\rho^\natural) = \perp_\mathcal{V} \\ e_2^\natural(\rho^\natural) & e_1^\natural(\rho^\natural) \in \{> 0, < 0\} \\ e_3^\natural(\rho^\natural) & e_1^\natural(\rho^\natural) = (= 0) \end{cases}$$

Fig. 10. Denotational and sign semantics of Num expressions.

Sign Semantics of Commands. We just provide the sign semantics of Imp-commands since Num-commands are a subset of those of Imp (Fig. 11). The carrier set is defined as $[\![com_1]\!]_{\mathscr{A}_1} \triangleq \mathsf{Env}^\natural \to \mathsf{Env}^\natural$. The poset $\langle \mathsf{Env}^\natural, \sqsubseteq_\mathcal{V} \rangle$, where $\rho_0^\natural \sqsubseteq_\mathcal{V} \rho_1^\natural$ if $\rho_0^\natural(x) \sqsubseteq \rho_1^\natural(x)$ for each $x \in \mathbb{X}$, is trivially a complete lattice $\langle \mathsf{Env}^\natural, \sqsubseteq_\mathcal{V}, \sqcup_\mathcal{V}, \sqcap_\mathcal{V}, \perp_\mathcal{V}, \top_\mathcal{V} \rangle$. We can then lift such a posetal structure defined on $\mathsf{Env}^\natural$ to the function space $\mathsf{Env}^\natural \to \mathsf{Env}^\natural$, thus making it a complete lattice $\langle \mathsf{Env}^\natural \to \mathsf{Env}^\natural, \widetilde{\sqsubseteq}_\mathcal{V}, \widetilde{\sqcup}_\mathcal{V}, \widetilde{\sqcap}_\mathcal{V}, \widetilde{\perp}_\mathcal{V}, \widetilde{\top}_\mathcal{V} \rangle$. In particular, the least upper bound operator is $\widetilde{\sqcup}_\mathcal{V} S = \rho^\natural \mapsto \sqcup_\mathcal{V}\{ f^\natural(\rho^\natural) \mid f^\natural \in S \}$, and the smallest and greatest element are $\widetilde{\perp}_\mathcal{V} = \rho^\natural \mapsto \perp_\mathcal{V}$ and $\widetilde{\top}_\mathcal{V} = \rho^\natural \mapsto \top_\mathcal{V}$, respectively. One can check that $F_{e^\natural, c^\natural}^\natural(f^\natural)$ is continuous, so that the *loop* semantics is well-defined.

$$\llbracket com_1 \rrbracket_{\mathscr{A}_1} \triangleq \mathsf{Env}^\natural \to \mathsf{Env}^\natural$$

$$\llbracket skip \rrbracket_{\mathscr{A}_1} \triangleq \rho^\natural \mapsto \rho^\natural$$

$$\llbracket assign_x \rrbracket_{\mathscr{A}_1}(e^\natural) \triangleq \rho^\natural \mapsto \rho^\natural[x \hookleftarrow e^\natural(\rho^\natural)] \quad \llbracket seq \rrbracket_{\mathscr{A}_1}(c_1^\natural, c_2^\natural) \triangleq \rho^\natural \mapsto (c_2^\natural \circ c_1^\natural)(\rho^\natural)$$

$$\llbracket cond \rrbracket_{\mathscr{A}_1}(e^\natural, c_1^\natural, c_2^\natural) \triangleq \rho^\natural \mapsto \begin{cases} c_1^\natural(\rho^\natural) \sqcup_\nu c_2^\natural(\rho^\natural) & e^\natural(\rho^\natural) = \top_\nu \\ c_2^\natural(\rho^\natural) & e^\natural(\rho^\natural) = (= 0) \\ c_1^\natural(\rho^\natural) & e^\natural(\rho^\natural) \in \{(< 0), (> 0)\} \\ \dot{\bot}_\nu & e^\natural(\rho^\natural) = \bot_\nu \end{cases}$$

$$\llbracket loop \rrbracket_{\mathscr{A}_1}(e^\natural, c^\natural) \triangleq \mathrm{lfp}_{\dot{\bot}}^{\sqsubseteq} F_{e^\natural, c^\natural}^\natural$$

$$F_{e^\natural, c^\natural}^\natural(f^\natural) = \rho^\natural \mapsto \begin{cases} \rho^\natural \sqcup_\nu f^\natural(c^\natural(\rho^\natural)) & e^\natural(\rho^\natural) = \top_\nu \\ \rho^\natural & e^\natural(\rho^\natural) = (= 0) \\ f^\natural(c^\natural(\rho^\natural)) & e^\natural(\rho^\natural) \in \{(< 0), (> 0)\} \\ \dot{\bot}_\nu & e^\natural(\rho^\natural) = \bot_\nu \end{cases}$$

Fig. 11. Sign semantics of Imp commands.

References

1. Ahmed, A., Blume, M.: An equivalence-preserving CPS translation via multi-language semantics. SIGPLAN Not. **46**(9), 431–444 (2011)
2. Amato, G., Meo, M.C., Scozzari, F.: On collecting semantics for program analysis. Theor. Comput. Sci. **823**, 1–25 (2020)
3. Arceri, V., Mastroeni, I.: Static program analysis for string manipulation languages. Electron. Proc. Theor. Comput. Sci. **299**, 19–33 (2019)
4. Barrett, E., Bolz, C.F., Tratt, L.: Approaches to interpreter composition. Comput. Lang. Syst. Struct. **44**, 199–217 (2015)
5. Benton, N.: Embedded interpreters. J. Funct. Program. **15**(4), 503–542 (2005)
6. Bjørner, N., Gurfinkel, A.: Property directed polyhedral abstraction. In: D'Souza, D., Lal, A., Larsen, K.G. (eds.) VMCAI 2015. LNCS, vol. 8931, pp. 263–281. Springer, Heidelberg (2015). https://doi.org/10.1007/978-3-662-46081-8_15
7. Buro, S., Mastroeni, I.: On the multi-language construction. In: Caires, L. (ed.) ESOP 2019. LNCS, vol. 11423, pp. 293–321. Springer, Cham (2019). https://doi.org/10.1007/978-3-030-17184-1_11
8. Buro, S., Mastroeni, I., Crole, R.L.: Equational logic and categorical semantics for multi-languages. In: In-press (Accepted for Publication at 36th International Conference on Mathematical Foundations of Programming Semantics – MFPS 2020) (2020)
9. Buro, S., Mastroeni, I., Crole, R.L.: Equational logic and set-theoretic models for multi-languages. In: In-press (Accepted for Publication at 21st Italian Conference on Theoretical Computer Science – ICTCS 2020) (2020)
10. Campbell, G., Papapetrou, P.P.: SonarQube in Action. Manning Publications Co., New York (2013)
11. Chisnall, D.: The challenge of cross-language interoperability. Commun. ACM **56**(12), 50–56 (2013)
12. Cohen, H., et al.: Handbook of Elliptic and Hyperelliptic Curve Cryptography. CRC Press, Boca Raton (2005)

13. Cousot, P.: Constructive design of a hierarchy of semantics of a transition system by abstract interpretation. Theor. Comput. Sci. **277**(1–2), 47–103 (2002)
14. Cousot, P., Cousot, R.: Abstract interpretation: a unified lattice model for static analysis of programs by construction or approximation of fixpoints. In: Proceedings of the 4th ACM SIGACT-SIGPLAN Symposium on Principles of Programming Languages, pp. 238–252 (1977)
15. Cousot, P., Cousot, R.: Abstract interpretation frameworks. J. Log. Comput. **2**(4), 511–547 (1992)
16. Cousot, P., Giacobazzi, R., Ranzato, F.: A^2i: abstract^2 interpretation. Proc. ACM Program. Lang. **3**(POPL), 1–31 (2019)
17. Cousot, P., Halbwachs, N.: Automatic discovery of linear restraints among variables of a program. In: Proceedings of the 5th ACM SIGACT-SIGPLAN Symposium on Principles of Programming Languages, pp. 84–96 (1978)
18. Furr, M., Foster, J.S.: Checking type safety of foreign function calls. SIGPLAN Not. **40**(6), 62–72 (2005)
19. Giacobazzi, R., Ranzato, F.: Completeness in abstract interpretation: a domain perspective. In: Johnson, M. (ed.) AMAST 1997. LNCS, vol. 1349, pp. 231–245. Springer, Heidelberg (1997). https://doi.org/10.1007/BFb0000474
20. Giacobazzi, R., Ranzato, F., Scozzari, F.: Making abstract interpretations complete. J. ACM (JACM) **47**(2), 361–416 (2000)
21. Goguen, J.A., Diaconescu, R.: An Oxford survey of order sorted algebra. Math. Struct. Comput. Sci. **4**(3), 363–392 (1994)
22. Goguen, J.A., Meseguer, J.: Order-sorted algebra I: equational deduction for multiple inheritance, overloading, exceptions and partial operations. Theor. Comput. Sci. **105**(2), 217–273 (1992)
23. Goguen, J.A., Thatcher, J.W., Wagner, E.G., Wright, J.B.: Initial algebra semantics and continuous algebras. J. ACM (JACM) **24**(1), 68–95 (1977)
24. Gordon, A.D., Syme, D.: Typing a multi-language intermediate code. In: Conference Record of POPL 2001: The 28th ACM SIGPLAN-SIGACT Symposium on Principles of Programming Languages, London, UK, January 17–19, 2001, pp. 248–260. ACM, New York (2001)
25. Gray, K.E.: Safe cross-language inheritance. In: Vitek, J. (ed.) ECOOP 2008. LNCS, vol. 5142, pp. 52–75. Springer, Heidelberg (2008). https://doi.org/10.1007/978-3-540-70592-5_4
26. Grimmer, M., Schatz, R., Seaton, C., Würthinger, T., Luján, M.: Cross-language interoperability in a multi-language runtime. ACM Trans. Program. Lang. Syst. **40**(2), 8:1–8:43 (2018)
27. JetBrains: Calling Java code from Kotlin. https://kotlinlang.org/docs/reference/java-interop.html
28. Juneau, J., Baker, J., Wierzbicki, F., Soto, L., Ng, V.: The Definitive Guide to Jython: Python for the Java Platform, 1st edn. Apress, Berkely (2010)
29. Kochems, J., Ong, C.: Improved functional flow and reachability analyses using indexed linear tree grammars. In: 22nd International Conference on Rewriting Techniques and Applications (RTA 2011). Schloss Dagstuhl-Leibniz-Zentrum fuer Informatik (2011)
30. Li, S., Tan, G.: Finding reference-counting errors in Python/C programs with affine analysis. In: Jones, R. (ed.) ECOOP 2014. LNCS, vol. 8586, pp. 80–104. Springer, Heidelberg (2014). https://doi.org/10.1007/978-3-662-44202-9_4
31. Liang, S.: Java Native Interface: Programmer's Guide and Reference, 1st edn. Addison-Wesley Longman Publishing Co., Inc., Boston (1999)

32. Mastroeni, I., Pasqua, M.: Hyperhierarchy of semantics - a formal framework for hyperproperties verification. In: Ranzato, F. (ed.) SAS 2017. LNCS, vol. 10422, pp. 232–252. Springer, Cham (2017). https://doi.org/10.1007/978-3-319-66706-5_12

33. Matthews, J., Findler, R.B.: Operational semantics for multi-language programs. ACM Trans. Program. Lang. Syst. **31**(3), 12:1–12:44 (2009)

34. Oracle: JNI types and data structures. https://docs.oracle.com/javase/7/docs/technotes/guides/jni/spec/types.html

35. Oracle: Nashorn user's guide. https://docs.oracle.com/en/java/javase/14/nashorn/introduction.html

36. Pasqua, M.: Hyper static analysis of programs - an abstract interpretation-based framework for hyperproperties verification. Ph.D. thesis, University of Verona (2019)

37. Patterson, D., Perconti, J., Dimoulas, C., Ahmed, A.: Funtal: reasonably mixing a functional language with assembly. In: Proceedings of the 38th ACM SIGPLAN Conference on Programming Language Design and Implementation, pp. 495–509. ACM, New York (2017)

38. Perconti, J.T., Ahmed, A.: Verifying an open compiler using multi-language semantics. In: Shao, Z. (ed.) ESOP 2014. LNCS, vol. 8410, pp. 128–148. Springer, Heidelberg (2014). https://doi.org/10.1007/978-3-642-54833-8_8

39. Ramsey, N.: ML module mania: a type-safe, separately compiled, extensible interpreter. Electron. Notes Theor. Comput. Sci. **148**(2), 181–209 (2006)

40. Rival, X., Yi, K.: Introduction to static analysis (2019)

41. Spoto, F., Jensen, T.: Class analyses as abstract interpretations of trace semantics. ACM Trans. Program. Lang. Syst. (TOPLAS) **25**(5), 578–630 (2003)

42. Tan, G., Morrisett, G.: Ilea: inter-language analysis across Java and C. SIGPLAN Not. **42**(10), 39–56 (2007)

43. Tennent, R.D.: The denotational semantics of programming languages. Commun. ACM **19**(8), 437–453 (1976)

Exact and Linear-Time Gas-Cost Analysis

Ankush Das[1]([✉])[iD] and Shaz Qadeer[2]

[1] Carnegie Mellon University, Pittsburgh, PA, USA
ankushd@cs.cmu.edu
[2] Novi, Seattle, WA, USA
shaz@fb.com

Abstract. Blockchains support execution of smart contracts: programs encoding complex transactions between distrusting parties. Due to their distributed nature, blockchains rely on third-party miners to execute and validate transactions. Miners are compensated by charging users with gas based on the execution cost of the transaction. To compute the exact gas cost, blockchains track gas cost dynamically creating its own overhead. This paper presents a static exact gas-cost analysis technique that can be employed to eliminate dynamic gas tracking. This approach presents further benefits such as providing miners with a trusted gas bound that can be verified in linear time, and eliminating out-of-gas exceptions. To handle recursion and unbounded computation, we propose a novel amortization technique that stores gas inside data structures. We have implemented our analysis technique in a tool called GasBoX that takes a contract as input and infers the gas cost of its functions automatically. We have evaluated GasBoX on 13 standard smart contracts borrowed from real-world blockchain projects. Our soundness theorem proves that the gas bound inferred by GasBoX exactly matches the gas cost at runtime and no dynamic gas tracking is necessary.

Keywords: Blockchains · Smart contracts · Resource analysis

1 Introduction

Blockchains such as Ethereum [43] and Libra [8] allow execution of complex transactions between distrusting parties through *smart contracts*. Smart contracts are programs typically written in a high-level language such as Solidity [16], Move [11] or Nomos [17] and compiled down to bytecode for execution on a distributed virtual machine. Smart contracts offer *transactions* (functions) that can be issued (called) by users to enforce such protocols, e.g. bidding in an auction, voting in an election, etc. Due to the distributed nature of blockchains, transactions are recorded by a large number of third-party entities, or *miners* (aka nodes) who are responsible for its execution. To prevent wastage of miner resources and compensate miners for their effort, users are charged for the execution cost of their transaction in the form of *gas units*.

© Springer Nature Switzerland AG 2020
D. Pichardie and M. Sighireanu (Eds.): SAS 2020, LNCS 12389, pp. 333–356, 2020.
https://doi.org/10.1007/978-3-030-65474-0_15

Gas is the fuel of computation on blockchains. A *cost model* assigns a fixed gas cost to each operation. Gas cost of a transaction is the sum of the gas cost of each operation executed during the transaction. Users are responsible for providing a sufficient *gas limit* along with the transaction to cover the execution cost. If a user fails to provide sufficient gas, the transaction fails after the execution runs out of gas, but the user is still charged for the gas used. The user then has to re-issue the transaction with a higher gas limit. Since users need to be aware of execution cost prior to issuing a transaction, there is a wide variety of analysis tools [5,6,17,23] to statically compute an *upper bound* on gas cost of transactions.

Unfortunately, upper gas bounds are inadequate. At runtime, if a user provides excess gas units, the leftover gas needs to be returned to the user. Thus, in existing blockchains such as Ethereum and Libra, a monitor function known as *dynamic gas meter* tracks the gas cost during execution. If the execution runs out of gas, the meter raises an *out-of-gas exception*, otherwise it returns the excess gas back to the user. Thus, despite the benefits of static gas analysis, blockchains still need to meter gas at runtime. Moreover, dynamic gas metering has its own limitations. First, it creates an execution overhead, inadvertently increasing the transaction gas cost (for the Libra blockchain, this overhead is about 20% of execution time!). Second, if the transaction runs out of gas, it does not provide any feedback to the user for transaction resubmission. Upper gas bounds can also be inadequate for miners. Blockchains often restrict transaction blocks using a *block gas limit*, i.e., the maximum gas consumption of transactions in a block. To estimate how many transactions a miner can fit in a block, miners need an *exact* gas bound; imprecise upper bounds are not sufficient. Thus, there is a need to *provide users and miners with a trusted exact gas bound that can be verified efficiently before accepting transactions*.

In response, this article describes a static analysis technique with two goals: *(i) exact* gas analysis to eliminate dynamic metering, and *(ii) efficient* analysis that can be employed by miners. These goals pose unique challenges, particularly in the blockchain domain. The gas cost of a transaction can not only depend on its arguments, but also on global state, i.e., data structures already published on the blockchain. This global state can also potentially be modified by other transactions. Since users and miners have no control over when their transactions are actually mined, they cannot exactly determine the global state during execution. Verifying exact bounds can further be challenging in the presence of branching since the gas cost may vary along different branches.

To this end, blockchains recommend implementing contracts and transactions in a way that the gas cost does not depend on global state. Realizing this, our analysis tool only verifies gas bounds that are a *constant*, i.e., do not depend on either the arguments or the global state. As a result, our analysis is very efficient, and is *linear-time* in the size of the program and thus, can be employed by miners with minimal overhead. This overhead is further compensated since the virtual machine no longer needs to meter gas at runtime.

To compute exact bounds in the presence of branching, we need to ensure that branches have equal gas cost. We establish this by introducing a special operation `Gas.deposit(n)` which deposits n gas units in the transaction sender's account at runtime. We augment the less costly branch with such an expression with n being the difference in the gas cost of both branches. This mechanism is sufficient to produce exact gas bounds and eliminates the need for gas metering, improving the overall hygiene of the virtual machine.

To handle unbounded computation such as recursion and iteration over data structures like maps, we utilize *amortization* [12,27,29,40]. We introduce $Gas(n)$ as a *first-class type* in the language to represent values with n gas units which can then be stored inside data structures. During a transaction, this stored gas can be consumed to pay for the transaction cost. Thus, users pay in advance while building up such data structures and later, iteration would effectively pay for itself! Thus, such transactions have a constant static gas bound which are automatically inferred by our analysis. We demonstrate that this amortization simplifies our gas analysis, prevents out-of-gas exceptions, and leads to more equitable gas-distribution schemes.

Although we have focused on constant gas bounds in this work, our analysis framework is general. Our key innovations of depositing gas in sender's account to obtain exact gas bounds and storing gas in data structures for amortization would still be applicable. The expressivity of the gas bounds can be enhanced by utilizing more sophisticated underlying logics, such as linear arithmetic [20] or SMT solvers [34]. However, such logics have a high computational complexity which would make the analysis inefficient, hampering its utility to miners. Although constant gas analysis precludes transactions that copy unbounded data structures such as lists and maps, we demonstrate that our tool can still analyze a large class of smart contracts.

We have implemented our analysis technique in a tool called GasBoX (GAS BOund eXact). The tool takes a function as input and automatically infers its exact gas bound by generating linear equalities and solving them via efficient off-the-shelf linear programming (LP) solvers. It can further take an initial gas bound as input and verify that it is exact or return the program location where the virtual machine would run out of gas. Thus, users can utilize GasBoX to infer gas bounds, while miners can utilize GasBoX to verify them in linear time. Our analysis framework is *compositional*, thereby efficiently analyzing functions in isolation. We have designed a simplistic programming language modeled on Move [11] to illustrate the analysis technique and tool. We conducted 13 case studies implementing standard smart contracts such as auctions, elections, bank accounts, tokens, etc. and inferred their gas bound using GasBoX. To the best of our knowledge, this is the first tool to compute exact gas bounds for smart contracts automatically.

Overall, we make the following technical contributions:

1. design of a linear-time and exact gas-analysis technique for smart contracts
2. introduction of a novel deposit operation to avoid gas metering
3. gas amortization to handle unbounded computation
4. implementation of an analysis tool that automatically infers gas bound using off-the-shelf LP solvers
5. case studies on standard smart contracts demonstrating its practicability.

2 Overview of Gas Analysis

The static gas-cost analysis is realized using a Hoare logic style reasoning with an abstract notion of a static *gas tank*. This gas tank symbolically represents the amount of gas available to the execution engine at a program location, and is denoted using a natural number. For a program expression e, we follow the rule

$$\{tank = \phi + \mathcal{C}(e)\}\ e\ \{tank = \phi \mid \phi \geq 0\}$$

Here, $\phi + \mathcal{C}(e)$ represents the initial value of the gas tank, and $\mathcal{C}(e)$ denotes the gas cost of expression e. The rule states that if the gas tank value is $\phi + \mathcal{C}(e)$ before execution, then gas tank value after execution is ϕ. Our analysis is naturally compositional since gas cost is additive: the gas cost for $e; e'$ is $\mathcal{C}(e) + \mathcal{C}(e')$.

$$\frac{\{tank = \phi + \mathcal{C}(e) + \mathcal{C}(e')\}\ e\ \{tank = \phi + \mathcal{C}(e') \mid \phi + \mathcal{C}(e') \geq 0\} \quad \{tank = \phi + \mathcal{C}(e')\}\ e'\ \{tank = \phi \mid \phi \geq 0\}}{\{tank = \phi + \mathcal{C}(e) + \mathcal{C}(e')\}\ e\ ;\ e'\ \{tank = \phi \mid \phi \geq 0\}}$$

2.1 Exact Bound Analysis and Runtime Overhead

We demonstrate our approach for exact gas analysis using an auction contract. Consider a function `addBid` which takes two arguments, `bidmap`: a reference to a map storing bids indexed by the address of their bidder, and `b`: a new bid to be added to the map represented using a `Coin` type.

```
fn addBid(bidmap: &Map<address, Coin>, b: Coin) {
  1. let bidder = GetTxnSenderAddress();
  2. if (Map.exists(copy(bidmap), copy(bidder))) then
  3.     tick(C_MoveToAddr); MoveToAddr(move(bidder), move(b));
  4. else
  5.     tick(C_MapInsert); Map.insert(move(bidmap), move(bidder), move(b));}
```

First, the bidder's address is computed and stored in the variable `bidder` (line 1). If `bidder` exists in the `bidmap` dictionary (line 2), then the bid is returned back to the bidder using the built-in `MoveToAddr` function (line 3). Otherwise, the bid is added to `bidmap` indexed by the bidder's address (line 5). For brevity, we allow a bidder to place a bid only once in this auction. Here, $move(v)$ moves the variable v out of scope by passing it to the callee while $copy(v)$ creates a fresh *deep* copy of v. This distinction is necessary from the gas analysis perspective, since the gas cost of $move(v)$ can be statically determined, while the cost of $copy(v)$ depends on the size of v (more details at the end of Sect. 2.2).

Gas cost of a function is defined w.r.t. a *cost model*. A cost model assigns a gas cost to each primitive operation. We simplify the analysis here by using the `tick` metric, which assigns a cost of n to `tick(n)`, and 0 to all other operations. Statically, our analysis follows the rule

$$\{tank = \phi + n\}\ \texttt{tick}(n)\ \{tank = \phi \mid \phi \geq 0\}$$

In the `addBid` function above, we have only instrumented the `MoveToAddr` and `Map.insert` functions with ticks for simplicity of exposition. In practice, our implementation takes a cost model as input, and inserts `tick` for all operations automatically (explained in Sect. 3.1) so its burden does not fall on the programmer. With this model, the gas cost of `addBid` is $C_{\texttt{MoveToAddr}}$ in the **then** branch and $C_{\texttt{MapInsert}}$ in the **else** branch. Since we cannot statically determine which branch would be taken at runtime, the worst-case gas bound of `addBid` is $\max(C_{\texttt{MapInsert}}, C_{\texttt{MoveToAddr}})$.

Since the statically derived gas bound is overapproximate, we need to dynamically meter the gas at runtime. Therefore, *despite the benefits of static gas analysis, we incur the overhead of metering the gas at runtime.* The gas meter will be responsible for returning the leftover gas back to the user at the end of execution. For the `addBid` function, if the initial provided gas is $\max(C_{\texttt{MapInsert}}, C_{\texttt{MoveToAddr}})$, the leftover gas at the end of execution would be 0 or $\max(C_{\texttt{MapInsert}}, C_{\texttt{MoveToAddr}}) - \min(C_{\texttt{MapInsert}}, C_{\texttt{MoveToAddr}})$, depending upon which branch is executed.

To avoid dynamic metering, we need to compute an *exact* gas bound. To achieve this, we mandate that both branches have equal gas cost. To ensure this, we introduce an expression `Gas.deposit(n)`. Statically, the gas cost of this expression is n. Dynamically, executing this deposits n units of gas in the account of the user who issued the transaction. The corresponding analysis rule is

$$\{tank = \phi + n\}\ \texttt{Gas.deposit}(n)\ \{tank = \phi \mid \phi \geq 0\}$$

Reimplementing the `addBid` function,

```
fn [C_MapInsert + C_MoveToAddr] addBid(bidmap: &Map<address, Coin>, b: Coin) {
  1. let bidder = GetTxnSenderAddress();
  2. if (Map.exists(copy(bidmap), copy(bidder))) then
         {tank = C_MapInsert + C_MoveToAddr}
  3.     tick(C_MoveToAddr); MoveToAddr(move(bidder), move(b));
         {tank = C_MapInsert + C_MoveToAddr - C_MoveToAddr = C_MapInsert}
  4.     Gas.deposit(C_MapInsert);
         {tank = C_MapInsert - C_MapInsert = 0}
  5. else
         {tank = C_MapInsert + C_MoveToAddr}
  6.     tick(C_MapInsert); Map.insert(move(bidmap), move(bidder), move(b));
         {tank = C_MapInsert + C_MoveToAddr - C_MapInsert = C_MoveToAddr}
  7.     Gas.deposit(C_MoveToAddr); }
         {tank = C_MoveToAddr - C_MoveToAddr = 0}
```

We have added the expression Gas.deposit($C_{\text{MapInsert}}$) in the then branch (line 4) and Gas.deposit($C_{\text{MoveToAddr}}$) in the else branch (line 7). With this addition, the gas cost of both branches becomes equal to $C_{\text{MapInsert}} + C_{\text{MoveToAddr}}$ as verified by the analysis (in blue). Since the gas tank value at the end of both branches is 0, we know that the *exact* gas bound of the addBid function is $C_{\text{MapInsert}} + C_{\text{MoveToAddr}}$ (described in blue along with the function declaration at the top).

Our analysis takes the function definition as input and infers its initial gas bound automatically. If it is already provided with an initial gas bound, it can further verify that the gas bound is exact or identify the location where the execution will run out of gas. Intuitively, if $\phi \geq 0$ at each program location during the analysis, the gas bound is sufficient. Otherwise, the first location where $\phi < 0$ is the point where the execution runs out of gas. Moreover, the gas bound is exact if $\phi = 0$ after the return expression(s) in the function body.

Advantages. Our analysis tool infers the exact gas bound automatically. The soundness of our analysis proves that if a user supplies this gas bound with a transaction, *there is no need for dynamic metering*. The Gas.deposit expression ensures that the user does not lose any gas units; *leftover gas is safely returned* to the user. Our analysis tool automatically instruments the program with the Gas.deposit operations, so its burden does not fall on the programmer. Furthermore, if the initial gas bound is not sufficient, the analysis identifies the program location where gas runs out, providing valuable feedback to the programmer.

One caveat here is that a programmer can still provide a high gas limit for a transaction and return most of the gas back to them using spurious Gas.deposit operations. To avoid this, we have augmented our analysis tool to detect spurious deposit operations. Minimally, deposit operations are only required at the join point of branches and only in one of the branches (the less costly one). Any other deposit operations are unnecessary and flagged by our analysis tool.

2.2   Handling Unbounded Computation

The auction contract also provides functionality for returning bids back to their respective bidders at the end of the auction. This is implemented with the recursive function below.

```
fn [C_MoveToAddr · sizeof(bidmap)] returnBids(bidmap : &Map<address, Coin>) {
  if (Map.size(copy(bidmap)) > 0) then
    {tank = C_MoveToAddr · sizeof(bidmap)}
    let (bidder, bid) = Map.remove_first(copy(bidmap)) ;
    {tank = C_MoveToAddr · (sizeof(bidmap) + 1)}
    tick(C_MoveToAddr) ; MoveToAddr(move(bidder), move(bid)) ;
    {tank = C_MoveToAddr · sizeof(bidmap)}
    returnBids(move(bidmap)) ; }
```

The function removes the first element from the map (remove first), storing the key in bidder and value in bid. The function then calls MoveToAddr which transfers the bid into the bidder's account. Finally, the function recurses. Since we incur $C_{\mathtt{MoveToAddr}}$ cost for each recursive call (due to the $\mathtt{tick}(C_{\mathtt{MoveToAddr}})$), the total cost of the $\mathtt{returnBids}$ function is $C_{\mathtt{MoveToAddr}} \cdot \mathtt{sizeof}(\mathtt{bidmap})$.

The analysis initiates with a gas tank value of $C_{\mathtt{MoveToAddr}} \cdot \mathtt{sizeof}(\mathtt{bidmap})$. The analysis then needs to verify that, in the $\mathtt{else}$ branch, $\mathtt{sizeof}(\mathtt{bidmap}) = 0$, thus the tank value is 0. In the $\mathtt{then}$ branch, the analysis needs to track that the size of $\mathtt{bidmap}$ decreases by 1 due to the $\mathtt{remove\_first}()$ function, and the gas tank value decreases by $C_{\mathtt{MoveToAddr}}$ due to $\mathtt{tick}(C_{\mathtt{MoveToAddr}})$. Thus, at the recursive call, we arrive at the invariant $\{>= C_{\mathtt{MoveToAddr}} \cdot \mathtt{sizeof}(\mathtt{bidmap})\}$. To express and verify such invariants, the analysis would need to track the size of data structures and their relation to the gas tank value. If the control flow involves deeper nested loops and recursion, the gas bounds would involve non-linear expressions and the analysis would require sophisticated techniques to synthesize such invariants [4,21,25]. Furthermore, blockchains discourage non-constant gas cost transactions since they are vulnerable to out-of-gas exceptions and denial-of-service attacks [23].

Gas Amortization. We instead propose a mechanism of *amortizing the linear cost* of $\mathtt{returnBids}$ over a series of bidding operations by *storing gas in data structures*. To pay for the gas cost of $\mathtt{MoveToAddr}$, we store $C_{\mathtt{MoveToAddr}}$ units of gas with the bid in $\mathtt{bidmap}$. This is defined using the type $\mathtt{GasBid}$ defined below.

```
resource GasBid {
  gas : Gas(C_MoveToAddr),    // C_MoveToAddr gas units stored inside GasBid
  bid : Coin }                // stores bid to be placed in auction
```

Our language allows declaration of two kinds of types: *structs* and *resources*. They are both analogous to classes in object-oriented languages, except that they differ in their treatment. Objects of struct types represent functional data structures: they can be moved or copied, whereas objects of resource types represent assets: they cannot be copied, only moved; they are treated *linearly* [22].

We introduce a new primitive linear type in the language $\mathtt{Gas}(n)$ where n is a constant natural number. Statically, a variable $v : \mathtt{Gas}(n)$ stores n units of gas. Constructing a variable of type $\mathtt{Gas}(n)$ consumes n gas units from the gas tank, while destructing it produces n gas units that are added to the gas tank. Formally, the introduction and elimination rules are described as

$$\{tank = \phi + n\}\; \mathtt{Gas.construct}(n)\; \{tank = \phi \mid \phi \geq 0\}$$
$$\{tank = \phi \mid v : \mathtt{Gas}(n)\}\; \mathtt{Gas.destruct}(v)\; \{tank = \phi + n\}$$

Amortized Auction. We reimplement the auction contract storing $C_{\mathtt{MoveToAddr}}$ gas units in the $\mathtt{GasBid}$ resource type. In this version, the bidder pays for the return of bids in advance.

```
fn [C_MapInsert + 2C_MoveToAddr] addBid(bidmap: &Map<address, GasBid>, b: Coin) {
  let bidder = GetTxnSenderAddress();
  if (Map.exists(copy(bidmap), copy(bidder))) then
```

$\{tank = C_{\texttt{MapInsert}} + 2C_{\texttt{MoveToAddr}}\}$
`tick(`$C_{\texttt{MoveToAddr}}$`); MoveToAddr(move(bidder), move(b));`
$\{tank = C_{\texttt{MapInsert}} + 2C_{\texttt{MoveToAddr}} - C_{\texttt{MoveToAddr}} = C_{\texttt{MapInsert}} + C_{\texttt{MoveToAddr}}\}$
`Gas.deposit(`$C_{\texttt{MapInsert}} + C_{\texttt{MoveToAddr}}$`);`
$\{tank = C_{\texttt{MapInsert}} + C_{\texttt{MoveToAddr}} - C_{\texttt{MapInsert}} - C_{\texttt{MoveToAddr}} = 0\}$
`else`
    $\{tank = C_{\texttt{MapInsert}} + 2C_{\texttt{MoveToAddr}}\}$
    `let g = Gas.construct(`$C_{\texttt{MoveToAddr}}$`);`
    $\{tank = C_{\texttt{MapInsert}} + 2C_{\texttt{MoveToAddr}} - C_{\texttt{MoveToAddr}} = C_{\texttt{MapInsert}} + C_{\texttt{MoveToAddr}}\}$
    `let gb = pack<GasBid> {gas: move(g), bid: move(b)};`
    `tick(`$C_{\texttt{MapInsert}}$`); Map.insert(move(bidmap), move(bidder), move(gb));`
    $\{tank = C_{\texttt{MapInsert}} + C_{\texttt{MoveToAddr}} - C_{\texttt{MapInsert}} = C_{\texttt{MoveToAddr}}\}$
    `Gas.deposit(`$C_{\texttt{MoveToAddr}}$`); }`
    $\{tank = C_{\texttt{MoveToAddr}} - C_{\texttt{MoveToAddr}} = 0\}$

```
fn [0] returnBids(bidmap : &Map<address, GasBid>) {
  if (Map.size(copy(bidmap)) > 0) then
    let (bidder, gbid) = Map.remove_first(copy(bidmap)) ;
    let (g, bid) = unpack<GasBid>(move(gbid));
```
    $\{tank = 0 \mid g : \texttt{Gas}(C_{\texttt{MoveToAddr}})\}$
    `Gas.destruct(g);`
    $\{tank = C_{\texttt{MoveToAddr}}\}$
    `tick(`$C_{\texttt{MoveToAddr}}$`) ; MoveToAddr(move(bidder), move(bid)) ;`
    $\{tank = C_{\texttt{MoveToAddr}} - C_{\texttt{MoveToAddr}} = 0\}$
    `returnBids(move(bidmap)) ; }`

The `bidmap` argument to `addBid` now has type $\&\texttt{Map}\langle\texttt{address},\texttt{GasBid}\rangle$. The `else` branch of `addBid` first constructs $\texttt{g} : \texttt{Gas}(C_{\texttt{MoveToAddr}})$ and then uses `pack` to create `gb : GasBid`. The `pack` expression takes the value of each field of a resource (or struct) and creates an object of that type. The object `gb` is then inserted and the remaining gas is deposited. The `returnBids` function first unpacks `gbid : GasBid`, storing the gas and bid in the variables `g` and `bid`. The gas is then destructed to pay for the cost of `tick(`$C_{\texttt{MoveToAddr}}$`)`.

The increased gas cost of `addBid` is $C_{\texttt{MapInsert}} + 2C_{\texttt{MoveToAddr}}$. Out of this, $C_{\texttt{MapInsert}} + C_{\texttt{MoveToAddr}}$ gas units are consumed for the cost of function execution, while $C_{\texttt{MoveToAddr}}$ gas units are stored in `bidmap` for future use. The gas cost of `returnBids` is now 0. It consumes $C_{\texttt{MoveToAddr}}$ gas units in every recursive call, which is provided by the gas stored inside `bidmap`.

Advantages. The advantages of amortization by storing gas inside data structures are manifold. First, it simplifies the analysis that *no longer needs to synthesize complicated invariants and track data structure sizes*. Second, blockchains such as Libra [8] and Ethereum [43] assign a maximum gas limit to transactions. The gas cost of the unamortized `returnBids` function is $C_{\texttt{MoveToAddr}} \cdot$ `sizeof(bidmap)`. This cost increases as the size of `bidmap` increases; if the size of `bidmap` increases beyond a threshold, the gas cost would *exceed the maximum gas limit* allowed for a transaction. The bids would then get stuck in the contract with no possibility of retrieving them [23]. Thirdly, this distribution of gas cost is more *equitable*. The bidders should be responsible for paying for both the cost of bidding as well as retrieving their bids from the auction. In the unamortized version, the user who issues `returnBids` bears the burden of paying for return of all the bids back to their respective bidders. Finally, the advantage of eliminating gas metering is also enhanced: the overhead of metering is linear in the execution time, while the overhead of static analysis is linear in the *program size*.

Move vs Copy. The distinction between move and copy operations is crucial for our static gas-cost analysis. Semantically, $move(v)$ corresponds to a shallow copy of v whose gas cost only depends on the type of v. On the other hand, $copy(v)$ corresponds to a deep copy of v, whose gas cost depends on the size of v. Since our analysis technique only handles constants, we disallow copy of unbounded data structures such as maps. Remarkably, we can analyze a large number of contracts despite this restriction (see Sect. 4) since we allow copy on primitive types and structs (and resources) containing them. Since we are working on an intermediate-level language, we require the move and copy operations to be explicit. However, they can be implicit in a source language, and be automatically inserted by a compiler, e.g. Move [11].

3 Formal Analysis

This section formalizes our source programming language, the static gas analysis and the formal gas semantics. We conclude with a soundness theorem connecting the static analysis with the semantics establishing that the gas bound verified by the static analysis is exactly matched at runtime.

3.1 A Simplistic Programming Language

Our language is modeled on Move [11], and provides an intuitive intermediate-level surface syntax on top of Move bytecode.

Types. The language features standard primitive types such as `int` and `bool` representing integers and booleans, respectively. It also provides a built-in map data type $\mathtt{Map}\langle \tau_1, \tau_2 \rangle$ where τ_1 and τ_2 are the key and value types, respectively. In addition, multiple values (with different types) can be packed together using `struct` and `resource` types. Finally, the language provides basic support for references, providing type $\&\ \tau$ to refer values of type τ. Although Move distinguishes mutable and immutable references, we consider all references as mutable since it is orthogonal to gas analysis. At runtime, references are represented by constant size addresses and do not pose additional challenges for gas analysis.

We also introduce $\mathtt{Gas}(n)$ as a first-class type in our language, where n is a constant natural number. This is used to store gas in data structures to share and amortize the gas cost of transactions, as demonstrated in Sect. 2. Thus, the type grammar for our language is

$$\tau \quad ::= \quad \mathtt{int} \mid \mathtt{bool} \mid \mathtt{Map}\langle \tau, \tau \rangle \mid \&\ \tau \mid V \mid \mathtt{Gas}(n)$$

V represents type names, denoting struct and resource types (e.g. `GasBid`). The syntax for declaring structs and resources is described later (end of Sect. 3.1).

Expressions. The expression language is expressed using the following grammar. Below, n is a constant integer, while v is a variable name.

$$e ::= n \mid \texttt{true} \mid \texttt{false} \mid \ldots (*\text{standard expressions for primitive types}*)$$
$$\mid \quad \texttt{pack}\langle\tau\rangle\{\texttt{f}_1 : e, \ldots, \texttt{f}_n : e\} \mid \texttt{unpack}\langle\tau\rangle(e) \mid \&v.\texttt{f} \mid \&v$$
$$\mid \quad \texttt{move}(v) \mid \texttt{copy}(v) \mid \texttt{g}(\bar{e})$$
$$\mid \quad \texttt{let } \bar{v} = e \mid v \leftarrow e \mid \texttt{if } e \texttt{ then } e \texttt{ else } e \mid e; e \mid \texttt{return } e$$
$$\mid \quad \texttt{tick}(n) \mid \texttt{Gas.construct}(n) \mid \texttt{Gas.destruct}(v) \mid \texttt{Gas.deposit}(n)$$

Our language features standard expressions for integer and boolean operations. These include binary arithmetic $(+, -, *, /)$, comparison $(>, \geq, <, \leq)$ and relational $(\&\&, ||)$ operators. Pack and unpack expressions are used to construct and destruct objects of struct (and resource) types, respectively. The expression $\texttt{pack}\langle\tau\rangle\{\texttt{f}_1 : e_1, \ldots, \texttt{f}_n : e_n\}$ packs together expressions $(e_1, \ldots, e_n)$ assigned to fields $\texttt{f}_1, \ldots, \texttt{f}_n$ respectively, and creates an object of type τ. Dually, $\texttt{unpack}\langle\tau\rangle(e)$ destructs object $e : \tau$ and returns the tuple $(e_1, \ldots, e_n)$ corresponding to each field. Additionally, we can reference the field $\texttt{f}$ of a variable v using $\&v.\texttt{f}$. References of a variable v can be taken using $\& v$. A variable v can be moved or copied using $\texttt{move}(v)$ and $\texttt{copy}(v)$ respectively. Function calls have the usual syntax $\texttt{g}(e_1, \ldots, e_n)$ calling function $\texttt{g}$ with argument expressions $e_1, \ldots, e_n$. We also provide standard map functions such as insertion, removal and checking size. Additionally, the function $\texttt{remove\_first}()$ removes and returns the first key-value pair in a map and is used to iterate over maps. The `let` expression evaluates e and assigns its value to a set of fresh variables $\bar{v}$. We use a set of variables because expressions `unpack` and `remove_first` return multiple values. The value of variable v is updated to the value of e using $v \leftarrow e$. Branches are created with `if` e `then` e `else` e, executing e_1 or e_2 depending upon whether e evaluates to `true` or `false` respectively. Expressions are composed using $e_1; e_2$ and returned using `return` e. Finally, we provide blockchain-specific operations and functions (similar to Move), e.g., `GetTxnSenderAddress` and `MoveToAddr`. These blockchain-specific expressions have a constant gas cost, and do not pose additional challenges w.r.t. gas analysis.

Cost Model and Gas Expressions. Our analysis needs to account for the gas cost assigned to each operation. We simplify the analysis by adding `tick` expressions [19,27] based on a cost model that assigns a constant gas cost to each primitive operation. Our implementation then automatically instruments the program by adding ticks for each primitive operation based on the cost model. We describe the rules of instrumentation with the convention that $[\![e]\!]$ represents the instrumented version of e (analogous cases skipped for brevity).

$$[\![\texttt{pack}\langle\tau\rangle\{\texttt{f}_1 : e_1, \ldots\}]\!] := \texttt{tick}(\mathcal{C}_{\texttt{pack}} \cdot \texttt{size}(\tau)) \,;\, \texttt{pack}\langle\tau\rangle\{\texttt{f}_1 : [\![e_1]\!], \ldots\}$$

$$[\![\texttt{unpack}\langle\tau\rangle(e)]\!] := \texttt{tick}(\mathcal{C}_{\texttt{unpack}} \cdot \texttt{size}(\tau)) \,;\, \texttt{unpack}\langle\tau\rangle([\![e]\!])$$

$$[\![\texttt{move}(v)]\!] := \texttt{tick}(\mathcal{C}_{\texttt{move}} \cdot \texttt{size}(\tau)) \,;\, \texttt{move}(v) \qquad (v : \tau)$$

$$[\![\texttt{g}(e_1, \ldots, e_n)]\!] := \texttt{tick}(\mathcal{C}_{\texttt{g}}) \,;\, \texttt{g}([\![e_1]\!], \ldots, [\![e_n]\!])$$

$$[\![\texttt{let } v = e]\!] := \texttt{tick}(\mathcal{C}_{\texttt{let}}) \,;\, \texttt{let } v = [\![e]\!]$$

$$[\![v \leftarrow e]\!] := \texttt{tick}(\mathcal{C}_{\texttt{asgn}}) \,;\, [\![v]\!] \leftarrow [\![e]\!]$$

$$[\![\texttt{if } e \texttt{ then } e_1 \texttt{ else } e_2]\!] := \texttt{tick}(\mathcal{C}_{\texttt{if}}) \,;\, \texttt{if } [\![e]\!] \texttt{ then } [\![e_1]\!] \texttt{ else } [\![e_2]\!]$$

$$[\![e_1 \,;\, e_2]\!] := [\![e_1]\!] \,;\, \texttt{tick}(\mathcal{C}_{\texttt{seq}}) \,;\, [\![e_2]\!]$$

$$[\![\texttt{return } e]\!] := \texttt{tick}(\mathcal{C}_{\texttt{ret}}) \,;\, \texttt{return } e$$

The costs $\mathcal{C}_i$'s above represent the cost model which we require the programmer to provide. The gas cost $\mathcal{C}_{\texttt{g}}$ of function $\texttt{g}$ is determined from the declaration of $\texttt{g}$ (described in the end of Sect. 3.1). The analysis is then completely *parametric in the cost model*, providing full flexibility to the programmer to specify their own cost model. The gas cost can also depend on $\texttt{size}(\tau)$, defined as

$$\texttt{size}(\texttt{int}) = 4 \qquad \texttt{size}(\texttt{bool}) = 2 \qquad \texttt{size}(\texttt{Gas}(n)) = 4 \qquad \texttt{size}(\&\tau) = 8$$
$$\texttt{size}(\texttt{Map}\langle\tau_1, \tau_2\rangle) = \texttt{size}(\tau_1) + \texttt{size}(\tau_2) \qquad \texttt{size}(V) = \Sigma_{i=1}^{n}\texttt{size}(\tau_i)$$

where V denotes a struct or resource type, and τ_i's denote the type of its fields.

We provide special syntax for creating and destroying gas variables. A variable v of type $\texttt{Gas}(n)$ (for a constant number n) can be constructed using $\texttt{Gas.construct}(n)$, while destructed using $\texttt{Gas.destruct}(v)$. We can further deposit gas in the sender's account with $\texttt{Gas.deposit}(n)$.

Program. A program is a sequence of (possibly mutually) recursive type and function declarations. Their grammar is

$$\langle decl \rangle ::= \texttt{resource } V \{\texttt{f}_1 : \tau, \ldots, \texttt{f}_n : \tau\} \mid \texttt{struct } V \{\texttt{f}_1 : \tau, \ldots, \texttt{f}_n : \tau\}$$
$$\mid \texttt{fn } [\mathcal{G}] \, F(v : \tau, \ldots, v : \tau) \rightarrow \tau\{e\}$$

Type declarations are used to define struct and resource types. The syntax $\texttt{resource } V \{\texttt{f}_1 : \tau_1, \ldots, \texttt{f}_n : \tau_n\}$ defines type V with fields $\texttt{f}_1, \ldots, \texttt{f}_n$ (with corresponding types $\tau_1, \ldots, \tau_n$ respectively). Structs have a similar syntax. Functions are declared using $\texttt{fn } [\mathcal{G}] \, F(v_1 : \tau_1, \ldots, v_n : \tau_n) \rightarrow \tau \, \{e\}$ defines function F with n arguments $v_1 : \tau_1, \ldots, v_n : \tau_n$, return type τ, function body e and gas bound $\mathcal{G}$ as a constant natural number. We store the definition of each type and function (with initial gas bound) in a *global signature* Σ. This signature Σ is referenced during tick instrumentation to obtain the gas cost of each function call. Our analysis takes a program as input and verifies that $\mathcal{G}$ is an exact gas bound for each function F in the program.

3.2   Static Gas Analysis

The analysis is formalized as a quantitative Hoare triple $\{\mathcal{G} \mid \Gamma\} \, e \, \{\mathcal{G}' \mid \Gamma'\}$. Here, e denotes the expression that will be *gas-analyzed*; Γ and Γ' store the context (type of variables in scope) before and after the execution of e; $\mathcal{G}$ and $\mathcal{G}'$ track the gas tank value as a natural number before and after the execution of e, respectively. As a convention, we refer to $\mathcal{G}$ and Γ as the *pre-gas* and *pre-context* together called *pre-state*, and $\mathcal{G}'$ and Γ' as the *post-gas* and *post-context* of e together called *post-state*, respectively. In the above judgment, there is an implicit invariant that $\mathcal{G}, \mathcal{G}' \geq 0$.

Expressions. We describe selected rules that update the gas tank.

$$\frac{\mathcal{G} = \mathcal{G}' + n}{\{\mathcal{G} \mid \Gamma\}\, \texttt{Gas.construct}(n)\, \{\mathcal{G}' \mid \Gamma\}}\ \text{I}_{\text{gas}}$$

$$\frac{\mathcal{G}' = \mathcal{G} + n}{\{\mathcal{G} \mid \Gamma, v : \texttt{Gas}(n)\}\, \texttt{Gas.destruct}(v)\, \{\mathcal{G}' \mid \Gamma\}}\ \text{E}_{\text{gas}}$$

$$\frac{\mathcal{G} = \mathcal{G}' + n}{\{\mathcal{G} \mid \Gamma\}\, \texttt{Gas.deposit}(n)\, \{\mathcal{G}' \mid \Gamma\}}\ \text{D}_{\text{gas}}$$

Constructing a variable of type $\texttt{Gas}(n)$ consumes n units of gas from the tank. Dually, $\texttt{Gas.destruct}(v)$ looks up the type of $v : \texttt{Gas}(n)$ in the context Γ and adds n gas units to the gas tank. The variable v is then removed from Γ since it is no longer in scope. $\texttt{Gas.deposit}(n)$ removes n units of gas from the tank and deposits it in the user's account.

$$\frac{\mathcal{G} = \mathcal{G}' + n}{\{\mathcal{G} \mid \Gamma\}\, \texttt{tick}(n)\, \{\mathcal{G}' \mid \Gamma\}}\ \text{tick}$$

Executing $\texttt{tick}(n)$ consumes n gas units.

$$\frac{\{\mathcal{G}_0 \mid \Gamma_0\}\, e_1\, \{\mathcal{G}_1 \mid \Gamma_1\} \quad \ldots \quad \{\mathcal{G}_{n-1} \mid \Gamma_{n-1}\}\, e_n\, \{\mathcal{G}_n \mid \Gamma_n\}}{\{\mathcal{G}_0 \mid \Gamma_0\}\, \texttt{pack}\langle \tau \rangle \{\texttt{f}_1 : e_1, \ldots, \texttt{f}_n : e_n\}\, \{\mathcal{G}_n \mid \Gamma_n\}}\ \text{pack}$$

Packing n expressions $e_1, \ldots, e_n$ requires analyzing each expression and composing the gas tanks and contexts together. The post-state of e_i becomes the pre-state for e_{i+1}. Unpacking an expression e corresponds to gas-analyzing it.

$$\frac{\{\mathcal{G}_0 \mid \Gamma_0\}\, e_1\, \{\mathcal{G}_1 \mid \Gamma_1\} \quad \ldots \quad \{\mathcal{G}_{n-1} \mid \Gamma_{n-1}\}\, e_n\, \{\mathcal{G}_n \mid \Gamma_n\}}{\{\mathcal{G}_0 \mid \Gamma_0\}\, \texttt{g}(e_1, \ldots, e_n)\, \{\mathcal{G}_n \mid \Gamma_n\}}\ \text{call}$$

For function calls, we analyze each argument, composing the gas tanks and contexts from left to right (similar to $\texttt{pack}$) since the expressions are evaluated from left to right at runtime. Note that there is no need to analyze the function body of $\texttt{g}$ since the cost of calling and evaluating $\texttt{g}$ is already accounted for by the tick instrumentation that inserts $\mathcal{C}_{\texttt{g}}$ just before the function call. *This observation is crucial to obtain a linear-time gas analysis.*

$$\frac{\{\mathcal{G} \mid \Gamma\}\, e\, \{\mathcal{G}' \mid \Gamma'\} \qquad \Gamma \vdash e : \tau}{\{\mathcal{G} \mid \Gamma\}\, \texttt{let}\ v = e\, \{\mathcal{G}' \mid \Gamma', v : \tau\}}\ \text{let}$$

For `let` expressions, we use an auxiliary judgment: $\Gamma \vdash e : \tau$ to mean that expression e has type τ under context Γ. The analysis first analyzes e with post state $\{\mathcal{G}' \mid \Gamma'\}$, determines e's type τ (second premise) and adds $v : \tau$ to Γ'. Our analysis relies on a type checker to determine the type of each expression.

$$\frac{\{\mathcal{G} \mid \Gamma\} \, e \, \{\mathcal{G}' \mid \Gamma'\}}{\{\mathcal{G} \mid \Gamma\} \, v \leftarrow e \, \{\mathcal{G}' \mid \Gamma'\}} \ \texttt{asgn}$$

The assignment expression $v \leftarrow e$ simply gas-analyzes e.

$$\frac{\{\mathcal{G}_0 \mid \Gamma_0\} \, e \, \{\mathcal{G}_1 \mid \Gamma_1\} \qquad \{\mathcal{G}_1 \mid \Gamma_1\} \, e_1 \, \{\mathcal{G}_2 \mid \Gamma_2\} \qquad \{\mathcal{G}_1 \mid \Gamma_1\} \, e_2 \, \{\mathcal{G}_2 \mid \Gamma_2\}}{\{\mathcal{G}_0 \mid \Gamma_0\} \, \texttt{if} \ e \ \texttt{then} \ e_1 \ \texttt{else} \ e_2 \, \{\mathcal{G}_2 \mid \Gamma_2\}} \ \texttt{if}$$

For `if` expressions, e is analyzed under pre-state $\{\mathcal{G}_0 \mid \Gamma_0\}$ resulting in post-state $\{\mathcal{G}_1 \mid \Gamma_1\}$. This state is then copied to both branches e_1 and e_2, which both result in post-state $\{\mathcal{G}_2 \mid \Gamma_2\}$. We mandate that the post-gases $\mathcal{G}_2$ after both branches are equal, thus ensuring that both branches have equal gas cost. This is exactly where `Gas.deposit` operation is used to equalize the cost of both branches. Our tool automatically instruments the cheaper branch with `Gas.deposit`(n) where n is the difference in the post-gas of e_1 and e_2.

$$\frac{\{\mathcal{G}_0 \mid \Gamma_0\} \, e_1 \, \{\mathcal{G}_1 \mid \Gamma_1\} \qquad \{\mathcal{G}_1 \mid \Gamma_1\} \, e_2 \, \{\mathcal{G}_2 \mid \Gamma_2\}}{\{\mathcal{G}_0 \mid \Gamma_0\} \, e_1; e_2 \, \{\mathcal{G}_2 \mid \Gamma_2\}} \ \texttt{compose}$$

Expression composition is standard; the intermediate state $\{\mathcal{G}_1 \mid \Gamma_1\}$ is the post-state for e_1 and the pre-state for e_2.

$$\frac{\{\mathcal{G} \mid \Gamma\} \, e \, \{\mathcal{G}' \mid \Gamma'\} \qquad \mathcal{G}' = 0}{\{\mathcal{G} \mid \Gamma\} \, \texttt{return} \ e \, \{\mathcal{G}' \mid \Gamma'\}} \ \texttt{ret}$$

We require that the post-gas of a return expression $\mathcal{G}' = 0$, thus ensuring the initial gas tank is completely used up for the function execution and the gas bound is exact. In case of branches, we require that the post-gas after each `return` expression is 0. The analysis rules for all other expressions are analogous and skipped for brevity.

3.3 Soundness of Analysis

We prove the soundness of the analysis by connecting the static gas analysis with the gas semantics. We define a program state σ as a mapping from variables to their values. We formalize the gas semantics as $\sigma \mid e \Downarrow_{\mu'}^{\mu} (v, \sigma')$ to define that the expression e evaluates to value v under program state σ with resulting program state σ'. The annotations μ and μ' denote the gas tank value (as a natural number) before and after the evaluation of e.

We describe selected rules that impact the gas cost.

$$\frac{}{\sigma \vdash \texttt{tick}(n) \Downarrow_{\mu}^{\mu+n} ((),\sigma)} \text{ TICK}$$

Executing $\texttt{tick}(n)$ consumes n gas units from the tank. The value of $\texttt{tick}$ is uninteresting and we use the convention that it evaluates to ().

$$\frac{}{\sigma \vdash \texttt{Gas.construct}(n) \Downarrow_{\mu}^{\mu+n} (n,\sigma)} \text{ CONSTRUCT}$$

Semantically, we treat gas values as natural numbers. Thus, a variable of type $\texttt{Gas}(n)$ evaluates to n. The gas cost of constructing is n, so the difference in the initial and final gas tanks is n.

$$\frac{}{\{[v \mapsto n],\sigma\} \vdash \texttt{Gas.destruct}(v) \Downarrow_{\mu+n}^{\mu} ((),\sigma)} \text{ DESTRUCT}$$

Destructing a variable with value n (i.e., of type $\texttt{Gas}(n)$) adds n to the gas tank. The value of destructing a gas variable is uninteresting and denoted by (). The variable is also removed from σ since it is no longer available.

$$\frac{}{\sigma \vdash \texttt{Gas.deposit}(n) \Downarrow_{\mu}^{\mu+n} ((),\sigma)} \text{ DEPOSIT}$$

Depositing gas into the user's account removes the same from the gas tank.

$$\frac{\begin{array}{c} \texttt{fn } [\mathcal{G}] \texttt{ g}(x_1 : \tau_1, \ldots, x_n : \tau_n) \to \tau \{e\} \in \Sigma \\ \sigma_0 \vdash e_1 \Downarrow_{\mu_1}^{\mu_0} (v_1,\sigma_1) \quad \cdots \quad \sigma_{n-1} \vdash e_n \Downarrow_{\mu_n}^{\mu_{n-1}} (v_n,\sigma_n) \\ \sigma_n \vdash e[v_1,\ldots,v_n/x_1,\ldots,x_n] \Downarrow_{\mu'}^{\mu_n} (v,\sigma') \end{array}}{\sigma_0 \vdash \texttt{g}(e_1,\ldots,e_n) \Downarrow_{\mu'}^{\mu_0} (v,\sigma')} \text{ CALL}$$

A function call to $\texttt{g}$ evaluates each argument, then evaluates the body e of $\texttt{g}$ with the value of each argument v_i substituted for the argument variable x_i. The body e of $\texttt{g}$ is looked up in the global signature Σ.

$$\frac{\sigma_0 \vdash e \Downarrow_{\mu_1}^{\mu_0} (v,\sigma_1)}{\sigma_0 \vdash \texttt{let } x = e \Downarrow_{\mu_1}^{\mu_0} ((),\{\sigma_1,[x \mapsto v]\})} \text{ LET}$$

The $\texttt{let}$ expression evaluates e to v with resulting state σ_1. It then assigns v to x and continues execution. The return value of the $\texttt{let}$ expression is (). A similar rule holds for assignments. For if expressions, we consider two cases.

$$\frac{\sigma_0 \vdash e \Downarrow_{\mu_1}^{\mu_0} (\text{true}, \sigma_1) \quad \sigma_1 \vdash e_1 \Downarrow_{\mu_2}^{\mu_1} (v, \sigma_2)}{\sigma_0 \vdash \text{if } e \text{ then } e_1 \text{ else } e_2 \Downarrow_{\mu_2}^{\mu_0} (v, \sigma_2)} \text{ TT}$$

$$\frac{\sigma_0 \vdash e \Downarrow_{\mu_1}^{\mu_0} (\text{false}, \sigma_1) \quad \sigma_1 \vdash e_2 \Downarrow_{\mu_2}^{\mu_1} (v, \sigma_2)}{\sigma_0 \vdash \text{if } e \text{ then } e_1 \text{ else } e_2 \Downarrow_{\mu_2}^{\mu_0} (v, \sigma_2)} \text{ FF}$$

If e evaluates to true with final tank μ_1, we evaluate e_1 with initial tank μ_1, otherwise we evaluate e_2 with tank μ_1.

$$\frac{\sigma_0 \vdash e_1 \Downarrow_{\mu_1}^{\mu_0} (v_1, \sigma_1) \quad \sigma_1 \vdash e_2 \Downarrow_{\mu_2}^{\mu_1} (v_2, \sigma_2)}{\sigma_0 \vdash e_1; e_2 \Downarrow_{\mu_2}^{\mu_0} (v_2, \sigma_2)} \text{ COMPOSE}$$

Expression composition is standard; σ_1 and μ_1 are the intermediate program state and tank value, respectively.

$$\frac{\sigma \vdash e \Downarrow_{\mu_1}^{\mu_0} (v, \sigma')}{\sigma \vdash \text{return } e \Downarrow_{\mu_1}^{\mu_0} (v, \sigma')} \text{ RET}$$

Finally, return e evaluates e. The semantics rules for the remaining expressions are analogous and skipped for brevity.

Theorem 1 (Soundness). *Given a function* fn $[\mathcal{G}]$ g$(x_1 : \tau_1, \ldots, x_n : \tau_n)$ *and a program state* σ, *if* $\sigma \vdash$ g$(v_1, \ldots, v_n) \Downarrow_{\mu'}^{\mu} (v, \sigma')$, *then* $\mu - \mu' = \mathcal{G}$.

Intuitively, the gas soundness theorem states that if a function call to g executes under program state σ with initial tank μ and final tank μ', the difference $\mu - \mu'$ is exactly equal to the gas bound $\mathcal{G}$. Thus, the static gas analysis provides an exact bound on the gas cost at runtime. The theorem is proved by induction on the gas semantics judgment.

4   Implementation and Evaluation

We have implemented a prototype for GasBoX in OCaml (2101 lines of code). The prototype contains a lexer and parser (334 lines), tick instrumentation engine (138 lines), pretty printer (185 lines), an arithmetic solver (258 lines), LP solver interface (239 lines), inference engine (284 lines) and gas analyzer (663 lines). The lexer and parser are implemented in Menhir [35], an LR(1) parser generator for OCaml.

Figure 1 describes the workflow of the GasBoX tool. First, as is standard, the source program is lexed, parsed, type checked and converted to an *typed abstract syntax tree*. We briefly describe the remaining two stages.

348 A. Das and S. Qadeer

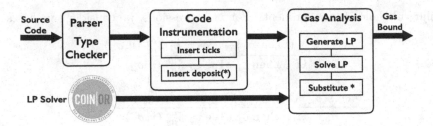

Fig. 1. Workflow demonstrating the various stages of GasBoX

- **Code Instrumentation:** The source code is first instrumented with `tick` expressions following Sect. 3.1. Since the tick amounts for `pack`, `unpack` and `move` depend on the size of the type being operated, we precompute the size of all types in the program. The instrumentation engine takes the sizes and the cost model (values of C_i's) as input and inserts the tick expressions. Programmers are free to specify their own cost model and the analysis computes the bound w.r.t. specified cost model. Next, all the join points in branches are instrumented with `Gas.deposit(*)` expressions. The value of these $*$ annotations are inferred in the next stage and described below.
- **Gas Analysis:** To support inference of gas bounds, the GasBoX tool allows programmers to use $*$ annotations in place of numerical values. To this end, we allow function declarations of the form `fn [*]` $F(v : \tau, \ldots, v : \tau) \to \tau \{e\}$ and type declarations to use `Gas(*)`. The gas analyzer first iterates through the program and replaces $*$ annotations with *gas variables*. Then, the analysis rules are applied while generating linear constraints for the gas variables. These linear constraints are then shipped to the inference engine that employs the Coin-Or LP solver [36]. The linear constraints are then solved while minimizing the value of the gas variables to achieve tight bounds. The LP solver either returns that the constraints are unsatisfiable, or a satisfying assignment, which is then substituted back into the program and pretty printed to the programmer.

  Our analysis tool is flexible in handling numerical values or $*$ for gas annotations. Thus, programmers can use $*$ for only the annotations they want inferred and numerical values for annotations they would like to fix. This can be used, for instance, if we want to fix the amount of gas stored in a data structure. If a programmer chooses to indicate a fixed exact gas bound for a function, GasBoX can verify if the bound is exact. In this case, we provide valuable feedback in terms of the exact program location where the execution would run out of gas.

4.1 Evaluation

We evaluate GasBoX by implementing standard smart contracts in our language, and inferring their gas bounds. We highlight some interesting examples, particularly the ones that involve amortization to handle unbounded computation. All our experiments use the cost model assigning $C_i = 1$ for all i. All gas annotations in the following examples have been automatically inferred using GasBoX.

Paying Interest on Bank Accounts. We implement a standard bank account contract, which provides the services of signing up to create an account, withdrawing and depositing money, and checking balance. The bank provides an additional facility of paying interest to each account holder periodically. The bank stores gas inside accounts to pay for the gas cost of paying interest.

```
resource GasBalance {
  balance : Coin,
  gas : Gas(65)        // utilized to pay interest periodically
}
resource Bank {
  nogas_accounts : Map<address, Coin>,
  gas_accounts : Map<address, GasBalance>
}
fn [201] recharge(bank : &Bank)
fn [29] payInterest(bank : &Bank)
fn [34] signup(bank : &Bank, amount : Coin)
fn [122] balance(bank : &Bank) -> int
fn [148] deposit(bank : &Bank, amount : Coin)
fn [187] withdraw(bank : &Bank, amount : int) -> Coin
```

The contract defines the resource type `GasBalance` for accounts containing gas. For our cost model, we need 65 gas units in each account for paying interest. The `Bank` type contains two maps: `gas_accounts` and `nogas_accounts` for accounts with and without gas respectively indexed by the address of the account holder. The contract provides a `recharge` function that replenishes gas in the sender's account, effectively removing it from `nogas_accounts` and adding it to `gas_accounts`. The `payInterest` function recursively removes an account from `gas_accounts`, consumes the gas stored in it to pay the interest, and adds it to `nogas_accounts`. Thus, it is the account holder's responsibility to periodically replenish the gas in their account by issuing the `recharge` function; the `payInterest` function only pays interest to accounts stored in `gas_accounts`. In addition, the contract provides the standard `signup`, `balance`, `deposit` and `withdraw` functions to create an account, check balance, deposit and withdraw money, respectively. The exact gas bound for each function is shown in square brackets [·] along with the declaration.

Since data structures that store gas inside them have a resource type, they are destroyed (using `unpack`) during iteration. Thus, using the same data structure multiple times would require a *recharge* function (similar to above) to restore the gas inside them. Thus, programmers need to be mindful of how often the contract data is operated upon.

The gas amortization provides the following benefits: (i) mitigating denial-of-service attacks since the gas bound of `payInterest` no longer depends on the number of bank accounts, (ii) equitable gas distribution since each account holder is responsible for covering the gas cost of paying interest on their account.

Voting. We implement a simple voting contract that provides two functions: a `vote` function to allow voters to cast their vote and a `count` function that counts the votes and computes the winner. The contract amortizes the cost of counting votes by storing gas inside the votes cast.

```
resource Votes {
  num_votes : int,
  gas : Gas(69) }        // utilized to count votes when election ends
fn [114] vote(elec : &Map<address, Votes>, candidate : address)
fn [55] count(elec : &Map<address, Votes>) -> address
```

The contract defines the resource type `Votes` used to store the votes for a particular candidate. The type contains two fields: `num_votes` denotes the number of votes for the candidate, and `gas` stores 69 gas units to pay for counting votes later. The `vote` function takes two arguments: `elec` contains the map storing the votes indexed by the address of the candidate, and `candidate` is the address of the candidate the sender wants to vote for. The function increments the number of votes in `candidate`'s name by 1. The `count` function takes `elec` as argument, iterates over the map, and consumes the gas stored inside it to compute the winner of the election. The exact gas bound for both functions is a constant and described alongside the declaration. This contract also provides the advantages of mitigating denial-of-service attacks and equitable gas distribution.

Table 1. Evaluation of GasBoX. LOC = lines of code; Defs = #definitions; Vars = #gas variables introduced; Cons = #linear constraints on gas variables; I (ms) = inference time in milliseconds V (μs) = verification time in microseconds.

Contract	LOC	Defs	Vars	Cons	I (ms)	V (μs)
auction	44	7	3	44	3.05	12.16
bank	138	14	11	254	3.97	54.12
ERC 20	101	11	8	91	3.45	56.98
escrow	140	7	9	213	3.29	61.03
insurance	43	5	3	43	3.02	9.05
voting	75	7	8	131	3.19	30.99
wallet	74	8	5	158	3.35	52.93
ethereumpot	259	13	13	332	3.94	101.08
puzzle	62	6	6	91	3.13	15.97
amort. auction	70	7	5	62	2.99	15.02
amort. bank	189	17	17	347	4.44	73.19
tether	382	29	30	842	26.14	365.01
libra system	124	12	12	170	3.38	45.06
Total	**1701**	**143**	**130**	**2878**	**67.34**	**892.59**

Other Contracts. We have implemented a total of 13 contracts in our language, and verified their gas bound with GasBoX. We briefly describe each contract.

1. **auction**: unamortized version of auction providing support for users to *pull* their bids out of the contract.
2. **bank**: naïve bank account with no functionality to pay interest.
3. **ERC 20**: technical standard for token implementation on Ethereum defining a list of rules Ethereum tokens should follow [1].
4. **escrow**: contract to exchange bonds between two parties.
5. **insurance**: contract processing flight delay insurance claims after verifying them with a trusted third party.
6. **voting**: election contract described earlier in this section.
7. **wallet**: standard contract allowing users to store money on the blockchain.
8. **ethereumpot**: standard lottery contract on Ethereum.
9. **puzzle**: contract rewarding users who solve a computational puzzle and submit the solution.
10. **amort. auction**: amortized auction described in Sect. 2.
11. **amort. bank**: amortized bank account paying interest periodically as described earlier in this section.
12. **tether**: stable coin contract allowing exchange of digital tokens pegged to fiat currencies e.g. dollars, euros, etc. [2].
13. **libra system**: standard library contract with recursive functions for configuration of third-party validators

The first 7 contracts are borrowed from the Nomos project [17], ethereumpot from the GASTAP project [6], puzzle from the Oyente project [32], tether from the Tether ERC 20 token contract [2] and libra system from the Libra blockchain [8] and reimplemented in our language.

Table 1 compiles the results of evaluating GasBoX on the implemented contracts. For each contract, we present the lines of code (LOC), number of type and function definitions (Defs), number of gas variables introduced (Vars) and number of linear constraints generated during gas analysis (Cons). The gas analysis time is separated into two components: the first phase of analysis generates the linear constraints which are then solved to infer the gas annotations (denoted by I (ms) in milliseconds); once the solutions are substituted back into the program, the second phase verifies if the bounds generated by the first phase are exact (denoted by V (μs) in microseconds). The experiments were run on an Intel Core i5 1.6 GHz dual-core processor with 16 GB DDR3L memory.

The evaluation demonstrates that gas bound verification is highly efficient with an overhead of less than 0.5 ms for all contracts. This indicates that GasBoX can be effectively utilized by miners to verify the exact gas bound. Moreover, this overhead is offset by the elimination of dynamic gas metering from the virtual machine. Gas inference is an order of magnitude slower but still acceptable, since it only needs to be performed once and stored in the gas signature for future verification. The programmer burden is low since they only need to indicate the data structures where gas is stored using the type Gas(*) and the remaining bounds are automatically inferred. Further, since the Gas.deposit operations were automatically inserted, programmers can remain oblivious of the exact cost model and difference in gas costs of different branches.

5   Related Work

Traditionally, resource analysis is grounded in deriving and solving recurrence relations, an approach introduced to analyze simple Lisp programs [42]. Since then, it has been applied to both imperative [3,7,21] and functional programs [9,15]. Amortization [40] was first integrated with resource analysis to automatically analyze heap usage of first-order functional programs [29]. In the context of functional languages, this technique has been applied to derive polynomial [28] and multivariate bounds [26] for first-order and higher-order programs [27] as well as programs with lazy evaluation [38]. For imperative programs, amortization has been utilized to derive bounds based on lexicographic ranking functions [39] and intervals [13], and has been extended to analyze object-oriented programs [30]. In contrast to the above works that focus on upper bounds, GasBoX verifies exact bounds for programs and is applicable to smart contracts.

Security analysis and safety verification of smart contracts have been extensively studied in prior work [10,24,31,32,41]. MadMax [23] automatically detects gas-focused vulnerabilities with high confidence. The analysis is based on a decompiler that extracts control and data flow information from EVM bytecode, and a logic-based analysis specification that produces a high-level program model. GASPER [14] is an analysis tool for EVM bytecode that relies on symbolic execution and the Z3 SMT solver [34] to identify 7 gas-costly programming patterns such as dead code, expensive and repeated computations in a loop, etc. GasBoX differs from these works by inferring and verifying gas cost, instead of identifying vulnerabilities related to gas.

Most closely related to GasBoX are languages and analysis tools for estimating upper gas bounds on contracts. Scilla [37] is an intermediate-level language which disallows loops and general recursion and infers gas usage of a function as a polynomial of the size of its parameters and contract fields in linear time. In contrast, GasBoX allows recursion and bounds are proven sound w.r.t. a gas semantics. Nomos is a programming language [17] based on resource-aware session types [18,19] that utilizes LP (linear programming) solving to automatically derive upper gas bounds on implemented contracts. GASTAP [6] infers gas bounds on contracts implemented in Solidity [16] or EVM bytecode in terms of size of the input parameters, contract state and gas consumption. The inference procedure requires construction of control-flow graphs, decompilation to a high-level representation, inferring size relations, generating and solving gas equations. GASOL [5] is an extension to GASTAP which offers a variety of cost models to measure the cost of, for e.g., only storage opcodes, selected family of gas-consumption opcodes, selected program line, etc. It further detects under-optimized storage patterns and automatic optimization of such patterns. Marescotti et al. [33] employ symbolic model checking to modularly enumerate all gas consumption paths based on unwinding loops to a limit. For each path, it then computes the environment state to force that path and simulates the transaction under the state to obtain an exact worst-case gas bound. GasBoX differs from these tools in its goal of providing miners with a trusted exact gas bound which can be verified in linear time and eliminating dynamic gas metering.

6 Conclusion

This paper presented a Hoare-logic style gas-analysis framework for smart contracts. This framework verifies exact gas bounds in linear-time and relies on amortization to handle unbounded computation. The verified gas bounds are proven sound w.r.t. a gas semantics. The framework has been implemented as a tool called GasBoX in the context of a simplistic programming language. The tool has been enhanced by integrating with the Coin-Or LP solver to infer gas bounds automatically. GasBoX has been evaluated on several standard smart contracts demonstrating its efficiency and expressivity.

In the future, we plan to use more sophisticated underlying logics such as SMT solvers, carefully weighing the balance of expressivity and efficiency of the gas-analysis framework. With more expressive solvers, we can store linear or polynomial gas in data structures. We would also like to handle copying of unbounded data structures such as maps. Since our approach requires updates to the virtual machine, it is most suited to newer blockchains. In the future, we plan to explore methods to integrate our approach into existing blockchains. Finally, we would like to extend our approach to traditional smart contract languages such as Solidity and Move, by transforming programs to our target language.

Acknowledgments. This article is based on research supported by the National Science Foundation under SaTC Award 1801369 and CAREER Award 1845514. Any opinions, findings, and conclusions contained in this document are those of the authors and do not necessarily reflect the views of the sponsoring organizations.

References

1. Erc20 Token Standard (December 2018). https://theethereum.wiki/w/index.php/ERC20_Token_Standard. Accessed 27 Feb 2018
2. Tether: Digital money for a digital age (Apr 2020). https://tether.to/. Accessed 29 Apr 2020
3. Albert, E., Arenas, P., Genaim, S., Puebla, G., Zanardini, D.: Cost analysis of java bytecode. In: De Nicola, R. (ed.) ESOP 2007. LNCS, vol. 4421, pp. 157–172. Springer, Heidelberg (2007). https://doi.org/10.1007/978-3-540-71316-6_12
4. Albert, E., Arenas, P., Genaim, S., Herraiz, I., Puebla, G.: Comparing cost functions in resource analysis. In: van Eekelen, M., Shkaravska, O. (eds.) FOPARA 2009. LNCS, vol. 6324, pp. 1–17. Springer, Heidelberg (2010). https://doi.org/10.1007/978-3-642-15331-0_1
5. Albert, E., Correas, J., Gordillo, P., Román-Díez, G., Rubio, A.: Gasol: gas analysis and optimization for Ethereum smart contracts (2019)

6. Albert, E., Gordillo, P., Rubio, A., Sergey, I.: Running on fumes. In: Ganty, P., Kaâniche, M. (eds.) VECoS 2019. LNCS, vol. 11847, pp. 63–78. Springer, Cham (2019). https://doi.org/10.1007/978-3-030-35092-5_5

7. Alonso-Blas, D.E., Genaim, S.: On the limits of the classical approach to cost analysis. In: Miné, A., Schmidt, D. (eds.) SAS 2012. LNCS, vol. 7460, pp. 405–421. Springer, Heidelberg (2012). https://doi.org/10.1007/978-3-642-33125-1_27

8. Baudet, M., et al.: State machine replication in the libra blockchain (2019). https://developers.libra.org/docs/assets/papers/libra-consensus-state-machine-replication-in-the-libra-blockchain.pdf

9. Benzinger, R.: Automated higher-order complexity analysis. Theor. Comput. Sci. **318**(1), 79–103 (2004). https://doi.org/10.1016/j.tcs.2003.10.022. http://www.sciencedirect.com/science/article/pii/S0304397503005279. implicit Computational Complexity

10. Bhargavan, K., et al.: Formal verification of smart contracts: short paper. In: Proceedings of the 2016 ACM Workshop on Programming Languages and Analysis for Security, PLAS 2016, pp. 91–96. ACM, New York (2016). https://doi.org/10.1145/2993600.2993611, http://doi.acm.org/10.1145/2993600.2993611

11. Blackshear, S., et al.: Move: a language with programmable resources (2019)

12. Carbonneaux, Q., Hoffmann, J., Reps, T., Shao, Z.: Automated resource analysis with Coq proof objects. In: Majumdar, R., Kunčak, V. (eds.) CAV 2017. LNCS, vol. 10427, pp. 64–85. Springer, Cham (2017). https://doi.org/10.1007/978-3-319-63390-9_4

13. Carbonneaux, Q., Hoffmann, J., Shao, Z.: Compositional certified resource bounds. In: Proceedings of the 36th ACM SIGPLAN Conference on Programming Language Design and Implementation, PLDI 2015, pp. 467–478. Association for Computing Machinery, New York (2015). https://doi.org/10.1145/2737924.2737955

14. Chen, T., Li, X., Luo, X., Zhang, X.: Under-optimized smart contracts devour your money. In: 2017 IEEE 24th International Conference on Software Analysis, Evolution and Reengineering (SANER), pp. 442–446 (2017)

15. Danielsson, N.A.: Lightweight semiformal time complexity analysis for purely functional data structures. In: Proceedings of the 35th Annual ACM SIGPLAN-SIGACT Symposium on Principles of Programming Languages, POPL 2008, pp. 133–144. Association for Computing Machinery, New York (2008). https://doi.org/10.1145/1328438.1328457

16. Dannen, C.: Introducing Ethereum and Solidity: Foundations of Cryptocurrency and Blockchain Programming for Beginners, 1st edn. Apress, USA (2017)

17. Das, A., Balzer, S., Hoffmann, J., Pfenning, F.: Resource-aware session types for digital contracts. CoRR abs/1902.06056 (2019). http://arxiv.org/abs/1902.06056

18. Das, A., Hoffmann, J., Pfenning, F.: Parallel complexity analysis with temporal session types. Proc. ACM Program. Lang. **2**(ICFP), 1–30 (2018). https://doi.org/10.1145/3236786

19. Das, A., Hoffmann, J., Pfenning, F.: Work analysis with resource-aware session types. In: Proceedings of the 33rd Annual ACM/IEEE Symposium on Logic in Computer Science, LICS 2018, pp. 305–314. ACM, New York (2018). https://doi.org/10.1145/3209108.3209146

20. Fischer, M.J., Rabin, M.O.: Super-exponential complexity of Presburger arithmetic. In: Caviness, B.F., Johnson, J.R. (eds.) Quantifier Elimination and Cylindrical Algebraic Decomposition. Texts and Monographs in Symbolic Computation (A Series of the Research Institute for Symbolic Computation, Johannes-Kepler-University, Linz, Austria). Springer, Vienna (1998). https://doi.org/10.1007/978-3-7091-9459-1_5

21. Flores-Montoya, A., Hähnle, R.: Resource analysis of complex programs with cost equations. In: Garrigue, J. (ed.) APLAS 2014. LNCS, vol. 8858, pp. 275–295. Springer, Cham (2014). https://doi.org/10.1007/978-3-319-12736-1_15
22. Girard, J.Y.: Linear logic. Theor. Comput. Sci. **50**(1), 1–101 (1987). https://doi.org/10.1016/0304-3975(87)90045-4. http://www.sciencedirect.com/science/article/pii/0304397587900454
23. Grech, N., Kong, M., Jurisevic, A., Brent, L., Scholz, B., Smaragdakis, Y.: MadMax: surviving out-of-gas conditions in Ethereum smart contracts. Proc. ACM Program. Lang. **2**(OOPSLA), 116:1–116:27 (2018). https://doi.org/10.1145/3276486. http://doi.acm.org/10.1145/3276486
24. Grishchenko, I., Maffei, M., Schneidewind, C.: Foundations and tools for the static analysis of Ethereum smart contracts. In: Chockler, H., Weissenbacher, G. (eds.) CAV 2018. LNCS, vol. 10981, pp. 51–78. Springer, Cham (2018). https://doi.org/10.1007/978-3-319-96145-3_4
25. Gulwani, S.: SPEED: symbolic complexity bound analysis. In: Bouajjani, A., Maler, O. (eds.) CAV 2009. LNCS, vol. 5643, pp. 51–62. Springer, Heidelberg (2009). https://doi.org/10.1007/978-3-642-02658-4_7
26. Hoffmann, J., Aehlig, K., Hofmann, M.: Multivariate amortized resource analysis. ACM Trans. Program. Lang. Syst. **34**(3), 1–62 (2012). https://doi.org/10.1145/2362389.2362393
27. Hoffmann, J., Das, A., Weng, S.C.: Towards automatic resource bound analysis for OCaml. In: Proceedings of the 44th ACM SIGPLAN Symposium on Principles of Programming Languages, POPL 2017, pp. 359–373. Association for Computing Machinery, New York (2017). https://doi.org/10.1145/3009837.3009842
28. Hoffmann, J., Hofmann, M.: Amortized resource analysis with polynomial potential. In: Gordon, A.D. (ed.) ESOP 2010. LNCS, vol. 6012, pp. 287–306. Springer, Heidelberg (2010). https://doi.org/10.1007/978-3-642-11957-6_16
29. Hofmann, M., Jost, S.: Static prediction of heap space usage for first-order functional programs. In: Proceedings of the 30th ACM SIGPLAN-SIGACT Symposium on Principles of Programming Languages, POPL 2003, pp. 185–197. ACM, New York (2003). https://doi.org/10.1145/604131.604148, http://doi.acm.org/10.1145/604131.604148
30. Hofmann, M., Jost, S.: Type-based amortised heap-space analysis. In: Sestoft, P. (ed.) ESOP 2006. LNCS, vol. 3924, pp. 22–37. Springer, Heidelberg (2006). https://doi.org/10.1007/11693024_3
31. Lahiri, S.K., Chen, S., Wang, Y., Dillig, I.: Formal specification and verification of smart contracts for azure blockchain. CoRR abs/1812.08829 (2018). http://arxiv.org/abs/1812.08829
32. Luu, L., Chu, D.H., Olickel, H., Saxena, P., Hobor, A.: Making smart contracts smarter. In: Proceedings of the 2016 ACM SIGSAC Conference on Computer and Communications Security, CCS 2016, pp. 254–269. ACM, New York (2016). https://doi.org/10.1145/2976749.2978309, http://doi.acm.org/10.1145/2976749.2978309
33. Marescotti, M., Blicha, M., Hyvärinen, A.E.J., Asadi, S., Sharygina, N.: Computing exact worst-case gas consumption for smart contracts. In: Margaria, T., Steffen, B. (eds.) ISoLA 2018. LNCS, vol. 11247, pp. 450–465. Springer, Cham (2018). https://doi.org/10.1007/978-3-030-03427-6_33
34. de Moura, L., Biørner, N.: Z3: an efficient SMT solver. In: Ramakrishnan, C.R., Rehof, J. (eds.) TACAS 2008. LNCS, vol. 4963, pp. 337–340. Springer, Heidelberg (2008). https://doi.org/10.1007/978-3-540-78800-3_24

35. Pottier, F., Régis-Gianas, Y.: Menhir Reference Manual (2019)
36. Saltzman, M.J.: Coin-or: an open-source library for optimization. In: Nielsen, S.S. (ed.) Programming Languages and Systems in Computational Economics and Finance. Advances in Computational Economics, vol. 18. Springer, Boston (2002). https://doi.org/10.1007/978-1-4615-1049-9_1
37. Sergey, I., Nagaraj, V., Johannsen, J., Kumar, A., Trunov, A., Hao, K.C.G.: Safer smart contract programming with Scilla. Proc. ACM Program. Lang. **3**(OOPSLA), 1–30 (2019). https://doi.org/10.1145/3360611
38. Simões, H., Vasconcelos, P., Florido, M., Jost, S., Hammond, K.: Automatic amortised analysis of dynamic memory allocation for lazy functional programs. In: Proceedings of the 17th ACM SIGPLAN International Conference on Functional Programming, ICFP 2012, pp. 165–176. Association for Computing Machinery, New York (2012). https://doi.org/10.1145/2364527.2364575
39. Sinn, M., Zuleger, F., Veith, H.: A simple and scalable static analysis for bound analysis and amortized complexity analysis. In: Biere, A., Bloem, R. (eds.) CAV 2014. LNCS, vol. 8559, pp. 745–761. Springer, Cham (2014). https://doi.org/10.1007/978-3-319-08867-9_50
40. Tarjan, R.: Amortized computational complexity. SIAM J. Algebr. Discret. Methods **6**(2), 306–318 (1985)
41. Tikhomirov, S., Voskresenskaya, E., Ivanitskiy, I., Takhaviev, R., Marchenko, E., Alexandrov, Y.: Smartcheck: static analysis of Ethereum smart contracts. In: 2018 IEEE/ACM 1st International Workshop on Emerging Trends in Software Engineering for Blockchain (WETSEB), pp. 9–16 (May 2018)
42. Wegbreit, B.: Mechanical program analysis. Commun. ACM **18**(9), 528–539 (1975). https://doi.org/10.1145/361002.361016
43. Wood, G.: Ethereum: a secure decentralised generalised transaction ledger eip-150 revision (759dccd - 2017–08-07) (2017). https://ethereum.github.io/yellowpaper/paper.pdf. Accessed 03 Jan 2018

Farkas-Based Tree Interpolation

Sepideh Asadi[1], Martin Blicha[1,2(✉)], Antti Hyvärinen[1(✉)],
Grigory Fedyukovich[3(✉)], and Natasha Sharygina[1(✉)]

[1] Università della Svizzera Italiana (USI), Lugano, Switzerland
{asadis,blicham,hyvaeria,sharygin}@usi.ch
[2] Charles University, Faculty of Mathematics and Physics, Prague, Czech Republic
[3] Florida State University, Tallahassee, USA
grigory@cs.fsu.edu

Abstract. Linear arithmetic over reals (LRA) underlies a wide range
of SMT-based modeling approaches, and, strengthened with Craig
interpolation using Farkas' lemma, is a central tool for efficient over-
approximation. Recent advances in LRA interpolation have resulted in
a range of promising interpolation algorithms with so far poorly understood properties. In this work we study the Farkas-based algorithms with
respect to tree interpolation, a practically important approach where a
set of interpolants is constructed following a given tree structure. We
classify the algorithms based on whether they guarantee the tree interpolation property, and present how to lift a recently introduced approach producing conjunctive LRA interpolants to tree interpolation in
the quantifier-free LRA fragment of first-order logic. Our experiments
show that the standard interpolation and the approach using conjunctive interpolants are complementary in tree interpolation, and suggest
that their combination would be very powerful in practice.

Keywords: Craig interpolation · Tree interpolation property · LRA
interpolation systems · SMT solving · Symbolic model checking

1 Introduction

Given an unsatisfiable first-order formula ϕ partitioned into two sets A and B,
a (binary) *Craig interpolant* [9] is a formula I that is implied by A, unsatisfiable
with B, and defined on the shared symbols of A and B. For certain applications
it is useful to consider sets of related interpolants obtained by partitioning ϕ in
different ways into A, B. Often these applications require further properties to
hold for the computed interpolants. For example, consider the following scenario
from *upgrade checking* of software [15]: a program with function calls is modeled
together with safety properties as an unsatisfiable formula. Once a programmer
introduces changes to the functions, it is often important to know whether the

This work was supported by Swiss National Science Foundation grant 200021_185031
and by Czech Science Foundation grant 20-07487S.

D. Pichardie and M. Sighireanu (Eds.): SAS 2020, LNCS 12389, pp. 357–379, 2020.
https://doi.org/10.1007/978-3-030-65474-0_16

Table 1. Validity of the tree interpolation property (TI) for the studied interpolation algorithms. The signs ✓ and × indicate, respectively, that the property holds and fails.

Interpolation algorithm	TI	Theorem
Farkas Itp^F	✓	1, 2
Dual Farkas $\overline{Itp^F}$	×	7
Decomposing Farkas Itp^D	✓	3, 4, 5
Dual Decomposing Farkas $\overline{Itp^D}$	×	Corollary 2
Flexible Farkas $Itp^{(\alpha)}$	×	6

same properties are satisfied by the new program. The key insight in the use of interpolants in this scenario is as follows. If each function is over-approximated by an interpolant, it is sufficient, under certain conditions, to check whether each new function is contained in the corresponding old function's interpolant in the logical sense. Such a check might be significantly lighter than re-verification of the whole program. However, if several functions were changed simultaneously, the resulting interpolants need to guarantee that no matter how the functions were changed, as long as the changes stay within the over-approximations, the program is correct. This requirement places restrictions on interpolants and ultimately on the interpolation algorithms.

It turns out that these conditions are guaranteed to hold if the interpolation algorithm satisfies the *tree interpolation property (TI)* (see Sect. 2). The property is useful not only in the above scenario, but also in many other applications, including solving constrained Horn clauses [16,27], and synthesis [13].

Many modeling approaches used in verification rely heavily on the use of linear algebra either by directly encoding arithmetic operations, or as part of an algorithm for more general arithmetic. As a result, over-approximation in linear real arithmetic (LRA) through interpolation is an active research area. *Farkas interpolation* [23] is a central class of algorithms for LRA interpolation and is widely used in verification tools. The idea underlying these algorithms is to first show a linear system unsatisfiable with a decision version of the Simplex algorithm. The *Farkas coefficients* computed as a side product can then be restricted to the linear system belonging to the A-part to obtain the interpolant.

Having different algorithms for interpolation is of great practical interest since the choice of a good interpolation algorithm may well determine whether an application terminates quickly or diverges. Up to now there have been few interpolation algorithms that guarantee TI in LRA, and we believe that this has severely limited their use in practical applications. In this work, we identify five variants of the Farkas interpolation algorithms and show that only two of them can be used as a basis for tree interpolation algorithms. Our results are summarized in Table 1.[1]

---

[1] The Farkas interpolation algorithm Itp^F guarantees TI (see, e.g., [7]). We show this for a stronger notion of tree interpolants.

The algorithm Itp^F, introduced in [23], produces a single inequality, whereas Itp^D [6] is a more recent algorithm based on *decomposing* the Farkas interpolants into conjunctions. Applying Itp^F in tree interpolation is relatively straightforward. However, for Itp^D, it is important to take the tree structure of the interpolation problem into consideration when constructing the decomposition. We show how the global tree structure can be brought to the binary interpolation problems through the use of *decomposition strategies*. A carefully designed strategy guarantees TI while still providing a rich variety of LRA inequalities in the resulting interpolants.

This work opens the possibility of using efficient proof-based interpolation portfolios in applications requiring TI. While a thorough study on the use of an interpolation portfolio in such applications is out of the scope for this theoretical paper, we verify experimentally that the resulting interpolants can differ in ways that have practical implications in their use in such applications. We show this by using two measures that we believe to be practical indicators of semantic difference on a set of quantifier-free first-order formulas obtained from software model checking.

Related work. The binary Craig interpolation has been extensively studied (see, e.g., [11,23,25,28,30]), and its practical success has motivated a line of research on tree interpolation [5,18,24,27] which we extend here. In particular, we identify five binary Farkas-based LRA interpolation systems from [1,6,23], classify them based on whether they can guarantee TI, and describe in detail a novel, nontrivial approach of adjusting the binary approach from [6] for tree interpolation. We believe that our approach can be applied in the analysis of other conjunctive binary interpolation approaches for LRA, such as the one in [8]. Similarly to us, [7] studies tree interpolation in LRA. Compared to [7], we extend the study by considering four other algorithms and strengthening the existing result. We base the propositional part of our results on the studies in [17,26,29], where tree interpolation is discussed in a purely propositional setting.

We mention here some applications that we believe to be relevant to our current work. In [13] the authors synthesize winning strategies by exploiting tree interpolants computed by the Z3 SMT solver [24]. The state-of-the-art Horn solver ELDARICA [19] uses tree interpolation to refine abstraction: it maps each (spurious) counterexample DAG to a tree interpolation problem. Finally, tree interpolants are also used in regression verification of evolving software. See, for example, [2,29], that use tree interpolants to over-approximate functions for incremental verification of program versions.

The paper is organized as follows. We first introduce in Sect. 2 the necessary background on tree interpolation and then, in Sect. 3, provide our main result that the decomposed interpolants guarantee TI. We prove the three smaller, negative results in Sect. 4. In Sect. 5 we show experimentally that the approach produces a range of interpolants not available through existing means, and finally offer conclusions in Sect. 6.

2 Background

Our context is that of SMT (Satisfiability Modulo Theories [3,10]) on quantifier-free formulas in the theory of linear arithmetic over the reals, LRA. A *term* in LRA is either a constant, a variable, or the application of a function symbol in LRA. An LRA *atom* is of the form $t < c$ or $t \leq c$, where t is a term and c is a constant. Given an LRA atom At, we denote by $symb(At)$ the set of variables in At. A *literal* is either an atom At or its negation $\overline{At}$. A *clause* cl is a finite disjunction of literals, and a *formula* in *conjunctive normal form* (CNF) is a conjunction of clauses. We interchangeably interpret a clause as a set of literals and a CNF formula as a set of clauses. We denote by Fla the set of all formulas in CNF. For a formula ϕ, we denote by $\neg\phi$ its negation. We extend the notation $symb$ to CNF formulas, writing $symb(\phi)$ for the set of atoms in ϕ.

A CNF formula ϕ is *satisfiable* if there exists an assignment to its variables so that each clause in ϕ contains a *true* literal. A *resolution refutation* (or *refutation*) of a CNF formula ϕ is a tree labeled with clauses. The root of the tree has the empty clause $\perp$, and the leaves have either *source clauses* appearing directly in ϕ, or *theory clauses* that are tautologies in LRA learned through an unsatisfiable conjunctive query to the LRA solver. The inner nodes are clauses derived by the *resolution rule*

$$\frac{C_1 \vee p \qquad C_2 \vee \overline{p}}{C_1 \vee C_2}$$

where $C_1 \vee p$ and $C_2 \vee \overline{p}$ are the *antecedents*, $C_1 \vee C_2$ the *resolvent*, p is the *pivot* of the resolution step.

The notion of interpolant goes back to Craig's interpolation theorem for first-order logic [9]. In this work we consider approaches where interpolants are constructed from proofs of unsatisfiability.

Definition 1 (binary interpolation). *Given an unsatisfiable CNF formula ϕ partitioned into two disjoint formulas A and B, we denote a binary interpolation instance by $(A \mid B)$. An interpolation algorithm Itp is a procedure that maps an interpolation instance to a formula $I = Itp(A \mid B)$ such that (i) $A \implies I$, (ii) $I \implies \neg B$, and (iii) $symb(I) \subseteq symb(A) \cap symb(B)$.*

If I is an interpolant for $(A \mid B)$, then $\neg I$ is an interpolant for $(B \mid A)$. This interpolant is called *dual interpolant* of $(B \mid A)$.

Part of our discussion combines Craig interpolation in propositional logic and LRA. For the propositional part, we use the Pudlák's interpolation algorithm [25], which we treat as an instance of D'Silva et al.'s labeling interpolation system [11]. The approach first constructs the refutation using standard SMT methods. The interpolation works then by labeling each clause with an interpolant starting from the leaf clauses towards the empty clause. The leaf theory clauses are labeled using an LRA interpolation after which the propositional labeling can be applied in a standard way. For lack of space, we refer the reader to Appendix A for details.

We in particular concentrate on *tree interpolants*, generalizations of binary interpolants, obtained from a single refutation.[2]

Definition 2 (weak tree-interpolation property). *Let* $X_1 \wedge \ldots \wedge X_n \wedge Y \wedge Z \implies \bot$. *Let* $I_{X_1}, \ldots, I_{X_n}$ *and* $I_{X_1 \ldots X_n Y}$ *be interpolants for interpolation instances* $(X_1 \mid X_2 \wedge \ldots \wedge X_n \wedge Y \wedge Z)$, $\ldots$, $(X_n \mid X_1 \wedge \ldots \wedge X_{n-1} \wedge Y \wedge Z)$, *and* $(X_1 \wedge \ldots \wedge X_n \wedge Y \mid Z)$, *respectively. The* $n+2$-*tuple* $(I_{X_1}, \ldots, I_{X_n}, Y, I_{X_1 \ldots X_n Y})$ *has the* weak tree-interpolation property *iff* $I_{X_1} \wedge \ldots \wedge I_{X_n} \wedge Y \implies I_{X_1 \ldots X_n Y}$.

We are now ready to define an instance of the tree interpolation problem.

Definition 3 (tree interpolation instance). *Let* ϕ *be an unsatisfiable SMT formula in CNF,* (V, E) *a directed tree with vertices* V *containing a unique root* $v_r \in V$, *and directed edges* $E \subseteq V \times V$. *Let furthermore* F *be a labeling function* $F : V \longrightarrow Fla$ *that maps vertices* V *to sets of clauses of* ϕ *such that* $\bigwedge_{v \in V} F(v) = \phi$ *and* $F(v) \cap F(w) = \emptyset$ *whenever* $v \neq w$. *We call* $\langle (V, E), F \rangle$ *a tree interpolation instance.*

Let E^* denote the reflexive transitive closure of E. We denote the nodes in the subtree rooted at a node v by $subtree(v) = \{w \mid (w, v) \in E^*\}$ and the complement of the subtree as $\overline{subtree(v)} = V \setminus subtree(v)$. We also extend the function F to sets of nodes as $F(U) = \bigwedge_{v \in U} F(v)$. With this notation we can define the *tree interpolant* for a problem $\langle (V, E), F \rangle$ as follows.

Definition 4 (tree interpolant). *A tree interpolant for a tree interpolation instance* $\langle (V, E), F \rangle$ *is a labeling function* $\tau\iota : V \longrightarrow Fla$ *that assigns a formula to every vertex in* V *satisfying the following conditions:*

1. $\tau\iota(v_r) = \bot$,
2. *for all* $v \in V$ *with children* $c_1, \ldots, c_n$, *the* $(n + 2)$-*tuple* $(\tau\iota(c_1), \ldots, \tau\iota(c_n), F(v), \tau\iota(v))$ *has the weak tree-interpolation property, i.e.,* $\bigwedge_{i=1}^{n} \tau\iota(c_i) \wedge F(v) \implies \tau\iota(v)$,
3. $\tau\iota(v)$ *uses only the common language of* $subtree(v)$ *and* $\overline{subtree(v)}$, *i.e.,* $symb(\tau\iota(v)) \subseteq symb(F(subtree(v))) \cap symb(F(\overline{subtree(v)}))$.

A tree interpolation algorithm $TItp$ *is a procedure that maps any tree interpolation instance to a tree interpolant* $\tau\iota = TItp(\langle (V, E), F \rangle)$.

We make the following observation that will be central in our discussion in Sect. 3:

Remark 1. Given a binary interpolation algorithm Itp, we can construct an algorithm $TItp_{Itp}$ that computes the labels of nodes v by iteratively applying Itp on a single resolution refutation for different binary partitionings as

$$\tau\iota(v) = Itp(F(subtree(v)) \mid F(\overline{subtree(v)}))$$

If Itp guarantees that for each node v and its children $c_1, \ldots, c_n$ the tuple $(\tau\iota(c_1), \ldots, \tau\iota(c_n), F(v), \tau\iota(v))$ satisfies the weak tree-interpolation property,

---

[2] For example in [7] this is called the *tree interpolation property.*

then the algorithm $TItp_{Itp}$ is guaranteed to produce a tree interpolant, that is, $TItp_{Itp}$ is a tree interpolation algorithm. As a subtle, important consequence, a certain interpolation algorithm class, called *decomposing Farkas interpolation algorithms* and discussed in Sect. 3.3, needs to be instantiated into actual algorithms using *decomposition strategies* that make the algorithms aware of the tree structure before they can be used as a component of a tree interpolation algorithm.

2.1 Linear Systems

The problem domain in this work is $\mathbb{R}$, the set of real numbers. The (column) vector of n elements is denoted by $\mathbf{v} = (v_1, \ldots, v_n)^\mathsf{T}$. The vector of all zeroes is denoted by $\mathbf{0}$.

A linear system S is a conjunction of m inequalities which we treat as a set $S = \{l_i \mid i = 1, \ldots, m\}$ involving the set of n variables $X = \{x_1, \ldots, x_n\}$ such that each l_i is of the form $\sum_j c_{ij} x_j \bowtie b_i$, where $\bowtie \in \{\leq, <\}$, $c_{11}, c_{12}, \ldots, c_{mn}$ are the coefficients of the system, and $b_1, \ldots, b_m$ are constants. We often fix an order for the system and denote it with the matrix notation $C\mathbf{x} \bowtie \mathbf{b}$, where C is the $m \times n$ matrix of coefficients c_{ij}, $\mathbf{x} = (x_1, \ldots, x_n)^\mathsf{T}$, and $\mathbf{b} = (b_1, \ldots, b_m)^\mathsf{T}$.

For the rest of the paper we use just $\leq$ instead of $\bowtie$. This does not affect the correctness of the proofs presented in this paper but greatly simplifies the presentation. Throughout the paper by system S we refer to a finite set of linear inequalities in the form of

$$l_1 \equiv \quad c_{11}x_1 + c_{12}x_2 + \cdots + c_{1n}x_n \leq b_1$$

$$\vdots$$

$$l_m \equiv \quad c_{m1}x_1 + c_{m2}x_2 + \cdots + c_{mn}x_n \leq b_m$$

Finally for the matrix C and constants $\mathbf{b}$ of system S, and a sub-system $S' \subseteq S$ we use the notations $C_{S'}$ and $\mathbf{b}_{S'}$ to denote the matrix and constants of the sub-system S'. Intuitively $C_{S'}$ and $\mathbf{b}_{S'}$ denote the restrictions of C and $\mathbf{b}$ where only the coordinates corresponding to the subsystem S' are kept. More formally, let $S := C\mathbf{x} \leq \mathbf{b}$ be a system of m linear inequalities, and $S' := ((C_{i_1}), \ldots, (C_{i_k}))^\mathsf{T}\mathbf{x} \leq (b_{i_1}, \ldots, b_{i_k})^\mathsf{T}$ be a subsystem of S with $k \leq m$ linear inequalities, where C_{i_j} is the $i_j{}^{\text{th}}$ row of C, b_{i_j} the $i_j{}^{\text{th}}$ element of $\mathbf{b}$, and $i_j < i_{j+1}$ for all $1 \leq j \leq k - 1$. We denote by $C_{S'}$ the matrix $((C_{i_1}), \ldots, (C_{i_k}))^\mathsf{T}$ and by $\mathbf{b}_{S'}$ the vector $(b_{i_1}, \ldots, b_{i_k})^\mathsf{T}$.

3 Tree Interpolation for Linear Real Arithmetic

In this section we show our main result, that the decomposing Farkas interpolation algorithm Itp^D guarantees the tree interpolation property. We first introduce a stronger version of tree interpolation property than Definition 2 that will be useful in the proofs and discussion.

Definition 5 (strong tree-interpolation property). [3] *Let $X_1 \wedge \ldots \wedge X_n \wedge$ $Z \implies \bot$. Let $I_{X_1}, \ldots, I_{X_n}$ and $I_{X_1 \ldots X_n}$ be interpolants for interpolation instances $(X_1 \mid X_2 \wedge \ldots \wedge X_n \wedge Z)$, ..., $(X_n \mid X_1 \wedge \ldots \wedge X_{n-1} \wedge Z)$, and $(X_1 \wedge \ldots \wedge X_n \mid Z)$, respectively. The $n+1$-tuple $(I_{X_1}, \ldots, I_{X_n}, I_{X_1 \ldots X_n})$ has the strong tree-interpolation property iff $(I_{X_1} \wedge \ldots \wedge I_{X_n}) \implies I_{X_1 \ldots X_n}$.*

It is easy to show that if a binary interpolation algorithm guarantees the strong tree-interpolation property, it also guarantees the weak tree-interpolation property because $Y \implies I_Y$. We use the term *tree interpolation property* without qualifiers when we refer to both its weak and strong versions.

Algorithms for solving linear systems in SMT solvers make use of the Simplex algorithm [12] and are based on the Farkas' lemma.

Lemma 1 (Farkas' lemma). *Let $C \in \mathbb{R}^{m \times n}$. $C\mathbf{x} \leq \mathbf{b}$ is unsatisfiable if and only if there exists a vector $\mathbf{f} \geq \mathbf{0}$ such that $\mathbf{f}^\mathsf{T} C = \mathbf{0}$ and $\mathbf{f}^\mathsf{T} \mathbf{b} < 0$.*

We refer to the vector $\mathbf{f}$ as the vector of Farkas coefficients. Given this vector it is possible to immediately compute two interpolants:

Definition 6 (Farkas and dual Farkas interpolants in LRA [23]). *Given an interpolation instance $(A \mid B)$ over a linear system $S = C\mathbf{x} \leq \mathbf{b}$ and its Farkas coefficients $\mathbf{f}$, the Farkas interpolant for $(A \mid B)$ is the inequality*

$$I^F := \mathbf{f}_A^\mathsf{T}(C_A \mathbf{x} - \mathbf{b}_A) \leq 0,$$

and the dual Farkas interpolant for $(A \mid B)$ is a negation of the Farkas interpolant for $(B \mid A)$:

$$\overline{I^F} := \neg\,(\mathbf{f}_B^\mathsf{T}(C_B \mathbf{x} - \mathbf{b}_B) \leq 0),$$

where $\mathbf{f}_A$ and $\mathbf{f}_B$ are the restrictions of $\mathbf{f}$ to the subsystems A and B, respectively.

Recently [6] introduced an algorithm to gain more control over the strength of LRA interpolants. The underlying idea is to not directly sum the inequalities in A-part, but instead split the sum into sub-sums. This yields an interpolant that is a conjunction (decomposition) of possibly more than one component of the Farkas interpolant. In the following, we formally define what type of decomposition is suitable for interpolation instances.

Definition 7 (proper decomposition for interpolation [6]). *Let $S = C\mathbf{x} \leq \mathbf{b}$ be a system of linear inequalities over a set of variables $X = \{\mathbf{x}_1, \ldots, \mathbf{x}_m\}$ and let $L \subseteq X$. Let $\mathbf{w} \geq \mathbf{0}$ be a vector such that all variables from L are eliminated in $\mathbf{w}^\mathsf{T} C\mathbf{x}$. We say that a set of vectors $\mathrm{Dec}(\mathbf{w}^\mathsf{T} C\mathbf{x}, L)$ is a proper decomposition for interpolation if it forms a decomposition of $\mathbf{w}$, i.e.,*

$$\mathbf{w} = \sum_{\mathbf{v} \in \mathrm{Dec}(\mathbf{w}^\mathsf{T} C\mathbf{x}, L)} \mathbf{v};$$

and for all $\mathbf{v} \in \mathrm{Dec}(\mathbf{w}^\mathsf{T} C\mathbf{x}, L)$, (i) $\mathbf{v} \geq \mathbf{0}$ and (ii) all variables from L are eliminated in $\mathbf{v}^\mathsf{T} C\mathbf{x}$.

---

[3] This property appears in the literature under names *generalized simultaneous abstraction* [17] and *symmetric interpolation* [21].

Definition 8 (decomposed interpolants and their duals [6]**).** *Let* $(A \mid B)$
be an interpolation instance in LRA, L_A *the local variables of* A *(those not
appearing in* B*), and* $\mathbf{f}$ *the vector of Farkas coefficients of the system. Let*
$\{\mathbf{f}_1, \dots, \mathbf{f}_k\} = \mathrm{Dec}(\mathbf{f_A}^\mathsf{T} C_A \mathbf{x}, L_A)$ *be a proper decomposition. Then*

$$I^D = \bigwedge_{i=1}^{k} \mathbf{f}_i^\mathsf{T}(C_A \mathbf{x} - \mathbf{b}_A) \le 0$$

is a decomposed interpolant *of size* k *for* $(A \mid B)$.

Similarly, for subsystem B *with its local variables* L_B, *if* $\{\mathbf{f}_1', \dots, \mathbf{f}_m'\} =$
$\mathrm{Dec}(\mathbf{f_B}^\mathsf{T} C_B \mathbf{x}, L_B)$ *then the* dual decomposed interpolant *for* $(A \mid B)$ *is the negation of the decomposed interpolant for* $(B \mid A)$:

$$\overline{I^D} \equiv \neg \left(\bigwedge_{j=1}^{m} \mathbf{f}_j'^\mathsf{T}(C_B \mathbf{x} - \mathbf{b}_B) \le 0 \right)$$

When the set of local variables is clear from the context we omit the second
argument of Dec. Note that *trivial* proper decomposition of size 1 always exists:
it is the Farkas interpolant.

Next, we illustrate the key difference between Farkas (I^F) and decomposed
Farkas (I^D) interpolants by an example that will serve as our running example.

Example 1. Consider S as the unsatisfiable conjunction of linear inequalities:

$$\begin{aligned}
\left. \begin{array}{r} x_1 + x_2 \le 0 \\ -x_1 + x_3 \le 0 \end{array} \right\} & X_1 \\[4pt]
\left. \begin{array}{r} x_1 + x_4 \le 0 \\ -x_1 + x_5 \le 0 \end{array} \right\} & X_2 \\[4pt]
-x_2 - x_5 + x_6 \le 0 \, \} & Y \\[4pt]
-x_3 - x_4 - x_6 \le -1 \, \} & Z,
\end{aligned}$$

where we will denote the inequalities by $l_1, \dots, l_6$, respectively. Consider the
following disjoint sets $X_1 = \{l_1, l_2\}$, $X_2 = \{l_3, l_4\}$, $Y = \{l_5\}$, and $Z = \{l_6\}$ as
shown above. The unsatisfiability of S is witnessed by the Farkas coefficients
$\mathbf{f}^\mathsf{T} = (1, 1, 1, 1, 1, 1)$. Let Itp^F be the Farkas interpolation algorithm. Consider
interpolation instance $(X_1 \wedge X_2 \wedge Y \mid Z)$, with $\mathbf{f}_{XY}^\mathsf{T} = (1, 1, 1, 1, 1)$ that eliminate x_1, x_2, x_5, the local variables of $X_1 \wedge X_2 \wedge Y$ with respect to the rest
of S. The interpolant $Itp^F(X_1 \wedge X_2 \wedge Y \mid Z)$ is $I_{XY}^F = x_3 + x_4 + x_6 \le 0$.
Let Itp^D be the decomposing Farkas interpolation algorithm. The interpo-
lation instance $(X_1 \wedge X_2 \wedge Y \mid Z)$ admits a decomposition of $\mathbf{f}_{XY}^\mathsf{T} C_{XY} \mathbf{x}$ as
$D = \{(1, 0, 0, 1, 1)^\mathsf{T}, (0, 1, 1, 0, 0)^\mathsf{T}\}$ that eliminates the local variables x_1, x_2, x_5.
The interpolant $Itp^D(X_1 \wedge X_2 \wedge Y \mid Z) = I_{XY}^D = x_6 \le 0 \wedge x_3 + x_4 \le 0$ computed
with respect to this decomposition contains two conjuncts and differs from the
Farkas interpolant.

3.1   Proper Labeling

We rely on resolution refutation that incorporates theory lemmas that are created by the theory solver and get propagated to the SAT solver. As theory solver provides a separate proof for each theory clause, we can compute an LRA interpolant for the negation of each theory clause. Once these are obtained, the final interpolant is computed using Pudlák's propositional interpolation algorithm [25].

The binary interpolation algorithms for linear real arithmetic discussed above require that the theory atoms be placed into exactly one partition. The origin of the partition is, however, the CNF partition, where it is common that atoms (as opposed to clauses) belong to several partitions. This can lead to subtle problems in the definitions and eventually implementations. We first illustrate the problem with an example before defining *proper labeling* in Definition 9 that we will use for resolving the problem.

Example 2. Consider the sets of clauses $X = \{a \leq b, (\overline{a \leq c}) \vee x\}$, $Y = \{b \leq c, (\overline{a \leq c}) \vee y\}$, and $Z = \{\overline{x} \vee \overline{y}\}$, and the theory clause $cl := (\overline{a \leq b}) \vee (\overline{b \leq c}) \vee a \leq c$ required for the refutation of $X \wedge Y \wedge Z$. The atom $a \leq c$ can be considered a part of both partitions X and Y when computing an interpolant for some binary partitioning of the theory clause cl. However, the strong TI is not guaranteed if we change the partition of $a \leq c$ between different binary interpolation instances. For example, placing $a \leq c$ in Y while interpolating $(X \mid Y \wedge Z)$ for cl yields the Farkas theory interpolant $I_X^F = a \leq b$. Placing $a \leq c$ in X while interpolating $(Y \mid X \wedge Z)$ and $(X \wedge Y \mid Z)$ for cl gives $I_Y^F = b \leq c$, and $I_{XY}^F = \bot$. Clearly using these interpolants violates the strong TI since $a \leq b \wedge b \leq c \not\Rightarrow \bot$.

We define a general version of this *proper labeling* of the theory clauses and argue that a fixed proper labeling must be used for a sequence of binary interpolation problems if tree interpolation property is to be guaranteed.

Definition 9 (proper labeling). *Let $X_1, \ldots, X_n$ be sets of clauses. We say that $X_1 \wedge \ldots \wedge X_n$ is a partitioned CNF formula F and we say that a function from atoms of F to partitions $PL : Atoms(F) \rightarrow \{1, \ldots, n\}$ is a proper labeling if for each atom At it holds that $PL(At) = i$ implies that there is a clause in X_i containing At (or its negation).*

Proper labeling is used in a resolution refutation of a partitioned CNF formula to determine the partitioning of theory clauses and consequently the input for theory interpolation algorithms. In the rest of the text we are going to assume that a refutation of a partitioned CNF formula always comes with some fixed proper labeling and we say that the refutation is *properly labeled*.

3.2   Tree Interpolation Property in Farkas Interpolation Algorithm

For the Farkas interpolation algorithm we first state and prove a simplified version of Definition 5 limited to three partitions and then generalize the result for an arbitrary number of partitions by an iterative application of Theorem 1.

Theorem 1 (strong TI in Farkas interpolation). *Let $X \wedge Y \wedge Z$ be an unsatisfiable partitioned CNF formula in* LRA *and let $\mathbb{P}$ be its properly labeled resolution refutation. Let Itp^{P+F} denote the interpolation algorithm that uses Pudlák's algorithm for the propositional part and Farkas algorithm for the theory clauses. Let I_X, I_Y, and I_{XY} be the binary interpolants $Itp^{P+F}(X \mid Y \wedge Z)$, $Itp^{P+F}(Y \mid X \wedge Z)$, and $Itp^{P+F}(X \wedge Y \mid Z)$, respectively. Then $(I_X \wedge I_Y) \implies I_{XY}$.*

Proof. We show using structural induction that for any clause cl in the refutation $\mathbb{P}$ and for all possible partial interpolants, property $(I_X \wedge I_Y) \implies I_{XY}$ holds.

Since a leaf in $\mathbb{P}$ could either be a source clause or a theory clause, we study each case separately. The proof has two steps: base case, and inductive step. The base case itself consists of two steps, depending on the nature of leaf clauses. Both the inductive step and the base case for source clauses are shown in [29] and are therefore given here as a sketch. Their full proofs are in Appendix A.

Base case (source clause, *sketch*). We can show one-by-one for the three cases $cl \in X, cl \in Y$, and $cl \in Z$ that the strong tree-interpolation property holds. See proof of Lemma 2 in Appendix A.

Base case (theory clause). Let $cl \equiv \bar{\ell}_1 \vee \cdots \vee \bar{\ell}_n$ from $\mathbb{P}$ be a theory clause in LRA, S the system of linear inequalities corresponding to $\neg cl$, and $\mathbf{f}$ the vector of Farkas coefficients witnessing the unsatisfiability of S.

As refutation $\mathbb{P}$ is properly labeled (Definition 9), each literal ℓ_i is uniquely assigned to either X, Y or Z. The LRA interpolants for the theory clause computed for the binary interpolation instances $(X \mid Y \wedge Z)$, $(Y \mid X \wedge Z)$, and $(X \wedge Y \mid Z)$ are thus $I_X^F = \mathbf{f}_X^\intercal(C_X \mathbf{x} - \mathbf{b}_X) \leq 0$, $I_Y^F = \mathbf{f}_Y^\intercal(C_Y \mathbf{x} - \mathbf{b}_Y) \leq 0$, and $I_{XY}^F = \mathbf{f}_{XY}^\intercal(C_{XY}\mathbf{x} - \mathbf{b}_{XY}) \leq 0$, respectively, where we denote by XY the subsystem corresponding to $X \wedge Y$. By construction, we have $\mathbf{f}_{XY}^\intercal(C_{XY}\mathbf{x} - \mathbf{b}_{XY}) = \mathbf{f}_X^\intercal(C_X \mathbf{x} - \mathbf{b}_X) + \mathbf{f}_Y^\intercal(C_Y \mathbf{x} - \mathbf{b}_Y)$. It follows that if $\mathbf{f}_X^\intercal(C_X \mathbf{x} - \mathbf{b}_X) \leq 0$ and $\mathbf{f}_Y^\intercal(C_Y \mathbf{x} - \mathbf{b}_Y) \leq 0$, then also $\mathbf{f}_{XY}^\intercal(C_{XY}\mathbf{x} - \mathbf{b}_{XY}) \leq 0$, which is exactly the desired result that $I_X^F \wedge I_Y^F \implies I_{XY}^F$.

Inductive step (inner node, *sketch*). By case analysis on the different binary interpolations in the nodes of the refutation $\mathbb{P}$ it is possible to show that each *partial interpolant* associated with the resolvent has TI (see proof of Lemma 3 in Appendix A). $\qquad\qquad\square$

The result of Theorem 1 can be generalized to prove that Itp^{P+F} guarantees strong (and consequently weak) TI.

Theorem 2 (generalizing strong TI in Farkas interpolation). *Let $X_1 \wedge \ldots \wedge X_n \wedge Z$, $n \geq 2$, be an unsatisfiable partitioned CNF formula in* LRA *and let $\mathbb{P}$ be its properly labeled resolution refutation. Let Itp^{P+F} denote the interpolation algorithm that uses Pudlák's algorithm for the propositional part and Farkas algorithm for the theory clauses. Let I_{X_1}, ..., I_{X_n}, and $I_{X_1...X_n}$ be the binary interpolants $Itp^{P+F}(X_1 \mid X_2 \wedge \ldots \wedge X_n \wedge Z)$, ..., $Itp^{P+F}(X_n \mid X_1 \wedge \ldots \wedge X_{n-1} \wedge Z)$ and $Itp^{P+F}(X_1 \wedge \ldots \wedge X_n \mid Z)$, respectively. Then $(I_{X_1} \wedge \ldots \wedge I_{X_n}) \implies I_{X_1...X_n}$, i.e., the tuple $(I_{X_1}, \ldots, I_{X_n}, I_{X_1...X_n})$ has the strong tree-interpolation property.*

Proof. We prove the theorem by induction. For the base case with $n = 2$ we may apply Theorem 1. Assume now that $n \geq 3$, and the theorem holds for $n - 1$. Using the induction hypothesis for the tuple $(X_1, \ldots, X_{n-1}, X_n \wedge Z)$ we get that

$$I_{X_1} \wedge \ldots \wedge I_{X_{n-1}} \implies I_{X_1 \ldots X_{n-1}}.$$

By applying Theorem 1 again for $(X_1 \wedge \ldots \wedge X_{n-1}, X_n, Z)$ we obtain

$$I_{X_1 \ldots X_{n-1}} \wedge I_{X_n} \implies I_{X_1 \ldots X_n}.$$

Combining these two implications yields the desired result $I_{X_1} \wedge \ldots \wedge I_{X_n} \implies I_{X_1 \ldots X_n}.$ □

By Theorem 2, the interpolation algorithm Itp^{P+F} guarantees the strong TI. We can use the technique described in Remark 1 to obtain a tree interpolation algorithm $TItp_{Itp^{P+F}}$ for computation of tree interpolants.

Corollary 1. $TItp_{Itp^{P+F}}$ *is a tree interpolation algorithm, that is, it computes tree interpolants.*

Note that while the result that $TItp_{Itp^{P+F}}$ is a tree interpolation algorithm is known from [7], our result that Itp^{P+F} guarantees the strong TI is new to the best of our knowledge.

3.3 A Tree Interpolation Algorithm Based on Decomposing Farkas Interpolation

In this section we consider the decomposing Farkas interpolation algorithm of [6], and show that if the decompositions satisfy a certain property, then the algorithm guarantees the tree interpolation property. We also show that if the condition is not satisfied, the tree interpolation property is not guaranteed.

A central difference between decomposing Farkas interpolation algorithm and Farkas interpolation algorithm is that the former is a template rather than a concrete algorithm. In practice this means that the algorithm is parameterized by the decomposition of the (restricted) vector of Farkas coefficients and can yield different interpolants for different decompositions. For tree interpolation one wants to relate interpolants computed by multiple binary interpolation instances over the same proof. Therefore also the decompositions need to respect this relation for the binary interpolation instances. We first show that tree interpolation property is not guaranteed in general for the decomposed interpolants, and then define a constraint on the decompositions that guarantees the tree interpolation property.

Example 3. Consider our running example of Example 1 and let $X := X_1 \wedge X_2$. Using the decomposing Farkas interpolation algorithm Itp^D, the interpolation instance $(X \mid Y \wedge Z)$ admits different non trivial decompositions of the restricted vector of Farkas coefficients $\mathbf{f}_X^T = (1, 1, 1, 1)$, for example $D_1 =$

$\{(1,0,0,1)^\mathsf{T}, (0,1,1,0)^\mathsf{T}\}$ and $D_2 = \{(1,1,0,0)^\mathsf{T}, (0,0,1,1)^\mathsf{T}\}$. Both D_1 and D_2 successfully eliminate the single X-local variable x_1, as required. The outcome of $Itp^D(X \mid Y \wedge Z)$ using D_1 is $I_X^1 = x_2 + x_5 \leq 0 \wedge x_3 + x_4 \leq 0$. When using D_2, the resulting interpolant is $I_X^2 = x_2 + x_3 \leq 0 \wedge x_4 + x_5 \leq 0$. Consider $(X \wedge Y \mid Z)$ that admits only a single non-trivial decomposition of $\mathbf{f}_{XY}^\mathsf{T} = (1,1,1,1,1)$ that eliminates XY-local variables x_1, x_2, x_5: $D_3 = \{(1,0,0,1,1)^\mathsf{T}, (0,1,1,0,0)^\mathsf{T}\}$. The interpolant computed with respect to this decomposition is $Itp^D(X \wedge Y \mid Z) = I_{XY} = x_6 \leq 0 \wedge x_3 + x_4 \leq 0$. Consider $(Y \mid X \wedge Z)$ where there is no opportunity for decomposition since its first part consists of the single inequality l_5. The computed interpolant is $Itp^D(Y \mid X \wedge Z) = I_Y = -x_2 - x_5 + x_6 \leq 0$. We can easily see that the strong tree-interpolation property ((Definition 5) is satisfied for $I_X^1 \colon I_X^1 \wedge I_Y \implies I_{XY}$. However, the property is not satisfied for I_X^2, since $I_X^2 \wedge I_Y \not\Rightarrow I_{XY}$. Since in this example $I_Y = Y$, the same is true for the weak tree-interpolation property (Definition 2).

Intuitively, the tree interpolation property might not hold when the subsystem's decomposition (D_2) does not agree with its supersystem's decomposition (D_3) (when restricted to the subsystem). More generally, the inequalities resulting from (the restriction of) supersystem's decomposition must be logically covered by the inequalities of subsystem's decomposition. The following *monotonicity* condition captures this formally.

Definition 10 (monotonic decompositions). *Let $S = C\mathbf{x} \leq \mathbf{b}$ be an unsatisfiable system of linear inequalities and let $(A_1 \mid B_1), \ldots, (A_n \mid B_n)$ be a set of binary interpolation problems over S. Let Itp^D denote the decomposing Farkas interpolation algorithm ((Definition 8). We say that Itp^D uses monotonic decompositions if whenever $A_i \subseteq A_j$, then for all vectors $\mathbf{w} \in \mathrm{Dec}(\mathbf{f}_{A_j}^\mathsf{T} C_{A_j}\mathbf{x}, L_{A_j})$ there exists $U \subseteq \mathrm{Dec}(\mathbf{f}_{A_i}^\mathsf{T} C_{A_i}\mathbf{x}, L_{A_i})$ such that $\sum_{\mathbf{u} \in U} \mathbf{u}^\mathsf{T}(C_{A_i}\mathbf{x} - \mathbf{b}_{A_i}) \leq 0 \implies \mathbf{w}_{A_i}^\mathsf{T}(C_{A_i}\mathbf{x} - \mathbf{b}_{A_i}) \leq 0$, where $\mathbf{w}_{A_i}$ is the restriction of $\mathbf{w}$ to the subsystem A_i.*

Now we can proceed to prove that Itp^D can guarantee the tree interpolation property.

Theorem 3 (strong TI in decomposing Farkas interpolation). *Let $X \wedge Y \wedge Z$ be an unsatisfiable partitioned CNF formula in LRA and let $\mathbb{P}$ be its properly labeled resolution refutation. Let Itp^{P+D} denote the interpolation algorithm that uses Pudlák's algorithm for the propositional part and decomposing Farkas algorithm for the theory clauses. Let I_X, I_Y, and I_{XY} be the binary interpolants $Itp^{P+D}(X \mid Y \wedge Z)$, $Itp^{P+D}(Y \mid X \wedge Z)$, and $Itp^{P+D}(X \wedge Y \mid Z)$, respectively. If Itp^D uses monotonic decompositions for every theory clause in $\mathbb{P}$ then $(I_X \wedge I_Y) \implies I_{XY}$.*

Proof (by structural induction). We only show the proof of the implication for a leaf with a theory clause. In the remaining cases the proof is the same as that of Theorem 1.

Let cl be a theory clause in LRA and let $S = C\mathbf{x} \leq \mathbf{b}$ be the system of linear inequalities corresponding to $\neg cl$. Let $\mathbf{f}$ denote the Farkas coefficients witnessing the unsatisfiability of S. Note that the proper labeling of $\mathbb{P}$ (recall (Definition 9) partitions cl into three disjoint sets of literals X, Y, Z. Let Dec_X, Dec_Y and Dec_{XY} denote the decompositions $\text{Dec}(\mathbf{f}_X^\mathsf{T} C_X \mathbf{x}, L_X)$, $\text{Dec}(\mathbf{f}_Y^\mathsf{T} C_Y \mathbf{x}, L_Y)$, and $\text{Dec}(\mathbf{f}_{XY}^\mathsf{T} C_{XY} \mathbf{x}, L_{XY})$, where XY denotes the subsystem $X \wedge Y$. We need to prove that

$$\left(\bigwedge_{\mathbf{p} \in Dec_X} \mathbf{p}^\mathsf{T} (C_X \mathbf{x} - \mathbf{b}_X) \le 0 \right) \wedge \left(\bigwedge_{\mathbf{q} \in Dec_Y} \mathbf{q}^\mathsf{T} (C_Y \mathbf{x} - \mathbf{b}_Y) \le 0 \right) \implies$$

$$\left(\bigwedge_{\mathbf{r} \in Dec_{XY}} \mathbf{r}^\mathsf{T} (C_{XY} \mathbf{x} - \mathbf{b}_{XY}) \le 0 \right)$$

It is enough to fix $\mathbf{r} \in Dec_{XY}$ and prove that $\mathbf{r}^\mathsf{T}(C_{XY}\mathbf{x} - \mathbf{b}_{XY}) \le 0$ is implied by the antecedent. As the subsystem XY consists of two disjoint subsystems X and Y, it holds that $\mathbf{r}^\mathsf{T} = (\mathbf{r}_X^\mathsf{T} \ \mathbf{r}_Y^\mathsf{T})$, $\mathbf{b}_{XY}^\mathsf{T} = (\mathbf{b}_X^\mathsf{T} \ \mathbf{b}_Y^\mathsf{T})$, $C_{XY}^\mathsf{T} = (C_X^\mathsf{T} \ C_Y^\mathsf{T})$ and $\mathbf{r}_X^\mathsf{T}(C_X \mathbf{x} - \mathbf{b}_X) + \mathbf{r}_Y^\mathsf{T}(C_Y \mathbf{x} - \mathbf{b}_Y) = \mathbf{r}^\mathsf{T}(C_{XY} \mathbf{x} - \mathbf{b}_{XY})$. Consequently, it is enough to prove that

$$\bigwedge_{\mathbf{p} \in Dec_X} \mathbf{p}^\mathsf{T} (C_X \mathbf{x} - \mathbf{b}_X) \le 0 \implies \mathbf{r}_X^\mathsf{T} (C_X \mathbf{x} - \mathbf{b}_X) \le 0$$

and

$$\bigwedge_{\mathbf{q} \in Dec_Y} \mathbf{q}^\mathsf{T} (C_Y \mathbf{x} - \mathbf{b}_Y) \le 0 \implies \mathbf{r}_Y^\mathsf{T} (C_Y \mathbf{x} - \mathbf{b}_Y) \le 0$$

We only show how to prove the first implication, the second one is analogous. According to our assumption, Itp^D uses monotonic decompositions. Hence for $\mathbf{r} \in Dec_{XY}$ there exists $U \subseteq Dec_X$ such that $\sum_{\mathbf{u} \in U} \mathbf{u}^\mathsf{T}(C_X \mathbf{x} - \mathbf{b}_X) \le 0 \implies \mathbf{r}_X^\mathsf{T}(C_X \mathbf{x} - \mathbf{b}_X) \le 0$. This is exactly what we need to finish the proof since

$$\bigwedge_{\mathbf{p} \in Dec_X} \mathbf{p}^\mathsf{T}(C_X \mathbf{x} - \mathbf{b}_X) \le 0 \implies \bigwedge_{\mathbf{u} \in U} \mathbf{u}^\mathsf{T}(C_X \mathbf{x} - \mathbf{b}_X) \le 0 \implies \sum_{\mathbf{u} \in U} \mathbf{u}^\mathsf{T}(C_X \mathbf{x} - \mathbf{b}_X) \le 0$$

$$\implies \mathbf{r}_X^\mathsf{T}(C_X \mathbf{x} - \mathbf{b}_X) \le 0.$$

$\square$

We first generalize the result of Theorem 3 to an arbitrary number of partitions, then discuss how monotonic decompositions can be achieved, and finally show that tree interpolants can be computed using the decomposing Farkas interpolation algorithm.

Theorem 4 (generalizing strong TI in decomposing Farkas interpolation). *Let $X_1 \wedge \ldots \wedge X_n \wedge Z$, $n \ge 2$, be an unsatisfiable partitioned CNF formula in* LRA *and let $\mathbb{P}$ be its properly labeled refutation. Let Itp^{P+D} denote the interpolation algorithm that uses Pudlák's algorithm for the propositional part and decomposing Farkas algorithm for the theory clauses. Let I_{X_1}, ...,*

I_{X_n}, and $I_{X_1 \ldots X_n}$ be the binary interpolants $Itp^{P+D}(X_1 \mid X_2 \wedge \ldots \wedge X_n \wedge Z)$, $\ldots$, $Itp^{P+D}(X_n \mid X_1 \wedge \ldots \wedge X_{n-1} \wedge Z)$ and $Itp^{P+D}(X_1 \wedge \ldots \wedge X_n \mid Z)$, respectively. If Itp^D uses monotonic decompositions for every theory clause in $\mathbb{P}$, then $(I_{X_1} \wedge \ldots \wedge I_{X_n}) \implies I_{X_1 \ldots X_n}$, i.e., the tuple $(I_{X_1}, \ldots, I_{X_n}, I_{X_1 \ldots X_n})$ has the strong tree-interpolation property.

Proof. The proof is done by induction, the same way as the proof of Theorem 2, here relying on Theorem 3. $\qquad\square$

To show how monotonic decompositions can be achieved, we first introduce a notion of *decomposition strategy* that determines the decompositions used for the related interpolation instances.

Definition 11 (decomposition strategy). *Let S be an unsatisfiable set of inequalities, $\mathbf{f}$ its witnessing vector of Farkas coefficients, and $\langle (V, E), F \rangle$ the related tree interpolation instance. The tree interpolation instance defines a set of binary interpolation instances $(F(subtree(v)) \mid F(\overline{subtree(v)}))$ for each $v \in V$. A decomposition strategy σ assigns to each vertex $v \in V$ some decomposition $\mathrm{Dec}(\mathbf{f}_{S_v}^{\mathsf{T}} C_{S_v} \mathbf{x}, L_{S_v})$, where $S_v = F(subtree(v))$. We denote the decomposing Farkas interpolation algorithm using strategy σ as $Itp^D(\sigma)$.*

An example of a decomposition strategy that guarantees monotonic decompositions is a *gradual* decomposition. The idea is to first decompose the larger subsystem and then, instead of computing independent decompositions for its subsystems, to decompose only elements of the decomposition of the larger system.

Definition 12 (gradual decomposition). *Given an unsatisfiable set of inequalities S, its witnessing vector of Farkas coefficients $\mathbf{f}$, and a tree interpolation instance $\langle (V, E), F \rangle$, a gradual decomposition GDec is a decomposition strategy defined inductively on $\langle (V, E), F \rangle$ from root to leaves as*

1. $\mathrm{GDec}(v_r) = \{\mathbf{f}\}$ *for root* v_r,
2. *otherwise*
$$\mathrm{GDec}(v) = \bigcup_{\mathbf{w} \in \mathrm{GDec}(par(v))} \mathrm{Dec}(\mathbf{w}_{S_v}^{\mathsf{T}} C_{S_v} \mathbf{x}, L(S_v)),$$

where $par(v)$ is the (unique) parent of v, and $S_v = F(subtree(v))$.

Intuitively, the gradual decomposition in a given node v decomposes each element $\mathbf{w}$ of the v's parent's decomposition separately, instead of independently decomposing $\mathbf{f}_{S_v}$, the restriction of the Farkas coefficients to the subsystem of v's subtree. Figure 1 compares the gradual decomposition and independent decomposition on the system from Example 3. It shows the tree structure of the three partitions X, Y, Z, and possible decompositions of the vector of Farkas coefficients for the corresponding binary interpolation problems $(X \mid Y \wedge Z)$, $(X \wedge Y \mid Z)$ and $(X \wedge Y \wedge Z \mid \top)$. The solid gray arrows labeled with a subsystem represent the restriction to that subsystem and the dashed arrows represent decomposition.

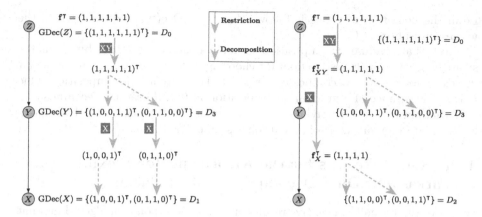

Fig. 1. A gradual decomposition (*left*) versus an independent decomposition (*right*).

The decompositions corresponding to vertices Z and Y (D_0 and D_3) are the same in both cases. The difference manifests when computing the decomposition corresponding to vertex X. On the *left*, gradual decomposition ensures that the decomposition D_1 agrees with D_3 by trying to decompose each (restricted) element of D_3 separately. In this case no further decomposition is possible, thus D_1 is equal to D_3 restricted to the subsystem X. On the *right*, if gradual decomposition is not used, then the decomposition corresponding to vertex X does not take into account what happens at X's parent Y and independently decomposes the restricted vector of Farkas coefficients $\mathbf{f}_X$. This can result in a different decomposition D_2 which, however, violates the *monotonicity* condition from (Definition 10 with respect to the decomposition D_3.

Theorem 5. *The algorithm* $TItp_{Itp^{P+D}(GDec)}$, *where decomposing Farkas interpolation algorithm uses gradual decomposition, is a tree interpolation algorithm, that is, it computes tree interpolants.*

Proof. Using the idea described in Remark 1, given a tree interpolation instance from (Definition 3 and a properly labeled refutation $\mathbb{P}$ of $\bigwedge_{v \in V} F(V)$, we define

$$\tau\iota(v) := Itp^{P+D}(GDec)(F(subtree(v)) \mid F(\overline{subtree(v)})).$$

Note that the proper labeling of $\mathbb{P}$ recreates the tree-structured partitioning of every theory clause in $\mathbb{P}$, which is required by the definition of the gradual decomposition.

The first and third conditions of tree interpolant automatically follow from our definition of $\tau\iota$. The second condition follows from Theorem 4 since gradual decomposition GDec ensures that the decompositions are monotonic. To see this, recall from the definition of monotonic decomposition ((Definition 10) that for each $v \in V$, its parent p, and for each $\mathbf{w} \in GDec(p)$, there must exist $\Pi \subseteq GDec(v)$ such that $\sum_{\mathbf{u} \in U} \mathbf{u}^\mathsf{T}(C_{S_v}\mathbf{x} - \mathbf{b}_{S_v}) \leq 0 \implies \mathbf{w}_{S_v}^\mathsf{T}(C_{S_v}\mathbf{x} - \mathbf{b}_{S_v}) \leq 0$.

From the definition of GDec it follows that $U = \mathrm{Dec}(\mathbf{w}_{S_v}^\intercal C_{S_v}\mathbf{x}, L(S_v))$ is the witnessing subset of GDec(v).   □

Note that gradual decomposition is not a concrete strategy, but rather a strategy scheme. It leaves freedom for choosing a decomposition in a particular vertex as long as the decomposition respects the parent's decomposition. One particular instance of a gradual decomposition is *trivial* gradual decomposition *Triv* that always uses the trivial decomposition of size 1. Since trivial decompositions result in Farkas interpolants, it follows that $TItp_{Itp^{P+D}(Triv)} \equiv TItp_{Itp^{P+F}}$.

4   Negative Results for the Algorithms for Flexible, Dual Farkas and Dual Decomposed Interpolation

We prove three smaller, negative results on binary interpolation algorithms that cannot be used as a basis of a tree interpolation algorithm. In particular, we show that the binary interpolation algorithms $\overline{Itp^F}$ and $\overline{Itp^D}$ discussed in Sect. 3, and an algorithm from [1] that we denote by $Itp^{(\alpha)}$, do not guarantee TI.

We first formally define the *flexible* interpolants from [1] in our notation.

Definition 13 (flexible Farkas interpolant [1]). *Let $(A\,|\,B)$ be an interpolation instance from a system $C\mathbf{x} \le \mathbf{b}$. Then the interpolants I^F and $\overline{I^F}$ are, respectively, $\mathbf{f}_A^\intercal(C_A\mathbf{x}-\mathbf{b}_A) \le 0$ and $\mathbf{f}_B^\intercal(C_B\mathbf{x}-\mathbf{b}_B) > 0$. The flexible Farkas interpolant $I^{(\alpha)}$ is defined as $\mathbf{f}_A^\intercal C_A\mathbf{x} + \mathbf{f}_B^\intercal \mathbf{b}_B - \alpha\mathbf{f}_{AB}^\intercal \mathbf{b}_{AB} \le 0$ where $0 < \alpha \le 1$.*

Flexible interpolants are useful in practice as they provide a more fine-grained approach than the Farkas and dual Farkas algorithms.[4] However, they cannot be used in general as a basis for a tree interpolation algorithm:

Theorem 6 *The flexible Farkas interpolation algorithm $Itp^{(\alpha)}$ for $0 < \alpha < 1$ does not guarantee the strong nor the weak tree-interpolation property.*

Proof Consider our running example from Example 1 and four binary interpolation instances $(X_1\,|\,X_2 \wedge Y \wedge Z), (X_2\,|\,X_1 \wedge Y \wedge Z), (Y\,|\,X_1 \wedge X_2 \wedge Z)$, and $(X_1 \wedge X_2 \wedge Y\,|\,Z)$. Let I_{X_1}, I_{X_2}, I_Y, and I_{XY} denote the interpolants from these interpolation instances. The strong tree-interpolation property is formulated as

$$I_{X_1} \wedge I_{X_2} \wedge I_Y \implies I_{XY} \tag{1}$$

and the weak tree-interpolation property is formulated as

$$I_{X_1} \wedge I_{X_2} \wedge Y \implies I_{XY}. \tag{2}$$

The flexible Farkas interpolants for the interpolation instance are

$$I_{X_1}^{(\alpha)} = (x_2 + x_3 \le 1 - \alpha) \qquad I_{X_2}^{(\alpha)} = (x_4 + x_5 \le 1 - \alpha)$$
$$I_Y^{(\alpha)} = (-x_2 - x_5 + x_6 \le 1 - \alpha) \qquad I_{XY}^{(\alpha)} = (x_3 + x_4 + x_6 \le 1 - \alpha)$$

The implications of Eq. (1) and Eq. (2) are both falsified with assignment $x_2 \mapsto 0, x_3 \mapsto 1 - \alpha, x_4 \mapsto 1 - \alpha, x_5 \mapsto 0, x_6 \mapsto 0$ for any $0 < \alpha < 1$.   □

---

[4] Farkas interpolation algorithm can be seen as the special case $Itp^{(1)}$, but dual Farkas interpolation algorithm is not a special case of the flexible interpolation algorithm.

We next show that also the dual Farkas interpolation algorithm cannot be used as a basis for a tree interpolation algorithm.

Theorem 7 *The dual Farkas interpolation algorithm does not guarantee the strong nor the weak tree-interpolation property.*

Proof Again in Example 1, the dual Farkas interpolants are computed as

$$\overline{I^F}_{X_1} = (x_2 + x_3 < 1) \qquad \overline{I^F}_{X_2} = (x_4 + x_5 < 1)$$
$$\overline{I^F}_Y = (-x_2 - x_5 + x_6 < 1) \qquad \overline{I^F}_{XY} = (x_3 + x_4 + x_6 < 1)$$

The implications of Eq. (1) and Eq. (2) are both falsified with assignment $x_2 \mapsto 0, x_3 \mapsto 0.5, x_4 \mapsto 0.5, x_5 \mapsto 0, x_6 \mapsto 0$. $\square$

From Theorem 7 we immediately get the following result.

Corollary 2 *The dual decomposing Farkas interpolation algorithm $\overline{Itp}^D$ does not have the strong nor the weak tree-interpolation property.*

Proof The interpolants computed by dual Farkas interpolation algorithm $\overline{Itp}^F$ are special cases of dual decomposed interpolants using trivial decompositions. Since Eq. (1) and Eq. (2) are not valid for $\overline{Itp}^F$, they are also invalid for $\overline{Itp}^D$. $\square$

5   Experimental Evaluation

This section provides experimental evidence on the usefulness of the decomposed Farkas tree interpolants obtained using the gradual decomposition algorithm from Sect. 3.3. In the experiments we use the SMT solver OPENSMT[20] for solving and interpolation. The solver implements a wide range of interpolation algorithms, including in particular both Farkas and decomposing Farkas algorithms [6]. These implementations allowed us to manually perform the required experiments also for gradual decomposition. In the following, for convenience, we use I^D and I^F for the tree interpolant resulting from the algorithm $TItp_{Itp^{P+D}(GDec)}$ and $TItp_{Itp^{P+F}}$, respectively.

To obtain benchmarks we used the tool FREQHORN [14] to create bounded model checking (BMC) [4] formulas from the Horn clauses available at https://github.com/chc-comp/chc-comp19-benchmarks/tree/master/lra-ts. We then applied both $TItp_{Itp^{P+D}(GDec)}$ and $TItp_{Itp^{P+F}}$ to the entire BMC formulas. In total the benchmarks consist of 514 LRA UNSAT formulas. We chose these benchmarks since they provide a natural tree structure that can be used by the gradual decomposition, the interpolants often have many non-trivial decompositions (up to 965), and are relatively big (up to 12k LoC).

Our goal in the experiments is to study whether the I^D are genuinely different from the I^F. We chose two example measures for difference of interpolants: (i) the number of top-level conjuncts, and (ii) the number of distinct LRA atoms. In (i), the number of top-level conjuncts is a measure of generalizability of the

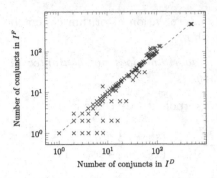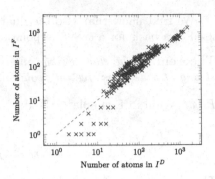

Fig. 2. Comparing decomposed Farkas and Farkas tree interpolants w.r.t the number of conjuncts (*left*) and theory atoms (*right*) in the interpolants.

interpolant. In some applications (see, for example, [14,22]) it is useful to further abstract an over-approximation, and in case the interpolant has several conjuncts, an easy way to achieve this is by dropping some of them. More technically, for formula f, we define this measure as $N_\wedge(f)$, where $N_\wedge(f) := 1$ if f is not a conjunction at the top-level, and $N_\wedge(f) := n$ if f is of the form $A_1 \wedge \ldots \wedge A_n$. In (ii), the number of distinct theory atoms indicates the complexity of the interpolant in the sense that an instance with more atoms represents a larger Boolean search space. Technically, we define this as the size of the largest subset of $Atoms(f)$ containing only theory atoms.

Figure 2 (*left*) shows the number of top-level conjuncts for I^F and I^D as a scatter plot. In 53% of the benchmarks I^D have strictly more conjuncts in comparison to I^F. Excluding the cases where the number of top-level conjuncts is the same in I^F and I^D, 91% of benchmarks (270 vs. 25) have strictly more conjuncts in I^D. While a non-negligible number of instances (219) have the same number of conjuncts in I^F and I^D, the majority of the instances are different.

Figure 2 (*right*) compares the number of unique LRA atoms in I^F and I^D. In almost one-third of the cases I^D contains fewer atoms, suggesting that the decompositions identify semantic structure that is shared between the LRA interpolation queries. We want to emphasize that this is, to the best or our knowledge, a new result that we expect to have practical impact. Based on the numerical results, and contrary to what the figure suggests, there are typically more atoms in I^D. Concretely, out of 514 benchmarks, 63% have fewer theory atoms in I^F. This is in particular because in 57 benchmarks there are two atoms in I^D and one atom in I^F, all represented by the single point (2,1) in the plot. This is somewhat expected, since on a single LRA interpolation query Itp^D is guaranteed to give at least as many atoms as Itp^F. In addition, in no case the number of theory atoms is the same in I^F and I^D, giving a strong indication that the interpolation algorithms differ in practice.

In conclusion, the results imply that a portfolio of the interpolation algorithms $TItp_{ItpP+D(GDec)}$ and $TItp_{ItpP+F}$ provides a range of interpolants that are substantially different from those available using only $TItp_{ItpP+F}$.

6 Conclusion

We identified five classes of interpolation systems for LRA based on Farkas' lemma, and investigated whether and under what conditions they can be used for tree interpolation. In addition to strengthening a known positive result for the Farkas algorithm, we showed that also the binary decomposing Farkas interpolation algorithm can be used as a basis for tree interpolation by using a novel method called *gradual decomposition*. We also showed that TI is not guaranteed by the dual Farkas, the dual decomposing Farkas, and a flexible variant of the Farkas interpolation algorithms.

We showed experimentally, based on two different measures, that Farkas and decomposed Farkas interpolants are often different. In addition, interestingly, it is not uncommon that the decomposed interpolants have fewer theory atoms than the Farkas interpolants, and that it is more common that the decomposed interpolants have more conjuncts also at the top-level of the formulas compared to Farkas interpolants. The existence of the decomposing Farkas interpolation algorithm for tree interpolation enables a liberty in the interpolant choice previously unavailable in the field. We are hopeful that the decomposed interpolants will become a powerful component of interpolation portfolios resulting in more scalable and general solving. In a future work we plan to implement the gradual decomposition in a more automatic way and experiment with the implementation in a more applied setting.

A   Appendix A

In this appendix we give auxiliary material for more formal treatment of the connection between propositional and theory interpolation. The propositional resolution rule state that an assignment satisfying the clauses $cl^+ \vee p$ and $cl^- \vee \overline{p}$ also satisfies $cl^+ \vee cl^-$.

Our propositional interpolation works on a refutation of a formula $A \wedge B$. We denote atoms of A and B as $Atoms(A, B)$. Note that each $At \in Atoms(A, B)$ may appear only in A, only in B, or in both conjuncts; Similarly to the notation in [11], we assign a *color* among $\{a, b, ab\}$ independently to each At, depending on whether At occurs only in A, only in B, or in both, respectively.

Table 2 describes the *Pudlák* interpolation algorithm, where the notation $p{:}\varepsilon$ indicates that a literal p has color ε.

Table 2. Pudlák's interpolation algorithm

Source clause: $C\,[I]$
$I = \begin{cases} \bot & \text{if } C \in A \\ \top & \text{if } C \in B \end{cases}$

Inner node: $\dfrac{cl^+ \vee p{:}\varepsilon\;[I^+] \qquad cl^- \vee \bar{p}{:}\varepsilon\;[I^-]}{cl^+ \vee cl^-\;[I]}$
$I = \begin{cases} I^+ \vee I^- & \text{if } \varepsilon = a \\ I^+ \wedge I^- & \text{if } \varepsilon = b \\ (I^+ \vee p) \wedge (I^- \vee \bar{p}) & \text{if } \varepsilon = ab \end{cases}$

Lemma 2 (source clause, base case) *The strong tree-interpolation property holds for Pudlák's interpolation algorithm Itp^P for source clauses.*

Proof Let cl be a source clause. There are three cases: $cl \in X$, $cl \in Y$, or $cl \in Z$. We consider the three interpolation instances $(X \mid Y \wedge Z)$, $(Y \mid X \wedge Z)$, and $(X \wedge Y \mid Z)$, and check whether TI holds, i.e., whether

$$Itp^P(X \mid Y \wedge Z) \wedge Itp^P(Y \mid X \wedge Z) \implies Itp^P(X \wedge Y \mid Z). \tag{3}$$

The relevant part in the algorithm is shown in Table 2 (*left*).

- $cl \in X$: When $cl \in X$, using Pudlák's interpolation algorithm and substituting the interpolants in Eq. (3), we have $(\bot \wedge \top) \implies \bot$, which is valid.
- $cl \in Y$: The case $cl \in Y$ is symmetric to the case when $cl \in X$, and thus valid.
- $cl \in Z$: When $cl \in Z$, we have again by substiting in Eq. (3) $(\top \wedge \top) \implies \top$, which is valid.

$\qquad\qquad\qquad\qquad\qquad\qquad\qquad\qquad\qquad\qquad\qquad\qquad\qquad\qquad\qquad\qquad\square$

Lemma 3 (inner node) *Let p be a variable. In refutation $\mathbb{P}$, if partial interpolants for nodes $cl^+ \vee p$ and $cl^- \vee \hat{p}$ satisfy the strong tree-interpolation property, then the partial interpolant for $cl^+ \vee cl^-$ satisfy the strong tree-interpolation property.*

Proof We show that for all resolvents in refutation $\mathbb{P}$, the implication $(I_X \wedge I_Y) \implies I_{XY}$ holds, where $I_X = (X \mid Y \wedge Z), I_Y = (Y \mid X \wedge Z)$, and $I_{XY} = (XY \mid Z)$.

we consider a node $cl^+ \vee cl^-$ representing resolution over a variable p with parent nodes $p \vee cl^+$ and $\bar{p} \vee cl^-$. From the inductive hypotheses, we have partial interpolants I_X^+, I_Y^+, and I_{XY}^+ for the node $p \vee cl^+$ so that $(I_X^+ \wedge I_Y^+) \implies I_{XY}^+$ and partial interpolants I_X^-, I_Y^-, and I_{XY}^- for the node $\bar{p} \vee cl^-$ so that $(I_X^- \wedge I_Y^-) \implies I_{XY}^-$.

We consider different cases of coloring of p. Depending on presence of p in the three partitions, i.e., X, Y, and Z, and also depending on interpolation instances $(X \mid Y \wedge Z)$, $(Y \mid X \wedge Z)$, and $(X \wedge Y \mid Z)$, p is colored a, b, or ab (Table 3).

Table 3. Coloring of variable p for each partial interpolant.

appearance of p	class of p for each partial interpolant		
	I_X	I_Y	I_{XY}
X	a	b	a
Y	b	a	a
Z	b	b	b
$X \cap Y$	ab	ab	a
$X \cap Z$	ab	b	ab
$Y \cap Z$	b	ab	ab
$X \cap Y \cap Z$	ab	ab	ab

In case of $p \in X$, based on Pudlák's algorithm 2, $I_X \equiv I_X^+ \vee I_X^-$, $I_Y \equiv I_Y^+ \wedge I_Y^-$, $I_{XY} \equiv I_{XY}^+ \vee I_{XY}^-$.

Using the inductive hypothesis, we have $((I_X^+ \vee I_X^-) \wedge I_Y^+ \wedge I_Y^-) \implies (I_{XY}^+ \vee I_{XY}^-)$, which is the required claim $(I_X \wedge I_Y) \implies I_{XY}$. The case $p \in Y$ is symmetric.

In case of $p \in Z$, we have $I_X \equiv I_X^+ \wedge I_X^-$, $I_Y \equiv I_Y^+ \wedge I_Y^-$, $I_{XY} \equiv I_{XY}^+ \wedge I_{XY}^-$. Using the inductive hypothesis, we have $(I_X^+ \wedge I_X^- \wedge I_Y^+ \wedge I_Y^-) \implies (I_{XY}^+ \wedge I_{XY}^-)$, which is the required claim $(I_X \wedge I_Y) \implies I_{XY}$.

In case of $p \in X \cap Y \cap Z$, using $sel(p, P, Q)$ as a shortcut for $(p \vee P) \wedge (\bar{p} \vee Q)$, we get: $I_X = sel(p, I_X^+, I_X^-)$, $I_Y = sel(p, I_Y^+, I_Y^-)$, $I_{XY} = sel(p, I_{XY}^+, I_{XY}^-)$. Using the inductive hypothesis and considering both possible values of p, we have $(sel(p, I_X^+, I_X^-) \wedge sel(p, I_Y^+, I_Y^-)) \implies sel(p, I_{XY}^+, I_{XY}^-)$, which is the desired claim $(I_X \wedge I_Y) \implies I_{XY}$. The other cases where $p \in X \cap Y$ or $p \in X \cap Z$ or $p \in Y \cap Z$ are subsumed by this case as $(P \wedge Q) \implies sel(p, P, Q) \implies (P \vee Q)$. $\qquad\square$

References

1. Alt, L., Hyvärinen, A.E.J., Sharygina, N.: LRA interpolants from no man's land. HVC 2017. LNCS, vol. 10629, pp. 195–210. Springer, Cham (2017). https://doi.org/10.1007/978-3-319-70389-3_13
2. Asadi, S., Blicha, M., Hyvärinen, A., Fedyukovich, G., Sharygina, N.: Incremental verification by SMT-based summary repair. In: Proceedings FMCAD 2020. IEEE digital library (2020)
3. Barrett, C., Sebastiani, R., Seshia, S., Tinelli, C.: Satisfiability modulo theories, Frontiers in Artificial Intelligence and Applications, (1 edn.) vol. 185, pp. 825 885. IOS Press (2009)

4. Biere, A., Cimatti, A., Clarke, E., Zhu, Y.: Symbolic model checking without BDDs. In: Cleaveland, W.R. (ed.) TACAS 1999. LNCS, vol. 1579, pp. 193–207. Springer, Heidelberg (1999). https://doi.org/10.1007/3-540-49059-0_14

5. Blanc, R., Gupta, A., Kovács, L., Kragl, B.: Tree interpolation in vampire. In: McMillan, K., Middeldorp, A., Voronkov, A. (eds.) LPAR 2013. LNCS, vol. 8312, pp. 173–181. Springer, Heidelberg (2013). https://doi.org/10.1007/978-3-642-45221-5_13

6. Blicha, M., Hyvärinen, A.E.J., Kofroň, J., Sharygina, N.: Decomposing Farkas interpolants. In: Vojnar, T., Zhang, L. (eds.) TACAS 2019. LNCS, vol. 11427, pp. 3–20. Springer, Cham (2019). https://doi.org/10.1007/978-3-030-17462-0_1

7. Christ, J., Hoenicke, J.: Proof tree preserving tree interpolation. J. Autom. Reasoning **57**(1), 67–95 (2016)

8. Cimatti, A., Griggio, A., Sebastiani, R.: Efficient generation of Craig interpolants in satisfiability modulo theories. ACM Trans. Comput. Log. **12**(1), 7:1–7:54 (2010)

9. Craig, W.: Three uses of the Herbrand-Gentzen theorem in relating model theory and proof theory. In: Journal of Symbolic Logic, pp. 269–285 (1957)

10. Detlefs, D., Nelson, G., Saxe, J.B.: Simplify: a theorem prover for program checking. J. ACM **52**(3), 365–473 (2005)

11. D'Silva, V., Kroening, D., Purandare, M., Weissenbacher, G.: Interpolant strength. In: Barthe, G., Hermenegildo, M. (eds.) VMCAI 2010. LNCS, vol. 5944, pp. 129–145. Springer, Heidelberg (2010). https://doi.org/10.1007/978-3-642-11319-2_12

12. Dutertre, B., de Moura, L.: A fast linear-arithmetic solver for DPLL(T). In: Ball, T., Jones, R.B. (eds.) CAV 2006. LNCS, vol. 4144, pp. 81–94. Springer, Heidelberg (2006). https://doi.org/10.1007/11817963_11

13. Farzan, A., Kincaid, Z.: Strategy synthesis for linear arithmetic games. PACMPL **2**(POPL), 1–61 (2018)

14. Fedyukovich, G., Bodík, R.: Accelerating syntax-guided invariant synthesis. In: Beyer, D., Huisman, M. (eds.) TACAS 2018. LNCS, vol. 10805, pp. 251–269. Springer, Cham (2018). https://doi.org/10.1007/978-3-319-89960-2_14

15. Fedyukovich, G., Sery, O., Sharygina, N.: eVolCheck: incremental upgrade checker for C. In: Piterman, N., Smolka, S.A. (eds.) TACAS 2013. LNCS, vol. 7795, pp. 292–307. Springer, Heidelberg (2013). https://doi.org/10.1007/978-3-642-36742-7_21

16. Gupta, A., Popeea, C., Rybalchenko, A.: Solving recursion-free horn clauses over LI+UIF. In: Yang, H. (ed.) APLAS 2011. LNCS, vol. 7078, pp. 188–203. Springer, Heidelberg (2011). https://doi.org/10.1007/978-3-642-25318-8_16

17. Gurfinkel, A., Rollini, S.F., Sharygina, N.: Interpolation properties and SAT-based model checking. In: Van Hung, D., Ogawa, M. (eds.) ATVA 2013. LNCS, vol. 8172, pp. 255–271. Springer, Cham (2013). https://doi.org/10.1007/978-3-319-02444-8_19

18. Heizmann, M., Hoenicke, J., Podelski, A.: Nested interpolants. In: Proceedings POPL 2010, pp. 471–482. ACM (2010)

19. Hojjat, H., Rümmer, P.: The ELDARICA Horn Solver. In: FMCAD, pp. 158–164. IEEE (2018)

20. Hyvärinen, A.E.J., Marescotti, M., Alt, L., Sharygina, N.: OpenSMT2: an SMT solver for multi-core and cloud computing. In: Creignou, N., Le Berre, D. (eds.) SAT 2016. LNCS, vol. 9710, pp. 547–553. Springer, Cham (2016). https://doi.org/10.1007/978-3-319-40970-2_35

21. Jhala, R., McMillan, K.L.: Interpolant-based transition relation approximation. In: Etessami, K., Rajamani, S.K. (eds.) CAV 2005. LNCS, vol. 3576, pp. 39–51. Springer, Heidelberg (2005). https://doi.org/10.1007/11513988_6

22. Komuravelli, A., Gurfinkel, A., Chaki, S., Clarke, E.M.: Automatic abstraction in SMT-based unbounded software model checking. In: Sharygina, N., Veith, H. (eds.) CAV 2013. LNCS, vol. 8044, pp. 846–862. Springer, Heidelberg (2013). https://doi.org/10.1007/978-3-642-39799-8_59

23. McMillan, K.L.: An interpolating theorem prover. In: Jensen, K., Podelski, A. (eds.) TACAS 2004. LNCS, vol. 2988, pp. 16–30. Springer, Heidelberg (2004). https://doi.org/10.1007/978-3-540-24730-2_2

24. McMillan, K.L., Rybalchenko, A.: Solving constrained Horn clauses using interpolation. Technical Report MSR-TR-2013-6 (2013)

25. Pudlák, P.: Lower bounds for resolution and cutting plane proofs and monotone computations. J. Symbolic Logic **62**(3), 981–998 (1997)

26. Rollini, S.F., Sery, O., Sharygina, N.: Leveraging interpolant strength in model checking. In: Madhusudan, P., Seshia, S.A. (eds.) CAV 2012. LNCS, vol. 7358, pp. 193–209. Springer, Heidelberg (2012). https://doi.org/10.1007/978-3-642-31424-7_18

27. Rümmer, P., Hojjat, H., Kuncak, V.: Disjunctive interpolants for horn-clause verification. In: Sharygina, N., Veith, H. (eds.) CAV 2013. LNCS, vol. 8044, pp. 347–363. Springer, Heidelberg (2013). https://doi.org/10.1007/978-3-642-39799-8_24

28. Rybalchenko, A., Sofronie-Stokkermans, V.: Constraint solving for interpolation. In: Cook, B., Podelski, A. (eds.) VMCAI 2007. LNCS, vol. 4349, pp. 346–362. Springer, Heidelberg (2007). https://doi.org/10.1007/978-3-540-69738-1_25

29. Sery, O., Fedyukovich, G., Sharygina, N.: Incremental upgrade checking by means of interpolation-based function summaries. In: Proceedings FMCAD 2012, pp. 114–121. IEEE (2012)

30. Sharma, R., Nori, A.V., Aiken, A.: Interpolants as classifiers. In: Madhusudan, P., Seshia, S.A. (eds.) CAV 2012. LNCS, vol. 7358, pp. 71–87. Springer, Heidelberg (2012). https://doi.org/10.1007/978-3-642-31424-7_11

Author Index

Printed in the United States
By Bookmasters

Printed in the United States
By Bookmasters